As our society gets ever more stressed and burned out, mental health professionals themselves are busier and more burned out than ever. Dr. Hersh has put together one of the best, most evidence-based yet accessible guides to restoring your health, mental health, and idealism as a mental health professional that I've encountered in years.

—Christopher Willard, PsyD, Psychologist and Consultant, Boston, MA

Matthew A. Hersh has given a tremendous gift to psychotherapists with his book on sustainable self-care. Born out of his personal experience with a life-threatening illness while he was still in training, this book provides an integrative and nuanced view of the critical importance of self-care to those who care for the mental wellness of others. His engaging style of writing and his self-care reflection breaks encourage the reader to actively participate in—rather than passively read through—this well-researched book. It offers important and meaningful wisdom for psychotherapists throughout their lives.

—Erica H. Wise, PhD, Clinical Professor Emerita, Department of Psychology & Neuroscience, University of North Carolina at Chapel Hill, Chapel Hill, NC, and Fellow of the American Psychological Association

Matthew A. Hersh has pulled together ideas from many wise people and integrated these with his own experiences as a psychologist, therapist, and cancer survivor. The result is a reflective guide to self-care for helping professionals and others who need skills for mindful coping. Readers will find a useful assortment of tools, guides, and wisdom to support themselves even as they strive to help others.

—Gerald P. Koocher, PhD, ABPP, Harvard Medical School, Boston, MA, and Former American Psychological Association President

The THRIVING
THERAPIST

The THRIVING
THERAPIST

Sustainable Self-Care to Prevent Burnout and Enhance Well-Being

Matthew A. Hersh

 AMERICAN PSYCHOLOGICAL ASSOCIATION

Published by
American Psychological Association
750 First Street, NE
Washington, DC 20002
https://www.apa.org

Order Department
https://www.apa.org/pubs/books
order@apa.org

In the U.K., Europe, Africa, and the Middle East, copies may be ordered from Eurospan
https://www.eurospanbookstore.com/apa
info@eurospangroup.com

Typeset in Charter and Interstate by Circle Graphics, Inc., Reisterstown, MD

Printer: Gasch Printing, Odenton, MD
Cover Designer: Nicci Falcone, Gaithersburg, MD
Cover Art: Joseph Falcone

Library of Congress Cataloging-in-Publication Data

Names: Hersh, Matthew A., author.
Title: The thriving therapist : sustainable self-care to prevent burnout
 and enhance well-being / by Matthew A. Hersh.
Description: Washington, DC : American Psychological Association, [2022] |
 Includes bibliographical references and index.
Identifiers: LCCN 2021059041 (print) | LCCN 2021059042 (ebook) |
 ISBN 9781433837845 (paperback) | ISBN 9781433840241 (ebook)
Subjects: LCSH: Counselors--Job stress. | Counselors--Mental health. |
 Clinical psychologists--Job stress. | Clinical psychologists--Mental
 health. | Self-care, Health. | BISAC: PSYCHOLOGY / Psychotherapy /
 General | PSYCHOLOGY / Practice Management
Classification: LCC BF636.64 .H47 2022 (print) | LCC BF636.64 (ebook) |
 DDC 158/.3--dc23/eng/20211213
LC record available at https://lccn.loc.gov/2021059041
LC ebook record available at https://lccn.loc.gov/2021059042

https://doi.org/10.1037/0000309-000

Printed in the United States of America

10 9 8 7 6 5 4 3 2 1

Contents

Acknowledgments

It feels like a nearly impossible task to adequately thank not only all those who have helped make this book possible but also those who have taught, supported, and loved me along the way. I am extremely grateful to the wonderful team at the American Psychological Association, in particular, to my editors, Emily Ekle, Ida Audeh, Gail Gottfried, and Elizabeth Brace, who compassionately and firmly guided me to make this book eminently more readable and the most helpful it could be. And to my external reviewers, who positively shaped this book in so many ways. To all those who took their precious time to be interviewed about their wisdom and experience with professional self-care, you helped to create and breathe life into this book. To Erica Wise, I owe you an enormous debt of gratitude for your graciousness and support. You opened the door for this book to happen, and I gladly accepted your invitation each time.

Countless mentors along the way have taught me about care and self-care in one profound way or another. To my wise and compassionate Duke University mindfulness-based stress reduction teachers, you helped illuminate the way toward self-caring possibilities I never knew existed. To Andrea Hussong, who showed me such patience and encouragement during graduate school and demonstrated such deep caring when I was gravely ill. The principles of stewardship and paying it forward couldn't be demonstrated more clearly than with the deep generosity offered to me by my internship supervisors and mentors, Eugene D'Angelo, Peter Hunt, Marcus Cherry, and Gary Gosselin. Their compassionate insistence that my self-care and healing be top priority was a priceless gift—a lesson in what ultimately matters.

I will always be grateful to my graduate school and internship classmates; to my friends and colleagues; and to Stephanie Eldringhoff and my energy psychology consultation group, Michaela Kohmetscher and Jeff Santee, for their enthusiastic support of this book. A special thanks to friends and colleagues Ariel Botta, Cory Chen, Marci Evans, Laura Ferrer, Thomas Richardson, Elizabeth Shepherd, Evan Waldheter, Miriam Waldheter, and Chris Willard, who supported this book from the beginning and were consummate cheerleaders and contributors in so many ways. And tremendous gratitude is due to my psychotherapy clients, past and present, who have taught me the abiding value of care and self-care as we've navigated a thousand joys and a thousand sorrows together.

To my surgeons and oncologists, who rooted out a foreign invader from my body so that I could live—I owe you my life. I am deeply grateful to Suzanne George, Ann Fiore, Kathy Polson, Mary Jane Ott, Chris Berlin, and Hannah Yzusqui-Butera, who constantly gave me hope and healing with humor, compassion, and mindful presence. I want to deeply thank my acupuncturist, Rong Zhang, who seemingly granted me miracle after miracle. And my hypnotherapist, Max Shapiro, who insisted that I was doing everything in my power to help myself while he did everything in his power to help me. I now understand exactly why he told me this during our first phone call. Caring and self-caring at that moment became inextricably intertwined.

Writing this book was an undertaking of grand proportions. It simply would not have been permitted without the undying love, support, and patience from my amazing family. Thank you to the Littles, who have supported me for over half my life. I am eternally grateful to my deceased grandparents for showing me unconditional love and support. To my aunt and cousin—you are two of the most caring and fun-loving individuals I know who embody the meaning of connection. To my awesome brother and his family for their sustained support and encouragement—Jerry, you can't possibly know how grateful I am for your presence, friendship, and hope, especially during the darker times. My deep gratitude extends to my parents whose support and love have been unwavering. You gave me permission to pursue what was most meaningful. Thank you doesn't cut it.

To my fantastic kids, Anya and Elan, who have such loving, creative, and fun-filled souls. You were as patient as you could be with a dad who grew busier and busier. Your support and humor have been invaluable. And finally, to my brilliant and beautiful wife, Carie. During so many times of doubting my abilities, you would remind me of who I am and what I was offering to my fellow therapists. There really aren't words to capture the endless forms of support, scaffolding, caring, and love that you gave during this time. You really made this happen. And last, a nod to myself, in the spirit of self-caring. I am grateful to you for persevering and having hope that this book could even be written, let alone serve those it was intended to support and inspire.

The THRIVING
THERAPIST

INTRODUCTION

It was 2006, and I had just begun my clinical psychology internship at Boston Children's Hospital/Harvard Medical School. Despite my feeling like an imposter and a virtual infant in the evolution of my professional training, our directors kindly insisted that we were the "cream of the crop" and that we could do anything we put our minds to. Skeptical but encouraged, I launched into the vast sea of psychotherapeutic training in one of the largest children's hospitals in the world.

Fortunately, I was embarking on this journey with six other compatriots with whom I would become incredibly close and entrust with my life. We ventured in and out of different rotations, some more brutal than others but all amazing learning experiences. Nothing, however, could have prepared me for what I was about to experience.

On April 3, 2007, my life dropped out from under me and would change forever. After several months of unidentified and unrelenting pain, several forms of unsuccessful therapies, and two grueling biopsies, I was diagnosed with an extremely rare form of cancer with which only 75 other Americans each year are afflicted. What ensued was a harrowingly surreal 8 months of intensive cell-killing treatments followed by two back-to-back 10-hour

https://doi.org/10.1037/0000309-001
The Thriving Therapist: Sustainable Self-Care to Prevent Burnout and Enhance Well-Being, by M. A. Hersh

surgeries and postsurgical radiation. My recovery, as one could imagine, was even longer than the course of treatment, and it's still ongoing in many ways.

It would be an understatement to say that I was suddenly thrust into what I would now consider a cosmically peculiar and intense experiment on self-care. Self-care became *self-caring*, a constant here-and-now endeavor rather than something planned for the future or done in reaction to my life getting too stressful. I tried to practice gratitude for the small victories, and I unknowingly signed up for crash courses in equanimity, radical acceptance, abiding presence, and unadulterated courage. Perhaps most importantly, I was supported in countless ways by loved ones, classmates, friends, and supervisors, all of whom figuratively and literally had my back.

From and through all my trials and tribulations that year, I learned the invaluable lesson of common humanity—that each and every one of us suffers and struggles. It became incredibly clear to me that because we're essentially no different from our clients or patients, we can harness that reality to empower ourselves for better preventive self-care and well-being enhancement over the rollercoaster journey of our professional and personal lives.

Although most psychotherapists, thankfully, will not be diagnosed with such a rare cancer, the vast majority of us have and will experience our fair share of everything else: illness, financial struggles, family conflict, loved ones lost, workplace inequities, addiction problems, depression, bigotry and racism, anxiety, insecurity, and relationship struggles and dissolution. Some of us will feel intense crises of identity and soul that sometimes spark feelings of hopelessness so profound that suicide becomes a viable alternative to living with such suffering. The bottom line is that psychotherapists are still human and need to treat ourselves as such.

PSYCHOTHERAPIST SELF-CARE: OUR RIGHT AND OUR MANDATE

Self-care is not just for the privileged. It's not just for psychotherapists who subscribe to any particular theoretical orientation. Nor is it just for "those" psychotherapists who "really" need it. Rather, self-care, like health care, is a universal right and need, and psychotherapists are invited to join the movement.

Allied helping professionals are also invited along on this journey. Although this book is written from the perspective of a clinical psychologist and is predominantly for fellow psychotherapists, many others share our way of helping, manage similar occupational stresses and strains, and are in need of the same self-care support and encouragement. Thus, I encourage helpers such as nurses and psychiatric nurse practitioners, physicians, addictions counselors, massage therapists, acupuncturists, hospice workers, child welfare workers, and wellness coaches (and many more) to walk this self-caring path as well. It's incumbent upon us all to be our own best advocates as well as to support and strengthen each other along the way.

The topic of professional self-care and occupational hazards awareness has been receiving a lot more academic and clinical attention in recent years. The American Psychological Association, Psychotherapy Networker, and National Register for Health Service Providers, to name a few, host powerful blogs, publish articles, and publicize resources for self-care and professional risk awareness and prevention. Over the last several years, major social media platforms have begun to attract highly specialized groups of mental health practitioners searching for community, support, and sharing of self-care resources to build their resilience and reduce occupational stress. Therapists now can benefit from podcasts and both online and live programs designed specifically for prevention of practitioners' burnout, management of stress, and cultivation of well-being (e.g., Greater Good Institute for Health Professionals, The Thriving Therapist's Self-Care for the Stressed Health Care Practitioner, Simple Practice, Compassion Fatigue Awareness Project, Fire Within Consulting).

There is good reason for such increased attention to psychotherapist self-care. Psychotherapy is not just about the faceless delivery of an intervention. *We* are the instruments through which our psychotherapeutic services flow. Every instrument needs calibration, tuning, and maintenance. We've all been there in our daily lives—with our cars, smartphones, and the beds and pillows on which we sleep. We tend not to tolerate (nor is it safe) driving a car that's depleted of brake fluid, using a phone that's run out of storage, or sleeping on a squeaky and unstable bed. We top off the fluid, clear out some storage space, and tighten up the beams on our beds. As our own instruments of psychotherapeutic change, empowerment, and healing, we deserve no less (and a lot more) than the inanimate tools we rely on in our everyday lives.

Thus, we can rest assured that there is quite the pragmatic rationale for bringing sustainable self-care into our lives as therapists. When we sleep better, we feel better and are less irritable and more tolerant of ourselves and our clients. When we eat well and stay adequately hydrated, we can sustain more mindful presence with clients' struggles and can feel more energized throughout long days. When we respect our own boundaries, we can feel less resentful when clients seem to demand our time and energy. Ultimately, we can feel more at ease taking care of ourselves without internal conflict or sense of self-judgment, and we propel ourselves forward with greater resilience and equanimity.

WHAT THIS BOOK CAN UNIQUELY OFFER

In stark contrast to well over 10,000 books published on various approaches to psychotherapy as well as on the ethics of psychotherapeutic practice, well under 50 books exist on self-care cultivation and occupational risk reduction for mental health professionals and trainees. That's about 0.5% of our psychotherapy training that's focused on taking care of ourselves. Some of the existing books focus on highly pragmatic daily self-care practices (e.g., *Simple Self-Care for Therapists*; Bush, 2015), whereas others like *Leaving It at the Office* (Norcross & VandenBos, 2018) are more principles based while offering integrative practices for optimal well-being and prevention of professional fatigue. These books and others like them have indeed provided an incredibly solid foundation on which I could create this book.

My aspiration in writing this book was to create a self-care framework that is at once integrative, holistic, and practical. My aim is to invite you, the reader, to be self-caring across your lifespan and career development rather than to "do self-care." Doing self-care is too often a reactive and piecemeal endeavor, whereas being self-caring is a proactive lifestyle for more sustainable well-being inside and out of the therapy room.

As human beings, we tend to begin with what appears most obvious. Larger societal messages convey that if X is good for you, then just do X. But starting a self-caring journey in this way might be like launching a business while feeling unworthy of making good money, jumping in without a business plan, or having very little internal motivational support to sustain oneself through the challenges of the process. Just as we treat our clients as highly unique individuals and consider their personal histories, learning styles, and conditioning to be of utmost importance for how we relate to them and what recommendations we offer, we too can become more deeply aware of the unique and idiosyncratic reasons and practices for taking the best care of ourselves over time. This book is an exploration of a self-evolutionary model of self-care in which growth in self-understanding begets a more fine-tuned sense of how to sustainably take care of ourselves professionally and personally and to the mutual benefit of our work and personal lives.

This book is dialectically oriented, with a focus on knowing ourselves more deeply and embodying and practicing self-care in alignment with that deeper knowing. We'll invite acceptance of who we already are (e.g., our strengths, challenges, blind spots) and move toward making the necessary changes within ourselves and in our environments for optimal health and healthy prevention. We'll welcome the notion of self-caring as an individualized developmental journey rather than a one-size-fits-all set of activities at any given time.

Therapist self-care is also inherently bidirectional and reciprocal, meaning that we're not doing self-care only at or for the office. Rather, how we relate to and comport ourselves in our personal lives influences our professional selves (e.g., competence, patience, mindful awareness, resilience, creativity), and how we think, feel, act, and react in our professional roles affect our personal lives. It would be unfair to our wholeness to completely separate these parts of our lives. And, of course, we can also assume that our professional and personal lives can remain distinct and be treated as such. From whatever angle we take, we can harness our professional and personal lives for mutual positive and preventive empowerment.

Before moving on, it's important to note something about the concept of self-care. Although this book is ostensibly about caring for the self, I don't intend for that "work" to be done completely on your own. That's too much to ask of any one psychotherapist. So much vital growth is done from within, but we still have to be buttressed, reminded, and validated from outside of ourselves. Thus, tones of a communitarian and stewardship ethos throughout this book encourage us to look out for one another and be each other's keepers.

HOW TO USE THIS BOOK

The book focuses primarily on two ways to approach self-care, risk prevention, and growth: (a) to ponder, pique curiosity, reflect, explore, discuss, invite, and give permission and (b) to experiment, practice, try out, try on, enact, decide, activate, and execute. With this dialectical framework, we can think, feel, and act our way into sustainable self-caring. I encourage you to take some time to explore each of the Self-Care Reflection Breaks with exercises, activities, or questions upon which to reflect and experiment. The appendices contain exercises and resources, and my accompanying website (https://www.TheThrivingTherapist.org) will house additional exercises that allow you to devote more concentrated time and energy.

The practices and reflection exercises throughout this book are designed to help you get curious, explore, and go deeper into the nuanced world of professional self-care. To be inspired, sometimes it's enough to read the words on the page. To make active change, sometimes we need to reflect intentionally on and radically invite in the tension or blind spots that might currently exist (or have existed) in our lives. Welcoming the confusion, internal conflict, feelings of burnout, or cognitive dissonance as well as our positive motivational states may be what we need at any given time. The timelessly insightful 13th century poet Jellaludin Rumi captured this invitation well in his famous poem, *The Guest House*:

> This being human is a guest house. Every morning a new arrival. A joy, a depression, a meanness, some momentary awareness comes as an unexpected visitor. Welcome and entertain them all! Even if they are a crowd of sorrows, who violently sweep your house empty of its furniture, still, treat each guest honorably. He may be clearing you out for some new delight. The dark thought, the shame, the malice, meet them at the door laughing, and invite them in. Be grateful for whoever comes, because each has been sent as a guide from beyond. (Barks, 1995, p. 109)

In the spirit of self-evolution and the development of sustainable self-care, I start with the theme of nourishing the roots of self-care: Part I focuses on the foundations of professional self-care and prevention. In this part of the book, I invite you to unpack and repack self-care conceptualizations, explore your occupational hazards, revisit why you became a psychotherapist and affirm what sustains you, and clarify your self-caring values. In Part II, Flexibly Grounded: Mindful Awareness of Habits, Patterns, and Needs, I encourage you to continue your self-caring journey by homing in on the habits in multiple domains of life that undergird your self-caring needs. Rather than a one-size-fits-all approach, this section encourages a personalized examination of how each reader can find opportunities to optimize self-caring and prevent unnecessary suffering in a variety of life domains.

Part II is the call to awareness of our personal and professional needs, and Parts III and IV are the skillful responses. Part III, Intrinsic Self-Care: Soft Strength, Hidden Resilience, provides an empirically supported toolbox of internal transformational practices that harness mind and heart skills. The last few decades have seen a surge in research on the benefits of these more intrinsic qualities that, when purposefully cultivated, can serve as powerful buffers of stress and burnout as well as facilitators of well-being and fulfillment. A beautiful aspect of these intrinsic self-care skills is that any therapist can cultivate and practice them anywhere and any time. The more observable and familiar counterpart to these intrinsic practices is Part IV, Extrinsic Self-Care: Powerful Practices, Transformational Habits. This section covers several practices, activities, and habits essential to all psychotherapists' self-care toolboxes. From basic biological and neuropsychological functioning to the navigation of relationships and external environments, Part IV offers suggestions to enact self-care in a pragmatic and sustainably supportive manner.

As we traverse the "what" of self-care, we must arrive at the "how." Part V, Thriving: Creating Sustainability of Self-Care and Well-Being, is about synthesizing our existing and recently learned knowledge to launch ourselves into a sustainable resilience and longevity of self-caring attitude and action. This section is about readiness and willingness to participate in self-caring, how to form long-term habits over the seasons and across development, and to integrate these habits in seamless and embodied ways on a daily basis. Finally, the book ends with a call for a communitarian ethos toward psychotherapist self-care. This is an invitation to look upon our roles as psychotherapists within a larger network of being one another's stewards and paying our gifts forward to the benefit of all.

To breathe life into the vital topic of self-care, you'll encounter my personal experiences as well as numerous anecdotes about therapists' real-life joys and struggles within the profession. Admittedly, it's quite a challenge to write about my own experiences through any other lens than my own—that of a White, male clinical psychologist in private practice in the Boston area who came of professional age in the early 2000s. Whenever possible, however, I've tried to include research and anecdotes that give voice to the diversity within the profession.

When I reference fellow therapists' experiences, some stories are about actual colleagues of mine. To honor and respect their experiences, I received their permission for their stories and names to be made public in this book. These colleagues are identified by first and last name. When I do not explicitly note that I'm discussing a real person, I've created a composite based on my experiences with different individuals over the course of my training and professional life. I have created (only first) names and backgrounds for such amalgamations that aren't necessarily associated with any given colleague I know.

Protection of confidentiality is of course paramount when discussing any clinical experiences with clients. Whenever I relay an anecdote about rewarding or challenging experiences that involved a client, I have sufficiently deidentified them by changing their name and facets of their identifying characteristics such as gender, ethnicity, socioeconomic status, diagnoses, presenting difficulties, and clinical experiences relevant to the client and my work with them.

I now invite you on this journey of affirming your place in the honorable world of being a psychotherapist. If the pitfalls to sustainable self-care for psychotherapists have innocently been created in your past, are accidentally maintained in your present, and will be unwittingly proliferated into your future, let's accept what has been and change what we can. I wish you much peace, success, and thriving in this noblest of endeavors.

PART I NOURISHING THE
ROOTS OF SELF-CARE

INTRODUCTION: NOURISHING THE ROOTS OF SELF-CARE

Whoever you are, no matter how lonely, the world offers itself to your imagination, calls to you like the wild geese, harsh and exciting—over and over announcing your place in the family of things.

—Mary Oliver

I have a Guiana chestnut plant (also known as a money tree) in my bedroom. I absolutely love it, and I feel peaceful every time I pass by this hearty and majestic-looking plant. I take pleasure in watering it, knowing that I'm actively contributing to its health and longevity. In fact, it responds so well to water and light that it's flourished over the months I've had it. Beyond reading the care instructions on the tag embedded in the soil, I have gotten to know how much light and water help it grow in optimal ways. I have learned what this particular plant needs, although my knowledge is far from complete, because if I took this plant to another location, I'd have to learn once again how to care for it under those new conditions.

This section, Nourishing the Roots of Self-Care, is where our self-care evolutionary journey begins. This book purposefully does not start with self-care practices or strategies. Rather, for self-care to become a truly sustainable force in our lives, we need to look to more foundational aspects of how to think about self-care and what it means to us. If self-care is primarily conceptualized as a reaction to aversive conditions, for example, then we can become victims of circumstance, and self-care becomes a reactive afterthought. If self-care is too narrowly or vaguely defined, then we're left adrift at sea searching for a life raft to keep us afloat in rough waters.

Nourishing our self-care roots also means that we more fully appreciate and validate what we're up against in this challenging and demanding but gratifying job. Our unique occupational stresses and hazards are to be understood and deeply honored for our professional and personal self-care to hold special meaning and to be cultivated in a sustainable fashion. But we must not forget to appreciate why and how we ended up in this profession in the first place. It's hard to weather the storms and maintain self-care over time if we don't take stock of what brought us here and is keeping us engaged and inspired.

As we explore the meanings of self-care and the hazards and rewards of our profession, we will also turn to our values to help guide our well-being. What really matters to us and why it matters can serve as our compass as we navigate the twists and turns of our personal and professional lives. Yes, there will be detours and roadblocks along the way. But if our own self-caring is perceived as a humanistic and ethical imperative, then we can more readily turn toward ourselves with the compassion we offer our clients. Psychotherapist self-care then stops being a luxury or burden and starts becoming a way of being, unquestioned and unstoppable.

1

EXPLORING PROFESSIONAL SELF-CARE

Myths, Mistaken Identities, and Meanings

The cure of the part should not be attempted without treatment of the whole.

—Plato

Joanna, an early-career licensed professional counselor and mother of two, has had her fair share of struggle. While she was working at a mental health clinic for several years, she and her husband found themselves unable to start a family on their own. After they adopted a 9-month-old boy, Joanna became increasingly aware that their son had significant reactive attachment difficulties. As these challenges were being formally discovered, Joanna became pregnant with a daughter who, now 6 years old, was recently diagnosed with autism.

Joanna had quit her job a few years back and devoted herself full time to her children, but because of significant financial struggles in her family, Joanna decided to reenter the workforce. She sees clients part time during the morning and early afternoon hours in an office she sublets from a colleague. She then rushes to her children's school by midafternoon to pick them

https://doi.org/10.1037/0000309-002
The Thriving Therapist: Sustainable Self-Care to Prevent Burnout and Enhance Well-Being,
by M. A. Hersh

up and start her "second shift." Joanna is no stranger to the earnest advice and urging from her mother, some of her friends, and a former supervisor: "Please take better care of yourself, Joanna. You seem so stressed."

We all might know a Joanna in our lives, or perhaps we are Joanna. Even if Joanna's situation doesn't resonate, we all can likely identify with the idea that life can be quite unpredictable, unforgiving, and even cruel at times. We can align with the feeling of having little choice in big matters; self-care might seem like the last thing on our minds as we struggle to keep our everyday lives operating in the most basic ways. Let's keep Joanna close in our minds and hearts as we enter the realm of self-care—its myths and mistaken identities as well as the healthy possibilities of how we can become our own best allies and advocates.

MYTHS AND MISTAKEN IDENTITIES OF SELF-CARE

You may have heard suggestions similar to those Joanna received from her well-intentioned colleagues and loved ones. But alas, sustainable self-care isn't that easy, nor is it always what it seems. The sheen our popular culture has buffed out has made self-care appear superficial at best and frustratingly unattainable at worst. Although the tide is certainly turning, for a few decades self-care had become a buzzword, a trend, and a fad. And like anything that floats through the media unchecked, the idea of self-care was often accompanied by misleading or unhelpful images and conceptualizations. These popularized self-care symbols have proven quite limiting and distracting.

As a teacher and practitioner of mindfulness meditation and energy psychology, I'm often on the lookout for how mind–body practices are portrayed. During the last two decades, as yoga and meditation have increased in their popular appeal, magazine covers have repeatedly featured (usually) thin, well-sculpted White women in yoga pants in a lush meadow or hovering above the ground with fingers arranged in a particular mudra. The innuendo is that meditation and yoga are reserved for only certain types of people and requires being somewhere special or wearing or doing something special. In fact, *Bad Yogi* (Howell, 2019) made a very strong argument to this effect, critiquing the 2019 January/February edition of *Yoga Journal* (and *Yoga Journal* itself) for this kind of biased, misleading, and noninclusive messaging.

If this type of branding of self-care can be considered too narrow and exclusive, the other end of the spectrum—overly broad and nondescript— is just as problematic. Ariel Botta, PhD, MSW, LiCSW, former director of group psychotherapy in the inpatient and outpatient psychiatry departments at

Boston Children's Hospital, spoke to the definitional and prescriptive dilemma that so many of us face (A. Botta, personal communication, September 2016). In meeting with hundreds of trainees over the last 2 decades, Dr. Botta noted that the vast majority of supervisees were never exposed to self-care training, and those who were exposed to some degree tended to be told to "do more self-care" and to "remember to take good care of yourselves because being a therapist is hard work." These trainees, however, weren't necessarily given a self-care model, a deeper rationale, practical guidance, space to explore barriers to implementation, or ways to integrate self-care into daily life. California State University social work professors Drs. Kathy Cox and Sue Steiner strongly echoed this sentiment as they noted how their social work students were unclear about the meaning of self-care, frustrated when encouraged to practice it, and insistent that there simply wasn't enough time (see K. Jackson, 2014).

Self-care has popularized itself with trendy notions of taking a well-deserved and much needed break. These well-intentioned offerings often involve luxurious bubble baths, indulging in a pint of your favorite ice cream, getting your nails done, and going away with friends for a spa day. The quintessentially supportive friend might compassionately suggest, "You deserve it, sweetie." If we're attentive to the subtle language often used when these self-care/pampering activities are suggested or justified, we also get a glimpse into the accidental disservice being done. "You deserve it," "You've worked so hard today; just take a nice weekend away doing nothing"— on the surface, these statements are perfectly reasonable, and they may be 100% true. However, the subtle implication of "deservingness" to engage in a self-care activity can create a conditional relationship between taking good care of yourself only when or because you've worked so hard and now can feel justified and guilt-free.

Lest this issue appear largely rhetorical, we can look directly to company and clinic policies that grant employees sick days or time off only after they've accumulated enough work time. Essentially, these policies reinforce the notion in very stark, sobering, and insidious ways that you're only allowed to be sick or to rest (and still be paid) when you've not been sick and haven't rested yet. There is a promising trend, however, for some companies to grant more flexible or even unlimited paid time off without needing to justify personal time to tend to self-care, take a short break, recover from an illness, or care for a loved one. In other words, these newer policies reflect a more compassionate view of reality. They suggest that tending to our personal lives matters for productive work and company well-being rather than work productivity serving as a justification that our personal lives and well-being matter too.

A good friend of mine and psychotherapist colleague works for a university counseling center. Although his job is quite stressful and busy, his sick days are unlimited, and he enjoys 4 weeks of vacation per year with unused days rolled over to the next calendar year. His former job in a large group practice, however, operated quite differently. Within a fee-for-service model, being sick or needing personal or family time meant immediate loss of income. Thus, his workplace policies placed contingencies and constraints on his ability to care for himself and his loved ones. We can already see how self-care isn't entirely a solo endeavor. It's supported or inhibited by the systems in which we're embedded.

WHY IS SELF-CARE SO SELFISH?

If you've ever heard or felt that self-care is selfish, you're in good company. Apparently self-care is also greedy, self-indulgent, weak, or even self-pitying. Self-care can also evoke a more flowery and new-agey sentiment of self-love, which can almost certainly cause some people (but not psychotherapists, of course) to run for the hills in disgust. If self-care is selfish or weak, for example, and we find it shameful to consider ourselves selfish or weak, then we're at risk of ignoring even our most basic needs in the service of not embodying those qualities.

Given the time, energy, and presence we devote to our clients, purposeful self-care can sometimes feel burdensome or unnecessary. I've heard many of the following attitudes uttered from fellow therapists themselves. I too may be guilty of one or two or five of these myself.

- I'm fine, and the work isn't *that* bad.
- I really do love my job. I can't be burned out.
- Self-care feels too much like a luxury at this point.
- I don't have many high-risk clients right now, so I'm not sure I need to take special care of myself.
- I plan really nice summer vacations, so that's my saving grace.
- I can't afford to be burned out and overwhelmed. I just don't have the time, energy, or money for that.

TOWARD MORE MEANINGFUL CONCEPTUALIZATIONS OF SELF-CARE

"And should the cabin lose pressure, oxygen masks will drop from the overhead area. Please place the mask over your own mouth and nose before assisting others." This famously heard *oxygen mask rule* is announced on almost every airline around the world. Why is this rule so important in an emergency like the loss of cabin pressure at 30,000 feet in the air, and why do psychotherapists in particular need to heed this counsel as an ongoing form of self-care? Even in emergencies, we must make sure we're as equipped as we can be to help others as best we can. This preparedness means having a steady flow of oxygenated air in the event of cabin pressure volatility. And it means having our wits about us in a moment of acute suicidality in our office or when chased around a therapy room by a highly disturbed teen in the midst of a manic episode.

Yasmine Jameelah, the founder of Transparent and Black, helps Black people heal from intergenerational trauma through her unique wellness collective. In her advocacy and teachings, she encourages us to heed the fact that "we are nothing to anyone if we cannot pour into ourselves first, and let our self-care overflow and extend to others as communal care" (Stessman, 2021). When we purposefully fill our cups, each hour, each day, and each week of every year, we are creating sustainable self-care.

It is quite true that we cannot pour anything from an empty cup. Psychotherapist, author, and speaker Robin Stone, LMHC, of Positive Psychological Associates in Manhattan noted, "if I'm exhausted, distracted, or in distress, I'm no good for my clients or myself. Making time and space for self-care is just as critical as knowing and applying effective psychotherapy interventions" (Stone, 2020). Embedded within this thinking is that therapist self-care is not a luxury nor is it a pursuit of perfection. It's the recognition of our common human condition and that psychotherapists must treat ourselves as humans first and psychotherapists second.

It may be self-evident but bears intentional expression: Self-care, in its most basic sense, is the act of an individual giving care to themself. This definition of course is overly simplified and not nuanced. However, in pursuit of expanding and creating more applied nuance to this self-care definition, we can look to Dr. Catherine Cook-Cottone, psychologist, author, educator, and yoga teacher, who described self-care as the "daily process of being aware of and attending to one's basic physiological and emotional needs" (see https://www.catherinecookcottone.com). Although we can always try to seek support from our environment and others around us, at the end of the day "it is absolutely an inside job in most cases, which is invaluable, because we are the person most available to us," said Aviva Chanksy Guttmann, LMSW, a couples and relationship therapist and energy psychology practitioner (Guttmann, 2021). Thus, the vast majority of this book is about self-assessment and self-practice, even if we are connected to others in pursuit of assistance, feedback, and guidance and still rely on others for support and fulfillment.

The self-care reflection break, Self-Care Definitions and Metaphors to Ponder (Exhibit 1.1), illustrates the diversity of ways we can think about (professional) self-caring. Having multiple perspectives on self-care grants us freedom to choose what resonates best with our unique life philosophy, sensibilities, and lifestyle at any given time. I believe that this approach ultimately paves a more easily accessible road to self-care sustainability.

EXHIBIT 1.1. Self-Care Reflection Break: Self-Care Definitions and Metaphors to Ponder

Self-care can be defined as a multidimensional, multifaceted process of purposeful engagement in strategies that promote healthy functioning and enhance well-being.
—Katherine Dorociak, PhD
(Dorociak et al., 2017)

Self-care is attending to a wholeness that we already assume is possible within ourselves. It's noticing what's absent in order to feel whole and feel content and then act to fill that void to flourish.
—Chris Berlin, MDiv
(C. Berlin, personal communication, October 2016)

Similar to a varied food diet, we can integrate a variety of self-care elements to sustain our functioning for both surviving and thriving. And we must evaluate what is missing from our self-care diet (e.g., creativity, self-reflection, mastery, interpersonal connection, etc.) for optimal health and thriving.
—Cory Chen, PhD
(C. Chen, personal communication, September 2016)

There are three important facets of professional self-care: 1) your own worthiness; 2) that self-care is a *nonnegotiable* part of your job; and 3) deep self-knowing—the capacity to discern your needs at any given time.
—Marci Evans, MS, CEDRD-S, LDN, cPT
(M. Evans, personal communication, October 2016)

Self-care is the dynamic process of remaining and returning to being whole within ourselves. Using deep self-awareness, we can experientially know what wholeness feels like so that when separation within the self occurs, we are better able to compassionately acknowledge this and then return ourselves to being whole once again.
—Thomas Richardson, LiAC, MA
(T. Richardson, personal communication, September 2016)

Self-care is anything we do to purposefully nurture ourselves on a regular basis (e.g., think about the foods we consume, notice when our bodies feel run down, cultivate bare awareness of internal and external experience, conscious breathing, etc.).
—Ariel Botta, PhD, MSW, LiCSW
(A. Botta, personal communication, September 2016)

Self-care includes three essential elements: 1) self-awareness, 2) self-regulation, and 3) balance. Self-awareness, however, is foundational in helping to cultivate better regulation and balance in our lives.
—Ellen Baker, PhD
(Baker, 2003, as discussed by E. Wise, personal communication, October, 2016)

As the absence of illness is not health, we must actively cultivate our well-being and make purposeful efforts to foster "the enduring quality in one's professional functioning over time and in the face of professional and personal stressors" (Coster & Schwebel, 1997, p. 5). Drs. Jeffrey Barnett and Erica Wise, two prominent psychologists at the intersection of professional ethics and self-care, echoed this sentiment, noting that self-care efforts in general should be positive actions that promote wellness and effective coping and involve the avoidance of negative coping behaviors (e.g., self-medication through alcohol and drugs, sexual boundary violations) that will likely exacerbate difficulties over time (Wise & Barnett, 2016). Moreover, Wise and Reuman (2019) suggested that we can indeed promote a competent and flourishing lifelong professional practice that incorporates deliberate self-care, values-based engagement, and positive and supportive relationships.

Broad-based conceptualizations of professional self-care have been unpacked, revealing several different facets. For example, Carroll and colleagues (1999) categorized self-care activities as a professional's inner work and growth, interpersonal support, professional development, and engagement in recreational activities. In an excellent review of mental health practitioner self-care, Posluns and Gall (2020) organized the empirical literature on professional self-care within six core domains: awareness, balance, flexibility, physical health, social support, and spirituality. Dorociak and colleagues (2017) identified five discrete, empirically derived domains of self-care among practicing psychologists parsed into: professional support, professional development, life balance, cognitive awareness, and daily balance.

Finally, Dr. Catherine Cook-Cottone, who developed the now widely researched Mindful Self-Care Scale (MSCS; Cook-Cottone, 2015; Cook-Cottone & Guyker, 2017), revealed 10 self-care dimensions in accordance with her attuned representational model of self (Cook-Cottone, 2006): nutrition/hydration, exercise, self-soothing, self-awareness/mindfulness, rest, relationships, physical/medical, environmental factors, self-compassion, and spiritual practice. In the abbreviated version of the scale, six dimensions have been empirically derived: physical care, supportive relationships, mindful self-awareness, self-compassion and purpose, mindful relaxation, and supportive structure. The MSCS has been shown to correlate positively with mental health practitioners' compassion satisfaction and negatively with burnout and compassion fatigue (Scaletta, 2021). Mindful self-care also appears beneficial for budding mental health trainees (Sünbül et al., 2018) and hospice workers (Hotchkiss, 2018), to name just a few important helping professional populations in need of appropriate, flexible, and enduring care of the self.

One of the more comprehensive and integrative approaches to psychotherapist self-care was promoted by Norcross and Guy (2007; see also Norcross & VandenBos, 2018) in their popular book *Leaving It at the Office: A Guide to Psychotherapist Self-Care.* They highlighted a number of core principles of which to stay mindful throughout one's career, such as focusing on rewards rather than failures and setbacks; fostering creativity, diversity, and growth at work; setting boundaries between therapists' professional and personal lives; nurturing relationships; and restructuring cognitions. In their approach, Norcross and colleagues employed a mix of tools for cultivating such self-care and lifestyle habits including mindfulness, cognitive behavioral methods, spirituality, positive psychology, and foundations of physical wellness. Norcross and VandenBos (2018) didn't mince words as they implored us to honor that "self-care is not a narcissistic luxury to be fulfilled as time permits . . . it is a human requisite, a clinical necessity, and an ethical imperative" (p. 15). Self-care is, as psychotherapist Dr. Zoe Shaw, PsyD, MFT, illuminated, "a continual reckoning with your soul where you make a declaration: I am worthy to be cared for!" (Shaw, 2020). Marci Evans, MS, CEDRD-S, LDN, cPT, registered eating disorder dietician, emphatically echoed this sentiment: "It is our non-negotiable priority" (M. Evans, personal communication, October 2016).

HOW DO PSYCHOTHERAPISTS TYPICALLY CARE FOR THEMSELVES?

To take good enough care of ourselves, personally and professionally, it behooves us to know who we are, as people and as the therapeutic instruments we're humbly aiming to keep in tune. Fundamentally, we must also keep in mind that all of us—no matter how advanced or expert at our craft and no matter how skilled we are at various aspects of life—are perfectly imperfect. We are all flawed, and that's simply the way it goes.

We bring ourselves into our practices, and our practices bring themselves into us. For example, if we become gently aware of the toll that an aging parent with dementia has been taking on our emotional well-being, we could become increasingly aware of our shorter fuse in everyday life. This awareness is crucial for how we operate in our professional roles, particularly if material in clients' lives triggers a sense of helplessness, loss, and emotional burden. Conversely, if we're working with several traumatized clients who have been recounting their childhood experiences of loss and powerlessness, we may end up taking these visceral feelings home with us. Purposeful self-care is thus necessary to prevent spillover from work to home and to protect against occupational stress syndromes.

So what do the data reveal about how psychotherapists tend to take care of themselves? Before reading on, what are your educated guesses about the go-to strategies, activities, or practices that your fellow practitioners employ for self-care? In a study of 400 practicing psychologists, Case and McMinn (2001) found that the most commonly used self-care strategies included the use of meditation and prayer, socializing with friends, maintaining a diversity of professional roles, maintaining relationships with one's family of origin as well as with friends, and engaging in relaxation activities to promote one's well-functioning. Mahoney (1997) found that mental health professionals endorsed previous-year self-care activities in a wide variety of areas, including (a) engaging in hobbies for pleasure, (b) taking trips or vacations, (c) attending creative and artistic events, (d) engaging in physical exercise, and (e) participating in peer consultation or supervision.

Cooper (2009) found an overlapping but distinct set of highly used self-care strategies in a sample of practicing psychologists who employed the use of humor (91.4%); relaxing activities such as meditation, yoga, and reading (85.6%); taking vacations (82.9%); exercise (75.2%); scheduling breaks throughout the day (67.6%); engaging in positive self-talk (66.7%); and use of email lists and professional affiliations (61.3%). Rupert and Kent (2007) conducted a large-scale survey of mostly married (75%), White (95%), mid-career (i.e., 18 years after licensure) clinical psychologists (83%). They found a similar profile of career-sustaining behaviors as the aforementioned surveys. Maintaining a sense of humor, self-awareness, and a values-based professional identity were rated as some of the most important. Following closely behind were balancing work and personal life, spending time with partners and friends, and maintaining a sense of control over work responsibilities.

In many ways the data from the four surveys fit fairly well into the aforementioned categorizations empirically derived by Dorociak and colleagues (2017) and Cook-Cottone and Guyker (2017) and proposed by Posluns and Gall (2020) and Norcross and VandenBos (2018). Interestingly, when psychotherapists (i.e., psychologists, social workers, counselors, and marriage and family therapists) were asked about what kinds of career-sustaining behaviors they used the most, the top five involved a somewhat similar but divergent set of strategies that practitioners use to stay afloat, engaged, and resilient: (a) maintaining a sense of humor, (b) viewing client problems as interesting, (c) renewing and relaxing with leisure activities, (d) maintaining objectivity about clients, and (e) seeking case consultation without fear of burdening colleagues (Kramen-Kahn & Hansen, 1998).

One of the most important takeaways from these self-care conceptualizations and survey-based data is the principle of being purposeful in our thoughts and actions. By adopting an intentionality to our self-care, we become actors in our own plays rather than audience members watching our lives unfold. Even if we don't have the "perfect" self-care plan (whatever that is), when we act with wakeful self-awareness we can choose what will ultimately be of best help across our development, career phase, and the inevitable ups and downs of life.

To understand ourselves and our current degree and quality of self-care in a variety of life domains, we can turn to three helpful self-assessments (which are by no means the only ways of gaining feedback about how we're treating ourselves and managing in the world). Exhibit 1.2 includes several thought-provoking questions that can foster a sense of ownership and accountability for self-caring actions. Notice how you are answering these questions. If you're feeling overwhelmed or disillusioned by these inquiries or are unable to say "yes" to many of these questions, you're likely in a particular state or circumstance right now (or have been for quite some

EXHIBIT 1.2. Self-Care Reflection Break: Self-Assessment of Your Current Level of Professional Self-Care

Do you (consistently enough):

- appear competent and professional?
- appear warm, caring, and accepting?
- regularly seek case consultation with another professional while protecting confidentiality?
- at the end of a stressful day, frequently utilize self-talk to put aside thoughts of clients?
- maintain a balance between work, family, and play?
- nurture a strong support network of family and friends?
- use healthy leisure activities as a way of helping yourself relax from work? If work is your whole world, watch out! You do not have a balanced life.
- often feel renewed and energized by working with clients?
- develop new interests in your professional work?
- perceive clients' problems as interesting and look forward to working with clients?
- maintain objectivity regarding clients' problems?
- maintain good boundaries with clients, allowing them to take full responsibility for their actions while providing support for change?
- use personal psychotherapy as a means of maintaining and/or improving your functioning as a psychotherapist?
- maintain a sense of humor? You can laugh with your clients.
- act in accordance with legal and ethical standards?

Note. From "Do You 'Walk Your Talk'?" by B. Kramen-Kahn, 2002, *The Maryland Psychologist, 44*(3), p. 12. Copyright 2002 by the Maryland Psychological Association. Adapted with permission.

time) that demands some extra compassionate attention and further exploration of the principles and practices found within the body of this book and other resources offered in the appendices. Conversely, you may be able to answer affirmatively to many of these items. Then you can check these "yeses" against how you're feeling from day to day, week to week. Is there a noticeable discrepancy between your answers to these questions and your gut-level assessment? What might that mean for you right now?

Second, we can explore our self-caring tendencies from a somewhat more historical and birds-eye perspective. In her book *Caring for Ourselves: A Therapist's Guide to Personal and Professional Well-Being*, Dr. Ellen Baker (2003) offered a compassionate mirror to reflect on why we entered this field in the first place, the kinds of professional expectations we hold, and coping approaches we enact to help keep ourselves in healthy balance (see Exhibit 1.3). Answering these questions as honestly as possible can offer us insight into what does and doesn't work very well in our professional life, and such authentic self-inquiry can grant us access into hidden resources and self-caring possibilities that we may never have contemplated.

The third powerful self-assessment resource for self-care, the MSCS (Cook-Cottone, 2015; Cook-Cottone & Guyker, 2017), comes in two forms. The 33-item online version (http://ed.buffalo.edu/mindful-assessment/scale/assessment.html) provides immediate feedback about six domain scores and a self-care total. Based on the range in which your scores fall, you'll receive feedback about tips and strategies to encourage paying more attention to what's missing from your self-care plate. The 84-item version of the MSCS (see Appendix A) incorporates more subdomains of self-care, such as

---

EXHIBIT 1.3. Self-Care Reflection Break: Self-Assessment of Self-Care Needs

What initially drew you to the field of mental health service/psychotherapy?

Briefly describe what makes a "good day" for you at work. In contrast, what makes a "bad day"?

What have been the significant periods/challenges during your career related to professional or personal stresses?

What would you say are your current professional concerns/stressors?

How do you know when you're under stress?

What do you consider your greatest challenge regarding self-care?

How does your work as a psychotherapist differ from what you expected?

What has been most helpful for you regarding taking care of yourself and maintaining resiliency in your professional and personal life?

Note. Adapted from *Caring for Ourselves: A Therapist's Guide to Personal and Professional Well-Being* (pp. 55–58), by E. Baker, 2003, American Psychological Association (https://doi.org/10.1037/10482-000). Copyright 2003 by the American Psychological Association.

nutrition, environmental factors, and rest. After completing this version by hand, you can tally these scores (instructions are given in Appendix A) and evaluate if any self-care domains have an average score under 3. Scores well under a cutoff of 3 indicate a need to pay particular attention to that arena of your life, which may be strained or compromised for a variety of reasons. Not all domains of self-care, however, can be tended to equally at all times. As self-caring is a constantly evolving process, these data are simply information about how you're doing in the last week or so, not necessarily how your life has been or will be in the future. Taking conscious action based on this self-assessment, however, can change your personal and work life for the better.

Finally, the *Self-Care Manual for Front-Line Workers* (OCHA, 2020; https://www.humanitarianresponse.info/en/operations/lebanon/document/lebanon-national-self-care-manual-enar) is a guide for crisis workers at high risk of occupational hazards, some like those we experience as psychotherapists. This manual is backed by the United Nations Office for the Coordination of Humanitarian Affairs (https://www.humanitarianresponse.info/) and the Republic of Lebanon's Ministry of Public Health (https://www.moph.gov.lb/). Within the manual is a treasure trove of guidance as well as two self-assessments well worth exploring. One assessment helps determine the frequency of self-caring behaviors across five life domains, whereas the other (i.e., Headington Self-Care and Lifestyle Inventory) helps us assess how often we've engaged in a variety of self-care actions within the month. This inventory provides a total score that we can compare to cutoff ranges that ultimately help us determine what we may need to modify.

PROFESSIONAL SELF-CARE: INTEGRATED VERSUS ADD-ON

If you've gotten a bit overwhelmed along the way reading about all the various ways in which psychotherapists engage in self-care, take heart and let's pause here. Self-care is not a competition to see who can use humor the most in client sessions to possibly stave off impending compassion fatigue. Self-care is not a race to see who gets to the self-awareness finish line first. And self-care certainly shouldn't feel like you're simply adding up activities to do, somehow tipping the balance toward well-being and away from suffering and burnout. Rather, we can think of self-care to be integrated, infused, embedded, and embodied for our professional and personal benefit. If going to the gym for a designated time each week helps you and is accommodated within your personal life, keep it up. If finding the time to do physical activity outside the house feels impossible right now, don't force it. Maybe you negotiate it with yourself or loved ones, or maybe you don't. Perhaps you watch (and do) a yoga DVD at home or use an app to do 8-minute high-intensity interval training three times per week. Or maybe you go for a brisk walk as often as you can, even for a few minutes.

Integrating such self-care activities during your workday is also a wonderful idea. Doing some wall stretches in between clients to open up the chest can help correct for the hunched postures many of us find ourselves in for hours. Doing a 60-second loving-kindness meditation before a difficult client enters and leaves the office infuses self-caring in an inspiring and uplifting way. Listening to a humorous podcast or video on your commute home can alleviate the heaviness of the day and help you transition to home. And mentally putting away your client files to engage in your personal or family life supports presence of mind and the nowness of your body. We will return to this notion of integrated self-caring throughout the book, focusing on some practical tips in the penultimate chapter on infusing and integrating self-caring into everyday life.

A WORD ON PSYCHOTHERAPIST SELF-CARE IN THE COVID-19 PANDEMIC

Where does one begin when discussing how COVID-19 has changed the face of the world in general and the ways in which psychotherapists have had to do our jobs and take care of ourselves? It would be one thing if we had been asked to "go remote" for a few months and then returned to our offices after a brief tele-mental health hiatus. But this has not been the case at all. The entire world shut down. Some of us got sick. Some of us know others who contracted the virus. And some of us heartbreakingly have lost loved ones, friends, neighbors, and clients to this viral siege.

Although many of us have been fortunate enough to continue to work, pay our rent and mortgage, and put food on the table through this trying time, some of us have struggled considerably as clients gradually faded from our weekly caseload and as schools, clinics, and treatment facilities shifted to remote-only or some hybrid type of support. In initially setting up our home offices, we worked out of our bathrooms, off of our beds, in corners of our living rooms or kitchens, and in tiny closets that we transformed into offices. And yet, some of us were required to continue to show up to our offices, hospitals, or schools. We were/are the frontline workers risking our lives to serve others.

It's not just our Wi-Fi bandwidths that have been challenged. Spouses and children were also on Zoom while we were trying to run our virtual sessions without asking clients to repeat themselves 20 times an hour. We've also been emotionally, physically, cognitively, and spiritually taxed beyond belief. Screen drain has depleted our energy, and our physical posture and eyesight have taken a hit. While counseling our highly anxious clients with obsessive-compulsive disorder on how to protect but not overprotect themselves from COVID, we too have been managing our anxieties about how to protect but not overprotect ourselves from COVID. In fact, the case could be made for an increased risk for experiencing a host of occupational hazards (e.g., secondary traumatic stress and vicarious traumatization) as we've listened to clients speak to their own harrowing experiences and living with painful uncertainty as the pandemic drags us forward. I have often found myself simply validating how hard this point in time really is while being at a profound loss to offer anything beyond radical acknowledgment.

As the months went by, I developed an internal policy never to directly advise someone with COVID anxiety on whether they "should" enter situations that they deem too risky. It is not my place, even within an anxiety-exposure or psychological-flexibility paradigm, to accidentally put a client (and their loved ones) in harm's way. I can help only to reconnect these clients with their values and the things that ultimately matter to them within the constant strain and struggle of this unprecedented and unrelenting pandemic.

Uncertainties about when life might return to some semblance of normalcy have become commonplace. Some of us, in fact, are in very high-risk groups, with compromised immune systems, heart conditions, and chronic illnesses. My one-lung status certainly isn't preferable when a horrific respiratory condition is literally floating through the air. My wife and I were forced to keep our children home, resulting in their being two of only a few remote-only students in their school. This situation has certainly taken its toll on their mental, emotional, and social development. When clients have asked me when we might return to in-person work, I have lamented that I wished it could be sooner but it's going to be later. Much later.

Psychotherapists Helena Colodro and Joe Oliver coauthored a book on practitioner self-care as it became clear that the pandemic had wormed its way into the foundation of our society and was burrowing fiercely and relentlessly. In *A Guide to Self-Care for Practitioners in Times of Uncertainty*, Colodro and Oliver (2020) offered several helpful principles and dialectics to hold in mind. They reminded us that we're not here to fix but rather to serve and support and that we're indeed all in this together (with colleagues and clients alike). Because the future is uncertain, we can all hold life a bit more lightly rather than clamping down on what "should" be. This approach has involved keeping an eye on impossible standards we set for ourselves (and our clients) and acknowledging that we're all grieving the loss of what was and what will (or won't) be. Colodro and Oliver also invited us to open up to and welcome new possibilities and opportunities given how the world essentially forced us to change anyway. Our strength through this pandemic may be measured more in how we flex and flow rather than how we cling to how things used to be.

Fortunately, we also had our own therapeutic organizations and businesses promoting self-care and ethical practice during the pandemic era and beyond. For example, when so many of us were thrust into teletherapy in 2020, Person Centered Tech, an innovative small business founded by the late Roy Huggins that synthesizes psychotherapy practice with technology and security, created an online conference, Thriving and Making Comfort. The conference included presentations on topics such as our collective trauma as mental health professionals, legal considerations for practicing during the pandemic, and reducing our personal–professional fatigue, to name a few. The longer we sit with the changes we are compelled to make, the more likely we will stand up to help ourselves and each other during this unprecedented time.

In this first chapter we've explored some foundational elements of what it can mean to offer ourselves care. The range of (professional) self-care conceptualizations is vast, but one of the most important aspects is to make your own meaning of the self-caring endeavor. Personalizing our own care allows for greater ease of sustainability and thus more opportunities for growth and thriving over time. This overarching principle is precisely what the balance of this book is all about.

We might ask, however, about why we should pay so much attention to sustainable self-care for therapists. Aren't we simply helping our fellow human beings? Sure, there can be a good deal of stress involved, but we work hard to change people's lives for the better. This is the real gift. But gifts can come with costs. You're now invited to hop in the boat with hundreds of thousands of other helpers like you who confront similar everyday struggles and strains and also the truly harrowing moments of working in this noblest of professions.

2 OUR UNIQUE STRESSORS, PRESSURES, AND CHALLENGES

We all make mistakes, have struggles, and even regret things in our past. But you are not your mistakes, you are not your struggles, and you are here NOW with the power to shape your day and your future.

—Steve Maraboli

> I have so much admiration for psychotherapists who do what you do. You sit with others' stress, suffering, and deep wish for a better life, hour after hour, day after day. And you still have your own life to live. I just don't know how you do it.

This compassionate statement of veneration came from a former client with quite the traumatic childhood. Echoing themes in her own life, she was in awe of how much we do for others while still needing to do for ourselves.

Psychotherapists occupy a highly unique role and an accompanying set of highly specified, sacred, and stressful occupational tasks. Unlike those in almost any other (helping) profession, including physicians, physical therapists, life coaches, and pharmacists, we can serve innumerable roles within

https://doi.org/10.1037/0000309-003

The Thriving Therapist: Sustainable Self-Care to Prevent Burnout and Enhance Well-Being, by M. A. Hersh

one therapy hour, in one psychotherapist "self" and for only one client, couple, family, or group. We are at once mindful listener, problem solver, curious inquisitor, supporter, perspective shifter, consultant, analyst, emotion processor, self-care advocate, diagnostician, validator, body coregulator, facilitator, relationship teacher, behavioral activator, memory reconsolidator, cheerleader, reframer, coach, guide, and healer. Then multiply that by however many hours you work each week. I would imagine that only a parent is within this range of varied and complex tasks within one role.

The complexities of our role as psychotherapist are emphasized here because our profession often gets oversimplified. Nuances are lost. We don't just "help people." We have been asked and have willingly chosen to accept an awesome set of responsibilities. We take care of the mental and mind–body health of people who were likely complete strangers before they entered our office, clinic, center, agency, school, court, hospital, or prison. We assess and guide whether couples can work it out or ultimately are on a path toward relationship dissolution. We help determine how seriously we should consider someone's thoughts of suicide, and then we must sit with or act on that knowledge. We listen and offer compassion to those grieving horrible loss and experiencing horrific trauma, and then we must say goodbye for the week only to say hello a few minutes later to the next client in need. We lend our warmth, abiding presence, and skillful guidance. Sometimes our observations, feedback, or recommendations are difficult to hear, and they're ignored or outright rejected. We help our clients to look inside their minds and bodies to become better friends with their inner cast of characters populating chaotic, confusing, or numbed interior worlds.

Some of the occupational stresses and pressures we may know all too well, while other aspects are largely unfamiliar. Some may be experienced acutely and sporadically, others more consistently and chronically. However you personally experience them, these tensions can be held with as much care and tenderness as possible. In fact, within the larger spirit of this book, you could imagine all of your fellow psychotherapists reading this chapter at the same time, nodding along with you knowing that we're all pretty much in the same boat.

HOW RESPONSIBLE ARE WE REALLY?

Psychotherapists are charged with sitting with some of the darkest parts of the human experience. Sometimes we bring a small candle and at other times a more luminous torch. When we say "yes" to working with that once complete stranger, we are entrusted to care not just for the thoughts they think and the feelings they feel. Their well-being and physical safety also become our purview.

Psychotherapists not only become responsible; a great many of us *feel* deeply responsible as well (Wise & Barnett, 2016). This sense of accountability can range from doggedly laissez-faire to a strong savior complex that can severely cripple our ability to remain balanced, grounded, and psychologically sound in relation to our clients' health and illness. In fact, Deutsch (1985) found that therapists' belief that "I must be totally competent and able to help everyone" was as significant a cause of stress as patients' troubling behaviors and as therapists' feelings of isolation in the workplace. Although we're implicitly charged with the task of helping people to feel and do better, we are not gods. Despite all the training we've gone through, all the continuing education courses we've taken, and all the consultation and supervision we've received, we cannot *cause* anything to happen for our clients even in their most desperate of hours.

Acupuncturist and traditional Chinese medicine practitioner Thomas Richardson noted that he explicitly doesn't label himself a healer for this exact reason (T. Richardson, personal communication, 2020). He knows that patients have to participate in their own recovery and wellness. If patients expect healing from him, the expectation he would hold for himself would necessarily be unrealistic and possibly detrimental. Rather, Richardson believes he is a facilitator of health, helping patients to move their subtle energies that they must then harness through their own self-caring actions.

The tension involved in how responsible we're really supposed to be comes quietly screaming out in the phenomenon of *imposter syndrome*, an experience many of us have known all too well during our careers. In *Sometimes Therapy Is Awkward*, marriage and family therapist Nicole Arzt (2020) artfully described our collective woes and wariness of being a clinician in today's world. Knowing our weaknesses as well as our strengths is a sign of strength, not weakness. As both our limitations and skills are ever evolving, we can take heart in knowing that nothing about our professional life is set in stone. In fact, feeling the need for deep authenticity as a therapist may belie the awkward reality of the necessary fakery many of us face every day (Goldman, 2007). Owning this inherent tension ultimately will serve us better than deluding ourselves out of it.

So what happens when progress is excruciatingly slow? What about no discernable change at all or degradation of functioning? In these cases, some therapists would consider the client or their condition to be "treatment resistant," whereas other therapists take a great deal of responsibility, beating themselves up along the way for missed therapeutic opportunities or failed interventions.

I once worked with a teenage boy who initially presented for therapy with social anxiety concerns. As we all know, when we take a good history and dig a bit deeper, we end up finding a lot more than we may have expected. This boy had a disturbingly uneasy sense of self and often had quite self-critical conversations in his head, yet he was very good at presenting as "just fine." Fast forward beyond some relatively successful therapeutic work on friendships and anxiety. This boy was then discovered to be pulling his hair out as a form of self-punishment for "being a bad kid." After relatively successful treatment of self-harm and addressing some of the underlying self-invalidation occurring below the surface, the boy turned to alcohol as his so-called "way out" of the incessant pain. Thus, despite more functional symptom abatement, crisis management work, and underlying self-concept exploration, the boy was contending with yet another manifestation of his deeper and more silent suffering.

How does a psychotherapist feel okay with what feels like spitting in the wind, watching certain clients continue to suffer despite our best efforts and even despite relatively successful work in some regards? Pragmatically, we try to step back and perhaps change tack. We seek consultation or supervisory support. We may refer the client to a colleague or specialist. But we, the theoretical agents of change, still must contend with our oversights, missteps, or just a plain ill-fated trajectory. We can take to heart, however, some of the simplest but most profound words ever shared to me by an intuitive/energy master I deeply trust: "You can help a lot of people. But you cannot help everyone. People come to you on their own journey. Try as you might, you simply may not be the one to change the course of their lives." This advice hurts because it can feel like failure, but it is actually a true gift in disguise.

OUR COMMON PROFESSIONAL STRESSORS AND PRESSURES

While some of our professional experiences may seem unique, personal, and isolated, they are, in fact, extremely common and woven into the fabric of our collective professional work (Norcross, 2000). First, it's important to note that the stresses delineated in this section aren't so cleanly compartmentalized and left sitting in our therapy chairs for the next day. Work demands and emotional exhaustion can in fact affect our home life, with deterioration in family functioning over time (Rupert et al., 2013). Fortunately, however, evidence suggests that the experience of greater control and mastery at work reduces work-to-family conflict, thus increasing family satisfaction at home (Rupert, Stevanovic, et al., 2012). We can also rest a bit easier in knowing that family support can increase work satisfaction through the reduction of family-to-work conflict (Rupert, Stevanovic, et al., 2012).

With these work–home crossover effects in mind, we can explore our most common challenges and experiences. Interacting with challenging clients tops the list, with virtually all of those surveyed (91%) endorsing it as a significant stressor (Cooper, 2009, as cited in Barnett, 2014; Mahoney, 1997). Not surprisingly, 91% also noted that record keeping and documentation were substantial hassles within the role of psychotherapist. A number of specific client behaviors have been identified as contributing to therapists' depletion and sadness. Clients' suicidal statements, hostility, agitation and depression, and apathy were all ranked among the highest stress-inducing and exhausting experiences (Deutsch, 1984; Farber, 1983; Farber & Heifetz, 1981). Psychotic and self-destructive behaviors, as well as personality-disordered presentations, also take their toll on the average psychotherapist (e.g., Wurst et al., 2010).

The suicidal elephant in the room must be acknowledged. It's not that most psychotherapists are unaware of the alarming and escalating rates of suicide in the world today (Stone et al., 2017) and that the grim possibility can show up at our door at any time. But it's the elephant tamers who often get left behind. The act of doing therapy with clients who are actively suicidal or have the potential to become so is among the most stressful and harrowing clinical work we do (Baerger, 2001). In fact, a staggering 50% of psychiatrists (and up to 30% of practicing psychologists) will lose at least one client to suicide over our careers (Chemtob et al., 1988; Pope, Sonne, & Greene, 2006; Pope & Tabachnick, 1994). It may be surprising to learn that the rates for psychiatry residents and psychology interns are not far behind. The trauma, loss, grief, and existential and professional crisis can be deeply profound (Pope, Sonne, & Greene, 2006).

Not long after I had completed my clinical internship, I learned that a supervisor's former client had taken his own life. I checked in with my supervisor a few times to make sure she was okay (enough), but I had no idea of the depths of her experience until years later when I too lost a client to suicide. In fact, this death occurred shortly after another active client ingested so much prescription pain medication that he theoretically could have died fairly instantly. This client survived but not without the unimaginable price anyone (and their family and friends) would pay for attempting to end their own life.

In the midst of such harrowing events, are we to assume that we weren't nearly as helpful as we could (or should) have been? Are we to conclude that we should have been "the one" to prevent such a horrific event, even if no one else could stop them either? Guided by the wisdom of Rabbi Laureate and author Harold Kushner (1997), we might ask ourselves, "How good do we think we really have to be?" This question is both a practical and spiritual one that begs our contemplation amid such crises of the human condition.

How do we cope with such devastation while providing comfort and solace, if appropriate, to the partner or family of the deceased? Some of us are never afforded the opportunity to speak to an aggrieved loved one, while others may feel ultimately responsible for not preventing the suicide, compelling us to want to hide or force ourselves to move on. As Wurst and colleagues (2010) suggested, nearly one third of therapists suffer severe distress from a patient's suicide. And how we immediately react to such a harrowing event predicts our future emotions and behavior up to 6 months into the future. Reaching out and accepting our humanity in such cases is undoubtedly a part of our healing.

It's not just client suicide that psychotherapists experience as a significant source of stress. The other side of that deeply disturbing coin is the act of being assaulted by a client. Between 35% and 40% of psychologists will be victims of a client assault during their careers (American Psychological Association, 2000), with 80% of survey participants reporting that they live in fear of such an act. Does this concern plague you, or does it linger inconspicuously in the corners of your mind? For individuals who have been physically or emotionally abused at some point, this fear of being aggressed upon may be a "live wire" in our bodies, easily triggered by a client's certain posturing or language.

Aside from the more harrowing events and conditions of psychotherapy are the more underacknowledged aspects with which most therapists can likely resonate. We really are flying blind with respect to knowing what lies in store for us when our clients walk through our (virtual) door each day. How often are you confronted with something you simply weren't expecting to show up in your clients' lives? Are you on guard or calmly prepared for the possibility that the next client on your schedule will come in with some news that may rattle you? The more seasoned a therapist you are, the more likely it is that you've heard it all. Perhaps nothing surprises you anymore, and yet your empathy, engagement, and concern for your clients' well-being still create distress and a sense of disruption in what we'd all like to perceive as a just and reasonable world.

In the TV show *Lucifer*, the devil, disguised as a very magnetically attractive Los Angeles nightclub owner, begins to meet with a psychotherapist. Notwithstanding the countless and obvious boundary and ethics violations that ensue, the therapist believes she is getting to know the "real" Lucifer as just another emotionally and relationally avoidant man despite his consistent attempts to tell her that he is the actual devil. When he finally reveals his true "devil face" to her, she is literally left catatonic for a week before beginning to recover from this surreal and traumatic experience.

Although hopefully none of us will encounter this degree of shock in our professional work, the average psychotherapist nevertheless endures stresses, pressures, and challenging experiences. The literature reveals five broad categories (Kramen-Kahn & Hansen, 1998), including business-related problems (e.g., economic uncertainty, record keeping), client-related issues (e.g., suicidal threats), personal challenges of the psychotherapist (e.g., constant giving, caring cycle), setting-related stressors (e.g., excessive workload), and evaluation-related problems (e.g., difficulty evaluating client progress). How do these categories play out in your actual experience as a psychotherapist? Are there some challenges that remain constants? Do some stressors show up predictably or more randomly? As we'll now explore, we are always contending with challenges in our personal lives that undoubtedly spill into our professional roles, whether we're aware of this or not.

OUR EVERYDAY LIVED EXPERIENCE AS MERE HUMANS

Stress is being felt at epidemic proportions. With 84% of Americans reporting that they feel some measure of afflictive emotions related to stress, it seems that most of us are wrestling with a tremendous daily burden (American Psychological Association, 2021). The vast majority of us are stressed about the future of our nation, the coronavirus pandemic, and political unrest and our political climate. Given that this level and quality of stress likely won't be vanishing any time soon, it's incumbent upon us to know our signature reactivities and get more familiar with our coping strategies.

What is your signature stress response? Do you curl up in a ball or stretch outward to the rest of the world? Do you accidentally engage in self-attack or attacks on others you love? How does it come out physiologically with your sleep, eating, and metabolic patterns? And how does the stress you feel show up in the therapy room? Let's pause here and take a look at the self-care reflection break (see Exhibit 2.1, Your Signature Stress Response) to elucidate this vital process further.

Despite insurance companies dubbing us "providers," and no matter how hard we try to be impartial helpers, we're still perfectly fallible humans and subject to the same struggles and vicissitudes of life as our clients (Wise et al., 2012), as well as the basic needs of any human being. However, the trouble is we can't necessarily let our hair down like our friends in other

EXHIBIT 2.1. Self-Care Reflection Break: Your Signature Stress Response

How would you describe your usual reactions to stress (actions, thoughts, feelings, relational habits, self-caring vs. self-denying)?

What are your external and internal triggers of stress?

What does it actually feel like to be in a chronically stressed state?

How might your stress affect client care?

• More distractable?

• Less patient and compassionate?

• More quick to advise vs. collaborate?

• More personal spillover of emotions from client to client?

• Fed up with clients who "won't change"?

Do you have a sense right now for how to help reprogram your habitual stress experience?

Note. From *Your Signature Stress Experience: Enhancing Your Mindful Awareness of the Sources, Experiences, and Impacts of Stress,* by M. A. Hersh, 2017 (https://s3.amazonaws.com/thrivingtherapistresources/Signature+Stress+Experience+Handout.pdf). Copyright 2017 by M. A. Hersh. Adapted with permission.

professions. One too many an awkward self-disclosure, and we're skating on ethical thin ice like the therapist I once heard about sharing her affinity for naked hot tubbing and how she felt such a strong friendship vibe with her client. Several poorly timed laughs or no laughs at all at clients' intended jokes can be (or be perceived as) insensitive at best and emotionally harmful at worst.

And yet we are human and continue to live our lives while trying to compartmentalize, regulate, and be as mindfully present as possible. Apparently debate on social media has focused on whether practitioners should even drink water, tea, or coffee during sessions (Turner, 2021). Some insist this isn't appropriate while others acknowledge our basic needs as needing to be satisfied. Here's my deep, dark confession. I drink a bit of coffee so I don't fall asleep from pandemic-anxiety sleep issues and my son's showing up in my bed with nightmares every 3 nights. I also consume plenty of water so I don't shrivel up like a raisin, lose focus, and have my contact lenses glued to my eyes. So, I guess I'm guilty as charged.

Erica Turner, LMFT, associate clinical director in the marriage and family therapy program at Virginia Tech and cofounder of Therapy Is Not a Dirty Word (https://therapyisnotadirtyword.com/), told of her longtime silent and stigmatized battle with obsessive–compulsive disorder, which wreaked havoc on her life (Turner, 2021). She was determined to out the beast, as it were, and fully embrace herself and her therapist self as a whole, fallible human being who struggles just like her clients and just like the rest of her fellow therapists. This destigmatizing, beyond mere knowledge of how we all struggle, seemed to save Ms. Turner from herself. As she powerfully questioned, "Who is this mythical therapist who has no pain, no fallibility, no body?" (Turner, 2021, p. 60).

Research suggests that as we sit with our clients, nearly half of us may be struggling with problems of irritability and emotional exhaustion (43%), insufficient sleep (44%), problems in our intimate relationships (38%), and doubts about our therapeutic effectiveness (42%; Mahoney, 1997). Other research shows that many of us experience uncertainty regarding whether we're using the best intervention for our clients (54%; Sherman & Thelen, 1998). Relationship difficulties, anxiety, self-esteem and self-confidence problems, attention-deficit/hyperactivity disorder, obsessive–compulsive disorder, posttraumatic stress, chronic fatigue, and chronic and acute illness all populate the lived experiences of so many of us (Johnson & Barnett, 2011; Pope & Tabachnick, 1994). Moreover, it may be surprising to learn that one study showed that 40% of psychologists are aware of colleagues whose psychotherapeutic work is affected by the use of drugs, while 60% know colleagues struggling with their jobs due to depression or burnout (Wood et al., 1985).

A very poignant series of articles on therapists' mental struggles in *The Psychotherapy Networker* (2021) reveal such trying experiences of vulnerability, emerging courage, and navigation of the uncertainty of our mental and emotional stability as we peddle our therapeutic wares to our often vulnerable and unstable clients. For example, trauma expert Dr. Janina Fisher learned over time to "[grow] muscles that said 'I'm not responsible for fixing everybody'" (p. 44). It had started when she got an urgent call in the middle of a therapy session from her sons' schools about how they had been expelled for selling drugs. George Faller—survivor of posttraumatic stress disorder, former firefighter, first responder on 9/11, and the founder of the New York Center for Emotionally Focused Therapy—acknowledged that "it isn't easy to learn self-care. Sometimes, you need to go through a fiery furnace to arrive at a place of centeredness" (p. 46).

Others, like trauma specialist Claudette Mestayer, LCSW, experienced not only severe postpartum depression but also the self-judgment of not having been able to help herself as well as she's able to help her clients (Mestayer, 2021). For Ms. Mestayer, throwing herself into her clinical work actually helped. But we should acknowledge that investing appropriate energy into our jobs isn't possible or helpful for everyone who is deeply suffering. In fact, for Michele Weiner-Davis, MSW, author and director of The Divorce Busting Center, the harrowing and long and winding journey with severe depression didn't allow her the ability to connect and be present as she had in the past (Weiner-Davis, 2021).

Whereas half of psychotherapists are known to have childhood histories of abuse and family dysfunction, research suggests that around one third of us may experience some form of abuse in our adult life (Pope & Feldman-Summers, 1992). In one study of therapists' experiences in their own therapy, well over half (61%) reported having had at least one episode of clinical depression, and close to one third (29%) disclosed experiencing suicidal ideation. A very sobering 4% of psychotherapists also reported attempting suicide (Pope & Tabachnick, 1994). Research by Gilroy et al. (2002) suggested a similar profile of suffering in a sample of counseling psychologists. Of respondents, 62% self-identified as depressed, and of that group, 42% reported experiencing suicidal ideation or behavior.

Even prior to becoming professional therapists, the majority of trainees surveyed during a suicide prevention workshop reported experiencing suicidal ideation (59%), and 5% had already attempted suicide (see Freedenthal, 2021, for reference to this study). The stigma against mental and emotional suffering in general and particularly toward mental health professionals, who are supposed to be shining beacons of health and well-being, suggests that we suffer in silence. Thoreau wasn't far afield in suggesting that the "mass of [wo]men lead lives of quiet desperation" (Thoreau, 1971, p. 8).

Let's take a moment to acknowledge and honor the realities of what we're up against. Just like you, your colleagues suffer too. And just like your colleagues, you are sometimes moving through life under a dark cloud. "But in the end," dear colleague, "it's only a passing thing, this shadow. Even darkness must pass. A new day will come. And when the sun shines it will shine out the clearer" (P. Jackson, 2002, 2:45:21). We must acknowledge our suffering and act compassionately unto ourselves. Whether it's obsessive–compulsive disorder, unresolved trauma, suicidal ideation, or a creeping alcohol problem, we're still just as human and worthy of support. Appendix B provides selected resources to support psychotherapists struggling with mental health challenges and includes other therapist and self-care support suggestions.

WHEN OUR HUMANITY ENTERS THE THERAPY ROOM

Perhaps not surprisingly, our natural human vulnerabilities combined with our professional stresses produce risk for compromised professional competence (Johnson et al., 2012). But this risk of reduced competence or even breaches in ethical behavior don't necessarily have to derive from therapists' distress or unusual circumstances. At baseline, therapists tend to see what they are conditioned to see as they navigate the rough seas of becoming and being a competent and ethical helper. Interestingly, as compared with the original research on the subject (Pope et al., 1987), contemporary therapists report that suspect and questionable therapist–client behaviors occur less frequently and tend to view such behaviors as less ethical than previously believed (Schwartz-Mette & Shen-Miller, 2018). These findings would indicate that to some extent we are, as Schwartz-Mette and Shen-Miller suggested, ships rising in the sea, lifted by changes in ethical codes and training over time.

But then, above and beyond our usual ways of perceiving our professional behaviors, we must consider therapists' experience of various forms of suffering as we're trying to help our clients with the same conditions. We are at risk of providing our prized services with diminished therapeutic fitness. We are not, in any way, shape, or form, blank slates on which to be projected. A variety of writers have long acknowledged that therapists' own mental and emotional ill health would have at least some impact on the therapeutic relationship and thus on clients' well-being and outcomes (e.g., Parloff et al., 1978). In surveying therapists' personal problems, Deutsch (1984) concluded that the vast majority of therapists who are personally stressed resign themselves to the fact that their professional behavior is somehow altered in the midst of a personal crisis.

This aligns with other research suggesting that the vast majority (74%) of practicing psychologists have experienced distress at some points during their work (Guy et al., 1989) and that more than one third of this group acknowledged that their distress negatively affected the quality of care they were providing. Pope et al. (1987) found that 60% of professionals end up working under enough distress that it would have a detrimental effect on the therapeutic relationship. In fact, in one study of psychologists, an estimated 5 to 15% demonstrated impaired behavior and delivery of care as a result of such distress (Laliotis & Grayson, 1985).

I know close colleagues whose children were killed, whose parents died unexpectedly, whose own therapists were killed in accidents, who were diagnosed with chronic illnesses, who went through marital dissolution and divorce, who had complicated pregnancies and postpartum psychotic depressive episodes, who have family members deeply suffering from physical and mental health issues (both acute and chronic), and who struggle with their own mental and emotional health conditions. These are not occupational hazards, per se, of being a psychotherapist specifically—these are the harsh realities of life. Period. And yet, these life events or chronic issues can become woven into the fabric of what it means to be a therapist working on others' behalf.

While we're taking care of the mental and emotional health of so many others each week, we may be contending with our own difficulties, which may pose serious obstacles to showing up for our clients with mindful presence, regulated emotions, sound decision making, and tempered countertransferential reactivity. Therapist, peacebuilder, and Sufi healer Dr. Sabrina N'Diaye experienced the mass death and destruction of COVID-19 that devastated the communities she inhabited. She noted that while doing grief work with her clients, her friends were dying all around her. On a break during an annual forgiveness retreat she was hosting online, N'Diaye learned that one of her dearest friends had died. Was she supposed to continue leading the retreat or take care of herself offline and suspend the meeting? N'Diaye decided to return to the retreat with her courage to be vulnerable as her saving grace. She was at once leader and participant, and she somehow knew to ask the fellow attendees for what she needed at that moment in time (N'Diaye, 2021).

As we become increasingly aware of the impact of our own struggles on our professional competence and on our relationships with our clients, we are sometimes forced to make very difficult decisions. Do we take extended time off to formally grieve the loss of a loved one? Do we share with our clients that we're facing a serious medical challenge and may need time off? What about individuals who become pregnant and need to figure out the right time to inform their clients or who have postpartum distress so severely that it affects everyday functioning? And what about the clients who are undergoing unsuccessful fertility treatments as you start showing? What happens when you're enduring major fertility problems and a client easily (or even accidentally) gets pregnant (Omin, 2020)?

As a matter of general course, we can tend to ourselves and our occupational hazards akin to managing chronic medical conditions wherein, for example, we take necessary medication, go to physical therapy, and know the limits of what our bodies can and cannot do. Hopefully, this lifestyle management approach can grant us the opportunity to be a few steps ahead (whenever possible)—preventing declining health, mitigating greater risk, and even thriving and living a valued life along the way.

MAKING SENSE OF OUR PROFESSIONAL ROLES

One of the more helpful frameworks for synthesizing the information presented in the previous section was offered by Dr. Leonard Pearlin (Pearlin et al., 1981). In his caregiving stress process model, Pearlin suggested that caregiver stress is a result of the dynamic interplay among five vulnerability and protective factors in therapists' personal and professional lives. Foundationally, we have *background and contextual stress*. For example, to what extent are we financially stressed or secure, and do we feel physically safe going to work every day? We then have our *primary role strain,* work stressors such as the issues that patients bring each week, whether traumatic material, aggressive posturing, suicidal ideation, and the like. The real-world impact of our primary stressors on our emotions and lived experience is our *secondary role strain.* For example, if you run a private practice and four patients cancel for the week (with enough advance notice), your income may take a significant hit, and you may feel this effect reverberate in your personal life throughout the month. Or your work with an actively suicidal client seen at 11 a.m. may send unsettling vibrations into your therapeutic encounters for the rest of the day, week, or month. Our external role strain can result in *intrapsychic strain,* the impact on our sense of self and mastery given the limited control and power we have over our daily therapeutic work. But all of this strain is mitigated and buffered by the *internal and external resources* we bring to our psychotherapist roles. For example, how proactive (vs. situationally reactive) is our coping, how supportive and available is our professional and personal network of connections, and what meaning do we make of the challenges and tragedies with which we're faced?

When we step back and look at how much is happening within and around us as we sit down to help our clients, we can hopefully appreciate that our particular helping role is quite special indeed. We develop a large toolbox of skills, we hone those skills over time, and we do our very best to use those skills to relieve others' suffering. And still, we are human and subject to the same pressures, strains, and hassles as our clients. Holding ourselves as lightly as possible in light of such stress is the ultimate form of self-care.

3 THE "BIG FOUR" OCCUPATIONAL HAZARDS

Burnout is what happens when you try to avoid being human for too long.

—Michael Gungor

Now that we've explored everyday stresses, pressures, and struggles, we turn to what we'll call the *Big Four occupational hazards*: burnout, compassion fatigue, secondary traumatic stress, and vicarious traumatization. These occupational hazards for psychotherapists are the most heavily researched and referenced. Although they have a good deal in common and sometimes are conflated with one another or considered interchangeable, they can be considered relatively distinct experiential phenomena and "syndromes." Importantly, they are not diagnostic or clinical phenomena, nor are they synonymous with depression, anxiety, or even everyday stress, although the experiential overlap is notable in many ways.

Although all four of these occupational hazards are indeed of great importance, the phenomenon of burnout is given relatively more attention. The rationale for this focus was based on utilitarian purposes more than anything

https://doi.org/10.1037/0000309-004
The Thriving Therapist: Sustainable Self-Care to Prevent Burnout and Enhance Well-Being,
by M. A. Hersh

else—that every single psychotherapist regardless of their workplace setting or populations they serve is at risk for burnout and that burnout is often identified as the most frequent stressful issue affecting therapeutic efficacy (e.g., Bearse et al., 2013). However, compassion fatigue, secondary traumatic stress, and vicarious traumatization should not be relegated to a status of relative unimportance. In fact, it is my hope that this chapter's treatment of the Big Four occupational hazards prompts further investigation of our own unique sets of therapeutic, workplace, and personal circumstances.

What the Big Four represent is what can happen (even) to highly dedicated, hard-working, well-intentioned psychotherapists who

- become emotionally depleted and interpersonally detached and feel a decreased sense of accomplishment over time because of an imbalance or mismatch between workplace demands and resources of the self (i.e., *burnout*);

- become more negative, cynical, distressed, and agitated from repeated empathic flooding and dissolution of interpersonal boundaries in the presence of clients' deep suffering (i.e., *compassion fatigue*);

- experience their own trauma symptomatology from exposure to clients' traumatic material (i.e., *secondary traumatic stress*); and

- take on a mental model of the world that reflects clients' suffering, trauma, or hopelessness (i.e., *vicarious traumatization*).

To what extent were these syndromes discussed in your professional training? Would you have become a psychotherapist if you had known that 40% to 56% of therapists report feeling moderate to high levels of burnout (e.g., McCormack et al., 2018)? If these occupational hazards were discussed in your trainings and professional development education, what precautions do you now take for yourself? Let's unpack each element of the Big Four so that we better appreciate what they are and what tends to predict them. Moreover, a nuanced understanding here will assist us for the balance of the book as we construct the most appropriate self-care practices and supports based on our particular occupational situations.

BURNOUT

As of 2017, there were well over half a million practicing mental health professionals in the United States alone (Bureau of Labor Statistics, 2017), approximately half of whom are likely experiencing moderate to high levels of burnout (Morse et al., 2012; Simionato & Simpson, 2018). Professional burnout, a term first coined in the 1970s (Freudenberger, 1975), is a syndrome (Maslach & Jackson, 1981) that involves decreased motivation and commitment to your work (i.e., *emotional exhaustion*), becoming interpersonally colder and more detached (i.e., *depersonalization*), and experiencing a depreciated sense of personal achievement and success (*personal accomplishment*). Burnout is not specific to the role of the psychotherapist, but it certainly is the most common Big Four occupational hazard that we experience.

The factors that can contribute to this trifecta of burnout experience involve a relatively insidious set of processes that build over time in which there is a mismatch between workplace demands and atmosphere and the therapist's resources and needs to meet those demands (e.g., Demerouti et al., 2001). Being relatively unaware of these possible tensions increases the chance that the symptoms of burnout will feel like they've sideswiped us from nowhere. Of the three burnout factors, emotional exhaustion is most common and seems more predictive of therapists' intent to quit than the job stress itself (see McCormack et al., 2018).

Similar to how one stressful event produces a wide variety of responses across different individuals, a work environment could certainly engender different experiences for different psychotherapists. For example, in a highly demanding group practice in which two therapists started their employment around the same time, Jamila, a midcareer therapist, may be feeling stressed but able to manage the workload whereas Jeff, an early career therapist, may be at his breaking point. There are of course many differences between them, but perhaps Jamila purposefully seeks out activities not related to psychology and supportive connections after work, while Jeff often does treatment planning by himself at home because he worries about lack of competence. In addition, Jamila may keep a relatively healthy distance between herself and her clients, whereas Jeff may feel an acute sense of responsibility for his caseload, quickly becoming overinvolved and overidentified with them (J. Lee et al., 2011).

Research tends to support these portrayals of Jamila and Jeff. Although being an earlier career therapist experiencing long hours, difficult clients, and piles of administrative tasks predicts multiple facets of burnout, positive resources such as maintaining a mindful awareness of needs, interpersonal support, and healthy professional boundaries all appear to help protect against it (Rupert et al., 2015). We can imagine that Jeff may fare better if he took his therapy skills to another group practice with similar caseload demands but with a different interpersonal atmosphere. Individuals and workplaces engage in a delicate dance, with some workplaces bringing out the "best moves" in the therapist while other workplaces engender an overload and confusion of dance steps that lead to missteps, faltering, and premature resignation of effort.

Potential mismatches between the therapist and the workplace can occur within a number of key domains: demand, control, reward, community, fairness, and values (i.e., areas of worklife model; Leiter & Maslach, 1999). Burnout is more likely to occur when the workplace does not provide what a given therapist may need at a given time. When these misalignments persist and cross a certain threshold for a particular therapist, undue emotional exhaustion, interpersonal detachment, and/or feelings of incompetence can result (e.g., Maslach et al., 2001). Sometimes, however, a workplace may be so egregious, for example in its demands or lack of fairness, that many employees will be on a path to burnout, even if they're not fully aware of it at the time.

A highly demanding, unrelenting work environment is probably the most common way to conceptualize the factors that contribute to burnout. The more hours we work, the more likely we'll feel the quintessential emotional exhaustion along with a more depersonalized interpersonal dynamic. The more our administrative and paperwork demand, the less our sense of personal accomplishment coupled with greater emotional exhaustion (see Rupert et al., 2015). In some ways, workplace demandingness is in the eye of the beholder. While some therapists feel that 20 clients per week is their absolute maximum, others are negotiating how to scale back a bit from 35. As I've scrolled through therapist self-care support forums and spoken with colleagues, it seems that when we're given a sort of moral permission from our fellow therapists to cut back on our work for the sake of our basic well-being, we more readily take action to support ourselves.

How much control you feel you have in your role as a psychotherapist also has a strong influence over your burnout risk. Being micromanaged, having little influence, and being accountable without any semblance of empowerment (Maslach & Leiter, 2005) are all forms of problematic low control in the workplace. Being able to exercise some degree of professional autonomy, however, is in itself burnout prevention.

When you think about your current job as a psychotherapist, how much influence do you perceive you have (and in reality get to have) over decisions that affect the way you work—client number and type, total and flexibility of hours worked, paperwork format, sick days and vacation time, and much more? Of course, working for someone else rather than working for yourself inherently creates more problems with control. However, companies, writ large, are increasingly aware of how lack of employee control can backfire and produce a host of negative effects including absenteeism, reduced organizational commitment, desire to quit, job dissatisfaction, lowered productivity, and impaired quality of work (Maslach & Leiter, 2016).

The presence or absence of rewards within our professional world can also contribute to burnout risk. "They don't pay me enough for all that I do." "No one sees how much I'm doing for this agency." The concept of rewards ultimately comes down to recognition of and valuing your worth, whether financially, socially, or institutionally. I know of a therapist who used to run a prominent program for a large network of mental health clinics. He painstakingly recruited patients into groups, supervised scores of trainees, designed new groups, and brought substantial revenue to the business. As these efforts continued to go relatively unrecognized year after year, he began to doubt whether it was all worth it in the end.

Burnout also feeds on a sense of an unsupportive or disconnected community, which can manifest as feelings of isolation, conflict, or disrespect from superiors, colleagues, and staff (e.g., Maslach & Leiter, 2005). What are your colleagues, supervisors, superiors, and supporting staff like? What is the tacit understanding within your workplace about "how to get along" with others? If you're in private practice, do you have an office in a suite with fellow health care practitioners or you are relatively isolated, never really seeing another soul day after day? In one of my previous office locations, I hardly saw or spoke to anyone. The sense of community within the small building in which my rented office was located was fractured and tacitly tense. Although some therapists may tolerate or even be able to ignore this type of atmosphere, others may find it uncomfortable or not meeting their needs.

In combination with our sense of job demands, control, rewards, and community, the principle of fairness cannot be understated. Do you feel decisions made on your behalf are morally just? Are workplace policies designed to benefit the bottom line or actually to care for the people who make the organization run, namely you and your colleagues? If you run a solo practice, how do your policies and standards for yourself measure up with respect to being fair and equitable? Do you grant yourself enough time off or opportunities to rest and rejuvenate with decent frequency, to diversify your professional activities, to reset between clients, to build support networks and community? Or does your professional life feel isolating, unrewarding, and underdiversified?

Finally, we can consider values as a contributor to burnout risk. Values speak to the ideals and motivations that attracted us to this profession more generally and to our current jobs more specifically. Identifying with our values allows us to better understand why we chose this field and what service we want to offer to the world. Values are a hidden magnetic force connecting therapist and workplace environment. For example, you may expect a sense of workplace openness and honesty, but your place of employment may tend to keep important policies and guidelines hidden and make excuses for why information doesn't flow freely. Your risk for burnout should you stay at that job will likely increase. Although not nearly as obvious as a highly demanding caseload, misalignments in values can slip under most therapists' radars, thus causing undue metalevel stress and disillusionment.

We shouldn't neglect the experience of client crises, which can also spark and stoke the fires of burnout (Sim et al., 2016). Cutting across many of the burnout domains discussed previously, even a small number of client crises demand the vast majority of our time, energy, and emotional resources. We lack control in these moments, and crises are often not terribly rewarding. It stands to reason that with repeated crises (and without a very helpful structure and collegial community of support), burnout and other occupational hazards are more likely to enter our experience.

It should be noted that the path toward burnout is a probabilistic process. As such, we can't assume that the same contributors to burnout will operate in the exact same way every time, even for the same therapist across their development. Thus, although the areas of the worklife burnout model are largely robust and provide a tremendously valuable framework to use in our professional lives, it is still up to us (and our support network) to evaluate our situation mindfully and to make decisions that reflect our highest good and deepest self-caring.

COMPASSION FATIGUE

"In our effort to view the world from the perspective of the suffering we suffer" (Figley, 2002, p. 1434). First introduced in the literature by Joinson (1992), *compassion fatigue* refers to a reduced capacity to feel compassion for those we serve and to whom we tend. Figley suggested that exhaustion, fatigue, disillusionment, and worthlessness set in over time as a result of absorbing so much distress and suffering from others. The unfortunate paradox of compassion fatigue may already be evident: The very nature of our work can produce the antithesis of the very nature of our work.

Like burnout, compassion fatigue doesn't arise from within a vacuum. Unlike burnout, however, compassion fatigue is about our relationship and emotional exchange with our clients and the material they present to us. Some would suggest that we're humbly asked to

> go where it hurts, to enter into places of pain, to share in brokenness, fear, confusion, and anguish. Compassion challenges us to cry out with those in

> misery, to mourn with those who are lonely, to weep with those in tears. Compassion requires us to be weak with the weak, vulnerable with the vulnerable, and powerless with the powerless. Compassion means full immersion into the condition of being human. (McNeill et al., 1982, p. 4.)

Although this statement is highly poignant, I don't believe that we must "cry out with those in misery . . . [and] weep with those in tears" to be compassionate and to offer compassion. In fact, this statement connotes so much identification with our clients' suffering that we may indeed fall into their lake of misery with them. Rather, I believe that our roles are more meant for us to bear witness to our clients' suffering so we're able to throw them a life raft of support.

In part through mirror neuron activity, we sense somatically and cognitively what our clients sense (Aubrey & Gentry, 2019). The problem with compassion fatigue is not that we can and do empathize with our clients, because we're doing this all the time and it is, in part, at the heart of psychotherapy. The potential risk for compassion fatigue lies in what happens downstream after we feel our clients' feelings, especially repeated feelings of deep suffering and frequently shared narratives of a traumatic past. At that point, we risk becoming overly identified and entangled in our clients' overwrought nervous systems.

After we have an empathic response to a client's troubling affect or material, we have a few choices or secondary response paths (Klimecki & Singer, 2012). We can continue to experience empathy without the felt sense necessarily bothering us. We can feel sympathy for the client, understanding what they're going through without having to feel it so strongly ourselves. We can experience and offer compassion, being willing to sit with and desiring to relieve the client's suffering. Or we can experience empathic overwhelm and personal distress. This last notion of empathic overwhelm may be what the literature continues to refer to as compassion fatigue. Figley (2002) even noted that (prolonged or intense) empathy is likely at the root of compassion fatigue, prompting Klimecki and Singer (2012) to suggest "empathic distress" rather than "compassion fatigue" as the appropriate label for this phenomenon.

Empathy, experienced over and over again, client after client, day after day, can take its toll. Feeling our clients' feelings and absorbing them rather than witnessing them can lead to overidentification and poorer therapeutic support than might occur without such empathic absorption. In fact, Kate Sheppard, PhD, RN, FNP, PMHNP-BC, FAANP, a clinical associate professor of nursing at the University of Arizona, suggested that this emotional overabsorption should be termed "professional emotional saturation" rather than compassion fatigue (as cited in Jablow, 2017). She has observed highly experienced nurses and physicians who still care deeply and want to make a difference in their patients' lives. And yet, their feeling "with" (vs. feeling "for") has been tapped out. These practitioners have in essence felt too much rather than had come to care too little.

What is commonly thought of as compassion fatigue is inextricably linked not only to our perceptions of our clients but also to our histories, emotion-based tendencies, sensory sensitivities, sense of responsibility and need for justice for our clients' welfare, and the depth with which we become immersed in our clients' suffering and wish for positive outcomes. Several personal factors have been shown to be related to reduced compassion fatigue, including mental health professionals' trait emotional intelligence, emotion management, and adaptive coping (Zeidner et al., 2013). In addition, research suggests that what contributes most to dysphoria in the helper is the perception that the client is suffering (Schulz et al., 2007), even beyond other ostensibly powerful factors such as clients' objective disabilities and the volume of work the helper faces. Perceptions of suffering in our clients are, in part, sourced from how (intensely and personally) we take in, feel, and process the emotions that our clients feel. As we'll explore later in the book, we have ways to reduce the risk of the fatigue and negativity we face from our clients' suffering.

SECONDARY TRAUMATIC STRESS

If we were first responders having to face the trauma of a natural disaster or mass shooting, we would certainly be at risk of developing the same trauma symptoms as the people directly affected by the traumatic event itself. Bearing witness and having close proximity to a traumatic event are well-known risk factors for developing posttraumatic stress disorder (PTSD). But what about sitting with traumatized clients, week after week? What about repeatedly hearing a client's trauma narrative as you see and feel their tearful and frightened affect?

Through whatever therapeutic approach you're using, you try to help clients access their resources, stay within their windows of tolerance, and process and resolve whatever traumatic material is causing them suffering. Such therapeutic work is not for the faint of heart. Some of us at some point will experience trauma symptoms about and as a result of our clients' trauma. In a large-scale study of social-work therapists, 15% met criteria for diagnosable PTSD as a result of their clients' traumas, and an even greater percentage experienced at least one major symptom cluster of PTSD (Bride, 2007). The most common symptom reported by these social workers was intrusive thoughts about the client and their trauma, with almost one third endorsing this symptom at least occasionally.

Secondary traumatic stress is essentially the spread of PTSD from client to therapist (Sodeke-Gregson et al., 2013). Thus, we may begin to feel symptoms of traumatic material, such as intrusion, avoidance, alterations in mood and cognition, and shifts in arousal and activity level. As you may imagine, experiencing such symptomatology while trying to help your clients (as well as the client[s] from whom you absorbed the trauma symptoms) is a very difficult endeavor. Professional psychotherapeutic support is certainly a warranted next step if these symptoms are occurring in your professional and personal life.

Having our own trauma history can prime us to absorb our clients' traumatic material more readily as our own (e.g., Price, 2001). When we bear witness to our clients' revelations about their traumatic pasts, we enter the stream of their troubled, unsettled, and hyperaroused system. When our stream has been disrupted with our own historical traumatic material as well, we may be all the more susceptible to the symptomatology that we're trying to help our clients alleviate.

And yet, there is hope. Some research suggests that our perceived coping ability can serve as a protective barrier against secondary traumatic stress (Follette et al., 1994). Furthermore, psychotherapists with secondary traumatic stress can find opportunity within the crisis. The relatively recently discovered phenomenon of *posttraumatic growth* is a source of positivity and possibility even within the most severely traumatized people (Collier, 2016). Posttraumatic growth is a positive condition that involves finding new meaning after hardships, newly viewing ourselves as resilient and capable, developing a sense of hope for the future, and valuing relationships in a meaningful manner. With appropriate support from trusted colleagues and loved ones as well as our own professional therapeutic assistance, we can transform trauma into thriving.

VICARIOUS TRAUMATIZATION

Leandra, a midcareer mental health counselor in a large group practice and a mother of two healthy teenage children, is quite emphatic that "life is just plain hard and then apparently you die." That wasn't always her philosophy, however. The last several years wore down her sense of hope, optimism, and vitality in her professional as well as her personal life. Although she isn't experiencing an obvious type of posttraumatic stress or depression and she is living a relatively healthy life, she certainly has experienced a more meta-level shift in her beliefs about and rules for how life is supposed to work.

Leandra has for many years worked with several adult victims of severe childhood abuse and neglect. Many of these clients feel incredibly precious to Leandra, and early on in their therapy she considered them part of her life. But as the sessions went by, as the therapeutic relationships strengthened and as her clients still suffered deeply, Leandra slowly became disillusioned with what life was supposed to offer. "How could parents do that to a child?" she would internally scream as her clients revealed layer upon layer of emotional abuse, physical aggression, and outright abandonment of the child versions of her now-grown clients. Her clients struggled with their pasts, presents, and their senses of future, and Leandra was now so tired of believing that life was unfair.

Leandra may very well be experiencing what McCann and Pearlman (1990) and Pearlman and Saakvitne (1995) called *vicarious traumatization.* Although it bears some similarities to compassion fatigue (Figley, 2002) and to secondary traumatic stress, vicarious traumatization is a syndrome characterized by a gradual disruption in a therapist's sense of self, others, and the world. Problematic shifts in the schema can be found in the realms of safety, trust, intimacy, esteem, and control (Baird & Kracen, 2006). The cognitive–emotional lens through which we make sense and meaning out of situations and interactions of the past, present, and future can become distorted and can cause increased suffering. Some evidence suggests that the repeated nature of the exposure to traumatic and difficult material and the profound suffering of our clients can alter our foundational belief system and the worldview we hold (Schauben & Frazier, 1995). The wily thing about vicarious traumatization is that it's insidious, gradual, and quite neglected as a potential occupational hazard to be mindful of in our roles as psychotherapists.

If we had caught Leandra as she was beginning to experience mild shifts in her core schemas, we may have been able to bolster her perceived coping capacities, as this factor may be protective against the development of vicarious traumatization (e.g., Painter & Woodside, 2016; C. M. Young, 1999). At this point, however, Leandra may need her own professional support, as it appears that her experience of vicarious traumatization has permeated much of her life. If she were in supervision or one-on-one consultation with a trusted mentor, she could work through the professional aspects of the dynamics within her caseload that lend themselves to an evolution of vicarious traumatization. Together with an effective psychotherapist well versed in trauma, her collegial support could help rewire her schemas for greater meaningfulness and resilience.

MAKING HOLISTIC SENSE OF OUR UNIQUE OCCUPATIONAL HAZARDS

With all of these occupational hazards, we come to appreciate the complex and dynamic nature of how the psychotherapist interacts with the environment to create a spectrum of well-being, struggle, distress, or full-blown experiential syndrome. Although we can make general risk predictions about "the average" psychotherapist, we need nuanced evaluation for a given therapist's unique life. Even given the most comprehensive research studies, we need to evaluate the complex interactions among attachment and adversity history, personality, coping style, career stage, supports, and workplace environment to accurately assess risk of and protection from the Big Four. Even across these major occupational hazards we find somewhat different sets of predictors and triggers. Thus, self-reflection and mindful awareness become key to our ability to protect ourselves against the hardship that may feel inevitable and to successfully mitigate what has already entered our experience.

As we've discussed thus far, the Big Four occupational hazards, together with subtle and underacknowledged processes of our psychotherapeutic roles, collectively create what we might call *psychotherapist role vulnerabilities*. These can be conceptualized as our cumulative and ever-evolving lived experiences that, because of our chosen profession, create unique sources and effects of stress. The sources of this stress are not ordinary, and the manifestations of this stress can be highly specific. Unlike individuals in other professions that may contend with what we all know of as stress, we as psychotherapists are uniquely positioned to and tasked with constantly caring for, sitting compassionately with, and doing our very best to help alleviate deep and palpable suffering in our clients. Can you think of another profession that is charged with this awesome power? And with that great power comes incredible responsibility for us to preserve and protect ourselves, as individuals and as a community.

With all of the everyday stressors, strains, and struggles and the unique occupational hazards we're up against, it stands to reason that we can be deeply and humanistically motivated to take the best care of ourselves and each other as possible. But this is not where our self-care mandate stops. We are indeed beholden to our ethical principles and codes to treat our clients with utmost care, respect, and promise. The next chapter thus helps us walk through the jungle of our ethical charges and imperatives within our challenging professional lives. Rather than instill more fear-based guardrails from such a discussion, it is my aspiration that we gain a sense of hope as we explore how our ethical principles can create abiding motivation to live and work with curiosity and honor for ourselves and those we serve.

4 OUR ETHICAL IMPERATIVE TOWARD SUSTAINABLE SELF-CARE

We are ethically obligated to care for ourselves: This, I believe, is incontrovertible.

—Craig Irvine

Imagine for a moment that James, one of your hardworking and dedicated social work therapist colleagues, is quite sleep deprived. He's functioning "OK," he says, but he's exhausted and acting less himself these days. Four months earlier, James' wife of 3 years suddenly picked up and left. James soon discovered that she had cheated on him and then moved in with another man. This situation was heartbreaking and hard on James, and then his father passed away from a tough battle with cancer. James was faced with deep grief for his father on top of his profound anger, hurt, and sense of betrayal by his ex-wife.

James received support from a local friend; they went out to dinner and had a few drinks. This was all it took to rekindle James's past problems with drinking, which peaked during his college and social work training years. In fact, James had received some warnings about his drinking behavior during

https://doi.org/10.1037/0000309-005
The Thriving Therapist: Sustainable Self-Care to Prevent Burnout and Enhance Well-Being, by M. A. Hersh

training when he showed up several times to his clinical practicum hung over and functioning somewhat sporadically. James was suffering profoundly, and his clinical work was suffering in turn. He was periodically showing up late to his agency job, forgetting to make collateral calls to colleagues, and essentially nodding off while with some of his clients. James was in jeopardy of serious reprimands with his agency and was possibly on the verge of several ethics complaints from clients.

STRESS-DISTRESS CONTINUUM ETHICS AND PREVENTION MODEL

James's deteriorating functioning fits squarely into the robust stress–distress continuum ethics and prevention model promulgated by the American Psychological Association (APA) Board of Professional Affairs Advisory Committee on Colleague Assistance (ACCA, n.d.). This model suggests an explanation for the ways in which stress can trigger a downward spiral of internal distress that, when overwhelming or mismanaged, can cascade into functional impairments and compromised competence. These functional impairments can result in ethically improper behavior.

Stress has been defined in this model as our body's reaction to the demands placed on us by internal (e.g., self-expectations, sense of responsibility, perfectionism) or external (e.g., client's anger at us, our own child's illness) sources. As these stresses come our way, we can experience distress, the subjective emotional response to such stress, challenges, and demands (Barnett et al., 2006). Importantly, the conversion of stress into distress is influenced by our histories of reactivity to similar stressors, by trauma, and by deeply held beliefs of empowerment or of helplessness and hopelessness.

If our distress becomes difficult to manage or spills over into our professional work, we may begin to see an objective change in how we interact with clients or colleagues and how we treat ourselves—not returning phone calls or completing reports in a timely manner, failing (or forgetting) to ask important questions to assess a client's safety, isolating ourselves socially, skipping meals, and so on (e.g., Margison, 1997). Lamb et al. (1987) summarized these forms of professional impairment as "interference in professional functioning in one or more of the following areas: (a) an inability and/or unwillingness to acquire and integrate professional standards into one's repertoire of professional behavior; (b) an inability to acquire professional skills to reach an acceptable level of competency; and (c) an inability to control personal stress, psychological dysfunction, and/or excessive emotional reactions that interfere with professional functioning" (p. 598). If the decline in the quality of a therapist's functioning persists, we would be likely to see consistently substandard performance (Coster & Schwebel, 1997).

In this downward spiral model, the resulting situation can involve improper professional behavior and starkly unethical conduct, such as breaches of confidentiality or sexual involvement with clients (e.g., Faunce, 1990; Sherman, 1996). Importantly, if therapists are unaware of this evolving downward spiral or do not take appropriate preventive or intervention-based action, unethical conduct can feel like a shock that has come out of the blue. A synergy of ongoing mindful awareness, professional and personal life relational support, and prevention efforts is vital to reducing the likelihood of ending up at the bottom of this downward spiral.

ETHICAL CODES

James's situation within the stress–distress continuum model is what many of us might conjure up when considering clinical competence degradations that could lead to ethics violations complaints from our professional organizations and licensing boards. APA's (2017b) *Ethical Principles of Psychologists and Code of Conduct* provides some aspirational yet enforceable codes of professional conduct to keep in mind. First and perhaps most fundamental is General Principle A: Beneficence and Nonmaleficence, which captures the motivational importance of making sure that we don't let our stress affect our ability to competently serve our clients: "Psychologists strive to benefit those with whom they work and take care to do no harm. . . . Psychologists strive to be aware of the possible effect of their own physical and mental health on their ability to help those with whom they work" (APA, 2017b, p. 3).

Directly linked to these aspirational principles are the related enforceable standards that in theory should hold us more accountable. Standard 3.04a, Avoiding Harm, dictates that "psychologists take reasonable steps to avoid harming their clients/patients . . . and others with whom they work, and to minimize harm where it is foreseeable and unavoidable" (APA, 2017b, p. 6). Standard 2.06, Personal Problems and Conflicts, is clearly focused on the potential negative impact that personal problems may have on professional competence and on protecting those with whom we work: "Psychologists refrain from initiating an activity when they know or should know that there is a substantial likelihood that their personal problems will prevent them from performing their work-related activities in a competent manner" (p. 5) and "when psychologists become aware of personal problems that may interfere with their performing their work-related duties adequately, they take appropriate measures, such as obtaining professional consultation or assistance, and determine whether they should limit, suspend, or terminate their work-related duties" (p. 5). Finally, Standard 2.03 directs that "psychologists undertake ongoing efforts to develop and maintain their competence" (p. 5).

As it currently stands, within this harm-reduction model and set of ethical principles and standards, prevention of this downward spiral becomes paramount. And it makes good practical sense for its importance and emphasis. However, if exclusively applied in a psychotherapist's life, the resulting efforts can inadvertently focus our attention on harm reduction at the expense of putting energy into upward spirals of well-being, internal resourcefulness, fulfillment, and job/workplace satisfaction (Wise et al., 2012).

In response to how our governing and licensing bodies have previously focused their attention almost exclusively on practitioner distress and reducing harm to clients (e.g., vis-à-vis effects of alcohol abuse or sexual misconduct), the last 2 decades have seen an increase in care and attention to psychotherapists' holistic well-being. Professional competence (Kaslow et al., 2004), as well as strengths and resilience (Bonanno, 2004; Kelley, 2005), has been increasingly emphasized for the betterment of both the therapist and the person within the therapist. Interestingly, APA's focus on strengths, resilience, self-care, and a healthy lifestyle seems to coincide with the public-facing evolution of positive psychology, beginning when Martin Seligman, as APA president in 1998, brought to life the concepts and supporting practices of flourishing, fulfillment, and living a good life.

To these points, we fortunately find that other professional organizations and their codes of ethical conduct pay some attention to psychotherapist self-care specifically. For example, within the *Canadian Code of Ethics for Psychologists*, Principle II.12, Responsible Caring, suggests that practitioners "engage in self-care activities that help to avoid conditions (e.g., burnout, addictions) that could result in impaired judgment and interfere with their ability to benefit and not harm others" (Canadian Psychological Association [CPA], 2017, p. 20). Similarly, Section C of the *ACA Code of Ethics*, Professional Responsibility, encourages that "counselors engage in self-care activities to maintain and promote their emotional, physical, and spiritual well-being to best meet their professional responsibilities" (American Counseling Association [ACA], 2014, p. 8).

Interestingly, the CPA code of ethics even goes so far as to have practitioners

evaluate how their own experiences, attitudes, culture, beliefs, values, individual differences, specific training, external pressures, personal needs, and historical, economic, and political context might influence their interactions with and perceptions of others, and integrate this awareness into their efforts to benefit and not harm others. (Principle II.10; CPA, 2017, p. 20).

These latter notions laid out by the CPA are explored in Part II of this book as we examine our developmental, career, personal, and therapist habits and patterns that create a unique set of self-care needs moving across time and context. Our particular needs and how they're met play out in both our personal and our professional lives. Paying attention to self-care in one domain will undoubtedly positively affect the other. After all, as secular mindfulness meditation pioneer Jon Kabat-Zinn (2005b) so aptly offered, wherever you go, there you are.

SELF-CARE–ORIENTED ETHICS

What were your ethics classes like? What kind of training did you receive regarding the intersections among professional ethics, competence, and self-care? Were these elements made explicit, or were they cloudy concepts that you had to divine on your own over time? In my own graduate training, my formal ethics class appeared to be all about what can go wrong in professional psychology activities and how to prevent wrongdoing. This risk management approach is traditional, and it's necessary but not sufficient.

We debated why would we make some decisions over others, what the legal statutes demanded, and how to determine if we would be in violation of legal and ethical standards. What was generally missing was an emphasis on "the human factors" of professional competence—what it was like to be a human being who then takes on a role of psychotherapist. We regrettably didn't delve into self-care and all its complexities, nuances, and associations with both competence and the larger ethical framework of being a practitioner of mental health.

With an expanded view of professional ethics to include self-care writ large, we could begin to incorporate aspirational principles as well as concrete suggestions for valuing the person within the therapist and honoring therapists' unique struggles and common hazards. Cultivation of self-caring attitudes and actions over time, however, aren't a one-size-fits-all endeavor. Rather, we can envision encouragement of every therapist (at different stages of their careers) to take personal and professional stock, much like Dr. Ellen Baker (2003) suggested in her popular book, *Caring for Ourselves: A Therapist's Guide to Personal and Professional Well-Being*. The Self-Care Reflection Break (Exhibit 1.3) in Chapter 1 is an example of such an inventory.

While honoring risk reduction and management perspectives, we could begin to include discussions about engaging in practices, internal and external, of upward spirals of well-being. This approach could involve an integrated constellation of mind–body–environment lifestyle choices (e.g., R. Walsh, 2011) as well as profession-specific soothing and energizing practices for our own betterment and for those we serve. We would essentially be resourcing ourselves (e.g., Hanson, 2018) to build greater and deeper resilience.

Fortunately, a positive ethics perspective (Handelsman et al., 2009) has been proposed and has permeated some of the writings on the intersection among ethics, self-care, and professional competence (e.g., Barnett et al., 2007; Wise & Barnett, 2016; Wise et al., 2012). Positive ethics can inspire us to think aspirationally, if not divergently and beneficially, while minimizing risk to our clients and protecting ourselves in the process. Welcomed into this aspirational thinking (and doing) is the art and science of self-care—of taking care of our whole beings, the very instruments involved in the work to which we have committed.

We cannot do this alone, however. Professional ethics is both a solo and a relational endeavor. It is indeed the case that most professional bodies (e.g., APA, NASW, the American Medical Association, ACA) stipulate, as a matter of both aspirational principle and ethical enforceable standards, that therapists *should assist their colleagues* in recognizing impairment to ensure prevention of harm to clients. For example, the ACA (2014) dictates that "counselors assist colleagues or supervisors in recognizing their own professional impairment and provide consultation and assistance when warranted with colleagues or supervisors showing signs of impairment and intervene as appropriate to prevent imminent harm to clients" (p. 9).

This notion of "keeping an eye out" for our fellow therapists is vital to promote best ethical practices and prevent undue harm to our clients (and to ourselves). Unfortunately, as Barnett et al. (2007) soberingly pointed out, practicing psychologists not only are loathe to refer themselves for help when truly needed (e.g., Barnett & Hillard, 2001; Pope et al., 1987) but also tend *not* to confront nor offer assistance to their colleagues when distress or impairment becomes a more obvious issue with which to intervene (e.g., Floyd et al., 1998). Ignoring the situation or taking no action (Good et al., 1995) are more common ways of handling the therapist driver who is showing signs of erratic or potentially harmful driving.

Understandably, it would be hard to imagine an enforceable code that created the case for an ethical violation if we didn't *actively promote* our colleagues' well-being. That kind of code may very well generate a wellness-oriented "big brother" scenario, and that's not what we would seek to promote.

Moreover, a fully interdependent worldview of professional ethics flies in the face of the individualism and litigiousness so deeply ingrained in our culture. So how do we keep a compassionate eye on our colleagues while not policing their potential harmful actions toward clients or over-monitoring their lifestyle for practices of well-being and wellness?

Part of our answer to this dilemma is found in the rationale for employing a communitarian approach to competence and ethics. Pioneers in the field of professional ethics, competence, self-care, and occupational hazards, Dr. Brad Johnson and colleagues (2012, 2013) made the case for paying attention to our colleagues' health (writ large) rather than just focusing on ourselves for maintenance of professional competence and enactment of self-care. The Dunning-Krueger effect posits that human beings are not very good at accurately evaluating their own competence (Dunning et al., 2004). Essentially, what is not within our (nonjudgmental) awareness, we can't possibly know about and reliably or accurately assess.

Not surprisingly, health care professionals are not exempt from this "perceptual error of being human," although we might feel as if we know how to self-assess better than the average person. For physicians and health care trainees, correlations between self-assessment and observer ratings are notoriously low (e.g., Eva et al., 2004; R. Gordon, 1991). This finding doesn't mean that others' observations of us are necessarily more accurate, but it does necessitate a curiosity and questioning of whether we are always the best judge of how we're doing or even what we ultimately need. In fact, closely held loved ones are likely better assessors of some aspects of our personality and social–emotional functioning than we are (Vazire & Carlson, 2011).

Can we adopt the view that we are all neighbors and striving to live the best possible life and to provide the best possible care for those we serve (Johnson et al., 2013)? If we're all in the same proverbial boat, each of us is subject to the same water, winds, weather, and whims of our minds and bodies. How we experience those elements will differ, but that should encourage us to form a community ethos, to take care of each other rather than only to turn inward.

Thus, stewardship would be the norm, and we would begin early in clinical training to practice being one another's keepers. Not out of threat nor out of fear of ethical violation but from a place of heartfulness and community, would we say to our colleagues, "Are you okay? Things look rough right now. How can we help?" As Johnson and colleagues (2012) offered in their seminal piece in *American Psychologist* on communities of competence, we must start on the ground floor. Through redefining our notions of ethical responsibility, reconfiguring our systems of education and training, and retooling our credentialing criteria toward a more communitarian ethos (MacIntyre, 1999), we may be able to achieve a new form of professional ethics that places all of us as interdependently accountable and mutually supportive.

We've now explored our ethical motivations to take adequate care of ourselves as well as to look out for one another's well-being. All this talk of stress, hazards, and ethical imperatives might have us wondering why we even entered this profession in the first place. And that's exactly what we'll delve into in the next chapter, which addresses why we became psychotherapists and what rewards and gifts this profession indeed offers us.

5 WHY WE BECOME PSYCHOTHERAPISTS AND WHAT SUSTAINS US

As you grow older, you will discover that you have two hands, one for helping yourself, and the other for helping others.

—Maya Angelou

"Whatever you do, don't tell the interviewer that you've 'always just wanted to help people.' You have to find a more personal reason." Did you ever get this advice as you were applying to graduate school or to your professional program? While wanting to help people is a perfectly (and socially) acceptable and quite valid reason for choosing this profession, it's likely not the whole story. Perhaps somewhat awkwardly, however, clinical psychologists (more so than psychiatrists and even psychoanalysts) often cite their original motivations for entering the field as a desire to "understand and help myself" (Henry et al., 1971).

Exploring your personal motivations, your particular life-course-shaping experiences, and the influential cultural forces at play ultimately can help us to become more compassionately aware self-advocates inside and out of

https://doi.org/10.1037/0000309-006
The Thriving Therapist: Sustainable Self-Care to Prevent Burnout and Enhance Well-Being,
by M. A. Hersh

the office. From these insights, we may ultimately foster a greater resilience to our occupational hazards while enhancing our potential for more lasting well-being.

ON BECOMING A PSYCHOTHERAPIST

Have you thought about it much, this question of why you became a psychotherapist? To do adequate justice to this question, let's imagine that you just grabbed some coffee or tea with Drs. John Norcross and Barry Farber, authors of a fascinating piece, "Choosing Psychotherapy as a Career: Beyond 'I Want to Help People.'" They might invite you to wonder why it is that you chose *this particular* helping career rather than working with the homeless, protecting the environment, teaching underprivileged youth, or engaging in some other noble and altruistic profession (Norcross & Farber, 2005). What was it about sitting with others' deepest and darkest and most aspirational secrets of living on this earth that attracted you so strongly? What do you think compelled you or turned on the gravitational force toward some of the most intimate, challenging, and humbling interactions you might ever have during your lifetime? Perhaps an unduly jarring thought, but you may in fact know your clients' psychological nooks and crannies better than you know those of your own partner, children, friends, or parents.

Perhaps you were a child with the raw materials to be an effective psychotherapist. You were a good listener, you had empathy in spades, and you could help problem-solve others' struggles (even if you had some trouble with your own). You may have been regaled with positive feedback about your innate skills. Throughout your schooling perhaps you took on volunteer positions like peer counseling or crisis hotline work. What others avoided or simply ignored, you saw as an opportunity to help. This feeling of wanting to support others therapeutically can certainly grow over time. As Dr. Zoe Shaw (2020), psychotherapist and relationship expert, noted, she started "studying" psychology as a 4-year-old sitting in her mother's psychology class. After a high school class in psychology and conversations with her mom, Shaw says she was hooked.

Findings from a small qualitative study of college undergraduates interested in careers in therapy (Hill et al., 2013) suggest some interesting ideas about motivations to pursue our humble profession. All the participants had experiences of and a passion for helping others and believed in the importance of giving back. They considered themselves empathic yet also conflict avoidant. And to echo what Henry et al. (1971) noted decades earlier, not only were they "other-oriented" but they also wanted to help themselves.

Chance events or influential relationships may have altered the direction of your life and career aspirations (see Norcross & Farber, 2005). Like Dr. Shaw, you may have already had the personal inclination or raw materials for psychological service, and the external events in your life helped to breathe life into these proclivities. These are the "situational imperatives *and* personal proclivities converg[ing] as interdependent shapers of life paths" (Norcross & Guy, 1989, as cited in Norcross & Farber, 2005, p. 941).

Maybe you decided to go back to school to become a psychotherapist after years of being steeped in one or more entirely different professions. I know therapists who were once attorneys, police officers, accountants, community organizers, yoga instructors, business owners, and teachers. The list is endless. These therapists may bring a unique set of skills to their psychotherapeutic endeavors and may even subspecialize in an area of their former expertise and experience. I once read about a financial advisor turned psychotherapist who now offers money coaching as part of his practice. He's now able to help his clients with trust and relationship issues around spending, saving, and allocating money in line with their deeper values.

Finally, some events shake people's foundations of what it means to be human. Perhaps you experienced your own trauma or witnessed traumatic events in the lives of loved ones. These crises can instill within us a sense of urgency and meaning about helping (ourselves or) a certain group of people to recover, heal, and thrive. You may have developed a passion and a mission for helping to alleviate mental illness or promote emotional and psychological health. Perhaps this urgency and importance has stuck with you this whole time.

We may feel from this discussion that our motivations and determinations for becoming therapists were seeded some time in childhood or that we somehow knew exactly what we wanted to do from the start. But we are evolving beings with the capacity to change course at any time, incorporating passions, interests, and skills we learned long ago or would like to integrate in the future.

EXPLORING THE "DARKER" SIDE OF OUR PROFESSIONAL MOTIVATIONS

"We all go into psychology to try to understand our mothers," a former graduate school supervisor only half-jokingly remarked. When surveyed and interviewed, psychotherapists tend to reveal similar themes related to the reasons they chose this helping profession. Many tell of their innate psychological mindedness as well as their childhood and familial pain. They also speak to cultural forces such as marginalization and alienation (Farber et al., 2005).

Compared with women in other professions, women mental health practitioners report greater histories of childhood abuse, family dysfunction, and parental alcoholism (Elliott & Guy, 1993). In one study, a staggering 70% of women psychologists (and 33% of men psychologists) reported histories of physical or sexual abuse (Pope & Feldman-Summers, 1992). Women practitioners are also more likely than others to have experienced the death of a family member and psychiatric hospitalization of a parent during their childhood. Either consequently or in its own right, many mental health professionals have served a parentified role in their families of origin (Racusin et al., 1981). Although it's perhaps quite difficult to ponder, do you imagine that any of these realities, if true for you, played an influential role in your becoming a psychotherapist?

Would these be *the* reasons you entered this profession, as some might suggest? Dr. Ned Hallowell (2018), psychiatrist, ADHD expert, and author, made an unambiguous and compelling argument in his autobiographical book, *Because I Come From a Crazy Family: The Making of a Psychiatrist.* Hallowell detailed his family's alcoholism and mental illness, which he notes pushed and pulled him to try to save them from themselves and in turn to become someone who could do for others what he couldn't do for his family.

Your family history and childhood, however, may have had a much more negligible effect on your choice of profession. Likely, if there were answers to divine to this question, they would be found within shades of gray. Even if we're not aware of the specific effects of our upbringing on our choice of profession, it's always healthy to raise a general awareness of what drives and motivates us to move in particular directions, particularly because we've invested so much blood, sweat, and tears into becoming mental health change agents.

I once had a client who was very interested in becoming a clinical psychologist or psychiatrist. He had struggled his whole life with issues of low self-worth, disturbed mood, and stress addiction emerging from a childhood of emotional neglect and diffuse family boundaries. This young man noted that he simply liked "how the brain works and how it goes awry." Was this young man not aware of what we all might suspect? Or did his challenges and upbringing have little to do with his interest in a clinical helping career? Would he be trying to *work through* the ills of childhood and the motivations that lie underneath (e.g., Barnett et al., 2007) if he pursued such a career?

There are many potential benefits of knowing one's own motivations for becoming and for being a psychotherapist. A deep understanding of these forces can help us understand how we tend to operate as therapists and the patterns of practice we typically engage in for ourselves. For example, do you gravitate toward or desire to avoid certain psychological, emotional, and social issues that emerge from your clients? When you were first training and learned in depth about certain psychiatric difficulties, did some compel you and some scare you away? Perhaps when you were growing up you knew someone in your family or school who was plagued by a mental health disorder. You may have *needed* to help this group of people or conversely may have less consciously pushed this population away in your mind as simply too much to handle.

Another major benefit to understanding our motivations to become and to continue to be psychotherapists is that we can learn how to take care of ourselves better. For example, if we have experienced significant trauma in our lives, we may be likely to experience secondary traumatic stress by virtue of our psychotherapeutic work (e.g., Delahanty & Nugent, 2006). If we were a parentified child (Racusin et al., 1981) or experienced subtle emotional neglect and invalidation (Webb, 2012), we may be more likely to adopt an inflexible role as caregiver or even fixer within our therapeutic relationships. This process may be quite unconscious but nevertheless may cause us to spend more time, attention, and energy helping others while we unknowingly tend less to ourselves. As physician and addictions expert, Gabor Maté, so poignantly wondered, "if our helper roles are taken away from us, or if in a crisis they're deeply challenged, then who are we? That's what we drag around" (Maté, 2021, p. 40) with ourselves, whether we know it consciously or not.

THE JOYS AND REWARDS OF BEING A PSYCHOTHERAPIST

Although psychotherapists experience more depression, anxiety, and burnout than their psychological researcher counterparts, therapists also more often report that their work is rewarding and feel more overall life satisfaction (Radeke & Mahoney, 2000). In fact, *compassion satisfaction* tends to grow as therapists get older and gain experience (Sprang et al., 2007). In support of how worthwhile the deed of being a psychotherapist is, Elliot Connie, internationally renowned trainer of solution-focused brief therapy, offered this stark but inspirational realization: "When I sit and think about it, I am still blown away that people trust me to help them in their darkest times. It's such an honor and privilege to be in that space" (E. Connie, personal communication, October, 3, 2020).

If you pause and reflect for a moment, what aspects of your professional life have you thoroughly enjoyed or found exceptionally rewarding thus far? Are there any aspects of being a therapist that have been positively surprising or awe inspiring for you? Reflecting with regularity or even sporadically on the grand as well as the subtle professional rewards is a vital form of self-care in and of itself (Norcross & VandenBos, 2018).

Let's now take a self-care reflection break to explore the extent to which you find a variety of professional rewards satisfying. Give a rating on the scale of 1 (*not at all*) to 7 (*extremely satisfying*) for each of the potential rewards shown in Exhibit 5.1. You can cover up the right-hand column while making your ratings and then compare your results to the average ratings for each item from a sample of mental health professionals across 37 states in the United States. With this assessment, you're comparing your ratings to a fairly even distribution of social workers, psychologists, marriage and family therapists, and professional counselors.

If you score much lower than the average for any given professional reward, don't worry. Your score is not an indictment of your capacity for joy or gratitude or an indication that your clinical practice is somehow failing. It is

EXHIBIT 5.1. Self-Care Reflection Break: Assessing Your Professional Joys and Rewards

How generally satisfying do you find the following potential rewards of clinical practice? Rate each item on a scale from 1 (*not all satisfying*) to 7 (*extremely satisfying*).

	Your rating	Average rating from sample of mental health professionals
Promoting growth in client		6.5
Enjoyment of work		6.0
Opportunity to continue to learn		6.1
Engaging in challenging work		5.9
Professional autonomy/independence		5.9
Flexible hours		5.7
Increased self-knowledge		5.6
Variety in work and cases		5.5
Personal growth		5.5
Sense of emotional intimacy		5.2
Being a role model and mentor		5.0

Note. Adapted from "Rafting the Rapids: Occupational Hazards, Rewards, and Coping Strategies of Psychotherapists," by B. Kramen-Kahn and N. D. Hansen, 1998, *Professional Psychology: Research and Practice, 29*(2), p. 131 (https://doi.org/10.1037/0735-7028.29.2.130). Copyright 1998 by the American Psychological Association.

simply a reflection of what you find more or less satisfying in your clinical work right now or in general. Your ratings can give you a sense of the areas of your work that could be enhanced and those that can continue to be integrated as sources of high satisfaction and fulfillment.

One of the large multistate surveys on the hazards and rewards experienced by mental health professionals (Kramen-Kahn & Hansen, 1998) revealed some interesting findings about the joys of our highly challenging work. Almost the entire sample (93%) of social workers, psychologists, marriage and family therapists, and professional counselors reported that *promoting growth in a client* was a treasured occupational reward. Was that item one of your most highly rated on the self-assessment you just took? As psychotherapy researcher and teacher Dr. Barry Farber eloquently offered, even the hope of helping our clients grow and gain more flexibility and freedom in their lives can be a career-sustaining aspiration (Farber, 1990).

How do you feel when you watch a client grow—when they take some action on their own behalf, when they use a skill you imparted, when they offer themselves a deep compassion that has been shrouded in shame, or when they make a leap of faith that they've been protecting against for decades? Do these actions inspire you? Do you allow the experience to flow through you, motivating you to continue the good work with that client? As Skovholt (2001) suggested, sometimes it feels incredibly good to "hit the bull's eye of success" with a given client, even if this success is short-lived or not yet generalized.

You may not find the bull's-eye metaphor particularly resonant with your personality or applicable to your clinical practice, but you've likely experienced what Csikszentmihályi (2008) dubbed *flow*. Flow occurs when we feel free to invest our attention in the moment or on future goals without resistance of having to strengthen some deficit or defend against some vulnerability. Think about your therapeutic encounters over the years and how you may have "lost yourself" in the pure and sacred act of helping another human being and bearing witness to their transformations, no matter how imperceptible to others they may be. How would you handle such experiences of inspiration or flow? Would you invite them to motivate you to become a better version of yourself?

Unfortunately, it can be far too easy to let these experiences pass us by although the majority of practitioners surveyed found it highly satisfying to have the opportunity to learn (76%), to grow personally (56%), and to increase their self-knowledge (61%; Kramen-Kahn & Hansen, 1998). When we feel inspired by our clients, we might be appealing to the human experiences of *awe* (Keltner & Haidt, 2003) and *elevation* (Haidt, 2000), both being morally and sensorially uplifting and expansive. In this spirit, the evolution of a client can prompt personal affirmation, self-fulfillment, and even a motivation to better ourselves. We may even gain a deeper appreciation and tolerance of the diversity of the human experience. Some of us might have noticed this growth within our relationships, making different and deeper meaning from our connections than we'd previously done. What transformative experiences have you had that changed your view of yourself as a therapist and/or your sense of purpose in this profession?

Survey data support such notions of being a psychotherapist as prompting betterment in our lives. Radeke and Mahoney (2000) found that a majority of the psychotherapists they surveyed endorsed items indicating that being a psychotherapist ultimately made them a better (94%) and wiser (92%) person, increased their self-awareness (92%), enhanced appreciation for human relationships (90%), accelerated their own psychological development (89%), increased tolerance for life's ambiguities (81%), increased their capacity to enjoy life (75%), felt like a form of spiritual service (74%), and resulted in changes in their core value system (61%). These data may indeed provide a reason that practicing psychologists find their jobs more rewarding and have more life satisfaction than their researcher colleagues do.

As maintaining a dialectical approach to life is often quite helpful, we can recognize the dual reality that occupational hazards (e.g., economic uncertainty, excessive workload, caseload uncertainties) can coexist with the highly satisfying facets of our clinical work. Interestingly, the majority (73%) of clinicians in the Kramen-Kahn and Hansen (1998) study found it quite satisfying to be challenged by their clinical work, thus inviting opportunities for gratitude within the struggle. This idea is especially salient for therapists who have the vast majority of their clinical caseload under third-party payment, requiring the therapist to engage in more administrative duties. These therapists enjoy career satisfaction when they purposefully reflect on the various satisfying aspects of their job. Interestingly, for therapists who have at least one fourth of their caseload as direct-pay clients, career satisfaction seems better predicted by the balance between work and home. As therapists engage in a rich and meaningful personal life, they may enhance their sense of fulfillment in their careers as well (Rupert, Miller, et al., 2012).

For now, let's take stock of the facets of being a psychotherapist that matter to you. See if you can stay connected to or come into better relationship with the rewards of your practice and to your higher purpose. This type of attunement is a wonderful "vaccine" for the stresses, pressures, and hazards that our challenging profession can bring (Kramen-Kahn & Hansen, 1998). Within any profession and any domain of life, the extent to which we approach it with a sense of purpose and meaning undoubtedly can help create a better quality of life, now and into the future. So let's ponder together what creative, purpose-driven, and expansive possibilities could create a brighter future and a more satisfying present.

In this chapter, we've explored our historical sources and personal motivations for the profession we've chosen. Even with decades of our own therapy, we may not fully understand why we became therapists, and that's perfectly okay. However, we can acknowledge what drives us toward less-than-healthy patterns (e.g., over-responsibility, diffuse boundaries) based on our personality, family-of-origin dynamics, or certain events that may have occurred prior to or during our professional development. These insights are a brilliant form of self-care as they give us permission to shift our mindset or action tendencies toward less resistance and greater well-being whenever possible.

We have also explored the aspects of our helping profession that fellow therapists find rewarding and satisfying. More fully appreciating (and practicing gratitude) for what brings us joy can certainly be its own reward. We can be encouraged by the interesting fact that the majority of therapists find it highly satisfying to be challenged in our professional roles. Of course staying within the scope of our practice and expertise, we might even say to ourselves, "bring it on" as we traverse the tricky and tangly world of helping our fellow human beings.

Taking on challenges and finding professional endeavors rewarding is in part a matter of our personal values. In other words, if we're living in accordance with what ultimately matters to us, then it becomes that much easier for us to walk toward (rather than retreat from) that which is difficult or even unknown. The next chapter is devoted to helping us identify what we find most meaningful in life, especially when it comes to how we can take the best care of ourselves as possible.

6 MAPPING OUR SELF-CARE VALUES

The most important thing is to keep the most important thing the most important thing.

—Donald Coduto

Jodi, 52, is a midcareer social work therapist who has been dedicated to helping others for 27 years. She has enjoyed a great deal of success mixed with a range of challenges working in community mental health, a college counseling center, and most recently her own private practice. She has a longtime yoga and meditation practice and often tries to incorporate mind–body–spirit work into her psychotherapy. Something, however, hasn't been sitting right. She has increasingly been feeling disillusioned with her work—the long hours, the relative lack of professional diversity, the hassle and energy drain of the insurance hustle, and the similarity of clientele who want quick fixes rather than deeper transformation. Jodi's work style has been weighing on her sense of lightness and joy inside and out of the therapy room. Jodi may very well be in need of a change. But what is her next step?

https://doi.org/10.1037/0000309-007
The Thriving Therapist: Sustainable Self-Care to Prevent Burnout and Enhance Well-Being,
by M. A. Hersh

At the heart of the psychological science of living a meaningful life is the process of identifying, clarifying, and living in accordance with one's values (e.g., Hayes et al., 2012). *Values* are chosen resonant beliefs and motivations about what truly matters to us and what we find deeply meaningful in life. They are, in effect, our life direction so that at any given moment our behavioral actions can align with what we've already determined as important. It is this very process that research consistently shows facilitates life satisfaction, sense of purpose, happiness, and well-being (e.g., Hayes et al., 2012; McKay et al., 2010). However, values don't necessarily make life easy. But they can certainly help life to feel less hard with deeper meaning, greater fulfillment, and a sustainability of spirit.

It's worth noting here that values are not equivalent to goals. As Dr. Steven Hayes, cofounder of acceptance and commitment therapy (ACT), likes to quip, you can't ever *achieve* north. Some years ago I was attending an exposure-based social anxiety treatment workshop. An audience member asked why the client would even do such difficult therapeutic work in the first place if they had conditioned themselves their whole lives to avoid social situations and the perception of others' judgment. The speaker replied that by setting concrete and manageable goals, the client would gradually expose themself to what had been avoided and the treatment should progress well. Dissatisfied with that response, the audience member wondered why anyone would move against the grain of their entire life's patterning, especially if the challenge of confronting that lived lifestyle would likely involve pain and suffering. The answer, in part, is that when we have our *why* (i.e., our consciously constructed, deeply held values) to guide, inspire, and fuel us, we end up more readily able to accomplish our *what* (i.e., measurable, behavioral goals). We need both whys and whats for ourselves to move in meaningful directions professionally and personally, accomplishing milestones that matter along the way.

Interestingly, making choices in line with our values allows us to face life's challenges with more confidence, whether from internal chatter, difficult memories, worries, afflictive interpersonal dynamics, or general stress. In her popular book on therapist self-care, Baker (2003) suggested that there is good value in periodically considering what we find most significant in our lives. She noted that the process of increasing our sense of meaning and purpose in life necessarily involves defining our version of "success" and then making tough choices in light of very real limits of time and energy.

Many writers of professional self-care and career-sustaining behaviors have discussed the importance of abiding by our values (e.g., Norcross & VandenBos, 2018; Wise et al., 2012), and it's found within many approaches, including ACT (LeJeune & Luoma, 2019; McKay et al., 2010), mindfulness, and positive psychology. Erin Olivo, PhD, MPH, former director of the Columbia University Integrative Medicine Program and author of *Wise Mind Living*, highlighted the notion that self-care isn't a list of activities (as cited in Tartakovsky, 2016). Rather, it's more about living your life in accordance with your values. As we develop our awareness of what self-care can mean to us, what our unique occupational stresses and pressures are, and what rewards and joys we derive from our work, we become increasingly ready to map (i.e., identify and clarify) what truly matters to us.

Values are not just about the direction in which we'd like our life to head; they are also about the qualities with which we move in that direction. For example, in the values domain of friendships, we would ask ourselves what *kind* of friend we really want to be? How would we embody and express our friendship qualities? What kinds of friendships do we ultimately want to build and maintain, and why would this ultimately matter to us anyway?

In your professional and personal life writ large, what qualities would you like to embody in a more consistent fashion or to continue to integrate into your life if they're already flourishing? We can now take a brief self-care reflection break (see Figure 6.1) to examine our desired qualities to embody and express. This diagram shows just a few qualities that could enhance our sense of well-being within ourselves and with loved ones, clients, and in our environment. As you take a moment to contemplate, imagine each desired quality and how it would show up in your life. How does it feel to see yourself in this capacity?

Although there are many life domains for which to consider our values (e.g., family, parenting, friendships, community involvement, health, self-growth,

FIGURE 6.1. Desired Qualities to Embody and Express

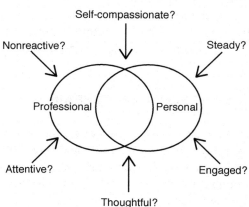

leisure, spirituality, work), mapping our professional and personal self-care values incorporates almost every other values domain within it. For example, our supportive interpersonal connections are an inherent part of how we take care of ourselves and nourish our well-being, and thus naturally they are part and parcel of self-care values. This value of fostering supportive connections can manifest at work with our colleagues and at home with our friends, partner, children, or others. If this valued life domain is strained, or we're not putting in the effort we once were, we may indeed feel this loss. Similarly, if we derive deep fulfillment in life through hiking, creative hobbies, and music, for example, then making sure our leisure time isn't overrun by our professional life is a fundamental form of self-caring. Being able to identify the values that contribute to our self-care can in turn help encourage us onto a path of more enduring professional and personal well-being.

As we return to Jodi, our social work colleague, we may realize that she would benefit from reconnecting with her values—what truly matters to her in the life she is living and wants to live for her future. Just like beautiful sea glass embedded within the grit of the wet sand, within Jodi's grievances of her current professional lifestyle she may find what deeply inspires and motivates her. She may learn the choices to make to take better care of herself while discovering more joy and vitality within her professional and personal life. Jodi can then turn to the mapping of her self-care values to move herself through choices and actions that help foster greater fulfillment and meaning.

Anytime we map something, we first need to get a "lay of the land" by understanding where we've traveled, what our experiences have been like along the way, and how we'd like to navigate new terrain in the future. Mapping our self-care values functions in a similar series of steps:

1. Map your existing self-care terrain.
2. Clarify what has and does currently matter about your own self-care.
3. Visualize your embodiment and expression of future self-caring.
4. Establish a self-caring compass as a tool for resilience.

MAP YOUR EXISTING SELF-CARE TERRAIN

In your life thus far, what has the terrain of caring for yourself been like? Has tending to your own needs been a rocky and jagged affair, or have you navigated a relatively smooth self-caring terrain? Perhaps your journey has been marked by large gaps in the care you've given yourself. Or maybe your self-caring is often thwarted despite your best intentions—other aspects of

EXHIBIT 6.1. Self-Care Reflection Break: History of Navigating Your Self-Care Terrain

Quality of Your Self-Care Boundaries

- Do your ideas of self-care end up being overly influenced by others and external forces?
- Do you maintain a rigid structure, not letting others influence you much at all?

Quality of Your Self-Caring Over Time

- Have you treated yourself with relative kindness and compassion?
- Have you struggled with how to care for yourself, or do you have a more nurturing and easeful self-relationship?

Consistency of Self-Caring Over Time

- Do you have long runs of taking good care of yourself and elevating your own needs to great importance?
- Are you pushed by certain stressful events to take better care of yourself, only to revert to poorer self-care after the acute stressor has passed?

life keep appearing as more vital or urgent than the priority of *you* and your well-being (see Exhibit 6.1).

In Chapter 7, we'll explore what often gets in the way of turning toward the establishment of self-care values and enacting the very habits that nourish us. For now, it's important to have a historical sense of your self-caring terrain so that you understand your past patterns of how you've related to your own well-being.

CLARIFY WHAT HAS AND DOES CURRENTLY MATTER ABOUT YOUR OWN SELF-CARE

How do you ultimately want to treat yourself so that you maintain a buoyancy of personal spirit and bring a vitality to your work? What do you want to stand for at the end of the day as well as at the end of your life? What follows is a (nonexhaustive) list of questions that can help spark greater clarity about what is truly meaningful within the broad domain of self-care for psychotherapists:

- What kind of psychotherapist do you really want to be, and how would you know when you're enacting this?

- What kind of self-caring is required to support being the therapist you desire to be? Greater flexibility of mind, more self-compassion, more intimacy in your personal life or connection to work colleagues, less identification and involvement in your clients' lives, more consistent down time, a more positive outlook and proactive coping?

- Do you tend to care for your own mental and emotional health as methodically and compassionately as you do your clients and/or loved ones in your life?

- How would your values in life domains such as leisure, self-growth, service, and friendships contribute to how you ultimately take care of yourself? Do you see these other domains as conflicting with your self-care, or are they inherently part of your self-caring mindset and behavioral actions?

- What qualities of mind and heart do you desire to live by so that your candle continues to burn brightly even in the strongest winds? Or to contemporize that metaphor, how do you desire to live your life so that you consciously recharge your batteries and are mindfully aware of what drains them?

- Why would it ultimately matter to you to take good care of yourself on a daily basis? Do you believe self-care really adds any true value? If so, why and how?

VISUALIZE YOUR EMBODIMENT AND EXPRESSION OF FUTURE SELF-CARING

Although figuring out how best to embody and enact your own self-caring is the theme of the entire book, it warrants some preframing in this chapter focused exclusively on values. Ultimately, the heart of any change process is doing things differently and then sustaining healthy habits in accordance with what truly matters to you, as a unique individual. And so as you're identifying and clarifying what is meaningful to you about taking care of yourself and the qualities you'd like to bring into your life that speak to your professional and personal well-being, it's worth beginning to note how this values-based self-care process might manifest in daily life. While it's not necessary to conjure up a perfectly clear vision, you can reflect on the feelings you'd like to experience based on a shift in how you would relate to your own care.

Right-brain exercises like visualization sometimes are more powerful than intellectual or purely verbal articulations of an idea. In your mind's eye, what do you see and sense you're doing as you go to bed tonight that fosters well-being and wellness? And when you wake in the morning, what does that self-caring look and feel like? How would you know experientially that you're caring for yourself in ways that truly matter to you? When you arrive at work (or if you are working remotely), how would you be living out your self-caring values? What would you be doing, saying, practicing, arranging in your environment? Take yourself through your clinical activities and administrative duties with the same loving attention to your own welfare rather than you being last on the list of things to take of.

If you experienced some resistance to this exercise, it's okay. You may have felt it almost impossible to imagine taking care of yourself as you'd really like because you have small children who demand your attention or because you are tending to extremely challenging cases right now. The point is to treat yourself as if you really matter and deserve grace regardless of what is happening around you. If that means you identify very small but powerful gestures of internal resilience (e.g., soothing self-compassionate voice, remembering to pack your lunch for the day), then that's exactly what you need at that time.

ESTABLISH A SELF-CARING COMPASS AS A TOOL FOR RESILIENCE

Values are like guides or compasses. They inform us of the direction we're headed and serve as reminders to correct course and adjust our bearings. Values help support our movements, actions, decisions, and resilience because they can powerfully whisper to us what matters and why. It's like we've audio recorded our values on our smartphones and then must press play again and again over time to remind ourselves of what's truly important.

Dr. Cory Chen—clinical professor in the Department of Psychiatry at New York University, Co-Chief of the Telepsychology Section, and director of the psychotherapy research and development program at the VA New York Harbor Healthcare System—has his own unique form of values check-in, which involves an Excel spreadsheet with values domains and their relative importance (C. Chen, personal communication, September 2016). Each values domain is explicated as to the qualities Dr. Chen desires to embody and express, and a set number of committed actions (or consciously conducted behaviors) are planned for each value. Although this practice ebbs and flows (because he's human), Dr. Chen checks in with himself periodically and reflects on how he is moving toward or away from each delineated value through his daily and weekly actions. He then adjusts his actions accordingly if too much or too little energy is being devoted to a particular value. Dr. Chen also notices his relative lack of attention to certain actions aligned with his core values when he begins to feel burned out or disconnected from his values. This particular method is much more structured than many of us might imagine for ourselves, but it provides a template for how we might consider holding ourselves accountable and making necessary adjustments to our physical actions to align with our deeper values.

It's important to note that values and their manifestations may change over time. For example, when we become a parent, we are charged with the 24/7 care of another tiny human being. Our priorities transform in a heartbeat. Dr. Chen noted that after becoming a father, he was forced to rethink what he truly cares about and how he spends his time (C. Chen, personal communication, March 1, 2021). Indeed, the kind of parent, partner, friend, therapist, or colleague you desire to be may shift with different stages of life and career. Sometimes, in fact, we feel lost like Jodi or need to reorient like Dr. Chen. With guidance and support from loved ones, trusted colleagues, and perhaps our own psychotherapist, mentor, or spiritual guide, we can evaluate our values at any stage and begin again to make the choices that we've identified as truly mattering to us.

We can also employ three other more graphically oriented self-care compass tools. First, the popular bull's-eye values exercise, created by Swedish ACT practitioner Tobias Lundgren, establishes the bull's eye on a concentric circle target as symbolic of living most in accordance with your values in various domains of life (Dahl & Lundgren, 2006; see https://www.actmindfully.com. au/free-stuff/worksheets-handouts-book-chapters/). The farther from the bull's eye, the more you've lost touch (mentally and most important behaviorally) with what truly matters. You can use this graphic to track your progress over time and spark reflection within yourself and discussions with others about the extent to which your everyday actions are values-aligned.

A similar but differently arranged tool is the "True North" Life Direction Exercise (Hersh, 2014; see Figure 6.2). This exercise can be as involved or as simplified as you like. For our visual purposes here, consider personal and professional self-care as distinct domains. Draw a long line in the middle of a blank piece paper, with an arrow pointing straight up (your "true north"). This is the direction of what truly matters to you personally and professionally and is all about your self-caring actions that would promote greater fulfillment and resilience. The specifics of what matters to you regarding your self-caring are derived from the steps described previously. From the bottom of the true north line, draw a separate dotted line representing how close you are to living your life aligned with your true north.

You can draw separate dotted lines for professional and personal domains, although these lines will likely overlap in considerable ways. For example,

FIGURE 6.2. True North Life Direction Exercise

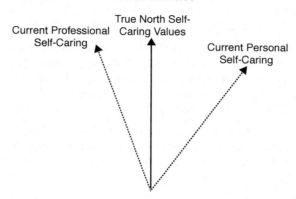

you might determine that you deeply value physical body vitality and energy. Thus, the dotted line on the left might represent healthy posture and stretching between sessions, while the dotted line on the right might represent behaviors such as getting high-quality sleep and doing some kind of bodily movement at least three times per week. How narrow the gap between the dotted lines and your true north signifies the degree of alignment of your daily actions with your deeper values.

A final popular resource to highlight is Dr. Kevin Polk's ACT matrix (Polk et al., 2016). Although the full multistep, highly interactive approach is beyond the scope of this chapter, I often use an abbreviated version in my clinical work and have used it in my own personal–professional life with good success. Draw one vertical and one horizontal line, intersecting in the middle. The Y-axis vertical line at the top represents what is real, what you can take in through your senses and manifest in the real world through action. At the bottom of this line is what is represented in your mind—your thoughts, feelings, imaginings, and so on. Neither is better than the other; they are just different aspects of our human experience. Discerning the difference between these "worlds," however, is a skill we can develop in the service of living a values-driven life.

The X-axis arrow toward the right represents ideas of who and what is meaningful to you (in the bottom right quadrant) and what committed actions you take (or could take) to align your real-world experience with what is deemed important in your mind (in the top right quadrant). The left arrow represents whatever is moving away from what is meaningful to you, which could be your fears, anxieties, and doubts that show up internally when you ponder what's important to you (lower left quadrant) and your more observable behavioral manifestations of those internal *away* feelings and thoughts (upper left quadrant).

There are several practical aspects of the ACT matrix, the primary one being our orientation toward (or away from) what truly matters to us. Being able to readily discern our real-world actions from our mental experiences becomes a vital skill as we do our best to align our behaviors with our deeper values. Importantly, the ACT matrix also serves as a powerful visual reminder of how much we might be getting caught up in mental or real-world activities that send us away from living a life that is ultimately meaningful and fulfilling. These *away* behaviors as well as more systemic barriers are explored more fully in Chapter 7.

As we've begun to map our self-care values, we may already have bumped up against blocks that may prevent us from moving forward with the least amount of resistance possible. It is the purview of our next chapter to illuminate such blocks, barriers, and objections and to provide some ideas for paving a smoother path ahead with fewer obstacles standing in our values-based way.

7 IDENTIFYING AND ADDRESSING THE BLOCKS TO BEING OUR OWN BEST ALLIES

Our task is not to seek for love, but merely to seek and find all the barriers within yourself that you have built against it.

—Rumi

The 13th-century mystic and poet, Jellaludin Rumi, seems to have been able to cut through time and space, echoing a sentiment that can gently but powerfully guide all human beings on their path forward. Many psychotherapeutic approaches that we often employ use this foundational concept—uncovering and gaining insight into the blocks we have constructed or internalized over the years and that often prevent us from living a more sustainably peaceful and fulfilling life. In fact, even if we've identified our core values, reflecting on what truly matters to us as self-caring and self-advocating therapists, we may nevertheless harbor (less than conscious) objections to moving in a desired and valued direction. However, when objections and barriers are shown the light of day and made more workable,

https://doi.org/10.1037/0000309-008

The Thriving Therapist: Sustainable Self-Care to Prevent Burnout and Enhance Well-Being, by M. A. Hersh

we find ourselves much better able to make and sustain changes that align with our deeper values.

Look back to Chapter 6 for a moment and focus on the self-caring and well-being values you've illuminated. You may have determined, for example, "I really want to relate to myself more compassionately. It matters to me that I truly listen to my intuition to guide my professional decision making." This set of values is honorable and can help guide and coach you in self-advocacy and toward more sustainable well-being. However, let's also imagine that much of your childhood was fraught with subtle questioning of your more intuitive self and that it wasn't too emotionally safe in your family to just "go with your gut" even if you felt something was right for *you*. So in this case, you may have developed both an overreliance on others' input and a self-doubting habit that detours you from the path you ultimately want and may need to travel. We could begin to think of many other examples of blocks, barriers, or objections (BBOs) that have some undue influence over our movement in the world, our habits of mind and body, and our acting in accordance with our deeper values.

To engage in sustainable self-care that becomes a meaningful way of life (rather than an obligation, afterthought, or acute reaction to crisis), it is itself a genuine act of care to acknowledge and nourish our sense of deserving-ness to live in a self-caring manner. Excavating and addressing our BBOs to adopt this self-caring lifestyle—both personally and professionally—also then becomes a de facto act of self-care. Throughout this chapter we'll explore therapist-reported notions about what gets in the way of living a more self-caring lifestyle, exploring from both a systemic and a personal perspective (Baker, 2007). And we'll illustrate some practical methods to support addressing and releasing the BBOs that you identify as influential.

It's important to note before we dive in that the following framework or heuristic around BBOs is not as clean in real life as it might appear on these pages. Thus, something that shows up as a systemic barrier may indeed be a long-standing personal block of yours. The opposite can be the case as well. It is also quite realistic to consider that systemic and personal BBOs have become intertwined over time, out of our conscious awareness. Through cultural and familial messaging, specific events and experiences, and interpersonal patterning, we have come to adopt various emotionally laden beliefs that may work in opposition to our best interest. So, we move forward with some acknowledgment that each unique person will likely read this section through a personal filter. In many ways, how could it be any other way?

SYSTEMIC BARRIERS TO ADOPTING SELF-CARE MINDSET AND ACTIONS

Systemic barriers can be as macro as the cultural atmosphere in which we all live and as micro as the rules and policies of the mental health organization for which we work. These blocks and barriers can make it feel as if we're swimming upstream. Although we may have identified and strongly resonate with the ways in which taking care of ourselves matters, atmospheric conditions may pull at us, push us sideways, or even turn us around completely.

Training Is Supposed to Insulate Us

Just because we've trained extensively and rigorously and have dedicated our careers to helping others, we are not insulated from occupational risks (Barnett et al., 2007) or the vicissitudes of life. Unwittingly, our training institutions may have inculcated the notion that we are separate from the people we serve. We're supposed to be the healthy and together ones, or so our training and cultural forces have insidiously led us to believe. We are, however, very much like our clients (Barnett et al., 2007), the majority of us struggling with everyday stressors, with loss and grief, anxiety and worry, low mood and disillusionment, and with poorer health than we want (e.g., Thoreson et al., 1989). However, we know that both the human condition and the courage to be vulnerable are paramount to accepting our ethical and humanistic mandate to be our own best advocates (Brown, 2018).

Attention to Self-Care and Risk Prevention Is Neglected

The myth of occupational risk insulation is just the tip of the iceberg. Psychologists have reported a lack or even total absence of attention to issues of occupational hazards and self-care within training programs and beyond (e.g., Schoener, 1999; Tart, 1992; Williams-Nickelson, 2001). Thus, trainees may not realize what risks and pitfalls lie ahead as well as the immense benefits of self-care and prevention. As Schoener (2007) noted, our field must devote resources and attention to the issue of self-care, at the formative training level and beyond.

Self-Care Is Selfish

"I'm very sorry; my caseload is full. But I can try to refer you to a colleague." Is that selfish? It may feel that way if you're used to accommodating your prospective clients over your own busy schedule. Or it may be a simple cut-and-dry situation, and there's no issue if you don't squeeze in a new client somewhere in your schedule. But what if your caseload isn't entirely full and you're fortunate enough not to have patient or client quotas to adhere to? Are you being selfish if you need or would like to reserve an hour one day a week for yourself?

The complexities of self-caring increase in proportion to the subtleties of our situations. If we're sick with the flu or can't speak due to laryngitis, we don't go to work (one hopes), and we rest. But what if we've been managing an acute phase of a chronically sick parent? Is this "enough justification" to warrant a *mental health day*, advocating for a bit more flexibility in our schedules, or demanding some much-needed rest and recuperation? Would intentionally taking some time off or resting feel selfish or even self-pitying? Unfortunately, the culturally propagated belief is that tending to oneself is somehow an egocentric act when done with purpose and perhaps self-pitying when done from a place of stress and vulnerability. As psychotherapists, we may even be made to feel guilty when we act with intention to take care of ourselves (Faunce, 1990).

Problems Are Emphasized at the Expense of Well-Being

Our culture is obsessed with problems and even manufactures them for commercial purposes. Your teeth are too yellow, hair too dull, lawn not green enough, house not big enough. To counteract such problems, we can spend countless hours and dollars and expend an inordinate amount of psychic energy on what can largely be considered running on the hedonic treadmill at best and becoming lost in empty and meaningless pursuits at worst. This is not to say that we shouldn't address the difficulties in our lives that interfere with the ability of our minds and bodies to function well. But attention to our problems can certainly be overblown and unfortunately manufactured by insidious cultural forces beyond our acute awareness.

Some research suggests that after social workers explain why they've neglected their own self-care (e.g., "I don't have time"), they will follow up with an assurance: "I will do it when I need it" (L. Butler, as presented in K. Jackson, 2014). Dr. Lisa Butler, associate professor in the School of Social Work at the University of Buffalo, painted a stark picture of a social worker waiting to brush their teeth until their gums were bleeding. But we brush our teeth because it produces health *as well as* prevents problems. We can bring to life our self-caring values for more uplifted well-being just as we've developed the habit of brushing our teeth for optimal oral hygiene.

Our Clients, Not Ourselves, Are the Ones Who Need Our Help

How strongly do you sense the implicit expectation that you work to serve others, not yourself? The more steeped we are in our professional work, the more we might act on such implicit notions. But, as Rabbi Hillel the Elder was thought to have said more than 2000 years ago, "If I am not for myself, who will be for me? And if I am only for myself, then what am I? And if not now, when?"

Almost every professional development and continuing education course that is offered is focused on how to help *others*. This is not only a statement of fact but also a symptom of a larger, more systemic problem that we all must face. How often have you thought about helping yourself and supporting your own life while participating in a continuing education course on nutrition for mental health, real-world dialectical behavior therapy skills for difficult emotions, or resilience skills for turbulent times? Do you feel awkward or selfish if your mind drifts toward your own life and not just focusing on how to help your clients?

How often have you attended workshops and seminars on professional self-care? If you've answered "never" to this last question, then you're not alone. Considering that we and the therapeutic relationship have been shown to be powerful agents of change for our clients (e.g., Flückiger et al., 2018; Karver et al., 2018), doesn't it make intuitive and even ethical sense that we are also the ones who need our compassionate and loving attention? In fact, because the therapeutic relationship predicts client outcomes independent of specific therapeutic methods (see Norcross & VandenBos, 2018), shouldn't the person within the therapist be a central focus of our collective attention (e.g., Ardito & Rabellino, 2011)?

We Are Expected to Be Productive and Responsible

A sobering fact of our current mental health system is that demand can be overwhelmingly high while supply languishes. Supply is us—our energy, time, skills, resources, and well-being. Unfortunately, the worldview and policies enforced within many companies and clinics (and even within our private practices) require that we work harder with fewer resources. Many (but certainly not all) cultural practices around the world seem to imply or even demand that to achieve great success we must work until we're close to burnout and that we must do it all to get ahead (Williams-Nickelson, 2006).

Burnout is of course perceived as a "bad outcome," but the ingredients that comprise the burnout recipe may not be recognized or addressed until therapists are pulled down that path of suffering. In fact, some social workers appear to neglect their own self-care because they perceive and believe that they must keep working and helping all the time at all costs (see K. Jackson, 2014).

Time Is at a Premium

There is perhaps no greater stress (and barrier to accomplishing things in life) than the feeling or stark reality of having little time to do the things you want or need to do. Time stress manifests particularly when we have pressures from our workplace, clients, family, and culture to "do more with less." Jon Kabat-Zinn (2013), one of the founding fathers of Western mindfulness meditation, wrote about time and time stress in *Full Catastrophe Living*. The perception (and reality) of not having enough time can, in general, strain our capacity to be productive, to relax, to connect, and to self-soothe. In fact, just feeling stressed about time is enough to excite the sympathetic tone of your nervous system at the expense of engaging your parasympathetic rest-and-digest, tend-and-befriend mode for optimal self-care enactment.

Difficulties Are Stigmatized in the Workplace

Quite unfortunately, psychotherapists working in a variety of settings have reported feeling a sense of stigma that prevents them from seeking help for their stress and their potential impairments. Most psychotherapists are reluctant to lean on their colleagues for personal support because they believe their colleagues will view them as untrustworthy and that they will be stigmatized for their problems (S. Walsh et al., 1991). Moreover, women therapists in particular have reported feeling judged and alienated if their colleagues learn that they are experiencing mental health issues such as depression (L. Carroll et al., 1999). Norcross (2000) noted that, despite such stigma and perceived barriers, more than 50% of psychotherapists reported that they participated in psychotherapy after their training program was complete, with the vast majority saying that their own personal therapy was quite fruitful. As Elman and Forrest (2007) poignantly implored, training programs need to communicate the message that self-care is just as important and respected as hard work. Internalizing this mindset from the beginning of our careers not only paves the way for self-advocacy (Dearing et al., 2005) but can also reduce stigma and increase stewardship of each other's well-being as we move through our professional development.

PERSONAL BARRIERS TO ADOPTING SELF-CARE MINDSET AND ACTIONS

While systemic barriers to integrating self-care into our lives can be powerfully influential, your constellation of personal blocks, barriers, and objections to a self-caring mindset and lifestyle can be equally as powerful and may even prime you to internalize the aforementioned systemic barriers more deeply.

Poor Self-Care Was Modeled During Childhood

To what degree and with what qualities did you experience your caregivers, older siblings, or other important adults in your life embodying a self-caring style? Did your parents directly and purposefully invite each family member to take time for themselves or encourage recuperation when exhausted and revitalization when drained? Was self-care modeled as conditional or perhaps a luxury, akin to the quality of pampering and indulgence we referenced in Chapter 1?

One of the most insidious ways of modeling something is to model the absence of it, as in childhood emotional neglect (Webb, 2012). For example, Rita, a midcareer psychologist in the Midwest, spoke of her early family life as a circus, with her four younger siblings always running around and her ever-exhausted mother never stopping to sit for more than a minute at a time. Her father, a self-declared workaholic, worked tirelessly outside the home and returned from his job just as Rita's mother was making dinner for the family. Rita, the oldest (and dubbed "mommy's best helper"), was always supporting her mother with household tasks and with babysitting her younger siblings. Rita noted that, although she was able to play a fair amount as a child, even the weekends seemed fraught with tension to complete some project, continue to clean, and get ready for the coming week. Rita lamented that she doesn't remember any conversations about taking breaks when tired or just lying around without some negative consequence. But she does vividly remember how utterly exhausted her parents were at every stage of her childhood. And it never seemed to change. What was your childhood modeling like with respect to self-care (mindset and action), wellness, and basic attention to your needs?

You Believe You Don't Deserve It

In a more existential and humanistic view of therapist self-care, Sapienza and Bugental (2000) likened our pursuit of self-care to that of keeping our instruments finely tuned. When we're disconnected from this notion, or have never really connected with it in the first place, then we encounter what might *feel* like a basic truth—that we're simply not supposed to take good care of ourselves. This experience can be a foundational deservingness problem, or it could be that we never really learned to see ourselves as valuable unless we were helping others. Earnestly helping ourselves in sustainable ways might feel like a foreign invader that we must ward off at all costs.

You're Not Fully Aware of Your Needs

How are we supposed to be aware of something of which we're not aware? This is quite the conundrum but one that is likely serving as one of your core personal barriers to fully adopting a self-caring mindset or implementing self-caring actions over time. Many of us have blind spots and a relative lack of awareness of our needs due to our upbringings, personalities, and training experiences (O'Connor, 2001). Thus, with less conscious attention to our personal pitfalls and work-related risk factors (Sherman, 1996), we may feel unnecessary distress and possibly engage in poor decision making that compromises our professional competence (Barnett et al., 2007).

You Hold Unrealistic Perceptions of Your Colleagues

"He's always so productive, well dressed, and never seems too stressed. He must really have his shit together. What's wrong with me, 'cause I'm such a mess?" Such an evaluation would undoubtedly generate and potentially sustain a *lesser than* feeling and one that promotes self-pity (and external anger or envy) rather than compassionate self-caring. But it should be clear by now that the majority of your colleagues have struggled and continue to struggle in various ways, just like you. Almost every therapist fears that one of their clients will commit suicide (Pope & Tabachnick, 1994). Half of your colleagues right now are likely to have client concerns affecting their daily functioning. It may be of some solace to acknowledge that the difference between being a client and being a psychotherapist simply depends on which chair you happen to sit in for that 50-minute hour.

You're Not Quite Sure What Self-Care Is Really About

"You really have to take better care of yourself." You may hear that as sage advice, but it may also vibrate as annoying or even as blaming. As colleague and self-care researcher Dr. Ariel Botta said about her clinical supervisees training at a large teaching hospital, "they've been told do more self-care but not about what to do or how" (A. Botta, personal communication, September 2016).

In some ways, knowing *what* to do for self-care is an internet search away. But the adoption of a self-caring mindset and the integration of a sustainable self-caring lifestyle is more than just referencing a list. Chapter 1 included numerous overlapping but fruitfully distinct definitions and conceptualizations of self-care. We can pore over the myths and meanings of self-care and find what speaks to us most readily. From there, we may even glance ahead at Parts III and IV of this book to see what self-caring practices, activities, and ways of being could look like. We could read a blog or another book on self-care to further expand our sense of the what and the how. We could have open-ended conversations with our peers and our loved ones, with mentors and trusted figures within wisdom traditions to which we might subscribe. Based on honest reflection of our unique needs and patterns, we could then experiment with a few ways of enacting self-care that resonate most strongly for the developmental phase we're inhabiting right now.

You Feel Excessive Guilt for Tending to Yourself

Although we've referenced guilt while discussing the BBO that self-care is selfish, it deserves its own treatment. Guilt is a very powerful emotion that can be triggered by real-world situations in which we've done something we *shouldn't have*. But many times guilt arises from our conditioned feelings of self-blame, over-responsibility, conscientiousness, and a rigid internal compass.

It's extremely important to address the guilt monster that can show up at inopportune times, almost compelling us to relinquish thoughts and actions toward helping ourselves in favor of taking on yet another client, project, or task. We may also feel a crushing guilt when we slow down to take a break. We may not necessarily believe that idle hands are the devil's workshop, but some of us can become fairly distraught at not doing something productive or helpful when we feel we should.

ADDRESSING BLOCKS, BARRIERS, AND OBJECTIONS TO BEING OUR OWN BEST ALLIES

It can be quite challenging to abide by our chosen values while experiencing the trials and tribulations of work and personal life. It can feel and be easier to take shelter and seek the safety of each ordinary day (McKay et al., 2010). Although quite difficult at times, fostering willingness is part of the answer.

As McKay and colleagues (2010) suggested, it's about accepting "everything that happens when we set off in a valued direction. Willingness is facing the cost of valued action—and doing it anyway" (p. 24).

It is not my intention here to imply that we would be able to move past any of these systemic or personal constraints simply from increased awareness and an unshakable willingness. Rather, through mindful awareness and genuine interest in self-growth, accompanied by ongoing dialogue with trusted others in your life, you may begin to peel the layers back to reveal what needs to be examined and duly addressed. Particularly for entrenched systemic barriers, successful mitigation or clearing of any blocks to becoming your own best ally may indeed take a village.

Rather than beginning with BBOs that may feel too insidious or organizationally constrained to effect direct change, it can be helpful to identify those that are obvious and within your reach. Let's start by reviewing the BBOs discussed earlier in this chapter. You may also discover that you experience your own BBOs, not mentioned previously but having personal relevance to your unique life. What stands out to you as you reflect more deeply now? Are there barriers or objections you've always known to be influential in your life, holding you back from taking better care of yourself in an ongoing fashion?

Let's do a pen-and-paper exercise right now that can get our BBO-tackling energies activated (see Appendix C: Addressing Our Blocks, Barriers, and Objections to Being Our Own Best Allies). Create three equal-sized columns. The left column is your brainstorming master list of BBOs. You can always add to that list; let it be a reference for you whenever you come back to this exercise. The middle column is simply to place the BBOs from the left column into a category (i.e., personal, systemic, combo, other). The right column is for you to rate (on a scale from 0 [*least*] to 10 [*most*]) how influential that particular BBO is your life, inhibiting your ability to do your very best to tend to your own care in a sustainable way. It's likely helpful to look back at Chapters 1 and 6 to remind yourself of what is most meaningful to you.

Once you've established the beginning of a master list and have categorized and rated the BBOs, you can take one BBO that stands out that you've rated as mildly to moderately influential. Much like with behavioral exposure hierarchies, finding a target that is workable and within your window of tolerance (i.e., not too mild but not too overwhelming) is often quite useful. Take a separate sheet of paper and create a heading with the selected BBO. Create three columns. The left column will be for ways in which this BBO behaviorally manifests itself in different facets of your life, personally and professionally. For example, if you've chosen the BBO "self-care is ultimately selfish," this feeling may reveal itself as never taking lunch breaks at work, skipping opportunities to relax during the weekend, or being bound up in tacit agreements with your spouse to give them breaks while you feel guilty for wanting to take your own.

The middle column is all about beginning to unpack the thoughts, feelings, actions, and reactions that (purposefully and accidentally) maintain the influential role of this BBO in your life. For example, let's say that you initially target *never taking a lunch break at work* because you feel guilty and selfish for taking time away from what you're "supposed to be doing." You can begin to dismantle this block by jotting down as many beliefs and feelings you currently hold that keep this behavioral pattern locked in place. What are your assumptions and expectations about what will happen if you do indeed take a lunch break? What feelings are perceived as too uncomfortable to experience but may have taken on an influential role in maintaining this lunchtime behavioral pattern of not taking a lunch break?

Incidentally, this BBO likely overlaps with systemic barriers related to productivity requirements as well as simply not having enough time to "get it all done." Therefore, even if the selfishness block is adequately addressed, other BBOs may continue to exert some undue influence on your relatively underdeveloped self-caring attitudes and actions. For this reason, it may be useful to conceptualize your self-care BBOs in a Venn diagram with spokes coming from each particular barrier to represent its real-world manifestations (see Appendix C). As you continue to work on dissolving the power of each BBO, you may visually get a sense of how the constellation or web of BBOs is arranged. This method may help you over time as you increasingly and actively address related issues that may have lain dormant if you followed only a master list.

In completing this particular writing exercise, the right column represents the possibilities for taking small but meaningful actions to test the waters or address head-on some underpinnings of that BBO. For example, if you determined from the middle column that you feel ashamed and guilty and that you are letting your clients down whenever you even think about taking a break for lunch, you could start shining some light on this darker set of sentiments by talking to a variety of colleagues and asking them how they manage this issue. Likely, you'll start to hear similar themes of "there's not enough time" and "it's hard for me, too." You may also hear "Yeah, even though it's really hard, I just commit to making the time. If I don't do it, no one will do it for me." Just hearing these responses firsthand from trusted colleagues could spill a bit of sunshine on the vampiric beliefs and feelings hanging out in the shadows. Shame and guilt love darkness, so any light you can shed on these issues is a powerful force of self-caring in and of itself.

Of note, other ways to break through and address particular BBOs are found within alternative approaches, such as energy psychology (see Chapter 27 for more detailed treatment of this topic). As a certified comprehensive energy psychologist, I frequently work with clients' beliefs and feelings that are holding them back from letting go of a problem or moving in the direction they desire. By activating (through thought and feeling) the very BBO in question, we can harness the use of specific acupoint tapping to remove or at least greatly mitigate the limiting effects of the BBO.

WARNING: OTHERS MAY WANT YOUR BBOs TO STICK AROUND

Releasing yourself from the effects of particular BBOs likely won't happen overnight. There may be blowback within yourself (see Neff & Germer, 2018, for a discussion of the concept of backdraft) or from others who unwittingly are counting on you *not* to change your ways. When you are not a so-called selfish person (i.e., you withhold your own self-care), for example, you unknowingly may benefit a vast network of coworkers, clients, family members, and friends.

Having candid discussions with those you most trust can kickstart softening some of the more rigid constraints already in place. To be sure, some of the people in our lives, including bosses, colleagues, spouses, children, and friends, may (feel like they) require us to be constantly selfless. They may say or do things to prevent us from tending to ourselves as we see fit. This situation is of course on the toxic end of the spectrum and may require professional and structured assistance to help you move the needle of your own self-care and well-being.

It is my hope that from these two chapters on mapping our self-care values and the obstacles to living in accordance with them that we feel both more knowledgeable and more energized. We can now take such an informed spirit into a deeper knowing of our professional and personal selves. Part II invites us to explore and discover who we are and how we work. We'll investigate our patterned ways of being and working and what we ultimately need for ourselves. These insights—whether clarified or gained anew—can set the stage for how to best care for ourselves while at work, at home, in the space between, and over the span of our careers.

PART **II**

FLEXIBLY GROUNDED:
MINDFUL AWARENESS
OF HABITS, PATTERNS,
AND NEEDS

INTRODUCTION: FLEXIBLY GROUNDED: MINDFUL AWARENESS OF HABITS, PATTERNS, AND NEEDS

It seems to me the beginning of wisdom of any kind, including knowledge of ourselves, is acknowledgment of the infirmity of our beliefs and the paucity of our knowledge.

—Mitchell S. Green

Like trees that need certain conditions to grow healthfully, we are creatures that need specific ingredients both to survive and to thrive. When we care for the greenery in our homes, we learn what each plant requires. Given the right nutrients and other environmental factors, that particular plant will likely flourish. Although certain hazards may influence healthy growth, the consistent care we provide that's based on working knowledge of that specific plant will likely foster good health.

Just as we benefit from our plants and with the human beings in our lives for whom we are accountable, we can benefit from learning more about our individual requirements for leading a healthy life, inside and out. Each of us will differ in our needs, however, based on our unique experiences across our own paths of development and throughout the phases of our career. Part II of this book encourages us to journey through the various domains of our needs, examining with curiosity and honesty our patterns and habits that affect the care we give ourselves.

Our "business" as psychotherapists is to know others' business—their needs, wishes, urges, traumas, aspirations, strengths, and resourcefulness. How do we learn about our clients' needs, patterns, and habits? We ask questions, and we listen. We attend to their stories, and we read between the lines. We look at the ways in which their bodies have kept the score and what's missing from their mannerisms and affects. Ultimately, we draw conclusions and hypothesize based on ever-accumulating data, humbly realizing that we may be off or even flat-out wrong and that the process of knowing is always a work in progress.

We now turn to do this process with ourselves in the service of hazards prevention and well-being enhancement. Although it may feel uncomfortable and even like a bizarre role reversal of sorts, it can be helpful for us to switch seats with our clients. Let's sit down on the proverbial couch and look inward. Let this needs exploration unfold at your own pace, and utilize the structure and guidance provided in a way that suits you.

The knowledge we gain about ourselves adds immense value to our capacity to give the best self-care possible over time and across context. Many writers and researchers who address psychotherapist self-care have drawn attention to self-awareness and self-monitoring as key tools to help us engage optimally in this challenging work (Baker, 2003; Coster & Schwebel, 1997; Stevanovic & Rupert, 2004). Realistic, ongoing assessment of our strengths and vulnerabilities becomes vital in assisting us to make sound and constructive decisions, personally and professionally.

Importantly, and of which we can be compassionately and repeatedly reminded, we inherently are *not* being selfish, egocentric, self-pitying, self-aggrandizing, or shameful if we pay mindful attention to identifying our needs and learning how to get them met in appropriate ways. Rather, this process of reflection, insight, and action is the cornerstone of flexible but sustainable self-care, which is the foundation of living and working with greater ease and competence.

In her attuned representational model of self, Dr. Catherine Cook-Cottone (2006)—clinical psychologist, yoga instructor, and eating disorder specialist—acknowledged this dual reality. We are all embedded within an ecological context (e.g., family, community, culture) but still need to embody a self-regulation that derives from awareness and maintenance of our unique needs. This dialectical synthesis is what Cook-Cottone called the *authentic self*. Deference to external demands, ideals, or pressures can cause a host of personal and professional problems. Only when we acknowledge outside forces but turn with deep respect to our interior dynamics is sustainable self-care truly attainable.

8 DEVELOPMENTAL AND CAREER-STAGE REALITIES

Self-care is a lifestyle that evolves with your needs.

—Lanie Smith

When we became professional helpers, we weren't automatically granted a magical shield to protect us from the whims of everyday living (Coster & Schwebel, 1997). Our being human first and psychotherapists second necessitates that we too experience success *and* failure, love *and* rejection, gain *and* loss, and pride *and* shame. We came to the business of psychotherapy already having to cope with and adapt to the changing tide of family life, gender roles, marital relationships, and economic conditions (Coster & Schwebel, 1997), to name just a few facets of our complicated lives. Over time, different phases of personal and professional development as well as differing ecological contexts (e.g., abruptly moving to a large city, being a psychotherapist of color in a mostly White town) will generate different constellations of demands, challenges, and self-care needs. Insofar as we're able to anticipate some of our upcoming developmental challenges, we can

https://doi.org/10.1037/0000309-009
The Thriving Therapist: Sustainable Self-Care to Prevent Burnout and Enhance Well-Being,
by M. A. Hersh

practice embracing what we encounter and rolling with the certain uncertainties. From this flexible stance, we ideally equip ourselves to move through our lives and careers with greater poise and resilience.

One of the most powerful ways of framing our developmental and professional needs is through the contribution of German psychologist, Dr. Paul Baltes. Baltes et al.'s (1998) *lifespan perspective* is a developmental and nonpathologizing approach to human aging emphasizing in part that development is a *lifelong* and *multidimensional* dynamic interaction among many aspects of our being, such as our emotions, physical bodies, and social development. Development is also *multidirectional*, as we are constantly engaged in a dance of often unpredictable steps forward and backward. Life is also *plastic*, and we are malleable, for better or for worse.

As we all know from our lived experiences, we do not develop in a vacuum. Our development is influenced by contextual forces, many of which are beyond our control. Although it's far too easy to insist that each individual is "ultimately in charge of their own destiny," the reality is that the cultural and historical forces of life are constantly shaping us just as much as we are shaping ourselves. So while this book is about *self*-care, it's actually more about locating our*selves* within the influences that not only restrict but also invite and promote therapist well-being.

Every therapist has been, is currently, and will be shaped by three major forces: normative age-related influences (e.g., puberty, completion of formal training), historical influences (e.g., 9/11 terrorist attacks, the COVID-19 pandemic, political and race-related tension and unrest), and nonnormative experiences (e.g., experiencing a rape, being diagnosed with a serious illness, going through a divorce, coping with the death of child). We also live within a larger cultural context (e.g., "I live in America"), but this simple statement likely falls short of helping to explain our unique lives at the intersection of various cultural and cohort forces (e.g., "They are a transgender man born in 1990, living on the West Coast of the United States, and working in a hospital clinic practicing psychotherapy with disenfranchised LGBTQ+ individuals"). From there, we can better understand what this therapist may need relative to a 55-year-old cisgender heterosexual woman born and living in London who works primarily with patients with anxiety and obsessive–compulsive disorder. Although they may have some overlap in self-care needs, they may also have significant and meaningful differences that would be wise to attend to with kindness, patience, and flexibility.

Keeping in mind this holistic lifespan developmental perspective, let's turn now to a framework for thinking about psychotherapists' professional development over time: formal training (FT) → early-career psychotherapist

(ECP) → midcareer psychotherapist (MCP) → late-career psychotherapist (LCP). Although painting psychotherapists' career development in this way can feel a bit broad-brush or overly compartmentalized, it can be helpful for discussion among colleagues and for your personal reflection. We can also purposefully integrate the lifespan developmental model into the career-stage heuristic to paint our individual pictures with fine-tuned and nuanced strokes. In addition, by harnessing this developmental long view, we increase the likelihood of identifying and then meeting our needs to take good care of ourselves at any point across our careers and lifespans. Even if you're well beyond your trainee years, it can be beneficial to reflect on your previous experiences. This self-reflection can generate empathy and compassion for your less senior colleagues, ideally increasing the chances of helping fellow therapists who may also be struggling to integrate self-care and find greater meaning and well-being.

THE FORMAL TRAINING YEARS

Each of us once sat in the classroom learning about how to help others with their mental and emotional struggles. After scores of courses and thousands of hours of clinical practica and supervision, slowly but surely we honed our skills. However, the evolution of our competencies came with a variety of costs. It wasn't just the total time and energy invested into these competence-building endeavors. It was also the seemingly impossible balancing act that many clinical students find themselves facing. As Pappas (2020) emphasized, the simultaneous juggling of coursework, clinical placements, teaching, research assistantships, and research and thesis writing can take its toll and result in undue stress, pressure, and overwhelm.

In a large-scale survey, the majority of clinical psychology graduate students endorsed time pressures, financial strain, and poor school–personal life balance as significant challenges and stressors (El-Ghoroury et al., 2012). These same students also lamented that lack of funds and time stand in the way of incorporating self-care into their lives. While schooling is our main mission, we are also living our personal lives, experiencing the joys and sorrows of relationships, family life, and financial uncertainties. It can sometimes feel like Greek hazing as we attempt to engage fully in schooling and clinical training while keeping our personal lives afloat. Years ago, a fellow trainee once lamented, "It's hard to pour yourself a nice cup of tea when your life raft has a hole in it."

As Wise et al. (2011) suggested, educators and supervisors may assume that they are providing sufficient guidance and structure as students begin the journey of psychotherapy training. However, many programs may be missing a key ingredient to student well-being throughout these years. When training programs fail to formally address trainee self-care, students' stress levels tend to increase (Dorff, 1997). Conversely, students who perceive self-care to be important within the graduate-school culture are likely to engage in self-care themselves (Zahniser et al., 2017).

Some of us may have experienced the developmental dyssynchrony of being in professional training programs for 2 to 7 years while many of our friends and former college classmates were already earning a living, potentially saving for the future, and generally "moving on with their lives." We most likely chose a formal training track to set ourselves up for future success in a field that matters to us, but the "grass is greener" developmental effect can still prove an insidiously powerful force.

Psychology students nearing the completion of in-house coursework, practica, teaching, and research begin the physically arduous, financially costly, and emotionally draining process of applying for internship. Although beyond the scope of this chapter to elucidate fully, it's fair to say that the application process alone is a massive test of one's resilience and stress hardiness. The day we step into our internships, we essentially become cheap labor. We work hard and learn a great deal. However, all that demanding work can come at quite the cost to our sense of self and cause us to question why we're on this professional track in the first place.

Dr. Laura Ferrer, a clinical psychologist in private practice and 20-year supervisor of clinical psychology interns at a major psychiatric hospital, spoke to the very professional identity struggles that interns experience (L. Ferrer, personal communication, October 2, 2020). Despite how talented, intelligent, and successful the trainees already are, they nevertheless are confronted with the culturally fueled worries—will their efforts and strivings be enough, and at what personal costs? Over the years, the interns have cited doubts about finding balance between their professional and their personal lives and have questioned whether they will be able to relax and enjoy themselves while walking a future professional path of success.

Dr. Ferrer has encouraged these trainees to find their voices and to bring their needs, preferences, and values to the foreground. In supervision and within an intern support group conducted over the years, self-care has found its way to center stage—the deeper elements of how to reconcile the professional shoulds with interns' personal coulds, wants, and needs. The evolution of interns' sense of who they are and how to listen to their own needs and preferences, said Dr. Ferrer, is a powerful and humbling site to behold (L. Ferrer, personal communication, October 2, 2020).

Ultimately, these years of formal education are excellent training grounds to unapologetically put ourselves first (Carter & Barnett, 2014). Adopting a self-caring lifestyle, however, does not mean shirking responsibilities, giving a proverbial finger to our professors or clinical supervisors, or becoming selfish. It simply means getting to know what we need and why, how to get our needs met appropriately and without guilt, and becoming our own best allies along the way.

However, these aspirations for self-caring do not let our training and educational institutions off the hook. Indeed, institutions can and should play a major part in how budding psychotherapists treat themselves and situate into the larger professional world. With bold attention paid to such vital issues, we can hope for student self-care and well-being to become part and parcel of how the next generation of psychotherapists will evolve. Table 8.1 points us to the questions we can ask ourselves and the recommendations we may consider with respect to self-care within our training years.

TABLE 8.1. The Formal Training Years

Questions to ponder	Recommendations to consider
Am I working/studying nonstop to the point of exhaustion?	Begin discussions and application of self-care in clinical practica, ethics courses, and professional seminars.
How well integrated am I into the social fabric of my training institution? (Can I reliably trust my peers and mentors as supports?)	Faculty and supervisors can model self-care disclosure and management of stress and occupational hazards.
Am I feeling worthy and deserving of being in this training program, even if I feel like an imposter for much of the time?	Cultivate the proactive and preventive nature of self-care.
Am I making adequate space for fun, rest, and a loving spirit?	Focus on self-awareness of needs and the art of balancing various school responsibilities with personal life tasks and enjoyment.
Do I have appropriate ways to manage my distress, negative thinking, and bodily pains?	Cultivate spirit of community support and student stewardship.

Note. Adapted from "Self-Care for Psychologists," by E. H. Wise and J. E. Barnett, in J. C. Norcross, G. R. VandenBos, D. K. Freedheim, and L. F. Campbell (Eds.), *APA Handbook of Clinical Psychology: Education and Profession* (pp. 218–219), 2016, American Psychological Association (https://doi.org/10.1037/14774-014). Copyright 2016 by the American Psychological Association.

EARLY-CAREER PSYCHOTHERAPISTS

The ECP stage has been characterized as the 10-year period directly after formal training (American Psychological Association [APA], 2017a). Although the ECP stage and terminology has largely been associated with graduate-school doctorates, we can also apply the general concept and timing of this stage to master's-level clinicians who completed, on average, 2-year training programs.

The majority of our new generation of ECPs (who are psychologists) are women (77%) and White (78%), and the median age is 37 (APA, 2017a). However, comparing across psychologist cohorts from late to early career, ECPs are much more racially diverse and have 30% more women than our LCP cohort. Regarding life stage, current ECPs who spent many years in graduate school have theoretically aged out of the emerging adulthood stage (e.g., Arnett, 2000) and are now "full-fledged adults." As such, many of the 21st century milestones that the average twentysomething achieves have often been put on hold for doctoral-level graduate students. Those in master's-level or other brief training programs (e.g., LCSW, LPC, MFT) who pursued their clinical training right after their undergraduate degrees find themselves newly minted professional psychotherapists in their mid-20s. This developmental-career experience carries with it its own set of identity struggles, of constantly needing *to become* a competent therapist at a relatively young age when all these young professionals may want to do is simply *to be* for a little while (Wise et al., 2011).

Dr. Kimberly Arditte Hall, chair of the ECP Committee of APA's Society for the Advancement of Psychotherapy, laid out some tough realities with which ECPs currently are confronted (Arditte Hall, 2018). Relative to their more experienced colleagues, ECPs tend to struggle more with the proverbial balancing act between professional and personal life combined with less regular engagement in self-care (Arora et al., 2017; Dorociak et al., 2017). Not surprisingly, burnout rates are typically higher for ECPs than for LCPs (Dorociak et al., 2017). ECPs tend to feel more emotionally exhausted and have lower job satisfaction than their midcareer counterparts do. ECPs also seem to feel less of a sense of personal accomplishment and more overwhelmed by their caseloads than their late-career colleagues. Combined with the existential doubting described previously (Arora et al., 2017; L. Ferrer, personal communication, October 2, 2020), these data certainly paint a less-than-rosy picture for those starting their careers in the psychotherapy world.

Some have suggested that ECPs may find themselves in job positions that don't actually suit them very well (Green & Hawley, 2009). Perhaps you had to move to a new city for your partner's work, and you have had trouble finding a clinical position you really like. Or maybe you realized that your particular clinical specialization isn't as marketable as you thought, and the group practices in your area are not interested in your skill set.

You may also experience too much financial strain from educational debt or a low entry-level clinical position that prompts you to "moonlight" just to make ends meet. The median total debt for early-career psychologists who were designated health service providers was a staggering $95,000 in 2016, and the cost of borrowing money continues to increase as the cost of living in many areas of the country skyrockets (Winerman, 2016). To make matters worse, the median starting salary of early-career professionals is $60,000, thus creating multiple tensions regarding spending, saving, starting a family, and purchasing a home. Depending on base income, some of us take adjunct teaching positions for an extra few thousand dollars each semester, while others sublet office space a few nights each week for supplemental income. Not surprisingly, these positions we take for extra cash often come with their own stress and hazards.

Why focus so much here on ECP financial strain, educational debt, and having to take other jobs to make ends meet? Green and Hawley (2009) suggested that early-career psychologists (but not necessarily early-career psychotherapists in general) are unduly burdened. In particular, 21st-century psychologists appear to be saddled with the most early-career debt, which is paired with lower starting salaries than any previous generation experienced (Michalski et al., 2011). These are dubious honors indeed! Quite sadly, the ECPs with the highest debt burden feel that the financial costs have outweighed the benefits of becoming a psychologist (Fagan et al., 2007).

Many of these identity and financial struggles are quite normative, and being an ECP is not all about stress. ECPs are generally enthusiastic, eager to apply their newly learned skillsets, and very willing to grow. However, this passion can be tempered at times by anxieties about ethical violations, said Dr. Stephen Behnke, former director of APA's Ethics Office (Behnke, 2009). With a hypervigilance around managing risk, some ECPs may ironically make missteps in their more extreme avoidance of doing something wrong, despite only 5% of psychologist disciplinary action occurring within the first 5 years following licensure (Hall & Boucher, 2003). But, as Behnke noted, these heightened ethical tensions in one's early career can provide the basis for sensitivity throughout the rest of one's career. An overly risk-avoidant style may make the psychotherapy endeavor quite stressful, with collegial relationships less flexible and meaningful than we might like to enjoy. Thus, ECPs can use their new experiences during this stage in their career as kindling to

TABLE 8.2. Early-Career Psychotherapists

Questions to ponder	Recommendations to consider
What has the ECP stage been like for you? What stressors, gifts, and challenges have you experienced?	Maintain and pursue supportive relationships from internship/graduate school and new collegial connections.
What do you anticipate as you transition into your midcareer stage? What would you like for yourself?	Seek out consultation groups, supervision, a colleague assistance program, and/or your own therapist. Avoid isolation by actively cultivating a support network.
Are you beginning to diversify your professional experience to prevent burnout?	Maintain awareness of life stress interacting with your professional role.
What are some ways in which you can better support yourself with what you currently need and anticipate needing for the near future?	Diversify professional experience as a burnout prevention measure, and cultivate lifelong learning aspirations.

Note. ECP = early-career psychotherapist. Adapted from "Self-Care for Psychologists," by E. H. Wise and J. E. Barnett, in J. C. Norcross, G. R. VandenBos, D. K. Freedheim, and L. F. Campbell (Eds.), *APA Handbook of Clinical Psychology: Education and Profession* (p. 219), 2016, American Psychological Association (https://doi.org/10.1037/14774-014). Copyright 2016 by the American Psychological Association.

spark how they would like to operate for years to come. Let's now turn to Table 8.2 to further explore how the ECP career stage is experienced and how to make the best of this period in your life.

MIDCAREER PSYCHOTHERAPISTS

You're anywhere between 7 and 20 years postlicensure, and memories of graduate and professional school have faded significantly now. You've begun to establish yourself as a generally knowledgeable, skilled, and confident therapist. However, you still may harbor some normative imposter feelings while expanding your skillset and professional identity.

Perhaps you've built a successful private practice in the decade since your formal training. Maybe you've become a senior staff clinician in a school, treatment center, clinic, or group practice. Some MCPs have taken on leadership and directorship positions, run trainings and workshops in their respective areas of clinical expertise, and supervise ECPs who could benefit from the experience and wisdom of a seasoned practitioner. Wherever you are and whatever position you hold, you likely have feelings of both stability and growth. Sometimes the stability can prompt the desire for more growth. We need routine and certainty but also crave (to varying degrees) expansion and diversity of experience.

MCPs seem to fall squarely in between ECPs and LCPs vis-à-vis trend lines of burnout, work–life experiences, and well-being. MCPs endorse greater perceived stress than their late-career counterparts do while experiencing lower burnout, greater job satisfaction, and less intent to quit than their early-career colleagues (Dorociak et al., 2017). As Dorociak and colleagues (2017) noted, MCPs may be somewhat difficult to characterize as a cohort given that the range of experience and years since licensure is so large (7–20 years). As the initial phase of career development is over, a great deal of *life* is happening for MCPs (Wise et al., 2011). Whereas ECPs, in general, may experience more day-to-day stressors, the general age cohort of MCPs tends to experience "overload" stress, juggling too many tasks and activities at the same time, as noted by psychologist Dr. David Almeida (as cited in Clay, 2003).

For example, this professional cohort falls into the so-called *sandwich generation*, comprising hardworking individuals who are generally raising their own children and simultaneously taking care of aging parents (Blustein, n.d.). Some MCPs will become empty nesters, prompting personal and familial identity shifts as now-grown children no longer require (as much) active parenting. These developmental shifts are all occurring as many MCPs are moving through menopause, and some are experiencing the proverbial midlife crisis, although this phenomenon is perhaps more rare than we might expect. Research indicates that, despite or perhaps because of all that's occurring for MCPs during this phase, self-care engagement (i.e., professional development, work–personal life balance, and daily balance) lags behind that of LCPs and is more aligned with that of ECPs.

Something else interesting is occurring, however, as psychotherapists transition into the midcareer stage. Whereas only 5% of disciplinary actions for ethical complaints occur within the first 5 years of licensure, national data reveal that nearly 57% of all actions against ethical violations occur mostly within the MCP range (Hall & Boucher, 2003). What is happening here? Is this related to professional life, personal life, or an interaction between the two? As a matter of course, MCPs are now further from their foundational clinical training than are ECPs. Perhaps ECP competence building gives way to MCP confidence, and this confidence accidentally promotes a more hands-off style as our guard insidiously slips further down. Interestingly, as many MCPs become clinical supervisors, consultants, and leaders, they may in fact be missing the guidance and oversight they once received as ECPs. So perhaps ironically as we mature into MCPs, we become professionally isolated and rely on others less for emotional support (Wise & Barnett, 2016).

TABLE 8.3. Midcareer Psychotherapists

Questions to ponder	Recommendations to consider
What has the MCP stage been like for you? What stressors, gifts, and challenges have you experienced?	Remain connected with your colleagues, and expand your support network as needed.
What have you learned about this part of your career that you can impart to trainees and ECPs?	Thoughtfully monitor caseload, particularly as you may take on more leadership and training roles in your area of expertise.
What learnings can you pay forward to yourself as you become an LCP?	Maintain awareness of midcareer life stress interacting with your professional role.
How are life events, stressors, and transitions affecting your personal and professional life?	Diversify professional experience as a burnout prevention measure, and continue to engage in lifelong learning experiences.
Do you continue to diversify your professional experience to mitigate occupational hazards?	

Note. MCP = midcareer psychotherapist; ECP = early-career psychotherapist; LCP = late-career psychotherapist. Adapted from "Self-Care for Psychologists," by E. H. Wise and J. E. Barnett, in J. C. Norcross, G. R. VandenBos, D. K. Freedheim, and L. F. Campbell (Eds.), *APA Handbook of Clinical Psychology: Education and Profession* (p. 219), 2016, American Psychological Association (https://doi.org/10.1037/14774-014). Copyright 2016 by the American Psychological Association.

The accrual of stress in the personal and family lives of MCPs may also play a role, as common developmental stressors interact with our unique professional role (Wise et al., 2011). The poignancy of saving for retirement, the constancy of raising a family and caring for aging parents, *and* the profound responsibility of helping our clients can combine to challenge our competence and create ethical risk. Given all that the MCP may have to address, let's turn to Table 8.3 for guidance on how we can support ourselves for optimal well-being during this time in our careers.

If midcareer experiences seem a bit despairing, it is quite interesting to note that LCPs fare more favorably than MCPs and ECPs on a number of indicators. Let's explore the final phase of career development of the now highly seasoned psychotherapist.

LATE-CAREER PSYCHOTHERAPISTS

We can thank Carl Rogers for a great many things, but his personal expression of humble wisdom is not often shared: "I have always been better at caring for and looking after others than I have been at caring for myself. But in these later years, I have made progress" (Rogers, 1995, p. 80). "Later years" can mean different things to different therapists. In general, after 20 years of psychotherapeutic service, we might consider ourselves an LCP (Lindstrom et al., 2011). This identity may feel strange if you're only 45 or 50 years old and entering the so-called *final* phase of career development, especially if you plan to work for another 25 years. Thus, the absolute time that has lapsed from the moment we received our clinical degree may not adequately capture our lived experience.

Because of significant changes in cultural expectations and in training requirements over the last few decades, today's LCPs likely had a different set of experiences in their earlier years than today's ECPs. For example, LCPs generally had a shorter tenure in their graduate and professional programs and less rigorous postdoctoral or post-master's requirements than today's generation of emerging psychotherapists have (Green & Hawley, 2009). Developmental trends reveal that people are now delaying marriage by several years, compared with several decades earlier, and educated women are choosing to have children in their 30s rather than in their 20s (Martinez et al., 2018). Thus, the LPC of today may have a different set of cultural and developmental experiences than therapists who will become LCPs a few decades from now. Because of these realities, it is important to acknowledge not only what career stage we're in but also the generation within which we're a part.

As today's ECPs are moving through their career stages, it stands to reason that as they approach the LCP phase they are more likely than previous generations to be still actively parenting their children, to be paying off educational debt, and to have had to delay more earnest retirement planning. In other words, the LCPs of today (and certainly of the future) compared with those of the 1980s, for example, appear to be at more financial disadvantage, to have a more demanding family life, and perhaps have aging and ailing parents to care for.

Encouragingly, however, research suggests that LCPs seem better poised to enjoy their professional and personal lives relative to ECPs and even to MCPs. Dettle (2014) noted that LCPs report greater frequency of self-care and coping self-efficacy than therapists in earlier career stages. Indeed, LCPs have been shown to experience greater overall well-being—lower levels of burnout, less stress, and fewer days of poor mental health (Dorociak et al., 2017). Relative to ECPs and MCPs, LCPs seem to employ more daily balance self-care strategies, to enjoy more work–personal life balance, and to engage in more professional development. It's also interesting to note, as a potential driver of some of these cohort differences, that LCPs were four times more likely to be in a private practice work setting than were ECPs (at the time they were surveyed). The relatively greater self-employment for LCPs may have also accounted for their endorsement of significantly fewer administrative and paperwork hours and fewer negative client behaviors, both known contributors to burnout (Rupert et al., 2015).

These cohorts also differed considerably based on racial identity and gender, with today's ECP cohorts including more women and people of color than today's LCP cohorts do (APA, 2017a). Specifically, 77% and 59% of women comprised the ECP and LCP groupings, respectively. And ECPs were twice as likely to be of minority racial status than were LCPs. It stands to reason that the research we're looking at is illuminating somewhat different experiences for a somewhat different make-up of psychotherapists based on cohort effects rather than the journey of the therapist through time.

For those LCPs who are closer to retirement, a different set of needs arise. Unlike the ECP who has their entire professional life (and identity to forge) ahead of them, the LCP's active career, for which they trained so vigorously and maintained with such dedication, is now in the rearview mirror. However, LCPs on the verge of retiring must still abide by the ethics of responsibly closing their practices, securely managing client files, and referring active clients to trusted others (Behnke, 2009). During this period of preretirement, LCPs may also be at risk for ethical violations to which their younger selves were not subject. Behnke noted that as we near the formal closing of our professional service, we may inadvertently bypass the usual ethical considerations as these are felt to (almost) no longer apply to us. Thus, vigilance of this possibility is a very wise self-care (and client care) strategy.

Reflecting on one's past and looking to an entirely new phase of one's life can bring a large mix of emotions. Loss and trepidation can populate the LCP's emotional landscape. Saying goodbye to a whole caseload of clients and transitioning from one's active professional identity, daily sense of purpose, and collegial relationships can certainly be a tremendous source of stress and existential anxiety.

However, psychotherapists may also feel a sense of excitement about this next phase. Dr. Erica Wise, psychologist and recently retired clinical professor and director of the academic training clinic in the Department of Psychology and Neuroscience at the University of North Carolina at Chapel Hill (UNC), realized quite poignantly that she has "retired from UNC, but . . . [has] not retired from psychology" (E. Wise, personal communication, March, 2021). Because of her love for the field of psychological service, Dr. Wise continues to engage in many facets of professional giving and has begun to endeavor in new ventures, but she is also happy to leave behind some previous activities. For example, Dr. Wise continues to provide ethical and legal consultations and to offer self-care and other continuing education workshops for psychologists.

She also began doing vital volunteer work with the American Red Cross, offering disaster mental health services. As is evidenced by Dr. Wise and so many others, retired psychotherapists can positively anticipate their newfound freedom and opportunity to participate in other meaningful activities that simply weren't available to them earlier in their careers.

The importance of meaning making during and beyond this phase cannot be overstated. A sense of purpose and living a values-driven life matter significantly at all stages of one's career and development, but LCPs soon to retire will be forging a new identity or at least settling into living in ways that they haven't for much or all of their lives previously. If you are closing in on retirement (even in the next 5 to 10 years), how do you want your life to look? How do you want to wake up each morning? How will your income be sustained as you are no longer actively working? All these factors can be considered fundamental forms of self-caring in this stage of your career and lifespan development. By spending some time examining Table 8.4, LCPs can further process their current experiences, reflect on how to make the most of this latter stage of their careers, and prepare for the type of retirement they would like to enjoy.

TABLE 8.4. Late-Career Psychotherapists

Questions to ponder	Recommendations to consider
What has the LCP stage been like for you? What stressors, gifts, and challenges have you experienced?	Continue developing and utilizing your supportive connections and competence constellation, especially if you're a solo practitioner.
How has it felt to have been a psychotherapist for much of your career thus far?	Make plans for transitioning to retirement.
What are you beginning to look forward to when you think about slowing down your practice?	Consider ways to maintain a sense of meaning and value through professional activities, service to community, and important relationships.
What would make this last portion of your professional life most enjoyable and fulfilling?	Pay it forward to graduate students and early-career therapists through workshops, lecturing, supervising, or serving as a mentor.

Note. LCP = late-career psychotherapist. Adapted from "Self-Care for Psychologists," by E. H. Wise and J. E. Barnett, in J. C. Norcross, G. R. VandenBos, D. K. Freedheim, and L. F. Campbell (Eds.), *APA Handbook of Clinical Psychology: Education and Profession* (pp. 219–220), 2016, American Psychological Association (https://doi.org/10.1037/14774-014). Copyright 2016 by the American Psychological Association.

STEPPING BACK TO LOOK ACROSS THE CAREER SPAN

It may help to step back right now and evaluate developmental career stages with some distance. We know from several lines of research that ECPs tend to be the most strained, most burnout-prone, least professionally satisfied, most likely to quit, and the most self-care-compromised of practicing psychologists. ECPs within other mental health professions (e.g., social work in particular) also experience early-career struggles that seem to spare later career therapists.

However, our knowledge of psychotherapist career stage across development is far from complete. As Dorociak and colleagues (2017) noted, we would benefit not only from more longitudinal research to better determine what's happening over time but also from more research on differences in psychotherapists' home environments, work settings, and self-care challenges across the career span. Take a moment to reflect on the intersections among your home, personal life, work life, and your career stage—what emerges for you as important? Do you see any patterns of influence? Are you the exception to the rule, or do you feel the data presented in this chapter are fairly consistent with your experience at this stage of your career?

It is true that we need different things at different stages of our personal development and our careers. If we leave life up to external forces, we can be left disempowered and too easily influenced by circumstance. However, consciously and mindfully walking through our professional and personal lives aligned with what truly matters is one of the best, foundational ways both to endure and to flourish.

9

LISTENING TO OUR BODIES

The human body is not an instrument to be used, but a realm of one's being to be experienced, explored, enriched and thereby educated.

–Thomas Hanna

My wife, now quite body aware, wasn't always that way. She sometimes tells the story of how she never realized that the food she ate actually affected how she felt. Being aware of this relationship wasn't exactly encouraged during her childhood. It wasn't until her mid-20s, she notes, that she began to notice patterns of fatigue, vitality and energy, or mental cloudiness after eating certain foods and related to the length of time between meals.

After my surgeries in 2007 that resulted in the majority of my left paraspinal muscles being removed, I was forced to become aware of my physical body in an entirely and shockingly new way. I could no longer take for granted sitting in certain postures, raising my arms above my head for longer than a few seconds, or being able to stretch certain muscles without painful consequence. I have made it part of my self-caring mission to pay attention to my

https://doi.org/10.1037/0000309-010
The Thriving Therapist: Sustainable Self-Care to Prevent Burnout and Enhance Well-Being, by M. A. Hersh

posture as I sit with clients and as I move throughout the rest of my nonwork life. This bodily awareness continues to present a moment-to-moment challenge, but one that is fueled by a deeper value of having a functional (enough) body for as long as possible.

Ella, a late-career social work therapist specializing in couples and trauma work, speaks of her breathing as an effective affect barometer. She had been working with Devon and Kip, a couple in dire need of emotion regulation and calmer communication. Every time Kip would draw a breath to speak, Ella would feel her own breath quicken. It didn't seem to matter what Kip was saying or even how he was saying it; Ella's body was detecting something threat related. As Ella continued her work with this couple, Kip eventually revealed that he was severely emotionally abused as a child and that his hypervigilance to avoid being attacked had him constantly on guard and on edge.

These anecdotes relate to our (a) energy and physical health state, (b) physical posture, and (c) breath. They all point to the sustainable self-caring habit of tuning into our bodies. Bodies are, after all, "endlessly fascinating— why not get to know them," noted Hannah Yzusqui-Butera, former engineer turned personal trainer, wellness coach, and certified yoga teacher (H. Yzusqui-Butera, personal communication, January 10, 2021). If our somatic awareness is strained or underdeveloped, or if we have a less-than-healthy emotional relationship with our physical bodies, then at best we're likely to miss vital cues that point us to some of our most basic needs for well-being and wellness over time. At worst, we might inadvertently exacerbate preexisting ailments or even create stress-based conditions born of our disconnection or hostility toward our physical selves.

Pema Chödrön, an American-born Buddhist nun and one of the most influential mindfulness teachers of our time, told us that one of the most important qualities of attention is precision (Chödrön, 2018). Being mindfully precise means directing our attention to a designated target (e.g., our posture or energy level in the moment) with as much caring exactness as possible. This process may feel like promoting a perfectionism of sorts, but this quality of attention, when mixed with compassion and curiosity, is an incredibly valuable way to get to know our bodies that often remain hidden in plain sight.

Rather than quickly determining that our body simply "feels bad" or "is fine," we can ask ourselves *what* we *actually* feel, where we feel it, what color and temperature it is, and so on. Is there stillness, stinging, numbness, ringing, heat, cold, tightness, tingling, floating, calm, relaxation, separation, wholeness, groundedness, levity? How would you add to this list to make your observations of what is happening within your body at any moment in time more precise?

Let's pause for a moment and do a 30- to 60-second body scan. Just hover your gentle awareness over your whole body. Then move to the top of your head, and traverse your body from head to toe as if you have a wand that compassionately illuminates the given area underneath it. See if you can sense the broad brush strokes within your awareness as well as more nuanced sensations wherever and whenever they may be arising.

When synthesized with precision, loving attention is the bedrock of how we can body-listen. Loving attention is a core facet of self-caring. Veteran mindfulness meditation teacher Dr. Jack Kornfield imparted that mindful attention equates to *loving* attention. In *A Path With Heart* (Kornfield, 1993), Kornfield spoke to the development of healing attention, the type of soft and allowing relationship that our minds can have with our bodies. Thus, when we lovingly, curiously, and with precision tune into our physical bodies, we can pick up quite useful information that not only can help prevent further "ailment" and promote general wellness but also can serve us well professionally.

Psychotherapists at different stages in their careers may have differing experiences and habits of listening to their bodies. For example, if you are an early-career therapist who just had a baby, your somatic awareness may be at an all-time high. Perhaps as an older late-career therapist you've been experiencing the effects of aging on your joints. At any age you may be struggling with an acute injury or a chronic condition that is firing off signals of discomfort, drawing your attention away from other aspects of the present moment, including your clients and the therapeutic relationship at hand.

Of note, by focusing on our bodies, we're not referring to our physical appearance or an exact "prescription" for how to look or what to do. Rather, the premise is about valuing our corporeal self and the wisdom it offers when we listen and relate to it mindfully. At the end of this chapter, we'll also dip into the realm of extending gratitude for our bodies exactly as they are and how they currently serve us.

SENSING OUR ENERGY AND PHYSICAL HEALTH

Nancy, a midcareer colleague who works in an outpatient psychiatric unit at a large hospital, once told me about her struggles with hypoglycemia. For years Nancy had no idea that her hidden insulin resistance issues were causing wild fluctuations in energy through the day. In fact, Nancy admitted to becoming so lethargic during her 2 to 4 pm client hours that she could barely keep her eyes open. She had resigned herself to the fact that she was "just getting older" and having to deal with more body-related struggles than when she was younger.

Nancy's explanation for her discomfort may seem like the whole story except for the fact that when she ran out of her stock of a particular granola bar she always ate at lunchtime, she no longer felt like her brain and body were shutting down each afternoon. She was still tired but nowhere close to the sheer exhaustion she had been feeling. Nancy finally learned that her favorite granola bar was packed with an inordinate amount of pure sugar. After this jolting realization, she took an inventory of the foods and the timing of her eating to better evaluate associations (more obvious and also more subtle) between what and when she was nourishing herself and how she would feel a short time later.

Nancy's awakening came as a shock to her, but Elliot, an early-career private practitioner and highly sensitive person, experienced a more gradual and subtle shift in their awareness of energy. It seemed as though Elliot experienced a similar midday drop in energy. Yet on closer inspection through a series of somewhat elusive epiphanies over the course of many months, Elliot discovered that their energy was more noticeably drained on some days and with certain clients. Whereas at first Elliot was fairly frustrated and somewhat disheartened with these energy drops (complete with hard-to-mask excessive yawning and reduction in motivation), the more curious and scientific they became, the more their afternoons became a setting for a sort of mindful observation game. Elliot soon discovered that they were affected by four clients in particular, all of whom shared a similar subdued energy and somewhat monotonous tone. Already quite exhausted from being a parent of a young child, Elliot became lulled into sleepiness when in the room with these clients' energies.

Nancy and Elliot are but two examples of helpful observation of energy patterns and an awakening of meeting one's needs in new ways. However, sometimes we have an obvious, contentious, or anxious relationship with how our bodies function. When this relationship persists or when ignored, not only can it affect our well-being, but we may also experience a countertransferential reaction if our clients present with similar health or energy issues. "I really think this is all about your sleep habits," you might somewhat abruptly advise a client with chronic fatigue. All the while, you may be dealing with longstanding sleep issues yourself. And so through a filter of relative hopelessness about your own situation, you may project a stoic but subtly dismissive stance toward your client. With greater conscious compassion to our ailments and chronic health struggles, we can at the very least release some of our internal struggle and lighten our unnecessary burdens.

NOTICING OUR POSTURE

Have you ever felt collapsed inward, like a star on its way out? Have you felt your chest sunken in, shoulders rounded, eyes downcast or distant, and an almost numbed, dissociated sense of the rest of your body? This posture both reflects and influences a deep belief, mood, or state of depletion, disillusionment, demoralization, or depression. If you've ever experienced this posture, what has it meant to you? Do you notice any inklings of this full-body manifestation when you're with certain clients or simply at the end of an exhausting day? Does your body want to collapse inward when you arrive home or come out of your home office?

Conversely, you may have moments when your chin is slightly raised, shoulders are back and down, chest is open, vertebrae aligned and stacked upon one another, and musculature is feeling strong and capable. Your eyes look out in a calm and expansive manner, and your jaw is relaxed. How does this posture feel? What would some modicum of this deportment mean to you? Do you ever notice this posture while at work, with certain clients, at home or in other parts of your personal life?

How we carry our physical bodies and how they carry us is an often-underexplored realm of self-care. But like how *the body keeps the score* (e.g., Van Der Kolk, 2015) for traumatic experiences, our everyday reactions, thoughts, feeling states, moods, and interpersonal interactions are tracked and expressed through our postural dynamics (Ogden, 2015). Let's reflect for a moment on how your body naturally carries itself, keeping in mind that your full-body posture may shift depending on variety of factors. Certain parts of our body may be arranged or carried differently from other parts. (Dynamically shifting) posture can be a beautifully decorated door through which to gain access to our inner workings. We just need to turn the handle and sense what's inside.

This *sensing into* our dynamic physical structure can benefit us in everyday life, just as it can facilitate our work with our clients and our self-caring offerings in the midst of our challenging clinical work. Our ability to intimately observe our posture as well as our capacity to change it at will can provide us with a newfound mind–body confidence. Through noticing and shifting posture we can better stabilize ourselves when shaky and activate ourselves when sluggish. We can honor certain postures for the signals they're sending and heed their call for self-caring action.

Importantly, we don't have to do this in front of a mirror, although doing so can certainly be helpful at times when we're somewhat disconnected from our physical selves. For the first several years after my surgeries, I had no idea how slouched I was or how I was virtually crumpled over toward my left side. I was prone to avoid the interior of my body for a long while, not wanting to place my mind on the areas at which so much trauma occurred. However, the friendlier and more curious I was about my insides and how they revealed themselves on the outside, the more comfortably embodied I became. What resulted was a relatively virtuous spiral upward, "seeing" myself from the inside out (Mischke-Reeds, 2018).

You may remember Joanna from Chapter 1. She is an early-career licensed professional counselor and mother of two young children with special needs. She was in desperate need of care, not just self-care. Stretched thin and depleted but needing to work to help support her family financially, Joanna felt buckled and shrunken. This feeling state and outlook manifested in a downturned head, downcast eyes, and a generally slumped posture. However, as Joanna's head was often lowered, she was forced to look upward when with clients or talking with colleagues, causing undue eye strain and fatigue. When working with her clients, Joanna would lean forward in her chair with rounded shoulders, her right elbow resting on her left leg that was crossed over, her hand propping up her heavy head.

One of Joanna's supervisors, Sandra, a friendly and caring late-career professional counselor who was experienced with sensorimotor psychotherapy and somatic psychotherapy, felt compelled to lend support and provide feedback about Joanna's posture and overall mental state. Understanding full well that this posture was both symptom and cause, Sandra worked with Joanna in real time to see what different postures felt like in her mind and body. They experimented with what somatic psychotherapist Manuela Mischke-Reeds (2018) called the *somatic strength posture*, wherein the head and chin are lifted up slightly, feet firmly planted on the ground, and arms are stretched out overhead. This deliberate pose and ones like it are supported by fascinating research on how certain open, expansive, and "power poses" of the body can affect confidence, emotional state, recall, self-evaluations, and the capacity to recover from unpleasant moods (e.g., Cuddy et al., 2018).

Incidentally, the original claim that 2 minutes of "power posing" could increase testosterone and decrease cortisol has been put on hold, but the cognitive and emotional benefits of posing in this way appear quite robust (Cuddy et al., 2018). Fortunately, Joanna could feel the difference quite immediately. She started to notice a bit less despair and depletion and a bit more hopefulness and vital energy as she embodied this pose. Although short, this meaningful session with Sandra sparked an increased awareness of how Joanna was carrying her physical body and how she could self-caringly affect her mood, motivation, and outlook from within.

Outside of the realm of posture as both reflector and influencer of one's mood, emotions, and outlook is the fact that how we carry our bodies matters for our musculoskeletal and overall physical health. If muscles are contracted all day as you hunch over in your chair, you're more likely to shorten those muscles over time. Shortened hip flexors, for example, tend to tug on the lower back. Lower back pain is one of the most prevalent discomforts of the American public (Rubin, 2007). Curious and caring awareness of your posture can indeed have subtle but profound implications over time for both how you feel and how you function.

OBSERVING AND EXPERIENCING OUR BREATH

Like our posture, the breath is a powerfully portable portal into what's happening within and around us. Attunement to our dynamically changing breath can allow us to track our emotional state, mood, stress, safety and safeness, relationship quality, anxiety, calm, and confidence, to name but a few experiential indicators. As an autonomic function, the breath naturally occurs. Fortunately, we don't have to lend any cognitive assistance to this process to stay alive. And so with this automatic (but malleable) process comes a unique opportunity for us to bring conscious, precise, and compassionate attention to multiple facets of our breathing—location, quality, and rhythm.

With approximately 12,000 breaths during your waking hours each day, how aware are you of *where* in your body the breath enters and exits? If that question feels confusing, you're not alone. So many of us, even as psychotherapists, are not optimally tuned into the dynamics and nature of the very thing that keep us alive. Do you often breathe from your chest, with your upper torso noticeably heaving up and out with every inhalation? Perhaps air so subtly traverses your nasal passages that your breath is almost undetectable. If someone asked you about your breath, would you be surprised that you've actually been breathing? It's something literally right under our noses, and yet sometimes it's so hard to find.

If you're predominantly an abdominal breather, you're recruiting a disciplined diaphragm muscle to expand to allow air in and contract to push air back out. This muscle, when strong but flexible, allows for the lungs to take in optimal levels of oxygen to then distribute through the bloodstream to the rest of our body. Even a few deep, diaphragmatic breaths can trigger the parasympathetic nervous system to begin its cascade of calm-inducing, digestion-prompting, immune-enhancing, safeness-producing, and stress-reducing effects. When we breathe in this fashion more often than not, we're literally breathing better mental, emotional, and physical health.

The location of our breath cannot, of course, be considered in a vacuum. *How* we breathe wherever we find the breath is quite important and has implications for everything from our anxiety level to our circulatory functioning and even down to the inner workings of our cells (Ramirez et al., 2012). The quality of our breathing consists, in part, of its depth, pacing, rhythm, fluctuation, and synchrony between in-breath and out-breath. What do you notice about the rhythms of your breathing? Are your breaths punctuated and jagged or more smooth and flowing? Is there any space between the in- and out-breaths, or does one breath abruptly begin before the previous one is completed? Do you feel like you're often *trying hard* to get more air or do your inhalations feel natural and automatic like the tide pulling in to get ready to settle back to shore?

Do you notice how deeply you tend to breathe? If you typically breathe more shallowly, then you're naturally more likely to be breathing more quickly. And this breathing pattern more often is located in the chest rather than in the abdomen, although it can happen anywhere, including more exclusively the nose. Shallow, fast-paced breathing in the chest is associated with anxiety and stress (e.g., Nestor, 2020) as a key indicator as well as influencer of this state of being.

One of the best ways to create a physiological and chemical *imbalance* in the body is to breathe out quickly in short but powerful bursts. Try it for about five breaths (unless of course you have a medical condition contraindicated for this exercise). It's actually quite easy to overbreathe and induce a hyperventilation effect. In these cases, it's less about the oxygen and more about the act of breathing out too much CO_2 too quickly. In fact, contrary to popular belief, in those moments of stress, distress, anxiety, or fear, we don't really need *more* oxygen. Rather, we need to keep the CO_2 in our blood or release it more slowly. A pursed-lip, slow, and elongated exhalation can be so beneficial in general and especially in the case of acute overbreathing. If you think of the paper bag remedy for hyperventilation, it starts to make sense. The bag collects some of the CO_2 and allows us to immediately breathe it back in, thus restoring our delicate but easily resettable blood chemistry.

One of the most profound scientific discoveries of the late 20th century is the polyvagal theory proposed by Dr. Stephen Porges (2018). According to this theory, which has wide application in a range of clinical phenomena and therapeutic interventions, the branch of the vagus nerve that wends its way through the abdomen and viscera can be stimulated reliably through the breath. When we breathe more deeply and slowly, with exhales longer than our inhales, we are in effect giving our vagus nerve a hug. This type of breathing puts the brakes on our sympathetic nervous system activity, calming our physiology, switching on our immune and digestive systems, and creating an emotional sense of safeness and connectedness (within ourselves and others). Thus, as we monitor our breathing throughout the day, we're assessing how simpatico our breath is with our vagus nerve, which is always working behind the scenes to keep us safe, protected, and connected.

This assessment of our breathing patterns and its varied effects can be of enormous benefit within the psychotherapeutic endeavor. Have you ever noticed that your breathing changes with certain clients? In fact, just thinking about a client who revealed suicidal ideation a week earlier may quicken your pulse and dysregulate your respiration. Perhaps it's less obvious: Your breathing pattern may shift subtly even before a particular client steps through your door.

Using our breath as both radio receiver and signal transmitter can serve us quite well. Just as with Ella, our late-career social work therapist described in the beginning of this chapter, our breath can reveal hidden depths of what's happening right in front of us. This breath-based internal locus of control undoubtedly empowers us to be a stabilizing force in the therapy room and as we leave for the day to be with ourselves and others in a variety of important capacities. We'll explore even more aspects of the breath in Chapter 24, particularly how to harness the breath for mind–body regulation.

ON RELATING TO OUR BODIES WITH GRATITUDE

Sometimes we can find opportunities for growth in someone else overcoming their own obstacles. Such is the case for my wife's lovingly *forcing* me to contact the personal trainer she had been working with for myofascial and musculoskeletal issues. I now feel extremely lucky to have begun a new relationship with my own body through the mindful guidance of Hannah Yzusqui-Butera. She is a consummate body explorer and a true facilitator of the body's natural ability to regain its strength, flexibility, and balance. Retraining of the body, however, only works when we first accept what our body can and can't do at any given moment. No need to push this or force that, she firmly but lovingly notes. No pain, no gain has no place in her work, and I have very good firsthand experience with this all-too-common philosophy backfiring almost every time.

Implied in all of her guidance is gratitude, or at least that's what I have come to feel even about my internally disfigured and Frankensteinian soma. When I occasionally complain to my wife about how my postsurgical body looks, she usually reflects a deep gratitude that I'm actually still alive and utters something like "your body is the result of a damn miracle. Look at what you can do! No one would ever know what you went through." I very often contemplatively nod my head and grow my appreciation of what I have and what I can do rather than what's missing.

Given how often we're either disconnected from our bodies or absorbed in disliking the way it works or looks, it can be invaluable to feel our bodies from the inside out. The intimacy of true interoceptive experience can feel quite foreign to many of us. If we pause for a moment, though, we might discover some simple pleasures from within. You might feel your expanding rib cage or the lowering of your diaphragm muscle every time you breathe in through your abdomen. Or you might close your eyes and begin to thank each body part for what it does for you, for how it helps you function in your daily life. Even if some aspects are causing some issues for you, ask yourself how those parts would want to be treated—harshly, indifferently, or with warmth and appreciation.

When it comes to befriending one's body in whatever condition it's in, we can turn to Dr. Jon Kabat-Zinn's loving reminder for us all: "If you're breathing, there's more right with you than wrong" (as cited in Halliwell, 2020). Being grateful for our physical bodies is tough work, but if we don't do it for ourselves, who will? As actress Jada Pinkett-Smith implored us, "Don't take your body for granted. Do something today that communicates to your body that you desire to care for it."

We now continue exploring our habits and needs by venturing into the realm of the mind and emotions. Because the mind is embodied, we should take care not to create an undue dualism between our mental and physical domains. However, it can be exceptionally useful in its own right to explore the habits of both our thinking and our emotions as they circulate within our physical selves. Let's now dive into this worthwhile endeavor.

10 KNOWING OUR HABITS OF MIND AND EMOTION

The mind is its own place, and in itself, can make a heaven of hell, and a hell of heaven.

–John Milton

The mind generates thousands of thoughts per day (Tseng & Poppenk, 2020), and the vast majority of those thoughts are both negative and repetitive. Familiarizing ourselves with our habits of thinking can undoubtedly assist us in caring for ourselves across time and context. In fact, many spiritual guides (e.g., Gandhi, Buddha) have implicated our thoughts, for better or worse, in the construction of the quality of the lives we live.

We can observe and familiarize ourselves with our emotional patterns as well. Although all humans cross-culturally may have a set of basic, hardwired emotions (Ekman, 1999), emotions are just the tip of the iceberg. One therapist's raw and brief experience of sadness may be another therapist's drawn-out and complicated despair. We each uniquely experience, express, and receive emotions based on our histories, cultures, and other current habits. Thus, basic

https://doi.org/10.1037/0000309-011
The Thriving Therapist: Sustainable Self-Care to Prevent Burnout and Enhance Well-Being,
by M. A. Hersh

emotions can manifest as habits of feeling and mood, vulnerabilities to experiencing emotional overwhelm or disconnection, and affective strengths and sources of resilience. The typical ways in which our thoughts and emotions repeatedly activate tend to create a structure of thinking and feeling that is worthy of our investigation.

As we well know, because it is our job to know, an unmonitored or underexplored inner world can wreak havoc on our sense of stability in the outside world and on our potential for healthy growth. Professionally, if we remain relatively cut off from or less curious about our inner workings we can unwittingly increase our risk of the occupational hazards that we're trying to prevent. For example, if you're prone to a pessimistic way of processing difficult situations but often don't realize this force is at play, you may be likely to experience negative ramifications of being repeatedly exposed to your more traumatized clients. Acknowledgment and observation of your pessimistic patterns, however, may readily allow for nonjudgmental reframing or a more hope-oriented meaning-making process. This type of mindfulness-based cognitive processing, in turn, could benefit both you and your traumatized clients as well as your friends and family, who may be unwitting recipients of your pessimistic style.

Ronald, a midcareer social work therapist, has had a long career in multiple clinical settings. In peer consultations over the years, Ronald has often lent slightly morbid perspectives and future predictions regarding his colleagues' cases. Although his guidance always seems to be helpful, it is nevertheless tinged with cynicism and suggestions that humans are basically powerless, subject to the whims of an unjust world.

For the last several years, Ronald has been serving as clinical director of a residential treatment facility for emotionally unstable young adults. Ronald feels a certain kinship with this population, perhaps linked to his own experiences during a childhood that he reluctantly describes as abusive. His clients, as well as those of his supervisees, not only share their trauma and abuse histories but also alternatingly reveal their overwhelmed and dissociative affect. All this disturbing material and somatic reactivity has been taking its toll.

One day Ronald began to complain to one of his colleagues (who didn't work directly with Ronald) about his supervisees' doubts and wariness of his guidance and feedback to them. When Ronald's colleague inquired about the nature of the supervisees' concerns, Ronald revealed that they felt more despondent and hopeless after supervision sessions. After much uncomfortable confrontation with his style of thought and emotion, Ronald sheepishly acknowledged that he was probably bringing everyone down. He knows he is a bit pessimistic, but he wasn't fully aware that his negativity was affecting his clinical work, supervisory style, and general helpfulness to his clients and colleagues. Moreover, this amplified pessimism has been spilling into his personal life and becoming especially problematic given that his family had thought he was gloomy and nihilistic for years prior. In fact, Ronald's wife noted that he had embodied this worldview since she first met him, before he entered graduate school.

How do Ronald's habits of mind and mood resonate with your own? If not pessimism and cynicism, are there other *isms* that run the show? How do you typically process unfamiliar situations, difficult events, annoyances, and the like? When you encounter negative client behaviors, which are strong predictors of burnout (Rupert & Morgan, 2005), how do you typically react? Do you tend to anxiously avoid or sidestep clients' expressions of suicidal ideation, anger, and cynicism, or do you perhaps confront them with subtle impatience or annoyance? Before you even take a full history from a client, are you already assuming the best or shouldering the worst?

HABITS OF THOUGHT AND THINKING

Well known at this point in the realm of psychotherapeutics is the notion of *cognitive distortion*, also known as *thinking errors, unhelpful thinking styles*, or *thinking traps* (Beck, 1976; Burns, 1980). I personally and professionally prefer using the terms "unhelpful thinking style" or "thinking trap," as "distortion" and "error" always sound a bit too pathologizing or punitive. Thinking traps are the ways in which humans engage in thoughts that unfortunately cause us undue stress and suffering. This type of thinking takes us away from the reality of the moment and exaggerates, distorts, and skews who we are, what the situation is actually like, and what's to come in the future. Regardless of our history—although history of course matters—all of us are prone to falling into these traps, which become conditioned through mere repetition as well as through feedback from our environment.

Sometimes, however, when we find particular thoughts relatively unacceptable, we begin to avoid those parts of our interior life. Unfortunately, the more we try to tamp down unwanted thoughts, the more they populate our mental landscape (Wegner, 1994), causing additional undue emotional stress. Sometimes this stress can occur at inopportune times, such as in our therapy sessions and at night as we're trying to drift asleep.

I once had a preteen client tell me that he expected he would die by suicide sometime before age 30. He was not actively suicidal but "simply" assumed he would end up killing himself several years down the road. This thought and image plagued me for a long while and, try as I might, I was not able to escort this unpleasantness from my mind–body so easily. Many of us have to contend with clients revealing incredibly harrowing events (e.g., being raped, witnessing their child die, being a victim of a natural disaster or car accident). Deliberately ignoring or suppressing simply doesn't allow for healthy processing of that kind of intrusive material. In fact, resistance can provoke persistence and even a spread of the initial ill-favored thought or feeling. Thus, tuning into our resistance to certain interior experiences can be a vitally important gesture of self-caring.

At this point, it's worth taking a brief look not at the *what* but at the *how* of our thinking. These patterned ways in which we tend to think are often at the root of at least some of our suffering. When such repetitive ways of thinking are modified, we can bless ourselves with a wonderful source of self-caring, stress relief, and enhanced well-being. As you read through the following (nonexhaustive) list of thinking traps, see if some of them resonate more than others. Reflect on when and how they occur, both at work and at home. You might even rate, on a scale of 1 to 10, how frequently you suspect your mind tends to process your experiences in these ways.

- *All-or-nothing thinking.* Absolutes abound with very little room for grays, sort ofs, and maybes.

- *Overgeneralization.* One negative event is viewed as a never-ending pattern, as if nothing could ever change in the future.

- *(Negative) Mental filter.* Your mind filters out positives or neutrals and just allows negatively valenced material.

- *Jumping to conclusions.* You tend to assume you know all there is to know about (a) others' negative thoughts about you (i.e., mind reading), (b) how a negative outcome came to be, and (c) what will happen in the future.

- *Magnification* or *minimization.* Two sides of the same coin—your mind tends to blow small things out of proportion or diminish the importance of something significant.

- *Emotional reasoning.* If you feel, it must be so. For example, "I feel so awful for what I did last session. I'm such a bad therapist. How could I have said that?"

- *Shoulding.* Your mind uses "shoulds," "shouldn'ts," "musts," "oughts," or "have tos," as if you or someone else were supposed to have followed one inflexible rule, but you didn't: "I should have asked my client another question about her suicidal ideation, and now look at what has happened!"

- *Labeling.* You essentialize your behavior and identify with your shortcomings rather than make statements about how you're feeling or thinking: "I'm such a terrible therapist" rather than "I feel like I really messed up."

- *Personalization* and *blame.* You feel more responsible for troubling events than is necessary or you blame others when not necessary.

Based on your rough self-assessment of the frequency with which you employ these thinking traps, note how they get in the way of your daily functioning. Do they interfere with how you cope with relatively benign events with clients? For example, when you step back into your home after work, do you tend to summarize your day in all-or-nothing terms or with personalization and blame so that you're left feeling even more depleted than you might otherwise be? Thoughts don't always precede feelings, but they certainly help build the case for certain feelings to arrive, reside, or potentiate themselves over time.

The Judging Mind

Any of the thinking traps described here can get us into more trouble than we bargained for if we frequently or indiscriminately engage in such habits of mind. And yet one of the most insidious mental patterns is that of judgment. The question is not whether we judge but rather how and how much. Judgment is a bit different than evaluation and discernment. It is tinged with affective reaction, preference, opinion, and prejudice. If our judging of others is strong and automatic, we may not fully realize the extent to which our judgments negatively affect our well-being and the quality of our therapeutic relationships. When we judge our clients for their actions, thoughts, and feelings, we can set ourselves up to view our clients as burdens, thus possibly potentiating rifts in the therapeutic relationship and compromised clinical competence. We may then start to dread seeing certain clients, which can certainly begin to weigh on our compassion satisfaction and overall professional engagement.

Similarly, when we judge ourselves, we risk alienating and invalidating the agent of change in the therapeutic endeavor. But perhaps more foundationally, we become estranged from ourselves as we're acting almost as an enemy rather than as an unconditional friend and companion. This self-judgmental process thus appears anti-self-caring and antithetical to the growth and service to which we may aspire.

Do you find that you tend to judge yourself or others? Does this judgment accidentally set you up for more distress? Do you tend to feel overly guilty for certain actions you've taken despite others having moved on? Perhaps you readily feel ashamed for ways you've behaved, as if you are a "bad" human being for the things you do, feelings you feel, and thoughts you think. This shame may be deeply rooted in earlier childhood experiences.

Perfectionistic Tendencies and Overcontrol

Judgment doesn't necessarily emerge in a vacuum. Often, we harshly self-criticize when we don't meet the nearly impossible standards we've set for ourselves. Research has shown that traits such as perfectionism and obses-siveness can be particularly problematic (Pica, 1998), especially when a therapist's workload is heavy (Fischer et al., 2007). Sometimes we harbor irrational beliefs that dictate we *must* be the most competent therapist at all times and able to help everyone we meet. One study showed that holding such a belief is as significant a cause of stress as our clients' behavior and the isolation of our workplace setting are (Deutsch, 1985). Let's sit with that notion for a moment. If your standards are extremely difficult to satisfy or simply feel that way, it can be much harder for you to feel joy and fulfillment as clients make their own versions of progress. The progress, in your eyes, may not feel good enough, may not have been fast enough, or may not have been linked enough to your own hard work as a therapist.

Very early in my career, I began seeing a very complex child. After numer-ous modalities of intervention, educational efforts, and my feeling that I had failed this child and her family, I finally referred the girl for a comprehensive neuropsychological exam. That one referral made a huge difference, com-passionately pushing the child onto a more hopeful trajectory. I needed to be reminded by my neuropsychologist colleague that sometimes it's the little things, like a referral, that make an enormous difference. Sometimes it's the kindness and compassion that we exude that deeply matter to our clients. We can't be all things to every client, and when we relax our standards for the work we're *supposed to do*, we may allow our work to be more rewarding and our well-being more supported.

The Worried Mind

How do you handle uncertainty in the therapy room? Do certain client actions, thoughts, or feelings tend to cause undue apprehensive thinking about disas-trous or untoward scenarios that could occur in the future? What is your thinking like in your personal life when things are a bit up in the air or when important plans need to made? The worried mind often has a mind of its own, habitually thinking about the future in ways that leave us feeling anxious and apprehensive, uneasy and unsettled. The function of worry is often seemingly to protect ourselves or others by running through scenario after scenario of how things *will be* in the future and how we can prevent those imagined negative occurrences from happening. Often the worried mind feels quite justified in its way of thinking because it's a well-worn groove with no other thinking track to present as an alternative or because the worry happened to serve us well at one point in the past.

HABITS OF EMOTION, FEELING, AND MOOD

Although others' affective experience is our area of professional expertise, we nevertheless may unwittingly neglect our own emotional lives in favor of habit and conditioning. However, increasing our familiarity with our experience, expression, and metacognition of our basic emotions can be an extremely fruitful self-caring enterprise. As discussed previously, emotions are raw materials—they're natural, automatic, chemical, electrical, universal, and usually brief (lasting for seconds to minutes). Feelings, somewhat more complicated, are a mixture of raw emotion(s) and thinking, memory, or experience. Two therapists watching the same video of a profoundly grief-stricken client may both feel sad, and yet one therapist may feel tenderness while the other may feel hopelessness. These different feeling states are secondary responses to the primary emotional experience, based on the two therapists' different histories and experiences with grief and loss or even with how they perceived the client to be expressing their sorrow.

Moods, composed of other inputs from the environment, memory, physiological states, and behavior, occur when certain feeling states become glued together through time and space. Maybe we wake up "on the wrong side of the bed" after a disconcerting dream that left us feeling unsettled and anxious for part of the day. Even being with a certain type of client can "put us" in a particular mood. If we're relatively unaware of this occurrence and we have enough experience feeling a certain way with that client, we may get thrust into that mood just by thinking of our upcoming session. This mood may last during that session and well beyond, affecting our lives upon returning home.

A helpful heuristic for our self-caring purposes came from one of the originators of emotion-focused therapy, Dr. Leslie Greenberg. We can think of our emotional responses as falling within four main categories (Greenberg, 2009):

• *Adaptive (healthy) emotional responses.* These are the emotions we feel, such as sadness or anger, in response to a loss or an injustice, respectively.

For example, we might feel a deep sadness on hearing that a client's dog died suddenly, or we might experience fear when we hear screaming from down the hall outside of our office.

- *Maladaptive (unhealthy) emotional responses.* Often conditioned from past traumatic or disruptive experiences, we experience a dysfunctional emotion or feeling that doesn't quite align with the situation. For example, we might feel wariness or disgust when someone does something nice for us.

- *Complex (reactive) emotional responses.* These secondary emotional responses are often layered on top of our primary experiences. For example, we might feel especially angry after finding out a child client for whom we've worked so hard attempted suicide. This response may be covering or mixed with our profound sadness at this situation.

- *Instrumental (manipulative) emotional responses.* When we learn that our emotions, feelings, and moods have an effect on others, we can use our expression of our experience to manipulate a person or situation. Crocodile tears, bullying, crying wolf, and feigned embarrassment are all examples of such instrumental emotional responses. Perhaps there are times when you're so upset from client interactions during your workday that you mope around the house later that evening trying to get your spouse to ask you what's wrong. Some of us might refer to this emotional process as *secondary gain*.

What meaning do you make of these types of emotional response? Do you imagine that one or more emotional responses dominate your emotional life? Do certain situations, people, or clinical scenarios engender a particular set of emotional reactivities? For example, do you end up taking a client's expression of anger toward you so personally that it becomes paralyzing to your professional identity and negatively affects your personal sense of safeness and safety?

Problematic countertransferential reactions are more likely when our emotional lives are underexplored. When we're unclear about the links between our past, our emotional filters, and our present moments, we're more prone to reacting in unhealthy or even in instrumentally unscrupulous ways. For example, we may have a client who demands a lot of help but is also rejecting help as we do our best to support them. Rather than address this dynamic directly, we may begin to withhold help or make subtle sarcastic comments about the client's progress. Our emotion-driven behavior may stem in part from how we were given support as children or how help was modeled by adults in our life.

Highly Sensitive Temperament

Many years ago, I realized something incredibly valuable that has served me well in the most fundamental self-caring fashion. Like approximately 15% to 20% of the population (Aron, 1997), I have a temperament high in sensory processing sensitivity, otherwise known as being a highly sensitive person (HSP). I'm now a proud card-carrying member of this special subspecies of human. These percentages suggest that approximately (but likely well over) 100,000 psychotherapists in the United States process and think about things deeply, get overstimulated by sensory stimuli, feel our own and others' emotions deeply and intensely, and easily detect (and can be overwhelmed by) nuances within our internal and external environments.

Most if not all of these facets are the makings of a pretty decent psychotherapist, right? However, as many HSPs can attest, we can be easily overwrought by troubling client behaviors, rattled by rifts or tensions in our therapeutic relationships, ruminative about complex client presentations, and quick to personalize situations that others can more easily just let be. If you identify as an HSP or if these descriptions ring true for you now, how do you imagine your temperament affects the way you do therapy, how you manage your personal life, and how you ultimately have come to take care of yourself? Chapter 16 includes additional discussion of how certain traits and characteristics play a role in your past and future choices of therapeutic engagement and workplace environment. Ultimately, understanding our internal workings is an act of self-caring in and of itself. This is truly the gift that keeps on giving.

Too Much Activity

Do you find it hard to *not* keep working? Are you the type of therapist who continues to see clients even when you're feeling really run down or even moderately sick? Does the thought of resting and sitting still cause more anxiety and restlessness than relief and relaxation? And what about having difficulty letting thoughts go or shifting your mental track to problem solve situations in more flexible ways? You may even detest making mistakes so much that you end up doing everything yourself rather than prioritize and/or delegate. In fact, the act of doing *something* is inherently more satisfying than doing nothing.

If you're nodding your head to most of these questions and suggestions, you may very well be entrenched in a brain–behavior pattern known as *too much activity* (TMA). Dr. Margaret Wehrenberg (2018), an anxiety treatment specialist, suggested that individuals with TMA have an area of the brain that is sort of stuck. Similar to that in people with obsessive-compulsive disorder, the anterior cingulate cortex in individuals with TMA has trouble not only regulating the limbic system for emotional response but also communicating effectively with the prefrontal cortex for healthy decision making and cognitive flexibility. Individuals who experience TMA are in *drive* mode much of the time, have difficulty letting things go, and are often tense, on edge, and not easily "relaxable."

You might already have figured out how a so-called stress addiction is implicated in both self-care and burnout prevention. Dr. Robert Wicks (2008), author of *The Resilient Clinician*, compassionately noted that although psychotherapists are often striving to do the right thing and perform their roles well, exhaustion and distress are often lurking right around the corner as therapists continue to invest in their helper and healer identities.

If resting and having fun are not readily on the radar *and* not really particularly welcomed, then a crucial ingredient of our self-caring recipe is compromised, and burnout is that much more likely to occur. For these individuals, small doses of rest, relaxation, and fun are better than big breaks of doing nothing. A "project" of relaxation breathing every hour, for example, may be more willingly entertained and executed than sitting for 15 minutes at a time. Active hiking may be more welcome than sitting on the couch as a form of respite and rejuvenation. This is not to say that individuals with TMA shouldn't look toward slowing down in some fashion, but it's important to recognize that the brains of these individuals are itching for activity, and when activity slows anxiety can increase. Loved ones and caring colleagues may need to help therapists with TMA to stay vigilant (but not too vigilant) to this pattern and to strongly encourage breaks and release from the constant pressure and productivity.

Getting to Know What's Under the Surface

Psychotherapist and artist Shelley Klammer (2020) provided a very simple way to get in touch what's happening for us on our emotional landscape. She referenced an exercise that Mindful Focusing founder David Rome (2014) illustrated in his book *Your Body Knows the Answer*. Klammer noted that Rome's exercise may be especially helpful if we tend to lose our way when we are with clients or if we get caught up in the stream of experience rather than observing the nuances of what we're really feeling. Let's now examine Exhibit 10.1 for a deeper dive into Rome's emotional exploration and clarification offering.

EXHIBIT 10.1. Self-Care Reflection Break: *Noticing "Something"*

1. Begin by simply asking yourself, "How am I?" Say whatever comes to mind. "I am fine . . . tired . . . sad . . . happy . . . excited" and write it down in your journal.

2. Now ask yourself, "But how am I really?" This time, ignore any words that arise quickly. Instead, hold in mind the question, "How am I really?" Allow there to be a gap, and sense into your body with an attitude of friendly attending.

3. Do not answer from your head—that would be what you already know. Look for a response to the question in your body. Find that unclear sense of "something." You might sense a strong sensation in a part of your body. You might see images, colors or symbols. Furthermore, you might hear music or words.

4. Don't rush. Go slow. Stay present. Be a friendly witness to what comes—even when nothing comes.

5. At first, feelings tend to be quite shy. They are not used to being seen and need time to feel safe enough to show themselves.

6. When you notice something, simply welcome it and be with it, and do not look for anything else to happen right away. Write down what you are experiencing.

7. After a while, ask for a third time, "How am I really?" and notice if the feeling alters, becomes clearer or disappears. Write down your felt-sense impression in your journal.

8. At any point in this process, you may experience a fresh insight, or something unexpected. These qualities come with a sense of Oh! or Aha! or Now I see! Make a note of your deeper insights in your journal.

Note. From *Your Body Knows the Answer: Using Your Felt Sense to Solve Problems, Effect Change, and Liberate Creativity* (pp. 18-19), by D. I. Rome, 2014, Shambhala Publications, Inc. Copyright 2014 by D. I. Rome. Reprinted with permission.

KNOWING OUR INNER STRENGTHS RELATED TO THOUGHT AND EMOTION

"Look. I know this is a really tough situation, and I realize that my client is engaging in really risky behaviors. I honestly feel like I'm doing the best I can with my direct service to her and with the other supports I've tried to put into place. Even though this might sound harsh, I simply can't save this woman from herself." This therapist has some core inner strength, and she is right. In the end, she cannot save her client from herself. That's not this therapist's job. In fact, that's not the job for any of us, even if it feels like it is or should be. What this therapist is saying signals an honest, acceptance-based reality check of what's happening with her risk-heavy client. She is sizing up the situation for what it is, not unfairly judging herself, and giving herself permission to detach from the outcomes in her client's life.

This is the *very tough* work of being a psychotherapist because we care, we empathize, and we're often trying really hard to improve the lives of those we serve. However, this difficult work can be made easier and even rewarding when we tap into our inner resources and resourcefulness. What have you been told are your strengths of mind and emotion? If you do an honest self-assessment, what is it about your thinking and affect regulation that allows you to bounce back from adversity and see the world more brightly and with flexible perspective?

One such inner resource is a simple awareness that's always worth remembering. As the parable goes, the Buddha once asked a student whether it would be painful if a person were struck by an arrow. The Buddha followed by asking if the person struck by a second arrow would experience even more pain. He went on to explain that the pain of life's circumstances (i.e., the first arrow) cannot necessarily be controlled. Yet we often shoot the second arrow at ourselves as a reaction to the first. We have some choice, however, in preventing an overcomplication of the initial pain. As such, His Holiness the 14th Dalai Lama is thought to have said that "pain is inevitable. Suffering is optional." If we take this wisdom as intended, we can hopefully find strength in knowing that we're all up against the trials and tribulations of a challenging life—the grief, loss, disillusionment, fear, and the like. How we respond to our human condition, however, can make all the difference for how we ultimately feel, live, and work.

Let's turn now to our awareness of our habits and needs within the relational realms of our personal and work lives. As with our bodies, minds, and emotions, when left underacknowledged or underexplored, our relational habits can cause undue stress and can drain our self-care resources. However, the more we welcome an understanding of our relational patterning, the greater ease with which we can harness our relationships for sustainable self-care and more durable well-being.

11 RELATIONAL PATTERNS AND FULFILLMENT OF NEEDS

The ultimate test of a relationship is to disagree but to hold hands.

—Alexandra Penney

It goes without saying that all of our psychotherapeutic endeavors involve relationships. Different types of clients present varying challenges for us yet also reveal particular strengths and skills within us. Some of our overt reactions and unexpressed feelings to certain clients can be considered countertransferential. Clients simply represent other human beings in the world with whom we might disagree, those we feel helpless or hopeless about, or those for whom we might have an unspoken affinity.

In this chapter, we'll explore our relational patterns and needs within both our personal and our professional lives. By tending to such patterns and meeting our relational needs, we can more readily observe how these interpersonal habits affect us for better or worse. Much as we experience the self-care benefits of maintaining awareness of our somatic, mental, and emotional habits, we are also demonstrating a deeply self-supportive stance by mindfully attending to our relationships inside and out of the therapy room. In Chapter 29,

https://doi.org/10.1037/0000309-012
The Thriving Therapist: Sustainable Self-Care to Prevent Burnout and Enhance Well-Being,
by M. A. Hersh

we'll dive more deeply into the pragmatics for establishing healthy interpersonal connections and maintaining appropriate boundaries in our social life and between work and home.

RELATIONAL PATTERNS AND NEEDS FULFILLMENT IN OUR PERSONAL LIVES

Since we were born (and even within the womb), we've been shaped and have been shaping the quality of our connections, just as a river shapes the earth around it and the landscape in turn signals the directional flow of the river. Our early experiences with caregivers helped to determine our attachment style (Ainsworth et al., 1978; Bowlby, 1982), the working model of how we experience ourselves, others, and the world. This process results in varying degrees of perceived safety and security, willingness to explore, assumptions about worthiness and deservingness, and the like. Our genetic predispositions and intrauterine environments contributed to the ways in which our biological temperaments took form and in turn how others interacted with us. Sometimes, in some families, it wouldn't have mattered what kind of temperament we displayed as infants. Our caregivers may have treated us in a particular way because of *their* attachment style and social-emotional legacy.

Beyond attachment theory, one of the more well-researched and agreed-upon paradigms for the ways in which our fundamental ways of being manifest in the world derives from the Big Five dimensions of personality (McCrae & Costa, 1987). We all have variable degrees of the traits of openness to experience, conscientiousness, extraversion, agreeableness, and neuroticism, remembered conveniently as *OCEAN*. Influenced by both genetics and epigenetic forces, these traits are relatively stable even through adversity (Rantanen et al., 2007), although it seems that with age people tend to experience more agreeableness and less neuroticism while being less open, conscientious, and extraverted (e.g., Marsh et al., 2013). If you're primarily a highly agreeable and extraverted individual who is fairly open to new experiences, you likely have a distinctly constructive and affirmative way of relating to others. In contrast, if you lean more toward the less agreeable, more neurotic, but more conscientious ends of those spectrums, you may expect poor behavior from others and interact in ways that are rigid and rule-following. A person with the same personality profile but with a greater degree of agreeableness may readily acquiesce, anxiously and scrupulously, to others' wishes or demands.

Tony Robbins—entrepreneur, motivational speaker, and psychotherapist without the degree—has spoken eloquently about humans' six basic needs or drives (Team Tony, n.d.-a). The more foundational needs he has articulated are (a) certainty or security; (b) variety or diversity; (c) significance or power; and (d) love, connection, and belonging. He has suggested two additional "greater-good" drives: (e) self-growth and (f) contribution to others. Many of these needs are inherently relational, with significance, connection, and contribution the more obvious ones. Robbins has emphasized that it's not just the strength or valuing of these needs or drives that matters; it's also how we get these needs met as we move through various life contexts. In many ways, life boils down to our patterns of interaction within ourselves and in the outside world to satisfy these particular needs and drives to feel and be human.

Setting aside the two greater-good needs for a moment, if you strip away even one of the other four basic needs, at best you'll find someone who is unfulfilled and at worst someone who feels broken. Unfortunately, millions of humans around the world suffer needlessly from being cut off from satisfaction of these basic needs even to a small degree. The COVID-19 global pandemic (still wreaking havoc as I write this book) has been one long and painful lesson in what happens when humans are denied opportunities to meet those needs. But there are countless other examples, in our contemporary era and throughout history, of denial of basic needs and of individuals and groups meeting their underserved needs in troubled ways.

If you were to rate each of the six needs listed above on a scale of 1 to 10, what would your profile look like (if you graphed your needs on the X axis and the rating on the Y)? Does your profile surprise you in any way? What meaning do you generally ascribe to each of those needs as well as your entire profile? With some honest self-reflection and the input from deeply trusted others, you can evaluate how you typically interact with others to fulfill these basic and higher drives. Realizations of this sort can help shed light on how you take care of yourself by meeting these needs and the ways of relating to the world that may accidentally backfire for your well-being. For example, if we have a strong need for importance or power and tend to steamroll over others, do we manifest this pattern in our therapy sessions or with colleagues? Or despite a strong need to feel important, perhaps we end up demurring to anyone and everyone else with a seemingly stronger opinion. With an accompanying strong need to feel as if we belong, this tendency to acquiesce may be detrimental to clients who might need to hear our guidance more clearly. This relational habit may also show up with colleagues or on a clinical team. You may go along with others' clinical judgments even if you intuit a different and more fruitful path forward for a given patient.

In graduate school I had heard stories of a recent graduate who was quite interpersonally loyal. Connection, love, harmony, and security within a relationship were very important to him. Whatever his attachment history, over time he had come to place enormous value on sticking together, being respectful, deeply trusting others, and giving a good deal of himself to the relational cause. These patterns served him quite well when relationships were harmonious and inherently reciprocal but had proven difficult with certain clients and with family, significant others, and friends who didn't necessarily display the reciprocity of connection and respect that he expected. In fact, his adherence to such loyalty had caused internal conflict and distress over the years, disrupting his sense of identity and comfort in the world.

Let's harness the reflections and understandings we may have garnered from this exploration and now turn our attention to our relational selves in the therapy room. Given that therapist qualities and the therapeutic relationship matter a great deal for client outcomes (Norcross & Lambert, 2011), let's see what habits and patterns are opposite the couch sitting in the therapist's chair.

YOUR RELATIONAL QUALITIES AS A THERAPIST AND YOUR WELL-BEING

"How dare you!" an irate mother of one of my young child clients forcefully questioned. As she stared daggers at me, she confronted me with extreme anger and disapproval about how I had communicated about her son's excessive behavioral dysregulation just days earlier. Mortified and dumbfounded, I felt my heart pounding in my chest, at once dizzy with my attempts to listen so carefully to every word this mother was yelling at me while trying so hard to listen carefully to the raw emotion underneath the words. I had no choice but to feel her anger.

How psychotherapists interpret and ultimately cope with such interpersonal breaches of normalcy and trust can make a significant difference not only in the "conversion" of these troubling interactions into our own distress but also into how our other relationships play out. Research suggests that negative client expressions such as unpredicted anger toward the therapist, sporadic limit testing, chronic lack of interest in partnering with the therapist, threatening behaviors, suicidal ideation and gestures, and instability emanating from personality and psychotic disorders can contribute to both compassion fatigue and burnout symptoms (Rupert, Miller, & Dorociak, 2015). These problematic expressions of patients with chronic or acute disturbances or clients periodically in extreme distress can set off a cascade of emotions and reactivities within us.

How do such client behaviors tend to affect you? Importantly for the focus of this chapter, how do these interpersonally oriented behaviors play into your ideas about relationships, thus reinforcing or challenging your notions of what it means to relate in the world? Do you expect others to behave in such offensive, threatening, or self-destructive ways? Are you surprised, disheartened, or even angry when these relationally unstable behaviors come into your atmosphere, whether in the therapy room or through a phone call, text, or email? Your relational style likely plays a role in whether you perceive these negative behaviors as violative or as stressful but manageable.

Because I don't want to let others down and have others think poorly of me (i.e., agreeable and conflict and shame averse), I'll sometimes go to lengths to try to make others feel comfortable. Perhaps I apologize in therapy more than I should or overexplain concepts in advance to make sure my clients or colleagues won't be upset by my poor communication. But of course, that overexplanation can be "too much" at times and may lead to poor communication or compromise of the therapeutic bond.

When your caseload is full and you need to turn prospective clients away, how do you manage? Do you overcompensate? Do you simply not return their phone calls or emails? Do you feel guilty for not doing so? In Team Tony's (n.d.-a) framework, which needs and drives are paramount for you in your clinical connections, and how do you typically fulfill those needs? What about through the lens of the Big Five personality traits or of basic attachment theory (i.e., secure, avoidant, ambivalent, or disorganized attachment styles)?

These types of relational patterns and the fulfillment of needs in these ways are the essence of what this domain of self-care awareness is all about. If interpersonal loyalty and deep connection are especially important to you but those who run your agency or large hospital clinic, for example, are more transactional and businesslike, how will you experience your work environment? If your work environment is interpersonally unfulfilling or even distressing for you, do you have other relational outlets that satisfy *your particular* connection-based needs?

Do you have long-held assumptions or rules about how people are supposed to treat you? Even if you acknowledge your role as therapist and that others are seeking your help *because* of relational and emotional issues, you may still feel uneasy when relationally or emotionally challenged patients say or do inappropriate things. Conversely, perhaps you expect to be treated unfairly within the psychotherapy endeavor, and thus so-called breaches of interpersonal decency simply don't phase you so much. Or they may even reinforce your internal working model of relationships that people inherently don't treat others well—and that you'll be mistreated somehow. These relational rules and assumptions can matter a great deal for your well-being and can make the difference between accumulating feelings of burnout or compassion disillusionment and experiencing more temporary, situational stress.

THE RECIPROCAL INFLUENCE OF WORK AND PERSONAL RELATIONSHIPS

Although more research needs to be conducted on the intersection between therapists' work and personal lives, we do know that as work demands pile up (e.g., hours and emotional exhaustion increase), our family satisfaction can decrease (e.g., Ford et al., 2007). For practicing psychologists specifically, work stress predicts somewhat worse family functioning over time (Rupert et al., 2013). However, when we have more control at work, we tend to experience less work-to-family conflict and thus have more family satisfaction. Importantly, having more family support reduces home-to-work conflict, thus increasing work satisfaction. In essence, how much control and support we experience at work *and* at home can spill over, both viciously and virtuously.

What are your tendencies with respect to giving and helping all day at work and then stepping foot through the door to reidentify as friend, sibling, child, spouse, parent, or combinations of these roles? Do you feel that you're in caregiver mode 24/7? This feeling may be accentuated if you're an active parent and have an elderly parent who is in need of care. All of this relational care can certainly overtax your system, tilting your mind–body toward sheer exhaustion and even resentment.

Perhaps your relationships at home are somewhat strained and you've come to rely too much on your therapeutic relationships for connection and your sense of relational self. I once had a colleague who was relatively isolated in his personal life and would relish the chance to see clients during the day and even later into the evening to keep himself *relationally attached*. On the other hand, a different colleague in private practice once discussed her need to end sessions on the early side of the evening so that appointments with men didn't inadvertently feel like a date.

When our nontherapeutic relationships are stable and sources of security and satisfaction, we may find ourselves more readily able to put our best relational selves forward in the therapy room. Mindful self-inquiry regarding our basic needs for connection—for stability, flexibility, boundaries, power, intimacy, and growth in our relationships—can prove immensely useful for illuminating how we operate in both professional and personal realms of life.

The next steps in our journey of self-discovery will involve bringing such mindful attention to the ways in which our brain functions, using an executive-control perspective. As executive functioning is often lurking behind the scenes as an important source of both success and well-being as well as challenge and heartache, it's incumbent upon us all to inquire with curiosity and compassion about how our brain is helping and harming in our pursuit to live and work with greatest fulfillment.

12

HOW'S YOUR FRONTAL LOBE DOING? AND OTHER EXECUTIVE FUNCTIONING QUESTIONS

Tell me and I forget. Teach me and I remember. Involve me and I learn.

—Benjamin Franklin

After hitting "2" on speed dial, my mother would frustratingly ask my now-retired radiologist father, "Are you finished yet?" I'd hear the same question every evening as my mom wondered how long it would take my dad to complete his work for the day. I would ask her which of my dad's two offices he was working at that day to figure out when he'd actually be home.

Fast forward about 15 years. I was newly married, and my wife would call my new, amazingly fancy flip phone, wondering if I'd be home soon from my long day in the Psychology Department. No matter what I was doing, it always seemed to take me three times longer than I thought it would or should and seemingly five times longer than my classmates.

Fast forward another 15 years to my private practice office. I text my wife, "I'm leaving in just a few minutes. I just have two more notes to finish up. And I'll pick up some chicken on the way home." It didn't matter

https://doi.org/10.1037/0000309-013
The Thriving Therapist: Sustainable Self-Care to Prevent Burnout and Enhance Well-Being, by M. A. Hersh

how hard my father or I worked, we were always lagging behind the clock. It's almost as if time has been taunting us, flaunting its ability to tick on by while it watches us struggle to meet deadlines and verbal commitments that we earnestly want but often fail to meet.

What's happening in all these examples is mostly about executive function (EF). Typically thought of as the seat of EF skills, the brain's frontal lobe (among other neural areas) is in part responsible for the constellation of skills that allow us to appropriately and effectively manage ourselves in the world. Our frontal lobe also has connections to our limbic system, and so a "well-toned and switched on" frontal cortex is quite important for helping us manage our emotions and moods throughout the day. For the psychotherapist moving in and out of both clinical and personal domains on a daily basis, these EF skills not only help keep us afloat but also can manage stress, support well-being, and promote professional thriving. Importantly, part of EF-related self-care is the capacity to evaluate these capacities with honesty and compassion.

Some research suggests that three core brain-based functions (i.e., inhibitory control, working memory, and cognitive flexibility; see Miyake et al., 2000) underlie and compose the variety of EF skills that are most often implicated in poor performance and health outcomes. From a practical perspective, we can assume that even if one of these core substrates of EF is challenged, we may find ourselves experiencing several real-world struggles in both the professional and personal realms of life. If two or three of these substrates are lagging behind, we may indeed feel overwhelmed with life, particularly when we have job and personal demands that overpower our internal EF resources.

HOW OUR EXECUTIVE FUNCTIONS HELP US MEET EVERYDAY DEMANDS

Lagging EF skills (see Table 12.1; Dawson & Guare, 2016) create undue stress and compromise our everyday functioning in many ways. If most of our EF skills are already (and perhaps more naturally) well-developed, we simply may be blessed with the capacity to address much of what life throws at us.

You can engage in a brief self-assessment of your EF strengths and challenges at https://www.buildingbetterprograms.org/2018/05/01/executive-skills-profile-2/. You'll be able to assess all domains of EF skills and derive your top and bottom three skills for better self-knowledge and application in the real world. If, for example, we have EF difficulties in time management/

TABLE 12.1. Self-Care Reflection Break: Executive Function Domains and Definitions

Executive function	Definition	Possible difficulty? (Yes/No)
Sustained attention	Capacity to pay and maintain attention despite low motivation and distractions present	
Response inhibition	Capacity to pause and think before reacting; to resist urges; to envision consequences before executing a task	
Planning/Prioritization	Ability to plan for the future and determine what steps to take next for a given task or project	
Time management/ Sweep of time	Discerning how long a task will likely take while mentalizing the deadline; ability to accurately detect and predict the passage of time	
Organization	Knowing where you've put things; capacity to create and maintain systems to keep track of both physical materials and mental information	
Task initiation/ Self-activation	Getting a task started without significant procrastination; starting tasks despite their feeling too tedious and/or challenging	
Working memory/ Remembering to remember	Capacity to keep active and manipulate information in your mind in a short-term timeframe; the capacity for prospective memory—to remind yourself to do a goal-oriented task at the right time in the future	
Emotional self-control	Keeping relatively calm even when frustrated; ability to experience feelings without necessarily acting on them	
Goal-directed persistence	Capacity to follow through with tasks even when challenging and/or tedious based on the goals you have set	
Stress tolerance	Managing stress without overwhelm	
Metacognition/ Self-monitoring	Capacity to monitor and assess your own performance and distractions from a birds-eye view as you progress with a task	
Flexibility	Ability to change strategies or revise plans when conditions change	

Note. Data from Building Better Programs (2022).

sweep of time and metacognition/self-monitoring, we may habitually run late and have a hard time tracking when our sessions should end or how long it's taking us to write a clinical note. Consequently, we may experience increased anxiety, time pressure, and disappointment from ourselves and others (especially if we're employed within an organization). The fallout might continue in the form of having less time for taking small breaks, keeping up with administrative work, eating, hydrating, or making important calls. Some of these "tasks" are basic forms of self-care, and without the appropriate time set aside to execute them, we needlessly neglect that which can ultimately support us.

Other common EF challenges involve organization, working memory, and planning/prioritization. These can manifest in having trouble keeping computer files and client records consistently organized or up to date; forgetting where we've put thumb drives, grocery lists, phone earbuds, or our favorite pen; and habitually handling our next set of tasks (e.g., progress notes, tidying up our office) in haphazard or time-inefficient ways. Consequently, we may fall behind in our work, miss deadlines, lose important documents, and fail to get important tasks done in favor of those that are or feel more urgent or appear "shinier."

Not surprisingly, these EF difficulties can generate a good deal of undue stress, anxiety, and overwhelm. Moreover, many of us may not realize that emotional control is indeed part of the constellation of EF skills. And so whenever something stressful comes our way, those of us with less control over our emotional experience are likely to feel the most overpowered by a given circumstance.

Let's take another look at the Self-Care Reflection Break (Table 12.1) and try to compassionately evaluate whether or not you have difficulty with each of the EF skills presented. Even if you say "yes" to one or two skills and "no" to all the others, consider how such challenges translate into your daily life. Perhaps a relative deficit in sustained attention, for example, manifests in multiple domains as you struggle to maintain adequate focus on your clients' narratives, colleagues' recommendations and feedback, and your family's stories about the day.

Not to overfocus on struggles, we should certainly examine our yes/no answers within Table 12.1 and determine which of those nonproblematic EF skills are indeed (hidden) strengths. If we move through the day staying decently organized and planful—remembering to take lunch and keep appointments for the day, consistently keeping our calendar or planner up to date, and prioritizing truly important tasks while outsourcing or automating others—we can own the fact that we have some powerful capacities to support our well-being. Recognizing these abilities as relative strengths can be seen and felt as an important form of self-caring in and of itself. We may even consider harnessing these strengths to help compensate for our less-developed EF skills.

To give ourselves a better sense of our relative strengths and challenges in the EF domain, we may choose to take screener questionnaires that can point us in a helpful direction toward awareness-building and possible remediation of lagging skills. The popular and evidence-supported online resource and magazine for attention deficit disorder and related issues, ADDitude, offers an online screener for EF challenges (https://www.additudemag.com/executive-function-deficit-adhd-symptoms-test-for-adults/). In addition, built and adapted from the extensive work by Dawson and Guare (2016), the Center on Budget and Policy Priorities and Global Learning Partners created an online resource and accompanying questionnaire designed to assess adults' EF strengths and challenges (http://www.buildingbetterprograms.org/2018/05/01/executive-skills-profile-2/).

It's important to note that we're exploring EF skills that each of us has to varying degrees. We're not evaluating clinical dysfunction or diagnosis of any sort. In fact, if we take a more dimensional and curiosity-based approach, we may learn (or perhaps confirm) some important information about the ways we interact with the world with greater or lesser ease.

Unfortunately, the EF challenges we experience can take their toll on our self-esteem and even self-worth. We may become (or already habitually are) disappointed in ourselves because such "simple" actions are hard to execute. Self-efficacy can wear down, anxiety and avoidance can increase, and our daily functioning can become even more compromised.

Recent work on the intersections among EF, poverty, stress, and oppression is showing that cultural-socioeconomic hardship can affect the brain in identifiable and pragmatic ways (see Daminger et al., 2015, for resources and citations in this area). Thus, not only might our brains more "naturally" tend toward certain EF strengths and challenges, but our frontal lobe can indeed suffer at the hand of inequities that many of us face (see Chapter 15, this volume, for additional insights into your own lived experience).

By assessing our EF capacities, we're evaluating a fundamental part of our broad-based self-caring effort to help prevent burnout and other occupational stresses as well as to cultivate well-being in sustainable ways. The stronger our EF skills, the more self-supportive we can be in the rest of our lives, personally and professionally. Strong EF skills are also implicated in healthy relationships

(Zelazo et al., 2016), thus making the case that good evaluation and intervention (where necessary) are both warranted and beneficial.

HOW DO YOU LEARN BEST?

Although outside the circumscribed realm of what we think of as EFs, our learning style matters a great deal for how we experience the world, express ourselves, and receive information from others. Thus, familiarizing ourselves a bit more with our primary modes of experiencing, expressing, and gathering information would likely help us to navigate our personal and professional lives with greater ease and confidence.

Theories abound for typologies of learner, but for our purposes we'll cover four basic types: visual (i.e., learning through images and graphics), aural (i.e., spoken word learning through conversation or audio recording), reading/writing, and kinesthetic (i.e., learning through interaction with the environment; Fleming & Mills, 1992). Some of these modes may reflect brain hemispheric dominance, but it's fair to say that some people learn well or comfortably through many channels or even through a synthesis of two or more channels.

Understanding your preferred (or most natural) modes of learning can have a profound impact on what type of job you choose and the type of work environment for which you may be better suited (see Sarkis, 2018). What happens when you're primarily a visual learner and yet half your average work week on a psychiatric inpatient unit is spent in auditory mode (e.g., morning rounds with rapid-fire talk about numerous patients, face-to-face chats with patient after patient, team meetings, and grand rounds)? Would this work environment cause undue occupational stress for you? In general, are your modes of learning relatively free of tension, and are those methods supported or well-matched to your work setting? If you're in a situation similar to that of the inpatient unit, how might you compensate for learner–environment incongruities? Determining your learning styles and preferences may not only help you accommodate to the different work environments you inhabit; it can also help you construct your life based on your inherent abilities.

Although this chapter may have felt like somewhat of a departure from what is typically considered self-care, it's important to broaden our perspectives on the various facets of what self-care can be. Just as knowledge of our career stage and habits of thinking, for example, contribute to how we can optimally tend to ourselves for a thriving life, so too does our knowledge of hidden brain-based functions like working memory and time management, to name just a few. Hopefully your curiosity has been piqued for the challenges you experience as well as the strengths you possess in the realm of EF. Chapter 30 allows us to connect the dots among the EF skills assessment in this chapter, ways to address any lagging skills we possess, and strategies to strengthen and harness our existing strengths.

We turn now to perhaps another atypical but quite vital aspect of self-care: our needs, beliefs, and habits related to money. Many of us don't like to talk about money, but when this integral aspect of modern life stays under-cover, we miss important ways both to manage our stress and burnout as well as to thrive.

13 MONEY

Our Unspoken Needs, Beliefs, and Habits

*Your relationship with money is like any other relationship. Check your
assumptions, be transparent and real, and give unconditionally.*

–Anonymous

Money can be quite the taboo subject. In more than one third of cohabit-
ing American couples, one or both partners couldn't identify how much the
other partner earned for a living (Fidelity Investments, 2018). Interestingly
if not shockingly, people surveyed about their financial habits indicated they
were more comfortable talking about nearly anything else, including sex,
addiction, health, politics, and race, than about money (Capital Group, 2018).
And that's exactly why we need to explore it here.

CULTURAL NOTIONS OF MONEY, WEALTH, AND EARNING

Quite surprisingly, only 13% of American millionaires consider themselves
"wealthy" (Herron, 2019). Not that psychotherapists are well-known for
their millionaire status, but this statistic reveals that financial standing is

https://doi.org/10.1037/0000309-014
The Thriving Therapist: Sustainable Self-Care to Prevent Burnout and Enhance Well-Being,
by M. A. Hersh

153

exceptionally subjective and dependent on the social comparisons we're making. Moreover, our level of happiness with our wealth is only as good as the reference group we're measuring ourselves against. For example, middle-income individuals were unsatisfied financially only if they lived in states with greater economic and earning inequality (Goldstein & Hastings, 2019). What are the social comparisons you tend to make around money? Do they serve you well or detract from your sense of security and stability in the world?

The United States is a society that hinges our value as human beings on our pay and how much we have in our bank accounts, said Dr. Caitlin Zaloom, an anthropologist at New York University (as cited in Pinsker, 2020). Even in the Hasbro board game "The Game of Life," a player wins as they finish the board at retirement after accumulating more money than their opponents. Family, occupation, and home only matter insofar as they are commodities for financial return. How aware are you of the extent to which money, worth, and life fulfillment are mangled together in your personal life?

THE DEVELOPMENT OF MONEY BELIEFS AND HABITS

What is also quite important in this discussion is how you, as an individual, feel about money. People attach meanings to money as a function of many variables in their lives, including culture, class, family patterns, gender, and personality (Estrella, 2010). What beliefs do you hold regarding the value of money and what money is supposed to signify? As Benjamin Franklin is thought to have said, "money never made a man happy yet, nor will it. The more a man has, the more he wants. Instead of filling a vacuum, it makes one." Similarly, we may resonate with financial sentiments like those of Franklin D. Roosevelt and Ayn Rand that highlight happiness in life as derived from our achievements and creative efforts rather than from money pushing and pulling us in ways we ultimately cannot control nor from which we can attain lasting well-being. The evil of being greedy is also made abundantly clear in this quote by Seneca the Younger (1917): "It is not the man who has too little, but the man who craves more, that is poor."

What is your relationship with money? We can think of it almost like an attachment style, with a secure and several insecure modes of relating to our financial self. Do you typically avoid thinking about or consciously inter-acting with money and its effects? Perhaps you have a love–hate, anxious-ambivalent relationship with money, at times befriending it out of worry and insecurity yet at other times showing a disdain for having to think about and manage its complexities. Some of us might even relate to money with extreme reactions of wild spending sprees and almost dissociative numbness to the fact that we have a relationship with the green stuff.

Just as we create internal working models of interpersonal relationships in childhood through patterned interactions and/or more troubling experiences, we also construct relatively unconscious beliefs about money as we develop. Financially oriented psychologists call these beliefs *money scripts*, and they can dictate, often out of conscious awareness, a myriad of financially driven behaviors, according to Brad Klontz, PsyD, director of research at H&R Block Dollars & Sense program and researcher at Kansas State University (as cited in Tartakovsky, 2012). Money scripts are formed from direct experiences, messages and stories, and attitudes held by parents and other influential people in our childhood. For example, our parents might have hammered in the idea that money is the root of all evil. Or, if we saved up our own money to buy a toy we wanted, perhaps we heard that we were being too greedy if we wanted another toy that was out of reach financially. "What, do you think money just grows on trees? We/you can't afford that, so put it back right now," we might have heard from a parent one too many times. A colleague of mine once told the story of how she vividly remembers tearing up a field trip permission slip because she already knew that her parents couldn't afford the fee involved in going. To this day she is cautious about spending and gets nervous about not saving enough.

Let's consider a few other money beliefs that Dr. Matt James, an integrative health psychologist and president of Empowerment, Inc., believes are toxic to our well-being and financial success (James, 2016):

- It's a dog-eat-dog world, survival of the fittest.
- I can't live a balanced life if I want to make money.
- You have to be in certain professions to make a lot of money.

Conversely, we may have been inculcated with a calming and grounding sense of what money can do and how we can relate to it with flexibility, respect, and appreciation. If we lost a prized possession, a parent may have empathized with our upset and then reassured us that the only thing that really matters is what you can't replace. Or perhaps you heard and saw modeled for you the idea that money is simply a tool. Just as you can use a Swiss Army knife for multiple functions depending on your purpose in the moment, so too can you use money based on many different reasons and goals. This type of money savvy is what clinical psychologists Joe Lowrance, PsyD, and Dr. Brad Klontz suggested when discussing financial wellness, which they posited is simply part of one's overall physical health and psychological well-being (as discussed in Tartakovsky, 2012). Lowrance and Klontz noted that financial wellness can include spending money based on one's values, keeping debt to a minimum, consciously saving money for future purposes, and having a dedicated back-up fund as a safety net for various emergencies.

What are your values around money? What truly matters to you about the money you have, earn, and spend willingly? Based on our exploration of values (Chapter 6) and the blocks to living in accordance with them (Chapter 7), are your self-care and holistic health values aligned with how you see and use money? Do your values facilitate a healthy financial self, and does your financial self facilitate healthy use of money? And as Klontz and Lowrance suggested (see Tartakovsky, 2012), do you consider your finances part of your overall health and well-being?

MONEY AND THE HARDWORKING PSYCHOTHERAPIST

When a colleague of mine had just begun building his fee-for-service private practice, he took just about any client at almost any fee. He felt pressure to build his practice no matter what. (He also felt guilty for not taking insurance but realized that playing the insurance game would have likely posed more risk for burnout than warranted.) However, several years later that fee structure translated into a perceived unfairness and frustration with himself (and inadvertently at the clients who were still paying low rates) as he increased his fees for new clients. He had a great deal of medical and family expenses to consider and wanted to diversify his professional roles, but the significantly lower fee that some clients were still paying was making it difficult for my colleague to move ahead.

Another example comes to mind of a social work colleague who worked within a large hospital system. She wore many clinical hats, she had served the hospital in numerous ways, and her resources were being worn thin. Pay continued to be low relative to her experience and expertise, and raises were hard to come by. Given that feeling (financially) rewarded is one component of mitigating burnout risk, we could imagine that this colleague was taking some hits to her sense of professional worth and overall well-being. This was indeed the case—she would remark that perhaps a different job entirely was in her (near) future.

So how are these notions of money related to psychotherapists' sustainable self-care and well-being? We can identify many examples of money wending its way into helping professionals' sense of identity, on the one hand, and practical financial solvency on the other. Let's look at the former aspect first so that we understand together how insidiously powerful the concepts of money, earning potential, and worth can be for a typical psychotherapist.

Many of us may recall being asked or hearing the smug or patronizingly rhetorical question, "well, you didn't think you were in this profession for the money, did you?" Think about that statement for a moment. Have you heard this sentiment spoken directly to you, and have you seen or heard it mentioned in blogs, articles, videos, or in interpersonal circles of fellow therapists? Now let's sit with that phrase for a few seconds. Lest I sound too "therapisty," how does that make you feel? If you experience a degree of moral outrage, uncomfortable resonance, or desire to dismiss the statement outright, your reaction wouldn't be uncommon.

But being a psychotherapist is our livelihood, and money is a top stressor for most people. In fact, in large surveys of stressors endured by practicing psychologists, 50% endorsed "financial concerns" (Cooper, 2009) while 42% noted "insufficient income" (Sherman & Thelen, 1998). In addition, Kramen-Kahn and Hansen (1998) summarized that one among five major domains of unique hazards of the mental health profession is business-related stress, including economic uncertainty. Whether you're steeped in a managed-care work setting or in fee-for-service private practice, money insecurity certainly can be present. If you operate an independent practice, you may be worried about how many clients you need to see that month to be able to pay the bills and other expenses. On the other hand, if you work for someone else, your salary—for better or for worse—is predefined, as are the expectations for direct clinical hours, paperwork, and other responsibilities that may overshadow the income you're earning.

Your income in general depends on your geographic region, insurance or managed-care involvement, how much your services typically are charged, and a variety of other factors. And how money-secure you feel with your own income also depends on whether you have a partner contributing to household revenue, medical insurance, and any other sources of financial support such as investments, family money, or other jobs. In fact, I have two colleagues earning almost the exact same income in similar enough clinical positions. One has a spouse who earns well over $200,000 per year while the other is single without any other family financial support to speak of. Clearly these are two incredibly different lived experiences while seemingly almost identical on the surface.

If you are currently in a position of relative financial freedom, do you feel this objective reality, or are you perhaps stuck in a previous financial mindset of lack and scarcity? A lack and scarcity mindset, a form of *money dysmorphia*, can develop in childhood but also may arise from financial struggles we've experienced within our evolving careers. For example, if you were used to receiving a very low stipend in graduate school or have been actively paying off educational loans from college or professional schooling, feelings of frugality and possibly running out of money might unconsciously dictate your financial decision making in the present day. Moving from one career and personal developmental stage to the next also brings different financial concerns and challenges. Psychotherapists who have their first child may experience an uptick in their expenses, leaving them in a different financial situation than they were just months earlier. As children approach college age, therapists may feel increased stress and financial burden in anticipation of new educational expenses (for both them and their children).

The balance of this chapter addresses the practical aspects of our relationships with money and our financial health. It's one thing to hold certain values about money and another thing entirely to be struggling to make ends meet despite working long hours in the emotionally demanding field of psychotherapy. How you arrange and manage your finances matters greatly. As mentioned at the outset of this chapter, money is a taboo subject. And yet bringing our financial health into the light of day is one of the best ways to learn what's really working for and against us. We're then better able to integrate how we think and manage our money into our self-caring attitude and enactments.

PRACTICAL DECISIONS BASED ON MONEY NEEDS AND HABITS

A whopping 45% of Americans reported having $0 in basic savings, and 24% have saved less than $1,000 (see Huddleston, 2019). Moreover, the average American's monthly expenses are $5,000, with indebted households owing more than $132,000 (Dautovic, 2021). Thus, it's safe to say that many of us experience financial situations marked by strain, tension, and disillusionment. But, as noted earlier in the chapter, how we *think* we're faring financially often has a lot to do with how we compare ourselves to others in our so-called reference group. So if other psychotherapists with whom you regularly relate are earning roughly the same income and are in approximately the same financial boat, you may not feel as strained as if you were surrounded by friends and colleagues who have much more financial freedom.

To this point, I vividly remember being quite angered that I was a psychology intern earning approximately $20,000 per year even after I spent the better part of a decade studying and training as a budding clinical psychologist. Not only was this amount quite dismal on its own, but in contrast to psychiatry residents—who were earning almost 3 times this amount while having significantly less psychotherapy training—the anger sometimes bubbled over. My fellow interns and I would circle back to this point of tension probably a little too often.

The inimitable Marie Forleo—life coach, entrepreneur, and motivational speaker—discussed how much she used to wrestle with her money demons, alternating between panic and avoidance of all the college debt with which she was once saddled (Team Tony, n.d.-b). Ms. Forleo noted that with so much debt she would often have trouble making ends meet. After a while of "playing that game," she felt compelled to commit to erasing her debt once and for all, no matter what. Although she often lived within the scarcity mindset, Ms. Forleo desired to connect with her values and decided to live a life in alignment with them—that there's enough to go around and that she could contribute to society in meaningful ways no matter what she was earning at a given point in time. We can follow exemplars like this, questioning our beliefs and habits around money in the service of our overall well-being. Having our financial house in order is a wonderful enactment of self-care.

One way to begin inspecting your financial house is through examination not only of your beliefs about money but how you actually manage it. In the service of this aspiration, you might become intimately familiar with several basic financial categories. If you find yourself anxiously avoiding one category or another, you likely need to put some extra loving care and attention to that category. While this framework may seem overly simplistic, it's really meant as a method of self-discovery and self-caring rather than as anything close to a full financial analysis.

- *Gross earnings.* How much money, in total, do you (and does your household) bring in? Exactly how much money you make each year *and* each month are key numbers to have as you determine the other indicators that follow in this list. Of note, if you operate a private practice and have fluctuating earnings by week, month, and year, it can be very helpful to pay yourself a regular paycheck or two each month so that you can feel confident during slow times. Earnings above these base paychecks can be saved for slow months in the future.

- *Net earnings.* Your net or "take home" is the money you actually get each month, after deducting all the various obligatory expenses such as health care, retirement plan savings, social security, and taxes withheld. Knowing this figure, especially as a private practitioner, can be exceptionally useful so that your gross revenue doesn't accidentally mislead you in some way.

- *(Un)usual expenses.* Knowing your typical household outlays can be an anxiety-provoking but ultimately self-caring exercise. From rent or mortgage and utilities to food, clothing, gas, entertainment, and out-of-pocket health costs, some monthly expenditures can be adjusted while others are fairly nonnegotiable. Atypical expenses such as car and home repairs can overwhelm many of us living on a tight budget or who haven't yet stashed money for emergencies.

- *Debts.* Given the amount of college and professional school debt that some of us may still be paying off, educational loans are often one of the biggest sources of expense. Many people feel quite frustrated and despondent about paying exorbitant interest on top of sometimes very large sums of money for education we got years ago. Credit card debt can also easily accrue, given imbalances in our net earnings, expenses, and spending habits. Having a structured plan for paying off debt can feel burdensome but also freeing in the long run.

- *Spending habits.* Are you fully aware of where and how your money is being spent each month? Are you often surprised by how much or little you still have in your checking account when you pay your bills? Based on our rough assessments in previous sections, you may have an avoidant financial style that creates anxiety and mystery around your spending habits rather than calm and transparency. Getting a hold of how your spending money is used can be a wonderfully helpful pragmatic self-caring tool.

- *Savings habits.* If you are part of the vast majority of the American population who struggle to save any money each year, this issue can be highly frustrating and disillusioning. If you typically don't save much but are able to save, it may be time to start paying yourself (and your future self) first. If it feels nearly impossible to save each month, figuring out how to transfer even a very small amount of spending money into saving money may help you feel better in both the short and long run.

- *Charitable donations.* It is said that the charitable spirit knows no financial bounds. Even if you earn much less than you'd like, giving a few dollars here and there to worthy causes is valuable for those to whom you're contributing and fulfilling to you as the donor. Then, as your income increases, your giving spirit more easily comes along for the ride.

At first blush it may have seemed like our money habits and beliefs don't necessarily have a place at the (professional) self-care table. However, hopefully we've identified some ways to better understand our financial selves for more sustainable personal and professional well-being.

Seemingly on the opposite end of the spectrum from money, spirituality is explored next as a potential form of deep and sustainable self-caring to bring meaning and soothing to the challenging life of the psychotherapist.

14 SPIRITUAL AND RELIGIOUS BELIEFS AND NEEDS

Being on the spiritual path means understanding that the source of your trouble and the source of your wellbeing are within you.

—Sadhguru

Although on the decline, religion continues to play an important role in American lives. Surveying religious and spiritual trends, the Pew Research Center (2014a, 2014b) found that although only one third of the American population frequently attend religious services, almost three quarters pray (as distinct from meditating) at least weekly. Interestingly, 59% of Americans "feel a sense of *spiritual* peace and well-being" at least once weekly, and of that group a staggering 84% also pray at least weekly.

Quite remarkably, the weekly experience of spiritual well-being differs significantly for individuals based on their parental and educational status and their income. Parents, individuals with postgraduate degrees, and individuals who earned more than $100,000 a year were all, respectively, much less likely than their counterparts who are childless and have substantially

https://doi.org/10.1037/0000309-015
The Thriving Therapist: Sustainable Self-Care to Prevent Burnout and Enhance Well-Being, by M. A. Hersh

less education and earnings to experience frequent feelings of spiritual peace and well-being. A similar finding was revealed regarding the importance of religion in one's life. Of those who believe religion to be "very important," only 9% have a postgraduate degree. That's us!

How do these opening statements resonate with you? Do these data align with your personal experience? If so, how? And if not, what are the ways in which your interior or exterior life operates in a way that is different from some of these findings? Religion and spirituality, as both concepts and practices, are not part of everyone's life. This chapter does not presuppose that they either are or should be. Rather, as some models of self-care delineate, if we tend to our spiritual selves, we may be more resilient, engage in more sustainable self-care, and experience well-being. And we can guard against unnecessary afflictive beliefs and emotions. Dr. Laronda Starling, psychotherapist and author of *Be Still: Spiritual Self-Care for Mental Health Professionals* (Starling, 2019), offered a therapist self-care model that incorporates many forms of spiritual strength, including knowing God, making space and time to pray, studying the scriptures, and reflecting on the good life. A belief in God and adherence to scripture, however, aren't necessary components of spiritual self-care of therapists. We can take a less religious and more spiritual perspective to self-care, integrating deep meaning making, our shared humanity, and a sense of connection to beyond what we can see and know.

For our purposes, let's conceptualize religiosity and spirituality as distinct but overlapping ideas and enactments. Religiosity, as opposed to particular religions themselves, is multidimensional and actually quite a complex notion. Although numerous models of religiosity exist, religious scholars Glock and Stark (1965) identified five major dimensions of religiosity: (a) experiential, (b) ritualistic, (c) ideological, (d) intellectual, and (e) consequential (see Holdcroft, 2006, for review). Essentially, within one's religion, we can *feel* our faith, *engage with others* in the practice of it, actively *identify* with religious beliefs and doctrine, *cognitively understand* the basic religious tenets and scriptures, and *integrate the benefits* of our faith into our lives and those of our community. Other scholars have noted that, for some people, religion can become the source of guidance for the rest of life's decisions, even down to the clinical training program you attend and the clientele you see. For others, religion fulfills an important but supportive role (see Holdcroft, 2006, for review).

Spirituality, although often part and parcel of religiosity, can be viewed as a somewhat distinct set of principles and practices. Although definitions and conceptualizations abound, spirituality is largely concerned with our connectedness to something larger than ourselves as we seek a deeper meaning and higher sense of purpose in living. Connecting to the divine within the self or to a higher power, communing deeply with nature, and practicing transcendence toward a broader and binding universal energy that is larger than oneself are all within the realm of the spiritual (Earl E. Bakken Center for Spirituality and Healing, n.d.). Humility, inspiration, deep gratitude, and ethical aspiration can all derive from one's spiritual pursuits.

RELIGIOSITY AND SPIRITUALITY IN PSYCHOTHERAPY TRAINING

Typically, religiosity and spirituality are not formally integrated into institutional psychotherapy training unless trainees are taking specific courses devoted to "special" topics or in supervision are discussing a particular client's background and coping. For example, a study of Canadian social work instructors revealed that although the majority of teachers favored inclusion of religion/spirituality into social work practice and course content, only one third reported that this type of content was included in program curricula. Furthermore, they noted that inclusion was largely up to the instructors' discretion (Kvarfordt et al., 2017).

How often did you explore or discuss your own religious practice or spiritual engagement while in graduate or professional school? Did it feel taboo to do so, or perhaps this topic was more openly discussed in some of your clinical training circles? I'm a bit ashamed to admit that during my early training years I would quietly question the benefit of discussing religion or spiritual beliefs as part of psychotherapy training. Apparently my support for diversity, equity, and inclusion stopped at the door of religion and spirituality. But given the Pew (2014a, 2014b) research findings described previously, it's clear that the majority of Americans hold some kind of religious or spiritual beliefs and engage in practices that require appropriate curiosity from therapists.

As if religion weren't implicated enough in the struggles people have to coexist, the last decade has seen an increase in legal and political action in some U.S. states (e.g., Arizona, Michigan, Tennessee) centered on religious freedoms within counseling, social work, and psychology training institutions. Essentially, these so-called conscience clause laws and bills (which have been introduced for a variety of reasons other than health care) give state legislatures jurisdiction over higher education institutions if a trainee refuses to treat a client whose religious or spiritual beliefs are uncomfortably discrepant from their own (American Psychological Association [APA], 2013). For example, if a trainee who opposes homosexuality for "religion reasons" simply stops seeing a client who reveals he is gay, the training institution legally would not be allowed to maintain control over the situation and could not "discipline" the trainee for such a refusal.

Many, including the APA, have made efforts to fight against such overreach by these states' legislative bodies as they try to dictate what our training institutions and their oversight credentialing and licensing boards can and cannot do (see APA, 2013). Undoubtedly, these issues will proliferate as our culture wars rage on and increasingly affect us all.

Whatever your experience with religion and spirituality and psychotherapy within your training years, how did you feel about and interact with such themes as you became an independent and experienced clinician? Do you tend to invoke religiosity and spirituality when in supervision, peer consultation, or in other clinical support settings? If these facets of life are important to you, do you feel comfortable letting them serve as sources of resilience, meaning making, positive coping, and hope?

For psychotherapists specifically, religion and spirituality can ostensibly be invoked through at least three lenses: (a) appreciation of the client and their lived experience, (b) the therapeutic relationship and how to best harness religious and spiritual engagement to enhance treatment outcomes, and (c) therapists' own self-care and well-being. For the purposes of this book, we'll focus mainly on the third lens, through which religiosity and spirituality enter therapists' lives.

HOW RELIGION AND SPIRITUALITY CAN SUPPORT OUR WELL-BEING

Although it's mentioned many times in this book, it always bears mindful and compassionate repeating: Our jobs are *hard*. This work is not light nor for the faint of heart. In fact, our hearts are "on the job" just as much as our intellects are. And when we start doubting ourselves as competent agents of change, become disillusioned with our work, or become overwrought by troubling client stories and behaviors that rattle our sense of self and of humanity, we can seek sources of soothing and perspective beyond our personal limits. The flexible roots of religion and spirituality can reach out to offer solace and helpful meaning making.

Think back, if you're comfortable enough doing so, to a tough situation in therapy. This situation could be highly disturbing in-session client behavior, a beloved client experiencing a psychotic break, or a longstanding client attempting or even dying by suicide. How did you make sense of that deeply difficult event in your professional life and in the lives of your clients and clients' loved ones? How did you offer yourself comfort and compassion when you left the busyness of work and returned home for the evening to act with some semblance of normalcy?

Perhaps you had a similarly traumatic or difficult situation in your personal life. I've known colleagues who have lost parents and children to cancer and to traumatic accidents, who have gone through highly contentious divorces, and who struggle to cope with chronic illness and unrelenting pain. And during the global pandemic that began in 2019, we've all had to find ways to manage both existential and acute anxieties that we've likely never encountered before in this form and to this degree. These situations are, no matter how painful, the human condition.

We can meet these situations in a variety of ways. As we've reflected on in Chapters 10 and 11, we may already have quite helpful and hopeful approaches to handling difficult situations. The benefits that religiosity and spirituality can bestow may guide, reinforce, buoy, or complement these patterned, positive coping tendencies. And yet our faith and connection to a higher power may provide solace that no human being, including ourselves, may be able to offer. Those who believe in God's loving presence or in a source energy bigger than all of us can't help but be swept up in the comforting hands of a larger force. However, some of us lean toward the pessimistic, anxious, or hopeless end of the stress response spectrum. We can become easily cynical at an unjust world and deeply disillusioned at all the suffering around us and sitting in front of us on a daily basis. For this group of therapists, invoking religious doctrine, spiritual connectedness, or the comfort of community can offer an optimism, hope, strength, and comfort that would be hard to muster on our own.

Acknowledgment of our precarious human condition and basic vulnerability as people and as psychotherapists is captured well by both contemporary and historical work. Dr. Brene Brown, a prominent social work researcher who has exposed the beauty and courage of being vulnerable, offered the comforting and inspiring notion that from a place of vulnerability we can create, innovate, and expand our sense of what is possible (B. Brown, 2010). We hear this echoed in more ancient wisdom from the Buddha, who asked us to consider that "every experience, no matter how bad it seems, holds within it a blessing of some kind. The goal is to find it." In addition, the *New Testament* also points us toward comfort within our vulnerability and depth of struggle:

> But he said to me, My grace is sufficient for you, for my power is made perfect in weakness. Therefore, I will boast all the more gladly of my weaknesses, so that

the power of Christ may rest upon me. For the sake of Christ, then, I am content with weaknesses, insults, hardships, persecutions, and calamities. For when I am weak, then I am strong. (Second Corinthians 12:9–10)

Just as every client who walks through our door is not spared a thousand joys *and* a thousand sorrows, so too are we subject to such vulnerability within the human condition. We sit with suffering all the time—our clients and our own. And we can look to sources and resources beyond ourselves and the present moment to offer us meaning, solace, and opportunity for growth. The 13th century Sufi mystic and poet, Jalaluddin Rumi, offered wisdom from beyond our current comprehension:

> This being human is a guest house.
> Every morning a new arrival.
> A joy, a depression, a meanness,
> some momentary awareness comes
> as an unexpected visitor.
> Welcome and entertain them all!
> Even if they're a crowd of sorrows,
> who violently sweep your house
> empty of its furniture,
> still, treat each guest honorably.
> He may be clearing you out
> for some new delight.
> The dark thought, the shame, the malice,
> meet them at the door laughing,
> and invite them in.
> Be grateful for whoever comes,
> because each has been sent
> as a guide from beyond. (Barks, 1995, p. 109)

Religion and spirituality, for the majority of people around the world, can serve as a compass of morality and a bedrock of resilience and hope. Thus, this is self-care in its most fundamental form. We resource ourselves by tuning into a higher power, a deep sense of something outside of us, or a community of like-minded individuals and families adhering to similar principles of love, connection, and faith in something bigger. Research shows that religiosity and happiness are positively associated (Bergan & McConatha, 2001). Those of us who express strong religious faith and involvement tend to report fewer stressful events and greater life satisfaction than do those whose faith and involvement is not as strong. Religious affiliation is also a significant predictor of overall belongingness and sense of purpose in life (e.g., Walker, 2003). In a study of health workers, Boero et al. (2005) found that spirituality plays a significant and positive role in quality of life; spirituality seemed to influence health workers' physical well-being as well.

So how do you integrate religiosity or spirituality into your personal and professional life? Is your sense of what's greater and more powerful infused into everything you do, or do you invoke a higher power as a resource primarily when times are difficult? Are religious or spiritual principles and practices familiar and comfortable companions, or do they seem like ideologies and rituals for someone else? Again, this chapter is not meant to bring religion or spirituality into your life if it hasn't been there so far. Rather, this chapter is more about asking and listening. Some aspects of your existing spirituality, for example, could be (re)awakened for productive meaning making and solace in the clinical work you do. These positive internal resources could serve to enhance your self-caring relationship and ideally foster resilience to prevent burnout, compassion fatigue, and other hazards of our profession.

Of final note, I would be remiss in not acknowledging that religion (and spirituality) for some of us has not been all positive. We may have wrestled (or we may still contend) with more restrictive doctrine, for example, that conflicts with our updated notions of fairness, equality, and decency. Scandals of various kinds throughout our modern era have created a great deal of disillusionment, frustration, and sorrow. And yet, we nevertheless can consciously orient toward what is most helpful and meaningful to us for our highest purpose and for the greater good of those around us.

15 CULTURAL INFLUENCES ON SELF-CARE AND WELL-BEING

We seldom realize, for example, that our most private thoughts and emotions are not actually our own. For we think in terms of languages and images which we did not invent, but which were given to us by our society.

—Alan W. Watts

When you hear the word "culture," what comes to mind? Do you get a clear notion of what it means to have your self-care needs influenced by the culture(s) around you? Unfortunately, culture is elusive and can evade even our best efforts to completely understand its impact on us. However, once we reflect on the ways in which culture manifests itself, we can more clearly see how it may influence how and why we (don't or can't) care for ourselves in the ways we do.

Some anthropologists suggest that culture is "simply" the knowledge that people use to live their lives and the varied ways in which they do so (Handwerker, 2002). Expanding on this definition, we can see culture as the full range of learned human behavioral and belief patterns—a multilayered,

https://doi.org/10.1037/0000309-016
The Thriving Therapist: Sustainable Self-Care to Prevent Burnout and Enhance Well-Being, by M. A. Hersh

complex phenomenon characterized by the ways in which different groups of people enact similar ways of living through similar-enough behaviors, ways of thinking, rituals, and symbols. But this definition may not grant us a personalized and nuanced sense of how the attitudes and actions of taking care of ourselves, especially as helpers, are shaped by historical, cultural, and societal forces. Just as the air we breathe goes unseen as it both sustains and complicates our lives, so too does culture operate insidiously and invisibly all around us at all times. In fact, as we'll explore in this chapter, cultural influences on the ways in which we tend to ourselves (and others) can become embodied and embedded into the very fabric of our being.

CULTURAL FORCES INFLUENCE NOTIONS OF WORK, REST, AND SELF-CARE

If we start unpacking some of the invisible cultural influences, we may find that the most fundamental notion of what it means to work is a cultural force that's hard to escape. As we explored the blocks to being our own best allies in Chapter 7, you may have noted several systemic barriers to self-care that have a shared undercurrent—work hard, stay disciplined (with little complaint), and earn your keep. Focus on problems after they arise rather than on prevention of issues in the first place.

As opposed to some European nations that allow for flexibility in the work week, the United States has, from its inception, fostered what Max Weber (2017) described as a Protestant work ethic, an ideological framework embodied in *Poor Richard's Almanac*: Time is money, and only through constant hard work is success (divine, social, or economic) earned. This ideology was partnered with a growing emphasis on values of independence, stories of rags to riches, and a capitalist system that pushes people to work harder, more efficiently, and more productively. Having babies is necessary to the success of the state, so long as having them doesn't interfere with work and productivity. Our policies are governed by our principles and our culturally created social and economic systems, and these pervade our whole culture. With the weight of ideology, socioeconomic structures, and pervasive value judgments about how hard we work and how we should spend our time, even the most service-oriented psychotherapist may be hard pressed to not walk this magnetic treadmill of hard work and earned income.

The ways in which Western work culture have been established and pre-defined can lead us down a path of intensity and constancy of work during the "work week" and respite only on the weekends. "Work hard, play hard" has become a source of pride in many circles, as if to play hard, whatever that really means, we need to work in a burnout-oriented fashion. This long-standing dichotomy really doesn't serve many of us very well because it insidiously promotes ill-attention toward self-care during our "up" work time only to finally pay attention to our down time when we've exhausted ourselves with intense, constant work.

CULTURAL FORCES AND THE HELPING PROFESSIONAL

Culture influences general notions not only of work but also specifically of being a *helping* professional. As our professional workforce is becoming increasingly diversified by race, ethnicity, and gender (American Psychological Association, 2020), we must take stock of how cultural forces affect how we live and work. Foundational virtues and values are often cultivated within our cultural backgrounds, and these need to be understood for us to treat ourselves well in the helping roles we occupy. For example, those of us who were raised within particular religious or spiritual backgrounds may have an especially strong sense of community, family, generosity, and responsibility to care for those in need. You may have been raised always to think of others before yourself. While this humanitarian ethos may be a defining aspect of many helping professions (e.g., social work), it may also be part of the recipe for burnout.

I once worked with an extremely thoughtful, generous, and kind client who had just begun his third year in medical school. As he described his all-too-common feelings of burnout, it became clear that his particular religious and familial upbringing promoted strong values to help others above all else. Although he had only just begun his clinical rotations, he invested an inordinate amount of time learning how to help each patient as if his (and their) life depended on it. Consequently, he felt quite guilty and ashamed with even the thought of taking time for himself to rest and recharge. When he did rest, he felt even more guilty because of it.

Does this resonate at all with you? Does any care for yourself trigger guilt? Did the community ethic in which you were raised suggest that you were selfish by tending to your own needs? What was it about your spiritual, religious, or familial guiding principles that points to this possible conundrum of feeling compelled to take care of others even when you needed to say "no" for legitimate reasons?

IDENTITY, OPPRESSION, AND FREEDOM FROM SUFFERING

Just as some cultural forces are hard to find and define, other influences are powerfully baked into our way life, to the hidden advantage of some and painful detriment of others. The concepts of *marked* and *unmarked categories* can shine a helpful light on how some identities (i.e., unmarked) are construed by the general culture as the "default." These identities (e.g., White, male, able-bodied) are generally not discriminated against and simply aren't given a second thought when it comes to policy, policing, housing, job hunting, securing employment, and the like. Marked categories, however, point to noticeable identity markers like non-White skin color, being in a wheelchair, having a strong accent, and having stereotypical male features as a gendered woman. As I was writing this book, a news story broke of an East London girl, Ruby Williams, who was repeatedly sent home from school because she supposedly violated the school's policy stating that "afro style hair must be of reasonable size and length." Imagine the effects on one's sense of self and the restriction on feeling the basic right to simply be and to care for and express oneself freely.

Unfortunately, some of us experience the negative consequences (even if subtle) of living from the position of one or more marked categories. And if we've never really been conscious of the consequences of marked and unmarked categories, we've likely had a depth and breadth of privilege in our lives that is well worth unpacking. *Privilege* is defined as "an advantage, immunity, or right held as a prerogative of status or rank, and exercised to the exclusion or detriment of others" (The Free Dictionary, n.d.). Recent but certainly not new inequities and disparities in the treatment of Black lives in America has shined a glaringly bright spotlight on the realities and effects of privilege of skin color, socioeconomic status, and gender. In *White Privilege: Unpacking the Invisible Knapsack*, Peggy McIntosh (2003) helped us see what is largely unseen. McIntosh powerfully noted that she "was taught to see racism only in individual acts of meanness, not in invisible systems conferring dominance on my group" (p. 1). It is exactly these hidden systems of oppression and discrimination that insidiously weave their way into our attitudes and actions and into those of the institutions for which we work, the colleagues with whom we work, and the clientele we serve.

Privilege comes in many shapes and forms, some of which are more obvious than others. Gender, race, skin color, hair, clothing, and accent tend to be some of the most outward-facing examples of privilege (and discrimination). Simply being a man (or child) who is Black, Hispanic, or Latino confers a much greater degree of risk of discrimination (Daniller, 2021) and even threat of bodily harm

(Khan, 2019) than being in an unmarked category does (e.g., White man). Recent hate crimes against Asian Americans only point to what Asian people in America have known from their experience of discrimination and hate for well over 100 years.

Being (obviously) male-looking is a form of privilege that many men have no idea they enjoy (McIntosh, 2020), and White males specifically tend to be ranked higher in the "pecking order" than women and virtually any other intersection of gender and racial identity. But many women already know and experience this inequity because they're not culturally privileged in the same way. In your employment as a psychotherapist, do you know if women earn less than colleagues who are men? Unfortunately, women in today's workplace (whether employed part-time or full-time) earn, on average, only 84 cents on the dollar relative to men (Barroso & Brown, 2021). That's well over 300 extra hours of work that women would need to do just to catch up to men's salaries. Quite sobering and maddening, women with psychology doctorates working in the health services field earn almost $40,000 per year less than their counterparts who are men (see Nigrinis et al., 2014). Within psychotherapy specifically, practitioners who are men typically report higher salaries than do clinicians who are women (Sentell et al., 2001).

Incidentally, this gender pay gap wouldn't affect women in private psychotherapy practice because we set our own rates, right? But then again, women have been culturally undervalued for so long that they're much less likely to ask for a raise and to receive one. This long-standing cultural influence on people's perceived value may translate into women's reluctance to set a higher fee for their useful services, although there are likely additional reasons for this type of hesitancy. Indeed, men have been found to charge higher fees than women charge for their clinical services (Sentell et al., 2001). Conversely, feminist and justice-oriented therapists (women and men alike) may want to keep their fees low to reduce the power differential between therapist and client (Zur, 2007). But again, this dynamic just highlights the effects of the cultural forces of living and working in a capitalist society with power differentials and inequalities.

In our capitalist and gendered societies, women are expected to and still do bear the brunt of the family management and unpaid care labor beyond the care they provide at work. As psychotherapists, constant caregiving is inherent in the job. And so, in general, women therapists may be taking care of children, planning meals, and keeping the house "in here" before and after they provide necessary caregiving and/or case management services to others in need "out there." Thus, when a well-intentioned friend suggests to a woman psychotherapist that she take better care of herself, cultural and familial restrictive forces may present a challenge and cause feelings of frustration. Some women may simply feel trapped. Of note, this discussion of unpaid caregiving labor at home is not reserved for just cisgender, heteronormative families. The issue of division of labor and family management can occur within any household. It may behoove you to reflect on the ways in which this dynamic functions in *your* particular household and to assess how some facets could be improved or strengthened to enhance your well-being and reduce the risk of burnout.

We can also extend this discussion to single parents and those who are earning substantially less than what they need or might expect for their level of training and expertise. Single parents tend to have even more on their plate, and individuals who earn low incomes may indeed feel financially trapped and in need of a second job just to makes ends meet. If we consider the *intersectionality* of a low-income-earning single parent of color working in an underfunded school system, for example, we might offer somewhat different self-care "advice" than we would for a White, married, upper class therapist in private practice. As noted later in the chapter, there are many sources of both privilege and burden, of which those with less privilege and more burden are already aware.

THERAPIST IDENTITY AND CULTURAL SELF-ASSESSMENT

As a sign of both changing demographics and awareness of how diversity and discrimination affect clinical work, contemporary clinical programs are likely to include diversity training within the curriculum. Does this mean that students of psychotherapy become mindfully aware of their categories of identity and indicators of privilege? If you are a therapist of color, LGBTQ+, of non-European heritage, with a strong "foreign" accent, or a woman in a predominantly man-oriented workplace, you already know full well what marked categories of your identity feel like and the privilege(s) you do not necessarily enjoy.

Dr. Dhara Meghani (2019) noted, in an article for the Society for Psychotherapy, that additional barriers and stressors for underrepresented trainees may be based on racial, ethnic, or language-based differences from majority students and faculty. For example, BIPOC (Black, Indigenous, and people of color) and LGBTQ+ students may feel an undue burden to carry the weight of their particular identity if they're in the minority based on numbers. This type of insidious expectation may lead to implicit or sometimes explicit messaging to be "representatives" of their race, ethnicity, gender identity, or sexual orientation. How training programs and the workplaces that trainees will occupy in the future handle such identity politics is an essential part of how minority professionals can become more unburdened from discrimination and ultimately feel valued, validated, and seen.

Fortunately, we have found ways to unlock the door to honest cultural self-assessment by "looking into the clinician's mirror" (Hays, 2008). Hays (2008) offered both a self-reflective and pragmatically useful framework for exploring one's own culturally dominant and nondominant identities that may confer privilege on us, knowingly or not. Hays used the acronym ADDRESSING to connote Age and generational influences, Developmental disabilities or Disabilities acquired later in life, Religion and spiritual orientation, Ethnic and racial identity, Socioeconomic status, Sexual orientation, Indigenous heritage, National origin, and Gender. This framework may not be exhaustive, yet it covers a reasonably large swath of categories reflecting the ways we might identify. Our lived experiences depend largely on context, with some identities perceived by others as assets, some perceived as liabilities, and others simply not considered as influential at all (see Exhibit 15.1).

EXHIBIT 15.1. Self-Care Reflection Break: Understanding Privilege

Privilege is contextual.	Privilege cuts people off from information and experiences related to minority groups. Thus, having privilege in certain areas necessarily means you may be less aware than those with less privilege.
Psychology itself is a privileged profession that reinforces many dominant cultural values.	Introspection, self-reflecting, reading, and research are necessary but not sufficient for increasing cross-cultural competence.
Our personal beliefs and lifestyles are often reflected in our values concerning therapy.	Critical thinking helps us turn mainstream sources of information into culture-specific learning opportunities.
Humor is a valuable tool in reducing conflict that often comes with cross-cultural relationships and interactions.	Peer-level intimate relationships with people of diverse identities are a rich source of cross-cultural learning (see Chapter 38 on stewardship networks).

Note. Adapted from *Addressing Cultural Complexities in Practice: Assessment, Diagnosis, and Therapy* (2nd ed., p. 62), by P. A. Hays, 2008, American Psychological Association (https://doi.org/10.1037/11650-003). Copyright 2008 by the American Psychological Association.

ASSUMPTIONS, PREJUDICE, AND BIGOTRY TOWARD THERAPISTS IN THE THERAPY ROOM AND BEYOND

You've trained for countless hours honing your craft. You may even be known in some circles as a resident expert in a particular issue or treatment approach. You greet a new client you've never seen before and begin your initial session with some pleasantries and assessment. But your client already is revealing some fairly incendiary prejudiced beliefs, and your being a bisexual and multiracial woman has you feeling quite uncomfortable. Like psychologist Dr. Lindsey Buckman, who identifies as a lesbian, noted, "Most people assume everybody is heterosexual . . . and people say things when they feel like you are similar that they wouldn't say if it was obvious that you are different" (as cited in Abrams, 2018).

This scene may not happen all the time, but it certainly happens. And if we live and work with privilege (e.g., as a White, male, cisgender and heterosexual practitioner), we may never encounter such an incident nor know remotely what it would feel like. In fact, in a *Monitor on Psychology* piece on therapists who face discrimination (Abrams, 2018), Atlanta-based clinical psychologist Dr. Jennifer Kelly, who is Black, discussed having been mistaken for "the help" while her White office manager was assumed to be the therapist. She reportedly endured outright hostility as well as a patient who refused to work with her because she was Black.

On the other side of the obvious hostility coin is the lack of acknowledgment for therapists' experience of prejudice and discrimination due to a variety of factors, including emigrating from a country with a different culture and a different accent, set of rituals and principles, and lifestyle. Living two lives as a therapist, as a native born to one country and as an immigrant in another country, surely is not to be ignored but rather to be honored and valued for both its challenges and its gifts.

Consider Maria, a second-generation Latinx psychotherapist in her early 30s with a Puerto Rican accent working in a mental health clinic in a predominantly White community of European descent in the American South. She often and readily feels her "difference" among the community she serves. Although she holds two master's degrees, one in public health and the other in social work, some clients and colleagues in the community assume she is "just a student trying hard to learn the ropes," as one physician she was collaborating with suggested. Several new clients Maria met over the years asked if she were really their therapist because they assumed she was "just part of the staff," similar to what Dr. Kelly (described previously) experienced.

Maria is gainfully employed, but her salary is quite low. Although Maria has friends where she lives, she feels beholden to her family in Puerto Rico. She video chats with them frequently and often feels guilty when she tries to forge a life of her own where she lives. Maria has long felt that she is bisexual, but she has yet to come out to her family, friends, or colleagues. She feels she has to keep her sexual and romantic inclinations secret despite having strong feelings toward a woman colleague.

Maria certainly tries to take care of herself. She does yoga at home a few times a week and watches her favorite shows. She tries to cook relatively healthy meals when she can despite long hours at the clinic. But there are numerous cultural influences that weigh on her, some she is quite aware of and others more hidden. The racism and implicit bias she experiences from her clients and coworkers eats away at her and sometimes keeps her up at night. She feels tethered to her family in Puerto Rico and guilty for not keeping in touch more frequently. Her upbringing instilled a strong sense of hetero-normativity that helped create both shame and fear when she thinks about expressing her true sexual attraction and love interest. For Maria, self-caring is complicated but not unworkable. It just looks a bit different than it might look for someone of marked identity but living in a more accepting or homogenous community or for someone in an unmarked identity category with a good deal of privilege.

There is no easy answer to the struggles that Dr. Kelly, Dr. Buckman, Maria, and so many others experience in their personal lives as well as with their clients and colleagues. Reflecting on the cultural assessment from Hays (2008), we, on the outside, can hopefully appreciate such lived experiences with more nuanced understanding and compassion. On the inside, Dr. Kelly, Dr. Buckman, and Maria may already feel the oppressive forces at play in their various forms—socioeconomic status, cultural heritage, language and accent, and sexual orientation. Appreciating the potency of these cultural forces doesn't make them go away, but it may help Maria feel more empowered through validation and other forms of support seeking and support offering.

Ideally, these therapists' colleagues could be better educated through workplace trainings on inclusion, sensitivity, diversity, and privilege (see Hays, 2008). It is incumbent on the workplace to help support and better understand the experiences of therapists with less privilege, including therapists experiencing struggles based on their skin color, backgrounds, sexual preferences, and the like. It is also critical that all therapists work to appreciate their own history of struggle, relative privilege, prejudice, and reactivity to the unjust world in which we live. We may even seek guidance from mentors, colleagues, and trusted others on how to handle unexpected, uncomfortable, and even repugnant interactions with the clients you've been charged to serve (Abblett, 2013).

Whatever the (sub)cultural body and world we inhabit, we do our best to help our clients while helping ourselves stay mindfully aware, grounded, and self-compassionate. But what happens when the jobs or workplaces we occupy are simply misaligned with our core strengths and basic personality? Chapter 16, the final chapter of Part II, helps us to explore the degree of resonance among our personal self, our therapist role, and the workplace setting(s) in which we find ourselves. When we're more aware of the degree of this resonance, we're more empowered to act consciously as our own best allies now and in the future.

16 PERSON-THERAPIST-WORK ALIGNMENT

If one does not know to which port one is sailing, no wind is favorable.

—Seneca the Younger

I didn't enter graduate school with a fascination for depression, schizophrenia, obsessive-compulsive disorder, or trauma. Rather, I had a long-held interest in how emotions work and how they're socialized in children. I carried this research and scholarly interest forward from the final year of undergraduate education all the way through my PhD dissertation. It may sound naïve, but I was quietly incredulous upon first hearing that some of my graduate school classmates had already done clinical work and were poised to conduct research with individuals with schizophrenia, autism, severe posttraumatic stress disorder, sociopathy, dementia, and chronic suicidality. Here I was, interested how children feel about and express their emotions while my fellow trainees were gearing up to learn about and treat some of society's most confounding and impactful psychological and relational challenges.

https://doi.org/10.1037/0000309-017

The Thriving Therapist: Sustainable Self-Care to Prevent Burnout and Enhance Well-Being, by M. A. Hersh

Many of my classmates and clinical internship peers went on to become experts in and program directors for a wide range of highly intense and complex populations. For example, some peers have directed programs for caregivers of elders with dementia, intensive outpatient programs for individuals with substance dependencies, and programs for inmates on inpatient units in prisons. Others have become comfortable and competent helpers for populations of youth who have committed sexual offenses and victims of child sex trafficking rings. Many of these colleagues couldn't imagine doing any work other than what they currently do. My forensic psychology colleagues love the world of child forensic evaluations no matter how utterly challenging and disheartening it can be. I know trauma specialists who deeply desire to help trauma survivors reclaim their lives, and so maintaining their focus on this arena is incredibly meaningful to them. This determination to pursue a particular path or niche interest, however, doesn't necessitate that we have blinders on to the realities of the stress and suffering that can accumulate with such a narrowed focus of work.

I look at my friends and colleagues with awe because I can't fathom how I would hold up in such settings and with such populations. Others can and do, willingly. I figured out fairly early on (despite implicit, self-imposed pressures to do otherwise) that something about my sensibilities, sensitivities, and strengths did not allow for the same clinical pursuits as some of my most respected friends and colleagues. These realizations about my intrapersonal qualities have carried forward into almost all of my professional decision making, which has in turn influenced my personal life. Such awareness and choice have, for the most part, helped create a more virtuous personhood–professional life cycle spinning across time and career development. It is my wish within the objectives of this chapter that we all find ourselves in a more virtuous cycle by acknowledging and honoring our gifts and our challenges and the ways in which they may or may not align with our work.

When we take a bird's-eye view of who ends up where and why, it can be quite interesting to learn how we all arrived at our current positions working with the populations we now serve. We can also project several years into the future and imagine the work contexts and professional activities that will facilitate our well-being, allow for optimal self-caring and positive resourcing, and grant us opportunities for fulfillment and meaning. In fact, the very act of optimally aligning ourselves with particular professional roles and settings is a beautiful enactment of sustainable self-caring.

This chapter is all about the *synergy* or *alignment* of you as a person, you as a psychotherapist, and the contexts in which you have chosen to work. However, you may not have freely chosen your specific job; rather, you may have ended up there out of necessity or a sort of forced choice. As we'll explore together, work setting and all its nuanced facets matter. Although we'll briefly discuss general factors of work demands, degree of autonomy granted, and personal resources—the core variables that contribute to burnout—we'll also explore how your personal self intersects with your therapist self to fit within a given work context. In this pursuit of higher purpose alignment, let's reference the chapters in Part II that speak to your unique personal and professional habits, patterns, and needs. We don't have to be rigidly defined by such habits to have them inform how we attempt to best align ourselves with our work.

WHO ARE YOU?

I've seen too many of my own clients and some of my clinical colleagues unhappy or downright miserable in their jobs, not because they chose the wrong career but rather due to poor alignment between their temperament, personality, and internal resources on the one hand and their work setting and type of daily work on the other. Psychotherapists may demand deliberate attention to this subject because of the very nature of our jobs. Because our work playground is situated in human suffering and hope for human potential, if we're less interested in or less equipped to interact with particular types of clients with certain types of struggles, we may very well be set up for all manner of our own personal suffering. Moreover, some types of clients may suffer as well, simply because they're not well matched to a therapist who could provide the best support or treatment.

What kind of person are you? This question is perhaps too broad and vague, but it just may elicit some measure of self-reflection about your temperament, strengths, weaknesses, proclivities, qualities, character, resourcefulness, ambitions, and even larger life purpose. If you took a piece of paper and wrote out this question and corollary inquires, how would you begin to free associate? (This exercise, incidentally, is not meant to diagnose, pathologize, or therapize. If it becomes distressing, simply stop as you try to acknowledge gently what may have triggered you.) Go ahead and give it a try, and then come back to the next paragraph.

This exercise can be useful in two core ways, the latter building on the former. First, we can see ourselves more clearly, both the bright and shadowy elements. We may hear whispers of "psychotherapist, know thyself" underneath this statement. You may benefit by getting a better handle on your countertransferential patterns and certain habitual reactivities. Hopefully your talents, strengths, and resources become more evident. Because individuals aren't terribly adept at self-assessment (Kruger & Dunning, 1999), you may want to have a very trusted other answer these questions about you and then compare their responses with yours.

The second way in which this exercise can be directly helpful is that it can set the stage for better alignment between you and *what* you have chosen to do, *where* you're doing it, and *why* you chose this path or position. This alignment, in part, is an essential ingredient in the recipe for mitigating occupational stress and cultivating sustainable self-caring. In previous chapters of this section, we explored our various patterns, habits, and needs related to our bodies, minds, feelings, relationships, and cultures. These explorations hopefully provided personalized data on what does and doesn't work for you with respect to self-care, well-being, and prevention of unnecessary suffering. These data can further enhance understanding of the (mis)match we currently experience between ourselves and our work. We're then that much better off for any future decisions we might make regarding taking on different types of clients, getting trained in a new approach, changing workplace environments, or possibly even changing professions altogether.

UNDERSTANDING OUR TEMPERAMENT, PERSONALITY, AND CORE STRENGTHS

Maybe you're a highly organized, internally managed, and conscientious go-getter. This set of characteristics may lead you down a different occupational path than the scattered therapist who tends toward procrastination and poor planning and is perhaps easily overwhelmed in the face of mild to moderate stressors. Yes, indeed, many of us would not be cast for superhero roles in the next Marvel Universe movie. That's perfectly fine because there isn't any sort of absolute standard we have to meet. Reducing burnout risk and enhancing our well-being is about alignment between what's on our inside and what's in front of us on the outside. It's like the advice clinical psychology students hear over and over again prior to applying to graduate school. "It's all about the match!" A good program is only as good as the mentor you'll be paired with and research topic in which you'll be investing thousands of hours of your precious time.

Temperament and personality may matter more than we think when it comes to work satisfaction, self-care needs, and reduction of occupational stress. For example, within a closed Facebook group for highly sensitive therapists (HSTs) are posts about how overwhelmed many HSTs can get when confronted with difficult client behaviors, enduring long work days, and arriving home to a relatively chaotic or busy family life. The HST may be particularly vulnerable to the elements of and from the workplace as well as to their own internal processes.

Although HSTs who have yet to declare themselves as such may try to soldier through, a HST may be at higher risk of burnout and many other occupational stress syndromes. Although we don't yet have data on whether HSTs are indeed more likely to experience occupational hazards, we do know from research on highly sensitive persons (HSPs) and sensory processing sensitivity that the HSP brain and body are indeed different from those of the rest of the public. Differences include how strongly we react to both positive and negative emotion, how deeply we process information, how over-aroused we can feel in everyday situations, how empathically attuned we can be, and how much we sense nuanced stimuli in our environments (Aron & Aron, 1997). As referenced earlier in this book, although HSPs make up about 15% to 20% of the population, the percentage for psychotherapists is likely much higher, given Aron's (2010) findings that HSPs readily gravitate toward careers within a variety of helping professions. However, quite poignantly Aron noted that HSPs are

> not suited . . . to entire careers that place them in almost hopeless situations—confrontations with truly cruel persons or working with victims so distressed that they simply cannot be helped very much, be they starving children or harpooned whales (all of which can serve to goad the non-sensitive into an optimal level of arousal for heroic action). (p. 173)

If you're an HSP, or if this description resonates with you in some way, you'll likely know on an intuitive level that your temperament is a glaring mismatch for some work environments and for some types of people with particular struggles. Some of us can't hack overstimulating environments. This limitation likely has little to do with our abilities, skill sets, training, or growth potential as a therapist and may have a lot to do with our (HSP) temperament and perhaps our executive function struggles (see Appendix D for selected resources on HSPs in general and for psychotherapists specifically). For example, fast-paced inpatient settings, high-stress and high-stakes forensics, and being responsible for a lot of employees would burn me out before I reached my first official sick day. But other people's constitutions serve them differently. Not that non-HSPs are immune from such burnout risk, but they may better handle occupational intensity and emotional uncertainty and in fact may welcome it with open arms.

Lest we assume from the focus of this section that all therapists were born with highly sensitive temperaments, we can expand our understanding of our personality and core strengths through popular and science-informed assessments, such as free online tests based on the Jungian Myers-Briggs Type

Indicator. You can use this type of assessment as a launching pad for further self-inquiry and discussions with trusted others about the kind of person you tend to be and how your profile syncs up with the world, including where, how, and with whom you work.

Another great online self-assessment is the Values in Action–Inventory of Strengths (VIA-IS, formerly known as the Values in Action Inventory). Created by and managed through the nonprofit VIA Institute on Character, the VIA-IS produces a ranked list of our character strengths within the broad categories of wisdom, courage, humanity, justice, temperance, and transcendence. More in-depth knowledge of what we stand for and the qualities that stand out as our strengths can undoubtedly assist us in finding the best fit between what drives us forward positively in life and the professional opportunities that can satisfy such drives.

THERAPIST STRENGTHS, SKILLS, INTERESTS, AND ORIENTATION

Paolo, an early-career social work therapist, is a highly creative person, enjoying and feeling inspired by painting, piano, and photography. During training and for several years post licensure, Paolo has been honing his skills as a child and adolescent clinician. Although he is quite creative and artistic and is deeply motivated to help ease young people's struggles, he discovered somewhere along the way, much to his chagrin, that he wasn't terribly skilled at working with children younger than 10 years of age. Paolo would quickly reach an impasse even with the most kind and well-mannered kids. After a few years of frustration and disillusionment, Paolo reconciled with himself. By leaving some kids out of his occupational picture, he was able to support the rest of his clients more effectively. Most important for our purposes here, Paolo was also giving himself a sustainable gift.

Paolo's story reveals that even if we're adept or interested in something in our personal lives, we may not have or be willing to show that same skill or motivation in our life as a psychotherapist. However, the converse may be true as well. We may naturally or in other ways feel the need to align our personal qualities and interests with our therapeutic professional ones for a deep coherence of self.

What are the qualities, strengths, resources, interests, and motivations that you identify in your personal life that align well with or are missing in your life as a therapist? For example, you may like to be active and *in* your body within your personal life, dedicating time every week for cardio, strength training, and yoga. You may desire to bring these interests and motivations into your therapeutic work by teaching and guiding clients through breathwork, energy movement, and yogic poses. This type of interest may be so pervasive in your life that you feel no real separation between outside and inside the therapy room.

At Southeast Psych, a large group practice with locations in North Carolina and Tennessee, Myque Harris, LPC and certified yoga instructor, sought to bridge one of her personal skill sets with her approach as a therapist (Chamberlin, 2017). With the support and accommodation of the group practice, Ms. Harris revamped her office space to accommodate mental health-supportive yoga offerings to several clients at once. Aligning the personal and therapeutic can unite what was formerly fragmented or perhaps yearning to be yoked.

When I brought my interest in acupressure and subtle energy into my clinical work, I gave voice to something that lay dormant for decades. My personal journey with energy psychology and energy medicine informs my clinical practice, and my clinical training in this field supports my personal life. Integrating energy psychology theory and methods into my professional life has since been one of the best and easiest decisions I've ever made. I did the same with mindfulness training as a graduate student. I fell in love (in a nonattached way of course) with what mindfulness and Buddhist psychology have to offer. Since then, my personal and professional trainings don't feel like labor, per se, and my training efforts have become inextricably part of how I operate as a therapist.

Similarly, my colleague Annabelle Coote, MA, LMHC, BC-DMT, has long had a deep love affair with the natural world and with dance. After obtaining her college degree in biology, she found her way back to dance and into counseling. In her private practice, Ms. Coote readily and enthusiastically integrates sensorimotor psychotherapy and other mind–body and movement-oriented approaches to help her clients live as fully and vibrantly as possible.

Given that stressful client behaviors writ large can be a drain on therapists' energy, we must look carefully at the type of clients we're interacting with on a daily basis. Therapists who routinely see clients with personality and psychotic disorders as well as those who are more aggressive or in suicidal crisis not surprisingly tend toward greater risk of burnout, more emotional exhaustion, and depersonalization (e.g., Ackerley et al., 1988; Ballenger-Browning et al., 2011; Rupert & Kent, 2007). However, some of us indeed thrive on handling crises or working with clients who have been traumatized, for example. We must all take care to know our limits and have appropriate outlets for releasing stress and seeking support.

Although we may think of the type of client we see as generating a good deal of job (dis)satisfaction, we can also explore the type of professional role we occupy and the tasks required of us on a daily basis. Are you in a primary therapist position (i.e., solo private practice) that compels you to be the sole decision maker on behalf of your clients? Are you readily and frequently part of a team, for example in an agency, clinic, treatment center, or school setting? Perhaps you "run the show" and are everyone's boss. Or you inhabit quite the opposite space, having very limited decision-making power and beholden to others' choices and clinical judgments all day long. These roles matter for the type of person you are and for the types of stress you can handle. Often enough, however, it's not a simple thing to conclude that being a private practitioner, for example, allows for ultimate freedom because the role also is accompanied by a fair amount of *responsibility stress* that someone in a team-based position doesn't have to contend with in the same way. Thus, weighing the pros and cons of the variety of positions out there and of course the one(s) you're currently occupying can be a very helpful process to ensure the best fit possible in your professional world.

ALIGNMENT OF PERSON, THERAPIST, AND WORK SETTING

When we think about Ms. Coote's and my respective interests, we can see how *not* incorporating such passions and curiosities might leave a void in our professional lives. That missingness may be subtle if we never had a taste of integrating our interests to begin with. But once they are a part of professional life, it may seem impossible or even existentially cruel to exclude something so core to the human spirit. After all, psychotherapy is ultimately about relationships—with each other and with ourselves. If we somehow feel disingenuous about how we're relating to our clients or how we're guiding our clients to relate to others and to themselves, then the whole psychotherapeutic endeavor can be compromised.

On the flip side of that coin are the facets of our work setting that can rub us the wrong way. Some workplaces may in essence mandate us to do therapy in a particular manner (especially if in an agency, clinic, or a specialized treatment facility). This type of professional expectation can generate a dissonance or lack of coherence with our personal values and sensibilities and/or therapeutic skill set or orientation. For example, I worked as a postdoctoral fellow at a research and clinical center that innovated and disseminated cognitive behavioral treatments for anxiety disorders. Although

I learned a great deal about diagnosis and treatment there, I was never one for overly protocol-driven, manualized therapies. I always felt a subtle tension and internal conflict, feeling the need to adhere to the center's mission on the one hand while staying true to my general therapeutic style on the other.

Consider if you're working for an institution of any kind that holds different values than yours or pushes a therapeutic agenda that significantly differs from your own. Sometimes an honest look at this arrangement, although potentially challenging and anxiety-provoking, can be the best catalyst for promoting your professional satisfaction and personal well-being in the long run. As Giovanni Dientsmann, meditation teacher and internet presence, suggested, "self-awareness is developed by reflection, meditation, and honest examination; courage is developed by daring to close your eyes and take the leap" (G. Dientsmann, personal communication, September 24, 2020).

It may come as no surprise that burnout rates are higher for those employed in agencies than for therapists in private or group independent practices (Rupert & Kent, 2007). Private practices, by design, offer more autonomy. Private practitioners experience more sources of satisfaction, fewer sources of stress, and more perceived control at work than therapists in agency settings. Time spent doing administrative tasks is almost double in agency settings than in private practices.

The takeaway is not to conclude that settings other than private practice are destined to produce burnout or that every therapist working in an agency, school, or clinic is mismatched with their work environment. In fact, if you are the type of person who, for whatever reason(s), needs less autonomy as a therapist and can handle administrative tasks more efficiently than other colleagues, then the relative lack of control granted in these settings may matter to you less. To this point, an interesting phenomenon seems to occur with therapists who work in settings that grant less discernable control, including more administrative load in addition to direct client hours. These therapists seem to enjoy more career satisfaction when they intentionally reflect on the facets of their job that are satisfying and rewarding (Rupert, Miller, et al., 2012).

However, for those whose executive function challenges and needs for autonomy and emotional stability take center stage, then agency or large hospital clinic work may wear them down in powerful and obvious ways. I wouldn't last two weeks in the hustle and bustle of the psychiatric inpatient unit where I did part of my internship. Part of my stark prediction is due to the overstimulation factor, but another part is the fast decision making that must happen in that setting. Clinical decisions often must be made on the spot or in quick verbal consultation with another team member. My brain operates a bit more slowly and deliberately, thus making private practice a much better match for my processing speed and decision-making strengths and limitations.

What is your work setting, and how would you describe it to a colleague? What about to a friend or acquaintance outside of the mental health field? When you describe your work setting, do you feel you're describing a place that brings out the best in your temperament and personality and allows for your therapist self the freedom to shine and grow? Indeed, "there is no greater joy than loving a job that also supports you well" (Aron, 2010, p. 174).

The importance of resonance among who we are, what kind of therapist we would like to be, and what type of workplace environment we inhabit cannot be overstated. To live a fulfilled personal life with the least amount of unnecessary suffering, we ultimately need a good enough match between our personality and values and that of our friends, partners, and communities. So too do we also need alignment in our professional life. It's not simply a matter of your supervisor or colleagues treating you well or your feeling duly rewarded and valued in your workplace. Those facets of course are vital to preventing burnout and cultivating well-being. But we must ask ourselves periodically how compatible we really are in our current role as therapist and in the environment in which we serve. This (self-)inquiry may require a lot of courage to be vulnerable in asking ourselves such tough questions, but what a meaningful gift of self-caring that can pay itself forward in the most durable way possible.

PART **III** INTRINSIC
SELF-CARE: SOFT
STRENGTH, HIDDEN
RESILIENCE

INTRODUCTION: INTRINSIC SELF-CARE: SOFT STRENGTH, HIDDEN RESILIENCE

In the end, only three things matter: how much you loved, how gently you lived, and how gracefully you let go of things not meant for you.

–The Buddha

Now that the foundations of self-care have been laid and the psychotherapist's diverse constellation of habits and needs have been explored, Part III focuses on the less observable, intrapersonal self-care processes that can powerfully transform our way of relating to ourselves and others. These are the processes that we often spend so much time encouraging in our clients and that we can turn lovingly toward ourselves for the benefit of all. In the therapy room, this intrinsic self-caring can serve to transmute afflictive energies into something more tolerable and workable. In our personal lives, we increasingly build resilience and resourcefulness as we softly but fiercely practice transforming our internal states einto traits of mindful awareness, wisdom, patience, self-compassion, and courage.

Although not all of the Part III intrinsic self-care skills pertain to the direct cultivation of positive emotion (Fredrickson, 2001), they have a constellation of themes in common: expansiveness, awareness, letting be and letting go of difficulty, and taking in what is wholesome and designed to benefit the greater good in (and for) us all. Another tie that binds these intrinsic self-care resources is that they are all inherently growable. Thanks to the discovery of neuroplasticity (i.e., that brain circuitry and structure can change as a result of naturally occurring experience as well as of our own purposeful doing; Fuchs & Flügge, 2014), we now fully acknowledge that we can transform a fleeting state or momentary demonstration of a skill into a sustainable practice and thus a set of resiliency characteristics (Hanson, 2018).

This section of the book begins with perhaps one of the most vital and foundational facets of intrinsic and extrinsic self-care, *mindful awareness and intentionality* (Chapter 17). Without experientially knowing what we're thinking and feeling and how we'd like to behave in any given moment, we're more subject to the whims and circumstances around and within us. From there, we turn to *acceptance, impermanence, and equanimity* (Chapter 18), three related principles and processes that help us stay grounded while remaining flexible in the sea of change. With these qualities on board, we can deepen our internal self-caring through the practice of *(self-)compassion* (Chapter 19). Whether working with the difficulties and suffering of others or tending to our self-relationships, compassion helps us soften the hard edges of what it means to live this life of challenge and uncertainty. When confronted with our own so-called failings or clients' offensive or harmful actions, *forgiveness* (Chapter 20) can serve as an antidote. This internal self-caring process not only can heal our minds, bodies, and relationships; it can also help us welcome other positive states and traits of resilience into our lives.

We then turn toward the *practice of gratitude* (Chapter 21) as one of the most powerful ways to protect against unnecessary suffering, strengthen our sense of self and of community, and encourage virtuous, upward spirals of emotion and generosity. In our quest to be as expansive as we can be in our notion and practice of self-care, we will also explore the ways in which we deliberately can bring more *laughter, humor, joy, and playfulness* into our lives (Chapter 22). Finally, we turn toward *optimism* (Chapter 23) as one of the most effective happiness- and resilience-boosting internal tools we have at our disposal.

It's important to note two features of these intrinsic self-caring tools. First, they can be powerfully cultivated through small, incremental steps of practice, a process further explored in Chapter 37. Second, these skills are not mutually exclusive. Purposefully building your optimism doesn't necessarily mean that you're not also working on self-compassion and forgiveness or that any other quality is any less important.

However, psychotherapists don't have to focus on all of these interior self-caring skills to enhance their well-being over time. In fact, deepening just one quality, for example self-compassion, could significantly improve the quality of your life. It stands to reason that some periods of your life may call for more attention to some self-caring skills than to others. And based on your self-knowledge, addressed in Part II of this book, you may have gained more insight into the practices that may be particularly beneficial and why.

17 CULTIVATING MINDFUL AWARENESS AND INTENTIONALITY

Attention needs somewhere good to go.

—Dr. Jeremy Hunter

The mindfulness tradition and the recent revolution of consciousness prompt us to live our lives consciously and on purpose. This is much harder and more complex, however, than we'd like to think. An untrained mind is like a puppy not yet able to stay or to go forth in a purposeful, regulated, and consistent manner. Our autopilot minds can be easily distracted and are often subject to the whims of what is happening around and within us.

But in a wakeful and intentional state, we are much more able and likely to make better decisions, regulate our emotions, and act in accordance with our deep values to willingly care for ourselves. When we are mindfully aware of our experiences, fed by both internal and external stimuli, we are essentially paying attention to the here-and-now with as much curiosity, nonjudgment, and precision as possible.

https://doi.org/10.1037/0000309-018
The Thriving Therapist: Sustainable Self-Care to Prevent Burnout and Enhance Well-Being,
by M. A. Hersh

Psychotherapists can harness the skills of mindful awareness and intentionality throughout the day in both personal and professional capacities. In fact, when these capacities are deliberately cultivated, we can be present with whatever is happening now as well as prepared to handle what is to come. This ever-changing dynamic of presence and preparation is constantly the case in psychotherapy, as we're never quite sure of the emotions, thoughts, or behaviors that will arise in any given moment. We must stay mindfully aware and flexibly connected to any given moment. By cultivating the skill of intentionality, we are able to direct our attention consciously toward what and where it may be most helpful rather than being swept along by our own internal waves and by the winds of our external surroundings. Intentionality then becomes a core element of sustainable self-caring that fosters behavioral alignment with what truly matters and experiential flexibility and resilience during challenging times.

AUTOMATIC PILOT MODE

Whether we like it or not, our pasts, our futures, and our nonconscious minds often dictate how we're living in any given moment. This *autopilot mode* is our well-worn constellation of neural and somatic pathways that tend to have a mind of their own (e.g., Uddin et al., 2009) and can cause us to feel like we're being driven rather than being the driver. Groundbreaking research into how and why we live on autopilot reveals that we're mentally checked out almost half of our daily lives (Killingsworth & Gilbert, 2010). Moment-to-moment analysis of thousands of adults suggests that our minds are very often wandering inwardly, remembering the past or projecting into the future.

With our minds wandering for nearly half our waking time, we might be curious about whether that's beneficial for our well-being. It turns out that when we're caught up in our thoughts, we can be doing almost any activity and find ourselves less happy than if we were connected directly (through our sensory apparatus) to our unfolding present moments (Killingsworth & Gilbert, 2010). Norman Farb, one of the pioneers of the field of affective neuroscience, suggested that we essentially have at least two distinct modes of neural circuitry (Farb et al., 2007). The *default mode* comes online when we're not tasked with anything in particular in the real world and when we're thinking about ourselves. This mode is active as we daydream, ruminate, recollect, and plan. It's also very much involved in "me," "my," and "mine," and it has a grooved, self-narrative storyline to it.

What can send us down a fruitless or even harmful path is spending too much time bathing in our narrative circuitry, inadvertently having our experiences (and even the clients in front of us) filtered through our own storylines. Likewise, if we're very often in narrative (vs. direct experience) mode, we can take our personal and home lives into the room with us. Sometimes this narrative mode intrusion can be of benefit, but other times it clouds our direct sensory experience of a client's life—their suffering, their aspirations, and their own moment-to-moment sensory experience.

On an average day at work, are you aware of the filter through which you're viewing your clients? If a client is recounting with helplessness a difficult memory about a traumatic car accident, how awake are you to your own sense of helplessness in an uncertain world? Do you know how much these personal feelings and beliefs might affect your responses in the moment and your feelings and thoughts after the session?

Unlike the default mode and narrative circuitry that is so automatically and easily triggered, our *direct experience network* can be activated both by external tasks and at will by intention. When embodying this real-world, experiential system, we become less constricted and caught up in our own filters of past habits, memories, expectations, and assumptions. We're thus better able to respond to events *as they actually are.* You might imagine the wide professional and personal applications of such a capacity.

Our clients' stories and behaviors can trigger many types of reactions and responses in us. Being mindfully aware of the tugs and pulls on our senses of fairness, safeness, predictability, and common decency, for example, provides us with wonderfully useful information. Rather than subtly (or even blatantly) avoiding this incoming data, we can observe it and even turn toward it with curiosity, kindness, and precision (Chödrön, 2018). Development of a keen sense of mindful awareness is, in part, an antidote to experiential avoidance on the one hand and overwhelm on the other (Hayes et al., 2012). Thus, being mindfully aware can reduce unnecessary suffering and foster the integration of healthy habits.

What we're essentially doing when we cultivate mindful awareness and intentionality is developing our responsivity over our reactivity. To respond is to build in a momentary pause after the stimulus "out there" or "in here." Responding is essentially a thoughtfulness of mind and heart rather than an impulsive reaction from nonconscious habit. When we're living mindfully with intention, we humbly serve our values and aspirations rather than our whims and circumstance.

PRACTICAL STRATEGIES FOR INCREASING MINDFUL AWARENESS AND INTENTIONALITY

There are hundreds of informal methods for cultivating mindful awareness and intention. This chapter highlights several everyday practices that you can easily integrate into your workday—before, during, and after sessions—as well as in your personal life before and after work starts and ends. The power of these practices is not only that they can assist us in the moment to regulate ourselves, but also that the more we integrate them into our daily routine the stronger our mindful presence, resilience, and stress hardiness will be.

Let's now follow Marcus, an early-career social work therapist who works in a large urban high school. We'll consider his usual workday to learn where and how he can practice the following mindful awareness exercises. Marcus's days often move at a frenetic pace as he juggles back-to-back counseling sessions with distraught teens, runs various mental health and prevention-based groups, meets with staff, holds phone-based consultations with parents, and collaborates with outside community helpers. Needless to say, it's sometimes quite the feat for Marcus to find time for lunch and a few snack breaks and to use the bathroom. And yet, therapists like Marcus may need brief but powerful reset buttons that can positively affect the mind, body, and spirit.

Recognize, Allow, Investigate, and Nurture (RAIN)

One of the most beneficial, straightforward, and practical ways to improve your mindful awareness is through the practice of RAIN, a dynamic, in-the-moment process made popular by mindfulness teacher and clinical psychologist Dr. Tara Brach (see Brach, 2020). RAIN—originally coined by Buddhist teacher Michele McDonald—stands for *recognize* (what's happening in the moment), *allow* (the experience to be there, as it is), *investigate* (the experience with interest, care, and precision), and *nurture* (yourself with self-compassion or other offerings of soothing). RAIN can be used quite informally or formally as part of meditation. Let's unpack the RAIN procedure, which can be very helpful as a guiding and foundational mindful awareness practice.

As you *recognize* and tune in to what you're currently experiencing, you can also name what's going on in that very moment (e.g., "My client, clearly very angry, just ended the session prematurely and walked out of my office"). You can name your internal experience (e.g., "I am so jarred by this guy! I'm so confused and hurt"). This naming or labeling can be done with a gentle whisper (Brach, 2020) or even through jotting some notes on paper to organize the thoughts, feelings, and behaviors that you notice are affecting you in those moments.

You can then take a few conscious breaths to help your mind remain tethered to your bodily experience, thus *allowing* this experience to simply exist for a few moments before you attempt to do anything else to investigate or regulate. You may even say to yourself while in your state of disbelief and discomfort, "Even though this feels horrible, and I'm so uncomfortable with what's happening, it is indeed happening and I'm here with myself." Or you may simply whisper to yourself, "It's OK" or "This is what I'm feeling, and it is what it is." The step of allowing is crucial as it invites us to develop the skill of psychological flexibility and counteract the omnipresent tendency to avoid unwanted internal experiences. Thus, we grow in our resilience to become larger than what we feel or think in any given moment.

From recognizing what's happening and then allowing our experience to be as it is, we have deepened our attention and created some space to *investigate*, with self-inquiry on a nuanced level, what is actually happening. Brach (2020) suggested that we ask ourselves what most wants attention in these moments: "How am I experiencing these thoughts and feelings in my body?" "What am I believing in this moment?" and "What is this vulnerable place in my mind–body trying to tell me?" Most important is the connection with our felt sense versus becoming "mind-y" and overly conceptualizing or intellectually analyzing.

In the last step of this process (although it's not necessarily strictly linear), we can turn to *nurturing* ourselves with self-compassion and other aspects of soothing. Brach (2020) offered many options of ways to relate to ourselves in this motivational state of nurturance. We can try to sense what this hurt, wounded, frightened, or angry place needs from us. Do we want to offer ourselves a simple gesture or word of reassurance (e.g., a nod, whispering "It's OK, [your name]")? Perhaps you would find it nurturing and soothing to place your hand lovingly over your heart. You might even consider imagery of a warm, soothing light enveloping you. With each in-breath, you take in more light. And with each out-breath, you distribute that light to all parts of you, especially the ones bearing the brunt of the emotional offense. If any of this imagery or gesturing is difficult to do for yourself, you might imagine a compassionate figure (i.e., someone or something that is wise, strong, warm, and compassionate) to appear by your side to help ease the suffering in those moments.

The 3-Minute Breathing Space

Developed by John Teasdale, Mark Williams, and Zindel Segal, the cocreators of mindfulness-based cognitive therapy (Segal et al., 2018), the 3-Minute Breathing Space exercise was designed to bridge the longer, more formal meditations of mindfulness-based stress reduction with the thoughts, emotions, and reactions of real-world situations. The idea of this on-the-spot practice is to pay attention on purpose in both broad and narrow ways. This dual focus of attention, of zooming in and out, not only can enhance your ability regulate your attention at will but also can help you to feel grounded in the moment. As the intention is to focus on several facets of your present-moment experience, you're developing your mindful awareness of what is as you consciously switch off the autopilot tendencies.

A very flexible and forgiving process, the 3-Minute Breathing Space can be done sitting or standing, wherever you are (except while driving of course, although at red lights it can be a true gift). Given that it's typically longer than a quick mindful check-in but often much briefer than a formal meditation, you'll likely want to use this technique outside of therapy sessions. In between appointments is a wonderful time to gain mastery over how our minds and bodies were reacting to the previous moments, thus facilitating ways to respond with intentionality to the next set of moments. After all, as Jon Kabat-Zinn said, "All we have are moments." How we respond to *this* moment affects the next and the next after that.

It can be helpful to conceptualize the breathing space practice as having an hourglass shape. First, our attention is broad, next it's narrower, and finally it's broad again. Over the course of 3 minutes (or more or less, depending on your situation), the instructions are as follows:

- *Becoming aware*: Purposefully direct your attention broadly to what's happening with your thoughts, emotions, and sensations. You can ask yourself what thoughts are present, what feelings you are experiencing, and what sensations you are detecting in various parts of your body. This step essentially can be done as a series of three scans (of thoughts, feelings, and sensations) over the course of one minute or so. As with the core tenet of any mindfulness practice, you can take care to simply acknowledge and turn toward what you're noticing as best you can. You can observe and honor if your mind wants to avoid or escape the moment.

- *Gathering and focusing attention*: In this second step, intentionally zoom your attention in on your abdominal area and begin to feel your breathing there. While the prior step was much more encompassing and allowed your thoughts, feelings, and sensations to fill your awareness, the gathering and focusing process invites narrower attention. Simply try to sense the rise and fall of your abdomen as each breath moves in and out of your body. You can also include in your awareness the sides and back of your abdominal area, as these parts of the body are likely expanding and contracting with the breath as well.

- *Expanding attention*: In this final step, see if you can broaden your attention once again, but this time the expansive focus is on your body as a whole. Include in your awareness your posture and your facial expression. Do you sense stillness or movement, tension or ease, and different temperatures within different parts of the body? Just notice what's there, and see if you can befriend all of it. You can whisper to yourself something like, "I'm here; this is what I'm sensing. It's all OK." In this last step of the breathing space, you can begin to prepare for reentering the stream of daily life. With this open and friendly awareness of your somatic self, you can now choose the ways in which you are best able to show up for yourself and others in the next set of moments. I have found that this process can bring a sense of dignity and self-respect as well as loving acceptance of what life has to offer without trying to force anything to happen.

The STOP Practice

STOP stands for *stop* or pause whatever you're doing or thinking; *take* a slow, deep belly breath; *observe* what's happening in this very moment (e.g., what sounds, sights, textures, smells do you notice? How do your breath and body feel?); and then *proceed* by continuing your previous actions or changing course based on new information. There are several versions of this informal, on-the-spot mindful awareness practice (e.g., Zylowska, 2012), which is quite simple yet effective. You can use STOP during an especially tough clinical moment, when talking with colleagues about a challenging case, or at any time that your personal life seems to be pulling you in unforeseen directions.

One Mindful Breath

This mindful awareness practice is an abbreviated version of the STOP practice. One Mindful Breath literally involves consciously taking one relatively deep and elongated in-breath and an even slower, more intentional out-breath. Within this one breath is a treasure trove of possibilities to tune into what's been happening within our mental and emotional landscape. We also can find that the perception of choice expands during the out-breath as we access and make room for other states of being. The deeper and lengthier breath out also serves as a source of activation for the parasympathetic nervous system, helping to reduce physiological arousal, broaden awareness, and reset calmer and more curious interpersonal engagement. Similar to the intentions of allowing and befriending found within the RAIN practice and the 3-Minute Breathing Space, One Mindful Breath encourages the mutual feedback to and from our bodies and our minds through the deliberate use of subtle bodily gestures (e.g., nodding, half smiling) and internal whispers of loving invitation to allow whatever is there to simply be there.

As Marcus awaits his next session, with a 14-year-old girl struggling with acute anxiety, he is transitioning from having sat with a 16-year-old boy who was depressed and passively suicidal. Meetings with this depressed boy often seem to have a strong impact on Marcus and his sense of power to help this teen. Marcus knows from his experience with such quick transitions that he needs some sort of reset for his mind and body. Marcus decides to do One Mindful Breath to help connect with his sensory experience as well as gather his sense of self. This single conscious breath helps bring Marcus into his present-moment self (rather than part of him being left in the previous session).

5-4-3-2-1 Grounding Practice

While many of the informal mindful awareness practices are often inwardly focused, there is great benefit to training the mind to pay curious, nonjudgmental, and precise attention to what's happening in the immediate environment, outside of our physical bodies. The 5-4-3-2-1 Grounding practice is an elongated version of the central theme of sensing one's immediate external environment through sight, sound, touch, smell, and taste. Please note that the sequencing of what to pay attention to is quite flexible, and you can also do an abbreviated 3-2-1 version of this practice. Essentially, it's not the *what* we're concerned about in this practice, it's the quality of *how* we're paying attention that matters the most.

First, bring your attention to your surroundings and, one by one, choose five different objects to sense through your vision. Just linger on each one for several seconds, describing in your mind (or whispering out loud) what you see. Really try to absorb yourself in the visual aspects of this object. After all five objects are "seen," move to your tactile sensory mode to touch and feel with your hands four different objects in your immediate environment. What does each object feel like? Turn it over in your hands perhaps while your eyes are closed, to enhance your sense of touch. Again, describe what each object feels like—is it smooth, rough, heavy, jagged, course, hot, cool, concave or convex, bumpy, angular? The possibilities are endless.

Move on to choose three objects that you can listen to with keen auditory attention. I'm reminded of one of my favorite children's books, *Listen Listen,* which I would read to my two kids when they were young: "Listen listen, what's the sound . . ." One by one, listen to each object with curiosity and patience. Perhaps all you hear is the whir of an air conditioning fan or privacy sound machine outside your office. If you're outside, maybe you hear birds, lawnmowers, car horns, people talking, or garbage trucks barreling down the street. When I've done this exercise with clients in the various offices I've occupied, I hear similar sounds but also distinct ones depending on my location, the time of day, and who knows what other factors that influence the sounds in those very moments. If this exercise were done 2 minutes earlier or later, perhaps the soundscape would be entirely different.

Penultimately, choose two objects to smell. Perhaps you can already smell something in the air. Maybe you ate a sandwich or have some coffee or tea sitting on your desk nearby. Or maybe you have to seek out something to experience through your olfactory sense gate. Smell is a powerful sense and is said to be connected directly to the limbic system. Thus, we may experience more emotion or quickly recall memories after smelling something poignant. Describe each of the two objects, one by one. Investigate and name what is really happening with the scents that you're experiencing with intention and curiosity.

Finally, choose one object to taste. If there isn't anything nearby to taste, skip this step of the exercise. However, mindful tasting and eating can be exceptionally interesting experiences and can slow down processes that are usually relegated to a quick bite, slurp, or gulp and then we've moved on.

Inside-Outside (Here-There) Mind Tuning

One of the most helpful, streamlined, and easeful ways to train both mindful awareness and intentionality is to practice deliberately toggling our attention back and forth between an internal and an external focus. In fact, we naturally and constantly engage in this process in our role as psychotherapist. We pay attention to our clients' affect, their breathing, their posture, their words. We shift our attention to the physical space between our clients' bodies and our own. We pay attention to our own breathing, our own posture, our own words, the heat or tingling in our feet from sitting in certain ways. While in session we can train this intrinsic awareness by purposefully taking care to sense what's "out there" and then what's "in here." The opportunities are endless within each client session, case consultations with colleagues, team meetings, and the like. This process, which can transpire over the course of just a few seconds or even minutes, can help us experientially understand how our exterior surroundings affect our interior experience and vice versa.

In a purposeful and perhaps slightly more formal fashion, we can practice this mind tuning for a minute or so before or after a session, before we step foot into our homes, when we wake up in the morning, or while we're eating or drinking. Bring your attention, with any sensory modality you'd like, to what's immediately outside of you. For example, as you awaken in the morning, perhaps focus on the ceiling or the light coming through the windows. Then bring your attention inside to your breath or perhaps to the sensation of your head on the pillow. If you stretch out your legs, what does that feel like? And then focus on anything else in your surroundings, such as the leaves of a plant in the corner of your bedroom.

The more we intentionally observe both here and there, the better able we are to shift from autopilot mode to a conscious, deliberate, and wakeful state of mind and body. This intrinsic skill can serve as a foundation for so many other facets of self-care we might be interested in tending to and cultivating.

Why Am I Talking? (WAIT)

WAIT (Warren et al., 2018) is a wonderfully simple but powerful strategy for mindful awareness and intentionality in the therapy room (but can certainly be used in everyday life as well). When sitting with clients, we practice noticing our urge to speak or gesture, and we pause with momentary wise discernment to reflect on whether we indeed "need" to be saying something in that moment. Perhaps we're trying to fill some uncomfortable silence, or we're reacting to something internal that is more "ours" than "theirs." Consider letting the urge pass, and practice interacting with your clients from a place of integrated wholeness.

The Mindful Check-In

The aforementioned mindful awareness skills-building practices all, to varying extents, rely heavily on sensory awareness. They are less conceptual–intellectual and much more experiential. The Mindful Check-In (see Appendix E), however, can operate in both ways, helping us to connect with our self-caring values and our vision for ourselves while also prompting a connection with what's happening in the here-and-now within our mind–body. This check-in exercise consists of prewritten questions to ask yourself, but the list can be modified or expanded as you expand in your knowledge of what will foster both stability and growth.

The following examples are from *The Thriving Therapist*, my online resource for therapist burnout prevention and self-care cultivation:

- What are my intentions for *how I'd like to be* in these very moments?
- Am I valuing myself enough in this moment to give myself the care I need?
- Are my moment-to-moment intentions and actions aligned with my values for what will bring me meaning, fulfillment, and sustainable wellness?
- Will it help me to "start over" in the next set of moments so that I don't proliferate feelings of fear, powerlessness, hopelessness, or resentment?
- Am I practicing self-compassion (e.g., going easy on myself) and self-forgiveness (e.g., letting be/go) as best I can?

You may notice that these questions are not specific to the therapist role or to the workplace, and that's purposeful. You can use these inquiries however the moment presents itself and for whatever purpose you deem important. At any given moment, you can use these questions to help guide you— to slow you down or speed you up, to help you ground down for containment or lift upwards for expansiveness, to help mend fractured self-parts or acknowledge your wholeness.

Jeremy Hunter, PhD, founding director of the Executive Mind Leadership Institute at the Peter F. Drucker Graduate School of Management at Claremont Graduate University, insists that "attention needs somewhere good to go" (1440 Multiversity, 2017). To live and work with integrity and on a path of success, we have to be intentional about the life we actually want to live. This way of being involves asking ourselves these tough questions about who we really want to be and how we would like to invest our energy and attention in wholesome, worthwhile, meaningful, and vitality-enhancing ways. In these ways, the Mindful Check-In is really all about intentional living. When we stop for a few moments to essentially ask ourselves, "What's up?," we are more consciously directing our next moves (i.e., thoughts, actions, observations) based on those qualities we would like to have in the driver's seat with us and those we'd prefer to hop in the back seat or even out of the car altogether.

The Mindful Check-In self-inquiry practice can be done with regular (enough) frequency or simply as an on-the-spot (re)orienting exercise. The predetermined questions are merely suggestions for making meaning of your current moments, helping you to gain perspective, facilitating a sense of grounding, or fostering a sense of expansion and growth. There are no right or wrong answers, and the sentiments you may feel during this self-inquiry can be held with as little self-judgment as possible.

The subsequent chapters on acceptance, self-compassion, forgiveness, and gratitude can offer further motivation and methods to help us enter increasingly frequent states of mindful awareness and the vital mode of soothing, softening, and grounding. This way of being can undoubtedly assist us in honest reflections on how we're treating ourselves and thus how to be as helpful to ourselves as we can.

18

FOSTERING ACCEPTANCE, EQUANIMITY, AND ACKNOWLEDGMENT OF IMPERMANENCE

To experience peace does not mean that your life is always blissful. It means that you are capable of tapping into a blissful state of mind amidst the normal chaos of a hectic life.

—Jill Bolte Taylor

Psychotherapists have the privilege and honor to be in the presence of clients' innermost worlds—their sordid histories, deepest wishes, and most frightening fears. This constant presence and caring, however, takes its toll. The costs show up in myriad ways as we often feel what our clients are feeling and work tirelessly to help alleviate suffering. We can do only so much; the deeper and more profound our acknowledgment of this foundational reality, the less burdened and burned out and more free we will be.

It is truly an act of radical self-caring when we offer ourselves opportunities to cultivate the qualities of *acceptance, equanimity,* and *impermanence.* All three of these internal-worldview skills have the quality of "clear seeing," allowing us to live in full recognition of *what is* rather than what should be. This skillset can go a long way to buffer the stress that is naturally generated

https://doi.org/10.1037/0000309-019
The Thriving Therapist: Sustainable Self-Care to Prevent Burnout and Enhance Well-Being, by M. A. Hersh

inside the therapy room and reduce the potential for burnout, distress, and fatigue that accompanies the life of the hardworking and empathic therapist.

ACCEPTANCE

When we let present reality be as it is, we are engaging in the powerful process of acceptance. As we come to terms with how each moment is unfolding, we are engaging in *willingness* of mind and heart, thus strengthening our muscle of psychological flexibility. In a practical sense, we are opening ourselves to a wide range of possibilities to support ourselves as well as our clients, loved ones, and even strangers who usually walk through our lives unnoticed.

The challenge with adopting an attitude of acceptance is that we're human. Human beings are born with a cognitive–emotional apparatus that over time becomes practiced at judging and at evaluating situations as good or bad, favorable or offensive, OK enough or worthy of rejection. A very common example of our struggle with acceptance is feeling physical pain. Not many of us would outright welcome the pain we feel, and we have become conditioned to resist it—to reject, deny, fight against, control. This effort to control creates undue struggle and suffering.

The Buddhist meditation teacher Shinzen Young (2016) has popularized a very practical "life equation" related to the principle and practice of acceptance. He suggested that the pain (e.g., emotional, physical, mental) we experience does not have to become a felt sense of suffering unless it is met with some degree of resistance. Thus, Pain (P) × Resistance (R) = Suffering (S). Resistance is wanting our experience (whether inside or outside of us) to be something it's actually not. We can experience resistance in many forms—as wishful thinking, avoidance, strong desires, fearful projections, and even subtle, seemingly benign judgments.

The equation $P \times R = S$ has two major implications, one quite promising and the other quite sobering. First, no matter how great our pain or stress, if we can substantially lower our resistance then we are less likely to suffer needlessly even if we're still in a great deal of pain. However, no matter how small our pain or stress, if we strongly resist our experience, then we are likely to suffer that much more. This dynamic process is what the Buddha was known to have labeled "the second arrow," whereby the first arrow to strike us is painful enough, but the second arrow pierces us in the form of rejecting our actual experience.

What does this skill of acceptance specifically have to do with sustainable self-care for psychotherapists? Therapists, unlike many other (helping) professionals, are in the business of sitting intimately with other people's emotional pain and suffering. When we're knee deep in a client's self-hatred, for example, we have the opportunity to hold our seat and simply acknowledge the reality of the present moment—this person is hurting badly, and we are there to bear witness to such suffering. Coming to terms with the stark realities of our job can grant us freedom to choose next steps wisely. Rather than either disconnecting or overidentifying with our clients' suffering, we can be with exactly what is. As a meditation teacher of mine once suggested, "neither add nor subtract anything."

Fortunately, the art of doing psychotherapy and of being a psychotherapist calls for hundreds of opportunities for acceptance practice every day. We actively employ and encourage acceptance all the time in our psychotherapeutic work as we attempt to help our clients accept reality so that they can make necessary changes and let be or let go of unproductive strivings that are causing more harm than good.

When we wake in the morning and feel ourselves sluggishly drag our feet from the bed to floor, we might observe this feeling exactly as it is: "Interesting, my legs are moving slowly right now." As we glance at our calendars and remind ourselves who is on our schedules for the day, we have a chance to observe our reactions as they're unfolding, whether positive, negative, or somewhere in between.

It's important to note that acceptance may be conflated with doing nothing or just giving up or giving in. Jon Kabat-Zinn, one of the founding fathers of secular mindfulness in the West, has long made the point that acceptance is not passive, nor does it have a quality of resignation. On the contrary, acceptance is active and sometimes radical recognition that things are the way they are (Kabat-Zinn, 2013). A therapist who is in the presence of an actively suicidal client isn't going to sit idly by and do nothing. Behaviorally, we may or should take certain actions when the situation calls for it. But psychologically and emotionally, we may meet the highly charged and fearful moment with more capacity to clearly see what is in front of us rather than seeing what we want to see or what is more convenient in that moment.

EQUANIMITY

I had been working with a 30-something man who had long been desiring a romantic relationship with a good friend. He was let down once when his efforts were rejected because intimacy fears overwhelmed his friend. But after many months, she asked him out. He was overjoyed and expressed his unadulterated excitement to me. However, I had a strong intuition (and some good previous evidence) that this relationship, in its newest form, would be quickly challenged and likely dissolved. In the face of my client's extreme positive emotion and hopefulness, I needed to stay centered. I validated his immense excitement while tempering my strong doubts. I needed to wait, be patient, and let my client's reality unfold as it would. I was not in control of this person's present moment, and despite my strong clinical hunches, I was likewise not all-knowing of his future.

As I endeavored to maintain "a balanced reaction to joy and misery, which protects one from emotional agitation" (Bodhi, 2005, p. 154), I was engaging in what is often referred to in Buddhist psychology as *equanimity*. This mindfulness-related quality of mind and heart allows us to bring an even-keeled and steady demeanor to situations, regardless of their emotional valence. We are neither overly attracted by the "positive" nor overly avoidant of or reactive to the "negative." With cultivated equanimity, our clients' emotional tides do not heave us upward, drag us down, or compel us to duck our heads.

It's one thing not to get swept up in the rushing river of your clients' excitement or joy and another thing to maintain a balanced demeanor in the face of clients' abject suffering. There aren't too many psychotherapists who are fond of hearing that their client is actively suicidal. This realization can produce feelings of fear, self-doubt, and helplessness in the therapist. So what would equanimity look like in the face of such distress? It would mean we do our best to stay physically grounded and rooted despite our emotional branches swaying strongly in the client's breeze. We would, as best we could, greet the reality of the difficult moment as it is, neither pushing away our fear nor getting swept up in it. We wouldn't try to force anything to happen or from happening, as we practice sitting with a patient and understanding heart (Pollak, 2017). In short, we wouldn't become emotionally entangled in this client's situation (Desbordes et al., 2015). We would act and make clinical decisions based on our training and compassion rather than out of impulse, fear, or grasping at something that may not be possible in that moment.

Indeed, equanimity has been proposed as a facet of resilience in that the more equanimity an individual has cultivated, the more likely they are to rapidly disengage and quickly recover from an emotional event (Desbordes et al., 2015). Psychotherapists are all too familiar with scores of emotional events within a workday or even within a single session, particularly if we are doing trauma resolution, anxiety exposure, or conflict-laden couples' work.

Cultivating equanimity is inherently difficult because we've been trained culturally to avoid what doesn't feel good and to seek what does. But as we know, this habit doesn't work so well in the therapy room. When sitting with clients, we can remind ourselves at the beginning of each session to remain poised and balanced no matter what shows up. This valuable reminder doesn't mean that we will, but it means that we're on a path toward this aspiration of equanimity. We can practice equanimity-based meditation, wherein we purposefully practice catching ourselves sensing and thinking toward or away from positive or negative experiences, respectively. We root ourselves in the here-and-now through our unfolding breath, and we commit to staying balanced and even-keeled with whatever is arising in each moment. We come back over and over again to our dedicated place of center whenever we feel ourselves swaying far from this space.

IMPERMANENCE

Human beings usually like a good measure of predictability and stability. And yet, as Greek philosopher Heraclitus once suggested, nothing lasts except change. No one is likely to step in the same river twice because they will not be the same person and it will not be the same river.

A clear vision of the universal quality of impermanence can be quite a challenge, especially if we struggle with our own foundational sense of self. But when we take a step back and observe the realities of the world, of our own minds and bodies, of our clients' lives, and even of the moment-to-moment process of psychotherapy, we quickly realize that it's all changing all the time. Attempting, consciously or not, to hold tightly to our personal and professional lives as stationary objects, frozen in time, will bring only more suffering.

Reflect for a moment on your last client interaction. Were you or your client in the exact same position (mentally, emotionally, relationally) as you were the session before? It may seem the same, and some elements may be more or less similar, and yet we may realize that much has changed. Although even the most severe forms of suffering in our own and our clients' lives may appear immutable, the principle of impermanence, like that of neuroplasticity, gives us hope that therapeutic change, no matter how small, is always happening or at least possible.

Looking for change is in itself a therapeutic strategy, and it's one that can sustain professional well-being more than we might know. "Interesting, Juan, just now you didn't seem as caught up in that obsessional loop as you had the last many weeks. Hmm, I wonder what changes have brought that about." Simply having on our radar the notion that change is always occurring can promote a sort of hopefulness about our professional encounters. Of course, we're not *overstriving* and forcing ourselves or our clients to do, think, or feel certain things. However, the principle of impermanence gives us permission to approach therapy with a type of expansiveness we might otherwise not have allowed.

As with equanimity and our cultivation of stability in the breeze, we can appreciate that impermanence means that good things change too. Perhaps you've been helping a client leave a very toxic work environment. They finally applied for a new job and were offered the position. All signs point to a positive transition, with the client leaving behind something that had drained their well-being for years. But positive change is still change, and it would be important to acknowledge for yourself the weathering of this job transition may still be quite stressful, with loss and gain both on the horizon.

Impermanence can also undergird resilience and spark growth in our personal lives. As change is inevitable, we can more fully embrace movement, shifts, and uncertainties in ourselves and in the world around us. We can use the paradoxical certainty of impermanence to help us look at ourselves as ever-evolving beings rather than as stuck where we are at any given time. For example, this realization can help us to break free of assumptions we've made about staying in a job that truly doesn't suit us. Or we may realize that some aspects of our personal life—such as caregiving for a challenging child or elder parent—are more subject to change than we think. And if we're on the lookout for small deviations, we may find more peace of mind than if we feel determined the situation will always be a certain way.

When we consciously integrate impermanence with acceptance and equanimity, we can concoct a powerful antidote to feeling beleaguered and overwhelmed in our work and personal lives. Purposefully looking for the temporary nature of our interior world as well as the one outside of us can help us to see reality as it is and remain poised amid the inevitable "thousand joys and thousand sorrows" of clinical work and everyday life.

With such principles elevated in our conscious awareness, may we ride with courage the waves of life, seeing what comes toward us without fear and with utmost compassion. And may we remain stable amid the shaking ground and take care to notice that all is not shaken nor lost.

19 NURTURING COMPASSION

*Compassion is not a relationship between the healer and the wounded. It's a
relationship between equals. Only when we know our own darkness well
can we be present with the darkness of others. Compassion becomes real when
we recognize our shared humanity.*

—Pema Chödrön

The young boy and his puppy were sprinting down the street, their paths
excitedly intertwining as they darted this way and that in a sort of blissful
dance. But what was in one moment pure happiness turned to a scene of
pain and tears. At full speed down the sidewalk the boy tripped and fell,
skinning his hands, knees, elbows, and nose. The boy was inconsolable. As
this boy's neighbor, you happen to witness this ordeal in real time. With no
other adult in sight, what would you do? How would you feel?

For many of us, compassion would drive this moment of decision and
action. We would wish to help alleviate this boy's pain and suffering, and
our compassion motivation would push us to act. Now imagine doing that

https://doi.org/10.1037/0000309-020
The Thriving Therapist: Sustainable Self-Care to Prevent Burnout and Enhance Well-Being,
by M. A. Hersh

many times in a row each day, several times per week, nearly 52 weeks per year. In our professional roles, we witness the pain and suffering of relative strangers (who become much more than that over time) and feel compelled to ease our clients' distress and act in ways that are designed to help. No wonder our profession is both highly rewarding *and* exceptionally challenging and hazardous.

Of course, we're not helping with overt physical injuries; we're tending to psychological and emotional wounds of all sorts. Sometimes, in fact, we're helping the 65-year-old, for example, who experienced one too many childhood situations like the one described at the start of the chapter but never received the necessary or good enough compassionate responses from those who mattered most. Because so many of our therapeutic encounters involve clients' unmet needs, our work in psychotherapy can be quite heartbreaking and requires both emotional and pragmatic intelligence, competently connecting with all types of human beings while we adeptly and compassionately sit with ourselves. We may take for granted how inherently challenging it can be to existentially tolerate and be resilient to others' suffering day in and day out. It is both a tremendous feat and a gift to continually offer our minds and hearts to help relieve others' states of dukkha—of sorrow, disillusionment, shame, fear, and longing (Kornfield, 2009).

THE CASE FOR OFFERING COMPASSION TO OUR CLIENTS

The Latin root of "compassion" ("com-pati") means "to suffer with," and yet as therapists we don't merely sit and feel our clients' misery and heartache. If we don't also extend our helping hands, using our emotional skills and varied therapeutic trainings, then we are at risk of experiencing empathy distress or emotional saturation. However, leading experts in the fields of compassion and contemplative studies have proposed that when we understand the depths and nuances of what compassion is and can do, we can dramatically lower our risk for compassion fatigue and can significantly mitigate the experience of empathy distress.

Chapter 3 discussed the relatively recent distinctions, made by neuroscientists and other compassion researchers, between compassion fatigue and empathy distress. These researchers have found that by doing loving-kindness and compassion meditations, we're stimulating reward, connection, and approach networks in the brain and body. Positive emotion becomes more, not less, accessible to us, and the hormone oxytocin is stimulated, helping us to feel more connected and safe rather than interpersonally detached

(Klimecki et al., 2013). Such findings have profound implications for the challenging and sometimes harrowing work that we do. Compassion training is shown to improve our outlook, awareness, capacity for empathy, and behavior toward others (Jazaieri et al., 2013).

Compassion, in its most fundamental form, is the aspiration to be as helpful, not harmful, as possible (Kaufman, 2019). This idea may seem trivial, and yet being of benefit to all humanity (including ourselves) as best we can sets us up not only to look for the good inside and outside of us but also to offer goodness whenever and wherever possible. Perhaps we need not be reminded so forcefully that our clients are struggling. That's what brought them to our doorstep in the first place. However, when we're worn down and irritated with certain clients, we must bring these mindful reminders back into view and to heart so that we don't further alienate ourselves from them or compromise our competent action.

As we orient toward being of greatest benefit, we can start to reflect on what compassion is really all about. It's a fully integrative experience of mind–body–brain–spirit–action. When we act with compassion toward a client, we are viewing them as a fellow human being in need. We get an internal infusion of oxytocin, the so-called bonding hormone. Our brain waves and neuroanatomy shift to represent both emotional pain and greater motivational energy to help and support others. Psychologically, we can experience the fading away of separateness of "me vs. them," and we recognize our common humanity. With adequate compassion motivation, we help others appreciate that this moment in time is one of difficulty, struggle, or suffering, and we are motivated to act with kindness and to help relieve that suffering in one way or another.

This compassion-based experience does not, however, have to involve overly identifying with *their* suffering or becoming one with their struggle. Rather, because we know generally what our own varieties of suffering feel like, we can *bear witness* with a deep feeling of shared humanity to that of our clients. We can remind ourselves of the heart wisdom that Pema Chödrön offered us in the chapter-opening quote. This reminder stands in subtle contrast to what some have suggested effective compassion should be, requiring us to "be weak with the weak, vulnerable with the vulnerable, and powerless with the powerless" (McNeill et al., 1982, p. 4.). I believe that we need to experientially know what psychological and emotional adversity feels like without the need to fully fuse with our clients' exact situations.

What happens when this heartfulness is challenged or breaks down? What do we do when we have a feeling of impending doom or perhaps irritation when we think about a particular client? Perhaps for a particular subset of our caseload, we've come to dread the encounter and constantly wish for that last-minute cancellation. What about when we're struggling to appreciate the work we've been doing and have become our own worst critic, to the detriment of our professional and personal functioning? Fortunately, we can turn to the nurturing, soothing, and strengthening force of compassion.

PRACTICAL HACKS FOR NURTURING COMPASSION PROFESSIONALLY

There are countless ways to cultivate external compassion, including meditation, empathy training, and charity work. Thinking outside the box, Dr. Christopher Willard, a psychotherapist, child and family mindfulness teacher, and author, created the Client Calendar Scan (C. Willard, personal communication, January 2019). This simple but powerful activity involves scanning your planner or calendar for the clients you're seeing for that week, or only for that day if a tighter time window feels more manageable. Glance at the name or initials of each client, pausing at each one to identify the emotions, thoughts, and reactions that arise within you. Which clients evoke a favorable reaction, which neutral, and which produce a drop in energy, annoyance, or even disdain for having to see them? Honesty with this exercise is quite vital. Deluding yourself into thinking that everything and everyone is always "just fine" and equally liked at all times may further suppress our opportunities and capacities for compassion. You can then harness this emotional data to nurture and replenish your compassion toward some of your more difficult clients.

What do we do when we notice emotional friction in thinking about some clients or when our compassion is worn down or depleted? Dr. Willard suggests the 3 × 3 Client Compassion Exercise (C. Willard, personal communication, January 2019; see Exhibit 19.1). This set of targeted questions can mitigate compassion fatigue, help revitalize a sluggish compassion system, and reorient us toward loving-kindness for clients we've come to feel jaded, annoyed, or overwhelmed by. We can ask ourselves and our fellow therapists these questions (in peer consultation, supervision, etc.) as a sort of intervention when we're feeling especially detached, cold, or annoyed. Yet we can also view this tool as a preventive one, keeping in mind such inquiries on a weekly or monthly basis. Committing to such a powerful exercise with some regularity can stave off relational tensions that build up within us but that can insidiously affect our sense of competence, genuine engagement, and job satisfaction.

EXHIBIT 19.1. 3 × 3 Client Compassion Exercise

Find 3 ways in which you're similar enough to your client.	Find 3 things you can admire about your client.	Find 3 reasons they're "doing their behaviors."
Example: We both have a tendency toward an anxious mind. I really do know what their struggle is like.	Example: They try and they show up as often as they can despite how much I perceive them as "overly needy."	Example: They were severely neglected as a child and are playing out what they never got yet desperately needed for so long.

Note. Copyright 2019 by C. Willard. Adapted with permission.

In the meditative sphere, we can engage in full or abbreviated compassion meditations. One of the more powerful compassion practices that can help generate feelings of mindful acknowledgment of clients' difficulties, shared humanity, and an orientation of basic kindness is the Just Like Me meditation. While there are many versions of this compassion practice, I'm fond of the one shown here, which can of course be expanded and individually tailored to your liking. Just reserve a few minutes of relative quiet, sit with intention to ease whatever relational tension might subtly or overtly exist, and then picture a particular client or set of clients in your mind's eye:

Just like me, this client [or my clients] is alive and breathing.
This client [or my clients] has thoughts, emotions, and urges, just like me.
Just like me, this client [or my clients] has struggled in some way during their childhood.
This client [or my clients] has been hurt by others, just like me.
Just like me, this client [or my clients] simply wants freedom from unnecessary pain and suffering.
I wish for you (keeping in mind the client[s]) the strength to move through these challenges with resilience.
I wish for you less struggle and greater ease, just like me.
I wish for you as much peace, happiness, and thriving as possible.

COMPASSION FOR OURSELVES AS THERAPISTS

The argument for psychotherapists' compassion for our clients' suffering may be relatively easy to make. But what about therapists' compassion for themselves? It has been suggested that the ability to be compassionate toward oneself is part and parcel of self-care (Gilbert, 2005). Without this offering to ourselves, the clinical and workplace challenges we face can seem even more unsurmountable and isolating, causing us to self-denigrate and self-alienate. Moreover, if we're often critical of our own predicaments and struggles, then we may develop a hardened interior reflecting as an inflexible and uncompassionate exterior when working with clients who "rub us the wrong way" with their particular brand of suffering.

Imagine attending a workshop in which the leader asks you to write down on a notecard three ways that your professional work has negatively affected you (see Saakvitne et al., 2001). After jotting these down, you're instructed to get up and meander around the room holding your card in front of you for everyone else to read. Each participant is doing the same, and the whole room ends up bearing witness to one another's suffering. What might have felt isolating or shameful becomes normalized and a shared experience. The common humanity in the room becomes undeniable, and everyone is seen and "heard."

Research on self-compassion training for psychotherapists shows quite promising findings with respect to our responses to self-criticism, depressive thinking, and the experience of stress and struggle (Neff, 2003). When we deliberately nurture our own compassion, we come to be more open to and moved by our own struggles, thus increasing our motivation to want to relieve our own distress and suffering. We turn toward ourselves with greater caring and kindness, develop nonjudgment of (perceived) failures and basic shortcomings, and recognize commonalities between our experiences and the whole of the human condition (Neff, 2003).

Before moving forward, we should clarify something quite crucial—what self-compassion is *not*. Self-compassion is not self-esteem. Rather than an air pump designed to inflate our sense of self, it's more like a cushion, a comforting blanket, a fundamental soothing agent, and a connector to humanity. Self-compassion is not self-pity or weakness. It won't demotivate us or cause us to "go soft." And nurturing self-compassion certainly won't just open the flood gates, permitting us to let ourselves off the hook for things for which we feel we should have been ultimately responsible.

Dr. Kristen Neff—self-compassion researcher, author, and training program developer—conceptualized self-compassion as three independent yet powerfully intertwined facets (Neff, 2015). First, being compassionate toward the self foundationally involves a *mindful acknowledgment* of the difficulties we're experiencing in any given moment. Without this component, we're more likely to end up lost or caught up in our struggle rather than gently but firmly greeting the issue for what it is in that moment. With this mindful observation, we then can recognize our *shared humanity of struggle*. As everyone suffers, we purposefully tune into all others in this world who feel some semblance of pain and difficulty in this moment. Rest assured, there is always at least one other person (but more like millions of others) right in this very second who feels lonely, like a failure, depressed, anxious, stressed, pressured, betrayed, and even horrified by something traumatic and incomprehensible. Finally, we offer ourselves some degree of kindness. As compassion includes kindness but is not defined by it, we act with compassion by extending ourselves a kind-hearted, gentle, soothing, or thoughtful word, image, gesture, or action.

PRACTICAL HACKS FOR NURTURING SELF-COMPASSION

Neff and Germer's (2018) Self-Compassion Break is a wonderful tool to use anytime and anywhere to help cushion the blow of something situationally distressing or perhaps harsh judgments we've been levying against ourselves. Following from the tripartite conceptualization of self-compassion, the self-compassion break is essentially a purposeful respite to practice soothing ourselves in times of particular need. For example, following a very challenging therapy session in which your client provided feedback that the therapy just wasn't helping and that they wanted to find someone new, you might take a mere 60 seconds to care for the "brokenness" you may feel within your mind, body, and spirit. "Wow, this is really shitty. I thought I was at least helping a little, but apparently not enough. This feels really hurtful" (mindfulness of the difficult moment). "I know it's hard to imagine, but I guess other therapists have also been fired by their clients. In fact, there are many articles written on the subject" (common humanity). "May I accept myself and this moment as best I can and be resilient as I feel the hurt, betrayal, and feelings of failure this is causing" (self-kindness).

Not that anyone would expect 60 seconds of on-the-spot self-compassion practice to change your entire experience for good, but the more you engage in a self-compassion break for this and other difficult situations, the more your mind–brain–body gets used to responding in a soothing manner. Of course, just as meditating in a hurricane is much harder than in the quieter refuge of your bedroom, so too is on-the-spot situation-based self-compassion harder than a more deliberate and meditative self-compassion break. For this reason, we now turn to two popular and effective meditations that can be powerful forces of self-compassion development.

Although *loving-kindness meditation* (LKM; i.e., *Metta* meditation) is not a self-compassion practice proper, it is a key ingredient in the recipe of self-compassionate responsivity (Salzberg, 2002). Just as cultivation of mindful awareness is vital for the development of self-compassion, purposeful generation of goodwill and unconditional friendliness is a foundation to finding freedom from suffering within ourselves. By conducting brief or spontaneous loving-kindness breaks or engaging in a structured LKM, we can intentionally nurture kindness, support, or protection from within.

One form of LKM is first to take your seat, place your hand(s) over your heart space, and breathe consciously and slowly for a few breaths. Then imagine someone or some entity from whom you can easily feel protection, support, kindness, or goodwill. Breathe in this caring energy through your heart space. Let this energy circulate throughout your entire body as you breathe in and out for several more breaths. Then you can turn your attention to offer this energy of goodwill back toward yourself in a purposeful, personalized, and poignant manner.

As Neff and Germer (2018) suggested, LKM that is self-oriented is all about asking oneself, "What do I need?" When we answer this question honestly, we may begin to generate several needs, such as courage, patience, protection, acceptance, validation, or connection. Design two to four phrases that make sense to *you* for this point in time. For example, "May I endure this pandemic with patience and love. May I be courageous even when I'm scared. May I see myself as a good enough therapist right now." You can repeat such phrases silently as a concentration practice over the course of a few minutes. Such phrases can also become reminders on your phone and written on sticky notes and posted on your office desk and by your bedside. You can offer them to yourself as you rise in the morning, before and after therapy sessions, and before bed.

LK and LKM are all about cultivation of goodwill and support through intention rather than willing into being something particular, such as specific emotions or an outcome to achieve. Thus, they are distinguished from self-affirmations or trying to manifest through the law of attraction, for example. Reminding ourselves of this basic notion can help take the pressure off and support sustainability to the practice.

Similar to the Just Like Me meditation, the Just Like You variation is a powerful force for cultivating self-compassionate energies. In this meditation, we're tapping into the second facet of Neff's (2015) conceptualization of self-compassion, common humanity. We're letting ourselves know that we have so much in common with the rest of the world, that we're not alone even in our darkest moments. We can think about and imagine our neighbors, our communities, the entire world, or our fellow psychotherapists. We might borrow the same or generate similar phrases as in the Just Like Me meditation:

Just like you, I am alive and breathing.
I have particular thoughts, emotions, and urges, just like you.
Just like you, I have struggled in some way during my childhood.
I have been hurt by others, just like you have.
Just like you, I simply want freedom from unnecessary pain and suffering.
I wish for the strength to move through my challenges with resilience.
I wish for less struggle and greater ease, just like you.
I wish for as much peace, happiness, and thriving as possible.

Ultimately, self-compassion is a way of relating to ourselves with wisdom, protection, care, support, and soothing. This manner of self-relating is not solely about language and thinking. It's also about how we care for our physical selves. Thus, we can nurture our self-compassionate selves through soothing gestures such as heart breathing and through conscious breaths that are deep, smooth, and nourishing.

Caring gestures of the body are a welcome form of self-compassion nurturance. For example, we might place our hands over our hearts, cradle our faces in our hands, gently stroke our hair, head, or arms, or cross our arms to give ourselves a gentle hug (Neff & Germer, 2018). The body responds well to soothing touch, just as others benefit from our compassionate touch and we benefit from theirs (Gilbert, 2013). Because compassion is often beyond words, such physical gestures can serve as a bedrock for the other aspects of how we practice treating ourselves with utmost care and concern. It should be noted that if you've endured sexual or physical abuse, certain physical touch gestures may not feel soothing for you. Finding your own soothing movements and self-relational gestures is vital to offering yourself the best care possible on your own behalf.

In addition to breathing and gestures, we can also generate *compassionate figure imagery* (Gilbert, 2013), conjuring up figures (real or imaginary, alive or deceased) that are wise, protective, caring, and strong. When I was going through a particularly rough time in graduate school, I would imagine being surrounded by all of my mindfulness teachers who had taught me in the previous few years. There they were, five of the most caring, thoughtful, and fiercely compassionate figures sitting in a circle with me. Just seeing them in my mind produced such a heartfelt and genuine sense of safeness and being held.

Whether we are engaging in compassionate imagery or breathing, meditations to foster goodwill and a sense of connection to community, or scanning our work calendars to (re)establish heartfulness with our clients and

EXHIBIT 19.2. Self-Care Reflection Break: Suggestions for Cultivating Self-Compassion for Sustainable Self-Care and Easing of Occupational Stress

- Compassion meditations
- Loving-kindness meditation
- Compassionate figure imagery ("perfect nurturer," compassionate figure, caring committee, compassion army)
- Compassionate gestures and movement
- Compassion letter writing
- Heart breathing
- Just Like Me meditation
- Just Like You meditation

colleagues, we are cultivating an incredibly vital competency for our professional and personal lives. Please see Exhibit 19.2 for a list of suggested practices that can support you on your compassion cultivation journey.

A NOTE ABOUT SYNERGISTIC FORCES OF COMPASSION AND EQUANIMITY

When compassion is accompanied by equanimity, we likely find ourselves with immunity to the side effects of working day in and day out with those who are suffering (Neff & Germer, 2018; Pollak, 2019), particularly those who have been traumatized. As illuminated in Chapter 18, equanimity is the quality of neither overstriving for what "should be" nor pushing away what "should not be." It's balanced awareness in the midst of pleasant or unpleasant emotions. When relatively equanimous, we are present, composed, and even-tempered in the face of struggle, difficult emotions, and challenge.

Our equanimity is often put to the test in our psychotherapeutic encounters, both when we're physically with our patients and when they live on in our minds and hearts after they've left our office or we've gone home for the day. How often have you lamented that you "should have done more to help," that "if only you would have asked that crucial question earlier your client would be in better shape now?" How often do you engage in self-attacks? They can seem very subtle and insidious, like a river slowly but steadfastly shaping the land through which it flows. Or perhaps the self-criticism and judgment are more like knives that puncture blatantly and deeply, causing damage to your senses of competence, confidence, and satisfaction as a therapist. When we experience difficult moments in therapy and frequently react with self-blame or criticism, we are programming our mind–body systems over time to react in this way. We become conditioned, and we become hooked.

What if there were an antidote to feeling and becoming overwhelmed by our clients' emotions, struggles, and suffering? What if we could shift the internal, conditioned chatter from "what's wrong with them?" and "what's wrong with me?" to "just like me, they suffer too" and "just like them, I suffer too?" If we put these compassionate aspirations in meditative form, it might look like *Tonglen* practice, a very powerful Tibetan meditation of giving and receiving. In this art form, which admittedly might require a bit more courage than many others, we purposefully breathe in that which is dark, tense, and painful and breathe out cool, calm, compassion. In other words, we use our breath as alchemy to help transform suffering (others *and* our own) into something beautiful for ourselves and others to receive and take back in. Since suffering already exists, and since we have the capacity to *want* to help, we use ourselves as conduits for desired transformation from misery to hope.

(Self-)compassion is a vast topic of discussion and real-world practice. It is my hope that this chapter helped spark a spirit and motivation to come home to a place of soothing compassion both for those we serve and for us, the servers of tireless support and aid. Compassion, however, should not stand alone as a soothing agent for what challenges us and sometimes steals our spirit. The art and practice of forgiveness is an extremely helpful companion to treat ourselves and our work with utmost care and respect. Let's now open the door to this essential self-care support to ease our suffering and enhance our well-being.

20

ENCOURAGING FORGIVENESS

Forgiveness is the fragrance that the violet sheds on the heel that has crushed it.

—Mark Twain

When was the last time you truly let go of the ill feelings you were harboring about a moral, emotional, or physical injury done to you or that you did to someone else? What about a series of untoward events or even the damaging way you were treated by someone for years? For those of us not accustomed to forgiveness or who have experienced offenses beyond the pale, this work may be the some of the hardest we do for ourselves. But there is very good reason to practice forgiveness not only of others but also of ourselves—for how we've treated our own mishandlings of challenging circumstances.

As we'll explore in this chapter, forgiveness heals. The practice of forgiveness spurs numerous health benefits, including elevated mood, bolstered optimism, and happiness. Forgiveness has also been shown to protect against experiences of unnecessary stress, anger, depressed mood, and anxiety

https://doi.org/10.1037/0000309-021
The Thriving Therapist: Sustainable Self-Care to Prevent Burnout and Enhance Well-Being,
by M. A. Hersh

(e.g., Toussaint et al., 2015). However we cultivate it, forgiveness can have a profound effect on how stress affects our mental health. Specifically, those of us high in forgiveness seem to be protected from the cumulative and negative effects of stress on mental health (Toussaint, Shields, Dorn, & Slavich, 2016). The practice of forgiveness can also directly affect stress in real time, with greater levels of forgiveness more immediately predicting less subjective stress (Toussaint, Shields, & Slavich, 2016). Less stress means fewer physical, mental, and emotional difficulties. In turn less burden frees us to be more of our best selves and to explore ways of being and doing that align with a higher purpose.

MYTHS AND MISCONCEPTIONS ABOUT FORGIVENESS

Although the word "forgiveness" is tossed around quite a bit, it's actually somewhat of an elusive process and likely misunderstood by many. It can be useful to start with what forgiveness is *not*. To forgive is not to forget. Those terms get lumped together, but they are certainly not the same thing, and forgiving someone doesn't mean you should or will forget what was done. Rather, you've internally transformed the ways in which you think, feel, and possibly behave.

Forgiveness is also not about letting others (including ourselves) off the hook for what they (or we) may have done. In fact, Everett Worthington, PhD, one of the leading experts on the science and process of forgiveness, noted that "forgiveness happens inside [our] skin" (Weir, 2017, p. 30). It doesn't have to be at all about reconciliation and seeking justice. Sometimes seeking resolution is warranted, wise, and beneficial, and other times it's not at all appropriate and may even be harmful.

A final common misconception is that forgiveness is weakness. However, we know that for those who practice forgiveness regularly, it can be one of the most empowering and character-strengthening internal acts we can do (Enright & Fitzgibbons, 2014).

FUNDAMENTALS OF FORGIVENESS AND ITS PRACTICE

So, what is forgiveness, and how do we cultivate it? Although there are somewhat different perspectives on how to conceptualize it and different methods for cultivation and practice, the fundamental notion is that forgiveness is about both *letting go* and *letting in*. We practice releasing resentment, bitterness, anger, and ruminative thinking about past transgressions. And we also practice offering something positive, whether it be understanding, empathy, or compassion toward the person who wronged or hurt you (Enright & Fitzgibbons, 2014).

Dr. Worthington and Dr. Bob Enright (Enright & Fitzgibbons, 2014; Worthington, 2008) have developed similar but unique phase-based programs for how to help people forgive. Worthington's method, REACH, is designed for forgiveness of another person and encourages us to

- *Recall* the hurt as objectively as we can and begin to make a decision to forgive. (In Enright's model, we would spend time in the *uncovering phase,* unpacking and understanding the untoward consequences of the offender's actions and the ways in which the offenses have affected our life. The *decision phase* would then involve gaining a more accurate understanding of what forgiveness entails and whether and how we're willing to forgive.)

- *Empathize* with the offending person. If the person isn't there to actively forgive, do some empty chair work, really letting them know how you've felt and still feel. Switch chairs and then try to take their perspective. Build an empathic alignment for why the other person may have hurt you in this way. This step and the next step of altruism are the heart of the forgiveness work and may be the hardest. Thinking differently about the offender may show up before feeling differently.

- *Altruistic gift-giving.* If you remember a time that someone forgave you for your trespasses and you felt much lighter afterward, you can unselfishly do the same for the person who offended you. This step can be done internally or with the other person.

- *Commit* yourself to express your forgiveness. You are more likely to sustain your feelings and acts of forgiveness by writing a note to yourself, writing in a journal, telling a trusted friend, or even letting the person who wronged you know about your forgiveness.

- *Hold onto the forgiveness.* When time passes, we can forget or doubt that we actually forgave someone, especially if they commit future offenses toward us or others who matter to us. As a reminder, we can reread the notes we wrote to ourselves.

I ended up informally and internally engaging in this type of forgiveness process for a client I had worked with for years. This young woman was suffering deeply after suddenly being fired from a job she had just come to love and feel valued at. I happened to be on the receiving end of her hurt, confusion, and sudden abandonment by her company: "I don't even think you give a crap about me now or really ever have cared." In those moments, all I could do was listen, validate, and gently but firmly let this woman know that my intention had always been to support her even if she hadn't felt that support and that I was here for her now.

After the session, however, I was quite offended and hurt. I replayed the scene over and over for days. I knew her words didn't represent any of our former interactions, but I couldn't shake how I was feeling. And so I began to consider how to release this friction from my system and to ensure that it wouldn't affect my therapeutic stance with her. Although she had returned to her usual receptive mode with me after a session or two, I could feel a lingering tension within me. I began to place myself in her shoes, imagining how utterly devasted this woman had been by her abrupt ejection from her company. My heart softened a bit. I reflected on her childhood of neglect and bullying. I softened a bit more. I went on to make a tacit agreement with myself that I would let this incident and its emotional fallout be in the past as it was rather than as I felt it *should* be from a place of righteous indignation. My irritation and offense gradually faded, and my pure presence returned to our therapeutic engagement.

THE CASE FOR FORGIVENESS AS SELF-CARE FOR PSYCHOTHERAPISTS

How does forgiveness fit into the toolbox of psychotherapist self-care? To be blunt, we screw up. We make clinical decisions too quickly or too slowly. We neglect to make a fairly obvious observation that a client points out later but that could have saved them weeks, months, or even years of heartache. We say things that cause discomfort and even harm to our clients.

Early on in my career I once said something to a client that I heard coming out of my mouth but couldn't stop. My client was at first extremely but quietly offended and angry. When they finally called me on it toward the end of the session, I was mortified. After profuse apologies, validation of my client's position and emotions, and my feeble attempts to bridge the growing divide between us, they walked out the door in a huff. To this day, that scene sometimes intrudes into my consciousness, and I hear a sharp-tongued voice whisper, "What were you thinking? How could you have said those things? Just, why?"

That particular client won't be coming back to work with me any time soon, despite my best efforts to make amends. When productive reconciliation isn't possible or even warranted, the internal practice of forgiveness—of beginning to release the tension-filled rope—is a very beneficial option. Left unforgiven, our blunders can have a tendency to build more and more tension (e.g., anger, bitterness, resentment, detachment, blame, shame) within ourselves.

The Buddha once said that holding onto anger is like drinking poison and expecting the other person to die. The sobering fact is that the client I wronged is not affected by my internal process. Only I am. But my lack of forgiveness of myself may evoke a certain constellation of afflictive emotions and cloud my clinical judgment when confronted with similar client behaviors in the future. Thus, the practice of (self-)forgiveness is one of the best ways to dissolve this often unspoken gravitational pull, let go of bitterness, and move on to reclaim our optimal competence.

WHEN CLIENTS MESS UP

As well-intentioned therapists, we're not on trial here. And we're also not the only ones who make mistakes. Client transgressions can be enormously egregious. They can also be so seemingly insignificant that even our colleagues, supervisors, and loved ones might think we're making a massive mountain out of the tiniest molehill.

An adult client might act abusively toward their spouse or treat their children with hostility and aggression. Regardless of any possible ethical and legal ramifications, we're still their therapist and are responsible to help them in the best ways we can. We still need to act with compassion. But how can we internally forgive this type of client or client behaviors and "move on" when such actions might evoke moral outrage in us? To complicate matters, one study indicated that roughly 50% of psychotherapists grew up with family dysfunction and abusive caregivers (Pope & Feldman-Summers, 1992). How do we readily forgive (and release resentments) toward an offending client if we haven't yet forgiven our past trespassers and perhaps even forgiven ourselves for the roles we think we played?

Clients can also seriously offend us or even inadvertently hold us psychologically hostage right there in the therapy room. They may express aggression or hostility toward us that can be very hard not to take personally. How do we not let such situations and transgressions sour our view of them? Regardless of the magnitude of offense committed by our clients, knowingly or not, holding onto the emotions of the offense (e.g., anger, resentment, ill will, betrayal) can harm us, our clients, and the therapeutic relationship in the long run.

The emotional backdrop of holding onto grievances in our professional lives can also affect our personal lives. This is a natural occupational hazard of working so intimately with other human beings' raw emotions, urges, wishes, and at times seemingly reprehensible behaviors. Our compromised acceptance and compassion from a resentment-soaked psychotherapeutic relationship may inadvertently seep into our ways of being at home. And if our loved ones don't know or don't understand our displaced emotions, we can harm our most precious relationships, including how we relate to ourselves.

WHEN WE MESS UP

We may be holding in or holding onto a harshness or a guilt for having done something of which we're not at all proud. We may feel guilty or even ashamed at the thought of having done something untoward with a client. But that's not what we do, and that's not who we are, right? We didn't train for decades to be good, honest, respectful, and effective psychotherapists and then make grievous mistakes with clients we were supposed to be helping, not harming. After all, the first and most important ethical aspiration embedded in our professional code of conduct is Do No Harm. But here we are, possibly losing sleep or having our (therapeutic or other) relationships tainted over something we said to a client that had a negative emotional impact.

Dr. Glenn Schiraldi (2017), author of *The Resilience Workbook*, noted that "forgiving the self is a critical aspect of bouncing back from things you've done and is as important as forgiving others" (p. 179). As the art and skill of bouncing back is integral to helping ourselves create sustainable self-care, self-forgiveness then becomes a natural extension of and contributor to our own self-caring.

This motivation to forgive ourselves for wrongdoing, however, is not so easily felt and often requires a good deal of courage to be vulnerable. It's similar to the motivation we need to extend compassion to ourselves during times of suffering. And this motivational spirit depends in part on our feelings of deservingness. Marci Evans, eating disorder dietician and self-care advocate, noted that turning toward the self with caring attitude and action in part requires worthiness. If we feel worthy or deserving of release from our own torment, then forgiveness can flow with greater ease.

Tina, a midcareer therapist specializing in anxiety and depression, once had a teen client who without prior discussion attempted suicide and came very close to killing himself. Tina had been working with this boy for several years and knew of this boy's deep suffering despite numerous interventions and supports. "I had such a hard time getting over this," Tina lamented. "I should have done more to help this kid. I know a lot about depression and suicide, but I just didn't see this coming."

When we make some fairly serious mistakes with clients, colleagues, loved ones, or even strangers, we can turn to the art and practice of self-forgiveness. Not entirely dissimilar from forgiving someone else for their transgressions, the self-forgiveness process can be a bit more involved, as many of us likely find it harder to forgive ourselves than to forgive someone else.

Thoughts like "I should have known better. What's wrong with me?" are good indications that self-forgiveness will be of benefit despite its challenging nature. Feelings of guilt, self-blame, and shame let us know that forgiveness might be a healthy next step. But just as we're not letting someone else off the hook for harm done to us, we're not irresponsibly sweeping our behavior under the rug in order to forgive ourselves. We must act with integrity and a sense of agency over our actions and their consequences.

Worthington (2008) suggested that we start with three steps before applying the REACH framework.

- First, try to receive some measure of forgiveness or compassion from a higher power or greater humanity. This process is akin to the facet of self-compassion practice that centers on connecting with our common humanity that is suffering *just like us*.

- Second, repair relationships as best you can under the circumstances. Even small acts of reparation can go a long way. If it's impossible to take such action with the other person or people you've hurt, you could extend a helping hand to others in similar situations or write an apology letter and not mail it.

- Third, rethink ruminations that might be holding you back from forgiving yourself. Dr. Schiraldi suggested that we drop the double standard we so often employ as we beat ourselves up while letting others off the hook (Schiraldi, 2017). In helping to rethink our ruminations, both Schiraldi (2017) and Worthington (2008) noted that perfectionism and letting our mistakes define us can be a huge barrier to moving on with ourselves in good conscience. Try reminding yourself of your common humanity, that every single human being makes an enormous number of mistakes in their lifetime.

Worthington (2008) suggested that, after rethinking your ruminations, you move on to the REACH model, then ending the self-forgiveness process by rebuilding self-acceptance and resolving to living as virtuously as possible. One could imagine that each time we forgive ourselves in this manner, we're cultivating an outlook of optimism and building a spirit of resilience. We strengthen the bond with ourselves, befriending the part of us that we'd often rather leave underground.

OTHER STRATEGIES AND SUPPORTS FOR PRACTICING FORGIVENESS

In his best-selling book, *How Good Do We Have to Be? A New Understanding of Guilt and Forgiveness*, Rabbi laureate Harold Kushner (1997) invited us to work through our existential guilt and offer ourselves forgiveness for simply being human. A forgiveness pact for psychotherapists (see Exhibit 20.1) can be a wonderful tool to remind us of our basic goodness and humanity despite the imperfections with which we're burdened. To borrow from conflict resolution expert Ken Cloke (2004), "forgiveness consists of releasing ourselves from the burden of our own false expectations" (p. 240).

Although the forgiveness pact for psychotherapists in Exhibit 20.1 may feel somewhat formal, read it to yourself and see what resonates. Let the words really sink in even if they feel uncomfortable at first. Reading this pact once a month perhaps can keep the self-forgiveness alive and well in your mind–body–spirit so that you don't forget the basic calling to be your own best ally and advocate on this challenging journey.

Another very potentially powerful practice we can use across a variety of situations is *Ho'oponopono*, an ancient Hawaiian spiritual practice of forgiveness and letting go. Ho'oponopono translates as "to make right, to make right" in English. Made popular in the contemporary era by clinical psychologist Dr. Hew Len, Ho'oponopono helps the individual to release burdens and resentments toward the offending world (including ourselves) by facilitating ultimate self-responsibility and ownership.

EXHIBIT 20.1. Self-Care Reflection Break: Forgiveness Pact for Psychotherapists

I, _____, a hard-working and dedicated psychotherapist, am first and foremost an imperfect human being. I have made mistakes that I regret and will continue to do so for as long as I work and live. If I don't do things that require forgiveness, then I've turned off my humanity. If I do things that require forgiveness, I know I continue to share the common experience of every other psychotherapist known and unknown as well as all other humans throughout time. When possible, I engage with myself with utmost compassion, patience, and wisdom to release accumulated and tightly held resentments, bitterness, anger, and contempt that serve to cloud my connections and judgment and that wear down my health and sense of self.

The practice, as it's been simplified in recent years, is similar to a loving-kindness meditation and involves repeating four key phrases while we focus on people we aim to forgive: "I'm sorry." "Please forgive me." "Thank you." "I love you." When I've done this practice with clients, they have shown a remarkable aversion as they struggle to identify with and offer such sentiments to the offending parties. Some ask, "Why would I say that I'm sorry when they've done me wrong?" Others declare, "I couldn't love that person if I tried." The flexibility of this practice allows us to adjust the aim of each sentiment to settle on a more palatable target. For example, if a client expressed a great deal of hostility toward you and it created a lingering hurt and resentment, you might first aspire to say to yourself, "I'm sorry *that we found ourselves in this situation.* Please forgive me *for whatever I may have contributed to this dynamic.* Thank you *for showing me what I need to practice.* I appreciate you *as a flawed human being, just as I am."*

We can use this four-phrase mantra type practice on the spot or as a deliberate and structured meditative exercise. Either way, Ho'oponopono is designed to untether us from toxic and burdensome ties that bind us to others "out there" or to the alienated parts of ourselves "in here" that we've come to ignore or even disdain.

ON HUMILITY AND APOLOGIES

Grandmaster Ed Parker, founder of American Kenpo Karate, respectfully suggested that "the humble man makes room for progress; the proud man believes he is already there" (Parker, 1983). Humility is crucial to human growth, and psychotherapists are certainly not exempt from this truism. In fact, humility seems to involve both internal and external qualities (Davis et al., 2011), and I would argue that when we are open to client feedback, supervisory and consultant offerings, and to our own musings, we can improve the ways we relate to ourselves, our clients, and the rest of the world.

Unfortunately, those of us low in humility and openness tend to take client feedback overly personally (although feeling easily offended can certainly result from a highly sensitive temperament too), in turn viewing the client as difficult and resistant (Davis et al., 2011) or even ignorant. One could imagine that the more closed off and self-protective we are, the more we avoid the reality of a situation or even of how we generally behave. Ultimately, this closed stance can backfire on us if our main mission is to treat ourselves (and others) with utmost respect, dignity, and fairness.

As we endeavor to care for ourselves with benevolence and grace, we might ask ourselves (or take the hint from trusted others or even our own clients) if we need a healthy infusion of humility. From there, apologies don't seem so scary or like breaches of some hidden contract we've made with ourselves. Apologizing then is part and parcel of good therapy and good self-care. As forgiveness can be seen as a vital form of self-caring, we might conjure up the imagery and embody the physicality of breathing out that which we no longer need to harbor within.

In the next chapter, we turn to the counterpart of letting out, the letting in of gratitude. Within this mind–body–spiritual state and quality of being, we deliberately invite into ourselves appreciation and thankfulness for the facets of personal and professional life that have bestowed some measure of positivity and growth upon us. Let's now explore how gratitude can assist us in our professional self-caring endeavor.

21 GIFTING GRATITUDE

Gratitude can transform common days into thanksgivings, turn routine jobs into joy, and change ordinary opportunities into blessings.

—William Arthur Ward

Think about yourself as a psychotherapist. Really dive into your role as helper and all the facets of your work. What stands out to you as something for which you're especially grateful? Are there particular clients, colleagues, or mentors you truly appreciate knowing and in whose presence you feel honored? Perhaps a more unfavorable painting of your professional life was framed by the soothing and expansive gift of gratitude (e.g., "Even though I've had so many difficult sessions lately and I feel so uncertain about the well-being of some of my patients, I know I'm doing what I can to help, and it feels good to realize that many patients are indeed holding steady or even improving under my care").

https://doi.org/10.1037/0000309-022
The Thriving Therapist: Sustainable Self-Care to Prevent Burnout and Enhance Well-Being, by M. A. Hersh

CONCEPTUALIZATIONS, BENEFITS, AND PITFALLS OF GRATITUDE

Gratitude is one of the most heavily researched psychospiritual topics of the 21st century. It has many conceptualizations—as a momentary state-like process, as a mood-based affective tone, and as a characteristic trait-like quality (i.e., being a grateful person; Emmons, 2008). However, well before the contemporary research, gratitude has long been extolled as a core human virtue. Heartfelt acknowledgment and thankfulness of that which we've received from others is then returned through some form of giving back. Conceptualized and practiced in this manner, gratitude helps keep interpersonal connections—in two-person partnerships and within larger communities—fluid and benevolent.

Dr. Robert Emmons, one of the leading scientific minds on gratitude, reinforced this point as he suggested that gratitude is very much a "relationship-strengthening emotion" as it compels us to appreciate what others have done us for us and then possibly to pay it forward in a virtuous and morally inspired spiral. Gratitude truly can be the gift that keeps on giving.

We might think of gratitude, however, as more than expressing thanks and appreciation for others and what they've bestowed to us. In contemporary gratitude practice, we can aim to pay mindful attention to what is and what we already have. For example, it's very easy to complain incessantly about the COVID-19 pandemic as I'm writing this book. However, I can explore my inner and outer surroundings for things to appreciate despite the challenges we're all enduring. I'm extremely grateful I get to walk down the stairs and see my family, even if I've been holed up my closet office all day. Even then, I get to easefully fill up my coffee cup between clients and do a few chin-ups on the bar outside where I work. As I'm writing these words, I actually feel a bit happier and more satisfied with how things are.

And that's exactly what regular gratitude practice and living a life of gratefulness can do for us. It's consistently associated with a number of psychological, emotional, and physical health benefits (Emmons, 2008). For example, the more gratitude one cultivates (or has at baseline), the more likely they are to feel satisfied with life, to report happiness, and to feel less materialistic. Stress hardiness increases, and our mental health ultimately benefits.

The effects of gratitude appear to function for relatively healthy volunteers as well as people who are struggling with mental (and physical) health issues. For example, in a large-scale study of adults seeking university-based psychotherapy services, the simple act of writing (but not necessarily sending) a letter of gratitude to another person once per week for 3 weeks had a profoundly beneficial effect on individuals' mental health, gratefulness, and neural activation 12 weeks after the gratitude letter-writing exercise, as compared with expressive writing or no writing at all (Wong et al., 2018). Interestingly, the beneficial effects seemed to accumulate over time rather than manifest immediately.

Emmons (2008) highlighted how gratitude can help us cope through difficult situations, build internal resourcefulness, and develop what he called a sort of psychological immune system to help cushion us through suffering. These are exactly the qualities we would desire in cultivating sustainable self-care resources.

However, some would caution against either offering too much gratitude or practicing gratitude in ways that disconnect from "reality," as if it's too Pollyannish of an attitude toward life. While ignoring something harmful by constantly orienting with appreciation and thankfulness may be a risk, this possibility may more likely occur if we're not taking a dialectical approach to life. In fact, it's a simple but powerful validation of our experience to acknowledge *both* the struggle *and* our gratitude for what has gone right, what's still working, and other positive aspects of our work. As Amie Gordon (2013) pointed out in *Berkeley Science Review*, it's helpful to be on the lookout for overdosing on gratitude, using it to avoid serious problems, exclusively orienting with gratitude for someone who is harming you, downplaying your own successes through excessive gratitude, and mistaking gratitude for indebtedness. Let's now translate this important research on gratitude into our lives as busy psychotherapists and address the stress and challenge we face on a daily basis and over the long term.

GRATITUDE IN THE LIFE OF THE PSYCHOTHERAPIST

Orienting the practice of gratitude and cultivation of the trait of gratefulness toward our professional lives can serve psychotherapists in numerous ways, inside and out of the office. However, if we're not used to approaching our daily lives with an attitude of gratitude, then it may be that much more challenging simply to "be grateful" for what we have and what has gone relatively well than it is to resort to focusing on the problematic nature of our work or even to give ourselves no feedback at all.

Psychotherapists are pretty smart folks. As discussed in Chapter 5, nearly all the participants in Kramen-Kahn and Hansen's (1998) survey of mental health professionals agreed it was quite rewarding to promote growth in their clients. Growth can come in all shapes and sizes. When we combine mindful awareness with gratitude practice, we start to look for things and moments of interaction to appreciate. We don't ignore "reality" by noticing aspects of life for which to be grateful. We're simply not letting the "good facts" (Hanson, 2009b) slip past us. It's too easy to do that, and too much cost is associated with it.

We can be grateful for the smallest of positive changes we see in our clients, whether stemming from their own resourcefulness, external circumstances, or the therapy itself. We might even be thanked for the work we do with a client, and we can practice with purpose taking into our mind and body the goodness and goodwill that is given to us.

We can be grateful for the training we've received thus far, propelling us forward in a confident and competent manner. We can turn toward our collegial connections with gratitude. Being a part of a supervision or peer consultation group can be extremely rewarding and beneficial. Acknowledging the gifts of wisdom, experience, and support received from our colleagues is a heartwarming practice that not only can fuel our own sense of being cared for through supportive connection but can engender a feeling in us of wanting to share and give back.

Unavailable to us not so long ago, connection through social media can be of great benefit to many of us. Notwithstanding the stressful and politicized elements of social media platforms, small closed groups of like-minded curious psychotherapists can be wonderful additions to our self-caring repertoires. I've seen enormous outpouring of compassion and wisdom on these platforms. Being a part of such groups can orient to how others in our boat are here to help us. And as we participate through a lens of gratitude, we can bolster our sense of well-being, resilience, and social connectivity along the way.

As you reflect on your sources of gratitude within your professional life (despite potentially enduring high levels of stress), what does your mind find? Toward what people, gifts, situations, or strengths and virtues within yourself does your attention gravitate? Sometimes we need to *zoom out* a fair amount to witness our entire professional life through a lens of gratefulness. What do you see when you look on your career as a psychotherapist thus far? On the other side of the coin, we may want *zoom in* considerably, to the moment-to-moment interactions that often pass us by or that we may take for granted. What small, seemingly insignificant moments can we mindfully catch flying by and observe through gratitude-tinted glasses?

In a study of health care practitioners who were asked to journal about work over the course of one month, the group who wrote in a work-related gratitude journal just twice per week were much more likely than those writing about work-related hassles and those who did no journaling at all to experience a reduction in perceived stress and depression over the duration of the study, and they maintained the enhanced effects on well-being 3 months after active journaling was done (Cheng et al., 2015).

I recall a similar reduction in stress and increase in my own happiness when I did a once-weekly gratitude (and loving-kindness wishes) practice with my former clinical mentor and a colleague. We simply emailed each other a few things we were grateful for in the past week along with wishing each other goodwill and wellness. I was actually quite surprised how different I felt after only a few weeks of doing this practice once every 7 days. The camaraderie may have accounted for some portion of the well-being effects, but even if that were the case, it just speaks to how important community and support also are in this endeavor.

Let's now explore several ways to integrate gratitude practice into our personal and professional lives, both when we're in the esteemed therapist's chair and when we've finally managed to peel ourselves off of it.

Counting Your Blessings

We can always bring more gratitude into our life in general. One of the best ways to do this is through the Counting Your Blessings activity at the end of each day. Some research suggests that less is better, and once or twice a week for many weeks in a row would benefit you more than a daily gratitude practice. I suggest that you experiment and see what works well for you over time. You can write your blessings in a journal, on a piece of paper, or on your phone, and you can even audio or video record yourself speaking truth for that which you're grateful.

This exercise goes by many names and has many variations on a theme, but the main idea is to take a few minutes to reflect on the goodness you've been bestowed, what is positive for you in this moment, or neutral objects that deserve your grateful awareness. You can turn your attention with gratitude toward anything you like, big or small, about the people in your life; surprising interactions you've had with strangers; things you've learned; your health; your ability to work; and even the sun in the sky or the breeze whispering through the trees. It's important to linger on each object of gratitude for 15 to 30 seconds. Ask yourself why you're taking this particular "object" into your system with appreciation. Breathe it in, and circulate the gratitude on your exhale to all parts of your body, down to all parts of yourself, from your cells to the protective energy around your physical body.

Given that the world continues to be filled with hate, negativity, and suffering, it is wise for us to live in a manner that counters this burdensome feeling with forces of good and gratitude. Otherwise, we can (depending on temperament, personality, and living situation) become a bit too bogged down in how the world is creating pain and misery rather than opportunity and love. These transformations almost always start within our own minds and bodies. Counting your blessings a few times each week is potentially enough to skyrocket your contentment and positive outlook and lower your stress and negativity. Please refer to Exhibit 21.1 for more suggestions about "objects" you could focus your gratitude practice on. Following are additional ideas to help us strengthen our heartful lens of gratitude.

Professional Gratitude Scan

You may already be familiar with the body scan, a mindfulness meditation practice designed to have us pay gentle but precise attention to each part of our physical body in a slow, gradual, and purposeful manner. The professional gratitude scan is similar in its orientation, but the objects of our attention are what we've been given and what we can be thankful for in our work life.

In a nonmeditative mode, start with a zoomed-out perspective to get a lay of the land for the different facets of your professional life. Elements include but aren't limited to office, physical workplace environment and amenities, commute, colleagues, supervision, consultation, clients, opportunities for

EXHIBIT 21.1. Self-Care Reflection Break: Gratitude Ideas

Progress (big or small) you have observed in yourself in last few days	Interesting parts of your job	Random acts of kindness you've done or someone else has done recently	Your clinical skills
Challenges or fear you have faced with courage	What you appreciate about where you live	The parts of your body that are working well	Aspects of your caseload
Others who have benefited you recently	What you appreciate about this time of year	Aspects of your colleagues you find especially helpful, supportive, or enjoyable	Any healthy or delicious food you've eaten recently
What you appreciate about where you work	This very moment (second, hour, or day)	The fact that you're breathing	Any sense of freedom or free will you feel

growth and learning, and diversity of professional activities. You might even create a Venn diagram of sorts to depict all the aspects of your professional life that hold at least some promise for your thankfulness and appreciation.

Then, on any day you choose to do this reflection practice, you can pick a domain and zoom in to look for something you can orient toward with thankfulness. For example, you might home in on your commute to and from work. One of my colleagues captured this spirit of gratitude beautifully: "I love that I can drive 10 minutes down the road, and I'm there. Parking is pretty easy, and I no longer have to wrestle with the 50-minute commute I once had. It's such a godsend." Another colleague had similar positive feelings about his commute, and yet he was driving 90 to 100 minutes each day. He reflected on how he finally had some time to listen to podcasts and audiobooks that were never an option in his former commute because of the loudness and busyness of public transportation and the need to stay fairly vigilant.

The professional gratitude scan can be done for any professional domain at any time. In fact, you can create a series of small, portable notecards, punch holes in them, and bind them with a ring. On the front might be the domain labels, and on the back can be up to five spaces for things you've scanned for gratitude in that particular domain. This exercise can be very helpful as a regular practice as well as on the spot as you catch something in your professional life for which you're grateful, savor it, and then allow it to infuse into your mind and body. In this way, building resilience never felt so good.

Gratitude Letter to a Special Mentor or Colleague

Gratitude letter writing is a widely used and highly effective practice for reaping the benefits of purposeful thankfulness. In the standard gratitude letter, writers choose someone, a benefactor of sorts, who has bestowed upon them something quite fulfilling and beneficial. For example, you could write a letter to a grandparent who gave you money for college tuition. You could write a heartfelt thank you, expressing all that the gift has allowed you to do and how much it and they have meant to you. If that person is still alive, you have the option of hand delivering it and even reading it directly to them.

My paternal grandfather, who has since passed on, had a life insurance policy that was divided up among myself, my brother, and my father. At the time, I was building my private practice and struggling to find the extra money to create a website. My wife encouraged me to use a bit of the money that my proud grandfather would have undoubtedly wanted me to use to help me on my professional path. I followed my wife's wise advice, and it felt so good to use the money he likely would have given me anyway if he were alive. I performed a bit of an informal ritual of gratitude to thank him for the gift—for several weeks, every time I looked at my newly developed website I would thank him for making that possible.

To create a gratitude letter to a special mentor or colleague, you can begin to think about who has *gifted* you something incredibly valuable in your professional training or experience. These gifts can come in hundreds of forms, including emotional support during an especially challenging time, wisdom and clinical acumen imparted during your training, instrumental assistance as you were acclimating to a new job, and the like. Although letter writing can be done multiple times over the course of months or years, start with just one benefactor. If you have many to choose from, practice some gratitude for that too.

Write the letter as if you really want to let that person know how much they've done for you at a single point in time or over the years. You can include facts and emotional sentiments alike. The beauty of this exercise is that you can email the letter, send it by mail, hand deliver it (to read to the individual or not), or simply read it out loud as if the person were there.

Sticky Notes of Gratitude for Clients

Perhaps it seems a bit strange to orient toward individual clients with gratitude. Our job is to help but not to become overidentified with them. However, it can be wonderfully beneficial to internally express appreciation for how certain clients engage with you, what they've taught you, and how they've grown and transformed. You can provide positive feedback to your clients regarding their own progress, which is very often a good idea. However, this exercise is about your appreciation for what clients unknowingly teach you about your life or how you can pay attention to them and your work with them through a lens of thankfulness.

Many times during the week, I'll experience brief moments of realization for how my clients are making progress toward something in their lives that I need to pay more attention to in my own life. I'm grateful for this opportunity to awaken to a new way of thinking about my parenting or lifestyle choices. For example, a client once told me about his conscious shift toward radical compassion for his child's challenging behaviors, and I ended up constructively reflecting on my struggles to provide what my children really need from me. Within your current caseload, how would you begin to orient with gratitude for what certain clients have taught you or even how they challenge you in positive, growth-oriented, and inspirational ways?

This exercise is called Sticky Notes of Gratitude because it's meant to be done as the moments of gratitude come to you and then can be jotted down on a sticky note to be stuck to your desk, for example. You could read the note(s) later, before you leave your workplace or in the morning as you start your workday. Just glancing at these sticky notes is a wonderful way to remind your mind–body of *the good facts* about your clients, your relationship with them, and what they've instilled within you. Ultimately, you can discard the notes (in a confidential way) and write new ones each day or as often as you'd like (still in a confidential way).

Gratitude is undoubtedly one of the more popular ways in contemporary society to build happiness and well-being. It's also a wonderfully powerful form of tending to the self while cultivating heartful connection with others and the world around us. If we're on a path toward burnout, empathically distressed, or experiencing secondary trauma, for example, we can rely on what we're thankful for in this life. Perhaps it might be a small but significant gesture of compassion you offered a client this week or the receipt of a "thank you for helping me today" text from a patient who has been struggling. And when all else feels too trying, you have the choice to mindfully zoom out to the indescribable bigness of the universe or curiously zoom in to the infinitesimal smallness of what comprises each of the trillions of cells in your body.

Practicing gratitude doesn't have to feel too serious though, as some of these discussions may imply. In fact, the vast arena of self-care can be infused with a very light and playful spirit, as we'll see Chapter 22 on inspiring laughter, humor, joy, and playfulness.

22 INSPIRING LAUGHTER, HUMOR, JOY, AND PLAYFULNESS

All work and no play makes Jack a dull boy.

—Proverb

The mirrored room was filled with 12 unassuming individuals. Some were dressed in casual weekend outfits and some in workout clothes. Her ebullient energy preceding her, the teacher walked in front of the class. "Welcome, everyone! Let's form a circle. Are you ready for some yoga?" The class began following their teacher's instructions to greet each other with big smiles and an emphatic set of joyful, welcoming body movements. Smiles were drawn prominently across the students' faces, although some were more reserved and cautious than others. They started some rhythmic movements of the hands on the torso. Then some bending and folding at the waist. As the class proceeded, so did their evolution of joy, laughter, and playfulness. Little chuckles turned into booming and boisterous guffaws. Cautious smiles gave way to inescapable cheek-to-cheek grins. By the end of the class, lightness and vitality were emanating from each individual as well

https://doi.org/10.1037/0000309-023

The Thriving Therapist: Sustainable Self-Care to Prevent Burnout and Enhance Well-Being, by M. A. Hersh

as from the room itself. Something powerful had transformed this group, and this group had transformed something powerful.

LAUGHTER AS THE BEST MEDICINE (AND THERAPY)

If we measured the interior of these 12 students' bodies before and after several classes like this, we'd find something fascinating. Positive emotions would increase by 17%, and negative emotions would decrease by 27%. Perceived stress would drop significantly (11%) with an accompanying massive reduction (28%) in cortisol, one of the best indicators of active stress in the body. (Incidentally, this large cortisol reduction has also been shown after energy tapping; see Chapter 27 for further descriptions.) Your heart rate would drop a bit and blood pressure (averaging systolic and diastolic) would be reduced by 5%. And oddly enough, your difficulty experiencing, tuning into, and naming your emotions (i.e., *alexithymia*) would be mitigated.

These data come from one of the original studies of laughter yoga (SVYASA, 2006), which included 200 information-technology professionals in Bangalore, India. After just seven sessions across 18 days, the subjective emotional states of the employees as well as their physiological, cardiovascular, and endocrine functioning dramatically improved, as compared with a nonlaughter yoga control group.

Laughter therapy has been promoted in the United States since the late 1800s, when Dr. John Kellogg (yes, of Kellogg's Corn Flakes), a physician turned wellness entrepreneur, recommended some of the same practices as offered in this book. Brought back to life in the 1993 movie *The Road to Wellville*, Dr. Kellogg insisted that frequent and purposeful laughter was good for the spirit, along with clean eating, good sleep, regular vigorous exercise, and fresh air and sunlight.

Fast forward to the 1970s as Norman Cousins, dubbed the so-called "father of laughter therapy," reportedly recovered from an incurable illness with the assistance of purposeful laughter and infusion of humor at any turn. Recent studies, albeit not without their limitations, support the notion that laughter may be some the best medicine we have and can create from within (Murray, 2009). Purposeful laughter (independent of humor) has been found to reduce hormones such as adrenaline (Berk et al., 2008), increase T-cell counts for enhanced immune functioning, release endorphins for pain management and feeling good in general, and increase circulation. Laughter can even dilate the endothelium, the inner lining of the blood vessels (University of Maryland Medical Center, 2005). All this research may feel a bit too serious, but let's see how a workplace laughter group helped transform employees' self-efficacy and self-regulation and had potential for reducing burnout risk and enhancing well-being.

The Promise of Leaning Into Laughter for Mental Health Professionals

Fortunately, purposeful laughter has been researched in both the nursing (Yazdani et al., 2014) and behavioral health arenas (Beckman et al., 2007). Aerobic laughter was studied in social workers, psychologists, nurses, and physicians at a behavioral and mental health center (Beckman et al., 2007). Perhaps you can envision yourself as you read this fascinating description. Imagine meeting in a conference room at a lunch break with several of your colleagues. For 15 minutes across a 2-week span, a laughter yoga teacher, much like the one in the original Bangalore study (SVYASA, 2006), leads you and your coworkers in incrementally more involved and engaging exercises in pure laughter, no humor required. The more you laugh, the more you may find things humorous. Thus, humor might naturally become a part of your experience during these groups. After 2 weeks *and* after 3 full months, your scores on a host of measures of competence have changed. You feel more self-aware, self-accepting, self-regulated, adaptable, motivated, optimistic, and assertive. You experience more positive emotion and easeful connection with others. Surprisingly, you even feel more at ease than usual while doing your paperwork and other administrative duties.

Although the Beckman et al. (2007) study has limitations that preclude from us from confidently asserting that laughter was *the* agent of change, the results were quite astounding, with moderate to large effects for most variables, *even after 90 days*. We also know that a host of studies continue to show the wide array of mental, emotional, physical, and relational benefits from engaging in purposeful laughter. Would you engage in a such a group for a few minutes each day for 2 weeks? If you knew that the average psychotherapist could reap benefits that would serve as a recipe for resilience and function as a form of sustainable self-care, would you sign up? What about the idea of laughing on purpose on your way to and from work? You don't have to ignore the tougher moments of the day, but you could intentionally invite your body for a few minutes to release and relax with the healthy laugh-induced vibration of your muscles and bones.

It's important to note that some of us who read the description of a laughter yoga group at their place of employment may have been skeptical at best and outright angry at worst. Perhaps our colleagues *are* part of our burnout risk, and to engage in a group like that with them would feel completely unrealistic, disingenuous, humiliating, or even preposterous. A workplace laughter group may also be impractical or feel inappropriate within a crowded clinic, small office space, or school. Patients, clients, and students could be within earshot of their therapists boisterously laughing for seemingly no reason. Thus, this type of practice within the workplace setting understandably may not be for everyone.

Ways to Laugh Just Because

Although certainly not exhaustive, the following list presents ways to get your laugh on. These can be done intentionally and planfully but also should allow for spontaneity. The last thing we want to do is become harshly robotic about laughter, commanding ourselves to "laugh now or else!"

- At your place of work (even if it's in your home), put up or have at the ready some photos, postcards, sayings, websites, videos, or other items that make you laugh. No explanations needed, no stories to be told. Those items simply cause you to chuckle or even let out a big belly laugh. I remember constantly finding a good friend and roommate in college chuckling to himself. When asked what was so funny, he would often say, "Oh, I'm just replaying a funny image in my mind. It always makes me laugh."

- If you relate well enough to some of your colleagues, perhaps you could let them in on your self-caring mission to laugh more at work. As laughter is quite contagious (see Zur Institute, n.d.), especially when we're not feeling too reserved or guarded, communal time for laughing can be both cathartic and a welcome respite from the day's challenges and emotional heaviness. Laughing together may even bring you and your colleagues closer and more trusting of one another.

- On the way home (if you're not commuting with others or on public transportation), just laugh. Maybe you have a sticky note on your dashboard that says "Just laugh on the way home." Perhaps you sarcastically but lightly remark to yourself, "Well, that was a tough day, am I right?" Then just start laughing. Maybe the laughter fizzles out after a few moments, or perhaps it continues as you navigate the streets or highways back home. If you don't have the luxury of your own car in which to freely laugh after work, you could allow for yourself to find or to let in humorous, laughter-producing elements at home. Even letting family members or roommates in on your laughter mission can be something funny in and of itself.

- As the workday fades, you can bring laughter to your personal life and time with family and friends. Creating a laugh-off competition or a home-based reality show in which each person tries to come up with the silliest laugh can be quite the scene. Of course, there's a time and place for those activities, and everyone should be on board as much as possible so that laughter doesn't turn quickly into anger. This effect would be quite the opposite of what we would be going for here.

Humor

If laughter is a physiological event, then humor is a cognitive–emotional experience (e.g., Mahony et al., 2002). We all experience humor differently. Some things make some of us laugh hysterically, while other things cause some of us to take deep offense. This reality of subjective difference is perhaps why therapeutic laughter yoga groups are purposefully designed to be humor independent. However, for humor to operate in *your* life as a source of both prevention of downward and support of upward spirals, all you need to know is what's funny, amusing, comical, and entertaining to *you*.

In their paper on work-setting differences in career-sustaining behaviors and burnout among professional psychologists, Rupert and Kent (2007) emphasized the need for strategies that keep work demands in perspective. Maintaining a sense of humor is one of those strategies, highly endorsed by a majority of respondents in several studies (e.g., Kramen-Kahn & Hansen, 1998; Rupert & Kent, 2007; Stevanovic & Rupert, 2004). In fact, 171 of 208 psychotherapists surveyed said that maintaining a sense of humor was a highly satisfying career-sustaining behavior (Kramen-Kahn & Hansen, 1998).

What does this mean to you? How do you maintain a sense of humor to sustain your well-being? Does it come naturally to you in everyday life? Is it something that needs a bit of assistance from others, or perhaps pleading from loved ones, "Can't you have a better sense of humor about this?"

Dr. Glenn Schiraldi suggested that we take our "humor temperature" by asking ourselves questions such as "Am I more serious than I need to be?" "Might I have more fun in my life?" "Can I try to find more amusement in the cosmically ridiculous nature of life?" and "Can I think of more ways to make others smile and laugh?" (Schiraldi, 2017). If we (or trusted colleagues or loved ones) determine that our temperature is low, we can ease off the seriousness and try to purposefully bring more humor into our lives. Attempts to integrate humor can be done as a characterological assessment as well as a regular check-in to make sure you are staying relatively buoyant rather than sinking with seriousness.

Psychotherapists, like many other professionals, can also "use" humor in therapy itself. Perhaps you feel as if you need to be more serious with the serious problems that clients bring to your doorstep. Whereas joking around with a client in a moment of deep hurt might violate our *do no harm* aspirational ethical mandate, we can feel free to infuse therapeutic encounters with lightness, humor, and playful banter that can be enormously beneficial to our clients, to the therapeutic relationship, and to ourselves.

A former therapist of mine once said, "It's always good to take the lighter things a bit more seriously and the serious things a bit more lightly." When we use humor with our clients, we reveal something more deeply human about ourselves than simply acting in a mechanistic or manualized fashion. This humanity in the therapy room can help remind us that we too are indeed human and need to laugh and find humor within the suffering. Such reminders of our humility can lighten our load as agents of change. It's a way of accepting the challenging work we do with greater levity and perspective than what the situation seems to demand of us and our clients.

Joseph, a 23-year-old man with a traumatic brain injury, was once again doubting the legitimacy of his existence. Joseph's guilt for simply being alive seemed quietly relentless. Moreover, one of Joseph's good friends had just sustained a major physical injury, which retriggered in Joseph a sense of powerlessness and survivor guilt. By the end of the session, however, we were cracking up together. I would not have thrown playful f-bombs into the air for a new or differently humored client, but I was fairly sure that this guy would receive my silly, therapeutically oriented, expletive-laden, compassion-softened projectiles as intended. Laughter soon filled the room, and the humorous way of holding this young man's suffering created a lightness of being that was illuminating the darkness for us both. My use of humor or the more playful interaction that ensued didn't resolve Joseph's survivor guilt and deep existential angst, but it placed his suffering and my holding of it in a different and more workable framework.

Seeking humor in one's mundane can be a gift of prevention, and finding humor in one's suffering can be a blessing of healing. How often do you reach for a trusted comedy movie to watch, something that you know will make you crack up and leave you feeling lighter and more softened than when you started? What about watching some funny YouTube clips in the middle of the day, perhaps some cats flying around on a ceiling fan and then somehow landing squarely on all fours? These videos can seem frivolous but may in fact be one of your best ways to self-regulate, pour yourself a cocktail of feel-good hormones, and generally lift up your spirits.

Humor and laughter are wily but sympathetic bedfellows. Although we often laugh when we're in the midst of something we find humorous, deep belly laughter isn't a requirement for finding benefit in humor. Simply lightening our spirits or finding the cosmic humor in something seemingly overwhelming can be a sustainable self-care practice that's seriously quite fun(ny) to employ.

JOY AND PLAYFULNESS

As if my smartphone were listening in on conversations I was having with my wife while writing this chapter, an article popped up in my newsfeed from a popular wellness magazine, *Well+Good*. Its headline, "20 Joyful Activities to Make Play a Priority in Your Self-Care Routine" (Garis, 2021), gets right to the heart of our mission here. Embodying a playful state and engaging in joy-producing activities are profoundly helpful for myriad reasons. They foster presence of mind–body, enliven our spirit, encourage more effortless and good-natured connection with others, and tether us to something beyond ourselves and our stress.

Joy is often described as a temporary feeling of delight, jubilation, excitement, or pleasure. It's a warmhearted sentiment that typically is *not* associated with craving (as with raw physical pleasure) or overstriving but rather is something almost peacefully uplifting. Joy is also often a choice. We can orient toward a situation with a joyful attitude or lean into the humor or levity of an interaction to feel a sense of joy from it.

The late and venerable Thich Nhat Hanh—Buddhist monk, mindfulness teacher, peace activist, and author—offered, "Sometimes your joy is the source of your smile, but sometimes your smile can be the source of your joy" (Thich Nhat Hanh Quote Collective, 2018). In this brief and unassuming offering, we can find something remarkably useful. The half-smile technique made popular in dialectical behavior therapy is a great example of this hidden gift, although its practical utility is more in line with self-regulation and relaxation. However, the underlying mechanisms are the same—we constantly receive feedback from our facial muscles and our posture. Our brains and bodies are just as much antennae in receiving mode as they are radios in transmission mode.

Give this a try right now: Think of something from your past that produced a good, joyful feeling. It may have been something you experienced by yourself or with other people—the joy of witnessing a beautiful sunset or perhaps children laughing and playing happily. When that scene has fully arisen in your mind, sense how it feels to you. Are you compelled to smile a bit? Does it help to intensify the joy of the scene by putting a deliberate smile on your face?

A wonderfully useful concept in Buddhist doctrine is that of *sympathetic joy,* quite the opposite of *schadenfreude* (i.e., joy from someone else's misfortune).

Stated simply, sympathetic joy boils down to rejoicing in the good fortune of others (McCormick, 2003). If you've ever heard the gleeful laughter of a young child being tickled, you may have delighted in their merriment. A big smile may have been drawn across your face, and the child's joy became your joy.

Sympathetic joy is not confined to humor, laughter, and glee. You can also rejoice in how well your clients have made progress on issues that seemed intractable to them (and even to you). You can help celebrate with a colleague in peer supervision who recently found a better work–life balance. And from there, perhaps this shared experience motivates you to reexamine the ways in which you think about and enact your self-care.

Intentionally being on the lookout for these types of experiences can be quite elevating. Orienting in this fashion is to be shifting one's perspective from "the usual" to greater curiosity and interest in generally positive deeds, news, and interactions in the world. In fact, a great practice for deliberately cultivating joy and a general positive outlook (that can counter the "doom-scrolling" that has taken over many people's lives) is to surf websites (e.g., https://www.PositiveNews.com, https://www.dailygood.org, https://Kindling.xyz) and YouTube channels (e.g., Some Good News) focused exclusively on positive news and others' wholesome and uplifting actions (Chapter 31 includes more about alternative ways to interact with media and mindful use of technology and [social] media).

Quite related but certainly distinct from laughter, humor, and joy is the mindset and behavioral characteristic of *playfulness*. You likely know someone in your life who is inherently a playful, spirited, fun-loving individual. Perhaps you are that person. What does it feel like to be playful or to be around someone who likes to frolic in the rain, is intentionally playful in nature or with food, or generally sees the world as a playground?

As they will with humor, others will often give you feedback about your relative degree of playfulness. And yet you may know for yourself how seriously you interact with yourself and the world. Do you give yourself opportunities to be frisky, light-hearted, bouncy, or even mischievous? If you have kids, do you play at their level, or do you feel compelled to let the playfulness rest in their hands while you maintain a more serious demeanor? Playfulness may not be second nature to you, and yet it's worth leaning into this way of being, both inside and outside of the therapy room. Becoming a bit more playful in your therapeutic approach or simply in how you relate to your clients not only can help you feel more lightness of being but also can help adjust the therapeutic relationship toward greater flexibility, freedom, and relaxed spirit.

In this chapter, we've explored how the lighter side of self-care—that of laughter, humor, joy, and playfulness—can facilitate states of mental and emotional well-being and physiological wellness. The fact that we can laugh just because we want to laugh is quite liberating as a deliberate way to reduce stress and bring some brightness to your life. We can also intentionally bring more of these qualities into our therapeutic endeavors, integrating a lightness of being that may ease our burdensome feelings while we boost our stress hardiness over time.

After reading this chapter, some of us might feel a bit skeptical that laughter and humor, for example, are really going to effect any significant change in our personal and professional lives. We might even hold a much more pessimistic view of the subject. However, as author and social investor Oscar Auliq-Ice is thought to have said, "Laughter is like a windshield wiper; it doesn't stop the rain but allows us to keep going." We turn now to optimism, a quality that we can cultivate for resilience and hope through the challenging moments that we face each day.

23 LEARNING OPTIMISM

In the midst of every crisis lies opportunity.

—Albert Einstein

"Optimism is tantamount to turning a blind eye to reality. It's ignorant and irresponsible." Although this was uttered by a self-declared *pessimistic* client of mine many years ago, perhaps it captures some degree of the skepticism some of us feel about this quality of mind. What do you think and how do you feel when you meet a self-declared optimist? Are you weary of how they *really* maintain such "unrealistic" hope amid all the suffering of the human condition? Do you consider yourself an optimist? Perhaps you're a realist? Or do you and others know you to be an unabashed pessimist?

Regardless of where we turn and what global or local crises we are asked to endure, we suffer because we're human. But that certainly doesn't mean that we must wade through such suffering (of ourselves, our loved ones, or our clients) without a sense of hope and psychological–emotional grit for

https://doi.org/10.1037/0000309-024

The Thriving Therapist: Sustainable Self-Care to Prevent Burnout and Enhance Well-Being,
by M. A. Hersh

getting through a crisis, learning and growing from the struggles, and potentially being better off because of it.

The COVID-19 pandemic has undoubtedly revealed a great deal about our mindsets and worldviews. How have you related to your clients as they've expressed grave doubt and fear on the one hand and hope and faith on the other? In many ways, therapists have been tested to think optimistically—to transform personal and collective suffering into opportunities to grow in meaningful ways. Optimism is in part about orienting with hope and an implicit expectation that things will turn out as favorably *as possible.* This perceptual stance does not mean optimists believe everything will be perfect or work out beautifully every time, nor does it mean simply thinking positive thoughts. The quality of realistic optimism allows us to appreciate that things may turn out more poorly than desired, but we may nevertheless maintain an attitude of hopeful resilience. Mr. Rogers, host of the widely popular and endearing children's show *Mr. Rogers' Neighborhood,* once quoted his mother for a powerful life lesson: "Look for the helpers. You will always find people who are helping."

Research shows that, compared with others, optimists are happier, have improved physical health, are more immune and resilient to stress and more satisfied in relationships, and show better performance in high-stress situations (e.g., Seligman, 2006). Clearly, there is something powerful and enduring in adopting an internal atmosphere of optimism. But how can psychotherapists harness this mindset skill in favor of sustainable self-care and longevity of well-being?

OPTIMISM, PSYCHOTHERAPISTS, AND PSYCHOTHERAPY

We know from decades of investigation that optimism can be learned (Seligman, 2006). It was once believed that there are pessimists and there are optimists. But we now know that optimism (like gratitude, compassion, and forgiveness) can be cultivated and evolved from a series of temporary states to an enduring and sustainable trait-like characteristic.

Many of us are probably optimists for our clients although we might not view ourselves and the world in as hopeful a manner. I've realized that I very clearly fall into this category. But many of us know what it feels like to coach and counsel our patients in the art of making (and taking away) the best of even the worst situations. What we're doing for our clients that's so helpful is assisting them in their explanatory styles—how they cognitively filter their experiences and then explain to themselves (or to others) the tough situations they're experiencing.

Explanatory styles for difficult situations can be personal, pervasive, and permanent (i.e., pessimistic) or external, specific, and impermanent (i.e., optimistic). In other words, every day in our professional lives we're likely helping others to see the suffering within themselves and in the world through a broad lens, as limited or circumscribed rather than pervasive, and as fleeting or even as malleable (rather than as permanent or unchangeable). If we have a personality style that leans in the optimistic direction or if we deliberately cultivate more optimism, we can find ourselves enjoying more career satisfaction (e.g., Lounsbury et al., 2003, 2008). It's really a win–win–win for our professional and personal lives and for the lives of our clients.

Optimistically, we can build a constructive and hopeful mindset for ourselves too. Think about the last time you encountered a very challenging situation in your therapeutic work. This situation could have been with a patient, a colleague, supervisor, or within the broad workplace context. Perhaps you overshared some of your personal life with a few clients in the past month, and one of your clients looked visibly uncomfortable by this sharing. What would be your automatic assumption about yourself be in this case? Would you personalize your behavior—blaming yourself and highlighting your flaws? Would you look for all the times in the past that you've made this kind error and then assume you'll be this kind of "oversharing" therapist long into the future? Or might you see the whole picture—what prompted you to overshare that day, with those clients in particular? And might you see this personal sharing as countertransferential and something that can be examined and changed? Paradoxically, an optimistic mindset helps us to take more responsibility for our actions because we're not pessimistically and negatively blaming ourselves or others and then clouding a situation that could potentially have been easily modified or supported.

OPTIMISM-BUILDING PRACTICES

We could all use a bit of assistance in building a more optimistic state of mind and body. For those who need a bit more support and encouragement, let's explore a few helpful ways that an optimistic spirit can begin to permeate your professional and personal life.

Hang Out With Optimistic People

Easy enough, right? Perhaps not, but as the saying goes, you rise to the level of those who surround you. If you're surrounded by one too many a negative Nancy, you might consider rethinking your network of friends and colleagues. Not that you need to abandon your existing connections, but seeking out a regular or deep connection with that optimistic colleague in your peer consultation group or that friend of a friend you just met could help to reinforce the mindset you're trying to cultivate.

Avoid Constant Negative News

It's fair to say that a lot of things happening in the world are extremely negative, threatening, and depressing—political incivility and lies, racial inequality and violence, global tensions and strained economies, and the worst health pandemic we might ever see in several lifetimes. We don't have to list any more current events to feel the slow burn both on a personal level *and* as a therapist sitting with others' suffering on a daily basis.

Understanding the detrimental impact of such news streaming through headlines, articles, videos, and social media posts can help us begin to shift consciously away from the 24/7 news cycle to more positive news as well as less news altogether. We don't have to lead ourselves to sheer ignorance of the world around us to reduce the negativity and pessimism we're likely infusing into our mind, body, and spirit on a constant basis.

Practice Generating Solutions

Because the brain has a built-in *negativity bias* that prompts us to protect against perceived threat rather than proceed confidently toward perceived good, we need to be quite aware of our natural tendency to see things more negatively than positively. We may complain much more than we solve. Following the 3:1 rule—that your mind–body requires three positive thoughts for every one negative—we can push ourselves toward optimistic thinking more of the time.

Optimism training is about cultivating a more hopeful, flexible, and solution-focused way of viewing oneself and the world. Perhaps with others' help, you can try to list a few solutions to every problem (no matter how small and seemingly insignificant) that comes into your awareness.

Recondition Your Learned Helplessness and Hopelessness

When we react with helplessness and hopelessness to a given negative event, we're usually thinking through a filter of "there's something about me that caused this" (personalization), "my whole life is ruined because of this" (pervasiveness), and "this negativity is going to last forever" (permanence). These three Ps keep the flower of optimism from budding.

We can challenge this thinking style by recognizing adversity (writ large) *doesn't have to* lead to a set of antioptimism beliefs that consequently *don't have to* lead to a negative or ill-fated consequence. We can use the tried-and-true ABC cognitive technique (Ellis, 1984) that Dr. Martin Seligman, positive psychology founder, made quite popular:

- Through the use of a small notepad, journal, or your smartphone, you can note any adversity that you perceive at any time. This is the *A* for antecedent.

- Then record how you're presently thinking about that adversity, specifically whether you're appraising the event through a personalized, pervasive, and/or permanent filter or whether there's a more optimistic flavor that would help you externalize (vs. personalize), think situationally (vs. pervasively), and ponder the temporary nature of an issue (vs. permanence). This is your *B* for your beliefs that almost always are the intervening variables between what's "out there" and how we consequently feel or act.

- Consider the effects that your intervening beliefs, rules, and mindset might be having on how the adverse event seems to have "caused" your hopeless feelings, for example. This is the *C* for consequences.

- Finally, you can reflect on and then jot down at least one way that the adverse event could be perceived as external, situational, and temporary or at least less pessimistically.

You may have quite a few adverse events each day, and thus you have more opportunity to practice. One of the biggest contributors to professional burnout is the overwhelm of adverse workplace events on our own resources. Cultivating a more optimistic thinking style is a self-care and burnout prevention resource that is well worth building.

If pen-and-paper exercises feel a bit too cumbersome or antiquated, you might consider a few online and smartphone-based resources. For example, the phone app Shine is a very comprehensive and overarchingly optimism-enhancing tool. You'll find practices, interactive opportunities, and reminders in the realms of kindness, compassion, and mindfulness. A wonderfully inventive online tool, ReFrame (see https://reframe.thnk.org/), allows for the user to be engaged and active in their processing of negative beliefs that can be turned toward greater optimism and health.

Whether through optimism, joy, gratitude, compassion, and forgiveness or the mindfulness pillars of intentionality, acceptance, and equanimity, we are blessed with such a wonderful treasure trove of interior qualities just waiting to be cultivated for a less burdensome and more resilient way of living. These growable qualities can often be seamlessly integrated into our commute to and from work, throughout the workday, and upon returning home for the balance of the day. We turn next to extrinsic self-caring resources and habits that harness our capacity for self-regulation, self-expansion, and connection with the word in flexible and meaningful ways.

PART **IV**

EXTRINSIC
SELF-CARE:
POWERFUL
PRACTICES,
TRANSFORMATIONAL
HABITS

INTRODUCTION: EXTRINSIC SELF-CARE: POWERFUL PRACTICES, TRANSFORMATIONAL HABITS

We have to find a balance between building up and breaking down . . . between activation and recovery, between being awake and sleeping, between exercising and resting. The body doesn't need one more than the other. It needs the balance between the two.

—Sten Ekberg, holistic doctor, former Olympic decathlete

As we segue from intrinsic to extrinsic self-care practices, this distinction might seem somewhat artificial. However, we draw out this difference as a helpful framework for qualities practiced "on the inside" and that even a proverbial fly on the wall wouldn't quite know about versus the more "seen from the outside" self-care enactments that are at least a bit more observable. When extrinsic self-care behaviors are done with healthy repetition, they can promote the qualities discussed in the chapters of Part III. Reciprocally, intrinsic self-caring qualities can become more infused into extrinsic practices we choose to endeavor and make habit.

It has become common knowledge that our wellness and well-being are significantly influenced by the daily habits in which we engage. Adequate sleep, good nutrition, regular exercise, and meditation, for example, all produce reliable (enough) impacts on our overall well-being over time. Research continues to confirm that our immune, endocrine, cardiovascular, and respiratory systems respond positively to such self-care and lifestyle practices. Moreover, the mental and emotional health benefits we experience, such as more balanced decision making, better emotion regulation, stronger impulse control, and more resilience to stress, create a positive feedback loop of engaging in these self-care practices and experiencing a wide array of mind–body benefits.

When we read about extrinsic self-care practices, many of them can be construed as "add-on" activities that may require extra time that we think (or actually) we don't have. It is my intention across these chapters simply to present options and opportunities that you can choose to bring into your life. Interestingly—and we've all probably experienced this phenomenon—once we've determined something really matters to us, we usually end up finding or making the time for it. After a little while, it becomes positive habit, and our lamenting the time it takes wanes or loses its power. Part V is all about readiness and willingness to do things differently and ways to install healthy habits that are workable and sustainable. So, as you read about these extrinsic skills, exercises, and practices, you can remind yourself that each one can be tailored to your needs and can become what you need it to be.

Another important aspect of most of these extrinsic self-care practices is that they require some degree of healthy boundary setting. Not that there should be a rigid boundary between your work and your personal life, but the ability of psychotherapists to demarcate their own space and time is absolutely crucial to the introduction and thus sustainability of any of these extrinsic aspects of self-care. And yet, making time for such extrinsic practices should not be an additional stressor, like an overly complicated medication regimen that's too difficult to follow each day.

Interestingly, two of the psychotherapists I've seen for my own benefit over the years were quite skilled at drawing boundaries around time they needed for rejuvenation and resetting in their own respective ways. One therapist would carve out one hour for self-care during each of his busy client-filled days. That meant several different things to him at different times, depending on what he needed and why. Another therapist liked to nap for roughly 30 minutes in the middle of the day, which helped his energy levels and supported his circadian rhythms.

Part IV of this book includes a wide variety of extrinsic self-caring practices, activities, and strategies. Two chapters address biological foundations of self-care: Chapter 24 focuses on sleep and breath, and Chapter 25 focuses on movement and nutrition. The next chapters present powerful mind–body integrative practices (meditation in Chapter 26 and subtle energy practices in Chapter 27) and are followed by ways to both connect and disconnect for health and restoration (rest and time off in Chapter 28 and supportive connections and healthy boundaries in Chapter 29). Continuing the theme of self-regulation as self-care, Chapter 30 addresses ways to strengthen executive functions, and Chapter 31 focuses on ways to approach (social) media more mindfully (Chapter 31). Chapter 32 presents several facets of personal grounding and growth that involve seeking creative, self-expansive, and self-healing endeavors. Mirroring this theme of growth in the professional realm, Chapter 33 addresses professional development, diversity of roles, and seeking consultation and supervision. Finally, two chapters include ways to optimally function within our workplace, navigating the existing challenges (Chapter 34) and consciously creating spaces of enduring wellness (Chapter 35).

24

BIOLOGICAL FOUNDATIONS OF SELF-CARE I

Sleep and Breath

Some doors only open from the inside, and the breath grants us access to those doors.

—Max Strom

I recognized the man in the computer monitor, but only vaguely. When I moved my head, his eyes tracked me. My yawning was growing incessant, and my narrowed field of vision felt veiled in thick clouds. But I *had* to submit my research paper, as I was already past the deadline. This was a draft of my soon-to-be master's project, and it had to be done. "Matt, are you OK? You don't look so good," a more advanced graduate student asked with concern. "Oh, I'm fine, just a bit tired," I replied, lying through my teeth. On the drive home, I saw long, drawn-out trails every time I blinked, my brain desperately trying to force sleep upon me.

This hallucinatory and dangerous situation was courtesy of essentially pulling two all-nighters in a row during my first year of graduate school. Unfortunately, I was no stranger to auditory and visual hallucinations from

https://doi.org/10.1037/0000309-025
The Thriving Therapist: Sustainable Self-Care to Prevent Burnout and Enhance Well-Being, by M. A. Hersh

massive sleep deficit—it happened in college as well. However, this type of experience is no longer a badge of courage, and "you can sleep when you're dead," a proud motto of one of my good college friends, was far in the rearview mirror. Our brains and bodies cannot handle this kind of sleep deficit, and they demand and crave sleep. It is a foundational biological necessity.

The extrinsic self-care section of this book begins with sleep and breath. Although we'd be wise to enact many other vital self-caring actions to prevent a host of occupational hazards and to live a relatively balanced and fulfilling life, if we're not sleeping and breathing adequately and consistently enough, then our entire system is quickly compromised. No other self-caring attitudes and actions matter all that much if we can't keep our eyes open during client sessions or if our sleep-deprived irritability and pessimistic outlook has pervaded our personal and professional lives.

SLEEP

Getting absolutely no sleep, such as in my graduate-school anecdote, is not the typical source of sleep deficit and tiredness. It's often more subtle than that. However, it's important to note that therapists who are new parents, particularly if their infant is a poor sleeper or feeder, will likely experience sleep deficits they never knew possible. Therapists in this position would be hard pressed to do responsible and effective psychotherapy on 4 to 5 hours of broken sleep each night for months in a row. Finding ways to reclaim any of that missing sleep is so crucial for a new parent but can be particularly vital for therapists (and other clinicians) who are looking after the mental health and well-being of others. Proactively seeking support from trusted others in your home, your extended network, colleagues, and mental and medical health care practitioners is essential during these challenging times.

Outside of normative experiences such as becoming a new parent or (hopefully) less frequent circumstances of enduring an injury or illness, how would you evaluate your sleep overall? Are you satisfied with the quantity, quality, and consistency of your sleep? Do you notice certain situations and habits that generate sleep difficulty? Unfortunately, disturbed sleep, insomnia symptoms, and diagnosable insomnia are quite prevalent among adults in the United States (Centers for Disease Control and Prevention [CDC], n.d.; Ram et al., 2010). Obstructive sleep apnea, often underdiagnosed, is another sleep disorder that can cause undue daily suffering as well as long-term health effects. Regardless of the source, sleep deprivation can exacerbate difficulties in concentration and focus, brain processing speed, and other executive functions, such as working memory (Goel et al., 2009; McCoy & Strecker, 2011).

Our particular habits around sleep, for example, how we wind down at night and what we eat before bed, are generally instilled at an early age, although this specific topic is beyond the scope of this chapter. Fortunately, such habits are malleable at any age. Biological sleep patterns, however, may be genetically influenced, as some of the new sleep chronotype research suggests (Breus, 2016). Evaluating your sleep chronotype (e.g., night owl, early morning riser) can assist you in determining optimal sleep and wake times, how much sleep is most beneficial, and when to engage in other habits for best daily functioning.

Given the premise that sleep is a biological necessity, we are reminded that regular, good-quality sleep can profoundly alter mind–body–brain functioning. It can not only restore our biological functions (e.g., coordination, temperature regulation, heart rhythm) from daily wear and tear but also build our capacity to self-regulate and manage psychological strain (Barber & Munz, 2011). High-quality sleep is essential for mood stability and immune support and even helps clean up and dispose of cellular debris and waste from our brains (Xie et al., 2013). Despite cultural pride in working our fingers to the bone and forgoing adequate sleep in the process, sleep is literally what keeps us both sane and alive.

Psychotherapists and Our Sleep

If you've ever (almost) fallen asleep while with a client, you know how utterly distressing and humiliating it can be. You might yawn incessantly but try to cover up signs of exhaustion through odd-looking facial gestures and a stealthy, strategically timed hand over the face. As your traumatized client is revealing some shameful aspect of their childhood never shared before, are you blinking so slowly with a wobbly head as to appear as if you're ignoring their pain? If you could keep a box of (padded) toothpicks in your desk drawer at work, would you? The plight of the overtired psychotherapist cannot be overstated.

We know that work stress (not necessarily specific to mental health professionals) is linked to poor sleep (Linton, 2004; Ota et al., 2009), particularly when employees perceive an imbalance of effort and reward, experience low social support, and have an overcommitment to their work. Poor sleep and chronic sleep problems are linked to low quality of life, including strained ability to focus, job dissatisfaction, and poor mental and physical health (Schlarb et al., 2012).

In a large study of German mental health professionals (Schlarb et al., 2012), nearly half of practitioners reported at least one symptom of insomnia, and over a quarter endorsed often or very often waking up tired. Practitioners' workload and specific job demands predicted their well-being, and symptoms of insomnia appeared to play a significant role in this relationship. This study might suggest that our work can negatively affect our well-being through the effects of disturbed sleep. We know, however, that experiencing poor sleep can lead to low productivity and low job satisfaction (Scott & Judge, 2006). Thus, our aim in this chapter is to help interrupt this vicious cycle and promote a favorable set of conditions for optimal nighttime rest and restoration.

Given the emotionally taxing work that we do, how mentally boundaried is your clinical work from your bedroom? In other words, do you not only take your work stress home with you but also find it keeping some part of you up as the rest of you is trying to turn itself down? Do you tend to ruminate about what went wrong with certain clients? Perhaps you're treatment planning for the next day. The self-care skills and resources found within the rest of this book can be of powerful benefit, as can those discussed within this chapter. The practices that help you release and let go of the day's stresses, seek more joy and creativity throughout your day, and truly wind down at night are all of potential support for more easeful and sound sleep.

Your Attachment Relationship to Sleep

It's quite useful to reflect on our attitudes and beliefs about sleep. In addition, we can ponder the quality of our relationship with sleep in general and our mindset when our sleep is suboptimal or highly problematic. As we do in other aspects of our life, we hold beliefs about sleep that can be limiting or benevolent. Using the language of attachment theory, ask yourself, are you securely attached in your relationship with slumber? Can you rest assured that you'll get good sleep and that sleep is an accessible resource in your life? Perhaps your partnership with sleep is strained, manifesting in preoccupations, anxieties, or a hostile sense that your body has somnologically betrayed you.

As you explore some of the tips and strategies for healthy sleep, you may notice yourself objecting or staring dumbfounded at the suggestion to go to bed and wake up at the same time each day/night, even on weekends and vacations. "But I deserve to sleep in!" you might demand. Slumped over in your chair you might wearily exclaim, "I'm so exhausted, I just have to catch up on some sleep." You do indeed deserve and need better sleep. In these cases, it's worth exploring your beliefs (or even the myths) about how sleep is *supposed* to be. You might find that some of your beliefs and habits are inadvertently maintaining a less-than-healthy slumber and sleep–wake pattern.

If we engage in *revenge sleep procrastination* (see Kroese et al., 2014), we may find ourselves delaying sleep because we simply crave some peace and quiet from a long, busy, and noisy day or want to escape the stress from challenging clinical work. Perhaps we feel we weren't productive or effective enough during the day, and as night falls we feel an urge to make up for our perceived laziness or incompetence by paying bills or catching up on some online continuing education course modules we've been neglecting. If any of these situations resonate with you, you're definitely not alone, and it's worth some further self-exploration and discussion with trusted others if you feel that would be of additional benefit.

Assessing Your Sleep Patterns and Habits

Before diving into what you might modify and how you might modify it, let's do a brief assessment of what your sleep patterns and habits are currently like. First and foremost, do you feel well rested most of the time, or do you readily know without much reflection that you need more or better quality sleep? Rather than relying solely on the amount of sleep the "experts" say you should get, make a subjective evaluation of how you feel. Your personal sense of your own sleep shouldn't be undervalued—it may be that your *less conventional* sleep patterns (e.g., timing, quantity) may indeed produce a more rested and vital feeling than might be experienced by someone who is following the guidelines in a more disciplined way. Thus, in harkening back to the idea of listening to our bodies (see Chapter 9, this volume), we can find both solace and value in tuning into our own subjective sense of ourselves.

With that said, we know that the average human being is better off with more than 7 hours of sleep per night on a relatively consistent basis. Less than this amount is associated not only with greater medical risk but also with mental health distress (CDC, n.d.). However, we also don't want to oversleep (e.g., well past 8 hours), as too much sleep has been found to disrupt your sleep cycle, increase fatigue, produce a type of brain fog that can follow us throughout the day, and much more (e.g., Youngstedt & Kripke, 2004). You're likely all too familiar with the exhausted feeling of getting (much) less than 7 hours per night if you have children, a puppy, very noisy neighbors, chronic pain, or constant worry, to name but a few sources of low quantity and quality of sleep. Approximately 70% of Americans have significantly disrupted sleep at least once per month (CDC, n.d.), and about 10% of Americans have chronic insomnia.

It's beneficial to know whether your sleep is simply shortened because of late bedtimes and/or early waking or if it's disrupted during the middle of the night even if you're going to bed and waking at reasonable times. Sometimes you may be facing both situations—shortened nights that are filled with overly light sleep and full-on, middle-of-the-night awakenings that cause undue distress. As we reflect on our habits, patterns, and circumstances that facilitate or detract from relatively consistent, high-quality sleep, we can turn to a tried-and-true approach for maximizing our chances of sound slumber.

Sleep Hygiene

I still remember a brown-bag lunch talk on sleep hygiene delivered by one of my knowledgeable classmates in graduate school. At the time, it seemed interesting and made good sense, but the information didn't feel pressing enough to take immediate action (despite my hallucinatory experiences from major sleep deficits). Sleep hygiene is ultimately about establishing and maintaining both an environment and a set of personal habits that *invite* healthy sleep—both to help fall asleep easefully and to stay asleep soundly.

There are many sources of information on good sleep hygiene, and we can reference Exhibit 24.1, composited from the CDC and the Sleep Foundation (Suni, 2020). Our task is to evaluate these reminders in the most self-caring and compassionate way. With honesty, good humor, and curiosity, note what resonates best with you, what you already implement in your daily life with relative success, and what could be points of improvement.

Sometimes it takes years to realize that your daytime fatigue and nighttime snoring and sudden awakenings are related to sleep apnea. Other times an aspect of your daily routine is hidden in plain sight (e.g., caffeine consumption too late in the day, a heavy meal or snack right before bed, unresolved interpersonal tension that elevates cortisol) and causing undue struggles with one or more aspects of sleeplessness. Medications are often inconspicuous culprits, especially if we take a dose of something long enough before bedtime that we are hard pressed to associate the medication with poor sleep. Pillow and mattress quality is underrepresented in many sleep hygiene surveys, so this is another arena you can evaluate for yourself.

Use of backlit electronic devices as well as simply playing, reading, and surfing on the computer and playing, surfing, and texting on the phone before bed also play a significant role in disrupting onset of sleep, affecting

EXHIBIT 24.1. Self-Care Reflection Break: Sleep Hygiene

Facet of healthy sleep habit and environment	Needs a lot of attention	Could be slightly modified	Going fairly well
Keep a consistent sleep schedule. Get up at the same time every day, even on weekends or during vacations.			
Set a bedtime that is early enough for you to get at least 7 hours of sleep.			
Don't go to bed unless you are sleepy.			
If you don't fall asleep after 20 minutes, get out of bed and do a quiet, nonstimulating activity away from electronics until feeling drowsy enough for sleep.			
Establish a relaxing bedtime routine.			
Use your bed only for sleep and sex, not writing progress notes or talking about clients with your partner, for example.			
Make your bedroom quiet and relaxing. Overnight, keep your room very dark and at a comfortable, cool temperature.			
Limit exposure to bright light in the evenings.			
Turn off electronic devices at least 30 minutes before bedtime.			
Don't eat a large meal before bedtime. If you are hungry at night, eat a light, healthy snack.			
Exercise regularly (but not too vigorously close to bedtime).			
Avoid consuming caffeine in the late afternoon or evening.			
Avoid consuming alcohol before bedtime.			
Make sure your prescribed medications aren't too stimulating. Reduce your fluid intake before bedtime.			

Note. Adapted from *Tips for Better Sleep*, by Centers for Disease Control and Prevention, 2016. In the public domain.

sleep quality, and causing difficulties getting up in the morning (Fossum et al., 2014). Some of us even sleep with our phones next to or under our pillow, further exacerbating our sleep difficulties. Could we even imagine this behavior only 15 years ago? Given the data on blue light and backlit device use before bed (Harvard Health Publishing, 2020) and the phone habits we may engage in before bed and upon waking, it can be an extremely useful practice to move the phone farther away from the bed. Plug it in at a far outlet, and make sure the volume is high enough if you need the phone alarm for waking. This setup may feel quite challenging at first if you have relied on your phone for a host of sleep-inducing (or accidental sleep-disrupting) activities.

Mind-Body Techniques for Better Sleep

If you've ever had a stressful day with clients (which all of us probably have), then you know that sometimes we have trouble letting go of things we said, did, or didn't do. Sometimes we hear clients' voices in our heads, echoing the suicide plans they have for themselves, just in case life doesn't work out the way they had hoped. At other times we had to manage an acute crisis at 7:00 p.m., and at bedtime we're somehow expected to turn our minds and bodies off for restful sleep. Or we may need to or have chosen to see clients into the late evening, not permitting enough transition time between our work self and our personal life self.

For these circumstances, as well as for other more normative ones, we can turn to a variety of mind–body approaches and techniques to help us fall asleep readily and stay asleep more soundly. The following list is not exhaustive but provides some useful techniques and practices to experiment with and potentially adopt for long-term sleep wellness.

- *Cognitive behavior therapy for insomnia* (CBT-I) has been recognized as a frontline, primary intervention for sleep problems (see Schutte-Rodin et al., 2008) and can be effective in up to 80% of individuals with chronic insomnia who stick with this program. It can be delivered in person as well as digitally (e.g., https://www.goodpath.com/learn/cbti-insomnia-treatment-program). CBT-I is a combination of tried-and-true cognitive strategies, stimulus control, sleep hygiene, relaxation training, and sleep restriction, to name five of the core components. Individuals practice identifying and reworking/reframing limiting beliefs and thoughts that tend to be antithetical to falling asleep with relative ease or staying asleep soundly (e.g., "What if I don't fall asleep quickly enough?" "What if I don't get the sleep I really need?" "I'll be an absolute wreck tomorrow if I don't get my requisite 8 hours!"). Stimulus control (Bootzin et al., 1991), sleep hygiene, and sleep consolidation/restriction (Spielman et al., 1987) all involve altering your relationship with the environment within and around you to create better biological sleep pressure and associations among you, sleep, and the bed that are more effective, efficient, and consistent. Benefits of CBT-I include less time to fall asleep, more time asleep, and waking up less during sleep time (Trauer et al., 2015).

- *Mindfulness* in general and *mindfulness-based therapy for insomnia* (MBT-I; Ong et al., 2008) are effective approaches to supporting optimal sleep. Through acceptance, letting go, and mindfully observing our thoughts and physical bodies, we can begin to change our relationship with sleep for the better. MBT-I in particular synthesizes mindfulness with other facets of sleep hygiene for a powerhouse intervention.

- *Guided imagery* and relaxing, nonlyrical music can be very effective alternative sleep aids. Sometimes we need less effortful ways to enact change in a systemic way. Guided imagery can answer this call as we plug in our headphones, lie down, breathe deeply, and listen to a trusted voice guiding us through sleep-inducing visualizations and sensory-based imagery. You could record a few minutes of your own voice on your smartphone or download one of many great sleep recordings from https://www.HealthJourneys.com, a trusted and well-respected source of guided imagery meditations. There are countless sleep music options on YouTube or reviewed on sites like https://www.verywellmind.com/best-sleep-music-apps-5115124. While it is the case that phone usage right before (or in) bed can serve to disrupt our sleep, consciously using our phones (or other non–Wi-Fi devices) for music or guided imagery can facilitate the sound sleep we desire.

- *Controlled breathing* can help regulate and slow your physiology and calm the mind. Starting before bedtime or while lying in bed, you can begin to slow your breathing by elongating the exhale through your nose or mouth. Gradually bring your breathing to a very comfortable, measured, and relaxed pace, simply focusing on the feeling of calm and restfulness. Give your mind permission to follow your breathing and the sensations of movement in your torso and abdomen.

- *Journaling* before bed can help on a few different levels. First, journaling allows us to download and express what has accumulated in our mind and body from the day. Second, it allows us to organize mind–body material that may feel confused or scattered. A variation on journaling is to jot down on a separate piece of paper a few things on our mind that we need to remember for the next day. When we hold those tasks mentally before bed, we may risk keeping ourselves up, trying to remember the items for the morning.

- *Practicing gratitude* is a wonderful way to wrap up the day and transition your mind–body for sleep. *How* we go to bed can partly determine how we wake. In other words, the quality of your mind and body as you lie down for bed matters for your motivation, attitude, energy, and outlook when your eyes open in the morning. A gratitude practice can help you acknowledge and infuse appreciation, thankfulness, and even joy into your system. So try experimenting with a simple practice of writing down three good things before bed each night. Reflect on each of them for about 20 seconds, inviting them into your mind–body through your in-breath and letting them integrate into your whole being on the out-breath.

- *Light therapy and supplements,* different forms of mind–body support, can certainly be beneficial when it comes to regulating our circadian rhythm and therefore our sleep. We may respond quite well to morning-time light (natural or artificial) that can stimulate production of serotonin (lifting mood and energy during the daytime) while delaying melatonin production until later in the evening for easeful sleep onset (see Pacheco, 2020). Melatonin can also be taken as a supplement at night just before bed to facilitate the secretion of this essential hormone. With either of these supports, it's important to check with a health care professional for any contraindications (e.g., artificial light may induce manic episodes in someone with bipolar disorder or seizures in someone with epilepsy).

BREATHWORK

If you recall from our exploration of listening to our bodies in Chapter 9, the breath is a dynamically unfolding and ever-changing process. It's both emotional barometer and signal transmitter. The breath is the profoundly miraculous intersection between an involuntary process of the brain–body and the voluntary, conscious control of our mind. While considering the breath as a barometer of our internal and external worlds (see Chapter 9), let's dive in to examine the various methods for using our breathing as influencer—as a tool of regulation, resilience, and restoration (see Nestor, 2020, for an excellent review of breathing and health and practical recommendations for cultivating the breath for wellness). Of note, controlled breathing of all sorts can be done on the spot in acute stress situations. More regulated and wellness-oriented breathing can become a way of life, part of a lifestyle shift. In this way, conscious and purposeful breathwork is foundational to sustainable self-care. Phone apps that may help you integrate healthy breathing include iBreathe (iPhone) and The Breathing App (Android), and some very helpful breathing videos can be found on James Nestor's website (https://www.mrjamesnestor.com/breath-vids).

Breathing to Calm (Down-Regulate)

Most of us are likely familiar with calming breath practices. We take calming breaths to slow our body and mind and to regain a certain stability and perceived safeness when we're thrown off balance.

Deep, Diaphragmatic Breathing

One of the most effective ways to calm and relax ourselves is to engage in slow, expansive, and regulated breathing through the abdomen rather than through the chest. In addition to the expansion of your abdomen as you breathe in, you may notice your intercostal muscles allowing for your ribcage to expand outward on the in-breath and relax as you breathe out. Deep, diaphragmatic breaths can quickly stimulate the parasympathetic nervous system, which is governed by the vagus nerve. As you breathe in through your nose calmly for a few seconds and breathe out through your nose or mouth for a bit longer, you signal to your entire body–mind that you are physically and psychologically safe and that you're willing to engage socially, including with yourself. Although there are many avenues for strengthening this ventral vagal pathway other than deep, diaphragmatic breathing (e.g., cold exposure, humming, singing), taking some deep breaths is one of the easiest and most portable methods that can be done anywhere and anytime.

If your breathing is nice and slow but is predominantly from your chest rather than your abdomen, you can try lying down on your back. This technique is often useful for encouraging healthy abdominal breathing. Placing one hand on your belly and the other on your chest can give you real-time tactile and proprioceptive feedback about the region of your torso that is moving most noticeably. Coaxing your abdomen to expand more than your chest is like focusing on gently blowing up a balloon that inflates right from your belly. If you've been a chest breather for much of your life, belly breathing can feel awkward. If you haven't been aware of how you breathe, now is a great time to start.

The effects of slow, deep abdominal breathing can be profound, from regulating blood pressure and heart rhythm to increasing healthy digestion and immune function. Abdominal breathing has emotional and psychological effects: It helps us to feel more grounded, less attentionally scattered, and less anxious and stressed. By breathing in this manner, we are, courtesy of the vagus nerve, granting ourselves access to playfulness, creativity, and interpersonal and intrapersonal connection. Thus, slow abdominal breathing can be done in the therapy room to bring yourself into harmony and balance and to connect with your clients with mitigated perceived threat and with presence, receptivity, and emotional safeness.

Alternate Nostril Breathing

Deep diaphragmatic breathing has become quite popular in the West and can be found in many a psychotherapist's toolbox for their clients and even for themselves. And yet for millennia, the Ayurvedic practice of *pranayama*, or breath control, has reigned supreme in many cultures and regions of the world. Anyone who has done yoga will likely be quite familiar with such breath control practices.

One of the most promising (and increasingly researched) pranayamic practices is alternate nostril breathing. The slow and measured breath through one nostril at a time almost automatically engages the diaphragm and abdomen. When one nostril is closed, air is encouraged to more gradually traverse the other nostril. With this method, you may find that you do not have to inhale more air to feel like you're getting more air. Research has suggested that slow alternate nostril breathing can improve markers of cardiovascular and respiratory function as well as lower perceived stress (Hakked et al., 2017; V. K. Sharma et al., 2013). Other benefits are improved focus and a reset, restoration, and balancing of the nervous system. As alternating nostrils stimulates the left and right sides of the body, the brain's two hemispheres are thus encouraged to better integrate and balance, and some evidence suggests that each nostril has a different set of effects on the body, with the right being more stimulating and the left more calming (Raghuraj & Telles, 2008; Telles et al., 1994). Alternating nostrils seems regulate our sympathetic and parasympathetic tones, thus increasing the positive marker of heart rate variability.

This breathwork practice has numerous variations. A popular version is to begin with a comfortable seated posture—spine straight, back strong, and belly soft. Place your right thumb on your right nostril and left ring finger on your left nostril. Rest your index and middle fingers just above the midpoint between your eyebrows as an anchor.

Begin to breathe in and out through both nostrils. When you're ready to inhale again, close your right nostril with your thumb, breathing in steadily and slowly through your left nostril. You will likely feel your abdomen expanding during this in-breath. Now close the left nostril so that both nostrils are momentarily closed on the top of the in-breath. Release your thumb from your right nostril, allowing for a steady and slow out-breath. Pause briefly at the bottom of the right nostril exhale. Now inhale through the right nostril only, closing both nostrils at the top of this breath. Finally, release your ring finger from the left nostril and release this breath steadily and slowly. You've just completed a full cycle. Even with this one progression, you may start to feel a calming or balancing feeling with a less scattered mental landscape.

Calming Breaths With Creative Spirit

There are many playful, creative, and outside-the-box ways to modify and support your calming breath practices. Designed for children but perfectly appropriate for all ages, *The Breathing Book* (Willard & Weisser, 2020) offers many artful and playful breathing adaptations. For example, you might engage in some *box breathing* wherein you breathe in, hold, breathe out, and hold for the same number of seconds. You might literally draw a box on a sticky note or trace your finger on your desk or in the air while breathing in this manner. In fact, this type of adaptation is a wonderful way to engage your attention more fully by using your body and proprioceptive functions.

Personally, I like a version of *triangle breathing* that involves breathing in, breathing out, and then gently resting (vs. holding) the breath—approximately 5 seconds each. Holding one's breath after inhalation can stimulate the sympathetic nervous system while helping the body through increased CO_2. Holding or resting one's breath after exhaling can be potentially less sympathetic-stimulating yet still beneficial because CO_2 accumulation is necessary for vital metabolic processes (see Nestor, 2020). Try experimenting with each of these methods and see which feels better to you.

Other modifications of calming breathing involve making particular soothing or spiritually meaningful sounds on the out-breath. For example, a simple "aaaah" or "ommm" or "sssssss" through the duration of the exhalation, although three potentially distinct experiences, can help guide your breathing and generate beneficial feelings and sensations. You might also loosely attach a calming word (e.g., "relaxed") or phrase (e.g., "breathing out I am calm") as you breathe slowly and steadily. This technique can be especially helpful when the mind is scattered or worried.

Calming breath variations can involve experimenting with the imagined quality of the breathing process. For example, Mischke-Reeds's (2018) *somatic psychotherapy toolbox* includes the *rounded calming breath*, slow and steady abdominal breathing that can be imagined as a "rounded wave" like "water going over a stone" or a "gentle wave cresting" (p. 186) upon reaching the top of the in-breath and then cascading down on the out-breath. Perhaps you might try it for a few breaths right now and sense how this feels to you and your well-being.

Down-regulating breaths can be done for several minutes at a time as a regular practice, much like meditation. The more you practice this type of breathing, the more your body and mind are conditioned for calm, balance, and resilience. However, sometimes we simply need to take the stress levels down in the moment, thus making more on-the-spot breathwork extremely helpful. During or after difficult sessions and before you head home for the day are strategically good times to calm your system and restore some balance for your next client or for your loved ones upon returning home.

Breathing to Activate (Up-Regulate)

Although many parts of our lives are probably fast-paced, stressful, and emotionally arousing, sometimes we're feeling sluggish, unmotivated, or disconnected and distant. In those instances, we may need to activate ourselves.

Fire Breathing

Another pranayamic breath practice, called *fire breathing* or *breath of fire*, can be exceptionally useful in these cases. Research suggests that consistent practice of breath of fire can lower perceived stress, increase focus, and strengthen the diaphragm muscle for better respiration (V. K. Sharma et al., 2013). It is paradoxically stimulating *and* stress mitigating. Quite promisingly, anecdotal evidence from hundreds of Koru mindfulness classes that my colleagues and I have taught all over the world suggests a noticeable shift in stress, focus, and healthy activation after only 3 minutes of breath of fire practice.

Unless you've already experienced breath of fire, it can appear and feel somewhat strange. The idea is to engage only your diaphragm muscle as you breathe relatively quickly only through your nostrils, mouth relaxed but completely closed. Your inhalation should take care of itself while your mental focus is on short but powerful bursts of exhalation through the nose. As you fire-breathe out you can feel your abdomen move inward while your diaphragm muscle moves back up toward your lungs to expel the stale air. Breath of fire is best learned with slow, deliberate breaths. Once you're acclimated to this feeling and movement pattern, you can increase the pace of your breathing. It's not necessary, however, to breathe at lightning-quick speed.

It's important to note that this form of breathwork isn't for everyone. For example, it's generally recommended that people who are pregnant, have heart conditions, or have high blood pressure refrain from breath of fire.

Interestingly, for a sample of 18- to 25-year-old health care students in India, a 12-week course of fast pranayama practice (e.g., breath of fire) did not increase vital signs of heart rate, respiration rate, or blood pressure but did significantly decrease perceived stress to the same degree as slow, deep breathwork practices such as alternate nostril breathing (V. K. Sharma et al., 2013).

Right Nostril Breathing

Unlike slow alternate nostril breathing, focusing only the right nostril can produce a charging effect to the mind and body. It is quite mind-blowing that we have nerve endings in the right and left nostrils that correspond to our sympathetic and parasympathetic nerve branches, respectively. Governed by our autonomic nervous system, each nostril has its time to dominate the flow of air through the nose, switching back and forth throughout the day in what is called a lateralized ultradian rhythm of the autonomic nervous system (Shannahoff-Khalsa, 1991). Thus, if we're interested in activating locomotor activity potential, testosterone, endorphins, and heart rate, for example, we can breathe in deeply through our right nostril for a few minutes. However, if you have high blood pressure or an elevated heart rate, this practice may not be the breathwork you want to do.

Restorative and Balancing Breathing Techniques

We now turn to breathing practices that can be considered balancing—both up- and down-regulating within one practice. This type of breathwork can be especially helpful when we're seeking to reduce stress, for example, while increasing our clarity of mind and vital energy flow within the body.

Heart-Focused Breathing/Quick Coherence Technique

Heart-focused breathing is a simple and very powerful technique that regulates the mind and body. It can generate both calm and peacefulness while increasing vital energy and cognitive clarity. Ultimately, this breathing practice trains heart–brain coherence, which results in an increase in heart rate variability, a marker of overall health and emotional resilience (Heart Math Institute, 2012).

Focus on the area of your heart (more in the middle of your chest) and begin to breathe in and out through this area. You can place one or both hands on your heart region to draw your attention there. Breathe a bit slower than usual, creating an ease of flow to your breath. Now, activate a positive feeling in your mind–body. This positive feeling could be from an experience you had that involved peacefulness, calm, or relaxation or perhaps care, generosity, kindness, or appreciation. Focus on the positive feelings and bring them into the present moment as best you can. Breathe in and out with your attention on these feelings. You could even place a small smile on your face to enhance the sensory experience. You can use this breathing technique whenever you're feeling frazzled or energetically depleted. It can be wonderfully restorative.

Polarity Breathing

This type of breathwork links mind and body through the breath and helps us tap into what we intend to take in and let go. Chris Berlin—Buddhist chaplain, mindfulness teacher, and instructor in Ministry and Spiritual Counseling at Harvard Divinity School—teaches that as we breathe out, we can direct our attention to releasing, discharging, expressing, and letting go whatever is not helpful to retain. As we breathe in, we can focus our attention on the opposite, the qualities we would find helpful to infuse and integrate into our being (C. Berlin, personal communication, October 2016).

For example, after a long day of seeing clients and doing administrative work, we might feel particularly overwhelmed, scattered, and depleted. We could take just a minute before we leave work or as we sit in our car or on public transportation. We would bring our attention to our breath as we feel it in our abdomen, gradually slowing our breathing until it's comfortable and smooth. We would then focus on the out-breath for the next several breaths, first acknowledging and honoring the difficulty of the day. We would assess whether any lingering energies could be released from our systems. We might find an overflow of tension and striving to have done a good job with our clients that day. On each out-breath, we imagine releasing any unnecessary tension and overstriving, letting those qualities flow right out on the breath to dissipate and vanish harmlessly into the air. Perhaps these qualities have a color or shape to them, and we could imagine that entity or energy being discharged from our mind–body. After several cycles of release, we would focus exclusively on the in-breath, gently taking in any qualities we find helpful and restorative. We might find it beneficial to infuse a calm but vibrant energy from all that tension and depletion of the day. Perhaps this energy has a color, and we could take in that color with each in-breath. We could then distribute and circulate this vibrancy on every out-breath thereafter.

In this practice, the breath can be a powerful vehicle for releasing and inviting. The structure is provided to us, but we, as individuals with our own needs, have the ultimate say as to what gets expressed outward and welcomed inward.

Hopefully, this chapter has given you some ideas of simple breathing practices that can help down- and up-regulate your nervous system and emotional tone as well as help provide balance and coherence to your entire system. Although there are literally hundreds of ways to consciously breathe for various effects, the idea is to find a few breathing practices that suit you for many different occasions, on the spot as well as for regular, habitual practice. Since the breath is as portable as the rest of you, it can be harnessed for sustainable self-caring action to prevent stress and enhance well-being wherever you go and whenever you are.

We've also explored our habits and quality of sleep. Beyond the oversimplified message of "just get more sleep" (if in fact we're sleep deprived), we can invite ourselves (and if applicable a partner) to investigate what is and isn't working in our efforts to get adequate amounts of sleep as well as the highest quality of sleep possible. Given that this biological function sets the tone for so much of the rest of our mental, physical, emotional, and relational health, it's perhaps one of the most vital forms of self-care we can offer.

We turn now to another vital set of foundational lifestyle themes, movement and nutrition, that can support our work and personal selves while nourishing myriad other extrinsic self-caring practices. As you explore Chapter 25, you may consider how the way you move and fuel your body is positively intertwined with the health of your sleep and breath.

25

BIOLOGICAL FOUNDATIONS OF SELF-CARE II

Movement and Nutrition

Take care of your body. It's the only place you have to live.

–Jim Rohn

How many times have we heard the advice to move more and eat better? I tend to repeat this to myself like a broken record (or glitching mp3 track) more than I'd like to admit. What is actually being advised when we hear such reminders? If we really take stock of our lifestyle, we can note some vital and sometimes hidden aspects of how we move our bodies and what we consume to fuel them.

We may already have an exercise or movement regimen that works really well for us. And we may already be eating in ways that balance the gut, enhance our energy and mental clarity, and coax wellness and well-being to our entire system one meal at a time. However, when these elements aren't integrated sufficiently into our daily lives or if things are simply off balance, we can look to some guidance from "out there." Ultimately, you'll be your

https://doi.org/10.1037/0000309-026
The Thriving Therapist: Sustainable Self-Care to Prevent Burnout and Enhance Well-Being, by M. A. Hersh

own guide "in here" to know how you feel, what you think, and what kinds
of healthy habits are most sustainable.

MOVEMENT

Humans were designed to move—forward and backward, left and right, up
and down, across the body, bending and jumping, twisting, running and
walking, and sweeping our arms and legs through air as if we were etching
circles in the sand. Our bodies desire stability in some regions (e.g., feet,
knees, shoulders) and require flexibility in others (e.g., ankles, hips, neck;
H. Yzusqui-Butera, personal communication, April 23, 2021). Our bodies
thrive in movement rather than in stagnation. In fact, regular physical activity
can help with a host of challenges that come with aging and living our modern
sedentary lifestyles of chronic stress (e.g., Anderson et al., 2005; Callaghan,
2004; Dishman, 2003; Lustyk et al., 2004; Ratey, 2008).

The physical component of self-care has been loosely defined as incorporating physical activity (L. Carroll et al., 1999), which in this context is characterized by bodily movement that results in the utilization of energy, which
can occur through exercise, sports, household activities, and other daily functioning (Henderson & Ainsworth, 2001). The intensity of physical activity and
the amount of time spent on it can vary dramatically, but the U.S. Department of Health and Human Services (2018) recommends at least 30 minutes of physical activity for most days throughout the week is necessary to
receive benefits.

Although physical activity has many specific physical health advantages
(Dishman, 2003), it also appears to have a mental–emotional benefit, with
symptoms of anxiety and depression decreasing (Callaghan, 2004; Dishman)
and overall quality of life increasing (Lustyk et al., 2004) as the volume and
frequency of exercise increase. For instance, physical activity has been shown
to increase women's satisfaction with their body functioning and their ability
to cope with daily stress (Anderson et al., 2005).

This chapter presents a broad view of physical activity, rather than the
general recommendation of 30 minutes of moderate aerobic activity four to
five times per week. Healthy movement in general can emerge from aerobic
exercise (see Ratey, 2008), strength training, high-intensity interval training,
Eastern energy movements and healing arts like QiGong and Tai Chi, yoga,
Pilates, dance, and basic stretching, to name just a few. These non-mutually
exclusive forms of body movement have been shown to have positive effects
on brain structure and function, emotional and mental health, cardiovascular

health, joint mobility, longevity, and psychological well-being. Of note, if we have chronic pain or other conditions that do not allow for full-body (or even moderate) movement, we can consult with a trusted health expert (e.g., primary care physician, exercise physiologist, personal trainer) to provide some guidance. In fact, we already know that we can do chair yoga or gentle medical Qigong, for example, to stimulate flow of lymph and blood without necessarily compromising other aspects of our body integrity. If you are at high risk of harm when you move more than is typical, a general rule of thumb is to start quite slow, experiment and note your experience, and then gradually build from there.

Neuroscience and epigenetics research have also demonstrated that through various forms of exercise we can increase human growth factor and brain-derived neurotrophic factor in areas of the brain responsible for regulating attention and emotion, strengthening problem-solving capacities, decreasing stress, enhancing peak performance, and alleviating depression and anxiety (see Ratey, 2008). Exercise increases dopamine, norepinephrine, and serotonin, neurotransmitters that are known to mediate nearly all mental and physical functions (e.g., Lin & Kuo, 2013). Moreover, exercise and movement of varying kinds is associated with heart rate variability, a foundational marker of vitality and health (e.g., Sandercock et al., 2005).

Psychotherapists' Relationship With Movement

Let's reflect for a moment on what our patterns of movement look like each day. Are you in a professional position that requires remaining seated for extended periods of time? How does this feel? Do you sense the need to decompress and almost unfurl your body after the workday is over? When in between clients, do you have or make time to stretch your muscles, flex your joints, and get your blood and lymph circulating? You may be in a therapist role that allows for much more movement. If so, do you notice what your mind and body feel like when you're more active, versus when you are more stagnant and sedentary? During an exploration of the ways in which you listen to your body (see Chapter 9), you may have discerned that your posture, breath, and energy are significantly enhanced when your physical body is active and dynamically flowing. If you haven't explored this relationship yet, now is a great opportunity to investigate how movement and exercise relate to how your body–mind feels and functions.

Do you conceptualize moving your body each day as simply part of how you care for yourself? Has it always been a part of your life, as a form of tending to your wellness and well-being? Do you assume that you deserve to take some time most days of the week to move your body in some purposeful way? Do you move every day as a matter of course, like brushing your teeth when you wake up and when you go to bed?

My friend, colleague, and former graduate school classmate, Dr. Cory Chen, once remarked that exercise, in one form or another, was a given in his life. He grew up with the notion that exercise was synonymous with healthy living. There was little negotiation on this matter. Fortunately, research suggests that, like Dr. Chen, 78% of mental health professionals surveyed reported engaging in some kind of physical exercise as a form of self-care in the prior year (Mahoney, 1997), although we don't know the frequency of this healthy habit.

Some therapists may not have exercise and movement on their radar. It may not feel important or like a part of self-care. Maybe exercise, fitness, and even basic movement were never modeled when you were growing up. Sitting (whether for work or entertainment) was perhaps more the norm than was moving around. Even still, exercise and purposeful movement may feel like something extra at best or like a burden or chore at worst. You may not even feel like you deserve to take 15 or 20 minutes a day, for example, to strengthen, stretch, or release your muscles or to condition your heart and brain through purposeful movement.

Some of us may hold a belief that our bodies can't or shouldn't exercise. This attitude may arise from having certain physical conditions or medical diagnoses or from assuming that we're not fit or in shape enough to exercise, despite exercise potentially helping us with those very conditions or experiences. A thoughtful examination of the beliefs you hold—expectations, limiting attitudes, and standards—can be well worth the time. In addition, consulting with a trusted physician, physical therapist, personal trainer, or someone else knowledgeable about your health history, risks, and limitations can be enormously valuable. It all starts with listening carefully to our bodies and being willing experiment with what does and does not work for us.

One of the most common grievances peppered throughout psychotherapist survey responses, as well as in self-care workshops and in discussions with self-care experts (e.g., C. Berlin, personal communication, October 2016), is *not having enough time*. This complaint isn't necessarily unique to psychotherapists, but it's echoed often enough when self-care is discussed among therapists. How to balance work and personal life often tops the list of psychotherapist stressors and barriers to implementing self-care. However, when therapists can harness the principle of *reciprocity*—"the process of dynamic exchange of beneficial lifestyle attitudes and practices between [therapist] and client" (Wise et al., 2012, p. 488)—they are potentially more likely to practice what they preach and preach what they practice. In fact, psychologists who recommend exercise to their clients tend to exercise themselves (McEntee & Halgin, 1996). This phenomenon is indeed what Dr. Roger Walsh, professor of psychiatry, philosophy, and anthropology, suggested as he noted that in contemplative disciplines, there has long been recognition that the health and maturity of the teacher is essential for cultivating the health and maturity of the student (R. Walsh, personal communication, October 27, 2011, as cited in Wise et al., 2012).

When we finish our day of tending to others' mind–body well-being, we have our personal and family lives to engage in as (mind)fully as possible. Sometimes, just the idea of fitting in the gym or attending an hour-long yoga class feels like adding more stress. More often than not, women psychotherapists who are in traditional gender roles and have children are especially challenged as they finish their "first shift" helping their clients and come home to their "second shift" managing their families. For many people who are coming home to more than just one other person, exercising may be the last thing on their mind. Fitting in a "workout" may feel pragmatically impossible and/or be perceived as less important than any number of other-oriented tasks and responsibilities.

Given your own personal and historical reasons as well as systemic and culturally circumscribed barriers to integrating exercise and planned movement into your daily life, you can remind yourself once again of one of the central premises and purposes of this book: to expand the definition and conceptualization of self-care to include a broad diversity of internal and external practices aligned with core values of self-care for sustainable well-being. Self-care is often defined or conceptualized too narrowly, thus restricting our ability to think outside the box. Or self-care hasn't been defined at all, and so we're left with an amorphous, slippery sense of self-caring and ways to integrate it into our busy days.

When we think about exercise and movement as more than just a gym membership that may take an extra 10 hours per week with workout and commute time, we can dismantle practical and logistical barriers and alleviate overwhelm and guilt. It is a good thing if you already have a workable existing gym routine or are currently building one into your life with relative ease. Our purpose here is to acknowledge that not every psychotherapist can make this happen for various reasons, including time constraints, physical limitations, family obligations, financial concerns, and other psychological–motivational issues. Even when woven into our lives in modest ways, exercise and purposeful movement can have profound benefits to our personhood and to our functioning as psychotherapists. Let's now explore several main categories of evidence-supported exercise that can fuel the heart, brain, and spirit of the hardworking therapist.

Ways to Move, Strengthen, and Energize

Aerobic movement is probably the most common and most recommended form of exercise in our popular society. Examples include walking briskly, riding a (stationary) bike, or using an elliptical machine. If we're so inclined, we can listen to music and dance. When done at a steady pace with mild to moderate intensity, we're engaging in a form of exercise that uses air relatively efficiently. Unless we've been sedentary for a while or have a medical condition, we likely wouldn't be terribly out of breath from this activity for 15 to 45 minutes at time. Aerobic exercise has many benefits for the cardiovascular system, brain health, mood brightness and stability, and anxiety and stress reduction (A. Sharma et al., 2006). Yet it's not the only form of exercise that has multiple benefits.

Seemingly at the opposite end of the exercise spectrum and highly valuable in its own right is *high-intensity interval training* (HIIT). HIIT became quite popular for many reasons, and the scientific support has been there along the way. Taking as little as 5 to 10 minutes a day, a few times a week, HIIT capitalizes on very short bursts (for approximately 30–45 seconds) of intense (80%–95% heart rate capacity) movement (e.g., running in place, performing squats, sprinting) with relatively equal time of partial rest at 40% to 50% heart rate capacity. This cycle is continued several times for up to 10 minutes. It's important to engage in a mild rest period so that you're not overtaxing your cardiovascular system in a long-term anaerobic fashion for the full duration of your workout.

Research on HIIT shows that our body quickly begins to produce brain-derived neurotrophic factor (Jiménez-Maldonado et al., 2018), which helps the brain form new synaptic pathways responsible for learning, memory, and overall brain function. These short bursts of higher intensity movements also stimulate human growth hormone, responsible in part for enhancing mood, building muscle, strengthening bone, and increasing energy. There are many other health benefits attributed to HIIT (e.g., helping decrease insulin resistance, lowering blood pressure) and the hormonal cocktail and cascade of positive changes that occur in the brain and body (e.g., Jelleyman et al., 2015).

Strength training, like HIIT, can produce some amazing body–mind changes (e.g., stress reduction, mood enhancement). Not only are we purposefully building muscle, but we're also enhancing the psychological qualities of grit and commitment. Whether we're using weights, bands, or our own body weight, we're often pushing ourselves beyond what we thought was possible. This sense of accomplishment can actually have a profound impact on one's sense of self.

Stepping away from the more vigorous forms of exercise, we move into long-standing traditional practices of *Tai Chi, Qigong,* and *yoga.* These ancient systems of healing arts and movement are physically demanding in their own right and powerful shapers of the mind, body, and spirit. Already known for their stress-mitigating effects, these practices can be effective for increasing energy and vitality, improving mood, attention, and resilience, and reducing anxiety and trauma symptomatology (e.g., Abbott & Lavretsky, 2013; Cocchiara et al., 2019). The physical health benefits, especially for those of us who sit all day conducting therapy, are particularly encouraging. These forms of movement encourage flexibility and resilience within the body, including within the cardiovascular and circulatory systems.

One additional form of movement that can greatly benefit psychotherapists comes from Dr. David Bercelli's *trauma releasing exercises* (TRE; Bercelli, 2005) and *somatic experiencing* (e.g., Levine, 2010). If you've ever seen a gazelle, for example, run for its life from a lion, you'll likely see something quite interesting after the crisis has been averted. The gazelle will shake. Its whole body will seem to convulse, discharging the traumatic experience built up in the nervous and musculoskeletal system. TRE helps us access this animal instinct of body-level-up healing from stress and trauma through a series of purposeful full-body shaking movements.

In an abbreviated and gentle form of TRE, you might set aside a few minutes after a long or difficult day with clients and begin a three-phase exercise (Mischke-Reeds, 2018) by standing up, legs shoulder-width apart. In the first step, *evoking,* notice your body and spine, let your arms hang down, and gently begin to move your legs rhythmically up and down, slightly bending them. You will be generating a gentle, wave-like motion through your spine. Continue with a rhythmic and comfortable shake, allowing this movement to feel natural and "second nature." In the second step, *moving through,* your body may now be "moving by itself." You may feel certain feelings; see if you can allow them simply to flow through. Your body's movements are therapeutic, and practice trusting them. The third step is *cooling down:* Gradually decrease your movement. It is normal to notice small tremors or sensations. Let the body come to a rest and stillness, and simply notice what's there or not there. Stand firm and still until you notice any waves of release subsiding. Once you feel calm, formally close the exercise. (See Dr. Bercelli and Donna Phillips's YouTube video that introduces the viewer to seven core exercises of TRE; https://www.youtube.com/watch?v=FeUioDuJjFI).

Whatever the form(s) of movement you're already engaging in or decide to try, it's important that you start where you are and not where someone else thinks you should be. If you are so pressed for time that 10 minutes three times per week feels overwhelming, then start walking around the inside of your residence for 60 seconds. Or walk up and down some stairs one time more than you normally would. Gradually build your movement habits from there (see Chapter 37, this volume, for further exploration of habit formation). Perhaps a phone app, YouTube video, or DVD could be of assistance as a reminder for specific movements or as a full-fledged guide to walk you through various poses, postures, and movements.

NUTRITION

In 2014, my wife underwent extensive allergy testing for a range of environmental and food allergies. As she moved forward with a painstaking elimination diet, she found herself at the point of removing gluten from her daily consumption. I decided to support her in this less-than-desirable experiment and committed to eliminating gluten from my diet as well. Although my wife unfortunately didn't notice any changes at first, I felt like a new man after only 3 days without gluten! (She's still a bit bitter about this.)

How does nutritional awareness and pattern change help us professionally? There are countless ways in which our diets writ large affect our daily and even hourly energy levels, mental clarity and attention, motivation, digestive comfort, muscular health, mood, and emotional reactivities. If you tend to feel sluggish after certain foods, then eating those foods will undoubtedly (but perhaps subtly) affect your therapeutic work for a period of time. You may respond to your clients more slowly, be less perceptive of nuances in their affects and narratives, sit with a slouched posture, or fall prey to slow blinking that borders on closed, sleeping eyes. Sometimes the foods we're eating (or not eating) may affect us at the same time day after day, week after week. For example, perhaps because of the lunches you tend to eat, you are a relatively slowed-down version of your 10:00 a.m. self when you meet your 2:00 p.m. clients.

It's important to note a few recent medical and public health trends. First, the word "diet" is not interchangeable with the act of "dieting." I refer to *diet* in this chapter as the types of foods and drinks you consume, when and how you consume them, and what is missing from this patterned consumption. I have no interest in promoting (certain types of) weight loss, and I don't intend to suggest that to care for ourselves through nutrition we have to *look* a certain way. Harnessing the power of nutrition to help our bodies (and minds) to *feel* a certain way and to *be* and *live* at our best is what we're really after.

Listening to Our Bodies for Nutritional Guidance

We can look to the wisdom found within Dr. Catherine Cook-Cottone's attuned representational model of self (Cook-Cottone, 2006; see the Introduction to Part II): Although we all need some guidance and regulation from "out there," we also can increasingly rely on the wisdom of the body from "in here." Sustainable self-care ultimately is facilitated when we turn toward ourselves with a deep respect of our unique interior dynamics and our own particular needs.

Although relatively new to the scene, health at every size (HAES; Robison, 2005) is a holistic and compassionate model that calls out our outdated and often toxic relationships with our (and others') bodies. Body size, shape, and percentage of fat, for example, are no longer synonymous with health when considered through the lens of HAES. "Proper" nutrition from this perspective doesn't presuppose that we must lose weight, be a certain weight, exercise specifically for weight loss, or adhere to some regimented diet that is likely doomed to fail. Rather, HAES promotes compassionate and truly self-loving notions of feeling good about one's body regardless of exact weight, size, and shape. We achieve such positive affirmation of our bodies and our health through engaging in sustainable routines of physical activity that are enjoyable and enhance quality of life and through attaining peaceful and relaxed patterns of eating according to hunger and satiety cues rather than through guilt, restriction, and externally imposed rules. As psychotherapists we are constantly encouraging this kind of self-relational frame for our clients. We can consider it for ourselves as well with utmost caring and concern.

One of my favorite research studies on self-acceptance and eating behaviors is affectionately referred to as "the donut–candy study" (Adams & Leary, 2007), designed to assess eating attitudes and self-regulation behaviors. College women were divided into three groups—two experimental and one control—and were told that the study was about eating experiences while watching TV. The experimental groups were asked to drink a glass of water and then eat a donut (which was predetermined to be considered relatively unhealthy) as they watched a short, neutral video clip. The control group just drank water. After the video, the participants in one experimental group were given a brief self-compassion induction involving reminders of self-kindness, nonjudgmental observation of their experience, and common humanity. After these procedures, participants in all groups were given three bowls of different and easily consumed candies they could snack on while completing questionnaires.

Although the study has its limitations, it is apropos of the HAES movement. The authors found that after eating the donuts, participants with higher self-reported restrictive eating attitudes ate half as much candy as the other two groups, but only if these participants were primed with self-compassion. In other words, eating the donut during the video didn't cause these self-compassion-primed but highly restrictive young women to rebound in their eating behaviors. In fact, this group also reported higher positive and lower negative emotion ratings during the experiment than the donut-eating group *without* self-compassion reminders. This effect has played out in various ways in other studies. For example, participants with rigid personal restrictions for alcohol consumption felt worse and subsequently drank more when they "broke their commitment" to their own consumption limits (Muraven et al., 2005).

In the spirit of sustainable self-care through nutrition, we can set ourselves up for both reasonable and healthy eating habits *while* feeling good about ourselves in the process. Consequently, the art and science of nutrition becomes less about some externally imposed set of rules that we feel we're supposed to adhere to "or else" and more about listening to our bodies in a friendly, compassionate, and attentive manner.

Intuitive Eating

A lifestyle trend in nutrition and dietetics, *intuitive eating* was developed in the 1990s by two dieticians, Evelyn Tribole and Elyse Resch. This trend promotes a similar set of principles as HAES does but may offer nuanced guidance about the food we can consume, how we consume it, and how we feel about ourselves in the process. First and foremost, intuitive eating is about rejecting or at least questioning the dieting mentality that was pushed fiercely in the 1980s and has continued feverishly since then. Unhealthy dieting is the strict adherence to a set of rules for what, how much, and when you should eat. Unlike guidelines or principles that can be followed flexibly, diets often promote eating rigidity and a restrictive attitude that we've noted can backfire, as in the donut–candy study.

Attitudes toward food and the body are important aspects of intuitive eating. Food is not the enemy: It shouldn't be policed, nor should it be dichotomized into "good" or "bad." Judgment and hypervigilance pits us against the foods we may enjoy but are told are "bad," thus exacerbating guilt and disinhibitory eating habits if we feel we've indulged in the so-called wrong foods. We experience discomfort and dislike of our bodies when we don't adhere to the ways we think we *should* be eating.

Flexibly Following Nutritional Guidance

Although we've focused thus far on internally derived guidance, it also bene-fits the average psychotherapist to tune into nutrition trends that favor holistic mind–body–brain health. Interestingly, diet trends in the United States since 2010 reveal a type of awakening to the inaccurate nutritional information "sold" to us decades earlier ("New Survey Shows Changes in American Diet Trends," 2018).

If we were to look to outside sources for specific nutritional support, we can find many reputable nutritionists, dieticians, functional medicine doctors, and allied professionals who take a holistic perspective on ways to keep our bodies healthy and prevent illness. For example, Dr. Mark Hyman is a well-respected functional medicine physician who promotes, among other things, the need for a healthy gut microbiome to support our brain–mind–body health. Food is his prescribed medicine. Thus, eating and hydration are viewed not as weight-loss tools or "shoulds" but rather as preventive and cor-rective medicine lifestyle habits. If you struggle with a particular metabolic disease like Type 2 diabetes, the right professional can help you construct a *diet* that helps support your metabolic process, controls your blood sugar, and reregulates your insulin. Because good nutritional support is also about other lifestyle habits, you would likely benefit from regulation of sleep, stress, and movement to balance your metabolic health.

The accumulating wisdom from such holistic health experts is now con-verging on a few basic principles that we can follow or at least keep in mind for long-term health and sustainability of nutrition-based self-care. These principles are supported by scientific data rather than marketing trends or popular fads that can easily take over and influence our entire ethos about nutrition and our bodies. The following guidelines are just that. They are not hard and fast rules that must be followed or else. Moreover, knowing your own unique body is key to making any nutritional self-care advice work for you. Let's explore these suggestions one at a time:

- *Eat organic foods when possible.* Organic foods, although not guaranteed to confer ultimate health benefits, are much less likely to be laden with toxins and genetically modified material that can interact with our bodies in known detrimental ways or in unknown ways. Whether you're making your own lunches to take with you to work or finding nearby restaurants or cafeterias in your clinic or hospital, you can consider whether organic options are available.

- *Reduce simple sugar and processed foods as best you can.* A staggering one of every three American adults likely has prediabetes, with blood sugar levels that are consistently high but not high enough to lead to the diagnosis of Type 2 diabetes (Centers for Disease Control and Prevention, 2020). Of this 33%, the vast majority (84%) have no idea of this situation. Simple carbohydrates and sugars harm our bodies in multiple ways, including negative mood effects (Knüppel et al., 2017) and full-body inflammation (Harvard Health Publishing, 2019). If you wrestle with any insulin resistance or reactivity issues, these carbs can quickly spike your blood sugar. Eating some version of these carbs throughout the day can keep your blood sugar higher than normal and keep your insulin pump working overtime. Some of us, however, may notice both blood sugar spikes and subsequent drops, resulting in fatigue, sweatiness, shakiness, and brain fog. These physical qualities certainly are not conducive to the subtle art of psychotherapy. If you don't regularly have blood sugar screening, getting your fasting blood sugar and hemoglobin A1C levels checked can be a move in the right direction.

- *Be mindful of your caffeine intake.* Although it likely pays to find a home-brewed coffee that is organic and mold free, generally speaking, coffee in moderation seems to have numerous health benefits, including boosts to attention, mood, and energy, as well as to the cardiovascular system. However, many of us are sensitive to the effects of caffeine. If you're particularly jittery, nervous, physiologically amped up, or experiencing insomnia, you could examine your caffeine intake—both quantity and timing. Those of us with highly sensitive temperaments will feel the effects of caffeine much more intensely than others who are less sensitive. Given that a substantial percentage of psychotherapists have this temperament, you may want to assess your intake and possibly scale back the quantity or alter the timing of your caffeine consumption to function better throughout the day and for better overall sleep.

- *Assess and address your vitamin, mineral, and electrolyte levels.* Many of us may walk around with subtle deficiencies or imbalances in vitamins, minerals, and electrolytes. These imbalances can lead to physical conditions or mimic psychiatric disorders. For example, depletions of magnesium can insidiously generate stress, while heightened stress can deplete magnesium (Pickering et al., 2020). If you don't already know your baseline levels from year to year, it may behoove you to assess a range of these easy-to-ignore health substrates. A well-rounded, vegetable-rich, healthy-fats diet often takes care of micronutrients, but sometimes our bodies continue to under-function. Supplements can help ameliorate certain conditions, enhance attention and energy, and improve our emotional health and resilience.

- *Good gut health is good (mental) health.* The research is increasingly clear. How well your gut (i.e., intestines) functions determines a large portion of your overall physical, mental, and emotional health (e.g., Harvard Health Publishing, 2021). Thus, learning about your gut health is one of the important things we can do for our present-day functioning and health for years to come. Gut health experts like Dr. Mark Hyman can help us better understand the ways in which our diet, lifestyle, and exercise patterns influence the promotion of positive health and overall resilience and resistance to disease (Hyman, 2018).

- *Practice being brutally honest with yourself about emotionally based eating habits.* Stress and eating aren't terribly good bedfellows. Or perhaps they are, because many of us eat more (or considerably less) when stressed, and that stress-based eating pattern then contributes to more stress or discomfort. When you have a hard day with clients, what do your food and drink intakes look like? How often will you eat? Are you often unaware that you're eating more or less of certain types of food (and perhaps alcohol) when stressed, tired, or deeply disillusioned? Once we own our emotion-based eating patterns, we can take better control. Of course, having alternative ways to reduce stress and to relax are crucial to this endeavor. Parts III and IV of this book provide such alternatives.

We've now had the opportunity to explore four foundational aspects of self-care (i.e., sleep, breath, movement, and nutrition) that are essential to sustainability of basic wellness and well-being. We turn next to the ancient practice of meditation that can produce remarkable changes in how we pay attention, think, feel, and act both at work and in our personal lives.

26 MEDITATION

Meditation means dissolving the invisible walls that unawareness has built.

—Sadhguru

The mind is now considered by many to be quite distinct from the brain. It's a *self-organizing process that regulates the flow of energy and information among the brain, body, and relationships* (Siegel, 2016). When harnessed appropriately and intentionally, it is a powerful sculpting agent of the structure and function of the brain and body itself. In other words, you can consciously use your mind to change your brain, body, and relationships. Meditation is one such powerful vehicle to enact these changes.

Dr. Evan Thompson, philosopher and Buddhist psychology scholar, suggests that the act of meditation can be a much more meaningful and expansive endeavor. Meditating itself can be part of a more conscious self-evolution to live a disciplined, wakeful, purposeful, and wholesome life. In fact, in *A Path With Heart* (Kornfield, 1993) and his other teachings, Dr. Jack Kornfield—clinical psychologist, former Buddhist monk, and meditation teacher—has invited us into the realm of spirituality and heartfulness through everyday

https://doi.org/10.1037/0000309-027
The Thriving Therapist: Sustainable Self-Care to Prevent Burnout and Enhance Well-Being, by M. A. Hersh

living. Meditation is there for us to strengthen the loving, wholesome qualities of heart and mind that we ultimately may desire to cultivate. In this way, meditation isn't reduced to merely a tool but rather is a practice and way of being on the path of more mindful, heartful living.

The many forms, traditions, and styles of meditation are too numerous to count and certainly too many to address in this chapter. For psychotherapists with the desire to cultivate a caring and wise relationship with the self (and thus also with others), our purpose in this chapter is to highlight a few forms of meditation that can benefit our professional and personal lives. Most forms of meditation share a foundational set of values and virtues. We meditate to help alleviate our suffering and to uplift our spirit. We meditate to steady the mind and to ground the body. We meditate to discover more peacefulness, ease, and lightness of our being. And we meditate to be in loving relationship with ourselves and the world around us.

THE RISE IN POPULARITY OF MEDITATION

According to the National Center for Health Statistics, almost one in six Americans in 2017 had engaged in some type of meditation (e.g., mindfulness, mantra-based meditation, or spiritually based contemplative practice), in contrast to only one in 25 in 2012 (Clarke et al., 2018). That's a 300% increase in only 5 years!

This rise in public popularity has followed and aligned with a vast proliferation of more formal, structured teaching of mindfulness to the lay public as well as to health professionals worldwide. Now considered one of the founding fathers of secular mindfulness in the West, Jon Kabat-Zinn, PhD, created Mindfulness-Based Stress Reduction (MBSR; Kabat-Zinn, 2013), an 8-week course that began in hospital settings in the late 1970s for patients with chronic pain who had fallen through the cracks of the health care system.

Kabat-Zinn (2013) and his colleagues have helped disseminate MBSR throughout the world to every population and setting imaginable. Prominent mindfulness teachers and peace activists like His Holiness the Dalai Lama, the late Thich Nhat Hanh, Pema Chödrön, Jack Kornfield, Ekhart Tolle, Tara Brach, Sharon Salzberg, and many others (some of whom also happen to be psychotherapists) have founded their own mindfulness and meditation centers over the years. With virtual teaching formats becoming increasingly popular, many online platforms like Udemy, Coursera, and edX host a plethora of brief teachings and longer courses and workshops. Through smartphone technology, 85% of Americans, for example, now have access to apps (e.g., Headspace, Calm, 10% Happier, Insight Timer; Pew Research Center, 2021) specifically designed to help us meditate, grow our mindfulness skills, and live with greater presence and peace.

THE WIDE-RANGING BENEFITS OF MINDFULNESS MEDITATION

The findings from the empirical research on mindfulness-based meditation are clear. As individuals intentionally and consistently train their attention and nonjudgmental awareness of the here-and-now experience, they bring their mental and emotional processes under voluntary control (e.g., R. Walsh & Shapiro, 2006). For adult populations across a broad array of cohorts and for a diverse number of presenting issues (for reviews, see Didonna, 2009, and Baer, 2006), mindfulness training through meditation results in a host of cognitive improvements, including better attention, increased information processing speed (Moore & Malinowski, 2009), decreased task effort and more on-task (vs. distracted) thinking (Lutz et al., 2009), greater cognitive flexibility (Moore & Malinowski, 2009), and improved working memory (Jha et al., 2010).

Mindfulness meditation tends to benefit our emotional system as well. We start to feel less stressed (e.g., Lazar, 2005) with a greater sense of well-being (Carmody & Baer, 2008), and we begin to react less intensely to our own emotions and to situations that provoke emotional responses (Ortner et al., 2007). Mindfulness meditation can lower anxiety and depressed mood and improve self-regulation (Keng et al., 2011) and can decrease the frequency of suicidal ideation (Luoma & Villatte, 2012).

Although all the aforementioned benefits are related to the self, mindfulness meditation enhances relationships as well. The more one person meditates, the better their relationship quality (Barnes et al., 2007; Wachs & Cordova, 2007) and communication capacity (Dekeyser et al., 2008). As we meditate more regularly, we may find ourselves protected against the impacts of stressful relationship conflict (Barnes et al., 2007). Mindfulness meditation also positively affects our physiology and immune functioning. We tend to sleep better, have lower blood pressure, and demonstrate an improved immunological response to viruses (Davidson et al., 2003; see Grossman et al., 2004, for a review of physical health benefits).

PSYCHOTHERAPISTS WHO MEDITATE

Studies within cognitive and affective neuroscience have revealed several important findings and significant implications for helping professionals who sit with fellow human beings' worst suffering and highest hopes. The amygdala, the brain's seat of threat detection and stress response, has been shown to decrease in size and activation after several weeks of consistent mindfulness meditation (Hölzel et al., 2011). The hippocampus, associated with contextual memory and emotion regulation, has been shown to improve in its functionality. Although trauma can significantly affect the structure and function of the hippocampus, mindfulness meditation can be considered a sort of antidote as it can facilitate neurogenesis and help grow new neurons in this region of the brain. In addition, evidence suggests that 8 weeks of MBSR training can significantly alter our neural responses to emotional stimuli, helping to create less reactivity and more stability of presence (Farb et al., 2010; Williams, 2010). These findings suggest that mindfulness meditation shifts people's ability to use emotion regulation strategies in a way that enables them to experience emotion selectively and that the emotions they experience may be processed differently in the brain (Farb et al., 2010; Williams, 2010).

As mindfulness meditation is practiced, a sort of protective shield is built within the brain's complex structure and network of functions. The more we meditate, the more we can disengage from the usual, automatic neural pathways that were constructed previously. Thus, present-moment input can be better and more flexibly integrated (Siegel, 2007), and automatic pilot is replaced by wakeful, conscious processing of moment-to-moment information.

These findings have profound implications for psychotherapist self-care and well-being, prevention of occupational hazards, and enhancement of clinical competence. Indeed, studies of mindfulness training for mental health and allied health professionals shows great promise for reducing psychological stress, rumination, and negative affect (Shapiro et al., 2007); mitigating stress, anxiety, and depression (Rosenzweig et al., 2003; Shapiro et al., 1998); enhancing empathy (Shapiro et al., 1998; Wang, 2007); and deepening spirituality.

With an eye toward how to reduce risk of psychotherapists' occupational hazards, we can harness mindfulness to enhance mental health professionals' compassion (Shapiro et al., 2005) and our nonreactivity and nonjudgment to difficult situations (Kingsbury, 2009). Mindfulness skills are even suggested to predict therapist perceived self-efficacy (Greason & Cashwell, 2009), a quality that becomes compromised during the process of burnout.

At its core, mindfulness meditation builds self-awareness (e.g., Grepmair et al., 2007), self-compassion, and insight, some of the most vital and foundational facets of sustainable self-care for psychotherapists. Awareness and insight can help us to minimize unhealthy countertransference, reflect on our own needs, and experientially know and better manage what is occurring in the present moment. Trainees (see Christopher & Maris, 2010) and licensed professionals alike tend to benefit when formal mindfulness-based meditation is a part of their personal or professional lives.

Although the research on the impact of therapist meditation on client outcomes is quite limited and somewhat equivocal, one seminal study shows exceptional promise. Not only did meditating practitioners increase in their self-awareness over the course of 9 weeks (as compared with nonmeditating counterparts), but the inpatients of the meditating clinicians displayed greater reductions in symptoms, experienced faster recovery, and reported more improved well-being than did the patients of nonmeditating clinicians (Grepmair et al., 2007).

Because the vast majority of well-controlled meditation research conducted in the past 20 years has focused on mindfulness meditation (and mostly concentration practices like breath awareness), we place the majority of our attention in this chapter on this topic. There are of course many meditative traditions and likely hundreds of meditation styles. Appendix F provides additional selected mindfulness and meditation resources.

THE PRACTICE OF MINDFULNESS MEDITATION FOR PSYCHOTHERAPISTS

Every job in this world requires some set of skills. Psychotherapists largely rely on having well-tuned *emotional equipment*, but we may be strained in empathy, experiencing compassion fatigue, misreading nonverbal emotion in our clients' faces and postures, reacting quite strongly to our clients' emotions, or lacking resilience within our (therapeutic) relationships to the point of spillover into the rest of our lives. Mindfulness meditation happens to address all these skills and may be one of the best all-around tools to sharpen our equipment.

Mindfulness meditation practice is just that, a practice. It is not a one-and-done endeavor, nor is it "achieved" once you complete an 8-week course or finish a 30-day challenge through an app you're using. While courses, programs, and challenges can be integral to acquiring the necessary mindfulness skills, and community (or *sangha*) is often quite invaluable to sustaining one's practice and getting the necessary feedback to deepen one's meditative skill, we can consider meditation to be an important part of what we do as often as we can do it. As we do when maintaining good dental hygiene, we don't overly romanticize meditation, but we also don't ignore its potential as a powerful self-care act with a diverse array of professional and personal benefits.

Since mindfulness is the awareness that arises from consciously and lovingly paying attention to the unfolding present moment, mindfulness meditation begins with the foundational practice of intentionally paying attention to the here-and-now with as much curiosity, acceptance, and patience as possible (Chödrön, 2018). Many supporting qualities make mindfulness, well, mindfulness, versus simply paying attention really well. What supports mindful awareness is a set of qualities demonstrating easefulness, stability, gentleness but firmness, lovingness, openness, nonjudgment, and wise discernment.

Whether we meditate seated or by walking, we purposefully direct our attention to an object that we can follow. It is through one simple objective—to make gentle, nonjudgmental contact with the present moment over and over again—that we begin to cultivate a breadth and depth of regulatory capacities. Through the instruction to be gentle and curious with ourselves, we further develop a kindness and compassion with all parts of us as well as with those around us. We begin to realize that through the training of loving attention as we meditate, we are training many of the intrinsic self-care qualities presented in Part III of this book.

Conveniently, the cultivation of making gentle, nonreactive contact with the unfolding moments of reality can profoundly affect our own well-being as well as our relationships with our clients. In fact, it is through our meditative training that we can become more mindful and effective agents of change and transformation in our clients. And we become our own best allies in the process, observing all facets of ourselves with as much kindness, compassion, and patience as possible.

What follows is a brief description of a select number of meditations that have been shown through thousands of studies to effect positive and lasting change. The more you put in, the more benefit you will likely find. However, mindfulness meditation is a practice rather than a competition or race. Starting where you are is far more effective than starting where you think you should be. If that means trying a meditation for 60 seconds each day for a 2-week period, so be it. Purposefully carving out time and space to sit down and meditate *is* self-caring in and of itself.

Breath Awareness Meditation

Find a time during which and a space in which you will be relatively undisturbed. Arrange yourself in a comfortable seated position, your body attentive and alert yet relaxed. Your head should be aligned with your neck and the rest of your spine. Imagine that you're allowed to take up the space you're embodying, thus inhabiting a self-respect and dignity. Close your eyes if you like, or keep them open and gaze out and down gently several feet in front of you. Just notice your physical body sitting there, all the points of contact between your body and what is supporting you underneath or in back. Feel into those junctures between your body and its surroundings. Then make a purposeful shift to begin earnestly paying attention to your breathing. Each breath in and out is its own experience. Each breath cycle is to be felt for exactly how it is rather than what it's supposed to be. Practice following your breath with your mind as the air flows in and reaches the top and then begins to flow out and reaches the bottom.

When (not if) thoughts enter your mind and feelings/sensations are felt in your body, this is your opportunity (over and over again) to strengthen your mindfulness muscle by acknowledging where your mind went and then gently but firmly bringing it back to the experience of your breath. Muscles that haven't been worked out need to be gradually exercised. Therefore, it may feel quite hard to let your breathing fill your whole awareness without distraction after distraction. That's normal and OK. For your allotted time (whether 1, 5, 10, or 15 minutes and beyond), just do your best to maintain an attitude of "I'm here for this meditation, and I'll do my best to stay on my breath, to know when I've drifted off, and to return to my breath." Thank yourself at the end of your meditation for the gift you've given yourself, no matter where your mind went.

Walking Meditation

It's quite hard to meditate in a hurricane but much easier in the light drizzling rain of spring. Walking is a wonderful way to bring meditation into an animated form, which is especially helpful when we're tired, restless, or agitated. Using the same principles as in breath awareness meditation, you can set aside a few minutes to walk without any other purpose except to pay gentle but firm attention to the movement of your body through space. Find a space that allows you to take at least five slowly paced steps back and forth in a straight line. Walk at a pace that is slow enough for you to focus on the swinging of each leg through the air while the foot of the other leg is planted on the ground. And then in an instant the weight shifts, and the swinging leg has landed with your heel hitting the ground while the other foot has launched your other leg to move through space. So much is happening in such a small space and short period of time. Our objective is to notice, without judgment, such movements.

You can synchronize your breath with your walking movements, but this isn't necessary. As in breath awareness meditation, when you notice your mind drifting away from the movements, gently but firmly bring it back. You may need to do this 100 times during a few minutes of walking meditation.

That's how it goes. Acceptance, patience, and generosity of spirit are all culti-vated by giving yourself permission to go through this process during your meditative practice.

Wheel of Awareness Practice

Created by Dr. Daniel Siegel, psychiatrist and pioneering mindfulness teacher, the wheel of awareness meditation (Siegel, 2018; https://www.wheelofawareness. com/) is an active method of training our purposeful attention to reach outward through our five senses, inward to our bodily sensations (sixth sense) and mental activities (seventh sense), and then outward again to the interconnec-tions with the world (eighth sense). Start with slowing yourself down a bit and perhaps closing your eyes. Imagine that your bare awareness is the center of the wheel, the hub. Just be aware that you are breathing, in and out.

From there, you can "send spokes" that contain the objects of our eight sense gates out to the rim of the wheel. Open your eyes for a moment and intentionally pay attention to something you see. Just notice it. Then come right back to the hub. Now send a spoke out to an object through your auditory sense gate. What do you hear? Just notice for few moments. After observing this sound, move your attention back to the hub, the still, silent place inside you.

Continue this process with the three other basic senses before moving back to your hub to be aware of your breathing, nothing more and nothing less. Now intentionally send a spoke of attention to the interior bodily sensa-tions that reside within your head and run down to your toes. This process is like a mini *body scan* found within MBSR courses. Progressively sense what it feels like within each bodily area. As you breathe in and out, feel your diaphragm expanding and contracting. Come back to your hub to be aware of your breath before moving on to deliberate attention to your mental activities, such as your thoughts and images. What's there? Just notice and label. Be receptive to what's there without getting caught up. Finally, after returning to your hub, you can send a spoke of attention to interpersonal connections in the world. Open your awareness to the fact that you are in the world with others. You are a child, perhaps a parent, maybe a sibling, a friend, many people's therapist, a colleague. Become increasingly aware of how interconnected you are.

Before wrapping up this meditative practice, you can wish for others in the world goodwill and freedom from suffering. You can wish this goodwill for yourself, and you can wish that everyone, including you, be happy, free from suffering, and able to live a meaningful and fulfilling life.

ADDRESSING THE FIVE HINDRANCES IN PROFESSIONAL LIFE THROUGH MEDITATION

When we meditate, we tend to run across what in the Buddhist tradition is called the *five hindrances*. These factors tend to hinder our progress to getting to know the mind and body more easefully. The five include (a) sensory desire; (b) ill will, aversion, and anger; (c) sloth, torpor, and boredom; (d) restlessness and worry; and (e) doubt. In other words, our mind–body says, "I want this so badly," "I don't like this at all," "This is so tedious," "I can't sit still, and my mind won't stop," and "What am I even doing?"

As you might imagine, these obstructive forces don't arise just in meditation; they inhabit all our lives at various times. By working with these hindrances as we meditate, we become increasingly adept at working with them off the meditation cushion too. In the therapy room, we're sitting there week after week with a client who perhaps is perceived as so boring that we yawn automatically and incessantly whenever they enter the room. Perhaps we yearn repeatedly for cancellations with a few folks in our caseload because we feel so inexplicably ineffective in their presence. Or maybe we almost squirm with an inner tension when we sit across from a particularly anxious client who just can't seem to regulate. And so as we meditate and greet whatever arises as it arises, we practice clearly and lovingly identifying what mental and bodily forces are present in that moment.

Paradoxically, the more we face such hindrances and see them for what they are, the less power they hold over us. Thus, we become our own best self-knowers and self-advocates as we increasingly confront *what is* on and off the cushion. Lest we get overwhelmed with which meditation to do, how much time it might take, and how so much other important stuff of life needs to be accomplished, let's consider the simple encouragement that only a few minutes of meditation practice each day can provide enormous benefit now and into the future. We likely impart this basic notion to our clients when we're fairly sure they would greatly benefit from therapeutic practice or homework. Surely, we can apply this to ourselves.

As meditation helps us move through life with less resistance and more acceptance, we can inhabit our lives with greater ease and flow. Such positive qualities of mind and body are precisely what the self-care and well-being approach discussed next in Chapter 27 offers us. The subtle energy practices found within energy psychology and energy medicine are increasingly revealing themselves to be effective mind–body tools for a wide range of challenges that we face.

27 SUBTLE ENERGY PRACTICES

If you want to find the secrets of the universe, think in terms of energy, frequency, and vibration.

—Nicola Tesla

Imagine sitting with one of your clients whose emotions are often intense and jarring to experience (for both of you). Your client is easily moved to tears of overwhelm; often catastrophizes relatively benign situations; makes grand, sweeping statements of hopelessness and helplessness; and periodically reveals acute suicidal feelings. What feelings arise right now as we conjure up this scene? You wouldn't be alone if you imagined or felt a sense of dread. Now let's imagine that a small but significant portion of your caseload generates such feelings within you at some point each week. Talk about unique occupational hazards and the need for powerful self-care and resilience-building tools.

https://doi.org/10.1037/0000309-028
The Thriving Therapist: Sustainable Self-Care to Prevent Burnout and Enhance Well-Being, by M. A. Hersh

Now let's envision that right after an emotionally overwhelming session you take a mere 180 seconds to tend to your hyperaroused state. After taking a deep breath, you assess the intensity of your emotions, sensations, and psychological upset (maybe on a scale of 0 to 10). You start tapping with mild pressure on a few designated points on your face, upper torso, and hands. Point by point you focus your attention on your hyperarousal, empathic distress, feelings of helplessness or hopelessness, or sense of dread to see that particular client again next week. You continue to tap, your mind focused on the sensations and feelings in your body while verbally expressing language that resonates with your particular inner experience.

As you near the end of your energy tapping self-care break, you increasingly focus on the intention of *releasing* any residual feelings and sensations that might still be quite powerful and negatively charged. You may even invite into your system some intention to embody and express the qualities you truly desire to experience—equanimity, calm, peace, resilience, compassion, confidence, and healthy emotional boundaries. After these several rounds of self-care tapping, you decide to check in with yourself (subjectively, on the 0-to-10 scale) to assess how you're feeling and the cognitive, emotional, and physiological changes that may have occurred.

ENERGY PSYCHOLOGY AND THE FOURTH WAVE OF THERAPEUTIC INTERVENTIONS

This clinically relevant and inherently self-caring practice described in the beginning of this chapter is an abbreviated version of *emotional freedom techniques* (EFT; Craig, 2008), colloquially known as "tapping," that sits under the larger umbrella of *energy psychology* (EP; Gallo, 1998). Some have dubbed energy tapping "psychological acupressure" because some points on the body that acupuncture and acupressure use are harnessed within these approaches for psychological (and somatic) transformative purposes.

EFT and other EP technologies are considered to be the "fourth wave" of psychotherapeutic approaches (see Stapleton, 2019), as they purposefully tap into the mind–body connection, the process of neuroplasticity, and memory reconsolidation to effect positive changes to one's entire system. An individual's psychology, emotions, cognitions, physiology, endocrine response, neurology, and even genetic expression can change under the influence of subtle energetic manipulation.

One of the first field research endeavors using *thought field therapy* (TFT; Callahan & Callahan, 1996), the precursor to EFT, was with Rwandan orphans. A significant percentage of these adolescents (100% based on caregiver report and 72% based on self-report) had severe posttraumatic stress disorder (PTSD) after witnessing their families being brutally murdered. Using a TFT trauma resolution protocol, researchers guided these Rwandan teens through a simple acupoint tapping sequence. At 1-year follow-up, only 8% (caregiver report) and 16% (adolescent report) of these youth met criteria for PTSD, paired with a 77% (caregiver report) and 54% (adolescent report) reduction in mean PTSD scores.

Since then, scores of clinical trials have suggested that EP approaches hold great promise for rapidly and sustainably altering our mind–body–brain patterned reactions to traumatic memories, anxiety, depression, pain, limiting beliefs, everyday stress triggers, and motivational states for optimal performance (Bach et al., 2019; Feinstein, 2019; Nelms & Castel, 2016; Sebastian & Nelms, 2017). Moreover, stress biochemistry, physiology, and neuroimaging studies have demonstrated very large reductions in cortisol (24%–43%; Church et al., 2012; Stapleton, 2019), increases in heart coherence and heart rate variability, lower blood pressure, improvement in brainwave patterning (Bach et al., 2019), and deactivation in certain brain regions associated with overeating, food cravings, urges, and emotional overwhelm (Stapleton et al., 2019). Researchers have even begun analyzing data from more than 250,000 worldwide users of The Tapping Solution smartphone app. Examining the effects of brief guided tapping sessions for experiences of stress and anxiety, Church et al. (2020) found highly significant reductions in stress and anxiety. Such findings show great promise for ease of energy tapping accessibility as well as emotional benefit.

EP approaches are derived in part from long and varied cultural traditions wherein health and well-being are accessible and modifiable through the subtle energy systems of the body (e.g., meridians, chakras, biofield). In the case of EFT energy tapping, we're relying on millennia worth of knowledge and successful use of acupoint therapies for hundreds of physical and mental health conditions (e.g., Au et al., 2015; M. N. Chen et al., 2013; Gach & Henning, 2004; Helmreich et al., 2006).

As pioneers such as clinical psychologist Dr. Roger Callahan began to experiment with tapping on certain acupoints to effect change in clients' severe anxiety struggles, a new system of psychotherapeutic intervention was born. What Callahan was intuiting as he had his clients repeatedly apply mild pressure to certain well-known acupoints on the face and upper torso (as they focused on their fears) has now been shown to produce local and brain-based electrical signals. Through mechanosensory transduction, local cells translate mechanical stimulation into electrical activity (Gillespie & Walker, 2001) that can rapidly disrupt what neurologically underlies a host of psychological and psychiatric symptoms (Stapleton et al., 2019). These signals are thought to travel at incredibly fast speeds (i.e., almost instantaneously) through the body's vast array of highly conductive connective tissue (see Stefanov et al., 2013).

Unlike acupressure or acupuncture for physical conditions, most acupoint psychotherapeutic approaches, as a form of either therapy or self-care practice, require our mindful attention on the issue we're trying to address. It's truly a cognitive–somatic or mind–body integrative approach. The mental targets of our physical tapping could be at the felt-symptom level, including feelings about the symptom, specific past experiences, or deeply held beliefs about oneself and the world. As we direct our attention to a designated area of our experience, we metaphorically point our acupoint tapping to what's needed. If our attention is scattered or dissociated, we may feel some degree of stress reduction as we tap but likely not the mitigation of the specific issues we may be interested in addressing.

Roger Callahan and other subtle energy practitioners refer to the *thought field*, the field of energetic activity stimulated by placing one's attention on an image, thought, feeling, or sensation in the body (S. Eldringhoff, personal communication, December 15, 2021). Although the term "thought field" isn't widely used, we're all familiar enough with the experience in which the mere thought of a distressing memory generates afflictive feelings, protective gestures, neurophysiological reactions, and related thoughts that comprise the memory's embodied network. *That* is the thought field.

Whether we're brought into a familiar thought field by a client's troubling behavior in the therapy room or we're struggling with our own difficult feelings, tapping on select acupoints while in this state will help organize, regulate, and balance the field of energy. Ideally, this regulatory tapping process rapidly and effectively relieves symptoms and can even reconsolidate traumatic memories and integrate new emotional learnings (Feinstein, 2019). As a comprehensive energy psychology practitioner, I see these kinds of full mind–body shifts all the time, even after a few minutes of tapping. There are other techniques for facilitating the sustainability of such changes, a few of which we'll entertain at the end of this chapter.

SUBTLE ENERGY PRACTICES FOR MITIGATING OCCUPATIONAL HAZARDS

Energy tapping, other EP approaches, and energy medicine (Eden, 2008) methods may have great potential for helping to depotentiate reactivities inside and outside of the therapy room. For example, imagine the client described at the outset of this chapter. Briefly applying energy tapping after several sessions of seeing that client and her particular constellation of affect, language, and posture may mitigate your distress in the future and allow you to be more equanimous and present, for yourself, for her, and for the clients you see after that client.

Colleagues who use EP methods have spoken about their wide-ranging utility. For example, Michaela Kohmetscher, LICSW, DCEP—colleague and peer consultee—noted that "EP techniques not only help me get grounded in between clients but also help me in closing out my day at the office before heading home" (M. Kohmetscher, personal communication, January 2021). These regulating and cleansing functions, not unlike those in polarity breathing (see Chapter 24, this volume), can be harnessed both for short- and long-term purposes. Kohmetscher also stated that EP methods have helped her "get out of [her] head and into [her] body." She uses EP methods to "ground [herself], calm [her] nervous system, practice self-compassion, and to gain a better understanding and acceptance of [herself]." In fact, EP can give us permission to feel worthy of self-care, something that can be a significant and underlying barrier to treating ourselves more fairly and lovingly.

Energy tapping can not only decrease the impact of daily stresses and pressures but can also be harnessed to mitigate the Big Four occupational hazards (see Chapter 3). Study after study conducted on the effects of EFT on posttraumatic stress have revealed very large reductions in trauma symptomatology, with symptom abatement holding steady at various follow-up times (Sebastian & Nelms, 2017). Given such powerful findings, it stands to reason that psychotherapists' secondary traumatic stress and vicarious traumatization could be readily addressed through energy tapping protocols.

We also have evidence that weekend EFT workshops can also produce lasting change in health care workers' distress, pain, and cravings, especially when tapping is practiced in an ongoing fashion (Church & Brooks, 2010). Both the intensity and the breadth of symptomatology were significantly reduced, and the gains maintained up to 3 months later. I have witnessed shifts like these in clients who are medical and mental health professionals. Not surprisingly, the more regularly (even if briefly) we apply tapping methods, the better the outcomes seem to be.

We could imagine that empathy distress and compassion fatigue also lend themselves easily to the therapeutic, resilience-building, and risk-protective effects of EFT tapping and other subtle energy practices. For example, I was once listening intently to a terrified client nervously talk about his wife's recent diagnosis of a malignant brain tumor. Although I've mostly resolved traumatic events surrounding my own cancer diagnosis in 2007, I was not prepared to hear this. As my client emoted, I could feel myself both increasingly overwhelmed and on the verge of dissociating. I took the reins in that moment and inconspicuously started to apply intermittent pressure to a few powerful acupoints in the EFT tapping protocol. I noticed a palpable shift in my overwhelm and feelings of disconnection. After the session, I took a few minutes to engage in a more comprehensive tapping sequence to help *clear out* any residual disruptions in my system. Although it continued to be quite difficult to hear this client's stories of his wife, I was much less empathically distressed and much more emotionally present.

The beauty of energy tapping as a self-care practice for psychotherapists is that it can be used on the spot or as a vehicle for ongoing self-work, healing, and growth. Perhaps you become overwhelmed by guilt and self-condemnation after learning that a client's romantic relationship fell apart despite your working hard to help the client preserve the relationship. It may help quite a bit to embody equanimity as best you can and lovingly remind yourself that this client's life is simply beyond your control. And yet, you may continue to feel plagued by doubt, guilt, and regret. Energy tapping in these instances could help you feel better able to move on from the grip of these afflictive emotions.

At the same time, the hidden power within EP approaches is that they can reveal associated psychological–emotional material that may be running the show behind the scenes. What is acutely felt as guilt and self-doubt about not adequately helping your client may give way to foundational experiences from your formative years. Perhaps you had experienced earnestly offering support to a loved one only to have it harshly rejected, or you tried to "save" a depressed friend who ultimately died by suicide.

As discussed in earlier chapters, research on clinical and counseling psychologists suggests that more than two thirds of women and one third of men have reported childhood histories of physical or sexual abuse (Pope & Feldman-Summers, 1992) and that women psychologists are more likely than non-mental health professionals to have experienced the death or psychiatric hospitalization of a parent (Elliott & Guy, 1993). Many of us have experiences like these that lay dormant, affecting our schemas and likely influencing how we receive clients' material. Doing subtle energy work on those core experiences may help reconsolidate the affectively charged nature of these memories (Feinstein, 2019) so that our present and future can be lived with less emotional reactivity and greater perceptual clarity and interpersonal ease.

EFT TAPPING PROTOCOL

The world of energy tapping and subtle energy practice is vast (see Appendix G). Although it's well beyond the scope of this chapter to cover all nuances and complexities, the foundational elements are presented here so that you're well-versed in helping yourself in a more streamlined but still quite powerful manner.

Each point in the tapping sequence corresponds to an acupoint on a given subtle energy meridian according to traditional Chinese medicine. All points can be tapped on with mild pressure for a minimum of eight taps. Referencing Figure 27.1 for the EFT tapping procedure (Bonnell, 2008; see TapIntoHeaven.com), begin tapping on the karate chop point or rubbing what is called the "sore spot," which should literally feel sore or tender when massaged in a circle.

In this initial setup phase, you're establishing the issue (e.g., symptom, difficult memory) to be addressed. You may acknowledge it out loud, or in your mind you may place an image or attach a verbal label to your experience. As you bring your attention to the issue at hand, you can say to yourself

FIGURE 27.1. EFT Tapping Procedure

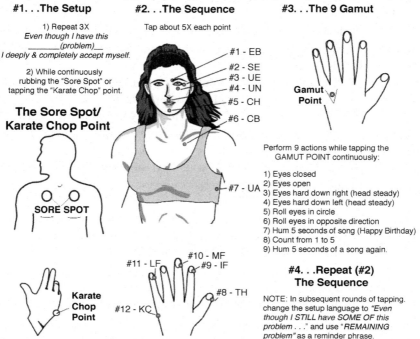

Note. From *Tap Into Heaven*, by Gwenn Bonnell, 2008 (https://www.tapintoheaven.com/charts/index.shtml). Copyright 2008 by Gwenn Bonnell. Reprinted with permission.

several times in a row something like "Even though I feel _____ [problem phrase], I deeply and completely love and accept myself [acceptance phrase]." Many people do not resonate with this version of the acceptance phrase. For this reason, you are encouraged to develop variations on this theme that align with what you need at any given time. For example, you may say, "I would like to accept myself deeply" or "I choose now to be willing to acknowledge how I really feel."

This setup statement and tapping the side of hand/karate chop point or rubbing the sore spot primes our energy system for the next step, although the setup phase is therapeutic and self-caring in and of itself. With your mind still attending to the issue or experience at hand, start traversing the face from the eyebrow point to the outer eye point and then the under eye point, followed by the under nose and chin points. Continue tapping on the collarbone and then the underarm point. The hand points, sometimes left out of other EFT protocols, are useful for several reasons. Theoretically speaking, these are acupoints along other important energy meridians. Practically speaking, you can hold or press these points in a session without your client really knowing what you're doing. It's your secret tool to help keep yourself regulated, balanced, and present. Ultimately, if you're doing subtle energy work with a client, you'll be doing tapping along with them, and no secret self-care work is needed.

After you've tapped on all the points listed, you've completed a *round*. Depending on the time you have and the issue you're exploring, you may do as few as one round or as many as it takes to help you feel more regulated, calm, clear, or present. It's always a wise idea to pause after a round or two and reassess how you're feeling and what you're experiencing. This brief check-in process helps guide you in your next step and directs where to place your mind's attention on your body's energy.

USING ENERGY TAPPING TO ADDRESS INTERNAL BLOCKS, BARRIERS, AND OBJECTIONS TO SELF-CARING

As discussed in Chapter 7, we may hold beliefs and be confronted with various barriers to taking the best care of ourselves as possible in a sustainable way. We can do EFT tapping (specifically on the side of hand point) for *psychological reversals* (see the previously described energy tapping protocol), our (less-than-consciously held) beliefs that often stand in the way of our moving in the direction we think we need or want to move but are having trouble doing so.

The big five energetic objections we often run across involve possibility, safety, deservingness, identity, and willingness. In other words, if you continue to have difficulties taking care of your own needs, you might use EFT tapping to address whether you believe that self-care is really possible, that it's truly safe for you to turn toward yourself in this way, that you deeply deserve it, that it might alter some part of who think you are, and/or that you're willing to make the necessary shifts toward self-caring.

As psychotherapist Michaela Kohmetscher noted, EP techniques "have given [her] permission to feel worthy of self-care, a psychological reversal that ruled and kept [her] in hustle and work mode" (Kohmetscher, personal communication, January 2021). Psychotherapists may also have idiosyncratic beliefs and rules that shape their relationships with self-care. As these beliefs and rules are explored, psychological reverse tapping can help to decrease their power and presence, thus inviting more freedom to relate to ourselves with greater ease and care.

INTEGRATING SUBTLE ENERGY PRACTICES INTO YOUR DAY

As psychotherapists, we have many options to integrate subtle energy practices into our busy days. Stepping outside of the EFT tapping protocol, we can look to tried and true acupressure points to press and hold for several seconds at a time while in a therapy session and certainly before and after. As acupuncturist and Eastern healing arts scholar Thomas Richardson, MA, LiAc, suggested, we may use two potent points opposite one another on the wrist (Pericardium 6 and Triple Heater 5; see Figure 27.2) to regulate interpersonal energetic and emotional boundaries with our clients as well as to decrease anxiety, stress, and a cloudy mind (T. Richardson, personal communication, September 2016).

One of my favorite subtle energy exercises is found within the comprehensive energy psychology approach, which is a cohesive series of steps and activities designed to address multiple systems of energy in the body. When we're feeling particularly emotionally overwhelmed from a difficult session, for example, we may take a minute to ourselves and engage in what is called the heart–brain dyslexia correction. Stephanie Eldringhoff, MA, LMFT, DCEP, TFTdx—a pioneer in EP as well as a certified energy medicine practitioner—developed a fast, effective, and soothing version of this technique: Place one hand over the heart, and use the other hand like a brush to smooth from the temple up and around close to the ear and down to the top of the shoulder. Repeat this motion several times, then switch to the other side of your head, using the same hand. Repeat this procedure switching the heart hand.

FIGURE 27.2. On-the-Spot Acupressure for Preserving Healthy Energetic Boundaries

Triple Heater-5
(Palm side down)

Pericardium-6 Acupoint
(Palm side up)

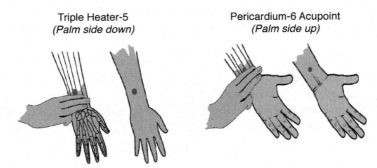

Note. From *Essential Mind-Body Practices to Ground and Rebound: Practitioners' Daily Self-Care Guide* (p. 7), by M. A. Hersh and T. Richardson, 2016, The Thriving Therapist (https://www.thethrivingtherapist.org/essential-mind-body-practices/). Copyright 2016 by M. A. Hersh. Reprinted with permission.

Technically, heart–brain dyslexia is not dyslexia as we know it. It was originally dubbed this because the emotional and mental energies were detected to be miscommunicating with one another. Doing this exercise puts them back in sync, very much like practicing ways to strengthen our wise mind, a process integral to dialectical behavior therapy. In addition, when we do this energetic correction, we're facilitating the organized flow of our systemic energy, not necessarily some single-point issue we're trying to resolve (although this technique can work focally too). Therefore, the more we engage in this corrective practice, the more we encourage our emotional mind and reasoning mind to connect in an organized and harmonious fashion.

Another favorite subtle energy practice is the *energy sweep*, developed by Eldringhoff and MacEwan (2005). Part of the more comprehensive *rapid relief process* (see https://stagefright.com/rapidrelief/), the energy sweep is a great tool for actively engaging your entire body in facilitating energetic movement throughout several subtle energy systems of the body (see Appendix H for full description, with illustrations).

Countless other subtle energy practices help to up-, down-, and interpersonally regulate one's mind and body throughout the psychotherapist's busy and stressful days. A set of powerful energy practices is the *5-minute Eden energy routine*, created by energy medicine pioneer, Donna Eden (2010, 2021). Linda Geronilla, energy medicine (EM) specialist, conducted an 8-week study of teachers (who are no strangers to stress and burnout) using a modified daily EM routine. Compared with a control group receiving no energy routine, the daily EM group reported improvements in memory, concentration, and energy levels while showing positive changes in several key brain areas associated with optimal neurophysiological and emotional performance (i.e., prefrontal cortex, cerebellum, temporal lobe, and anterior cingulate gyrus; Eden & Feinstein, 2008).

Although this brief but powerful daily routine has received only limited empirical attention, I have found it invaluable as a sustainable self-care tool. It has helped me to prevent the onset of physical illness as well as to maintain a sense of vital energy and self-regulation throughout my stressful days. When I don't remember to do it, I feel its absence. When I do remember, I'm very grateful I did.

All of this discussion of actively doing things on behalf on our own professional and personal well-being may produce a bit of overwhelm. When do we get to simply rest, allowing ourselves to rejuvenate and restore a healthier balance between doing and relaxing? That's exactly what we'll explore in Chapter 28, which focuses on rest, time off, and how to recharge our batteries.

28 REST, TIME OFF, AND RECHARGING OUR BATTERIES

Almost everything will work again if you unplug it for a few minutes, including you.

—Anne Lamott

Greg, an early-career clinical psychologist, was constantly working. He was employed at an independent group practice, and although his billing was done by a specialist, Greg was responsible for all other facets of his caseload. He also liked to do research and teach and was always interested in taking on new and exciting opportunities in his specialization of young adult depression. Greg admired his (more experienced) colleagues, who also maintained very full caseloads as well as professional side gigs that they enjoyed. However, Greg's partner, Jimmy, was growing increasingly concerned and frustrated at Greg's workaholic tendencies. After many conflicts with Jimmy, constant sicknesses year after year, and the emerging threat of contracting the COVID-19 virus, Greg waved his white flag. He knew he had to slow down.

https://doi.org/10.1037/0000309-029
The Thriving Therapist: Sustainable Self-Care to Prevent Burnout and Enhance Well-Being, by M. A. Hersh

The recuperation of our precious energy can be a deliberately chosen self-caring act. Time specifically spent *not working* can give us a temporary break from overworking, overcommitting, and inviting higher burnout risk, and it can facilitate long-term scaffolding for our physical, emotional, mental, and relational health. The aunt of one of my clients apparently used to say that how you spend your downtime shapes how you spend your uptime.

Physically resting and not doing much at all for a few hours is of course quite different from taking time off to go skiing, sightseeing in a new city, or taking an extended weekend hiking on some nearby trails. Any of these active breaks is still a respite from our professional lives and can provide necessary revitalizing energy to our system. Conversely, we might desire a discernable slowdown as we choose to literally just sit around, perhaps sipping some coffee and reading a book or two or 10. (If this sounds like an idyllic scene, maybe you could plan one of these coffee and book afternoons in the near future, even if it's for 20 minutes in your kitchen, bedroom, front step, or back porch.) Regardless of the particular form of respite you choose, one of the core tenets of this chapter is to consider time off and downtime as a purposeful and sustainable enactment of genuine self-care.

It's quite healthy to consider the various outlets we may seek for our downtime. Asking "What's my particular cup of downtime tea?" can help push us toward more intimate knowledge of how we typically (and atypically) like to relax and recuperate. Some days, weeks, or months you may want something very familiar or routine, whereas at other times you may need diversity or adventure. Creating a menu of downtime and rest options can therefore be very helpful.

GIVING OURSELVES PERMISSION TO REST

Many of us are embedded in a very fast-paced, frenetic culture of doing more with less. We are, as Dr. Ned Hallowell wrote, overstretched, overbooked, and about to snap (Hallowell, 2007). Some of us have clued into this cultural phenomenon and have made conscious decisions to slow down, move our residences to less bustling environments or into more natural surroundings, or build in downtime as part of our work week. Highly sensitive therapists, in particular, are strongly encouraged to "figure out how [to do] less to accomplish more." As the "basis of good work is being rested, when [we're] rested [our] sensitivity will help [us] find ways to be more effective" (Aron, 2010, p. 179).

How many of us truly allow ourselves to rest and recharge, let alone invite such a recuperative spirit into our lives in a purposeful and meaningful manner? We might see deliberate rest as a sign of weakness or as a luxury, as if we're supposed to be working hard and constantly productive or else we're not proving our worth. Perhaps we worry that if we rest, we'll never get back into productivity mode. We might have had real-world struggles with this phenomenon, and we're now fearful of confronting this challenge again.

Recalling the discussion of knowing our habits of mind and emotion (see Chapter 10, this volume), we can imagine that a tendency of the brain–body toward too much activity (Wehrenberg, 2018) would prompt us to be more or less constantly in *drive mode* (Gilbert, 2005), an ever-changing mental, physiological, hormonal, and behavioral state of movement toward goals, achievement, and productivity of some sort. Resting and relaxing then would ostensibly be unwelcome visitors in a vast sea of things to be done, along with a perceived lack of time in which to relax.

On the other hand, for some of us, resting and taking time off may be welcome sources of recharging our batteries and simply doing something (or even nothing) for ourselves. Resting and kicking back may be pleasurable and desirable, thus creating a paradoxical drive to not be so driven for a little while. Dr. April McDowell, a colleague and a couple's therapist, noted how much more compassionate she is with herself if she "needs to do something more passive for self-care like binging on Netflix or spending hours on good books" (A. McDowell, personal communication, March 10, 2021). Those of us who readily enter this realm of respite and relaxation know full well how restorative it can be and how much we may ultimately seek and benefit from this self-caring motivation and state of being.

Although regular or at least periodic rest a good thing, it's important to note what we're taking a break from. When we utter the words "I need a break," are we aware of how much or how hard we've been working? We don't need to justify rest, and yet acknowledging what we're resting from gives us an even deeper understanding of the patterns of work and respite that possibly contribute to our feelings of burnout on the one hand and upward spirals of well-being on the other.

SEEDING THE HABITS OF WORK, STRESS, AND REST

Although our temperaments lay the foundation, so much of our attitudes and behavioral coping responses to stress and work can depend on how we were raised. Our caregivers were constantly modeling, mostly out of our conscious awareness, how to feel about and engage with work, time off, and time itself. In fact, being exposed as children to parents' high levels of stress can affect the expression of our DNA (Essex et al., 2013).

Do you remember how different family members managed the stress of work or of raising a family? Did you regularly witness a parent taking time for themselves or declaring that the family needed some down time? Did you have parents who insisted that you went to school even if you were sick? Or perhaps they let you stay home simply because you said you needed a day to recharge and reset. Did your family take vacations, even if they were brief and inexpensive? How did you learn how time could be apportioned? How were your own childhood experiences with chill time differentially reinforced or punished (in the operant conditioning sense of the words)? What happened when you were quite productive with your schoolwork? Perhaps breaks were encouraged, or maybe you constantly felt the need to keep working or keep helping the family.

I have a counseling psychologist friend whose mother would constantly mock her for "just being so lazy" when she slept in an hour or two later than what the mother expected from her. This dynamic continued well into graduate school, when the friend returned home for the holidays and other brief visits. Indeed, our mindset and relationship to rest and purposeful rejuvenation is also powerfully shaped throughout our adult life—during our formal professional training years, within our new independent life with a partner or family perhaps, and from the invisible cultural forces outside of us.

HAVE A GREAT VACATION, BUT PLEASE DON'T LEAVE

Unlike other professions (even research-based positions that many of our compatriots might hold), psychotherapy contains within it a very unique relationship. And within this relationship can arise feelings from the client about their therapist taking time off. From the client's perspective, therapist vacations can signal abandonment, relief, indifference, annoyance, or even devastation (Howes, 2010). If you are highly attuned to your clients' needs and feelings, you may experience an empathic distress around taking time off and leaving and feel driven to continue to work on their behalf.

We may also find that we're saddled with the feelings (and deep-seated beliefs) of needing to help our clients at all costs and at all times. We may indeed be consummate "people pleasers" (see Chapter 11 for discussion of relational patterns and needs) wherein our relationships are marked with conflict avoidance and placing others' needs above ours. When this patterning happens within our psychotherapeutic relationships, we may feel guilty that we're somehow abandoning our clients in their time of need when we take an hour, a few days, or even a few weeks to ourselves. This guilt may be linked to a larger belief that as psychotherapists we are beholden to (and responsible for) fixing, mending, healing, or even saving a client.

When I work with other therapists and nurses as my clients, they implicitly understand the need for time off. Some will almost attempt to get me to skip a week if I'm searching for a new time to reschedule them because of *their* scheduling conflict. "Please," they will say, "you deserve your Friday off too. No worries. I'll see you next week."

HEALTHY WAYS TO NOT WORK

Let's now explore four core ways to build rest, time off, and recharging time into your professional and personal life. The idea is to broaden our view of rest and time off so that we can choose from a menu of options rather than feeling railroaded into perceiving downtime in only one way or another. We'll proceed from the most commonly held notion of rest, the *vacation*, and end with more subtle and everyday ways of recharging and resetting, *daily self-care breaks*.

Vacations

I once knew a colleague who was so committed to her psychotherapy practice that the thought of taking extended time off never really crossed her mind. This mindset may seem unusual, and not entertaining the thought of taking a vacation may indeed seem rare. In fact, according to one survey, 83% of psychologists reported "taking vacations" as a form of purposeful self-care (Cooper, 2009).

What does this look like for you? Do you plan and budget for one or more vacations a year? Giving yourself a gift of a vacation, even if it's many months down the road, can exercise vital muscles of self-care and well-being. In fact, planning and getting excited about a vacation can be almost as important as the vacation itself.

When your vacation(s) finally arrive, how do you spend them? In other words, is your mind allowing the rest of you to be present in this nonwork atmosphere? Are your thoughts oriented more toward the vacation or more toward what you're leaving behind and having to come back to? You may even have a hard time unwinding for much of the vacation, signaling a highly stressed and tense mind–body patterning.

Many productivity and lifestyle coaches suggest that easing into and out of a vacation can be quite useful and healthy. Thus, having many hours or even a full day to complete your packing and finalize your trip itinerary can be a much less stressful way of entering the stream of a vacation than meeting your family at the airport would be, for example, after working 9 hours seeing clients. Similarly, it can be an act of purposeful self-caring to build in a day of recuperation on the tail end of your trip. Some of us may feel, however, that our vacation *was* our recuperation time, and hence we don't need or even deserve more time to ease back into the swing of things. Or perhaps we desire to maximize the time away as much as we're able. Thus, we believe that we're cutting our vacation short by one day and shortchanging ourselves. However, if we conceptualize this final day of vacation as part of the vacation itself, we may support ourselves in shifting modes—from nonwork to work—more easefully.

I vividly recall when my father, a now-retired physician, decided to build in Sunday, the last day of vacation, as his time for reset and transition. We would drive or fly back from a trip on Saturday evening so that he could wake up in his own bed and start his Sunday with less transition stress. My current family and I have followed this self-caring habit to varying degrees. And I have noticed that when I don't build in enough transition time, the vacations seem to end with the greatest amount of stress and most amount of dread to return to work.

Staycations

Staycation, a relatively new term dating back roughly to 2005, is all about deliberately taking extended time off but not necessarily going anywhere special or costly. A staycation could literally be hanging out in your home for a few days, doing whatever you'd like (to whatever degree that's possible). You can be quite creative with this time, for example, discovering new local outdoor activities or sightseeing around your local town or city. The money you spend can be extremely low, or you could save a bit to indulge in food and activities that you normally would never splurge for. The main idea is that you're not working. You've taken time off from work, whether you're employed or self-employed. Acting as if you're going on a cruise somewhere halfway around the world is a good way to look at a staycation. Either way, your *vacation responder* is set to "on," and you've gotten someone to cover for you because you're *not working*.

Mental Health Days

Taking a mental health day may seem like a frivolous thing or something constructed to let kids off the hook from school when they didn't want to do their work. Around in the vernacular since approximately 1971, the term "mental health day" is defined as a "day an employee takes off from work in order to relieve stress or renew vitality" (Merriam-Webster, n.d.-a). Taking some time to and for yourself in such a way seems pretty relevant to values-driven, purposeful therapist self-care, right?

The prospect of a mental health day doesn't mean that we need to wait until we're at our wits' end or burned out to take a day off. Rather, it's a beautiful way to consciously engage in a *pattern interrupt*, to positively jostle the usual way our minds, brains, and bodies have been operating. Instead of recovering from a bad cold in bed or taking care of a sick loved one during a conventional sick day, we are acting proactively on our own behalf, and we're doing what we would like (although we also might throw in a load of laundry during our day of respite). The idea is to revitalize ourselves in meaningful ways so that we're much better able to return to our psychotherapeutic work with a fresh mind and body, more present and more grounded.

Daily Self-Care Breaks

Taking time off and resting does not have to be an all-out endeavor. It can be free, brief, and frequent. Taking downtime in a conscious way throughout the day can be a very fruitful form of self-caring that is supportive of your well-being over time. In fact, spontaneously taking small breaks through the day and intentionally scheduling a half or full hour of downtime here and there are incredibly proactive and burnout-preventive acts. You're telling yourself that you matter enough to rest, take some deep breaths, get some fresh air, text a friend, meditate for 5 minutes, move your body, read for pleasure, listen to music, or talk to some colleagues who might also be free at that time. In this way, we don't have to wait 11 months until the next vacation to feel like we're purposefully resting and recharging.

MAKING TIME FOR THE DOWNTIME

Perhaps the trickiest aspect of any kind of purposeful downtime is making the time for it. We may be or feel so swamped by our current caseload or work schedule that we couldn't fathom building in even 5 minutes of respite. I have several colleagues who work in hospital clinics, schools, inpatient units, and community agencies, and they all say something similar: "I simply can't do it. There's literally no time."

Sometimes a solution to time scarcity is a matter of building a nonworking lunch into your daily schedule. You may have slipped into a mode of doing paperwork while you hurriedly shove some reheated leftovers into your mouth. Perhaps the integration of daily self-care breaks requires more of an interpersonal negotiation with your direct supervisor, boss, or director. And still, there may be much larger systemic issues at play that demand concerted effort from a group of like-minded psychotherapists to the larger organization.

That may not be your battle, however. Yours may be to discern what is within your power to enact. If it's a feeling of undeservingness to take some time off, that emotional belief must be lovingly confronted. If you've tried 10 different ways to get a break from work and your workplace will not permit any of them, it may be time to look for another place to work. I've seen this counsel compassionately offered by fellow therapists on some of the closed Facebook groups of which I'm a member. The advice is empathically firm: "You must take care of yourself and make the time. You deserve this. You can do this."

A NOTE ON NATURE

Discussion of rest, time off, and recharging our batteries wouldn't be complete without a few words on nature. Although this book doesn't include an entire chapter devoted to this topic, spending time in nature has been well-documented (e.g., R. Walsh, 2011) as having powerful mind–body restorative effects and is recommended practice for psychotherapists (Norcross & VandenBos, 2018). You may be at the beach, letting the water and sand swirl around your naked feet, infusing your body with restorative free electrons (e.g., Chevalier et al., 2012). Or perhaps you're hiking in the woods and letting the raw beauty and wisdom of the trees and the sun-tipped leaves permeate your being. Some of us are mountain folk and love to climb and traverse challenging terrain. Dr. Rick Hanson—author, neuropsychologist, and mindfulness teacher—often speaks of his love for climbing and how he gets a charge from the challenge and thrill of scaling such awe-inspiring natural formations of the earth. Quite the opposite in terms of thrill, I've come to enjoy what my daughter has lovingly dubbed "dethatching my way to peace." As a relatively new homeowner, I have surprisingly found lawn care both interesting and quite restorative.

My family and I have been fortunate to make a yearly tradition of taking a few days in a now-beloved area of the northeastern United States. This destination has a small town on one side of the road and a large national park on the other. Being among the centuries-old trees, gazing out at the majestic mountains, and losing myself in the sun reflecting off the brilliantly blue lakes has been extremely calming, awe-inspiring, and revitalizing all at once. At night, I have a tradition to walk from our motel to the water's edge, sit down, and simply look up. Sometimes I spend a good 30 minutes just gazing at the night sky, as if I expect something magical to happen. In fact, one year I was lucky enough to catch a glimpse of shooting stars, scores of comets burning up in the atmosphere and producing brief and bright glowing trails across the sky. Whatever we're most drawn to about nature, we can welcome that facet of rejuvenation and revitalization into our lives.

CHOOSING YOUR MODE OF DOWNTIME AND REVITALIZATION

There is something so freeing *and* so challenging about being able to say at any moment, "I will stop now. I need a break." As psychotherapists who find ourselves at relatively constant work on behalf of others, we must declare our downtime so that the uptime doesn't always declare itself first. Within this declaration at any given time, we can also choose to some degree what type of rest we need or can get. You can ask yourself the 3R question (see Exhibit 28.1): "What kind of relaxation, revitalization, or recuperation do I need right now and into the future?" Determining the quality of your downtime can then prompt some options for what to do (or not do) to help you toward this goal.

Rest and time off are essential forms of self-care and powerful forces in the prevention of accumulating stress and burnout risk. We likely already know this intellectually and even from firsthand experience. However, consistently creating the time and space to recuperate and restore your vital energy and mental–spiritual vibrancy is another story. Healthy inquiry into both the barriers and the easefulness of resting your precious self is therefore well worth the skillful effort.

EXHIBIT 28.1. Self-Care Reflection Break: Ideas for Relaxation, Revitalization, and Recuperation

Spending time in nature or going for a walk	Watching a good TV show or movie	Writing for pleasure	Talking/hanging out with partner, friends, and beloved family
Painting, drawing, collage, scrapbooking, other visual arts	Listening to or playing music	Cooking	Daydreaming just because
Taking pictures	Going for a walk, hiking, or other forms of relaxing or rejuvenating movement	Drinking/eating comfort food and drink	Napping (before midafternoon)
Knitting, sewing, embroidery, and similar activities	Reading a book	Sightseeing, traveling, journeying	Working on a puzzle or other intellectually stimulating but relaxing activity

29 SUPPORTIVE CONNECTIONS AND HEALTHY BOUNDARIES

Don't set yourself on fire trying to keep others warm.

—Penny Reid

We are all social beings. All we have to do is reflect for a moment on some of our most troubled clients. How are their relationships? Are they strained and filled with conflict or emptiness? Do our patients long for deeper, more trusting, more equitable, and more consistent relationships with their loved ones, friends, coworkers, and families of origin? Is our patients' loneliness consuming them? Our job, in part, is to help our patients connect more skillfully, love and trust more deeply, and to create and maintain healthier boundaries as they navigate the unpredictably rocky terrain of interpersonal life. It's almost as if we're unwittingly hired to mend and fortify broken hearts caused by disaffected relationships, emotional neglect, and interpersonal betrayal.

Are we any different? We too must attend to our connections and the boundaries within and between them. Two frequent points of guidance emerging from the psychotherapist self-care literature are (a) to cultivate healthy and

https://doi.org/10.1037/0000309-030
The Thriving Therapist: Sustainable Self-Care to Prevent Burnout and Enhance Well-Being, by M. A. Hersh

supportive relationships and (b) to maintain healthy boundaries between yourself and others and between your professional and personal life (Norcross & VandenBos, 2018; Wise & Barnett, 2016). Building on your understanding of your relational needs and patterns (see Chapter 11, this volume), this chapter addresses the pragmatic ways in which healthy relationships and boundaries can serve as a concrete practice to support sustainable self-caring and longevity of well-being.

SEEK AND CULTIVATE NOURISHING RELATIONSHIPS

If you're a securely attached, strongly extraverted, highly agreeable, and socially adept person, you probably have little difficulty in the social realm. Meeting new people, establishing friendships and collegial relationships, and enjoying the connections you've made may be second nature to you. Whether it is or not, all of us could benefit from putting some good energy into nurturing the relationships that serve us well and skillfully mending or possibly disconnecting from those that unnecessarily drain us. In fact, if you are a consummate extravert and a loyal friend or colleague, for example, you may struggle with drawing firm boundaries between you and the rest of the world. This pattern could become just as problematic as the almost-pure introvert and/or highly sensitive soul who has "naturally" already drawn social lines in the sand.

Being in touch with your general proclivities for how (and how much) you spend time with others is a crucial self-care awareness skill. If you are fueled by others' energies, for example, but operate a solo practice in a relatively isolated office space, this setup is likely not the best option for you in the long run unless you derive the majority of your interpersonal satisfaction outside of work. How then do you satisfy your needs for interpersonal connection if your working hours matter significantly to your relational health? Making sure that good-enough relationships are cultivated and maintained would be paramount and a vital form of sustainable self-caring. On the other hand, the isolated office setup might not have such a negative impact for a more introverted and highly sensitive therapist. Relationships of course still matter, and if you have a reliable partner, trusting friendships, and/or close collegial relationships, then taking care of these precious relationships becomes taking care of yourself.

When relatively healthy, our relationships can help physiologically soothe, bolster our sense of worth and compassion, create emotional stability, spark hope, and shift cognitive perspective, to name but a few important effects. When strained, our relationships can compromise our ability to function, create feelings of alienation and isolation, and challenge the very notion of the person we thought we were or should be.

The goal of this chapter isn't to help you resolve all relationship challenges or to coach you to make new friends or to find a partner. Rather, given how important social connection and meaningful relationships are to our well-being and health, we can examine the relationships that currently support us, consider ways to strengthen them, and reflect on when to "tap out" when those connections are simply not working.

Who Has Your Back?

How do you evaluate your underlying relational attachment patterns (e.g., Chapter 11)? How warm, good-natured, and supportive are your connections in your personal and professional life? Psychotherapist self-care experts John Norcross, James Guy, and Gary VandenBos would encourage you to ask, "Who has my back?" (Norcross & Guy, 2007; Norcross & VandenBos, 2018). As a pragmatic strategy, it can very useful to identify who is in your supportive social sphere (see Exhibit 29.1).

Take a moment to ask yourself who you feel closest to and trust the most in your personal and professional life. Perhaps you determined that some people

EXHIBIT 29.1. Self-Care Reflection Break: Who Has My Back?

Write the names of your connections, and label each with a "W" for work connection and "P" for personal connection, if appropriate. Names closer to the bullseye are those you trust most, feel most comfortable around, and/or are most supportive in your life. If there are potentially supportive people you would like closer in your orbit, consider what steps may be necessary to forge a different kind of relationship with them in the future.

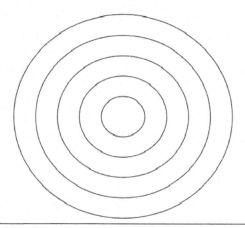

are quite close, some relationships you'd like to deepen or strengthen, and some relationships are in fact detrimental. If you drew concentric circles with you in the center, who would be in your inner ring? With whom are you closest and most trusting in your personal and your professional life? With whom would you like to strengthen the relationship because it and they matter to you?

Who inadvertently becomes countertransferentially reflected in your therapeutic relationships? For example, I once worked with a very challenging adolescent boy who had a previous therapist with a very challenging daughter. The parents of my client recounted many stories of the previous therapist's making catastrophized predictions about their son's future while that therapist was struggling with his own parenting woes. The fact that the parents learned of this therapist's own family issues is not insignificant and fits squarely into the discussion of healthy boundaries.

Sometimes psychotherapists end up viewing their clients as primary relationships or at least as sources of connection and apparent support. One colleague once told me that although she was fairly lonely at work, she at least had her clients. I also learned over the years (from current clients who had former therapists) that many psychotherapists shared their deeper selves with their clients, some even stating they'd really love to become friends. This type of boundary blurring can confuse and possibly harm the client emotionally as well as maintain a distorted sense of self and relationships for the psychotherapist.

Being given support from trusted and well-intentioned others is of course essential. How well you receive this support is another story. If you've determined that you struggle with receiving assistance and caring offered from friends and colleagues, then this theme would certainly be a key target for personal growth (whether through your own growing-edge endeavors or in personal therapy or coaching). In fact, I know several people in my life who have a good deal of (potential) support around them but have served their whole lives almost exclusively in the role of helper rather than also in the role of support receiver. The nursing profession is said to attract people into this type of helper role. How does our profession of psychotherapy fare here? Although it is beyond the scope of this book to unpack that dynamic, suffice it to say that the roles we occupy in life are sources of both strength and confidence as well as challenge and depletion. Familiarizing ourselves with such role patterns and habits is a powerful form of self-caring.

Types of Relational Support

In my first year of graduate school, I spent countless hours in my research advisor's lab coding different forms of social support offered and received between college student dyadic friendships. Over time, I learned why this endeavor was so important. Within one conversation we can give and get tangible, financial, emotional, moral, intellectual, and motivational support. Across interactions, over time different forms of support wax and wane. And across different people in our lives we may give and receive numerous constellations of support. A colleague who has never directly offered motivational or moral support may be quite adept at providing very pragmatic advice on how to manage ethical issues within challenging cases. Perhaps friends outside of your professional life cannot readily understand or are not equipped to offer practical assistance to your clinical woes but can lend you some emotional and moral support because you are burned out or conflicted about asking your director for more flex time in your work schedule.

Both giving and receiving support can enhance our well-being in numerous ways, both personally and professionally. Being able to discern the degree of reciprocity of your friendships and collegial relationships is a highly valuable skill you can cultivate. Quite troubling is the realization that your closest relationships are indeed somewhat unrequited. The opposite can occur as well, with friends or colleagues looking to you for support while you maintain a relative aloofness or desire to keep your distance for one reason or another.

I might argue that relationship reciprocity detection is a secret but powerful form of sustainable self-care. Holding out for a decade-long nonreciprocal collegial relationship to (magically) turn reciprocal unfortunately may be a continued drain on your precious energy. Conversely, not putting enough energy into maintaining a relatively reciprocal relationship may cause it to turn less reciprocal and potentially to end up dissolving as a once-trusted source of support and nourishment for you.

Conscious Cultivation of Healthy Connections

Ultimately, if you look at the range of your relationships in the mirror, how would you evaluate what's staring back at you? This earnest assessment of both the quantity and (more importantly) the quality of these connections can lead you to make healthier decisions even if it is quite challenging to do so. Consciously putting your relationship energies where they're best suited is an investment in your long-term well-being. Of note, if your early attachment relationships helped to create an overinvolvement, detachment, or ambivalence within relationships, then you may be likely to view continued disloyalty from a romantic partner as always reparable, or sporadic and benign annoyances from a colleague as water that easily breaks the bridge.

Nourishing and nurturing healthy relationships takes mindful awareness, skill, and patience. Our job is not to create and maintain the perfect constellation of relationships and connections. Those do not exist, as far as I know. Rather, we can aspire to elevate social connection to the level it deserves and to the degree that it truly nourishes our spirit. As Norcross and VandenBos (2018) reminded us, peer support (Coster & Schwebel, 1997) and spending time with one's spouse or partner (Rupert & Kent, 2007) are two of the highest rated and most highly prioritized career-sustaining behaviors for psychotherapists.

However, Norcross and VandenBos (2018) cautioned against friendships that are exclusively with clinical colleagues, as these have the potential to naturally revolve around work themes and could easily end up becoming peer consultation sessions. Ultimately, each therapist's relationships with different people in their lives will behave differently and serve different roles. That's OK and in fact expected. The preservation of energy for these social and connection-oriented endeavors is a general offering of caring we can give to ourselves.

As the language within acceptance and commitment therapy would have us phrase these sentiments, what committed actions will you engage in that align with what truly matters to you? Consider your self-caring values (e.g., Chapter 6). If you articulated some version of "nurturing relationships," then you likely find relationships meaningful and worthy of pursuing for greater fulfillment in your life. How you nurture and nourish those connections is a wide-open field. Perhaps you text your partner or a friend during a quick break at work, plan and actually go on date nights with your partner (even if the dates are in your own home), reach out to trusted colleagues more often, spend quality time with your kids with your phone in a different room, offer support to a colleague simply to be a friendly presence in their life, scribe a letter or write an email to an old friend to reestablish a forgotten friendship, or take a few minutes here and there to show love and affection to those you most truly value. There are numerous other ways to forge, maintain, and deeply nurture the connections in your life. Taking some time to give this arena some concentrated attention and energy is a good place to start.

ESTABLISHING AND MAINTAINING HEALTHY BOUNDARIES

Work–life balance. Say the words out loud slowly. We see them everywhere, even in articles and on surveys on psychotherapist self-care and stress. Do you notice anything in particular? What I tend to observe in myself is a frustration and an impossible standard to be met.

I realize that work–life balance is shorthand for "work life—personal life," but by condensing this phrase, we lose something incredibly meaningful in translation. This abridged version connotes that life is lived outside of work and that work is its own entity. While it is true (and is partly the premise of this chapter) that maintaining healthy boundaries between work and our personal lives is a form of self-care and preservation of our sanity, it may be misleading and potentially demoralizing to suggest that work is just that thing we go to while the rest of life waits for us until we step across the threshold. We can indeed bring "life" into work for our own betterment.

Another reason this phrase bugs me is that the word "balance" connotes two or more objects being a similar enough weight as to manifest as an equilibrium or stability (Jamie Stack, personal communication, 2018). If you imagine a scale being balanced, then the two objects on either side of that scale weigh roughly the same. So are we to assume that work sits on one end of the scale while the rest of life sits on the other? How are we supposed to think about these two all-encompassing parts of our lives as needing to be balanced?

Dr. Gemma Leigh Roberts, a U.K. psychologist with a keen eye on the accidental back-firings of our aspirations for achieving balance, proposed a sort of *blending* instead (Roberts, 2021). Blending ultimately can be based on mapping your values and ideal lifestyle, assessing your priorities and your current support of them, embracing flexibility, communicating your needs and wishes, and regularly reviewing your status at any given time. Thus, blending different facets of our life is akin to the healthy differentiation and then integration of disparate parts that Daniel Siegel, MD, promoted in his work on interpersonal neurobiology and the mindful brain (e.g., Siegel, 2007). Thinking of our work lives and personal lives and all the facets of them within a Venn diagram may ultimately be more helpful than imagining a scale we have to try to keep always in balance.

Whether we like it or not, we take our personal lives to work and our work lives home. Our typical ways of thinking, feeling, behaving, and responding don't necessarily get checked at the therapy room door like coats at a cocktail party. We bring our personalities and our stresses wherever we go, and the environments through which we travel can influence our actions, thoughts, and feelings.

Dr. Urie Bronfenbrenner, renowned for his ecological systems theory (Bronfenbrenner, 1977) and revised bioecological model (Bronfenbrenner & Ceci, 1994), powerfully suggested that the individual is mutually and dynamically influenced by and influencing of the larger systems (e.g., family, work, media, culture) in which they are embedded. If, for example, we work within an agency or clinic that basically calls the shots, our work and personal life are inherently shaped by such policies and philosophies, whether we're conscious of this process or not. Those of us who can compartmentalize relatively well (based on temperament, personality, a solid support network within and outside of work, etc.) will enjoy the relatively lower degree of spillover between work and home and vice versa. But it can be quite challenging to fully compartmentalize if, for example, your own ill child is at home being cared for by your babysitter who is moving out of town soon and you realize that you have only one more sick day that your agency will grant you.

And the opposite occurs too. We can be prone to take the emotional fallout from work experience home with us. As Barnett (2014) highlighted in his treatment of the role of balance in burnout prevention, no real lines are drawn in the sand to fully separate our work from our personal lives. They are of mutual influence, for better or worse (Pipes et al., 2005). When we don't attend with care and concern to each domain respectively, one may dominate or drain energy from the other. In fact, as Rupert and colleagues (2012) showed, having more control at work predicts less work-to-family conflict, which then improves family satisfaction. In a potentially virtuous cycle, having more family support reduced home-to-work conflict, thus increasing work satisfaction. In essence, how much control and support we experience at work and at home can spill over, both viciously and virtuously.

Establishing interpersonal boundaries, as well as boundaries between work and our personal lives, is easier said than done. A powerful and foundational healthy boundary setter is the art and skill of demarcating the *here* from the *there* and the *now* from the *then*. For example, it's Friday evening, and you're at home talking to a friend on the phone. You've just ended a long and stressful day with clients, hours earlier having engaged in nonurgent but highly stressful discussions of two separate clients' suicidal ideation. Are you *here, now* with your friend, or are you still *there, then* at work? Are your physiological and emotional energies still caught up or revved up by the charged conversations you had earlier in the day? Just by asking yourself these questions you can begin to differentiate the then from the now and the there from the here.

If it were that easy, however, we wouldn't keep having the same conversations about the importance of boundary setting. In fact, it's not easy at all. Let's look at a few ways to help facilitate drawing some healthy boundaries between our professional lives and our personal lives. In *Leaving It at the Office*, Norcross and VandenBos (2018) offered valuable guidance. The following list is nonexhaustive but represents some of the more powerful boundary setting strategies:

- Work under 90% capacity so that family and personal life responsibilities, including your own self-care, can be regularly accommodated. To this point, two of the three psychotherapists I've personally had in my life deliberately carved out an hour during the day each day for various personal tasks, including a power nap, making personal calls, and de-stressing.

- Take some time to reflect on how accommodating you really are to certain clients and their issues. If going above and beyond is in fact draining your energy or cutting into your personal or family time, it may be time to reconsider what constitutes being a "good therapist." Occasionally I have offered to periodically text certain clients (with either executive function challenges or motivational consistency struggles), providing brief reminders of the work they're aspiring to do in between sessions. While I've gotten very positive feedback from several clients about this tactic, when left undefined or undercircumscribed, I find myself violating my own boundaries. I'll hold those clients and their struggles in my awareness well beyond their sessions and take time from my personal life to send these reminders. Perhaps this form of between-session support feels manageable and is "no big deal" with one client, but what happens with two or three or more?

- Demarcate the daily transition from work to nonwork. This boundary-setting tactic can be done with regular healthy rituals such as listening to music, exercising, showering, changing clothes, participating in yoga and meditation, energy tapping, and engaging in deliberate breathwork. A friend and colleague who worked very long hours at a large bustling hospital often talked about the shower ritual in which she engaged after walking through her door after work. She physically cleansed and used the shower as a time for emotional and mental release from the day's stressful therapeutic encounters.

Following Chris Berlin's *polarity breathing* (explored in Chapter 24), take a minute at the end of your workday and breathe out what you would like to release and dissipate from your mind–body (C. Berlin, personal communication, October 2016). For several breaths, breathe out any unnecessary and residual tension, stress, frustration, helplessness, or lost hope. For several more breaths, breathe in what you'd like to integrate and infuse into your being. This in-breath positive aspiration could be calm, hope, peace, stillness, balance, stability, levity, and the like. You may also try alternating the intention of releasing and infusing on each in-breath and out-breath respectively within each breath cycle. I have practiced this exercise for just a few breaths when getting into my car after leaving my office. Shortly after that I clicked on a favorite YouTube channel and started listening (but not watching of course) to the politics of the day. While some (including myself) could argue that listening to political news is not a great way to decompress from doing therapy all day, I have found this particular channel fairly uplifting, inspiring, and quite humorous as well. There can, however, be too much of a good thing.

- Determine, request, and then preserve nonwork time as best you can. Chapter 28 includes discussion of why resting and restoring our minds and bodies is vital. Whether you set an hour aside during the workday, negotiate a half or full day off each week or on a biweekly basis, or go on a full-on vacation, knowing that you need and deserve some measure of nonwork time is foundational to self-caring. Preserving that time can be challenging as we may be pulled to (and feel guilty if we don't) make clinical calls, check work email, attend online meetings we didn't *really* need to attend, and the like. Protecting nonwork time extends to making sure you get adequate coverage while on vacation (whether you're away or staying at home). Nothing says "vacation over" more than getting a crisis call from a client that takes up half your day and spills over emotionally into the rest of your time off. Even knowing that someone could call is enough to put your amygdala on higher alert.

Just as important as setting boundaries between work and personal life are the boundaries and limits we set within our professional life itself. The following strategies are related to keeping your work life more manageable and your work self more resilient.

- Through clear communication about your policies up front, practice establishing expectations for how and how much you typically work with clients. These conversations, which can be part of the informed consent process, can save you an enormous amount of confusion and spillover stress in the future.

- Practice being an assertive therapist. Saying "no thanks" can be a true asset for preventing overload beyond the point of no return. Even if we really desire to take on that next client, project, presentation, or task, we may ultimately be better off by respectfully declining. Depending on your relational and emotional style, saying no may be harder or easier when you're your own boss in private practice. In that case, the only person you really have to say no to is yourself.

  I purposefully added the word "thanks" to the frequently recommended boundary setting tactic of saying an outright "no." Some of us feel horribly guilty for refusing to help. The word or sentiment "no" itself may be too hard to say and then sit with. It may even conjure up untoward feelings from childhood. But we might think and then say something like "You know, I would love to help in that way, but I just can't right now. I'm swamped as it is, and I'm already feeling a bit burned out. Hopefully when I have more time and energy in the future, I'll be able to do that." This response may seem overly drawn out, apologetic, or justified. And yet, some of us may need to practice rehearsing such self-caring sentiments to experience what it feels like to be our own best advocate and to draw lines more clearly. Why we're saying no seems just as important as the act itself of saying no.

- Demand enough income (from yourself or employer) to make ends meet, at minimum. Request enough income to be able to live more comfortably and/or to save for the future. Be wary, however, of the hedonic and revenue treadmill, as it insidiously may keep us fixated on earning more income while ignoring our other needs in the process. Private practitioners may be especially vulnerable to this slippery-slope process, taking "just one more" client to earn a bit more and a bit more after that.

- Establish cutoffs for how many direct service hours you'll commit to on a weekly basis. Realizing that your time commitment is much less under your control if you're not in private practice, it may still be a negotiable element of your job if you emphasize this issue to your supervisor or director as deeply important to you. If you own your own practice, you 100% determine how many clients you're willing to see. As Arzt (2020) aptly suggested, working past 25 clients per week is a slippery slope toward more stress and exhaustion. Negotiating with yourself regarding income, up time, and down time is a vital part of owning your own practice. As owner, you decide. As employee, you decide. Hopefully owner and employee get along well with one another.

- If relevant to your situation, try to include at least one quarter of your caseload as private pay. Interesting research (Rupert, Miller, et al., 2012) suggests that career satisfaction is enhanced when we take in more income and reduce the negative aspects involved in relying on third-party payments.

Norcross and VandenBos (2018) offered many other helpful boundary setting strategies, and one of them in particular stands out as especially poignant. They discussed establishing a professional bill of rights—reflecting deeply on what you consider to be your inalienable rights as a psychotherapist. At first blush this idea may seem a bit strange. Do we really need to engage in such a formal process or create a structured document? As discussed in the first section of this book, at the heart of therapist self-care is the establishment of a different kind of relationship with yourself. This relationship is ideally one of self-deservingness, preservation of your own humanity, and creative possibility. Try drafting your own bill of rights, and see what kinds of nonnegotiables emerge. Even as a thought exercise, this activity will almost definitely get your self-caring juices flowing.

30

SUPPORTING OUR FRONTAL LOBE FOR SUSTAINABLE SELF-CARE AND WELL-BEING

I have not failed. I've just found 10,000 ways that won't work.

–Thomas Edison

We all know that thinking about doing something and actually doing that thing are two completely different things. This chapter presents some empirically based frameworks and strategies to best support our executive functions (EFs), the foundational brain-based capacities we all have to varying degrees that help us to get things done, keep distractions at bay, remember our clients' pertinent information, end sessions on time, hold clients' trauma stories in mind while also remembering components of our intervention, refrain from impulsive self-disclosures, keep our files organized, and remember to pick up (three, not two) cartons of eggs on the way home. By enhancing your EF skills, you'll hopefully feel more on top of things on a daily basis and over time, thus lowering your stress level and increasing your stress hardiness within both clinical work and your personal life, as well as between these two realms.

https://doi.org/10.1037/0000309-031
The Thriving Therapist: Sustainable Self-Care to Prevent Burnout and Enhance Well-Being,
by M. A. Hersh

Self-knowledge of both your more prominent and your hidden EF challenges and strengths (see Chapter 12) is key to the self-care practice of remediating deficits, maintaining strengths, and boosting EF effectiveness for the future. Do your current job and your workplace environment support your EF skills, or do they inadvertently bring out the worst in your frontal lobe functioning? How do your current EF skills hinder or bolster your work functioning? You may find that your work and your personal life affect one another based on how well your executive control center is functioning.

It is a common misconception that EF difficulties are the domain only of people diagnosed with attention-deficit/hyperactivity disorder (ADHD). In fact, EF struggles also show up in individuals with depressive disorders, learning disabilities, autism spectrum disorder, certain personality disorders, cognitive disorders, chronic pain, and posttraumatic stress disorder (Sarkis, 2018). Thus, for both our clients and our fellow psychotherapists, EF struggles of various kinds are likely more common than we think. Ignoring even subtle EF difficulties can make our lives unnecessarily hard, whereas addressing those compromised capacities can bring greater peace of mind and less stress, better quality relationships (Hallowell & Hallowell, 2010), and enhanced clinical competence.

Addressing your EF difficulties is generally a beneficial thing. Letting poor planning, impulsivity, and forgetfulness, for example, run the show isn't likely to feel very good, nor will it get you where you might want to go. However, life is not about absolutes or one-size-fits-alls. It may feel that way sometimes, and so much about one's culture would have us believe we're all supposed to be and live according to a certain standard. But as Ned Hallowell, attention-deficit disorder (ADD) expert and prolific author, compassionately asserted, individuals with ADD and other EF challenges have gifts and not just challenges (Hallowell & Ratey, 2021). Once we realize these gifts—such as creativity, exuberance, and emotional sensitivity—we can help transform and become more agentic in our work (and personal) lives rather than being victim to them.

If your EF profile causes you undue stress in your current job and workplace environment, is this all "on you" to remediate or fix, or can your workplace become a better match to your strengths and challenges? If your EF profile is simply a poor match with your specific job or workplace environment, and neither you nor your employer (including yourself as a private practice owner) is willing to compromise or accommodate, perhaps that's not the place to be. There are other oceans for the same fish to swim. Although changing jobs is likely something more serious to contemplate, you almost always have a choice.

I was quite sincere when I mentioned in Chapter 16 that I wouldn't last 2 weeks on a psychiatric inpatient unit. Partly that's due to my sensory processing sensitivity (i.e., highly sensitive person temperament), but it's also because of my EF challenges. I just wouldn't be able to keep up for very long organizationally, with time management, or with the quick decisions always having to be made. My relatively slow and deep processing of information compels me to need more time, and I feel as if I have thrived in my own relatively slow paced and quiet private practice. Over the years I've been surrounded by a few kind-hearted colleagues rather than 20 to 30 staff or managing several clients at once without fully getting to know them and what makes them tick. However, I don't mistake quieter and slower paced for dull and lacking in challenge because I'm very often given a run for my money, so to speak.

Much has been written about intervention for EF skills deficits (e.g., Allen, 2001; Honos-Webb, 2018; Sarkis, 2018; Tuckman, 2012), including numerous well-respected books on ADHD (e.g., Barkley, 2020; Hallowell & Ratey, 2021; Tuckman, 2009; Zylowska, 2012). Thus, the aim of this chapter is to elucidate how various experts currently think about coaching EF skills and then to apply this intervention knowledge to the role of psychotherapist—to benefit us at work, in our personal lives, and in the crossover between the two. This chapter includes two main frameworks and then presents a set of specific tools and supports that can help a busy psychotherapist manage time and resources as efficiently and effectively as possible.

ACCOMMODATE AND MODIFY TO EASE AND COMPENSATE FOR EF DIFFICULTIES

A classic approach to helping with EF difficulties is to offer accommodations for better EF management and to create modifications within the environment that ease the burdens of everyday challenges. Within this general framework, the goal is to harness compensatory strategies and shifts in the environment to facilitate better and smoother functioning. Training and enhancement of EF skills comes indirectly through the use of different technologies, practices, and environmental changes, but the proof is in the daily functioning and tension-reduced pudding. When the right accommodations and modifications are made, we feel less friction and stress and are better able to manifest our strengths and gifts in other domains as well.

Cora, a late-career counseling psychologist who worked for a large community mental health agency, was well respected for her clinical competence and ability to work flexibly with a wide diversity of clients, families, and community systems. One thing that Cora knew about herself, however, was how far her EF capacities lagged behind her clinical capabilities and interpersonal adeptness. Given Cora's breadth of experience and depth of expertise in her agency, she took on more administrative and project management responsibilities as the years went on. Although she loved creating programming to connect her agency with the community, her relatively disorganized approach often resulted in much greater stress for herself (and for her colleagues and community stakeholders) than she was willing to admit. She tried to hide these challenges as best she could, but it was clear that the more she took on, the deeper into the EF hole she sank. This dynamic reverberated to Cora's home life because she had to take home administrative work that she did not finish while at the agency.

Fortunately, within the framework of accommodations and modifications are many ways that someone like Cora could support herself and create greater ease of mind, body, and action. As you read about Cora's navigation of her EF challenges, see whether any of these constructive supports might help you in any way. If Cora did some EF self-assessment (see Chapter 12), she might discover that she is challenged by planning, prioritization, and organization. Cora first examined the system she was using to help her manage all the information and planning responsibilities she had and discovered that she never really used a "system." Her stellar auditory memory was her organizational system, but as the cognitive load and set of responsibilities increased, she got too overloaded and felt the ill effects.

Because Cora had a hard time managing and tracking meetings with colleagues within and outside her agency, she began to use the calendar app on her phone, which she took everywhere she went. Recurring meetings can be created in less than 10 seconds, and a colleague showed her how to color code her appointments and tasks for greater ease of management and tracking. As Cora was at her computer a good portion of each day, she also found it helpful to have her phone and computer calendars synced.

Cora also sometimes took handwritten notes during meetings, but she never filed them away using a system and thus was not readily able to retrieve when she needed them. Notes with vague headings were stacked on top of one another, and Cora sporadically opened folders that were created for different projects while trying to put away or take out relevant documents. File folders were strewn about on her desk and even on the floor beside her. Cora would eventually find the files she needed or, if pressed for time, she would simply take notes from scratch rather than reference information that came before. Although her auditory memory prowess allowed her to continue in this way for some time, she eventually needed a more comprehensive and consistently used system to accommodate the number of projects, tasks, and meetings she managed.

Cora was encouraged by her husband and grown children to discuss with the director an agency-wide change in the ways that clinicians and administrators take, keep, and use notes. The agency was operating on a manual, handwritten clinical records system with confidential files housed in a records room. This system proved to be a nightmare for Cora, as each clinical note just piled on top of the other, waiting for some magical day when she would file them all in their respective charts.

After many theoretical and budgetary discussions, the agency decided to purchase a multiclinician software package for managing electronic health records (EHRs). Although it took several weeks for Cora to feel relatively comfortable, the benefits of a cloud-based system became clear to her. She no longer felt she had to keep her desk filled with clinical notes, just in case. Her clients were accessible with a quick log-in. She also realized that she typed her notes much faster than she could handwrite them. This one systemic change added some time back to Cora's day, helped her stay on top of her clients' progress, and decluttered her desk for greater peace of mind.

Prior to the purchase of the EHR software, Cora would often sit down to work on administrative tasks for the nonclinical aspects of her job and find her clinical work intruding. One of her biggest distractions was remembering important elements of a session that she never recorded. The moment Cora began her admin work, she began to think about the clients she saw that day. Thoughts about one client led to reflections on another. Conversely, the moment Cora would sit down to write her progress notes for the day (usually during a free nonclinical hour), she would unconsciously engage in productive procrastination and begin doing more pressing admin tasks.

The new software led to one of the most important personal changes during Cora's day: a new process for writing very *streamlined* progress notes into the agency's cloud-based EHR system *immediately after* each session. Cora found her narrative-based progress notes (which reflected the way her mind usually worked) becoming more effective and efficient. Within her EHR system, she even had the option to choose among three different note-writing formats, thus providing her both freedom and structure. Cora's own progress with her progress notes took a good deal of effort at first, but some of her most trusted colleagues were there to "enforce it" when they would inquire about how the note writing was going.

Another change that Cora made was to her planfulness. Cora realized that she and her husband often had dinner leftovers that she was intent on taking to work the next day for lunch, but she rarely put the food into a portable container after dinner. Instead, she either rushed to pack up the leftovers in the morning or would buy less-desired lunches at a sandwich shop down the street from work. Cora and her husband thus made a simple change: They bought new portable Tupperware and began to put their dinner leftovers into it as they cleaned up in the evening. Immediately afterward, Cora would place an especially large and bright sticky note on the inside of the front door as a reminder, (mostly) ensuring she would turn back to the fridge if she began to leave without her lunch.

Individuals, psychotherapists included, may have trouble recognizing when it's time to take care of ourselves in basic but important ways. If we forget to eat, drink, or take breaks, for example, we are accidentally depleting our reserves while exacerbating a dysregulated system. Simple acts such as stretching, eating a small snack between clients, and drinking water or tea throughout the day can be built into our daily routine by posting a "stretch now" sticky note on the computer, leaving a snack out on the desk, or having a refillable water bottle in a highly visible and convenient location at all times. Other EF supportive practices for the workday include the following:

- Position several (functioning) clocks around your office that you can easily see from all angles.

- Do your best to take a few minutes between clients to regain your composure and write a brief progress note, if possible, or establish a note-writing time each day so that it becomes routine to finish your charting that day rather than letting the notes accumulate and generate unnecessary stress.

- Plan ahead for times of the day when you're predictably less energetic and attentive. Move your body, have a snack, or get some fresh air in advance.

- Use technology (e.g., calendar, reminder app, GPS) when appropriate to facilitate time management, remember important obligations and tasks, and release the burden of having to hold everything in memory for some future date. Automate as much as you can to reduce the inevitable stress of a high cognitive load on your daily functioning.

- Schedule a break each day to give your brain a rest. If your EF difficulties involve attention and emotion dysregulation, for example, then having to be compassionately present all day can significantly drain your system.

- Adopt a cloud-based visual workflow or task management system (e.g., Trello) for work and personal-life projects and tasks. While some of us thrive on simple checklists, others need graphically oriented, prioritization-friendly, and easily manipulatable "cards" that we can move around from a "master list" to a "to do this week" column to an "actively doing" pile and finally to a "done" column.

GIVE YOUR FRONTAL LOBE A FITNESS WORKOUT

There are many ways to enhance your EF skills, both directly and indirectly. A recent approach that holds great promise for enhancing your EF is mindfulness training with meditation (Sarkis, 2018; Zylowska, 2012), which is essentially strengthening our attentional and regulatory capacities one breath at a time. People who regularly meditate show development in the brain regions associated with attention, self-monitoring, and emotional processing (Lazar, 2013).

The act of doing mindfulness-based meditation helps us deliberately use the mind to change the brain. When we purposefully, nonjudgmentally, repeatedly bring our minds to a neutral object of attention even when we get distracted by our own thoughts and feelings, we are training skills that can benefit our everyday lives. Mindfulness meditation improves our inhibitory functions (e.g., Gallant, 2016) and thus allows us to stop, think, and choose rather than getting pulled in whatever direction internal or external circumstances might dictate.

Mindfulness training has also been shown to decrease the size and activation of the amygdala, the threat detection area of the brain, and to strengthen the connectivity between the prefrontal cortex and the limbic system (Hölzel et al., 2011). People feel subjectively less stressed when they engage in meditation practice, and stress cannot be overstated as a significant source of EF struggles.

Think back to a time when you were particularly stressed or had to juggle multiple tasks at once. Where was your mind? Were you distracted by the stress and diverted from your important tasks? When there's stress in our systems, working memory and response times can be negatively affected (Sliwinski et al., 2006), decision making is compromised, and we can become more reactive. Reactivity may be one of the most unfortunate consequences of strained executive control, and stress exacerbates reactivity. Fortunately, mindfulness meditation is somewhat of an antidote to this cascade of deleterious effects.

Sometimes we can become emotionally overwhelmed, feeling as if things in the moment are just too much to handle. This process happens frequently enough with individuals who have ADHD or other EF struggles. Fortunately, we can turn to a wonderful on-the-spot practice for emotion regulation that Sarkis (2018) called "managing the too much." The idea is to slow down the flow of experience by taking snapshots of your physical (and/or emotional) landscape with your eyes. Close your eyes and connect with your breath for a moment. Then open your eyes and close them again quickly, taking a circumscribed snapshot of the area around you. What details did you notice; what was your experience like? Open and close your eyes quickly two more times, being curious about whatever you saw and perhaps describing it briefly in your mind. Take deep belly breaths throughout the brief process to add to the regulatory effect, as you're actively engaging your parasympathetic nervous system to soothe, relax, clarify, and create an increased sense of exterior safety and interior safeness.

Our brains and thus our EF skills don't change only when we directly influence them through conscious actions such as meditation, doing active brain-stimulating and synchronizing activities (e.g., BrainGym), or playing brain-training apps (e.g., Lumosity). We can also indirectly but significantly affect our frontal lobe functioning and thereby affect our well-being through integrating other practices and habits such as those discussed earlier in this book. For example, sleep that is of adequate length, high quality, and consistent is probably one of the most fundamental mechanisms for helping your brain's executive center to function optimally. We've all likely experienced the ill effects of being sleep deprived as we drive our cars absentmindedly, process and remember material with clients slowly, and have trouble doing basic tasks in our personal lives. The negative effects of poor sleep on our brain power not only emerge from significant sleep deficits but can also snake their way in through inconsistent sleep patterns, broken REM and deep restorative sleep cycles, and untreated sleep disorders.

Exercise and movement are also crucial for helping to support your EF capacities (Ratey, 2008). Through certain forms of movement, we increase a host of neurotransmitters (e.g., dopamine, endorphins, serotonin, norepinephrine, GABA) that are partly responsible for or at least supportive of a large constellation of EF abilities and overall functioning of the body and brain (Durston, 2010). Research suggests that even short bouts of exercise can help improve EF (MacIntosh et al., 2014) and that 20 to 30 minutes of exercise can improve performance on EF skills tests (Wigal et al., 2013). We also know that exercise and certain forms of movement help decrease levels of depression and anxiety, thus freeing up our brain's capacity to function without such hindrances.

Although there is a lot of advice on what forms of exercise are the "best," we're likely safe in concluding that any movement and exercise is better than no movement to help your brain function more optimally (unless it's actually harmful or contraindicated from a particular condition you have). Research continues to demonstrate that, for different reasons and for a different range of benefits, moderate low-intensity aerobic exercise, high-intensity interval training, and strength training can all be excellent for overall brain–body health. Martial arts, including tai chi, and yoga have also been shown to support, train, and improve EF skills (e.g., Converse et al., 2014; Marquez-Castillo, 2013). Tai chi, qigong, and yoga specifically are known for their stress-mitigating effects (e.g., Abbott & Lavretsky, 2013), among other amazing benefits, and so incorporating even simple versions of these ancient practices can help.

The power of proper hydration cannot be overstated. When our bodies are not adequately hydrated, our mood and cognitive functioning can be disrupted (Procyk, 2018). A fairly reliable way to test for good hydration is to see if your urine is clear. In general, the darker the urine, the more water you need. But as Wittbrodt and Millard-Stafford (2018) found, as you approach the feeling of thirst, you're already likely to have compromised attention, EFs, and motor coordination. Making sure good-tasting water and/or low-caffeine tea are a frequent enough part of your daily routine could enhance your mind–body–brain functioning, even if you're compelled to take a few more trips to the bathroom each day.

Nutrition, including adequate hydration, is another important part of maintaining and even enhancing the functioning of your frontal lobe. There is some evidence that omega-3 fatty acids support effective neuronal activity (e.g., Bauer et al., 2014), improve ADHD symptoms (e.g., Hawkey & Nigg, 2014), increase EF performance in older adults, and improve processing speed and attention in individuals with age-related cognitive decline (Mazereeuw et al., 2012).

CHECK PROCRASTINATION AT THE DOOR NOW, NOT LATER

Those of us who procrastinate frequently know all too well how it feels to delay important tasks in favor of doing something else, anything else. The allure of productive procrastination or just plain avoidance is strong. What seemed like a good strategy or simply a way to avoid tough decision making or unpleasant feelings can unfortunately backfire. Although procrastination is initially a reprieve from stress, we end up contending with distressing and sometimes panic-inducing experiences.

Ned Hallowell, MD—ADHD expert and author—summed up this deal with the devil with an understanding that in the eyes of individual with ADHD or other EF challenges, there's only "now or not now" (Hallowell, 2019). But "not now" soon becomes a pressing and distressing "now!" Although minimizing the procrastination in your life may not seem like a self-care strategy proper, it can be one of the best gifts we can give ourselves, operating behind the scenes to keep our lives smoothly humming rather than bumping along in stressful fits and starts.

Some of us who are chronic procrastinators—roughly 20% of the American population—may feel that we're lazy (American Psychological Association, 2010). Incidentally, I would argue that the word "lazy" is simply pejorative without any substance, as it belies what's underneath people's tendencies to either delay doing what they need to do or not do it at all. Dr. Elizabeth Lombardo (2014), clinical psychologist and author of *Better Than Perfect*, offered some sound insights about the nature of procrastination and what to do about it. What many of us might conclude is a time management problem is likely also or even more of a distress tolerance and task aversion issue. The perceived unpleasantness of a given task (e.g., boring, painful, challenging) gives way to avoidance. Thoughts about our relative ineptitude, lack of support, or history of not being able to accomplish similar tasks can weigh us down and hold us back. For that reason, a comprehensive, values-oriented set of strategies can be very helpful.

Using the framework by Lombardo (2014), we can explore several strategies that can be quite fruitful when kept in the front of your mind, on your calendar, taped to your wall, on coping codes in your pocket, or with a trusted other who has your back:

- *Keep your catastrophizing and perfectionism in check.* Tasks that are perceived as "unbearable" or "hellish" are simply less likely even to be considered than are tasks that are "workable" or "manageable." An all-or-nothing, perfection-or-failure attitude can often accompany the perception of tasks as overwhelming. Tasks don't get started or completed nearly as easily if something has to feel perfect in order to proceed. Thus, "good enough" or "done is better than perfect" can replace "yes, but it has to be . . ."

- *Focus on values and incentives.* When we know our "why" for doing the things we do, we can build intrinsic motivation and fuel our purpose for taking action sooner rather than later. For example, imagine that a client is expressing appreciation that you emailed them a few referrals they've been waiting for. This imagery may provide just enough values-oriented push for you to take the extra few minutes right now for the task. Similarly, most of us need some kind of incentive to get things done. Rather than co-opting the "fun" activities as distractions, use them as immediate rewards for getting the delayed tasks done in a timely fashion.

- *Schedule your tasks, and then do them at the designated times.* One of the most common ways we delay is by contingency planning—"When I have time, then I'll do it." Think about how well that works in your life. Scheduling tasks like we schedule clients is often an effective way to accomplish all the business we have to get done in our lives. "I can just get to it later" is another very common trap. But as Lombardo (2014) warned, be *realistic* about what and when you can do those tasks. If you're simply not a morning person, perhaps don't schedule important tasks for 6:00 a.m. just because you saw a YouTube video with an overly compelling and attractive person who shouts from the rooftops that it's the best thing she's ever done and has changed her life forever. (Please note that I've never done that.)

- *Chunk it to dunk it.* You'll be much more likely to tackle a project or big task if it's not looming large and seemingly unmanageable. Related to the potential for catastrophizing and perfectionism is the idea of breaking down tasks into component parts to reduce their overwhelm and increase your empowerment and confidence. Twenty-six progress notes to catch up on from the week can be quite daunting and cause more procrastination. However, let's say you can write efficiently at 3 minutes per note, totaling a little over 1 hour of note writing. You could be done catching up on your notes for the week in less than three 30-minute work periods (even saying "three 30-minute work periods" might *sound* more workable than "almost 1.5 hours of progress notes to do"). Chunking also gives you milestones, whereas a big unmonitored task doesn't allow for rewards along the way nor obvious feelings of accomplishment.

- *Keep an eye on those excuses.* If you've ever uttered the words "I need to be in the right mood to work" or "I work best only when it's ___ time of day," then you might be operating under the pretense that work can *only* be done or done well when all necessary conditions are met. Finding good environmental support and a clear-enough head to do your work are of course wise, but we can easily get caught up in an "if–then" excuse fest. Waiting and waiting for the right time or mood is often a surefire way of ensuring it never gets done.

- *Partner up and get accountable.* Sometimes we need basic interpersonal connection, feedback, shared goals, and accountability to get things done in a timely way. One of my clients began to make considerable progress on his goals when I offered a coaching technique of checking in by text every few days simply to ask him how he was doing with respect to what mattered. On my own behalf, I accelerated my gratitude practice once I partnered up with my former graduate school supervisor and another former student of hers. Each week, we shared through email what we were grateful for and even added some loving-kindness wishes for each other. This experience produced one of the most palpable shifts in my well-being during the month or so that we endeavored it.

- *Design your environment for success.* Industrial and organizational psychology research points us in the direction of optimizing productivity, performance, and wellness while we're on the job. If you're trying to work on your computer but your phone notifications are buzzing away and your 15 other tabs are slowing your processing speed while enticing you to look at them, it may be time for an environment optimization check. For 30 minutes of uninterrupted work, perhaps you might turn your phone to airplane mode (or at least turn notifications off), close down but save all your active tabs (perhaps using an amazing extension for the Chrome browser called OneTab), get a glass of water and a small snack, and let others know you'll be in another room (if available) finishing some work. This set of strategies isn't failsafe, but it sure beats sitting at your slow computer with a YouTube video paused on a visible window while your stomach rumbles and your mouth feels as dry as a desert.

- *Forgive yourself.* When all else "fails," try your best to let be or let go. Beating ourselves up for poor or delayed productivity usually just demoralizes us and sets us up for the same or worse feelings next time. Forgiveness can ease procrastinatory tendencies and enhance your optimism. You can also use procrastination awareness to your advantage by learning what got in the way the first time and then modifying those variables for future endeavors (Lombardo, 2014).

Hopefully, this chapter shed some light on how to support an often-hidden set of brain-based capacities that can both help and hinder our everyday functioning. Because we may not be aware of subtle deficits or the EF strengths we possess, we can do our best to draw compassionate attention to this facet of our lives. Our professional and personal selves will thank us for this far-reaching form of self-caring.

As we take a closer look at how to enhance our everyday functioning, we must also elevate our awareness of what draws and drags our attention away from what is most important to us. (Social) media is one such source of mental and emotional influence, and it has an increasingly powerful presence in our lives. Chapter 31 focuses on ways to consume media in the most mindful and balanced way possible to support our overall health and sense of stability in an ever-changing and unstable world.

31 MINDFUL USE OF TECHNOLOGY AND MEDIA

The growing influence of technology on the human condition is vast and varied. We must be mindful of even the best it has to offer.

—Anonymous

When you were a child perhaps you imagined growing up in a fantastical future filled with flying cars and talking robots. Well, the future is now. In fact, as I was working on the revisions of this book, I saw a news headline touting the construction of the first functional flying car. Millions of us own robotic vacuums, devices that listen and talk to us, and incredibly powerful computers that we carry around with us like appendages. On these computers are gateways to everything and anything we can imagine. We can do a crossword puzzle, get a social media "like," post a photo of our index finger for hundreds of people to see instantaneously, select someone to date, buy furniture, watch videos strung together like DNA, deposit money in our bank, transfer rent to our landlord, and scroll through endless comments from people we've never met and likely never will. Like Pavlov's dog, we can begin to feel urges to engage in (or avoid) such activities simply at the sight of our devices.

https://doi.org/10.1037/0000309-032
The Thriving Therapist: Sustainable Self-Care to Prevent Burnout and Enhance Well-Being, by M. A. Hersh

How we interact with our smart devices can have profound implications for experiences of stress, anxiety, mood, self-worth, energy, and overall outlook on the world. As I pen these words, we're still caught in the middle of one of the world's most devastating pandemics, and racial and ethnic tensions continue to be a fever pitch with no signs of relenting. This perfect storm is where social media and incredibly stressful circumstances meet.

Our news apps, YouTube, and social media platforms all feed us minute-by-minute updates of real, semi-real, and doctored stories and footage of what's happening around us. As Wise and Barnett (2016) noted, a vital facet of therapist self-care is raising awareness of our global tendency toward "exposure to contexts of hyper-reality and media immersion" (p. 10). Our threat detection and protection systems are often on high alert, and constant media updates and notification pushes likely do not help us to "stand down" and engage our soothing systems for pausing, seeking refuge and calm, and offering ourselves and others compassion.

YOUR SMART TECH INTERACTIONAL STYLE

We typically don't stop to think about how we're right- or left-handed. We just favor one or the other and procedurally use the favored arm and hand in functional ways each day. If our smartphones have indeed become attached like appendages, however, we may function on relative autopilot without thoughtful reflection before speedily entering our passcodes and consuming the latest news buzz, social media commentary, or endless video posts.

A 2017 global survey revealed some staggering statistics on the *how* and *how often* of smartphone usage (Deloitte, 2017). We check our phones a sobering 47 times per day, with 93% of us using our phone while shopping and 89% on our phone *while* we watch TV. Half of us check our phones within 15 minutes of waking up, and almost 58% are on our phone 30 minutes before bed. Some of us even check our phone during the middle of night, with 50% of young adults and approximately 15% of older folks engaging in this behavior.

Do you carry your phone around with you 24/7 and feel highly unsettled if you discover it's not on your person? Do you commit to phone-free time when engaged in meaningful activities or try to limit your usage by setting reminders, deleting apps, or putting your phone away for a period of time? What about between clients or at the start or end of your clinical day? Perhaps you feel you can't be without your phone in the bathroom, using it as a virtual newspaper, book, TV, or the Sunday crossword. The fact that you may have half your library of books on a reader phone app would indeed make it difficult to separate from your device at the time you might like to use it the most.

How often to do use your phone as a bedtime companion and as a morning cup of joe served piping hot with other people's news before your head even lifts off your pillow? Understanding our patterns and habits is part of the solution to helping us use our devices and interact with (social) media in the most helpful, informative, uplifting, and balanced ways possible.

HOW SMART TECH AND SOCIAL MEDIA CAN BENEFIT US

As discussed throughout this book, relational support and a sense of connection are vital facets of self-care and prevention aids for dis-ease. Being a significant source of support for clients' emotional and mental health is a serious and complex task. As therapists, we need trusted outlets and ways to release, reconnect with humanity, and reset ourselves. Social media in particular is a spectacular method for such self-caring aspirations. We can quickly see a comment from a friend or post something silly to our network and get some relatively immediate (and hopefully supportive or funny) responses in return. We can reconnect with old friends and quickly befriend acquaintances we met at a conference a year earlier.

Over the years, social media and networking sites have increased the feasibility of their platforms to benefit niche groups in a relatively safe and secure manner. The advent of closed, moderated professional development groups for psychotherapists is a seemingly beneficial product of this movement. Through various platforms, such groups offer to mental health professionals all types of support, including professional growth, decision making, balanced living, private practice building, and self-care.

In fact, some highly specialized groups target niche populations of psychotherapists, like highly sensitive persons (HSPs). Being relatively hidden in plain sight and often stigmatized for feeling "too much," HSP therapists can come together in one virtual place and support one another's professional and personal lives. This camaraderie and support also occurs on social media for therapists with other conditions such as obsessive–compulsive disorder and attention-deficit/hyperactivity disorder. These types of groups could not have existed without ever-expanding social media platforms.

HOW SMART TECH AND SOCIAL MEDIA COMPROMISE OUR WELL-BEING

The pace of technological advances is staggering. Books on self-care written 15 years ago had only a small glimpse of the ways in which smartphones and social media would come to dominate our mental, emotional, relational, and physical landscape. Experimental research suggests that attention and cognitive performance can be compromised by the mere presence of a smartphone, even when the user attempts to ignore it (Wilmer et al., 2017). The social implications are not to be underestimated. In fact, spouses can get a bit testy when their partners are "listening" more to their phones than to them (Golem, 2018), a recently dubbed phenomenon called *partner phubbing* (Roberts & David, 2016).

As Dr. Chris Willard—mindfulness teacher, author, and psychotherapist—noted, the instant we click that button or log in, "we are drinking from a firehose of emotional stimulus" (Willard, 2016). Like no other phenomenon on the planet, interacting with a social media platform can insidiously and simultaneously produce self-doubt, social disgust, envy, hate, frustration, satisfaction, lust, reassurance, inspiration, demotivation, and increased motivation. These feelings can all occur in just a few minutes or even seconds of scrolling through Facebook or Twitter, for example.

The news is no different. If we click on one article about racial unrest and violence and begin to feel helpless, angry, or sad, then we feel compelled to click another link that leads us to so many other previous incidents of racial violence. We then watch three short clips of an innocent person being harassed, threatened, or even killed. Before we know it, we're flooded. The unsettling nature of this kind of news might be disheartening and jarring within an average instance of scrolling through the news, but some of us may read or listen to news of this type just before or after seeing clients. How are we supposed to compose and ground ourselves and ignore what we just took into our systems? We would be justified in acknowledging that we're asking too much to ask of ourselves—to be *containers* of our clients' struggles, our own strains, and the world's suffering.

Psychotherapists, unlike so many other professionals, are already dealing with so much emotion as a matter of course. Trauma, hopelessness, or suicidal ideation, for example, don't often reveal themselves in a car dealership or at the accountant's office. But those experiences are sometimes spilled into our occupational laps when people come to see us for those very conditions of mind, heart, and spirit. Thus, it behooves us to avoid the unnecessary dread, hopelessness, anger, or uncertainty by nonconstructively being connected to (certain) social media and news sites.

However, I do not take the view that all phone use and social media should be avoided. Rather, we have to make very mindful and informed decisions based on who we are and how we process rapidly generated and often jarring information. If I read my phone news updates in the morning and happen to run across a horrific news story, my mood undoubtedly will be affected for minutes to hours. I will sometimes be aware of this effect, while other times

I'm likely ignorant of the subtle damage that's been done to my outlook and mental state for that period of time.

If we work to know our habits of mind and emotion (see Chapter 10), we can reflect on whether news scrolling or "visits to the social media shop" temporarily alter our emotions, transform our feelings, or modify our moods for an even greater length of time and depth of intensity. The balance of this chapter focuses on how to stay our most mindful selves as the news, social media, and general phone distractions swirl around us.

HOW PSYCHOTHERAPISTS CAN MINDFULLY CONSUME AND DIGEST (SOCIAL) MEDIA

So how do we stay connected and informed, if those are our goals, while not getting unnecessarily and negatively affected by social media and other media-based doom-scrolling experiences?

- *Set limits*. This advice runs counter to how most of us use social media and check the news on our phones or computers—largely on a whim, when bored, or just out of habit. This autopilot checking occurs often when our phones are in our pockets or set in front of us, rather than when they are stashed away or charging somewhere else. Limit setting can come in many forms:

  - Commit to *not* looking at news or social media feeds for at least 30 minutes before bed and after you wake up.

  - Set a time limit for reading the news or scrolling through/posting on social media platforms. You can set a timer on your phone or download one of the many apps designed to help people curb the overuse of smartphones.

  - Give yourself permission to refrain from checking your work email (in particular) after dinner and before breakfast (if you indeed eat breakfast). Even if you don't see a client's or a colleague's email, opening up your inbox serves to prompt your mind–body–brain toward work, productivity, stress, and responsibility. These are the *drive mode* effects that we're interested in soothing toward the end of the day and hopefully interested in slowly and deliberately revving up in the morning, rather than being jarred into a feeling via an innocent check of our email.

- *Sort out the emotional effects*. Media in general, and social media in particular, can produce a wide range of emotions in a very short span of time. We would thus benefit from practicing careful awareness of the ins and outs of what we're consuming. If we were reading a funny article on how comedians have dealt with the COVID-19 pandemic and then autopilot-clicked on a U.S. Centers for Disease Control and Prevention report on the potentially grave risks of large indoor social gatherings, we would be lifted up and slammed down all within a few minutes. If we weren't keenly mindful of this yo-yo effect, we might take our confused anxiety into the next portion of our day, including our therapy sessions. At the very least, we might need to give ourselves a bit of space between media consumption and media digestion so that we know if the news went down just fine or if we'll be uncomfortably emotionally bloated for the next several hours, in need of some affective Pepto.

• *Build in the pause.* Practice pausing long enough to ask yourself what your intention is as you begin to read an article, watch a video, or mop up scores of posts and comments on social media. If you're reading comments that were based on previous comments based on prior comments, you might be far enough down the comment rabbit hole. If you typically aren't aware of how much time you're spending engaged in (social) media, you would likely benefit from a conscious media engagement approach. Asking yourself "What am I about to do and why?" might initially feel like an overly stilted question, but it could benefit your peace of mind and sanity along the way.

• *Consume positive news to counteract everyday media consumption.* From watching the "nightly news" or the daily updates (refreshed seemingly every 5 minutes), we might conclude that the earth is literally on fire or on a collision course with Mars (which will then be populated with a special race of humans created by Elon Musk). News is not neutral. News catches fire because it's next to other news that's already burning. And like a moth to flame, humans are attracted to the light. There's nothing particularly uplifting, inspiring, or soothing about what is typically thrust in our face on an hourly basis. We must consciously choose alternative news sources that can help remind us of the good in most of us. You can check out lists of positive news sites at https://www.top10.com/good-news-websites. From there, you can choose a few favorite sites to routinely peruse to remind yourself that a lot more good than evil is brewing in the world.

A NOTE ON TELE-MENTAL HEALTH AND "ZOOM FATIGUE"

Those of us who endured the practice of psychotherapy during the COVID-19 pandemic became intimately if not frustratingly familiar with staring at our computer screens for hours on end. We logged on to our platform of choice (or one that our agency or clinic decided to use) and tried our best to stay connected in more ways than one. Sometimes our (or our client's) Wi-Fi signal was weak, and we strained to hear or see our client amid the broken stream of sounds and sights. We became strained to connect emotionally as well, feeling increasingly exhausted as the days, weeks, and months went by.

Pandemic-inspired research from Professor Jeremy Bailenson, founding director of the Stanford Virtual Human Interaction Lab, pointed to some reasons why (Bailenson, 2021). First, it is quite unnatural to have prolonged and excessive amounts of close-up eye contact. It's too intense, and humans aren't really built for this type of interaction. But the virtual platform "allows" for or even encourages this unnatural connection, although our brains and bodies are not prepared for such engagement. Second, since when do we watch ourselves when we do therapy? Video chat platforms, when left to their default settings, force us to glance or even stare at ourselves all day long. This "mirror mode" can be incredibly fatiguing and can create much more self-consciousness than is typical for the average human, even for the exceptionally humble psychotherapist. Third, although many of us aren't typically too active within most psychotherapy sessions, there's much less opportunity for mobility during virtual appointments. This stagnation can impede cognitive performance and can certainly encourage more tiredness and sleepiness than usual. Finally, in-person engagement allows us to interpret nonverbal and ideomotor cues relatively effortlessly and fluidly. Video platforms can make us work hard for this vital data streaming into our subconscious mind. We have to strain to send and receive the usual signals of good therapy. Moreover, some gestures you or your client make may be therapeutically meaningless (e.g., your client staring off camera because their dog is barking), but similar behaviors (e.g., a side stare) could be quite concerning when in person.

Bailenson (2021) recommended a few strategies to minimize fatigue. For example, you can reduce the size of your client's face (staring you in the face) by minimizing the video platform screen. You can also attach an external keyboard to "pull yourself back" from the screen. Relatedly, you can hide the "self view" that always shows your face and torso next to your client's face. Just looking at your client is enough for the hour.

To allow for mobility, you could directly invite movement to your sessions by making it "allowable" to move around and shift your eyes as needed. If you're a body-oriented or movement-based therapist, you can push your screen much farther back so that your client can see you fully standing if you need to stand for your therapeutic work. As nonverbal gestures and ideomotor cues are quite important for the psychotherapeutic endeavor, you'll want to cut yourself some slack if you miss some little cues you might otherwise have caught. You can also look less intently at your client's face for the entire session. This strategy may ultimately help with facial image burnout session after session.

THE TELETHERAPY MOVEMENT: CHANGING THE FACE OF OUR PROFESSION ONE ZOOM LOG-IN AT A TIME

It is almost certain that the discussion of telehealth strategies is only the beginning of the conversation about ways to work more effectively within an evolving virtual psychotherapy model. The COVID-19 pandemic has shed light on teletherapy not only as a necessary part of how we can serve our clients but also as a viable option to be integrated into everyday practice and professional development. We've seen agencies, clinics, hospitals, and treatment centers rely to some extent on remote methods for therapy sessions, supervision, staff and research meetings, and the like. The pandemic has also interfered with inpatient, partial hospital, and residential treatment programs, causing some to resort only to virtual programming to *try* to meet patients' needs. In the realm of professional development, workshop and conference organizers to some extent have been compelled to switch their delivery of content to an all-online format.

These changes to therapeutic, support-oriented, and continuing education content delivery have been a boon, as therapists have been able to provide essential assistance, connect with like-minded therapists through the click of a button, and learn a vast amount of information from the comfort of their own homes. However, given all the challenges inherent in doing only virtual therapy, we may be neglecting vital aspects of how we do our jobs. In addition, as we perform the nondirect service and professional development aspects of our work, networking, hands-on skills building, and fundamental in-person and face-to-face contact are compromised. These new realities have been extremely difficult on some of us who rely on live and experiential work to learn, teach, and help.

None of us were at all prepared for this. Even if we had experience with teletherapy or an occasional video or phone meeting, these methods likely weren't woven into the fabric of how we worked. The pandemic has compelled these ways of working and relating to become normative. It's now expected that some of us take crash courses in the ethics and pragmatics of telehealth as a matter of survival and to thrive in this new age (see Breslin, 2020, for telehealth best practices at https://www.GoodTherapy.com; see also *Mastering Telehealth & Anxiety Treatment in the Age of Social Distancing* at https://catalog.pesi.com/). Whatever your workplace and treatment delivery circumstance, it is probably safe to assume that the various faces of telehealth are here to stay. It will be up to us as individuals but also to our workplace environments and professional culture to help us acclimate to this new normal.

Technology writ large of course will not stop advancing. Social media of some form certainly isn't going away. The news will likely keep its main focus on strife and tragedy, with less on what's going well and who is making the world a better place. The pandemic has been slow to recede, and we may be burdened as a society and planet by other such scourges that affect the ways we work and live. So, the question is not about *whether* but *how* we'll need to adjust to such challenges now and over time. This confrontation of stark reality is not meant to bring us down. It's meant to invite us to realize that we may have more influence than we think. We can turn off our devices earlier than we normally do. We can download more "peace-loving" apps than our phones might natively offer us. We can consciously consume social media and really know what and who we're clicking on rather than slipping down the rabbit hole after one or two unfortunate scrolls.

Part of how we can conquer these technology- and media-based realities is through making space for other endeavors that feel expansive, bring us joy, and inspire a variety of opportunities to thrive. Chapter 32 addresses such invitations for both grounding and growth.

32

PERSONAL GROUNDING AND GROWTH

Making Space for Creative Endeavors, Self-Growth, and Pursuing Our Own Therapy

The most regretful people on earth are those who felt the call to creative work, who felt their own creative power restive and uprising, and gave to it neither power nor time.

—Mary Oliver

Seeking ways to engage your creative self can be an enormous gift. Through hobbies like music, art, writing, baking, learning languages, hiking, athletics, or other hands-on endeavors, we can complement our professional lives in meaningful and fun ways. We can also seek to thrive, grow, and expand in ways that we don't currently experience. Professional growth (explored in Chapter 33) is one thing, but a focus on your personal development and evolution can be a beautiful and worthwhile pursuit in and of itself. To evolve (and to heal), sometimes we need assistance from a coach, group, or individual practitioner. Pursuing therapeutic endeavors of our own can be exceptionally useful to remediate difficult conditions, cope with challenging circumstances, support our own self-care, and gain freedom toward a more fulfilling life.

https://doi.org/10.1037/0000309-033
The Thriving Therapist: Sustainable Self-Care to Prevent Burnout and Enhance Well-Being, by M. A. Hersh

CREATIVE ENDEAVORS OUTSIDE OF WORK

Creativity can mean different things to different people, and the more expansively we can think the better. And so you may reflect on creativity as signifying creating or constructing new "things" or being innovative, for example by writing your own music, creating a painting, or authoring a blog post on your photography adventures. But this type of creativity might be overly narrow and restrict us from brainstorming the variety of ways in which we can be active participants in hobbies rather than passive receivers (e.g., watching TV, listening to a podcast). Thus, we can take the broad view and consider that creative endeavors outside of your professional world can stretch as far outside the box as you'd like. After all, engaging in hobbies has been a highly endorsed strategy for getting away from the demands of clinical work and building a rewarding personal life (Rupert & Kent, 2007).

We weren't always therapists, even if we long had the qualities and necessary ingredients to occupy and perform well in this role. What did you like to do before you became a therapist? Did you find yourself captivated by making things with your hands? Maybe you sew, knit, crochet, or embroider. Perhaps you scrapbook, do collage, or fancy yourself a photographer or amateur movie maker. Do you like to bake, cook, garden, or landscape? Were you on your way to becoming a serious musician, dancer, or athlete? Not that I had the advanced technical skills at the time, but toward the end of college I seriously contemplated devoting myself to jazz piano. I loved jazz and played piano. As may be evident from this book, I chose psychology. But my musical self is still inside, and I have to make sure to coax him out more often to bring fulfillment and joy to my life.

I have a colleague and friend, Jen Earls, who is an active professional dancer. Dance is "so much a part of who she [is] and a pathway to [her] wholeness" (J. Earls, personal communication, October 2, 2021). Ms. Earls used to operate her own life coaching and career counseling practice and would use "movement, dance, and mindfulness when [she] was coaching to help [her] clients feel more fully aligned and thereby access their own creativity and empowered choices in ways they couldn't from where they started or from traditional, solely mental or linear approaches." Ms. Earls noted that "coaching others on following their dreams in this way inspired [her] to fully pursue [her] creative, entrepreneurial vision and path." She went on to found Dance for Humanity, a sustainable dance community and business that aims to enhance dancers' and viewers' well-being as well as to raise funds for ecosocial causes. Ms. Earls's story is one of values, wholeness, and courage—deeply knowing what compels us into easeful alignment and allowing inspiration to fuel what truly matters.

Another colleague and friend of mine is a denominational counselor of Buddhism and instructor in ministry and pastoral counseling by day and a musician by night. In fact, he harnessed his passion for and education in Buddhism to cofound a contemplative music group that merges chanting, acoustic folk tradition, and Buddhist practice. For this colleague, the music he writes and creates is designed to inspire spiritual exploration and the qualities of well-being, compassion, freedom, and sense of community. In fact, he is *in community*, with creative others, and engaging in meaningful and spiritual practice as he creates and performs his music. Thus, he likely experiences many benefits by making space for this one creative endeavor outside of his work.

Of course, not all creative endeavors in your down time have to involve some element of your up time. During graduate school, a dear friend and colleague trained vigorously in martial arts and *leaned back* into some creative relaxation through painting. He noted that martial arts, in part, helped him to release and harness energy with his physical body that he was unable to address adequately with his verbal self. Painting allowed him to explore themes, feelings, and the odd beauty of the world that couldn't be captured in any other way for him. This friend inspired me to remember some of the creative passions that I had forgotten during the first 2 years of my graduate school tenure (and that I continue to have to keep on the front burner lest they get relegated to the, well, back burner). My first 2 years of graduate school were so incredibly work intensive, and I certainly would have been more seriously burned out by the middle of graduate training had I not rediscovered my love for music. I began to play guitar again, and I reinvigorated my interest as a songwriter. I played open-mic nights and equitably allocated my time and energy to include writing, playing, and performing music as well as training as a psychologist and psychotherapist.

To pause, to really listen to your needs for creative outlets, and to make space for what calls to you actually takes some courage. Some of us are quite driven, perfectionistic, or addicted to the intermittently rewarding hum of working, striving, and helping. If this experience resonates at all with you, then it's even more important to slow down and tune into the "white space," as life coach and former art therapist Lanie Smith articulated (Smith, 2016).

How do you view creative endeavors in your life? Do you make space for them? Are you perhaps unaware that something is missing? What beliefs do you hold regarding creativity outside of your professional life? Some therapists consider their professional roles as secondary and their roles outside of work as primary. When we map our self-care values in this way (see Chapter 6), we put our larger selves first and our work selves second. But this prioritization is not so easy, and we may find ourselves for many reasons—financial, emotional, physical—less able or less willing to intentionally carve out this time for our more creative selves.

Look back to Part II of this book. What did you divine regarding your tendencies to move and carry your body, to think about yourself and the world, to relate to others, to manage yourself in the flow of time? Further reflection on these patterns and the needs that arise from your honest self-assessments can tell you something quite important about if, what, and how you engage your creative side. If you're frequently intellectualizing, worrying, or planning, you may be in particular need of tapping into your capacity to simply *do* something with your hands. In this case, perhaps creativity would *not* involve thinking creatively but rather would simply involve making things with your hands or moving your body in unstructured and unfiltered ways.

Some creative hobbies and activities simply give us a break from our work selves and help regulate our mind–body–brain, while others offer a vital boost to our sense of life fulfillment and purpose. Dr. Jean Shinoda Bolen, Jungian analyst and psychiatrist, appeals to us on a spiritual level: "When you recover or discover something that nourishes your soul and brings joy, care enough about yourself to make room for it in your life" (see https://www.jeanbolen.com/). The activities that help us to expand our sense of self can be considered self-evolutionary and ultimately can contribute to a more enduring self-caring and well-being-oriented lifestyle.

The next section of this chapter addresses personal growth and development as a form of self-caring. Even the belief that we are capable of self-expansion and growth frees us from a caged feeling and into a more open and charged life (Burchard, 2012).

SELF-GROWTH AND DEVELOPMENT

The personal development and self-help industries are worth a staggering $40 billion worldwide. People devoured self-help books in the 1980s and 1990s, but contemporary self-growth and development looks a lot different. Online courses, personal growth YouTube channels, and life coaching have added entirely new dimensions to how we seek to advance ourselves in pursuit of something greater and deeper.

Brendon Burchard (2012)—entrepreneur, motivational speaker, and author—offered us a thought-provoking framework for how to think about our lives as we currently inhabit them. As you read through the following descriptions, see which best fits your life right now. Burchard noted that we can live either a caged life, a comfortable life, or a charged life. In a *caged life*, we tend to be dictated by the past and by others' expectations of us.

Achievement is what's already happened in the past rather than something that is grown on purpose in the future. In a *comfortable life*, we're oriented toward our lives with engagement and gratitude, and we find meaning and purpose in what we do. Finally, cultivating a *charged life* is about practicing contentment for what is but never being satisfied with what has yet to be. Charged lives are lives of inspiration, to ourselves and to others. We pursue things authentic to ourselves, not to others' views of us. We're constantly hungry to stretch our capacities and to even find new abilities we never knew we had.

As Burchard (2012) directed us, each of these three types of lives is fully attainable, and we get what we ask for. It's up to us which type of life we live. Charged lives are not necessarily easy in the traditional sense of the word. In fact, you're likely going against the grain in many respects, and you may necessarily be challenged along the way. However, as with living a values-driven life, this kind of living ultimately allows us to be fulfilled and find life meaningful in spite of the struggle or even because of it.

Reinforcing the guidance from Burchard, Dr. Joe Dispenza (2007) reminded us that we can't expand our lives when we repeat the exact same habits every day while entering the exact same contexts in the exact same way. We have to step back and begin to do and think things differently. We then start to embody these changes and feel the feelings that result from our conscious choice to have changed our mundane into something more extraordinary.

How would you evaluate your own life at this moment in time? What if you reflected on the last 3 years and envisioned how you want your next 3 years to be? Money and socioeconomic status should have little do with whether you decide to live a caged, comfortable, or charged life. Such lifestyle choices are much more about mindset and the small things you do rather than financially backed endeavors that require particular privileged resources. With that said, of course it's often a lot easier to go against others' expectations and "do your own thing" when you have the financial, racial, and gender-based freedom and privilege to do so.

Whatever "type of life" we're living now, we can pay attention to what brings us fulfillment and what helps us push the envelope toward being more enlightened, self-aware, joyful, and generous. As noted in Chapter 11, master motivator Tony Robbins offered us a template to use when we think about our needs and the ways in which we get them met in the real world (Team Tony, n.d.-a). His two high-level needs/drives are all about self-growth and contribution to others.

Not surprisingly, we're already steeped in contributing to others' well-being as part of our professional roles. However, we may decide to engage in other forms of giving, almost as if they tap a different well of inspiration and energy within us. For example, a neuropsychologist colleague has volunteered at Planned Parenthood for years. This longstanding volunteer position meets a self-growth need of hers while providing a wonderful service to an entirely differently population than the clients she typically serves. Another colleague volunteers at an animal shelter, and one volunteers at a horticulture center. These therapists recognize the importance of accessing other parts of themselves that deserve to be seen and given a voice.

Of course, not all personal growth and service-contribution needs have to be met through volunteer work. You may desire to learn how to play an instrument, take care of your house and yard in a particular manner, use your hands in a skillful and creative way, or be more savvy with how to handle your emotions. As a parent, you might desire simply to be more present and attentive to your children. As a friend, you might work on reaching out more and replying more consistently to friends reaching out to you.

I have long had a clear aspiration to serve as a better brother. Not just because my brother was there for me in the most supportive way possible when I was ill, but also simply because it's good for me and for our relationship. Hopefully, it's good for him too. For those of us who seem to let (important) correspondence slip by, this type of personal and relational growth enactment can truly be a challenge. It's one, however, that we can prioritize and elevate in our conscious awareness. It goes without saying, but engaging in what is meaningful pays us back in the currency of living a meaningful and honorable life.

PURSUING YOUR OWN THERAPY

Eight of us, eager and wet behind the ears, gathered in the main conference room of the clinical psychology department. This room would become all too familiar over the next several years as it hosted our academic courses, brown-bag seminars, clinical practica meetings, and research experiments. In fact, I administered my master's project surveys to a room full of undergraduates in this room.

One thing I still remember vividly amid the partial blur of graduate school—our director of clinical training handed us a list of psychotherapists in the local Chapel Hill area who were willing to provide therapy on a substantial sliding scale for interested students. His invitation to us was essentially one of self-care, self-inquiry, growth, and cultivation of well-being.

I distinctly remember thinking something at that moment that I now look back on with sadness and regret. For all my courage to be vulnerable and my desire to become a clinical psychologist, I inconspicuously but somewhat smugly balked at the idea of needing therapy for myself. I was fine. I was in graduate school to help *other* people. But *I* was OK.

This was not my proudest moment, for sure. Fortunately, it was only a moment in time; by the next year I had reached out to a local therapist to begin work on some past issues affecting my present. At the same time I became extremely interested in mindfulness-based stress reduction (MBSR). My immersion throughout graduate school in MBSR courses facilitated a life-long engagement with the teachings of Buddhist psychology and the practice and teaching of mindfulness meditation to help me relate to myself and to my environment with greater ease and compassion.

Many graduate and professional programs in clinical psychology used to require students to be in their own therapy during training. This requirement was not punishment but rather an expected and standard part of becoming a good therapist. "Physician, know thyself" should also be translated for budding psychotherapists. If "psychotherapist, know thyself" were integrated into graduate and professional programs that train psychotherapists, we might very well have a different culture among those whose main job is to help others with their well-being. We would come to view the therapist as both person and helper and as simultaneously distinct and intertwined. Student therapists would begin to know themselves—in shadow and in light, in group and indi-vidual modalities—more intimately and with greater loving awareness.

If you haven't engaged in your own therapy, it may be well worth the time, energy, and cost. Jeff Guenther, MS, LPC, operates many small businesses that support therapists' well-being and professional proficiencies and has a wonderfully helpful list of reasons to go to therapy (that you [perhaps] haven't considered before; Guenther, 2021):

- Get reparented.
- Meet your greatest cheerleader.
- What if there's a sudden crisis?
- Talk to someone who knows you better than you know yourself.
- Practice being different.
- Get called out in the most compassionate way ever.
- Experience the weirdest, most intimate relationship you'll ever have.
- Have a super grounding force in your life.

If you consider that you're a multidimensional vulnerable human being first and a psychotherapist second, Guenther's list seems quite reasonable and inspiring. We can certainly pursue therapy to grow, in positive and expansive ways. We may also need our own psychotherapy to remediate conditions and cope with circumstances that are quite troubling. Many of us live with undue suffering as we struggle with obsessive–compulsive disorder, depression, suicidal ideation, domestic violence, parenting stress, marital dissolution and divorce, burnout, and the like.

As discussed in Chapter 2, psychotherapists are not immune to the extreme existential and depressogenic doubts that plague far too many humans. Four of every 100 therapists have attempted to kill themselves (Pope & Tabachnick, 1994), and suicidal ideation is even more prevalent. For fundamental self-relational issues like these, it would seem imperative for therapists to seek counsel and have a trusted therapist of their own. However, real and perceived barriers exist, such as lack of time and difficulty finding an appropriate therapist (Bearse et al., 2013) as well as the stigma and financial strain that one's own therapy can create. Whether any of these stresses and conditions show up acutely or are lifelong struggles, it behooves us to mitigate the unnecessary strain on our sense of self, relationships, and future.

Certainly, there are vital personal reasons for psychotherapists to pursue their own therapy during training *and* across the career span (Ziede & Norcross, 2020); psychotherapy can help to diminish the influence of occupational hazards and workplace strain. It can be an integrated tool in the toolbox of therapist sustainable self-care. Weekly sessions of our own mixed in with the therapy we offer to others can serve as a grounding and stabilizing force, not letting everyday stress accumulate to uncomfortable levels. We can also work through bigger, deeper, or more chronic issues that may be holding us back both in (Bonovitz, 2009) and out of the therapy room while helping to cultivate intrinsic qualities of resilience and self-compassion. Thus, both stability and growth, both softness and strength can be fostered as we sit humbly in the client's chair for a change.

EXPLORING COMPLEMENTARY THERAPIES

Personal growth and pursing one's own therapy aren't just relegated to psychological change and to the context of psychotherapy. Growth and development come in hundreds of forms, including something as seemingly simple as cooking healthier meals or relating to your family in a more peaceful manner. You may discover that some therapeutic modalities in particular help you to tend to your whole being. For example, if you have decided to treat your body more like a temple than like a machine, you may commit to viewing food as wholesome medicine—making healthy, metabolically resonant meals as an act of self-care and self-evolution. Or you may choose to get a massage once per month, not perceived as a luxury but regarded as essential to your enduring wellness and well-being.

Acupuncture, reiki, craniosacral therapy, massage, physical therapy, hypno-therapy, foot reflexology, energy medicine, mindfulness and yoga classes—the list is endless for the sort of mind–body therapeutic modalities available to us for a wide variety of conditions and issues. The beauty of such approaches is that they can serve as stand-alone support for some issues and comple-mentary to more Western conventional treatments for others. Most major cities and bigger towns have many of these types of practitioners available to help.

Perhaps you've struggled with attention-deficit/hyperactivity disorder (ADHD) your whole life and decide you want to up your game to manage the fallout from your frontal lobe falling down on the job so frequently. Joining an online or in-person ADHD support group or securing a one-on-one ADHD coach could be invaluable for helping you reduce stress and reach new heights.

Sometimes it takes a push from a loved one, and other times we require tapping into a courage to be vulnerable with ourselves. We ask this brave honesty of our clients all the time, and we make space for them to heal and grow. Don't we owe it to ourselves to do the same? In whatever form(s) it takes, seeking out our own sources of support is a gift waiting for us to unwrap.

As we've explored in this chapter, seeking grounding and growth in our personal lives can not only enhance and enliven our nonwork time but also bring a joyful resilience to our work lives. In the next chapter, we turn to a variety of self-caring facets of professional development to bring us both stability and growth in our challenging roles as therapists.

33 PROFESSIONAL GROUNDING AND GROWTH

Seeking Professional Development, Diversity of Experience, and Consultation/Supervision

I've learned that you shouldn't go through life with a catcher's mitt on both hands; you need to be able to throw something back.

—Maya Angelou

We trained hard for years. Coursework, practica, more coursework, and more practica. We completed externships and internships. And we've participated in hundreds of hours of supervision overseeing thousands of hours of client contact. After studying for weeks or months on end, we passed our licensing and ethics exams. Finally, we received a small piece of paper officially declaring us the very thing we set out to train for years earlier. Little did we know (or perhaps some of us were already quite savvy) that this was only the beginning.

CONTINUING EDUCATION AND BEYOND

Continuing education (CE) and professional development are baked into our occupation, as they should be. These growth-oriented objectives not only benefit our current and future clients through increased competencies

https://doi.org/10.1037/0000309-034
The Thriving Therapist: Sustainable Self-Care to Prevent Burnout and Enhance Well-Being, by M. A. Hersh

but also can strengthen existing capacities or foster new ones for psychotherapists' own sake. In fact, the merger of professional ethics, competence, and self-care is a burgeoning area of scholarly work that is being translated into how training programs operate as well as how therapists can conduct themselves across the career span (e.g., Neimeyer et al., 2019).

As is too often done, using the terms "CE" and "professional development" synonymously does our profession a disservice. CE, as a licensure-based requirement, is simply one aspect under the larger umbrella of continuing professional development. We can take a few courses or read a few books every few years to fulfill our CE credits, but this doesn't necessarily mean that we're on a meaningful path of professional development or engaged in adequate competence and self-care assessment (see Neimeyer et al., 2019). Engaging in peer consultation and/or supervision, for example, is part of our professional development just as much as attending a series of workshops on a new therapeutic approach might be.

Beyond our formal training institutions and "prescribed" growth experiences within the therapeutic approach to which we subscribe or the forms of suffering we're treating, we may find it increasingly difficult to place a meaningful structure around the CE and overarching professional development opportunities that we seek and that would be fruitful to our work (see Neimeyer et al., 2019, for a discussion of these themes). When licensure renewal is fast approaching, we may scramble to squeeze in our balance of CE credits rather than having planned out what would ultimately be competence enhancing, beneficial, and fulfilling. Conscious and planful engagement in pursuits of professional development is thus a foundational element of sustainable self-caring and of cultivating and maintaining a competent clinical practice. In their piece on the trials and tribulations of assessing professional learning, self-care, and competence across professional psychologists' careers, Neimeyer and Taylor (2019) spoke to how professional development tools (e.g., Commitment-to-Change Assessment, Jefferson Scale of Psychotherapists Lifelong Learning, Professional Self-Care Scale, Professional Competencies Scale) could help us, our colleagues, and our supervisors provide structured and validated feedback on how we're faring in these domains over time.

Given the rapid pace and development of technology, neuroscience research, pharmacologic interventions, and mind–body approaches, for example, it may be quite frustrating that our knowledge acquisition during our internship, early-career phase, and beyond may quickly become obsolete (see Neimeyer et al., 2019). But alas, as we mature as people and as therapists, we have the capacity for awareness of the maturation of our profession around us. Hopefully, along the way we are consulting with colleagues, former and current supervisors and mentors, and friends and family to achieve clarity and supportive backing for how we learn, grow, and advance ourselves as competently as possible throughout our careers.

Perhaps one of the most sorely needed but unrepresented facets of professional development writ large and CE specifically is that of self-care for the therapist. Professional self-care is increasingly recognized in larger national conventions, but it nevertheless seems to be relegated to the back burner. Even though self-care for the psychotherapist pays dividends "behind the scenes" and in more obvious ways, training in certain approaches always gets the lion's share of our professional development attention.

Fortunately, as we respond thoughtfully to the COVID-19 crises in physical and mental health (and that of the mental health clinician), we are taking our own health and well-being more seriously. For example, the American Psychological Association (APA) invited Dr. Leisl Bryant, a trauma specialist and professor of psychology at Tulane University, to lead a two-part workshop on mental health clinician self-care (Bryant, n.d.). Dr. Bryant spoke to how, now more than ever, we have to turn toward ourselves and our fellow colleagues with utmost compassion, self-awareness, and a self-caring spirit.

Similarly, Dr. Leigh Ann Carter of the Professional Practice Committee of APA's Society for the Advancement of Psychotherapy invited Dr. Erica Wise, self-care and psychology ethics expert, to speak about the state of our challenges and the promises and necessity of self-care in a peri- and postpandemic society (Carter & Wise, 2021). State associations as well as hospitals around the United States are increasingly hosting workshops and grand rounds, respectively, on self-care. As institutional resources have been stretched thin and clinicians' burnout risk has increased exponentially during the pandemic, institutions of all sorts have recognized the need to help the helpers more earnestly and in more tangible ways.

PURSUING A DIVERSITY OF PROFESSIONAL EXPERIENCES

One of the most rewarding experiences I've had the privilege to engage in each semester is teaching mindfulness meditation to college students. Not only do I look forward to the activity of small-group teaching, but I'm always eager to learn from each new group of students. I also have the honor of working with other dedicated mindfulness teachers and wellness professionals within the university and beyond. These individuals always open my eyes to new avenues for imparting mindfulness to emerging adults, and their unwavering commitment to serving their students is both humbling and inspiring.

Side professional activities like small-group mindfulness meditation instruction can serve many purposes. For me, they are healthy diversions from the heaviness of the clinical workday, day in and day out. I relish the opportunity each semester to reach out to the new group of college students, eager for some stress relief skills and ready to join a group of like-motivated peers. Mindfulness teaching is not *yet another* clinical job, however, despite my teaching skills to stressed-out people. I have found over the years that this experience allows me to tap into different strengths and take on new challenges that I don't necessarily have the opportunity to express in individual psychotherapy. Although I'm doing a bit more work each week, this additional professional activity is, in part, just what the burnout prevention doctor ordered.

Many psychotherapists are interested in sharing their skills, expertise, and experience with the public. In our contemporary age, it has become infinitely easier to promote one's ideas through the written word, live spoken word, and video. With a simple click of a few buttons or email to your website manager, you could be up and running with an active blog within a day. Consistently writing enough material that will serve your audience is another story, but professional blogging could become a fun, stimulating, and fulfilling weekend project that doesn't have to consume *too* much of your time. Depending on your areas of expertise and interest, you can find other outlets and platforms (e.g., state and national associations, credentialing bodies, organizations with an online presence, local newspapers) for your writings. Particularly if you've been wrestling with the feeling that you are not reaching as many people as you'd like in your current role as psychotherapist, this form of outreach can be rewarding to all involved.

Some psychotherapists have created podcasts or YouTube channels within their professional expertise and comfort zones. Although quite a bit of work to create, build a faithful audience, and maintain a meaningful presence, podcasts and video channels can be incredibly fulfilling professional activities. A good example of someone pursuing this type of professional experience is Rebecca Wong, LCSW-R, who has promoted her own niche specialty area through a strong web presence and podcast on the relational process of connectfulness. She has significantly expanded her meaningful and positive impact on her professional colleagues and helped scratch an itch to diversify her helping role.

Depending on your goals, you can also create and (co)host workshops, presentations, or small classes that can be live or online. These can be one-off events (in collaboration with different institutions) or recurring offerings. Unlike a fledgling podcast or YouTube channel, workshops can bring in some extra revenue, depending on your audience. The beauty of such offerings is that once you have a few successful events, you can more easily offer more. You can help train or offer support to fellow professionals within your area of expertise as well as share your knowledge with the general public or with particular populations in need.

Still others will create and administrate closed Facebook groups on topics with which they have a good deal of experience. A great example is Lynn Louise Wonders, LPC, RPT-S, CPCS, who created one of the first closed Facebook groups for therapist self-care and support. In his closed Facebook group and podcast *Selling the Couch*, Melvin Varghese, PhD, had a mission to help other mental health professionals *grow our impact and income in and beyond the therapy room* (Varghese, 2015–present). Not only does Dr. Varghese appear to be fulfilling this mission for himself, but he is facilitating fellow therapists' ideas for creating their own diversity of ways to positively affect others and serve themselves along the way.

Other therapists have successfully created niche closed groups for highly sensitive therapists, something that is of special meaning to therapists who feel and think deeply while trying to help and support others with their suffering. I've seen websites of therapists who are artists, photographers, poets, and dancers, for example, and who incorporate in big and small ways their artistic crafts into their professional lives.

Yet other colleagues I know record meditations for websites and meditation apps to serve far more of the general audience than they could ever reach through their one-on-one or small-group therapeutic contacts. There are countless other ways that you and your colleagues can extend and expand your professional selves—perhaps your brainstorming list will spill off the page.

Alternative professional activities don't necessarily have to be strictly within your exact therapeutic or professional skill set. These types of activities can be fulfilling and meaningful, regardless. I know several colleagues who volunteer at food pantries, homeless shelters, and Planned Parenthood. These organizations support underserved and underrepresented populations, and these colleagues feel that their underlying motivation to serve others is satisfied within these volunteer positions. Sometimes it's the act of diversifying how, why, and with whom we interact that can make all the difference for burnout prevention.

Although exploration of alternative professional activities is often done outside of your current job or workplace, you may find a diversity of activities within your current position. Drs. Jason Luoma and Jenna LeJeune, husband and wife co-owners of Portland Psychotherapy, actively weave research into the fabric of workplace culture and activity of their clinic and training center (Chamberlin, 2017). They've chosen to use at least 10% of their revenue to support in-house research studies on the effectiveness and mechanisms of various clinical interventions. Thus, Drs. Luoma and LeJeune not only are fulfilling their own aspirations of both diversity of professional experience and integration of clinical and research endeavors but also are affording their staff to avail themselves of such opportunities.

THE UNASSUMING POWER OF PEER CONSULTATION

Jonathan, an early-career psychologist, was growing increasingly fatigued. He had joined a small group practice 3 years earlier after graduating from a clinical psychology program with a specialization in youth trauma treatment and research. Upon graduation he briefly served as a trauma-oriented therapist on a locked unit at a psychiatric hospital. The high turnover there didn't allow Jonathan to develop the long-term therapy skills he so desired.

Jonathan's current caseload felt enormous, in both volume and the type of clientele he was seeing. Despite his best efforts to find a group practice that offered a specialization in trauma-related services or at least had a few trauma specialists, he found himself in a practice as the sole trauma-informed practitioner, quickly and unintentionally becoming the "resident expert." Unfortunately, Jonathan's experience translated into well over 50% of his caseload (30 clients per week), mostly filled with deeply emotionally disturbed teens within highly challenging family systems. Moreover, his group practice colleagues came to him when they were struggling with highly anxious and depressed clients with morbid histories of trauma.

Jonathan felt like an imposter, supposedly offering top-notch trauma therapy (and consultation to colleagues) but actually feeling like he was doing his clients and their families a huge disservice. He didn't want to rock the boat, given how little time he'd been at the practice. His previous attempts to request support from the group practice director were met with well-intentioned validation but very little pragmatic changes to help stave off Jonathan's slow burn. Jonathan became desperate for help and relief on many levels. Should he ask to scale back his caseload despite the group practice's strict quota for direct client contact? Perhaps he could sign up for more trainings on ways to deliver more effective trauma treatment.

On the advice of some of his graduate-school classmates with whom he still kept in touch, Jonathan began to look for a peer consultation group in his local area. Facilitated by contacts through his state psychological association, he found a small group of more experienced trauma therapists who had room for another colleague. Although it was quite challenging to make time each month and although his caseload remained the same, Jonathan soon found the weight of his imposter syndrome and emotional exhaustion lightening. His new peer consultation group provided reassurance and validation. They helped offer checks and balances against his perception of having to "cure" his clients and profoundly change their life trajectories. His new colleagues with whom he met monthly helped directly with his tougher cases while reframing his tougher therapist moments and lofty expectations of being an early-career trauma therapist. Jonathan also had the opportunity to support his peers, sharing new mind–body trauma treatment perspectives and offering compassion and empathy for their struggles. Finally, Jonathan was able to talk candidly with his new peers about how to reconcile his personal and work life, something he regrettably felt uneasy doing within his group practice.

Therapy consultation writ large is a nonlegally binding sharing of professional and personal support. Unlike formal supervision, consultation can be thought of as informal guidance and advice. This doesn't mean, however, that consultative arrangements are any less valuable. It simply means that your fellow consultants bear no formal or legal responsibility for your actions or development as a therapist. And as a consultee, you have no ethical obligation to adhere to the guidance provided by your peers with whom you're consulting.

As part of conceptualizing self-care as an expansive idea and set of practices, we can view consultation as but one key facet of tending to our personal and professional selves in ways that help us simultaneously stabilize and grow. If you already engage in consultation, how does it contribute to your sense of grounding? What about your growth and sense of evolution of previous versions of your professional (and personal) self? Are you ultimately better off because of your consultative relationships?

Dialectical behavior therapy (DBT) consultation groups are a great example of an integrated form of directed support woven into the fabric of the treatment. Not only are therapists continually learning DBT principles and practices, but they're also fostering the grounding skills needed to survive the frequent emotional ups and downs of this type of clinical practice. If you're in such a consultation group, how does it benefit you, and what are the challenges? If you're not, could you imagine yourself feeling a greater sense of equanimity and growth from such a group?

Types and Purposes of Consultation

What type of consultative relationships do you maintain? Are they regular discussions or one-off consults based on a particular need in the moment? Are your needs met within these relationships, or do you feel that these relational dynamics could be improved in a significant way? Do others reach out to you? Do you lead consultation groups based on your expertise in one approach or arena of psychotherapy?

Psychotherapists generally seek consultation for two main purposes and within two main modalities. One central purpose is to get some help with a tough case or difficult choice points within that case. You might reach out to a trusted colleague who often provides beneficial and reassuring feedback. Or perhaps you have a go-to colleague who is particularly adept at navigating ethical issues. The other main purpose is to establish an ongoing professional relationship or set of relationships with colleagues who share a particular theoretical orientation or perhaps who all work with children and teens with difficulties of overcontrol, for example. These consultative relationships can have a sense of camaraderie and a feeling of belonging to a trusted professional network rather than serving a more problem-focused need.

No matter the size of a consultative group, the structure is likely either a lateral peer-to-peer or a vertical consultant–consultee structure. The hierarchical structure may closely resemble a supervisory relationship save for the legal and ethical responsibilities involved. If you're thinking about joining a consultation group, you would likely benefit from clarifying the structure and expectations of each group member so that you're not caught off guard or disappointed down the road.

If you don't already have a regular, established consultation arrangement, you can call on a trusted colleague on an ad hoc basis. The need might arise in times of professional crisis or acute struggles with particular clients, when your professional activities are significantly affecting your personal life, or when your personal life is influencing your professional role. This type of consultative experience is typically a one-off endeavor that ebbs and flows with how you're feeling and doing as a therapist. Alternatively, you may have a long-term, regular consultative relationship that you can confidently rely on at any time. In this predictable relationship or set of relationships are expectations that colleagues meet with and/or reach out to one another on a regular basis.

The two main modalities of consultation arrangement are *individual* and *group*. With each modality, you could either maintain a regular, ongoing commitment or reach out to a colleague (reciprocally or not) as needed. Ostensibly, you could have a few different individual colleagues (who don't even know each other) who constitute your network of trusted consultants. For example, one colleague could be well-versed in DBT while another might be a relative expert on teen anxiety.

Joining (or forming) a peer consultation group can also provide exceptional benefits in a different way. A consultation group is a bit like a group of friends or a (hopefully harmonious) family system. Each colleague may have a different area of expertise or training background to share with the rest of the group. Opinions and perspectives of course can differ, but ideally the group has each member's best interest at heart, and each member is acting in the best interest of the larger group.

At times, consultation groups may form around one therapeutic approach. I used to rent my office in a suite of expert emotion-focused couples therapists. They would host regular consultation group meetings in the suite conference room as they brought together like-minded couples therapists practicing roughly the same approach. They would talk, share cases, watch videos, and train together. My more expert and seasoned colleagues would offer a great deal of guidance while receiving invaluable feedback from their peers.

I am fortunate to be part of a consultation group whose central focus is the integration of energy psychology into the larger psychotherapeutic endeavor. Three group members (including myself) initially had sought the consultative services of the fourth member, an expert in all things subtle energy related. She assisted us in achieving our diplomate status in comprehensive energy psychology and then continued as lead consultant and group facilitator. Sometimes we learn about new energy psychology methods, and sometimes we discuss the trials and tribulations with these approaches.

Our meetings, however, often expand well beyond energy psychology methods and into the often-explored realms of tough cases, therapist burnout prevention, and the influence of life at large on our professions and vice versa. During the COVID-19 pandemic, we talked a lot not only about how to help our clients through this trying time but also about how to support ourselves with basic self-care practices as well as energy medicine and psychology exercises that can be highly effective in keeping the mind and body "tuned up" and switched on. I now consider each of these consultation group members my trusted colleagues despite their being in different states and our only having met through video chat.

Practical Considerations in Forging Consultative Relationships

How you reach out and in which ways you get support likely depend on a few factors. Your temperament and personality matter. If you lean toward extraversion, for example, you may seek out the company of several colleagues with whom you can regularly discuss cases and even personal–professional life balance. However, if you tend to keep to yourself and prefer one-on-one relationships, then a tight, less relationally involved network of consultative relationships may work better for you.

Logistical considerations, such as location and scheduling, also may affect how you choose your consultative support. If you've joined a promising group that meets biweekly but your drive time is 25 minutes in traffic in each way, you may be adding to your stress rather than finding relief from it. Of course, you'll have to weigh the costs and benefits for your own individual situation. However, the potential burnout prevention, emotional grounding, and challenging case support provided by the group may overshadow the inconveniences of traffic, long travel times, and lost income.

Sometimes we stumble upon our gifts serendipitously. Several of my go-to consultative relationships over the years emerged when I was least expecting it. This is not to say we should rely on chance to support ourselves professionally but rather that we may need to expand our awareness of the relationships we already have or are currently forging. From there, we may choose to develop a meaningful set of collaborative and consultative connections that can benefit us for years to come. We may also seek out consultation groups via more formal channels such as our state psychological association, any professional organization of which we're a member, and our training institutions. Informally, we can "ask around"—colleagues in different circles will always have ideas worthy of pursuing. We just have to inquire.

What to Avoid With Consultation

If this book had been written a decade earlier, we would have had very little to say about the strong and pervasive influence of social media culture on our professional and social lives. Today's reality paints a very different picture. Given that there were 3.6 billion users of social networking sites in 2020 (Statista Research Department, 2021), it is very likely that psychotherapists use at least one social media platform for personal use.

However, we still don't have good data on the percentage of psychotherapists who engage with social media for professional purposes of various kinds. It is true that scores of closed Facebook and LinkedIn groups cater specifically to mental health professionals, focusing on marketing, building a private practice, telehealth practices, and self-care. Within these groups, we must monitor ourselves carefully and not overstep both professional ethical boundaries and our own personal ethics regarding how to conduct ourselves in this vast and dynamic social space.

As a member of some of these amazingly helpful virtual groups, I have felt the allure both of responding to someone's plea for help with a particular situation and of posting something that was particularly challenging in my own professional world. But as Rebecca Wong, LCSW-R, wrote, ". . . when it comes time for actual case consult and those nitty gritty details. . . . Not Facebook. Please just say no to social media TMI (too much information) when it comes to your caseload" (Wong, 2015).

In truth, there is no way to discern who is who on a social media platform, despite the semblance of authenticity we would expect and assume within a virtual group of fellow psychotherapists. Even if every group member were who they said they were, we would still be sharing information in a relatively unsecure, public forum to folks whose personalities, specific situations, and nuanced needs remain largely hidden. Patient confidentiality becomes relatively quickly compromised if we are disclosing clinical accounts or any kind of protected health information that could be identified. These factors are essential ingredients to consider for a solid consultation recipe, whether we are more informally consulting or receiving true professional consultation.

Seeking more information, however, on how and with whom to consult is a great use of these specific social media groups. Moreover, these groups can be tremendously useful for sharing ideas about private practice development, marketing, changing jobs, diversity of professional activities, how to seek support from your clinic boss, and self-care and personal development, for example.

What reasons might you currently have or could have in the future for utilizing consultation? The list of possible themes and issues for which to consult are endless, but some of the main domains include

- resolving ethical dilemmas
- tweaking or fine-tuning a method or delivery element within a given therapeutic approach
- exploring difficult material a client is presenting
- mitigating feelings of overwhelm from a given client or from a particular session
- managing transference and countertransference (including sexual, aggressive, and noncompassionate feelings)
- coming to terms with patients who don't seem to be able to change or want to make progress
- understanding how to integrate professional and personal life
- pondering change of careers or change of focus within one's psychotherapy career
- seeking help and guidance for burnout and other occupational hazards

Unfortunately, despite acknowledging all the logical reasons for seeking consultation, we may harbor misconceptions or objections about the consultative process. For example, we may believe that

- peers are going to judge us as inadequate
- we will feel embarrassed or ashamed about needing consultation
- we fear we'll be seen as less capable than our peers rather than as their equal (Alexander, 2019; Brickel, 2015)

It is normal to feel that "I don't need this." We may have a protective impulse to guard ourselves against the appearance of "doing things wrong." The downside is that this fear cuts us off from what we need in order to do the best for our clients and our profession—each other's experience, expertise, and support.

SEEKING SUPERVISION FOR GROWTH AND EMPOWERMENT

Unlike the relatively informal arrangements of peer (or even expert) consultation, which are not required by any licensing board or credentialing body, supervision is a formal, (sometimes) mandated, and legally binding relationship that is part and parcel of professional training programs and within hierarchical structures of clinics and group practices. Supervision facilitates one's professional development, competence building, and path toward licensure and credentialing. Different professional licensing bodies have different requirements, but most licensed professionals after a certain number of supervised hours are no longer obligated to be supervised.

Supervisory relationships, of which there may be many over the course of our careers, are ideally supposed to instill trust, safety, and a sense of freedom for growth within the supervisee. Hopefully we've all had at least one of these relationships in our professional careers thus far. Ultimately, supervision is designed to help shape our clinical acumen, tune our wise discernment between intuition and fear, hone our ethical mind, teach and refine particular therapeutic approaches, enhance our mindful presence and cultural sensitivity with a diversity of patients, and foster attention and care of the person within the therapist.

Think for a moment about the best supervisory or mentor relationship you've had the pleasure to be a part of. How did you feel when you met with this person? Did you come out of most sessions feeling either more stable and grounded or more expansive, challenged, and curious? Perhaps you experienced both stability and growth within a given supervision meeting. In many ways, supervisory relationships can *and should* be a bedrock of self-care development for therapists in training.

As we grow as therapists, wouldn't we benefit from a coach, teacher, or parent-like figure to give us feedback on how we're doing, how we're developing as a clinician, whether we're overloading ourselves, and if we're somehow blocking our own potential? Supervisors, when doing a good job, allow us to safely explore and experiment with various parts of ourselves to ultimately evolve into the therapists they hope we can become and that we aspire to be. Interestingly, as clinical psychologist and long-time supervisor

Dr. Cory Chen noted, it's more concerning when supervisees don't question their competence. In fact, "uncertainty about their competence represents an appropriate degree of humility and recognition of the complexity of the work that we do" (C. Chen, personal communication, March 1, 2021).

Conversely, where supervisees see outright failure, supervisors hopefully see potential and promise. They hold our hands when needed and yet allow us to sail farther and farther away with an increasingly lengthy anchor. Just like good-enough parenting, good-enough supervision can help us trust in ourselves, know when to seek additional support, and internalize a sense of self-caring and professional–personal balance beyond the supervisory relationship.

Although supervision of many kinds is required throughout one's formal training years (which can last up to a decade depending on our unique experiences), a licensed psychotherapist may also seek supervision later in their career, such as when they're attempting to become more expert in a new therapeutic approach or modality. For example, becoming a trauma therapist or couples and family therapist would likely necessitate learning directly from a more experienced and knowledgeable practitioner in that area of practice. Supervision in this case could be conducted in either individual or group format depending on many factors, including the number of interested therapists for any given supervisor and whether the supervisor is part of a larger institution offering these kinds of professional development trainings.

Supervision, like consultation and even our own psychotherapy, can allow us to drop our guard and express the conflicts and struggles, hopes and wishes of our professional and personal lives. During the middle of my graduate training, I began to experience a tremendous number of physical symptoms that I couldn't explain and that were causing undue stress and anxiety. Catalyzed by other stressors, I began to experience full-blown panic attacks in some of my client sessions. As you could imagine, this was incredibly disturbing, disheartening, and disruptive, although I was somehow *fairly* adept at hiding my physiological overwhelm from my clients.

One of my main clinical supervisors, Dr. Erica Wise, was there as my trusted guide through this unsettling time. Both compassionate and pragmatic, Dr. Wise validated my experience, explored with me its origins and impacts, and helped craft a plan designed to mitigate my stress and the effect it was having on my therapeutic encounters. Like a valve releasing accumulated pressure, my supervision sessions left me feeling significantly less trapped and more willing to tolerate my discomfort. I went on to experience similar humanity, validation, and pragmatic support from several supervisors while on my clinical internship when I was diagnosed with cancer.

An effective and trusting supervisory relationship can uniquely grant us permission to share our deeper fantasies in the supervision room so that they're appropriately handled in the therapy room. Two such examples that are by no means rarities in the realm of psychotherapy are psychotherapists' own sexual fantasies about their clients and our self-disclosures to clients. These phenomena may not stem directly from underdeveloped self-care or therapists' strained well-being, but left unchecked and underdiscussed they can certainly have the potential to compromise therapist competence and jeopardize the integrity of the therapeutic relationship.

In many cases, crossing physical and emotional boundaries may violate ethical mandates and enforceable codes (APA, 2017b). Given that up to 90% of therapists report being attracted to at least one client in their careers (e.g., Pope, Keith-Spiegel, & Tabachnick, 2006) and that various types of therapist personal disclosures are a common experience, supervision can help us sort out what is appropriate to feel but not say and to experience but not act on.

Even if the thought of seeking out a supervisor at this stage in your career feels awkward or even shameful, rest assured that supervision at any career stage is an acceptable and welcomed endeavor. In fact, supervision not only can help you work through personal–professional blind spots and difficult therapeutic processes but also can support and strengthen your gifts, skills, and aspirations for the direction of your career.

Good supervisors also pay particular attention to supervisees' self-care. The act of being in supervision is a form of therapist self-care to begin with, but for a supervisor to instill within the supervisory relationship a sense of self-care as vital and valued takes this concept to the next level. Ultimately, self-care in supervision shouldn't be an afterthought. It should be part and parcel of the overarching experience.

It's important to acknowledge, however, that finding the right match can be difficult. If you're in the physical location where you did your clinical training, it may be fruitful to reach out to former supervisors and professors who are in the know. Current colleagues may be in supervision and have good leads. If you're learning a new therapeutic approach and need more focal supervision, that training or credentialing organization can potentially provide avenues to secure supervision for this specific goal. Licensing boards and professional organizations associated with your particular helping profession may also provide assistance. Finally, some psychological science and clinically oriented associations take pride in supporting professionals at various stages of career development and with a variety of professional needs. In short, there are many potential ways to find the right match to bolster your skills and find the appropriate supervisory support you desire.

As we've just explored, both professional grounding *and* growth are essential forms of self-care for therapists. The ways in which we seek such stability and expansion for ourselves may differ across phases of our lifespan and career. Thus, it's important to remain open and curious about opportunities that may arise as a function of where we work, how experienced we've become, what our preferences and interests may whisper, and how our personal lives are faring at any given time. In the spirit of this book, it would benefit us to take a personalized and needs-based look at what we truly require and want across our professional development. From these insights, we can more deeply know which facets of our profession could continue as they are and which could be altered to enhance our competence, well-being, and sense of flourishing.

Consciously creating our own path for healthy professional development is sometimes impeded by the work environment in which we find ourselves. In the next chapter, we turn to the pitfalls and rewards of our places of work and how to navigate these environments for optimal well-being over time.

34 NAVIGATING OUR WORK ENVIRONMENT

A team is not a group of people that work together. A team is a group of people that trust each other.

—Simon Sinek

Zora, now a midcareer marriage and family therapist, once worked for a large group practice employing 32 clinicians. The clinic housed a variety of psychotherapists, including psychologists, social workers, marriage and family therapists, and licensed professional counselors, as well as a handful of psychiatrists, psychiatric nurse practitioners, and a neuropsychologist. Four full-time administrative staff managed scheduling, initial client inquiries, billing, and insurance reimbursements.

The director of the clinic, an older male clinical psychologist with an MBA, also saw a several clients each week. He had a reputation for running a "tight ship" and liked to keep the clinic bustling. As such, the waiting room was always full, clinicians and staff were always moving up and down hallways and in and out of offices, and required meetings were plentiful.

https://doi.org/10.1037/0000309-035
The Thriving Therapist: Sustainable Self-Care to Prevent Burnout and Enhance Well-Being, by M. A. Hersh

Clinicians were also expected to "meet their numbers," as it was unaffectionately referred to during meetings. When therapists dipped below their quota for 2 weeks in a row, they were supposed to meet with the group practice director to bump their numbers back up.

How did you feel reading this description? Were the atmospheric conditions and productivity expectations familiar to you? Were you a bit overwhelmed, or perhaps you perceived this clinic as fairly normal and even as desirable? Whether obviously or covertly, we are tasked with navigating the challenges of our workplace culture and structure, relationship dynamics, caseload burdens and freedoms, and the opportunities for supporting self-care, growth, and diversity of professional experience.

WORKPLACE CULTURE

What is the general atmosphere in your workplace? Does it feel mostly welcoming and supportive, overly controlling and demanding, or perhaps laissez-faire? Is it relatively even keeled and predictable or on the mercurial end of the spectrum? What about a healthy synergy of productivity with a relaxed flexibility, seriousness mixed with elements of fun, humor, and enjoyment? Are professional autonomy and creativity encouraged in meaningful ways, or are these qualities subtly or overtly discouraged? Given that control and autonomy are such important resources for work-related outcomes (e.g., Rupert et al., 2009) as well as for reducing work-to-home conflicts (Rupert et al., 2012), a workplace culture that grants some degree of flexibility and decision making is likely quite beneficial for therapists' overall well-being.

Work environments are systems like any other. An entirely closed system doesn't welcome feedback or agency of its employees, whereas a completely open system may feel chaotic. How would you assess your current workplace for its openness of communication and feedback loops? Being left to your own devices to assess how and what you're doing can be quite a strain on job satisfaction and thus overall well-being. Openness of communication also includes a spirit of teamwork and camaraderie rather than an atmosphere of every colleague for themself (even if subtly encouraged). Feeling bound by common purpose, common stresses, and communal support is often a tacit but incredibly powerful source of professional well-being.

A supportive culture is one that fosters good communication among its employees. In fact, anxiety can be lessened and motivation enhanced when employees of any organization are part of a workplace culture that values and acts on clear, direct, and consistent communication (American Psychological Association, 2011). Being duly informed about your workplace policies, expectations, and activities and having a sense of ownership and responsibility over your professional future can facilitate more effective coping with the stresses and demands of the job. In effect, as your sense of agency increases, your risk of burnout decreases. Research on burnout supports this idea, as several studies show that greater sense of control is related to lower levels of emotional exhaustion and depersonalization and a higher sense of personal accomplishment (e.g., Ackerley et al., 1988; J. Lee et al., 2011).

Sharing in the values, beliefs, assumptions, and guiding principles that, in part, contribute to your workplace culture may also indicate how well you're resonating in that atmosphere. Some of us may like our specific job but find ourselves at odds with how the particular clinical setting treats its clients or the therapeutic approaches it readily advocates using. This element can make a significant difference for how accepted you feel and how eager you are to return to work each day.

Threats of aggression and violence in clinical settings can significantly affect a therapist's basic sense of safety, although some psychotherapists are affected more than others. How your workplace views such potentials and handles the actual incidents matters a great deal. A colleague who worked for years on an adolescent inpatient psychiatric unit at large urban hospital was confronted many times with threats, aggression, and violence from various patients. How quickly and effectively this colleague was assisted by fellow staff was at times likely a matter of serious injury or worse. And the extent to which she received adequate debriefing and support was subsequently a matter of her well-being and mitigation of posttraumatic stress symptomatology. What is your workplace policy and support around such incidents, both for acute crises and as prevention? Ultimately, do you feel safe in your own office or in the facility in which you work?

For those of us who are private practitioners, evaluation of the culture and atmosphere of the practice setting might seem a bit strange. Consider how welcoming or warm you are to yourself. Have you established fair policies, reliable and easily implemented protocols, and predictable systems of communication for yourself that keep your practice humming smoothly? Do you feel safe in your space, and do you have ways to protect against potential aggressive acts from clients? As discussed in this chapter, being both your own boss and employee lowers risk of burnout in so many ways but can also increase feelings of isolation and lack of support.

INTERPERSONAL WORK DYNAMICS

When it comes to how we evaluate the stresses and supports of our job, how often are we thinking of people *other* than our clients? Bosses, supervisors, fellow psychotherapists, other allied professionals, office or clinic staff, and even referral sources and outside professional collaborators are the people with whom you relate within your work environment. Workplace leadership (e.g., owner, director, supervisor) tends to set the tone for the work environment—whether through overt actions or through personal qualities—even if much of their influence is behind the scenes.

How you perceive your boss also matters. Do you feel valued, even if you don't have a lot of direct contact? When you have problems or need extra support, is your boss available to listen, validate, and problem solve? Perhaps you get a lot of lip service, but changes you feel need to happen never actually happen. If the roles are reversed and you are in charge of a number of other therapists, it's quite useful to reflect on the degree of fairness, enjoyment, validation, humility, and openness that you embody and express. Bosses are not superhuman and more effectively lead from a place of courageous vulnerability (Brown, 2018). However, given the differential power they hold, it's very important for that influence to be aligned with the larger mission of the workplace setting and be adequately supportive of the psychotherapists who serve that mission on a daily basis.

A number of tips and strategies are available for negotiating professional relationships, and they are especially useful if you go to work each day anticipating and avoiding interactions with a "difficult" boss or supervisor. According to many experts in the field of occupational wellness, it's wise to ascertain if difficult behaviors from leadership are situational and/or malleable or if they reflect a deeper and more consistent pattern of personality structure that is responsible for troubling or stress-inducing actions (e.g., Puder-York, 2005). Sometimes bosses are flagrantly narcissistic, overly demanding, neglectfully oblivious, or even downright abusive. In any of these cases (and of course with other variations on this theme), therapists can first seek counsel with and validation from trusted colleagues, colleague assistance programs, union reps if applicable, human resources if potentially helpful, and friends and family.

Peer and collegial dynamics in the workplace can be a source of both occupational support and stress, even at times from within the same relationship. Fortunately, social support specifically from coworkers has been found to be effective at reducing burnout (McCormack et al., 2015). With greater support comes less emotional exhaustion and depersonalization and more of a sense of personal accomplishment (Ben-Zur & Michael, 2007; Rupert et al., 2015). What only our colleagues can truly understand and appreciate may provide us with the most meaningful support. In fact, workplace support has been shown to be the only positive resource associated with therapist's sense of personal accomplishment (J. Lee et al., 2011).

A great example of the process and benefits of coworker support is found within an inpatient hospital setting. I once heard of a highly creative and morale-boosting therapist who would conduct mini video interviews with their coworkers about what they were grateful for and what inspired them about their jobs. This type of interview was not intended to ignore the stresses and strains of the highly challenging jobs everyone performed each day. Rather, this form of support highlighted in part why we entered these jobs in the first place and how we can all find rewards and joys even amid the struggle. Not surprisingly, morale, sympathetic joy, and inspiration were boosted among the coworkers and even within the therapist who was spreading the good feelings.

Let's come back to those in private practice for a moment. Such therapists may simply not have any colleagues from whom to seek support, for whom to provide assistance, and with whom they can participate in a wonderful workplace satisfaction-enhancing practice. Not surprisingly, research shows that solo practitioners indeed have lower levels of workplace social support (Rupert & Kent, 2007). As McCormack and colleagues (2018) considered, however, it may be interesting to reflect on how the support that private practitioners' both need and perceive may be dependent on their experience, work setting, and level of training. On average, we know that burnout risk decreases with age and/or career stage (e.g., Scaletta, 2021), and so maturity and experience may be protective factors for people who are relatively isolated within a solo psychotherapy practice.

I recall the feeling of isolation and stark lack of support when I moved from a thriving research and clinical center in the downtown Boston area to subletting two different office spaces for a year. I interacted with very few other professionals during that year. When I made the move to rent my own office space, which was a gift in many ways, I quickly experienced the noninteractive, noncollegial tenor of the small house of only nine other independent practitioners of varying sorts, including an attorney and a small nonprofit agency. On the basement level with only one other clinician's office and a waiting room big enough for 1.5 chairs, I occasionally passed by my "colleagues" on the way to the bathroom like ships in the night. This workplace environment certainly didn't help my case for holistically supporting my well-being at the outset of my career as a psychotherapist.

The transition to renting an office within a three-person independent group practice held much more promise for the perception of support, if not the full-on experience of it. I immediately felt a fellowship with the other clinicians even if they were fully established amongst themselves. We have shared some cases, made reciprocal referrals, and maintain a friendly supportive spirit. Although I'm more introverted and a highly sensitive person, this social upgrade seemed to make a world of difference for my mental and emotional health.

What are the strengths and challenges right now of your collegial relationships? What is the general tone of your interactions with your peers? Do you have the opportunity to talk, meet, or have lunch with your colleagues, or is everyone moving through their day independently with their head down? What is the quality of your relationships and pattern of interactions with your colleagues? Does anything need to change on your end? Perhaps you realize that you feel both uplifted and grounded when you see some colleagues more than others. Can you consciously make these interactions more plentiful? Similarly, skillful lessening of your investment in draining interactions can lighten the load and save your precious energy for strengthening other relationships of deeper value and meaning.

What do we do when our colleagues are difficult to work with? Dr. Glenn Rolfsen, a Norwegian clinical psychologist and specialist in occupational well-being, addressed a very insidious and toxic dynamic bordering on bullying that he highlighted as "backbiting" (Rolfsen, 2016). When colleagues essentially gossip and complain about their coworkers behind their backs, a subtly tense and damaging atmosphere is created and often unknowingly perpetuated. The "talked about" coworkers may be treated differently, with increased bias and disrespect, while the backbiting individual(s) now may feel justified in the gossip and may spread more harmful untruths about their colleagues.

Lest we lament that nothing can be done about such a toxic interpersonal culture, Rolfsen (2016) offered some hope. In his work as psychotherapist, corporate counselor, and leadership consultant, he has helped transform this type of atmosphere in hundreds of companies. Through larger company meetings, employees are asked three basic questions to harness the spirit of group-level change. In the triple-filter test, we can ask ourselves (or trusted supervisors or peers can ask us), regarding communication *about* others, is it true, it is good, and is it useful? If you answered "not really" to one or more of these questions, you might need to reconsider sharing information about a colleague with another colleague.

Rolfsen (2016) advised that the group be asked a simple question: "Would you like to work in a place where there is no backbiting?" From there, workers then agree, through formally signing a document, to join this new initiative to keep the workplace free from backbiting, with reminders posted in various locations and weekly check-ins for several months about how the project is going. This type of mini-intervention, Dr. Rolfsen reported, will result in the reduction of absenteeism, minimization of interpersonal tensions, and increases in productivity.

The complexities and uniqueness of each therapist's workplace environment call for a flexible, resilience-building framework to support well-being in a sustainable manner. In her RESET approach, Dr. Kristen Lee (2014)—behavioral science and resilience expert—suggested that we first consider our primary appraisal of and reactivity to a given situation before making any decisions. In other words, trying to make reasonable decisions when emotions are running hot often backfires. With a more *wise mind* online, we can appraise a situation from multiple perspectives and draw on the resources we already have available to us. We could reach out to colleagues, mentors, and friends outside of our workplace. Fresh takes on a long-standing problem can often be exactly what is needed in these situations.

WORKPLACE STRUCTURES

Whether you work for someone else or for yourself, you know the value of well-oiled operations and internal structures of your workplace. The administrative duties you're responsible for and supported on are likely more tangible and trackable than your workplace culture and atmosphere, and they matter a great deal. How user-friendly and consistently operational your electronic health records system is can make all the difference for daily frustration levels and feelings of satisfaction in your workplace. The volume and manageability of your paperwork and the requirements related to diagnosing for billing can also press on therapists with significant weight. A very large survey of practicing psychologists revealed that 68% endorsed paperwork as a primary stressor in their professional lives (Sherman & Thelen, 1998), and burnout risk not surprisingly increases when practitioners work more and log more administrative paperwork hours (e.g., Rupert et al., 2015). It's probably fair to say that no psychotherapist got into this helping profession to write progress notes and manage billing and insurance complexities.

How we manage ourselves with these administrative tasks is a continuous act of self-caring. Despite disliking and sometimes being overwhelmed by our paperwork, it is a necessary evil that we all must face and make the best of. How does your workplace build in supports for you in this endeavor?

How do you typically handle your workplace guidelines and policies for the administrative duties for which you're responsible? Influenced by many factors including your work style, conscientiousness, perfectionism, and executive functioning, addressing your paperwork and other important administrative tasks may feel like such a burden that you avoid it at all costs or attempt it diligently but can't seem to get a hold of it. The accumulation of your progress notes and other tasks may quietly but powerfully follow you around and into your home after work is officially over for the day.

Divining for yourself (or with the help of trusted colleagues or your workplace leadership) how to reduce the negative impact of your administrative responsibilities can be an incredible gift of sustainable self-caring. Interestingly, some of my colleagues and I became significantly more proficient and efficient in note writing during the pandemic because there was no real divide between looking at the computer screen to see a client and viewing your computer- or cloud-housed records for that client at the same time. Doing your best to make sure your sessions end on time allows for the extra few minutes to write an efficient note. If note writing during or immediately after a clinical encounter is unworkable for you for personal or workplace reasons, making sure you set aside your own administrative task time during your day is essential to mitigate burnout risk. Talking with colleagues about their best methods for the most efficient note writing or other administrative tasks can save you a great deal of unnecessary stress and can help make your work experience more of what it was designed for—helping others and being the best clinician you can be.

Although tele-mental health services have been increasing exponentially in the last several years, the COVID-19 pandemic brought telehealth into great relief in a dramatic and immediate fashion. Almost every if not all psychotherapists (at least temporarily) abandoned their physical offices for virtual workplaces. How well private practices, clinics, agencies, schools, and treatment facilities managed this necessary transition was an obvious source of stress and/or support for many. We all were required to adjust and accommodate, and how open and flexible your workplace was might have made a significant difference for your well-being during this highly challenging time.

Prior to and well after the pandemic, however, is the general notion that workplace operations should, when running smoothly, be out of our conscious awareness to a large degree and serve not only to prevent extra workplace stress and demand but also to enhance our degree of work satisfaction. Workplace operations that ideally would run effectively behind the scenes include reliable high-speed internet (for regular and telehealth uses), user-friendly fax or secure e-transmission mechanisms, email, security and privacy measures, hassle-free booking and scheduling systems, accessible and up-to-date documentation and forms, and billing and insurance interfaces or helpful staff management of such administrative nightmares.

Although private practitioners are often executing many or all of these tasks themselves, it behooves us to evaluate how well our workplace and business systems are operating. In what ways would you fix or enhance the current workplace structures and operations so that your business runs smoothly and you can focus on doing psychotherapy rather than struggling with internet connectivity issues or billing hassles, for example? Reliable cloud-based practice management software can be a relatively inexpensive way to help cover many of these areas. Another fundamental self-caring act as a private practitioner is using a separate business phone line. I've met too many practitioners who have one phone number for both their personal cell and their work lines. This set-up can cause boundary confusion for both therapist and client and may accidentally lead to work–personal life spillover. Free services like Google Voice can be accessed directly from your smartphone, and VoIP services that may offer additional functionality and features require a high-speed internet connection.

We can also gain so much wisdom and practical guidance through dedicated therapy practice forums on social media, free or low-cost offerings from practice management software companies like SimplePractice, state and provincial associations and colleague assistance programs, and small but highly influential entrepreneurial endeavors like Person Centered Tech (which marries psychotherapy practice with technology and security), The Private Practice Startup, Practice Academy, and TherapyDen.

CASELOAD BURDENS AND FREEDOMS

At the intersection of workplace culture, interpersonal dynamics, and structure is a psychotherapist's caseload. Classical burnout theory suggests that high demand, low control, and depleted resources all contribute to risk of burnout. As such, when you consider your caseload, you're also reflecting on how much control you have over the volume, type, and variety of clients you see. How demanding is your caseload overall? Do 20% of your clients take up 80% of your energy and time, like the rule somehow seems to play out so reliably? Are your personal and social resources and competence levels sufficient for the caseload you manage?

Even if we are in private practice, we might feel that we have little control over who we see. Intersecting with savvy marketing, a good business model, and our unique financial situation is the influence we feel we have over which clients to take and which ones to decline or refer. At the outset of establishing her private practice many years ago, a colleague took all prospective clients who called her, and she charged whatever they said they could afford. After a while, not surprisingly, this caseload and fee structure wore on this therapist. Shortly after recognizing that this way of practicing was unsustainable for both her business and her mental health, this colleague became more selective and increased her fees, thus significantly contributing to her overall work satisfaction. If you work in an environment whose culture is oriented strictly to the "bottom line" despite its mission to serve others, you'll likely feel this tension quite acutely. Does your boss or supervisor (subtly or overtly) levy demands that you meet your direct contacts quota each week even if you've expressed how stressed or overwhelmed you might be? We know that number of hours worked, regardless of workplace setting, translates into higher burnout risk (e.g., Rupert et al., 2015).

The question then becomes how open and flexible are the systems within which we work. Does your work culture allow for open and honest communication about your workload and risk of occupational hazards, and would your director truly listen to your experience and needs? There are many great examples of group practices that place as much value as possible on the professional autonomy of their employees while still forging an atmosphere of community and mutual support. These guiding principles then extend not only to caseload decisions but also to employees' internal conflicts and to other workplace dynamics that require fairness and swift resolution.

Negotiation, whether with yourself in private practice or with a superior, is a necessary task and a skill worthy of cultivating. If 60% of your caseload is moderately to severely depressed middle-aged White men, perhaps you would benefit from some kind of caseload diversity before a degree of cynicism sets in and your effectiveness with this population wanes. How open is your workplace to accommodating your particular needs? Are you simply required to take whoever walks through the door? If you're a therapist in a residential treatment facility or on inpatient psychiatric unit, for example, you would by default have much less control than would a therapist in a large group practice or in business for themself. Trauma therapists and practitioners of dialectical behavior therapy, for example, may be at high risk for secondary traumatic stress and vicarious traumatization by virtue of the nature of their caseloads as well as the particular material and affect that are presented to them on an hourly basis. In these cases especially, development of fine-tuned coping and reliance on trusted peer and supervisory supports become quite essential self-caring enactments. Ideally, your workplace would account for such occupational risks and hazards in part through flexible caseload management and through carrying each therapist's well-being in mind and heart.

We can consider Zora once again; she had quite strict "numbers" goals to reach each week. Although Zora tried to negotiate the sheer volume of clients in her caseload and the quota she was required to meet, she was essentially told to keep at it. This lack of flexibility eventually contributed to Zora's deciding to leave that group practice for another setting altogether. That option is *almost* always there for us, even if it feels like it isn't. After careful consultation with trusted colleagues, friends in the know, and colleague assistance associations available to you, you may end up deciding to move on to save your sanity and get a taste for what another environment could offer.

WORKPLACE SUPPORT FOR WELLNESS, DIVERSITY OF PROFESSIONAL EXPERIENCE, AND THRIVING

Dr. Jeff Santee—clinical psychologist, Diplomate of comprehensive energy psychology, and co-owner of Summit Clinical Services outside of Chicago, Illinois—is no stranger to managing the joys and complexities of running a medium-sized group psychotherapy practice. With an initial vision to be multidisciplinary and comprehensive, Dr. Santee helped create a full-service and administrative staff-supported group practice that was designed to provide for maximum professional autonomy for its clinicians. Clinicians can choose either part- or full-time employment, and each clinician is given a voice on at least one practice or operations committee for more enhanced engagement and decision making. The practice has an active blog that clinicians can contribute to, thus enhancing clinicians' diversity of professional engagement and potential job satisfaction.

Although his colleagues were initially unfamiliar with energy psychology, Dr. Santee noted that he felt supported in openly integrating these methods into his practice (rather than keeping this aspect of his professional life a secret; J. Santee, personal communication, January 2021). Given that some of us may struggle to find coverage during our precious time off, Dr. Santee feels fortunate that he can take vacations with the peace of mind that he (and his clients) are adequately covered by his colleagues while he's away.

Summit Clinical Services is just one example of a workplace that values some of the central themes of this book. Although we're exploring *self*-care, we're also speaking about being seen and feeling whole within our psychotherapeutic community. Having opportunities to grow and contribute in unique ways while still maintaining a sense of connection to a larger whole is ultimately supportive of one's own caring and well-being over time. No one likes to feel like a cog in a machine. Psychotherapists, doing some of the most challenging and human-oriented work in existence today, are no exception.

Not every therapist is only a therapist. Some of us enjoy research and writing, community outreach and pro bono work, workshopping, and teaching, to name a few forms of professionally diverse experience. Are these types of experiences readily available within the scope of your employment, or would you have to manage these endeavors on your own time? If you're a private practitioner, carving out the time for endeavors that inspire, motivate, and expand your professional self becomes an area of negotiation with yourself. Not putting all your eggs of talent and skill in one professional basket can allow us to feel more whole, revitalize the soul, and spread any stress across activities rather than accumulated within one role.

Not all supplemental or even complementary professional activities can be accommodated within a given workplace, but some models for this type of employment have caught the eye of the American Psychological Association (Chamberlin, 2017). Around the country some group practices subscribe to a more scientist–practitioner model (LeJeune & Luoma, 2015). Alvord Baker & Associates (in Maryland) and Portland Psychotherapy Clinic, Research, and Training Center (in Oregon) are two standout examples showing how research is built into the group practice model, with in-house research directors and assistants to support a variety of research projects more fully. Psychotherapists who have trained as researchers and have long-standing interests in pursuing some measure of a research career would likely find these hybrid roles quite appealing.

Research, however, isn't the only facet of a clinician's experience that a workplace can value, support, and encourage. Creativity, flexibility, community involvement, professional development, and in-house mentorship are all examples of how some group practices make the workplace highly inviting and rewarding. Some group practices, like Southeast Psych in North Carolina and Tennessee, embrace therapists' complementary skill sets. For example, one therapist who was a certified yoga instructor was able to expand her office space and practice model to accommodate large yoga sessions for mental health support. Other practices, like IntraSpectrum Counseling in Chicago, recognize staff's basic needs by keeping the communal pantry stocked with food and drink to grab between clients. Supplying quick and easy nourishment can seem so basic as to accidentally ignore, but I can attest firsthand to the incredible effect that my office suite's coffee maker has had on my well-being over the years.

Professional development is both a necessary and often desired element of any psychotherapist's job and journey, but when continuing education (CE) opportunities are always left to the individual therapist, they can feel a bit isolating and frustrating. And when CE courses or books are boring, professional development can feel uninspired. Workplaces that integrate professional development into the job description are helping breathe life into a sometimes perfunctory task. Some group practices offer lunchtime talks for CE credit, while others have established a mentorship system for staff to develop their careers and discuss issues around managing both their professional and personal lives.

IntraSpectrum gives new meaning to workplace togetherness and professional–personal life integration by encouraging staff to engage in activities like bowling and cooking classes together outside of work. Southeast Psych has a similar approach, reserving a few hours on the last Wednesday of each month to incorporate play, fun food, and entertainment. As you read about such innovative workplaces, do you imagine that your work environment could benefit from infusion of a spirit of camaraderie and wellness? What would happen if you and a few colleagues experimented with such themes and then proposed these ideas to leadership? If you're a director or owner of a group practice, clinic, or agency, do you think there's room for more enjoyment, creativity, and togetherness in your workplace? How could you incorporate even a little of this fun-loving spirit into your culture?

Our discussion of how workplace environments influence our ability to care for ourselves with relative ease wouldn't be complete without a mention of health care, sick leave, and vacation policies. Even if you work for yourself, how would you evaluate your values and policies related to keeping yourself well and taking care of yourself when you're sick? (These, as we likely know, are two separate endeavors and should deserve somewhat distinct workplace efforts.) If you're part-time, does your place of employment offer benefits, or do you have to shop around and find them elsewhere, likely for much higher cost? How much sick time are you afforded?

In one clinic where I worked, employees had to work for a designated period to earn 1 day of sick leave. This type of policy is not uncommon, but how flexible are your workplace policies, and how guilty do you end up feeling for calling out sick? If you have children and need to stay home, how does your workplace handle this? Is this an added stressor, or do you feel taken care of and supported? The extra societal burden cannot be overstated. Sometimes all the "best" self-care in the world doesn't make up for a lack of external support or workplace neglect of our health and wellness. At the very least, we can find company in such suffering and begin to let go of any extraneous emotional burden. At the very best, we may see (or help bring about) changes in the ways our workplace treats its employees, for our and our colleagues' betterment and thriving.

Self-care is a two-way street. That is, we can certainly modify our mindset and actions to be our own best allies. But we must also look to the ways in which our workplace environments support us in this endeavor. Employees of massive corporations who earn minimum wage and work 60 to 70 hours per week just to make ends meet obviously have very little time to do anything extra to tend to themselves. Thus, self-care somehow must be integrated into their day. Similarly, if you're expected to meet a very high quota for direct service hours each week, you may be hard pressed to find any pockets of time to slow down, breathe, eat, and do other necessary things for your basic wellness and well-being.

Workplace culture and practices matter. How open, flexible, and employee-centered the workplace is can contribute both directly and indirectly to employees' satisfaction and morale. But if we stay focused on cultural atmosphere and interpersonal dynamics, we might miss another important source of therapists' wellness, that of the more physical and sensory aspects of our workplace environment that can easily slither under the radar but nevertheless affect our sense of comfort and well-being. In Chapter 35, we explore the often ignored facets of our physical atmosphere and ways that we can modify our work spaces for our enhanced wellness over time.

35 ENHANCING OUR WORK SPACE FOR BETTER HEALTH

The question of what you want to own is actually the question of how you want to live your life.

—Marie Kondo

"I'm sorry, could you repeat that?" My small and unassuming desk fan was blowing out more noise than air, and I was constantly straining to hear my clients' voices clearly. The oddly regulated temperature in my office (relative to other offices in my suite) often threw me off my game, causing more stress than was necessary. Theoretically, I *should* have been clued in to the fact that not only did this fan produce more noise than power, but it also didn't oscillate, thus blowing air directly into one specific area of the office at a time. This didn't satisfy me or my clients, and when a given client asked for "no air," I often directed it to blow on me during the hot summer days, drying out my contact lenses and irritating my throat and making it scratchy. A colleague in my suite was kind enough to lend me her oscillating standing fan, which was quieter, and my heat and hearing problems quickly vanished. Of course,

https://doi.org/10.1037/0000309-036
The Thriving Therapist: Sustainable Self-Care to Prevent Burnout and Enhance Well-Being, by M. A. Hersh

I could have gone out and purchased a relatively inexpensive fan of this type as a proactive self-care response.

Are there potentially more vital things to address than a fan for our well-being? Absolutely. Is the choice of an office fan for the summer or portable heater for the winter of negligible importance? Absolutely not. I partly ranked clinical internship sites on "feel" of the environment, favoring brighter more active surroundings over the more drab, windowless, and sparsely populated places in which I would be training. We make decisions like this all the time, from how certain clothes look to a house we're looking to buy.

This chapter will help us assess and address our immediate workplace surroundings for optimal well-being and wellness. The idea is to consciously build into your environment elements of sustainable well-being that you can "set and forget" and "adjust without fuss." We'll discuss both aesthetics and function, thus covering facets of wellness that nourish the soul and support the body. After all, we spend nearly one third of our lives in the workplace (including home offices or makeshift spaces we may have settled into during the COVID-19 pandemic era). Shouldn't we consider our immediate surroundings a vital facet of self-care, prevention of unnecessary stress, and a source of our well-being?

It should be noted that some therapists have much more control and influence over their immediate work space than others do. Therapists who share a small office, work part-time in a hospital clinic or community agency, are employed within a school system, work in a residential facility, or do home visits are often less likely to have a say in what their therapeutic space looks like. Those of us who sublet an office have little if any "official" control over how that office looks or functions. We should also recognize that some therapists are moving in and out of different work spaces throughout the day—running a group in one room, seeing a few individual clients in the office, attending meetings in a conference room, talking with colleagues in the hallway, and so on. These therapists may feel as if they are blowing in the breeze with the constantly changing microenvironments. And yet, there is always something we can do to make the most of where and how we work. With that note of optimism, let's explore your work surroundings.

AESTHETICS: ENHANCING YOUR EMOTIONAL WELL-BEING THROUGH A MULTISENSORY APPROACH

The Center for Workplace Mental Health at the American Psychiatric Association Foundation found that 37% of employees surveyed said that their work environments affected their mental health (Agovino, 2019). The relationship between environment and well-being could certainly involve the interpersonal aspects of the workplace as well as the multisensory stimuli around us and the ways in which we, as unique individuals, take it all in.

Our physical environments are also quite slippery in the sense that we're often unconscious of the effects our surroundings have on us. Research from the Princeton University Neuroscience Institute revealed that a chaotic or disorganized environment tends to affect the brain negatively in ways that engender more irritability, distractibility, and stress than clutter-free surroundings do (Peelen & Kastner, 2014). Having a pile-up of papers or a high density of objects laying around is particularly detrimental. This type of environment can affect mood, self-esteem, and even cortisol levels, particularly in women (e.g., Arnold et al., 2012). On the flipside of this coin is the notion that your physical surroundings are a reflection, to some degree, of your inner life. If you struggle with certain aspects of executive functioning, does your work desk look like a clutter elf darted in, dropped a stack of mismatched papers, folders, and envelopes, and then quickly fled the scene?

How would this research translate to your workplace surroundings (and even to your car and your home)? If you took a snow globe assessment (i.e., 360 and up and down) of your immediate work surroundings, how would you viscerally feel? Do you experience hyper- or hypoarousal when in your office space for longer than a few minutes? What are the smells, sights, sounds, and textures? Is it cluttered or disorganized? Is there are layer of dust you can see on your bookshelves? What do the walls, ceiling, and floor look like? How about noise? Do you hear conversations or outside construction or is your office relatively soundproof? What about the aesthetic of the furniture and accessories? Do you have wall hangings and greenery that are both pleasing to you and calming for your clients?

Do you enjoy looking at and being in the space in which you spend a good portion of your day? Does it cause you some measure of tension, frustration, or ill feeling when you step into that space? Do you have enough natural light during the day? Are your lamps and light fixtures the right luminosity and temperature to suit your eyes, brain, and energy? Perhaps different rooms you occupy throughout the day give off different vibes, some generating more subtle well-being than others. Becoming increasingly curious about such variables is an essential step to reducing unnecessary stress (no matter how subtle) and improving the quality of your work life.

An office I occupied many years ago had an unresolved sewer smell that affected the quality of my work life fairly significantly. Much to the dismay and frustration of the tenants in that small building, the source of the smell was never appropriately fixed. I would apologize to clients who would sit in the waiting room absorbing toilet odors until they were relatively safe in my office. But still, hints of sewer seeped in, and I could never fully ignore that noxious smell despite an army of candles and essential oils.

Noise pollution was also a factor. Despite a standard sound machine that most therapists (or clinics) own, voices of louder therapists traveled through the thin walls. Bathroom noises were heard. And sporadic booming thumps from the floor above would jostle me and my clients in our seats. Not the best situation for either highly anxious individuals or a highly sensitive therapist.

When I transitioned to a new office, embedded in an independent group practice suite, I was in relative heaven. In the waiting room was a water cooler, coffee maker, and even a vacuum I could use for my office whenever needed. A small kitchenette off of a conference room housed a fridge and microwave. The suite even had a bathroom that didn't smell of sewer gas. Although the bathroom was adjacent to my office and sounds were slightly more noticeable than desired, the physical proximity of the bathroom didn't cross my threshold for potentially interrupting my therapy sessions with sounds of someone peeing behind a wall just a few feet to my left.

I was fortunate to have so much freely bestowed upon me when I took over the lease for that office. I enjoyed the built-in bookcase that I quickly filled, a couch and two chairs, a small but functional desk, a lamp, and a lovely large plant. With the help of my wife, I readily noticed what was missing (or needed to go) to help support my emotional well-being and to enhance the functionality of the physical space I used every day. I brought in two framed landscape photographs that had helped cultivate a subtle easeful-ness in my previous office and a relatively inconspicuous rolling bookshelf to accommodate more therapeutic "stuff." Although I have kept a second chair for aesthetic purposes to balance the room's furnishings, it's quite non-functional and not so comfy as it forces people into a sort of blast-off posture when they sit back. When the lovely large plant somehow got infested with tiny bugs, I removed it.

Let's take a moment to brainstorm the possible ways that you can influ-ence the emotional tone of your work space to minimize unwanted stress and maximize easefulness, joy, peace, and focus. Especially if you're a highly sensitive person, you may crave soft textures, pleasant and calming aromas, plants of varying sorts, images that soothe or inspire, and a certain brightness and temperature of light. There are likely many categories of office space modifications that you could consider. Take another minute and see what comes to your mind. Perhaps this is an exercise in visualizing (or photograph-ing or sitting quietly in) your office and then *feeling* what you feel. Decisions to keep, discard, or change some aspects of your office can follow with con-fidence as you bring a mindful curiosity to this endeavor.

You may also get inspired by colleagues' solicited (and even some unsolicited) suggestions. Closed social media groups that allow for photo posts showing how other therapists are arranging, furnishing, and decorating their offices can also be quite useful. Two of the most inspiring offices I've ever seen were on opposite ends of the spectrum—one, situated in an older building, was earth-toned and filled with plants and antique-looking furnishings while the other, housed in a large office building, was grey-white themed with a sleek and modern yet wholly inviting aura.

If your situation is not as simple as "I decided to hang a new photograph or poster on the wall and so I did," then it's very useful to brainstorm the subtle ways you can effect change in your immediate work space. If you feel joy, calm, or inspiration by regularly seeing certain photos but you sublet or float between offices throughout the day, you could purchase a relatively inexpensive and slender digital photo frame that you take with you along with your planner, phone, or notepad. For aesthetic and emotional purposes, fake plants are also a lovely alternative to the real deal. Some are small enough for you to store in a corner or small box in someone else's space. The first office I ever had was a sublet for a few hours per week. My subletter, a local psychiatrist and friend, let me use a storage ottoman to store some things I didn't want to transport every week. Had I thought about the plant idea back then, I might have kept some fake succulents in that ottoman. Fake plants don't need light, right?

Our immediate work environment can influence us in numerous ways, and we can also influence our environment. This section has focused on the aesthetics and emotional tone of your surroundings, which by no means are peripheral or frivolous. These factors are quite essential to our well-being, particularly as many of us occupy our work spaces for scores of hours each week. Similar to how we might modify our bedroom for optimal sleep, we can consider making sensory-based changes to our work space for optimal wellness.

MAINTAINING OPTIMAL FUNCTIONALITY OF YOUR WORK SPACE

A good friend and colleague of mine who works in a youth forensic mental health setting has a bowl of chocolates perched welcomingly on her desk. Coworkers will conveniently stop by for a chocolate and a quick commiserating chat. This is one deceptively simple way of enhancing professional atmosphere and building community, although my friend sometimes contends with colleagues' inadvertent spillover of stress as a parade of allied professionals (e.g., judges, attorneys, probation officers) passes by her office to unload their woes. Creating a wellness-oriented work environment is one of the more direct forms of extrinsic professional self-care, and it's one that's worth exploring.

Because many of us spend roughly half of our waking life in our work space, how we functionally interact with the various facets of our space matters. Reflect on your experience listening to your body in Chapter 9. What did you divine about your posture, energy, and breath throughout the day? These signals of the body can be readily linked to the furniture, accessories, and amenities of your workplace. Such facets of the physical environment help create conditions for emotional grounding as well as physical wellness.

How long do you sit each day? Your seated posture may perhaps be one of the more underestimated facets contributing to your mental and physical health. If you happen to be one of the estimated 90% of the U.S. population who leans forward with their necks (D. Brown, 2010) and one of upwards of 80% of Americans who complain of back pain (Rubin, 2007), then you know how important it is to mind your body for prevention of pain and dysfunction and for optimal wellness.

The chairs we sit in day in and day out can greatly facilitate or hinder appropriate posture for both short- and long-term functioning of our muscles, fascia, joints, spine, gut health, breathing, focus, and emotions. Our lives cannot be completely transformed by sitting in the right chair in wellness-supportive postures, but the ergonomics of sitting are not to be undervalued. When you sit in your main work space chair (the one in which you spend the majority of your time), how is your body arranged? Are your knees accidentally higher than your pelvis, or are your hamstring muscles cut into by the edge of the chair? Do you sink back, or are you thrust forward? Do you notice if the chair feels too soft or too firm? If your chair has arms, are they at a height that forces your shoulder muscles to contract, holding unnecessary tension session after session?

One important way to enhance the ergonomics of your seated sessions is to find a comfortable chair that provides good lumbar support and chair arms that don't force your shoulders toward the ceiling. Some chairs have built-in lumbar support, but you may consider purchasing a lumbar-specific pillow to place behind your lower back. When you test chairs, find one that allows for your pelvic area to be slightly higher than your knees. Otherwise, you will be constantly shortening your hip flexor muscles, thus ultimately creating more tension and strain on your lower back. Tight and shortened hip flexors, including your deep psoas muscle (the only muscle that traverses the front to the back of your body, through your lower abdomen), can also affect gut health (Northrup, 2019). Thus, taking care to sit in a chair that allows for lengthened hip flexors could do wonders for your back, gut, and overall well-being.

Although the chair is indeed a vital part of maintaining optimal functionality of the work space, the desk—either inherited or purchased—is also quite important. If you do a good deal of paperwork or have telehealth sessions, how does your desk suit you? Are you craning your neck to look down at a laptop, and are your arms bent over a 90-degree angle? These signs suggest a desk setup that is not ergonomic and therefore worth modifying. More subtle than craning your neck to work on your laptop is the slight downward or sometimes upward positioning of the eyes. Ergonomics experts strongly recommend that we position our computer screen so that it allows for an upright head aligned with the rest of our spine with our eyes maintaining minimum tension by looking directly in front of us.

Movement and wellness coach Hannah Yzusqui-Butera highlighted the vital importance of creating work spaces that do the work for us (H. Yzusqui-Butera, personal communication, April 23, 2021). If the desk is too high, the chair too low, hips overly contracted, or shoulders constantly tensed, there's unfortunately not much hope that you can "just relax" or "just stretch" those parts at the end of each session, only to plop down 5 minutes later in the same poorly postured position for the next session. We can put in some initial effort so that our work space functional setup can become effortless and health-producing in the long run.

We can consider a few other modifications to your immediate office space that might contribute to your overall wellness. Depending on the relative humidity in your geographic region and the given season, having a humidifier can be a true gift. Some research suggests that indoor humidity, whether too low or too high, can subtly contribute to a number of issues, including respiratory vulnerability to molds and mites and contracting certain airborne viruses and bacteria (e.g., Arundel et al., 1986; Lowen et al., 2007). Humidity well below 40% can contribute to dry eyes, cracked lips, a bloody nose, nasal congestion, and an irritated throat. Some people feel palpably fatigued if the humidity is too low or too high. If you're able to have some influence over this wellness factor, adjusting the relative humidity of your office air to 40 to 60% can be of potential benefit. Air purifiers with HEPA filters can also enhance the air quality of the spaces in which we spend so much time and improve our peace of mind as our clients cycle through our offices throughout each day.

Relatedly, drinking enough water throughout the day is a fantastic way to prevent the effects of relative dryness in the air. The creation of a wellness-oriented workplace may involve the addition of clean, healthy, and freely accessible drinking water. For those who drink coffee or tea, a coffee maker or hot water maker can also be a lifesaver and can keep us awake and our spirits lifted (even without caffeine).

Although the list of ways to optimize the functionality of your work space for greatest well-being benefit is potentially endless, here are several more ideas for your consideration:

- *Use a privacy sound machine.* Sound machines are essential for confidentiality and privacy on behalf of our clients, and they can give us the peace of mind to speak at a normal volume. They can also allow us not to feel tense and hypervigilant when louder clients speak. Unfortunately, I've known some psychotherapists who rent offices in buildings that don't allow for this standard tool of our trade. It's like telling a painter they're not permitted to bring a paint tray.

- *Set up well-positioned clocks around your office space (or wherever you're doing your therapeutic work).* An easily readable clock positioned on an end table and directly behind and just above where clients usually sit can be of subtle but enormous benefit. It stands to reason that you're more likely to end sessions on time, look less obvious as you mark time toward the end of each session, and feel more confident that you're managing yourself fluidly over the course of the day.

- *Declutter and organize your materials.* Clutter is something that affects peace of mind and emotion. Disorganized materials may be a result of simply not having the appropriate furnishings for storing books, file folders, and other important supplies. Do you have adequate bookshelf space, filing cabinets, and supply storage? If you work in an agency, clinic, school, or residential facility, are adequate supplies readily accessible, or do you have to requisition them and wait a month for a notepad?

I would be remiss if I didn't address the COVID-19 pandemic in this chapter. During the first few months of the pandemic, I read many accounts of therapists literally working out of bathrooms. They angled their laptops from the toilet and sat on the floor. Or they sat on closed toilets and propped up their laptops on small tables. Some figured they could sit up in bed and run their sessions this way, worrying along the way though that their clients might perceive them differently as they soaked in their bedroom atmosphere. Other therapists were fortunate enough to have small office spaces, separated from a main room or nestled in a corner of a bedroom, for example.

Therapists were making it work somehow, even if the conditions they had to work with were far less ideal than desired and expected. As the weeks became months and months became years, many therapists realized that we were in this for the long haul and that setting up some semblance of a home office space was a necessity. Applying many of the principles and concrete suggestions for work space setup have enhanced many therapists' professional *and* personal lives, especially given that the boundaries between work and home are often almost completely blurred.

In this and the previous chapter, we've explored the ways in which our workplace environments matter to our well-being and overall functioning. It might appear at first blush that we're at the mercy of where we work. However, how we perceive and manage our environments, whether the complex interpersonal dynamics or the chairs we sit on every day, can make a noticeable difference to our mental, emotional, and physical health. Let's now make a call to action to begin to integrate the principles and practices that we've explored thus far in this book. The next steps on our journey toward greater sustainability of self-care and enduring well-being await us.

PART **V** THRIVING: CREATING SUSTAINABILITY OF SELF-CARE AND WELL-BEING

INTRODUCTION: THRIVING: CREATING SUSTAINABILITY OF SELF-CARE AND WELL-BEING

The bamboo that bends is stronger than oak that resists.

—Japanese proverb

As the leaves were falling vigorously one fall in the Boston area, I received profoundly beneficial guidance from a meditation and spiritual teacher from whom I was seeking counsel for existential anxiety and mortality salience. She told me that I should follow the leaves. Follow the leaves down, as they drift from branch to ground. I should listen to the crunching underfoot and make deliberate movements to swirl the leaves up around my feet only to watch them patiently as they dance to the ground. I have tried to heed this call to action every autumn, as it helps me to remain present with what is, to follow the beauty of cyclical decay, and to connect with the earth as a stabilizing force.

If building our self-care foundation in Parts I and II is akin to establishing a sturdy but flexible root system and trunk, and Parts III and IV are the branches and flowering buds, then the call in this final section for sustainable self-care is all about how we nourish to flourish. This last part of the book is about ways to keep your garden thriving, based on the practices that best resonate with you as a gardener and best suit the greenery you desire to maintain. It's about watering adequately, tending to the soil and leaves, removing weeds, and pruning back overgrowth that can crowd meaningful development. Moreover, just as different weather and seasons tend to prompt different needs and growth patterns of the trees and plants around us, we too can listen to environmental cues that may signal the need to pace, promote, and protect ourselves in different ways at different times.

Joan Borysenko, PhD—a Harvard-trained cell biologist, behavioral medicine specialist, and psychoneuroimmunologist, as well as licensed psychologist—has long been a pioneer in the field mind–body medicine. Within her many teachings, she advocates for individuals not only to heed their own guidance systems but also to look to outside forces such as seasonal changes to help determine what resources are needed and to be used at any given time. Drawing from traditional Chinese medicine (TCM), Dr. Borysenko highlights that winter, for example, is often a time of natural slowing, rest, and inner reflection. Spring and summer, on the other hand, are more about reactivating ourselves and the possibilities for flourishing. As summer gives way to autumn, we can begin to gather our resources in preparation for resting once again. We can turn to different meditations, physical movements, objects of gratitude, and ways of relating and coping as we interact with different seasons throughout the year.

As if TCM and the Old Testament were sharing ideas at the same table, Ecclesiastes 3:1–8 tells us that "to every thing there is a season, and a time to every purpose under heaven. . . . A time to be born, and a time to die; a time to plant, and a time to pluck up that which is planted. . . . A time to weep, and a time to laugh; a time to mourn, and a time to dance" (*King James Bible*, 1989). (It may help some of us to be reminded of the song penned by Pete Seeger and made popular by the 1960s group The Byrds.)

Thomas Richardson—an acupuncturist, Eastern healing arts scholar, and medical qigong teacher—similarly suggested that "self-care is the dynamic process of remaining and returning to being whole within ourselves. Using deep self-awareness, we can experientially know what wholeness feels like so that when separation within the self occurs, we are better able to compassionately acknowledge this and then return ourselves to being whole once again" (T. Richardson, personal communication, September 2016). This recognition and experiential awareness of our wholeness as well as the times we feel fragmented can be our compass as well as our permission-granter to pace ourselves based on the world around us.

What are some of the ways in which your needs and self-caring habits shift with the seasons or with particular events (like the COVID-19 pandemic, tumultuous election cycles, racial unrest, or natural disasters)? Do any practices serve you well year-round? What in your environment, natural or otherwise, helps to remind you that you deserve to care for yourself and to receive care from the elements around you?

Because the basic premise of this book is that self-care is not a one-size-fits-all proposition, each of us would benefit at any point in our lives to slow down and reflect mindfully on our uniquely painted canvas. This individually tailored reflection can include our points of professional support and challenge, personal stressors and reasons for gratitude, and our unique needs that arise from where we are developmentally and in our career. For example, did you just have a baby and have basic needs for sleep, rest, and nourishment of yourself and your child? Or perhaps your children are grown and have launched out of the house, and you're now feeling freedom to expand yourself professionally or, conversely, to begin simplifying and streamlining your life. Maybe you have been caring for an ill child who is now grown but still in need of a tremendous amount of support. Perhaps you're not with a partner or have no children, and you're used to meeting your needs through other avenues—friends, colleagues, and your own resources and resourcefulness. Maybe you've experienced profound loss of connection and love, and you have foundational needs for healing the trauma of separation as well as forging new community or rekindling old relationships. Are you in a particularly overloaded and overwhelming period of time at work?

Our aspirations at any given time must be evaluated against the backdrop of our unique situation. What is *your* temperament and personality? What are *your* particular needs? And what are *your* particular habits and patterns of striving for success, for example, even if your strivings inadvertently place you further down the path of burnout and exhaustion? If we take an even bigger step back from any potential challenge we're facing, what are the aspects of your life right in this moment to which you can orient with gratitude, appreciation, and savoring? What have you handled relatively well despite the odds or the circumstances? What "small wins" can you count and breathe into your being? It's important that we routinely check our status along the *surviving–thriving* spectrum to identify what we need at any given moment.

As a poignant if not harrowing example, the COVID-19 pandemic has served as an opportunity for mindful acknowledgment of how steeped many of us have been in survival mode. In conversations with many other psychotherapists during this time, a common theme emerged. Therapists wanted to help more, whether through taking on more clients, adjunct teaching to help out fellow faculty, or offering workshops and presentations to serve lay folk and fellow professionals alike. Our drive to contribute positively to others' health is in large part why we signed up for this professional life. But some of these psychotherapists also have felt exhausted, demoralized, scared, and desirous of wanting to hunker down and tend to themselves and their families—their physical safety and psychological safeness during this pandemic of health, economics, and basic human decency.

While considering myths, mistaken identities, and meanings of self-care in Chapter 1, we got a taste of seven different working definitions of professional self-care. Interestingly, the vast majority acknowledge as foundational a basic awareness of our needs and the status of our well-being so that we can make informed decisions about our own caring and ways in which we can orient outwardly to the world. We can "notice what's absent in order to feel whole and content" (C. Berlin, personal communication, October 2016), "evaluate what's missing from our self-care diet" (C. Chen, personal communication, September 2016), "discern our needs at any given time . . . through deep self-knowing" (M. Evans, personal communication, October 2016), "use deep self-awareness . . . to experientially know what wholeness feels like" (T. Richardson, personal communication, September 2016), cultivate bare awareness of internal and external experience (A. Botta, personal communication, September 2016), or engage in "self-awareness . . . as foundational in helping to cultivate better regulation and balance in our lives" (Baker, 2003, as cited by E. Wise, personal communication, October 2016).

We are acting with wisdom and deep self-caring when we mindfully check our drive or striving to do more even though we may not have met our basic needs. Basic needs can include sleep and basic nutrition, paying our rent or mortgage, staying out of the red financially, and making sure our mental and physical health are managed decently. Otherwise, our striving to "be better" or "do more" can feel disingenuous at best and frustratingly impossible or shaming at worst. During times of extreme biological, relational, cultural, emotional, or financial crisis, our primary needs may demand most of our attention. And that is perfectly honorable and respectable.

Lest this discussion of discernment between surviving and thriving feel demotivating, it's important to take a hopeful turn to look at our professional and personal well-being through a positive psychological lens. Within this perspective, we can begin to embody the notion that thriving is really about growth. We can grow even within harsh conditions because, unlike the plants and trees around us, we always have our internal consciousness and will that are unaffected by the weather. As mindfulness teachings sagely offer, our conscious awareness is like the sky. Even the most terrible storm cannot taint the purity of the sky itself.

In the realm of positive psychology, flourishing is a process. It's not static or immutable, nor is it a characteristic or a trait. It's a multidimensional, multifaceted set of principles and practices that become integrated and infused into one's daily life. It's *lifestyle psychology*. As professional educator Lynn Soots noted, flourishing is thus derived, in part, from the "product of the pursuit of engagement of an authentic life that brings inner joy and happiness through meeting goals, being connected with life passions, and relishing in accomplishments through the peaks and valleys of life" (Soots, n.d., as cited in Ackerman, 2021).

The idea of thriving or flourishing is also one of *possibility*. Now famous for her hundreds of studies on mindset, Stanford University psychologist Dr. Carol Dweck teaches us that a *growth mindset* fosters actual growth well beyond what a *fixed mindset* tends to keep more locked in place (e.g., Dweck, 2007). A simple word like "yet" can promote expansiveness and possibilities in which our future has *yet to be determined*. As we think about cultivating self-care and enhancing our well-being, we may whisper to ourselves "and it hasn't happened *yet* the way I truly need. It's always a work in progress."

36 WILLINGNESS, READINESS, AND MOTIVATION TO INTEGRATE SELF-CARE

Happiness is not the belief that we don't need to change; it is the realization that we can.

—Shawn Achor

Jeffrey Siegel—a Harvard-affiliated international speaker, personal trainer, life coach, and mindfulness teacher—has written eloquently about "the why" and "the how" of finding ourselves taking up a self-care practice such as mindfulness meditation. Siegel (2019) suggested that sometimes "we're *pushed* by something [in our lives] that shook [us] to the core, and other times we're *pulled* by the potential benefits [of a practice] such as greater tranquility, focus, and peacefulness." I consider this push/pull distinction to be of such potential benefit as we ponder what self-care really means to us and how we can sustainably enact it for our own unique lives.

https://doi.org/10.1037/0000309-037
The Thriving Therapist: Sustainable Self-Care to Prevent Burnout and Enhance Well-Being, by M. A. Hersh

MOTIVATIONS TO CHANGE

What have your motivations been in the realm of caring for yourself? Reflecting on what you currently do to take care of yourself, do you have a sense for how you came to those self-caring enactments? Were you pushed by some harrowing events or by some interesting catalyst? Maybe you've been pulled by the positive effects that you aspire to see and feel for yourself? One of my colleagues, Dr. April McDowell, a couples and relationship-oriented therapist, recently experienced what Siegel so aptly suggested:

> The pandemic gave me time to tighten up my business practices and just about forced me to get better at self-care due to the mental stress of it all. I've never taken my self-care as seriously as I do now, and that's a direct result of the pandemic. For this, I'm truly grateful! I feel more confident that I'm serving my clients well because I'm taking way better care of myself. (A. McDowell, personal communication, March 10, 2021)

What sets humans apart from just about every other animal is our powerful ability to question our conditioning. Just because we've been doing things one way doesn't mean that we *have to* continue doing those things the same way in the future. We are infinitely malleable, and we have neuroplasticity on our side. Rick Hanson, PhD, perhaps one of the foremost authorities on *positive neuroplasticity*, has spoken about our inherent capacity for transformation of momentary good experiences into lasting characteristics (e.g., Hanson, 2018). These desired qualities become part of a newly wired network of neurons that fire together for better health, affecting the everyday experience of our minds, bodies, and relationships.

What also sets humans apart from other animals is that we often require willingness, psychological readiness, and motivation to live our lives differently. Why even orient our professional lives any differently if we perceive things to be going "just fine" and not too stressful most of the time? Or despite warning signs of burnout or repeated empathy distress, why do we continue to walk down a familiar path toward more entrenched suffering? Do we imagine conscious shifts in attitude and acts of self-caring will actually do anything for us, beyond what we're already doing or are able to do for ourselves? The answers to these questions are derived in part from the knowledge we've acquired from Parts I and II of this book.

As we explored numerous internal skills and external habits in Parts III and IV, some practices and activities may have resonated more strongly than others. Perhaps these chapters felt too overwhelming, as if you're supposed to incorporate all these self-caring qualities and activities into your life because it's *supposed to be* worthwhile to do so. Quite the contrary, these self-caring qualities and activities are not just laundry lists of things you "should" do for yourself; rather, these chapters and the entire premise of the book illustrate that we're given a template onto which we can place our unique awareness, values, needs, mindset, and self-care behaviors. This is your personalized map that when thoughtfully layered can take you into realms of well-being and sustainable self-care that you may not have thought possible.

Now is the time to begin exploring your personal *motivations* to be your own best ally as you are inevitably confronted by challenging work situations—harsh client behaviors, highly traumatized patients, client suicidality and actual suicide, burnout-prone high-volume caseloads, difficult communications with colleagues, and the delicate dance of integrating work with personal life. Now is the time to begin in earnest considering how your personal life—your patterns, habits, joys, and stresses—both uplifts and dispirits your professional life. Now is the time to begin evaluating your *willingness* to make shifts, some subtle and some more obvious, in support of your well-being now and into the future. Do you feel *ready enough*, right now, to begin to move the self-caring needle even in the most subtle way imaginable? How prepared do you feel to begin to identify what you'd like your life to look and feel like, even with its ups and downs? How would you like your self-caring mindset to sound and feel as you embody this mindset in everyday practices and behaviors designed to serve you as well as you serve your clients?

STAGES OF CHANGE

If you don't feel completely motivated, willing, or ready to begin making meaningful changes in your professional and personal life to support your well-being and wellness, you're not alone. Only about 20% of populations needing to make important changes are actually prepared to take action at any given time (Velicer et al., 1995). In fact, you may feel quite unwilling, unready, or unmotivated to shift anything about your current situation or the ways you relate to yourself, to your work, and to others. Despite having clarified your self-caring values and explored ways to remove important blocks, barriers, or objections to living in accordance with your values, a sobering reality may remain: you may simply not feel like you need, want, or are able to take on anything new or different in your life right now. You may even resent the implication that you're supposed to find more time to incorporate more self-care. If this sentiment resonates strongly, stay tuned for Chapter 37, which includes discussion of how to integrate facets of self-caring into your life in ways that feel more easeful and nonburdensome.

On the other hand, the 80% of individuals who aren't quite prepared to take action to change some part of their lives may have a strong desire to make meaningful change. It's just that their cognitions, affects, and behavior are not aligned to see it through. Does this sound familiar to you? Do you have the best of intentions to make some changes on your own behalf, only to fall back to your old, familiar patterns after a little while? For example, you may have been wanting to scale back your private practice caseload, only to find yourself the next month taking on just one or two or three more clients. Or perhaps you've been truly meaning to carve out "me time" each week so that you can rejuvenate and recharge. But the usual stressors seem to demand your time and attention so powerfully that you resume old patterns of wanting, denying, resenting, and ultimately feeling disillusioned.

Enter the *transtheoretical model* (TTM; Prochaska & DiClemente, 1983), one of the most widely researched and utilized approaches to behavior change that exists. Instead of having someone tell you (or telling yourself) that "you should just get more sleep and exercise, take more breaks, or just say 'no' to taking on more clients or projects," each of us would likely better serve our needs and self-care aspirations by acknowledging which *stage of change* for a given behavior we're embodying at this time.

For sustainability of self-care, we also benefit from knowing just what we're aspiring to do differently on our own behalf. Simply saying that we "should do more self-care" will only get us so far. What specific aspects of self-care and facets of your well-being are in need of the most care at this moment? Which facets have been ignored or neglected in the past? Which are likely to be "missing from your self-care diet" in the future (C. Chen, personal communication, September 2016)? This is a good time to strategically capitalize on the explorations in this book to discern what you most need to shift away from and/or move toward.

The genius of TTM as a comprehensive change technology is that it harnesses multiple facets of cognition, emotion, and behavior as they unfold over time in a relatively predictable sequence. Successful "self-changers" tend to employ different strategies and processes at different stages of change. Let's say that you have a close colleague who has commented with concern about your tendency toward perfectionism, overwork, repeatedly seeing many of same type of high-needs clients, and generally taking on too much in the precious time you have. In fact, the people who have your back are worried that you're burning out. They lovingly want you to slow down and adjust your priorities (I imagine it would ultimately be a true gift to have such people in our lives).

Together with your concerned colleague, you might create a *decisional balance sheet* (Janis & Mann, 1977) to organize your thoughts and motivations. What would your decisional balance sheet of comparative losses and gains look like? You could note the pros and cons of both changing and not changing your current pattern of behavior, thought, and feeling. This exercise can go a long way to illuminate what's really going on underneath your daily grind. If you're in the *precontemplation stage,* you may stack up the reasons and the ways you've been operating in favor of continuing that same pattern. In that case, despite what concerned others say, you would quickly shut down the conversation and likely would continue to live your life as it has been. Within the precontemplative mind would be minimal acknowledgment or outright denial or unawareness of the losses you're currently experiencing or will experience should you continue to engage with work in this way. The gains you'd make if you made changes in your professional life would likely be underappreciated or simply not on your radar.

Altering that way of engaging professionally may also produce a deep fear that you'd rather not confront. If you slowed down and backed off the intensity of your work, you could be introducing a "threat" to your preexisting identity and behavioral patterning that has been well-wired. For therapists who are quite driven, challenges to our usual way of being can feel unnerving. In fact, independent lines of work by Dr. Paul Gilbert and Dr. Stephen Porges suggest that a driven-ness (or "drive" mode, which has its own constellation of physiological, neurotransmitter, and hormonal responses; Gilbert, 2013) that is threatened is likely to induce a wave of reactions in the brain, mind, and body—reactions that are designed to protect and defend. Polyvagal theory (Porges, 2018) suggests that our nervous system at that point is on edge, on guard, closed off to curiosity, and feeling relatively insecure. This is likely especially the case if we have an underdeveloped *soothing* system. Thus, we would greatly benefit from exploring this perceived threat of backing off and slowing down our work. From there we could engage in soothing and decatastrophizing practices to take steps toward meaningful change. Sitting with (rather than avoiding) the feelings and sensations of such perceived threats to enacting change would also provide us a way to gain ground in this area (Strosahl et al., 2012).

The *contemplation stage* is the thinking, feeling, and behaving that lie between "I'm not even entertaining the need to streamline my professional life," for example, and "I'm actually gearing up to make these changes." You may have a discernably different decisional balance sheet and a stronger feeling of efficacy about making needed changes. You are getting ready. The benefits of slowing down or carving out more time for yourself may begin to overshadow the costs. But just as important in this example is the need to evaluate the benefits of keeping your driven-ness and busy schedule against the costs of slowing down or scaling back, for example. Without this acknowledgment and assessment of "why would I even keep myself so busy?" we can too easily gloss over how this mental–emotional–behavioral pattern became instantiated in the first place and why it may be so difficult to alter.

I once had a client who was a therapist struggling with long-standing workplace conflicts; he had been experiencing a slow burn for years. In fact, when he came to see me, he was showing all the signs and symptoms of classic burnout. As if to pay direct tribute to Prochaska and DiClemente (1983), he described moving through precontemplation and contemplation to arrive at the *preparation stage* by the time he scheduled his first appointment with me. He detailed almost 3 years of tension, disrespect, and invalidation when trying to communicate with his treatment facility director. But he had very little recognition that this pattern was changeable and that he had quite a bit of power to enact change. In fact, in our first session, he was already gearing up mentally and emotionally to make his life less stressful. Together we realized that some of his professional identity was tied up his current workplace, given how long he had worked there and how established and respected a presence he had become. This identity entanglement needed to be addressed before concrete and meaningful action was to be taken.

As this client more deeply acknowledged that his worth was not tied to this particular treatment facility, where so much of his expertise was nurtured but also so much of his conflict generated, the *action stage* began to flow almost on its own. This therapist started looking for other jobs, finally owning the irreconcilable differences between him and the director. These differences didn't make him any less of a respectable therapist, and he could take his experience and expertise into other professional realms. I did not have a chance to witness the *maintenance stage* of this therapist's change process, but I can imagine that he kept both internal and observable processes alive and working on his own behalf. Validating his own worth, reflecting on what was meaningful to *him* and not just the workplace at which he employed, and constantly reminding himself of his own empowerment were three major processes that were hinted at during our work together. Continuing to foster such cognitive–emotional resources would undoubtedly help this therapist walk a professional path worth traveling.

Let's now pause for a moment and reflect on something in your professional or personal life that could be different in the service of greater self-caring and well-being. It could be something you'd create, increase, or integrate into your life. Or it could be something you'd take out, decrease, or dissolve from your life. It may even be something that needs just a small modification rather than a significant change. What are the perceived benefits and costs of changing and of not changing? What would your decisional balance sheet look like for an important self-caring mindset or set of actions you could potentially integrate into your professional or personal life? How confident do you feel that you could make these changes? In values-speak, why would this change even be worth your consideration and energy to enact it?

Look back at Part II of this book. Do you have mindsets or behavioral patterns that are in need of shifting? What about finding a better match between your temperament and the professional or personal environment around you? Have you come to realize that you've been neglecting certain aspects of what makes you whole (or simply less stressed and more satisfied)? Have Parts III and IV of this book provided ideas about the skills, practices, and changes you could integrate in your life? Are you already engaging in relatively consistent and healthy self-care that promotes your well-being as best it can?

Whatever your current self-caring "status," that's simply where you are at this point in time. No need to lament that it's any other way than it actually is because you got here through a series of fortunate and unfortunate events and decisions that have all culminated in *right now*. And right now is the only time we have to make change. How will you tend to your now?

37

INTEGRATION AND EMBODIMENT OF SELF-CARING INTO EVERYDAY LIFE

Be patient with yourself. Self-growth is tender: It's holy ground. There's no greater investment.

—Stephen Covey

Stephen Covey, author of the international best-seller *Seven Habits of Highly Effective People*, is indeed onto something. Self-growth most definitely requires patience and is a delicate beast. Evolving oneself toward greater self-caring—whether better emotion regulation, humility, sleep, self-compassion, movement and exercise, boundary construction, or down time—demands something unique. We must not only know what we want to change and how to change it but also become intimately familiar with how to keep ourselves "on the path." This steadfastness requires investment of energy, persistence, clarity, acceptance, hope, and community, among other helpful qualities. It also requires smart strategy and sound tactics.

https://doi.org/10.1037/0000309-038
The Thriving Therapist: Sustainable Self-Care to Prevent Burnout and Enhance Well-Being, by M. A. Hersh

Jaime, a midcareer colleague, often lamented the long hours of "endless clients who all seem so broken." This sentiment certainly smacks of high burnout risk and/or compassion fatigue risk or indicates that Jaime is already experiencing such occupational hazards. While Jaime's income, skillset, and experience were generally quite solid, her morale was relatively porous. Jaime had lost the sense of buoyancy and resilience that characterized her earlier career. Clients seemed to annoy her more than ever before, and even those with whom she used to enjoy working felt burdensome. These feelings felt was largely unacceptable to Jaime, as she took pride in her clinical work and in her identity as a therapist.

In her personal life, Jaime increasingly felt a developmental dyssynchrony—a disconnect with her colleagues and friends as they experienced their children mature and make their way through college. Jaime did not have children and had gone through a divorce abruptly initiated by her ex-husband. Experiencing a life quite different from those of her midcareer colleagues was producing a general disillusionment and fracturing of Jaime's sense of fulfillment. Ultimately, Jaime knew she needed something to change.

Jaime got in touch with an old friend, someone who could have been a stellar psychotherapist herself. As Jaime and her friend spoke across several conversations that involved some informal motivational interviewing, Jaime seemed to reignite her sense of purpose as a psychotherapist and what it meant to her to turn toward herself more compassionately despite feeling guilty for turning away from her clients. This was the ultimate paradox for Jaime: The caring attention she paid to herself in order to feel whole engendered feelings of selfishness and fear of further disconnection from her clients. However, the more compassion and forgiveness Jaime offered herself, the more she was able to engage warmly and effectively with her clients and reclaim her identity as a helpful therapist.

Because Jaime is a relatively religious and spiritual person, she chose to pray more frequently (for strength and forgiveness) and attend church more regularly (to be part of a close, supportive community and to feel more purposeful in her life). This type of engagement inherently made sense to her and resonated deeply as both intrinsic and extrinsic practices to try to integrate into her life, not just as activities but as lifestyle changes that truly meant something to her. Jaime also felt her physical sluggishness and mental cloudiness as impediments to living out her potential. She desired to increase her vital energy and move toward a clearer mind. Deep down she knew that moving her body in various ways was a key to the vitality that was in greater abundance just a few years earlier.

First and foremost, it's vital for psychotherapists, who are spending hours on end each day serving others' needs, to tap back into themselves. In fact, we may need to "tap out" on some of our unhealthy patterned ways of operating even if it feels like we're "copping out" (C. K. Chen, 2016). As we've been compassionately but perhaps uncomfortably confronted with many times over in this book thus far, turning toward ourselves for *our* needs and well-being is not inherently selfish. It's not inherently self-aggrandizing, narcissistic, or self-pitying.

Whatever the internalized voices in your head—introjected from childhood or constructed during your training and throughout your adulthood—can be disentangled, made less implicit, and faced with a fierce acceptance. From these more flexible, more explicit, and healthily reframed beliefs about how we, as psychotherapists, are supposed to operate, we can unravel the string to our self-care kite to give it a chance in the blowing wind. Held too tightly, it never flies. Held too loosely, it can get tangled up in the branches as boundaries become increasingly diffuse. In the middle zone of a flexible relationship with ourselves we ultimately serve ourselves (and others) in optimal ways.

So how does a therapist like Jaime get herself back on track, coaxing herself into the realm where (self-)compassion meets committed action? Through her informal work with her friend and following some of the guidance presented in previous chapters of this book, Jaime is more poised to begin to integrate the attitudes, mindsets, practices, and activities that can facilitate living in accordance with what truly matters *to her*. Recognizing and constantly reminding herself with utmost compassion and acceptance that she has entered a new *developmental season* in her life, Jaime can begin to figure out what she needs to feel more whole, professionally and personally. It is interesting to note that often when we fill one missing part of our lives, a cascading effect of healing and awakening can occur.

Jaime places a high premium on dissolving her icy and irritated feelings about her clients. She knows that these negative perceptions are affecting her workday, her professional identity, and her therapeutic relationships. And this pervasive feeling is spilling over into her personal life. Jaime is also aware that the disillusionment and judgment from her recent personal trials and tribulations is affecting her clinical work. She has resolved to start reclaiming a more mindful life by softening her stance on both herself and her clients through some of the (self-)compassion and (self-)forgiveness practices she has learned. Let's take a look at how Jaime used a promising new set of change technologies to install and sustain new self-caring habits into daily life.

FORMING HABITS ONE MOMENT AT A TIME

Jaime's new self-caring journey begins with the influential work of James Clear, author of *Atomic Habits* (Clear, 2018) and creator of the online platform, The Habits Academy. While we acknowledge the many habit formation books and systems that have recently shown promise, Clear has developed one of the most hopeful new systems to sustainable habit formation, built on decades of behavior change research alongside insights from neuroscience and psychology. Jaime can flexibly adhere to Clear's foundational principles and the actionable components that undergird formation of healthy habits and renunciation of unhealthy ones. Clear's three powerful tenets and four tactical methods can set psychotherapists like Jaime on a path toward healthy habit integration over the long haul.

The Power of 1% Compounding

If you've ever (patiently) watched your money grow in the stock market or in a CD through your bank, you know the value of compound interest. Each new incremental gain, added to the ever-evolving foundation of previous gains, makes a special kind of impact. Over the long term, compounding doesn't simply result in linear growth. Rather, the longer we stick with a habit, the more growth and more sustainability we enjoy. Moreover, we might even experience a greater range of behavioral possibility and opportunity over time. But if we give up too soon, we'll likely miss opportunities for habit integration right around the corner.

As Clear (2018) provocatively suggested, "habits are the compound interest of self-improvement" (p. 16). Jaime could engage for a few minutes each day in compassion and forgiveness practices regardless of the results that these practices are producing on any given day. This approach requires a purposeful delay of gratification, but this mindset of patience and perseverance will ultimately help Jaime much more than assuming that each day that she intentionally offers herself and her clients compassion should deliver an exact and direct benefit.

I noticed this principle in action at a certain pivotal point during at-home work during the COVID-19 pandemic. As I noted earlier in the book, I was interested in building in the habit of doing chin-ups on the bar I had installed in my bathroom doorframe across the hall from the small office my family and I had created in what was previously my bedroom closet. After some sessions, I would pop out of the office and do a few chin-ups. I didn't notice much improvement for a while until one week it was just easier. I found myself able to pull myself up and even hang there more effortlessly. This progress helped produce more impetus to keep going. If I gave up too early, none of those gains and future progress would have been within reach.

Dr. Rick Hanson—mindfulness teacher, neuropsychologist, and neuroplasticity expert—has suggested that a similar phenomenon is occurring with positive neuroplasticity and building resilience (e.g., Hanson, 2018). Each drop in the bucket matters even though it may feel as if it doesn't. Jaime could imagine that although each hour she fills her compassion bucket may not make a perceived difference, the bucket is indeed being filled. After a certain period of time, Jaime could subjectively begin to feel a weightier bucket when compared to the day or week before. Said more accurately, Jaime will likely begin to feel the lightness and warmth from her compassion practice as long as she sticks with the practice itself. This powerful idea of compounding leads nicely into the next foundational principle: Drop goals in favor of systems.

Focus on Systems Instead of Goals

The master points patiently at the moon. The student studiously attends to the master's finger. Sometimes we believe we're focusing on the right thing but end up wasting our time and energy on the wrong object of our precious attention. In Clear's (2018) *Atomic Habits* approach, goals (set and followed poorly) can mislead us and cause our energy unfortunately to backfire. Goals can end up acting like the proverbial finger that the student continues to look at rather than studying the moon itself.

Imagine you're on a sports team. Your coach sets goals that the team should achieve a certain score or higher during each game and in turn win a certain number of games each season. You and your fellow players become increasingly disillusioned when you don't obtain "the right" score and when you aren't winning the "appropriate" number of games along the way. Unfortunately, while in pursuit of specific goals, the team suspends happiness and satisfaction until a particular goal is reached. If those goals aren't reached, morale sinks, and the team may begin to lose more. The score became the main attraction rather than the by-product.

We ultimately have more control over the systems we build to take action than we do over the achievement of a specific goal at a specific time in a specific manner. In the movie *Field of Dreams* (Robinson, 1989), Ray Kinsella hears a voice in the corn field that captures this sentiment well: "If you build it, he will come." In place of goals, we can construct enduring systems that allow the scores to take care of themselves. Clear (2018) noted that "the purpose of setting goals is to win the game. The purpose of building systems is to continue playing the game" (p. 27).

Jaime doesn't have to focus much on the number of times she practices compassion or decide that she "should" achieve a certain amount or quality of practice by a certain date. Rather, Jaime can build a system for herself that allows for a relatively seamless integration of daily compassion practice. The system Jaime constructs is the underlying mechanism for how she'll practice compassion in a fairly reliable way. Any time she misses a practice or feels as if practice didn't go well, she can borrow from principles of mindfulness-based relapse prevention (Bowen et al., 2010) and recognize that this is a blip along the path toward more sustainable self-caring. Self-judgment can be relaxed as Jaime compassionately reminds herself of her system rather than of exactly how often she's supposed to hone her compassion skills. Practicing self-compassion is the ultimate self-compassionate and self-caring act.

Like Jaime, I use Clear's (2018) principle of focusing on systems rather than goals for my physical wellness and mental well-being. Toward the end of writing this book, my personal trainer taught me a technique that allowed for my spinal muscles and connective tissue to release the excessive tension they've been holding for years since my surgeries. "Let be, let go, just release," I say to myself as I lie on the floor, breathe mindfully, and encourage the gradual softening of my spinal musculature. My only goal is to do the exercise, but I created a conditional system: After I put my kids to bed and finish cleaning the kitchen, I go upstairs to my bedroom, lie down on the floor, and do the exercise. My wife knows I'm taking 10 minutes or so to do this. I haven't yet felt guilty, and I have let the system work for me.

Make the Habit Your Identity

Often enough, we rely on our obtained results to inform us about who we are. In other words, we tend to put the outcomes cart before the identity horse rather than having our identity guide and shape our habits and thus the outcomes achieved over time. During the first summer of the COVID-19 pandemic, my then 11-year-old daughter decided to learn American Sign Language (ASL). She wanted to learn mostly because she thought it was an incredibly interesting and innovative way to communicate. Instead of relying on how well she was doing to determine how much she would stick with the habit and thus identify with being an ASL speaker, right out of the gate my daughter simply said, "I'm learning ASL. I already learned how to communicate 10 words and three phrases" (A. Hersh, personal communication,

June 5, 2020). It was clear that my daughter had "preowned" the fact that she was going to communicate using ASL.

Turning back to Jaime, we can imagine that instead of waiting to feel how much more compassionate she was feeling toward herself and her clients, Jaime could simply reclaim her sense of herself as an engaged and compassionate therapist. She could reconnect with the meaning that being a compassionate therapist offered her. In essence, she wouldn't need to see the results of her habit to enact her habit day after day. She could precommit to what she wanted and what was meaningful to her. By activating and maintaining her habits based on identity resonance (vs. outcomes management), Jaime would be that much more likely to stick with her compassion practice, thinking of it as part of her lifestyle rather than some "thing" to add on and have to practice.

FOUR POWERFUL TACTICS OF SUSTAINABLE BEHAVIOR CHANGE

Now that we have our core principles of habit formation, we can turn to the particular methods that can help facilitate the changes we're seeking. The following four tactics certainly will be familiar to behaviorists (and dog owners) and are likely used to some extent by most of us in daily life in one capacity or another. We will purposefully harness such change methods to help weave our self-caring aspirations into the fabric of both our professional and our personal life.

Cuing

Answering the question "How can I make this obvious?" is the first step toward building a positive habit. At least since graduate school, I can remember having a very difficult time wrapping up my sessions on time. I later figured out that this difficulty was due in part to my undiagnosed attention-deficit disorder or at least to my host of executive function challenges, which made it hard to assess the sweep of time. For a long time, the clocks in whatever clinic room or office space I was occupying or subletting were positioned in a way that made it just difficult enough for me to glance comfortably at the time. I wouldn't allow my eyes to see the clock lest it look like I was *trying* to see what time it was. My worry that clients would detect my clock-watching tendencies combined with my relatively poor sweep of time resulted in many late sessions. As you could well imagine, late to end, late to start, and so on and so forth.

One day I was lamenting this issue to a colleague. I told her that I wanted to set better boundaries with and for my clients. And from this one lingering habit, regrettably I was maintaining a low-level hum of stress at work and inhibiting my ability to access the brief but vital time I desperately needed in between clients. I wanted to harness my drive for better self-care that could be seamlessly integrated into my workday. In under 10 seconds, my colleague had solved the environmental cue problem of the insidious habit I wanted to kick and the new habit I wanted to install. She simply and rhetorically asked, "Why couldn't you just place several clocks around the office at different eye levels to ensure you can always easily see what time it is without your clients detecting your eye movements?" And there it was. I was well on my way to integrating a positive habit in the service of better therapeutic relationship boundaries, lowered stress, and greater self-caring. This simple cuing shift allowed me more frequently to preserve the 10 minutes between clients so I could take some deep breaths, do some energy tapping to self-regulate, make sense of tougher moments so I didn't accidentally spill that energy into the next session, jot down some notes, and possibly pee.

Cuing is essentially about making the enactment of the healthy habit as obvious and clear as possible and encouraging cues for a unhealthy habit to become more invisible. What would this cuing look like in your life with a positive self-caring habit that you would like to integrate? How can you arrange your environment so that you are more "naturally" exposed to cues for what you want or need to do while the cues for unhealthy habits remain (or become) more hidden?

For Jaime's aspirations of bringing more compassion into her workday, she could cue herself in several ways. Since Jaime usually arrives to work before her first client, she can establish a system and routine of setting up her computer, using the bathroom, and sitting in her therapist chair and perhaps offering compassion to imagined clients sitting in front of her. This doesn't have to take long; it just has to be included.

Dr. B. J. Fogg—Stanford University professor, director of the Behavior Design Lab, and originator of the *Tiny Habits* approach—has a very straightforward but powerful method for the tactic of cuing: Link the new behavior to an existing anchor activity that you already do each day (Fogg, 2021). The new habit enactment should be implemented immediately after the existing activity to ensure that the new habit has a chance to see the light of day. Something Jaime already does after each client is use the bathroom. Since she drinks tea during her sessions, that's already an established habit. And she almost always needs to pee after each session (I have heard that even the most skilled and experienced psychotherapists have to pee and may even feel like they need to end the session early to run to the bathroom). So as soon as Jaime comes out of the bathroom and walks through her office door, she can sit down in her favorite chair and spend a few seconds to a few minutes practicing compassion.

Since remote-only sessions during the COVID-19 pandemic were the norm for me, I chose to link four small but meaningful habits to the anchor activity of finishing each session. As soon as I'd say goodbye to the client and finish my progress note, I would open up the next client's progress note page. Now I was ready to go as soon I returned to my bedroom closet-turned-office. Next, I would do five chin-ups on the bar I had installed in my bathroom doorframe years earlier. This pull-up bar was 3 feet from my makeshift office, so the cuing and ease of enacting this action was quite manageable. I would then take my glass of water downstairs and refill it. I can get dehydrated fairly easily; my eyes become uncomfortably dry, and I feel more fatigued than I normally would. So just this one tiny habit makes a world of difference for my wellness, well-being, and effectiveness as a therapist. Finally, I would make the rounds to each family member available at the time to kiss, hug, or just say hi to them. I was relatively conscious of all these habits when I initiated them, but they became easefully and easily cued by and anchored to the existing activity of ending a session and stepping foot out of my home office. In fact, each tiny habit conveniently and seamlessly cued the next. However, when life got very busy and when my wife went back to work and my kids went back to school in person, my cuing changed, as did my self-caring efforts. I had to draw on the principle of impermanence and evolve with the changing times.

Craving

Answering the question "How can I make this attractive?" is the second step toward building a positive habit. When we watch something exciting on TV, when we eat something we crave (or even simply crave something we like to eat), or when we think about or actually have sex, we get boosts of dopamine to our system. This is normal, natural, and healthy. The unfortunate thing about implementing new habits is that they can be perceived as chores, thus generating very little dopamine activation. Thus, just thinking about engaging in the habit may produce the opposite effect of what we're going for. This dynamic is in part why the *craving* element is so helpful. If doing the habit has an appeal to it—some reward-based stimulation or values-based aspiration—you're more likely to stimulate some dopamine, thus further enhancing your activation energy and likelihood of pursuing and thus engaging in your healthy habit.

As Jaime visualizes herself doing her compassion practice and as a more engaged and compassionate therapist, she may enter a mode of being that feels safe, comfortable, and regulated. From this cognitive–somatic space, Jaime may be even more likely to feel the appeal of integrating her compassion practices into her workday. Interestingly, the habit doesn't necessarily need to be highly attractive, but the act of doing it can be made to have some degree of gravitational pull. As an avid tea drinker, Jaime likes to sip hot tea during her therapy sessions. This habit helps keep her hydrated, awake, present, and calm. She therefore decided to bring her tea drinking into her compassion practice. It may seem subtle or even insignificant, but it's effective for Jaime because it added an element of calming ritual that she had always found appealing. Moreover, she was able to synch an appealing activity (i.e., tea drinking) with the enactment of the new compassion practice habit.

Responding

Answering the question "How can I make this easy?" is the third step toward building a positive habit. This facet of sustainable behavior change and habit integration is all about making the *doing* of the habit as easy as possible. Essentially, we want to reduce the friction for healthy habits and increase the difficulty for unhealthy ones.

In *Atomic Habits*, Clear (2018) offered the example of meditation. If we desire to instill a habit of meditating (or of becoming a meditator), we can establish, at least at first, the most workable way to bring this action into our daily lives. If we follow conventional wisdom and commit to meditating 20 minutes per day, we might stop before we start. It's not that we don't have 20 minutes each day to do something healthy, but if we perceive 20 minutes as too much or too inaccessible, then we're much less likely to initiate the habit. Sustainability of that self-caring action would then be a moot point. Simply doing some small version of the habit will be much more important than the exact amount or length of time engaged in that habit at each step along the way. Of course, for some habits we'll want to increase the time if duration of that activity or practice indeed matters.

Dr. B. J. Fogg (2021) has similar suggestions to install new habits into our lives. The core tenet of his approach is to intentionally make the new habit small and brief enough to do with great ease, with almost no feeling of a hurdle to jump or wall to scale. As a psychotherapist, if you're interested in bringing creative endeavors into your life to spice things up and to expand your sense of self beyond that of constant helper, *start tiny*. Sit down at your piano for a minute and just play something, anything. Get used to hearing yourself play again. Order a book about photography to come straight to your home. When it arrives, look through it while you snap a few photos of random things around your home. Make it easy.

This process of scaling the habit down to bite-size pieces may also remind us of the 1% compounding principle. If we're putting some action into our new habit on a *regular enough* basis, we will begin to feel and see the cumulative effects, but if we set the bar too high or get overly frustrated at not engaging long enough or practicing the habit frequently enough, we likely are setting ourselves up to give up prematurely. This experience may be especially relevant to those of us who lean toward perfectionism or engage in all-or-nothing thinking. What we can do is quite simple: Commit to making it as simple and smooth as possible so that you can get the habit underway. Meditate for literally 60 seconds. If it helps to view the interval as one minute (vs. 60 seconds), then do that. While some of us may perceive a 10-minute meditation as too high of a hurdle to jump, we all have literally one minute to sit or lie down to tend with care to our mind, body, and spirit.

Clear (2018) would encourage Jaime to practice compassion in an easeful fashion so that she almost guarantees herself to do it as often as possible. Perhaps at first Jaime would imagine a client for whom it's easy to feel compassion. She could say out loud something like "I want to offer so-and-so my understanding and kindness during all the tough times he has been going through. I would like to sit with him as he is suffering and to stay present with a kindhearted warmth." For all her clients but especially for the tougher ones, Jaime could harness Dr. Chris Willard's 3 × 3 compassion exercise (see Chapter 19, this volume). For example, with a client in mind, she could identify one thing she has in common, one thing she admires, and one reason that the given client acts as they do. Even though the exercise is designed to have us generate three things for each category, Jaime knows to reduce the friction and make the practice as easeful as possible. She could even start by identifying just one aspect within one category. The overarching idea here is to get the ball rolling. Once it's rolling, it's more likely to keep rolling. A modified version of Newton's first law is on our side.

Rewarding

Answering the question "How can I make this satisfying?" is the fourth step toward building a positive habit. According to Seth Godin (2014), entrepreneur and lifestyle guru, "The best way to change long-term behavior is short-term feedback." We need an immediate "hit" of reward (and dopamine in the system) that gives us a sense that what we're doing for ourselves is enjoyable in the moment (as well as knowing it's likely beneficial in the long run). Long-term changes, like the kind we want to see or embody 6 months or 2 years from now, are so subject to delayed gratification that we would stop right in our tracks if our focus was only on that distant future. However, when we zoom right in to the present moment, today, tomorrow, and the next day, we can reward ourselves in the immediate for a step taken toward instilling a positive habit or ground held firmly as we practice refraining from a negative habit.

Even just checking off a box or crossing an item off a list can feel rewarding (enough). If you're keeping a journal of your self-caring practices, looking back on what you've already accomplished can help you feel validated. We need to give ourselves the proverbial pat on the back for at least practicing what we believe will ultimately help us. Journals, apps, audio recordings you can make for yourself, and even reward charts for adults can be of service. And we can remind ourselves that we're not necessarily rewarding goal-driven achievements but rather simply the act of showing up and engaging in our preframed identity and predetermined system.

DISTINGUISHING IMPORTANCE FROM URGENCY

Author Charles E. Hummel, in *Tyranny of the Urgent*, highlighted a far too frequent and humbly sobering part of the human condition. What we deem important unfortunately gets limited airtime and limited conscious attention, particularly when what we perceive as urgent takes center stage or feels especially pressing (Hummel, 2013).

It can be surprisingly helpful to spend a few minutes to reflect on the *time management matrix* that Stephen Covey (2020) brought to popular light. Originally offered by Dwight D. Eisenhower, this matrix features a four-quadrant template for helping people to better understand for themselves what is important, urgent, both important and urgent, and neither important nor urgent. It stands to reason that if our daily lives are filled with (what we perceive as) relatively urgent matters, by extension the truly important actions, tasks, and activities have a much lower probability of being executed. In fact, the urgency of tasks combined with general autopilot tendencies may lead to values-based tasks never fully arising within our conscious awareness.

A visual metaphor I like and have found quite helpful, relayed to me by a good friend in graduate school, is that of a big jar and a pile of large rocks, pebbles, and sand. The large rocks represent what we ultimately deem important. They are essentially our core values. The pebbles are somewhat important and may or may not need to be attended to with some urgency.

The sand represents everything else that simply begs for our attention, time, and energy. We have to get those things done, but we may be able to automate some of those hassles and daily chores or even outsource them somehow. If we put the sand into our jars first, we will never have room for our more meaningful rocks. The physics makes it impossible. Lest we let the sand come to define what we do and eventually who we are, we must first tend to our large rocks and make sure we place them in our jars with mindful awareness and care. See if you can bring this metaphor to life by grabbing a decently sized jar, some bigger rocks, some pebbles, and some sand or even salt. Experiment with filling your jar in a variety of ways, and note how you feel with each trial.

EMOTION VERSUS MOTIVATION FOR SUSTAINABLE HABITS

While it is a popularly held notion that proper motivation must precede action, this idea has been called into question by contemporary habit researchers and behavior change experts. This is not to suggest that the motivational models highlighted in Chapter 36 should be disregarded. One's motivation to change or incorporate new ways of being, writ large, is still quite worthy of reflection. However, capital *M* motivation can be distinguished from lower-case *m* motivation.

In *The Motivation Myth*, Jeff Haden (2018) suggested that while we often believe that we must have motivational energy or inspiration to take appropriate action for a habit or task, it's actually the other way around. Taking a small, simple action can generate motivation, which then leads to more action. That virtuous cycle can continue as long we're not convinced that we must have the right amount of motivation to initiate a task. Once the first steps of enacting a habit are begun, we've opened the door for myriad additional opportunities. The habit can then be done for a longer duration, and enhanced creativity and inspiration are more likely to flow.

Both Fogg (2021) and Clear (2018) strongly suggested that positive emotion needs to be paired with the healthy activity you're trying to incorporate into your day. Dr. Rick Hanson (2018) also noted the importance of elevating positive affect when practicing the integration of resilience-building activities of any kind. I'm reminded of a meditation teacher who encouraged his students to flash a little smile while meditating. He noted that meditation doesn't have to be so serious, that we can bring some lightness or simple joy to the practice of training our minds and bodies to pay attention with curiosity and acceptance.

ESTABLISHING A CLEAR VISION FOR SELF-CARING HABITS

Some change experts will also suggest keeping your vision of how you'd like things to look as clear as possible (e.g., Clear, 2018). This type of clarity can come in the form of mental imagery, word-based language, or having what some call *vision boards* to keep your aspirations for the future in sharp, vivid focus. We know from recent neuroscience research and the principle of neuroplasticity that when we repeatedly imagine doing a task, we're firing neural networks as if we did the task itself. So it may be well worth the extra few seconds every now and then to conjure up an image of yourself executing a newly acquired positive habit. Close your eyes and imagine yourself doing this task and experiencing the healthy changes that occur in those moments and over time. Really see and feel what this would be like for you. Jaime could envision herself becoming less and less irritable with her clients and increasingly engaged with feelings of warmth and unconditional friendliness. She could mentally link this ever-evolving outcome to her very brief practice of compassion that she aims to integrate into her workday.

Clear (2018) discussed how our identities—who we believe ourselves to be—are shaped by the very evidence that our daily actions, practices, and habits provide us. The more evidence we have for a belief, the more likely we are to believe it. If you meditate, for example, for 20 minutes per day, 7 days per week, every week each month, and every month each year, not only will your consistent efforts likely pay off by way of results, but you'll also be much more likely to consider yourself *a meditator*. It's hard not to identify in this way when meditation becomes your integrated, embodied, daily practice. No longer a mere habit, it is simply part of what you do and how and who you are. Within Clear's approach, it's not about the behaviors at all; it's about the identity we'd like to embody through enacting those behaviors. In this way, it's very much about your values and what ultimately matters to you for how you live your life.

Small habits and little choices are transforming us all the time anyway, so as we reflect on how to create and integrate sustainable self-care into our lives for our long-term betterment, we need to think simultaneously small and big. The *big think* is all about the grand vision of ourselves, what we desire to become. If you truly value a more peaceful, less frenetic work life, what would it look like? Paint a picture of it in your mind. See and try to feel it happening in your mind's eye and in your body. Envision it as you're falling asleep, when your alpha and theta brain waves are most prominent and your mind is most "programmable."

The *small think* is in the mini actions (both subtle and observable) we take each hour of every day. When your vision is clear in your mind's eye, begin with what's obvious, attractive, easy, and satisfying. That habit will evolve, and you'll evolve with it. Appendix I provides numerous examples of the tiny habits we can do as we start the day, as we navigate throughout our workday, and as we end the work day and transition to our nonprofessional life. Some of these activities you may already do but would like to do more mindfully. Others you might consider integrating without much hassle but with an invigorated sense of self-caring intention. The idea is to infuse our days with self-caring actions and attitudes that keep our vital energies humming soundly and well-tuned. When we notice disruptions in our vibration (e.g., too high, low, loud, quiet, erratic), then we can examine our actions and mental habits and adjust accordingly. Sometimes, however, circumstances are just difficult and our day is just long. When we're operating from a self-caring needs-based perspective, we can lovingly ask ourselves what we need and then listen patiently for an answer (see Appendix E for mindful check-in questions).

As we gather the big vision and the small habits together, we can synthesize them into a self-care plan and calendar created by licensed professional counselor Lynn Louise Wonders, a yoga and mindfulness instructor and active psychotherapist self-care advocate (L. L. Wonders, personal communication, March 5, 2021). Appendix J includes a mindful self-caring plan and calendar that can help put your vision into action and sculpt your actions into a larger vision. Ms. Wonders emphasized that we benefit deeply from paying attention to our needs on a daily and weekly basis as well as on monthly, quarterly, and annual timeframes. Using this simple but powerful self-care planning device can help you to move the self-care needle while holding yourself compassionately accountable.

Healthy self-caring habits aren't formed overnight. They take wise discernment of what we're aspiring to build into our lives and why. They require some perseverance, grit, and patience. They demand self-acceptance and self-compassion. And they certainly are facilitated by the right support and resources, both from out there and from in here. Appendix K provides a sample of apps, books, and websites catering to the formation of healthy habits and integration of values-based actions that can benefit you as a person and a therapist now and for years to come.

The final chapter of the book presents a (more utopian) vision of how support from fellow therapists and a network of supportive others can indeed be a form of sustainable care in and of itself. By incorporating a profession-wide expectation that we all care for one another just as we're theoretically supposed to be caring for ourselves, we can make our envisioned lifestyle of self-caring that much more easeful, beneficial, and enduring.

38

THE GIFTS OF STEWARDSHIP AND PAYING IT FORWARD

A Communitarian Approach to Helping Our Fellow Helpers

If I am not for myself, who will be for me? If I am only for myself, what am I? And if not now, when?

–Attributed to Rabbi Hillel the Elder

The tired but eager practitioners broke into several groups. The task was to share ideas, experiences, and challenges of engaging in self-care as forensic mental health workers. Dr. Elizabeth Shepherd, my cofacilitator, former internship classmate, and a Boston-area child forensic mental health expert, knew from years of firsthand experience that her fellow forensic practitioners within this unique and sobering field were taxed and overwhelmed. Forensic mental health may be one of the most stressful and burnout-susceptible helping professions, and these practitioners could use all the help they could get.

One of the most humbling experiences I was fortunate to observe during this small group activity was experienced clinicians sharing wisdom with helpers at earlier stages of their careers. Senior practitioners spoke of the

https://doi.org/10.1037/0000309-039

The Thriving Therapist: Sustainable Self-Care to Prevent Burnout and Enhance Well-Being, by M. A. Hersh

need for balance, seeking support, not taking things too personally, and making time for oneself no matter what. You could almost imagine the advanced practitioners taking the early-career helpers by the hand and whispering, "It doesn't have to be *this* hard. Here's how to suffer less." Of course, the less experienced helpers had plenty of insight and wisdom in their own right, but there was something so inspiring about watching how freely the self-care knowledge and experience was being paid forward. It felt like a true gift willingly bestowed and received.

CONCEPTUALIZING STEWARDSHIP AND PAYING IT FORWARD

According to Merriam-Webster (n.d.-b), *stewardship* is defined as "the conducting, supervising, or managing of something; especially the careful and responsible management of something entrusted to one's care." The need for stewardship within the realm of the psychotherapy profession cannot be overstated. Going it alone in our helping profession is an unnecessary burden at best and a recipe for profound personal and professional suffering at worst. This sobering reality is, in part, why we are entrusted and entrust ourselves to the care and oversight of our training institutions, more experienced supervisors, continuing education opportunities, niche social media groups and forums, peer consultation groups, state and provincial associations, and colleague support and assistance organizations (e.g., the Advisory Committee on Colleague Assistance of the American Psychological Association), to name a few.

Stewardship over each other's clinical competence as well as overall well-being has been powerfully discussed within the *competence constellation model* (CCM), a communitarian approach to supporting professionals in maintaining their competence over time (Johnson et al., 2013). This notion of competence involves not only essential clinical skills and career growth but also the vital personal resilience and self-caring skills that help support being a whole person *and* a thriving therapist.

Quite starkly, part of the human condition involves blind spots in assessing our own abilities, weaknesses, and areas of need. In general (Dunning et al., 2003) and as health care professionals specifically (Davis et al., 2006), we are often quite inaccurate in our self-assessments of competence (e.g., Eva et al., 2004). Unfortunately, we tend to overestimate our own prowess relative to how our familiar peers observe us. As the quip goes, we can't all be above average, can we? This confrontation with reality begs the question of why we tend to rely so heavily on our own (biased, misguided, or flawed) evaluations to serve our own (self-care) needs.

Johnson and colleagues noted this problematic phenomenon as a vital area of investigation and transformation (e.g., Johnson et al., 2013). Recognizing the overvaluation of self-assessment and acknowledging the interdependent nature of human functioning provide the foundation for mutual stewardship of competence and care. This model does not replace the trifecta of self-awareness, self-evaluation, and self-care. Rather, a communitarian approach both complements and augments the self-assessment and self-caring process, honoring how difficult (and even unfair) it can be to rely solely on ourselves to be our own best allies. In fact, Oana Tomescu, MD, PhD, of the Perelman School of Medicine at the University of Pennsylvania, made the need for a communitarian ethic of care for our helpers plainly clear: "It's critical to realize that this epidemic [of compassion fatigue] is a shared responsibility. Individuals are not going to 'resilience their way' out of this" (Jablow, 2017).

How do we attempt to take care of each other? Practicing psychologists, for example, are loathe to intervene when they detect a competence problem with a fellow therapist (e.g., Barnett & Hillard, 2001). Collectively, we have to shift away from the notion of intervening only when problems arise. In fact, the spirit of this entire book promotes an aspiration to be aware of what we (and others) might need *before* we find ourselves in too deep, burned out, or in trouble.

Psychotherapists could aspire to form networks of colleagues and organizations that are oriented toward both prevention and growth. The qualities of these networks would be marked by care, concern, and support with integrity and honesty. By nature, these relationships would be *ongoing*. Similar to the entrepreneurial Mastermind groups made popular by entrepreneur Napoleon Hill in the 1920s and 1930s, this type of peer-to-peer collegiality would offer a unique combination of brainstorming, accountability, ethics management, and numerous kinds of support. In addition, these stewardship networks would help normalize and remediate the challenges of professional and personal development as well as serve as a source of joy, growth, and thriving.

Rather than relying on traditional measures of the "success" of mentorship groups or supervisory relationships, stewardship networks for psychotherapists could have broad notions of benefit to a given therapist. They could be oriented toward relational, holistic, and self-evolutionary processes and outcomes. Psychotherapists could both offer and receive from their colleagues wisdom and experience, honest feedback, and general support for overall wellness and well-being. These dynamic experiences could involve discussions about personal issues (e.g., raising children, difficult relationships, finding creative outlets), professional development (e.g., therapists' diversity of activities, income issues, finding the best workplace match for one's personality and career aspirations), and the inextricable and reciprocal relationship between the two.

In this vein, Dr. Kristen Lee, author of *Mentalligence*, has encouraged individuals and workplaces to approach usual difficulties in a new way. Dr. Lee (2018) said that by adopting a model of *collective efficacy* that is less I-focused and more we-focused, we can turn problems with individual burnout and resilience on their head. No longer would we have a set of individual therapists all experiencing the same issues but not communicating or assisting one another. A more we-focused mentality simultaneously places no one in the spotlight nor in the dark. Just imagine a willingness of collective problem solving that would help alleviate stigma and cultivate connection.

If we look back to the chapters of Part II that invite us to examine the type of person we are behind the therapist and the environments for which we're likely best suited, we can acknowledge the relative ease or difficulty with which we would reach out to form or join and then sustain our own stewardship network. We must be careful not to rule out the whole concept of stewardship networks for our fellow therapists who are less relationally oriented, more introverted, or temperamentally highly sensitive. To this end, we can address the notion of stewardship with a broad, multitiered conceptualization.

At the most fundamental but still vital level, stewardship could be as simple as having a relatively close colleague with whom you feel comfortable seeking and giving support. Sometimes that relationship may feel somewhat lopsided as you text them several times in one month in desperation for words of wisdom about struggles you're having with your cases. Or perhaps you hear from them about their professional impasses or that their personal and work life are not cooperating with one another. At other times, however, the relationship may feel quite reciprocal, one of mutual stewardship. Ultimately, the mutuality of support and honest feedback between you and one or more colleagues serves as the foundation for sustainable (self-)care.

Some psychotherapists may already have established or want to build a more extensive and diverse network beyond this first tier. In their competence constellation model, Johnson et al. (2012) suggested that the more varied and culturally diverse one's network, the more sustainable and effective it will be. Variation of professional identity, personal background, and cognitive worldview can contribute positively to one's performance and problem-solving opportunities (Page, 2007). But the relationship wouldn't be defined only by this type of exchange. You could reach out to your colleague to check in on them. Without provocation, you could ask how they've been, what's going well, and what's been challenging lately. Without jealousy, you could inquire about how your colleague is being supported by others—colleagues, friends, and family alike (e.g., Johnson & Ridley, 2008). In other words, you would be merely one, albeit important, part of their constellation of stewardship, and they would be one of many important figures in your network (see Figure 38.1).

IT STARTS AT THE BEGINNING: STEWARDSHIP WITHIN TRAINING INSTITUTIONS

Interestingly but perhaps not surprisingly, the more that psychologists-in-training *perceive* their programs to value self-care, the more likely trainees are to engage in self-care themselves (Zahniser et al., 2017). Simply by fostering an atmosphere that places a premium on the need for students to care for themselves—to seek and receive support, to take time off, to build appropriate coping strategies, to cultivate mindful awareness—the more students will gravitate toward those self-caring attitudes and enactments. Practicing psychotherapists, in part, learn how to be responsible and healthy members of their helping professions through their initial training programs. Thus,

FIGURE 38.1. Sample Stewardship Constellation Between and Within Colleagues

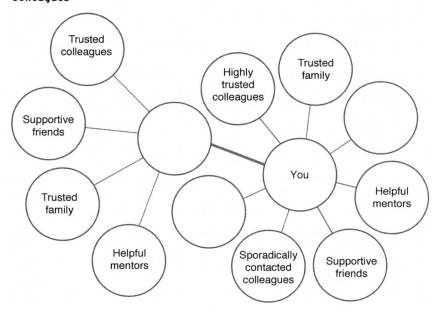

in some ways (as with all early attachment relationships), learning how to care for ourselves *and* one another begins when we step through the doors of our institutions.

One of the most poignant examples of the roots of stewardship comes from the kindergarten classroom in my children's school. Among the many small but important jobs the children are responsible for executing each week is the role of *empathy doctor*. If the child who is empathy doctor for that week sees a classmate in emotional or physical need, the empathy doctor can ask what's wrong, provide assistance, or seek support for the child in need. I was blown away by the fact that 5-year-olds are learning this vital social-emotional skill, which is the cornerstone of all healthy relationships, communities, and psychotherapeutic engagements.

We might consider that empathy doctors are in fact *compassion doctors*, as this term perhaps captures the role more precisely. We see someone in need, and we are motivated to reach out to help to alleviate their suffering. We may first feel what they feel and thus be moved to act based on this empathic sentiment. Or we may inherently come to know that "they" are just like "me," and "I" am just like "them." The boat glides across the water when we all row in concert but spins around and around when only one of us cuts our oar across the waves.

As we evolve through our professional training and careers, we could, ideally, learn to embody the role of empathy/compassion doctor for all our classmates, partners in training, colleagues, supervisees, and less experienced contemporaries. At Loyola University in Chicago, Illinois, Patricia Rupert and her students have taken a keen interest in investigating burnout and self-care for practicing psychologists. Not only is it important that students build awareness of their needs and signature reactions to stressors; the construction of professional support systems has also been determined to be of significance to students' well-being and self-reported progress throughout their graduate training (Zahniser et al., 2017). This creation of a *culture* of self-care de facto becomes a culture of caring more broadly. Sustaining that culture, however, is something else entirely.

Training programs across the globe are beginning to take self-care and stewardship of their trainees more seriously, thus helping to create a simultaneous culture of helper self-care and care for our fellow helpers. A great example of this both/and endeavor is at Fordham University Graduate School of Social Service. During her time as a student, Rev. Jade de Saussure, MSW, OMC, observed that students were well taught how to care for their clients but not necessarily how to care for themselves. She was intent on helping to create a culture of self-care (K. Jackson, 2014). Forged from this compassion-doctor inspiration was a bimonthly continuing education course on stress reduction skills for professionals, stand-alone self-care workshops addressing burnout and compassion fatigue, and an offsite self-care program facilitating these types of trainings to other agencies.

At McLean Hospital, one of the most prominent stand-alone mental health facilities in the United States, Dr. Laura Ferrer facilitated a psychology intern support group for a full decade. Psychology interns are at a crucial crossroads in both personal and professional development as they increasingly assume the role (and identity) of relatively independent clinicians (L. Ferrer, personal communication, October 2, 2020). Helping these trainees and soon-to-be licensed professionals to sort through and express their fears and aspirations can be considered a vital service to each and every individual but also to the larger network of students. In fact, this support group serves multiple purposes and can be thought of as stewardship on many levels.

By facilitating such a group year after year, Dr. Ferrer was *paying it forward*. She was actively contributing to the well-being and (self-)caring of future psychotherapists (although not all group members become practicing psychologists). She also learned a great deal from her trainees within these networks, growing in her understanding and compassion for the silent suffering that many of us continue to endure.

BESTOWING ACCUMULATED WISDOM WITHIN CONTINUATION EDUCATION

What if at every workshop, conference, or training we attended, we were able to both share and receive the personal and collective self-care wisdom from our fellow psychotherapists? Sometimes these events are intentionally structured to offer this mutual exchange, and other times sharing self-caring knowledge is sort of an accidental by-product of the focal training itself. Yet at other times, psychotherapists' well-being and self-care needs are totally neglected, even if unintentionally.

Trainers and workshop leaders could purposefully facilitate a spirit of camaraderie and support. Leaders and trainers could become each other's keepers (MacIntyre, 1999), demonstrating compassionate caring for the future well-being of those who are learning from them. Rather than disseminating only a new therapeutic approach, leaders could integrate the ethics of self-care and career-sustaining behaviors into their trainings. What if these themes became the norm for how we all related to one another? What if we no longer pretended that we're all fine all the time?

Three examples of self-care built into trainings include comprehensive energy psychology, dialectical behavior therapy, and various trauma-centered therapies. For such trainings as well as for the treatment approaches themselves, therapists are taught to help regulate themselves, cultivate nonjudgmental awareness, and establish mindful presence. Understanding one's boundaries and limits at any given time is essential to maintaining optimal and ethical delivery of clinical services and is of utmost importance to sustainable care of the therapist.

Within trainings and conference events, early-career psychotherapists (ECPs) could be paired with midcareer (MCPs) and late-career psychotherapists (LCPs) so that they could learn about the experiences—joys, challenges, and surprises—of traveling along the psychotherapists' path. ECPs could hear directly from their more experienced counterparts that burnout risk tends to decrease as more opportunities arise, more experience is gained, and as evolving ECPs intentionally prioritize themselves in value-driven ways. MCPs and certainly LCPs could feel not only a sense of *generativity*—pride in expressing care as they contribute in meaningful ways to their less experienced colleagues—but also a humbled excitement about learning how ECPs overcome their struggles in innovative and creative ways. Looking out for one another could become expected and commonplace, as we're all experiencing such similar struggles anyway. In fact, we don't have to rely on a hierarchical mentorship-type exchange; any set of colleagues can look out for each other at any time.

BUILDING NETWORKS OF STEWARDSHIP AND IMPARTING OUR WISDOM

During the writing of this book, I had several phone conversations with Dr. Chris Willard, my colleague and friend. At the time of this writing, both Dr. Willard and I are probably somewhere in the beginning of the MCP stage. We're both in private practice, we each have two young children and a wife in academia, and we have similar sensibilities and senses of humor. Needless to say, it's an easeful friendship even if we remain busy in our own personal and professional lives. As we listen to each other's thousand joys and thousand sorrows, we not only empathize and sympathize but can become each other's keeper. It doesn't necessarily have to be an explicit or obvious thing in the moment.

As we share our stories that resonate, two important *caring* opportunities arise. First, we can be on the lookout for the other's well-being—listening, validating, or providing constructive feedback. If something sounds like an undue burden, we can ask some poignant questions, share our own stories of hardship and resilience, or compassionately sound the awareness alarm. Second, as we listen to the struggles and triumphs of the other, each of us can pause to reflect on our own state of being and our personal and professional integrity. Thus, caring and self-caring can arise from a single exchange, and we can become increasingly accountable to and for our fellow helper(s).

Stewardship networks and opportunities to pay our wisdom and kindness forward abound. While the specific types of opportunities may depend on the individual practitioner and their work setting, establishing *mentoring programs* may be an effective means of supporting ECPs (Dorociak et al., 2017). Other opportunities can be found within group practices. For example, an owner or clinic director may help to create an atmosphere of such camaraderie and collegiality that it would be hard not to feel wanted and part of a cohesive team.

Within more intimate relational contexts, supervisors and consultants can make sure they're paying careful attention to the whole person within the therapist and not just the delivery of certain interventions. This may be a tall order for supervisors, and yet, as Dr. Cory Chen noted, "supervision can and should help a trainee make sense of their . . . strengths, weaknesses, and blind spots [in the service of] the trainee's development as a therapist" (C. Chen, personal communication, March 1, 2021). Even if some supervisors draw a hard boundary between supervision and what smacks of personal therapy, it still behooves the supervisor–supervisee team to acknowledge what is needed to help the supervisee to feel and be whole.

Outside the intimate realm of supervision is a much broader mode of stewardship. Lynn Louise Wonders—licensed professional counselor, play therapist, and mindfulness and yoga teacher—has significantly expanded her meaningful and positive impact on her professional colleagues. In 2014 she founded one of the first closed Facebook groups for mental health professionals, titled "Therapists' self-care support: For mental health professionals to give and gain encouragement to attend to self-care." With nearly 5,000 psychotherapists exchanging ideas, offering support, and being in community, this group is a wonderful example of a broad stewardship network that devoted participants can rely on.

And finally, paying it forward can come in the form of a simple phone chat with a mentor. Nearly one decade ago, I had the pleasure of talking to my former graduate school clinical supervisor and mentor, Dr. Erica Wise. She invited me and another former supervisee to join her to write about ethics and self-care for practicing psychologists. Unbeknownst to me at the time, the seeds for this book were planted. In fact, Dr. Wise so graciously paid forward to me this gift—the opportunity to write a book on therapist self-care that she herself was offered but decided to decline. She referred a few editors my way, and the rest, they say, is history.

Stewardship and the art of paying it forward remind us that we are not ever in this alone. Self-care is only dubbed in such a way because ultimately no one else can think, feel, and act for us. And so we must in some ways take matters into our own hands. And yet, interconnectedness is our truth (Nhat Hanh, 2020). We are a collective of human beings who trained to become helpers. We know how hard this profession is. Let's make it a bit easier for ourselves by making it more easeful for each other. From the wisdom of the 15th-century Indian mystic poet and saint, Kabir, "In your veins, and in mine, there is only one blood, the same life that animates us all! Since one unique mother begat us all, where did we learn to divide ourselves?"

To close, I would like to offer a blessing to us all adapted from the wisdom and compassion of Jack Kornfield (2009):

> May we love ourselves just as we are.
> May we sense our worthiness and well-being.
> May we trust the world.
> May we hold ourselves in compassion.
> May we meet the suffering and ignorance of others with compassion. (p. 306)

I wish each and every one of you, as well as our collective professions, the very best right in this moment and far into the future. What will come to pass is not yet known, but we can turn toward ourselves and each other with as much caring and compassion as possible. This, fellow therapists, will make all the difference.

Appendix A

MINDFUL SELF-CARE SCALE–CLINICAL VERSION

Instructions for completing the scale are found below. To arrive at interpretable scores, please tally your subscale scores carefully, paying attention to reverse-scored items. When you derive your subscale and total scores, you can compare them against the average score, 3.0. If any subscale is (much) lower than 3.0, pay close attention to what this score means for you at this time. Suggestions are found at http://ed.buffalo.edu/mindful-assessment/ scale/assessment.html and within this book. Subscale scores 3.0 or above indicate an easeful form of self-caring for you, a strength, or something you're working hard to integrate into your life. Keep up the great work!

From *Mindfulness and Yoga for Embodied Self-Regulation: A Primer for Mental Health Professionals* (pp. 297–311), by C. P. Cook-Cottone, 2015, Springer Publishing. Copyright 2015 by Springer. Reprinted with permission.

Mindful Self-Care Scale – Clinical

Please Cite as: Cook-Cottone, C. P. (2015). *Mindfulness and yoga for embodied self-regulation: A primer for mental health professionals.* New York, NY: Springer Publishing. (See text for a detailed description of the measure)

The Mindful Self-Care Scale – Clinical is an 84-item scale that measures the self-reported frequency of behaviors that measure self-care behavior.

Self-care is defined as the daily process of being aware of and attending to one's basic physiological and emotional needs including the shaping of one's daily routine, relationships, and environment as needed to promote self-care. Mindful self-care addresses self-care and adds the component of mindful awareness.

Mindful self-care is seen as the foundational work required for physical and emotional well-being. Self-care is associated with positive physical health, emotional well-being, and mental health. Steady and intentional practice of mindful self-care is seen as protective by preventing the onset of mental health symptoms, job/school burnout, and improving work and school productivity.

This scale is intended to help individuals identify areas of strength and weakness in mindful self-care behavior as well as assess interventions that serve to improve self-care. The scale addresses 10 domains of self-care: nutrition/hydration, exercise, soothing strategies, self-awareness/mindfulness, rest, relationships, physical and medical practices, environmental factors, self-compassion, and spiritual practices. There are also three general items assessing the individual's general or more global practices of self-care.

Contact information: Catherine Cook-Cottone, Ph.D. at cpcook@buffalo.edu

Circle the number that reflects the frequency of your behavior (how much or how often) within past week (7 days):

Never (0 days)	Rarely (1 day)	Sometimes (2 to 3 days)	Often (4 to 5 days)	Regularly (6 to 7 days)
1	2	3	4	5

Reverse-Scored:

Never (0 days)	Rarely (1 day)	Sometimes (2 to 3 days)	Often (4 to 5 days)	Regularly (6 to 7 days)
5	4	3	2	1

The questions on the scale follow.

1

Mindful Self-Care Scale – Clinical

Nutrition/Hydration (NH) – 7 items

I drank at least 6 to 8 cups of water	1	2	3	4	5
Even though my stomach felt full enough, I kept eating *reverse scored*	5	4	3	2	1
I adjusted my water intake when I needed to (e.g., for exercise, hot weather)	1	2	3	4	5
I skipped a meal *reverse scored*	5	4	3	2	1
I ate breakfast, lunch, dinner, and, when needed, snacks	1	2	3	4	5
I ate a variety of nutritious foods (e.g., vegetables, protein, fruits, and grains)	1	2	3	4	5
I planned my meals and snacks	1	2	3	4	5

Total _____

Average for Subscale = Total/# of items _____

Exercise (E) – 7 items

I exercised at least 30 to 60 minutes	1	2	3	4	5
I took part in sports, dance or other scheduled physical activities (e.g., sports teams, dance classes)	1	2	3	4	5
I did sedentary activities instead of exercising (e.g., watched tv, worked on the computer) *reverse scored*	5	4	3	2	1
I sat for periods of longer than 60-minutes at a time *reverse scored*	5	4	3	2	1
I did fun physical activities (e.g., danced, played active games, jumped in leaves)	1	2	3	4	5
I exercised in excess (e.g., when I was tired, sleep deprived, or risking stress/injury) *reverse scored*	5	4	3	2	1
I planned/scheduled my exercise for the day	1	2	3	4	5

Total _____

Average for Subscale = Total/# of items _____

2

Mindful Self-Care Scale – Clinical

Self-Soothing (S) – 13 items

I used deep breathing to relax	1	2	3	4	5
I did <u>not</u> know how to relax *reverse scored*	5	4	3	2	1
I thought about calming things (e.g., nature, happy memories)	1	2	3	4	5
When I got stressed, I stayed stressed for hours (i.e., I couldn't calm down) *reverse scored*	5	4	3	2	1
I did something physical to help me relax (e.g., taking a bath, yoga, going for a walk)	1	2	3	4	5
I did something intellectual (using my mind) to help me relax (e.g., read a book, wrote)	1	2	3	4	5
I did something interpersonal to relax (e.g., connected with friends)	1	2	3	4	5
I did something creative to relax (e.g., drew, played instrument, wrote creatively, sang, organized)	1	2	3	4	5
I listened to relax (e.g., to music, a podcast, radio show, rainforest sounds)	1	2	3	4	5
I sought out images to relax (e.g., art, film, window shopping, nature)	1	2	3	4	5
I sought out smells to relax (lotions, nature, candles/incense, smells of baking)	1	2	3	4	5
I sought out tactile or touch-based experiences to relax (e.g., petting an animal, cuddling a soft blanket, floated in a pool, put on comfy clothes)	1	2	3	4	5
I prioritized activities that help me relax	1	2	3	4	5

Total _____

Average for Subscale = Total/# of items _____

Self-Awareness/Mindfulness (SA) – 10 items

I had a calm awareness of my thoughts	1	2	3	4	5
I had a calm awareness of my feelings	1	2	3	4	5
I had a calm awareness of my body	1	2	3	4	5

3

Mindful Self-Care Scale – Clinical

I carefully selected which of my thoughts and feelings I used to guide my actions	1	2	3	4	5
I meditated in some form (e.g., sitting meditation, walking meditation, prayer)	1	2	3	4	5
I practiced mindful eating (i.e., paid attention to the taste and texture of the food, ate without distraction)	1	2	3	4	5
I practiced yoga or another mind/body practice (e.g., Tae Kwon Do, Tai Chi)	1	2	3	4	5
I tracked/recorded my self-care practices (e.g., journaling, used an app, kept a calendar)	1	2	3	4	5
I planned/scheduled meditation and/or a mindful practice for the day (e.g., yoga, walking meditation, prayer)	1	2	3	4	5
I took time to acknowledge the things for which I am grateful	1	2	3	4	5

Total _____

Average for Subscale = Total/# of items _____

Rest (R) – 7 items

I got enough sleep to feel rested and restored when I woke up	1	2	3	4	5
I planned restful/rejuvenating breaks throughout the day	1	2	3	4	5
I rested when I needed to (e.g., when not feeling well, after a long work out or effort)	1	2	3	4	5
I took planned breaks from school or work	1	2	3	4	5
I planned/scheduled pleasant activities that were not work or school related	1	2	3	4	5
I took time away from electronics (e.g., turned off phone and other devices)	1	2	3	4	5
I made time in my schedule for enough sleep	1	2	3	4	5

Total _____

Average for Subscale = Total/# of items _____

4

Mindful Self-Care Scale – Clinical

Relationships (RR) – 7 items

I spent time with people who are good to me (e.g., support, encourage, and believe in me)	1	2	3	4	5
I scheduled/planned time to be with people who are special to me	1	2	3	4	5
I felt supported by people in my life	1	2	3	4	5
I felt confident that people in my life would respect my choice if I said "no"	1	2	3	4	5
I knew that, if I needed to, I could stand up for myself in my relationships	1	2	3	4	5
I made time for people who sustain and support me	1	2	3	4	5
I felt that I had someone who would listen to me if I became upset (e.g., friend, counselor, group)	1	2	3	4	5

Total _____

Average for Subscale = Total/# of items _____

Physical/Medical (PM) – 8 items

I engaged in medical care to prevent/treat illness and disease (e.g., attended doctor's visits, took prescribed medications/vitamins, was up to date on screenings/immunizations, followed doctor recommendations)	1	2	3	4	5
I engaged in dental care to prevent/treat illness and disease (e.g., dental visits, tooth brushing, flossing)	1	2	3	4	5
I took/did recreational drugs *reverse scored*	5	4	3	2	1
I did _not_ drink alcohol	1	2	3	4	5
I practiced overall cleanliness and hygiene	1	2	3	4	5
I accessed the medical/dental care I needed	1	2	3	4	5
I did not smoke	1	2	3	4	5
I did not drink alcohol in excess (i.e., more than 1 to 2 drinks [1 drink = 12 ounces beer, 5 ounces wine, or 1.5 ounces liquor])	1	2	3	4	5

Total _____

5

Mindful Self-Care Scale – Clinical

Average for Subscale = Total/# of items   _____

Environmental Factors (EF) – 9 items

I maintained a manageable schedule	1	2	3	4	5
I avoided taking on too many requests or demands	1	2	3	4	5
I maintained a comforting and pleasing living environment	1	2	3	4	5
I kept my work/schoolwork area organized to support my work/school tasks	1	2	3	4	5
I maintained balance between the demands of others and what is important to me	1	2	3	4	5
Physical barriers to daily functioning were addressed (e.g., needed supplies for home and work were secured, light bulbs were replaced and functioning)	1	2	3	4	5
I made sure I wore suitable clothing for the weather (e.g., umbrella in the rain, boots in the snow, warm coat in winter)	1	2	3	4	5
I did things to make my everyday environment more pleasant (e.g., put a support on my chair, placed a meaningful photo on my desk)	1	2	3	4	5
I did things to make my work setting more enjoyable (e.g., planned fun Fridays, partnered with a co-worker on an assignment)	1	2	3	4	5

Total   _____

Average for Subscale = Total/# of items   _____

Self-Compassion (SC) – 7 items

I noticed, *without judgment*, when I was struggling (e.g., feeling resistance, falling short of my goals, not completing as much as I'd like)	1	2	3	4	5
I punitively/harshly judged my progress and effort *reverse scored*	5	4	3	2	1
I kindly acknowledged my own challenges and difficulties	1	2	3	4	5
I engaged in critical or harsh self-talk *reverse scored*	5	4	3	2	1
I engaged in supportive and comforting self-talk (e.g., "My effort is valuable and meaningful")	1	2	3	4	5
I reminded myself that failure and challenge are part of the human experience	1	2	3	4	5

6

Mindful Self-Care Scale – Clinical

| I gave myself permission to feel my feelings (e.g., allowed myself to cry) | 1 | 2 | 3 | 4 | 5 |

Total _____

Average for Subscale = Total/# of items _____

Spiritual Practice (SP) – 6 items

| I experienced meaning and/or a larger purpose in my _work/school_ life (e.g., for a cause) | 1 | 2 | 3 | 4 | 5 |

| I experienced meaning and/or a larger purpose in my _private/personal_ life (e.g., for a cause) | 1 | 2 | 3 | 4 | 5 |

| I spent time in a spiritual place (e.g., church, meditation room, nature) | 1 | 2 | 3 | 4 | 5 |

| I read, watched, or listened to something inspirational (e.g., watched a video that gives me hope, read inspirational material, listened to spiritual music) | 1 | 2 | 3 | 4 | 5 |

| I spent time with others who share my spiritual worldview (e.g., church community, volunteer group) | 1 | 2 | 3 | 4 | 5 |

| I spent time doing something that I hope will make a positive difference in the world (e.g., volunteered at a soup kitchen, took time out for someone else) | 1 | 2 | 3 | 4 | 5 |

Total _____

Average for Subscale = Total/# of items _____

General (G) – 3 items

| I engaged in a variety of self-care strategies (e.g., mindfulness, support, exercise, nutrition, spiritual practice) | 1 | 2 | 3 | 4 | 5 |

| I planned my self-care | 1 | 2 | 3 | 4 | 5 |

| I explored new ways to bring self-care into my life | 1 | 2 | 3 | 4 | 5 |

Total _____

Average for Subscale = Total/# of items _____

7

Mindful Self-Care Scale – Clinical

Total Score Summary
Be sure you have correctly scored your *reverse scored* items

Averaged Score	Subscale
_____	Nutrition/Hydration (NH)
_____	Exercise (E)
_____	Self-Soothing (S)
_____	Self-Awareness/Mindfulness (SA)
_____	Rest (R)
_____	Relationships (RR)
_____	Physical/Medical (PM)
_____	Environmental Factors (EF)
_____	Self-Compassion (SC)
_____	Spiritual Practice (SP)
_____	General (G)

Shade in your average score for each subscale below:

5											
4											
3											
2											
1											
Scale	NH	E	S	SA	R	RR	PM	EF	SC	SP	G

8

Appendix B

SELECTED RESOURCES FOR PSYCHOTHERAPISTS' PROFESSIONAL DEVELOPMENT AND WELL-BEING

Purpose/organization	Source
General professional development	
American Psychological Association, NASW, ACA, AAMFT, American Psychiatric Association	https://www.apa.org, https://www.socialworkers.org, https://www.counseling.org, https://www.aamft.org, https://www.psychiatry.org
Psychotherapy.net	https://www.psychotherapy.net
Psychotherapy Networker	https://www.psychotherapynetworker.org
PESI continuing education	https://www.pesi.com
Therapist self-care support	
University of Buffalo School of Social Work Self-Care	https://www.socialwork.buffalo.edu/resources/self-care-starter-kit.html
Self-Care in Social Work	http://www.socialworkblog.org/practice-and-professional-development/2020/04/the-art-of-self-care-for-social-workers/
Mindful Self-Care Scale (Free online)	https://www.catherinecookcottone.com/research-and-teaching/mindful-self-care-scale/
TEND Academy for Compassion Fatigue	https://www.tendacademy.ca
Compassion Fatigue Awareness Project	https://www.compassionfatigue.org
Training programs for professionals who treat trauma	http://www.figleyinstitute.com/
Compassion Fatigue Prevention & Resiliency Fitness	https://www.youtube.com/watch?v=RppP5z7AXLQ (Eric Gentry, PhD, powerful excerpt from the program)
Fire Within (mental health professional mind–body support)	https://www.firewithinconsulting.com (Annabelle Coote)
Self-relationship support	https://www.connectfulness.com

Purpose/organization	Source
Simple self-care practices	*Simple Self-Care for Therapists* (Bush, 2015)
	https://www.wonderscounseling.com/51-simple-self-care-practices/
Comprehensive therapist self-care	*Leaving It at the Office* (Norcross & VandenBos, 2018)
	The A to Z Self-Care Handbook for Social Workers and Other Helping Professionals (Grise-Owens et al., 2016)
Self-care for frontline workers	*Self-Care Manual for Front-Line Workers* (https://www.moph.gov.lb/en/Pages/6/553/nmhp)
Burnout prevention	*Anti-Burnout Card Deck* (Warren et al., 2018)
Psychotherapy memes	https://www.psychotherapymemes.com/
Therapy Is Not a Dirty Word	https://www.therapyisnotadirtyword.com/
Mental health support	
National Alliance on Mental Illness	https://www.nami.org
Attention-deficit/hyperactivity disorder support	https://www.chadd.org
Obsessive-compulsive disorder support	https://www.iocdf.org; *Everyday mindfulness for OCD* (Hershfield & Nicely, 2017)
Anxiety and depression support	https://www.adaa.org/
Trauma support	https://www.traumasurvivorsnetwork.org
	https://www.attachmenttraumanetwork.org
Alcohol treatment support	https://www.niaaa.nih.gov/publications/brochures-and-fact-sheets/treatment-alcohol-problems-finding-and-getting-help
Suicide prevention	https://www.suicidepreventionlifeline.org
	https://www.crisistextline.org
Psychotherapist support groups/forums	
Mental health professionals meet-ups	https://www.meetup.com/topics/mentalhealthpro
Online group therapy for therapists	https://www.grouptherapycentral.com/online-groups-for-therapists
Therapists' Self-Care Support (Facebook closed group)	https://www.facebook.com/groups/caringfortheself/
REAL Self-Care (Facebook closed group)	https://www.facebook.com/groups/realselfcare
Highly Sensitive Therapists (Facebook closed group)	https://www.facebook.com/groups/Support.for.HSTs

Purpose/organization	Source
Professional administrative/therapy delivery support	
Simple Practice (EHR)	https://www.simplepractice.com
Therapy Notes (EHR)	https://www.therapynotes.com
Therapist Aid (Worksheets/Tools)	https://www.therapistaid.com
Psychology Tools (Worksheets/ Tools)	https://www.psychologytools.com
Private practice support	
Selling the Couch	https://www.sellingthecouch.com
Abundance Practice Building	https://www.facebook.com/ abundancepracticebuilding
Private Practice Builders	https://www.facebook.com/groups/private. practice.builder
The Private Practice Startup	https://www.facebook.com/ theprivatepracticestartup

Note. NASW = National Association of Social Workers; ACA = American Counseling Association; AAMFT = American Association for Marriage and Family Therapy; EHR = electronic health record.

ADDRESSING OUR BLOCKS, BARRIERS, AND OBJECTIONS TO BEING OUR OWN BEST ALLIES

BBO master list

Master list of BBOs	BBO category (systemic, personal, other)	Rating (0-10) of blocking influence on your self-care manifestation
Example: I often tend to put out fires instead of focus on prevention (proactive self-care is an afterthought)	Personal	5

Addressing the BBO: "My spouse is so busy, my kids have special needs, and so it's very hard to focus on myself."

Behavioral manifestations of the BBO	Thoughts, feelings, actions, reactions that maintain the BBO's role	Possible meaningful actions to address BBO
Example: I pick up the slack that my partner leaves due to his work schedule—I do most of the household tasks and family management in addition to my clinical work; I tend to my children's special needs whenever they need me.	I feel resentful that I have to manage nearly everything. But I also feel and would feel guilty for demanding more time for myself. That's not how I was raised. The pattern never gets broken.	Have a candid conversation with my partner about my concerns; consider qualified babysitter for even one or two afternoons per week.

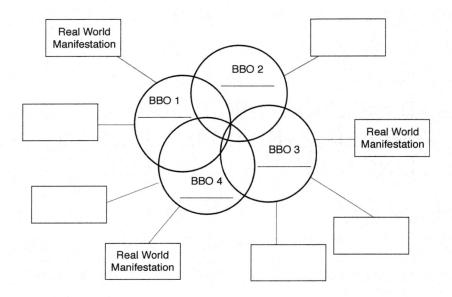

SELECTED RESOURCES FOR PSYCHOTHERAPISTS WITH A HIGHLY SENSITIVE TEMPERAMENT

Books

The Highly Sensitive Person (Aron, 1997)
Making Work Work for the Highly Sensitive Person (Jaeger, 2005)
The Highly Sensitive Person's Survival Guide (Zeff, 2004)
Psychotherapy and the Highly Sensitive Person: Improving Outcomes for That Minority of People Who Are the Majority of Clients (Aron, 2010)
Brain Training for the Highly Sensitive Person: Techniques to Reduce Anxiety and Overwhelming Emotions: An 8-Week Program (Bjelland, 2017)

Websites

https://www.hsperson.com
https://www.hsperson.com/resources/just-for-highly-sensitive-therapists-and-coaches/
https://www.highlysensitiverefuge.com/
https://www.hsperson.com/therapists/seeking-an-hsp-knowledgeable-therapist/
https://www.highlysensitive.org/

Social Media and Podcasts

https://www.facebook.com/groups/Support.for.HSTs/
https://www.facebook.com/highlysensitivepeopleIlseSand/
https://thehspexperience.libsyn.com/
https://podcasts.apple.com/us/podcast/hsp-sos/id1221116848
https://highlysensitiveperson.net/hsppodcast/

Appendix E

MINDFUL CHECK-IN

Suggestions for Optimal Benefit: Print this handout for work and home. Write one or two questions on a sticky note for your night table at home and your desk at work. Just by glancing at the questions, you'll remember to practice treating yourself well. Rotate the questions every few days to spark mindful presence and a wellness orientation in a variety of ways.

What are my intentions for "how to be" in these very moments?

Are my moment-to-moment intentions and actions aligned with my deeper values for what can bring me greater meaning, fulfillment, or sustainable well-being?

Am I valuing myself enough in this moment to give myself the care I need?

Will it help me to "start over" in the next set of moments so that I don't proliferate feelings of fear, powerlessness, hopelessness, or resentment?

Can I address self-care barriers right now without grasping, avoidance, or defensiveness?

What can I do for myself in this moment that promotes stability, growth, or both?

Is my work environment resonating with my temperament, sensibilities, and needs? If not, what can I do within my control to enhance this resonance?

Am I practicing self-compassion (i.e., going easy on myself) and self-forgiveness (i.e., letting be/letting go) as best I can?

Can I identify and relax the overstriving for needing to "do it all"?

Am I being as honest with myself right now as is humanly possible?

SELECTED MINDFULNESS AND MEDITATION RESOURCES

Books

Wherever You Go, There You Are: Mindfulness Meditation in Everyday Life (Kabat-Zinn, 2005b)

Mindfulness in Plain English (Gunaratana, 2011)

The Miracle of Mindfulness (Nhat Hanh, 1999)

The Power of Now (Tolle, 2004)

10% Happier (Harris, 2019)

Buddha's Brain (Hanson, 2009a)

Coming to Our Senses (Kabat-Zinn, 2005a)

When Things Fall Apart (Chödrön, 2016)

Meditation for Fidgety Skeptics (Harris, 2018)

The Mindful Way Through Depression (Willams et al., 2007)

The Mindful Way Through Anxiety (Orsillo & Roemer, 2011)

A Path With Heart (Kornfield, 1993)

Lovingkindness (Salzberg, 2002)

The Art of Happiness: A Handbook for Living (H.H. The Dalai Lama & Cutler, 2020)

Radical Acceptance (Brach, 2004)

Radical Compassion (Brach, 2020)

Practical Meditation (Dientsmann, 2018)

Awake at Work (Caroll, 2006)

Real Happiness at Work (Salzberg, 2013)

Buddha at Work: Finding Purpose, Balance, and Happiness at Your Workplace Pandit, 2020)

A Year of Living Mindfully: Quotes and Weekly Mindfulness Practices (Fields, 2012)

Mindful Self-Compassion Workbook (Neff & Germer, 2018)

Mindful Parenting (Race, 2016)

Self-Compassion for Parents (Pollak, 2019b)

Websites

https://www.mindful.org
https://www.liveanddare.com
https://www.mindfulleader.org
https://www.heartmath.com
https://www.brain.fm
https://www.tinybuddha.com
https://www.zenhabits.net
https://www.mindfulnessexercises.com
https://www.urbanmindfulness.org
https://www.franticworld.com
https://www.pocketmindfulness.com
https://www.instituteformindfulleadership.org
https://www.tarabrach.com/guided-meditations/

Apps

The Mindfulness App
HeadSpace
Calm
MyLife Meditation
Insight Timer
Buddhify
Sattva
Breathe
10% Happier
Inscape
Meditation Studio
Waking Up
Oak
Let's Meditate
Happy Not Perfect
The Tapping Solution
Happify
Omvana
ZenHabits

Appendix G

SELECTED SUBTLE ENERGY RESOURCES AND PRACTICES

Organization/resource	Website
Association for Comprehensive Energy Psychology	https://www.energypsych.org
Resources for Resilience (subtle energy based self-help techniques)	https://www.r4r.support/
Thought Field Therapy (TFT)	https://www.tftfoundation.org/
Clinical EFT (Gary Craig, founder)	https://www.emofree.com
EFT Universe—EFT trainings and resources	https://www.eftuniverse.com
EFT Tapping Training Institute	https://www.efttappingtraining.com
The science behind energy tapping	https://www.petastapleton.com https://www.sciencedirect.com/science/article/pii/S1550830718303513
EFT for general audience (The Tapping Solution)	https://www.thetappingsolution.com
Energy medicine	https://www.edenmethod.com
5-Minute Eden Energy Routine	https://www.edenenergymedicine.com/donnas-daily-energy-routine/
Tapas Acupressure Technique	https://www.tatlife.com
Chakras and psychology	*Eastern Body, Western Mind* (Judith, 2004)
Quantum physics, epigenetics, and healing	https://www.lynnemctaggart.com https://www.brucelipton.com https://www.drjoedispenza.com https://www.bengstonresearch.com

Note. EFT = emotional freedom techniques.

Appendix H

THE RAPID RELIEF ENERGY SWEEP

The Rapid Relief Energy Sweep™

developed by Stephanie Eldringhoff, MA, LMFT, DCEP and Marti MacEwan, MA, LMHC, DCEP
contact: Stephanie Eldringhoff, Stephanie@stephanieeldringhoff.com
Marti MacEwan, Marti@stagefright.com

This technique uses the subtle energy from your own hands and fingertips to correct imbalances and strengthen the natural energy flow in your subtle energy systems. It has been shown to clear and balance many energy systems including the meridians, chakras, radiant circuits and auric field. It unscrambles energies, gets them moving the right direction and crossing over.

You "sweep" by spreading your fingers and passing your fingertips and palms over your body. Exercise can be done with hands touching the body or just off the body (maybe 2 inches).

Part 1 — Sweep the Body

1) Sweep up the inside of the legs to just below the chin. (breathing in)

Rub your hands together. Then starting at the inside of your big toes (Spleen 1), move up the inside of your feet and legs, across the front of your hips and up your torso to your chest.

Intentionally bring energy up from the earth through the bottoms of your feet.

2) Sweep across the chest and down the inside of the arm. (breathing out)

Take one hand and move it across your chest and down the inside of the opposite arm. Continue off the palm and fingers, being sure to cover all the fingers.

Do the same on the other side.

3) Sweep up the back of the hand, top and outside of the arm, dipping behind your shoulder over the shoulder blade, and back up to the neck. (breathing in)

Turn your palm over and trace over the back of your hand, covering all fingers. Move across the back of the hand and over the top and outside of your arm, behind your elbow, behind your shoulder, up to your neck.

Do the same on the other side.

4) Sweep up over the face and head, and down the back, off the outside edge of the feet. (breathing out)

Place your palms back on your chest. Spread the fingers and move them up across your face and over your head. Trace behind the backs of your ears with your thumbs. Continue down your back as far as you can reach on your shoulder blades. Bring your arms down and reach around to continue the path down your back, tracing your sides with your thumbs. Continue over your hips, down the back and outside of your legs, and off your little toes.

Intentionally send energy down into the earth to ground through the bottoms of your feet).

This completes one cycle. Repeat for three cycles, starting again coming up from the inside of the big toes.

Part 2 — Collect the Energy

As if you were beginning another cycle of the sweep, come up the inside of your feet and legs, across the front of your hips and up your torso to your chest

Spread your arms, palms up, and "collect" energy into your palms and through the top of your head.

Place one palm over your heart chakra (the center of your chest) and then the other palm on top of that one.

Hold that position and "breathe into the ground" through your feet.

Part 3 — Clearing the Auric Field

Bring your hands into the prayer position.

Move the hands up vertically over your head.

Open your arms wide, sweeping down the auric field to the sides of your body, resting on your thighs. Palms face either up or down as you prefer as you sweep your auric field.

Bring your palms together in front of your thighs with your fingertips facing downward.

Bring your hands up the midline of the body to over your head and again open your arms wide, sweeping through the auric field around your body

Do this several times if you like and return to finish, palm over palm, at the heart chakra.

Repeat any or all parts of the EFA Energy Sweep as many times as you like.
Often you will feel a tangible change immediately. Sometimes you will see a more subtle, cumulative effect.

Using the Energy Sweep to Clear a Thought Field

You can use the Energy Sweep to correct the subtle energy systems in the face of a particular intention or "Thought Field." The exercise helps you reinforce positive goals, and/or clear the emotional charge of a problem and move past it.

- First "tune in" to a problem or positive goal and notice its quality and intensity.
- As you do the Energy Sweep, "hold onto," observe and monitor the focus of your thought.
- It might help you to jot down a few words representing the issue or goal you are holding in your energy field and place it on the floor between your feet.
- Include an action verb, such as "releasing..." or "increasing...." That way you will be concretely reminded of it each time you pass this point in the cycle.

If it is helpful, you can rate it on a scale of 0-10. If you are focusing on a problem, as the energy field of the problem dissipates the number will go down. If you are strengthening a positive, the more the plausibility of the desired state comes into your awareness, the number will go up.

Appendix I

SELECTED SELF-CARE PRACTICES TO INTEGRATE THROUGHOUT THE (WORK)DAY

Starting the day

Engage in mindful stretching and an easeful transition from bed	Do a subtle energy routine to boost vital energy	Take an invigorating hot or cold shower
Set daily intentions and/or visualize your "best effort" emerging	Hug your loved ones (if you're able)	Know ahead of time your "white space" and downtime for the day
Plan and pack nutritious lunch, snacks, and/or hydration for day	Allow for enough time to transition from home to work	Drink enough water to rehydrate from overnight

During the day

Mentally prepare for your next client or clinical activity	Practice relaxing your jaw and dropping your tongue*	Remind yourself how challenging our profession really is
Do a 3-Minute Breathing Space practice	Do a wall stretch to open your chest	Prep for next (difficult) client through compassion reminder (e.g., they're just like you in many ways)
Mentally note your feelings after each session and then do energy tapping, breathwork, or movement to invite a release or clearing	Watch a short clip of something funny or inspiring	Tidy or spruce up your work space for optimal sensory input
Drink good tasting, clean water between and during sessions	Remind yourself of your intention to help	Splash some cold water on your face (to stimulate your vagus nerve and to reinvigorate you)

Ending the day and/or on weekends

Practice gratitude (with others or in a journal) for the good facts of the day	Read a print book and give your "screen eyes" a rest*	Be in nature or watch a nature video (get some *porch time**)
Practice *polarity breathing* (breathe out tension, breathe in feeling state and qualities you desire)	Reach out to trusted others for support or "just because"	Be and laugh with friends and/or family
Practice radically accepting the realities of the day	Give thanks at dinner with yourself, family, or friends	Use your hands or do something creative
Meditate (even if for 60 seconds); do yoga or other present-focused mind–body activity	Engage in sensory soothing activities (e.g., warm blanket, calming music)	Use your voice other than for therapy (e.g., sing, hum, chant)

Note. Items marked with * reflect practices from Wonders (2020). Reprinted with permission.

MINDFUL SELF-CARING PLAN AND CALENDAR

Part I: Begin by appreciating that you indeed need various things to function and to be well (e.g., downtime, movement, food, interpersonal connection). Start with the daily needs box and write down what you know or suspect you need to be well (enough) on a daily basis. Circle the needs that definitely feel doable (at least) right now. Move to weekly, monthly, quarterly, and annually, writing down particular needs that you're fairly sure should be met to not just survive but even to thrive.

Part II: After you've brainstormed your daily through annual needs and circled what you feel you can almost guarantee you can execute, get out your calendar and schedule your circled needs like you would schedule a client. Place daily and weekly needs in your calendar at particular times that enhance the likelihood of your fulfilling that activity. Flip/scroll to monthly view to write in the needs further down the road. Honor this new calendar mixed with *your needs* as best you can. It may benefit you to revisit this plan periodically to update your needs and their prioritization. You may also find it beneficial to have a trusted loved one or colleague help hold you accountable to your plan.

Daily		Weekly	
Monthly	Quarterly		Yearly

Appendix K

SELECTED RESOURCES FOR HEALTHY HABIT FORMATION AND BUILDING A MEANINGFUL LIFE

Books

Atomic Habits (Clear, 2018)
Tiny Habits (Fogg, 2021)
The Power of Habit (Duhigg, 2014)
Habit Journal from James Clear
The Tapping Solution Planner (Ortner, 2020)
Mindset: The New Psychology of Success: How You Can Learn to Fulfill Your Potential (Dweck, 2007)
The 7 Habits of Highly Effective People: Revised (Covey, 2020)
Drive (Pink, 2011)
Resilient (Hanson, 2018)
Grit: The Power of Passion and Perseverance (Duckworth, 2018)
Get Out of Your Mind and Into Your Life (Hayes, 2005)
The Happiness Trap: How to Stop Struggling and Start Living: A Guide to ACT (Harris, 2008)

Websites

https://www.jamesclear.com
https://www.bjfogg.com
https://www.thefoundationsofwellbeing.com
https://www.rickhanson.net/the-science-of-positive-brain-change
https://www.theminimalists.com/

Apps

Habitica
Simple Habit

Mood Trackers
MetaFi (Be Your Best Self)
Shine
HabitBull
Goalify
Google Calendar
Productive Habit Tracker
Streaks
Grow Habit Tracking
Routines

References

Abblett, M. (2013). *The heat of the moment in treatment: Mindful management of difficult clients*. W. W. Norton & Co.

Abbott, R., & Lavretsky, H. (2013). Tai chi and qigong for the treatment and prevention of mental disorders. *The Psychiatric Clinics of North America, 36*(1), 109–119. https://doi.org/10.1016/j.psc.2013.01.011

Abrams, Z. (2018). When therapists face discrimination. *Monitor on Psychology, 49*(4). https://www.apa.org/monitor/2018/04/therapists-discrimination

Ackerley, G. D., Burnell, J., Holder, D. C., & Kurdek, L. A. (1988). Burnout among licensed psychologists. *Professional Psychology: Research and Practice, 19*(6), 624–631. https://doi.org/10.1037/0735-7028.19.6.624

Ackerman, C. E. (2021, January 25). *Flourishing in positive psychology: Definition + 8 practical tips*. Positive Psychology. https://positivepsychology.com/flourishing/

Adams, C. E., & Leary, M. R. (2007). Promoting self-compassionate attitudes toward eating among restrictive and guilty eaters. *Journal of Social and Clinical Psychology, 26*(10), 1120–1144. https://doi.org/10.1521/jscp.2007.26.10.1120

Advisory Committee on Colleague Assistance. (n.d.). *The stress–distress–impairment continuum for psychologists*. American Psychological Association. https://www.apaservices.org/practice/ce/self-care/colleague-assist

Agovino, T. (2019, August 3). Mental illness and the workplace. *SHRM*. https://www.shrm.org/hr-today/news/all-things-work/pages/mental-illness-and-the-workplace.aspx

Ainsworth, M. D. S., Blehar, M. C., Waters, E., & Wall, S. (1978). *Patterns of attachment: A psychological study of the strange situation*. Lawrence Erlbaum Associates.

Alexander, A. (2019). I would never do that! Examining sexual boundary violations. *Psychotherapy Bulletin, 54*(3), 49–52. https://societyforpsychotherapy.org/i-would-never-do-that/

Allen, D. (2001). *Getting things done: The art of stress-free productivity*. Penguin.

American Counseling Association. (2014). *ACA code of ethics*. https://www.counseling.org/Resources/aca-code-of-ethics.pdf

American Psychological Association. (2000). *Division 12, Section VII report on education and training in behavioral emergencies*.

American Psychological Association. (2010). *Psychology of procrastination: Why people put off important tasks until the last minute* [Press release]. https://www.apa.org/news/press/releases/2010/04/procrastination

American Psychological Association. (2011). *Managing your boss*. https://www.apa.org/topics/managing-boss

American Psychological Association. (2013). *The "conscience clause" in professional training*. https://www.apa.org/ed/graduate/conscience-clause-brief

American Psychological Association. (2017a). *Career stages of health service psychologists: Special analysis of the 2015 APA Survey of Psychology Health Service Providers*.

American Psychological Association. (2017b). *Ethical principles of psychologists and code of conduct* (2002, amended June 1, 2010, and January 1, 2017). http://www.apa.org/ethics/code/index.html

American Psychological Association. (2020, November). Psychology's workforce is becoming more diverse. *Monitor on Psychology, 51*(8). http://www.apa.org/monitor/2020/11/datapoint-diverse

American Psychological Association. (2021, February 2). *APA: U.S. adults report highest stress level since early days of the COVID-19 pandemic* [Press release]. http://www.apa.org/news/press/releases/2021/02/adults-stress-pandemic

American Psychological Association's Board of Professional Affairs Advisory Committee on Colleague Assistance. (n.d.). Advisory Committee on Colleague Assistance. https://www.apa.org/practice/resources/assistance

Anderson, R. T., King, A., Stewart, A. L., Camacho, F., & Rejeski, W. J. (2005). Physical activity counseling in primary care and patient well-being: Do patients benefit? *Annals of Behavioral Medicine, 30*(2), 146–154. https://doi.org/10.1207/s15324796abm3002_7

Ardito, R. B., & Rabellino, D. (2011). Therapeutic alliance and outcome of psychotherapy: Historical excursus, measurements, and prospects for research. *Frontiers in Psychology, 2*, Article 270. https://doi.org/10.3389/fpsyg.2011.00270

Arditte Hall, K. A. (2018). Assessing the needs and interests of our early career psychologist members. *Psychotherapy Bulletin, 53*(2), 49–52. https://societyforpsychotherapy.org/assessing-the-needs-and-interests-of-our-early-career-psychologist-members/

Arnett, J. J. (2000). Emerging adulthood: A theory of development from the late teens through the twenties. *American Psychologist, 55*(5), 469–480. https://doi.org/10.1037/0003-066X.55.5.469

Arnold, J. E., Graesch, A. P., Ragazzini, E., & Ochs, E. (2012). *Life at home in the twenty-first century: 32 families open their doors*. The Cotsen Institute of Archaeology Press. https://doi.org/10.2307/j.ctvdjrr2c

Aron, E. N. (1997). *The highly sensitive person: How to thrive when the world overwhelms you*. Broadway Books.

Aron, E. N. (2010). *Psychotherapy and the highly sensitive person: Improving outcomes for that minority of people who are the majority of clients*. Routledge.

Aron, E. N., & Aron, A. (1997). Sensory-processing sensitivity and its relation to introversion and emotionality. *Journal of Personality and Social Psychology*, *73*(2), 345–368. https://doi.org/10.1037/0022-3514.73.2.345

Arora, P. G., Brown, J., Harris, B., & Sullivan, A. (2017). Professional development needs and training interests: A survey of early career school psychologists. *Contemporary School Psychology*, *21*(1), 49–57. https://doi.org/10.1007/s40688-016-0108-8

Arundel, A. V., Sterling, E. M., Biggin, J. H., & Sterling, T. D. (1986). Indirect health effects of relative humidity in indoor environments. *Environmental Health Perspectives*, *65*(March), 351–361.

Arzt, N. (2020). *Sometimes therapy is awkward: A collection of life-changing insights for the modern clinician*.

Au, D. W., Tsang, H. W., Ling, P. P., Leung, C. H., Ip, P. K., & Cheung, W. M. (2015). Effects of acupressure on anxiety: A systematic review and meta-analysis. *Acupuncture in Medicine*, *33*(5), 353–359. https://doi.org/10.1136/acupmed-2014-010720

Aubrey, T. E. R., & Gentry, J. E. (2019). *Unlocking the code to human resiliency: Building professional resiliency against burnout, traumatic stress and compassion fatigue*. XanEdu Publishing.

Bach, D., Groesbeck, G., Stapleton, P., Sims, R., Blickheuser, K., & Church, D. (2019). Clinical EFT (Emotional Freedom Techniques) improves multiple physiological markers of health. *Journal of Evidence-Based Integrative Medicine*, *24*, Article X18823691. https://doi.org/10.1177/2515690X18823691

Baer, R. (2006). *Mindfulness-based treatment approaches: Clinician's guide to evidence base and applications*. Elsevier.

Baerger, D. R. (2001). Risk management with the suicidal patient: Lessons from case law. *Professional Psychology: Research and Practice*, *32*(4), 359–366. https://doi.org/10.1037/0735-7028.32.4.359

Bailenson, J. N. (2021). Nonverbal overload: A theoretical argument for the causes of zoom fatigue. *Technology, Mind, and Behavior*, *2*(1). https://doi.org/10.1037/tmb0000030

Baird, K., & Kracen, A. C. (2006). Vicarious traumatization and secondary traumatic stress: A research synthesis. *Counselling Psychology Quarterly*, *19*(2), 181–188. https://doi.org/10.1080/09515070600811899

Baker, E. (2003). *Caring for ourselves: A therapist's guide to personal and professional well-being*. American Psychological Association. https://doi.org/10.1037/10482-000

Baker, E. K. (2007). Therapist self-care: Challenges within ourselves and within the profession. *Professional Psychology: Research and Practice, 38*(6), 607–608.

Ballenger-Browning, K. K., Schmitz, K. J., Rothacker, J. A., Hammer, P. S., Webb-Murphy, J. A., & Johnson, D. C. (2011). Predictors of burnout among military mental health providers. *Military Medicine, 176*(3), 253–260. https://doi.org/10.7205/MILMED-D-10-00269

Baltes, P. B., Lindenberger, U., & Staudinger, U. M. (1998). Life-span theory in developmental psychology. In W. Damon & R. M. Lerner (Eds.), *Handbook of child psychology: Theoretical models of human development* (pp. 1029–1143). John Wiley & Sons.

Barber, L. K., & Munz, D. C. (2011). Consistent-sufficient sleep predicts improvements in self-regulatory performance and psychological strain. *Stress and Health, 27*(4), 314–324. https://doi.org/10.1002/smi.1364

Barkley, R. A. (2020). *Taking charge of ADHD: The complete, authoritative guide for parents* (4th ed.). Guilford Press.

Barks, C. (1995). *The essential Rumi.* Harper.

Barnes, S., Brown, K. W., Krusemark, E., Campbell, W. K., & Rogge, R. D. (2007). The role of mindfulness in romantic relationship satisfaction and responses to relationship stress. *Journal of Marital and Family Therapy, 33*(4), 482–500. https://doi.org/10.1111/j.1752-0606.2007.00033.x

Barnett, J. (2014, December). Distress, burnout, self-care, and the promotion of wellness for psychotherapists and trainees: Issues, implications, and recommendations. *Society for Psychotherapy.* http://www.societyforpsychotherapy.org/distress-therapist-burnout-self-care-promotion-wellness-psychotherapists-trainees-issues-implications-recommendations

Barnett, J. E., Baker, E. K., Elman, N. S., & Schoener, G. R. (2007). In pursuit of wellness. *Professional Psychology: Research and Practice, 38*(6), 603–612. https://doi.org/10.1037/0735-7028.38.6.603

Barnett, J. E., & Hillard, D. (2001). Psychologist distress and impairment. *Professional Psychology: Research and Practice, 32*(2), 205–210. https://doi.org/10.1037/0735-7028.32.2.205

Barnett, J. E., Johnston, L. C., & Hillard, D. (2006). Psychotherapist wellness as an ethical imperative. In L. VandeCreek & J. B. Allen (Eds.), *Innovations in clinical practice: Focus on health and wellness* (pp. 257–271). Professional Resources Press.

Barroso, A., & Brown, A. (2021). *Gender pay gap in U.S. held steady in 2020.* Pew Research Center. https://www.pewresearch.org/fact-tank/2021/05/25/gender-pay-gap-facts/

Bauer, I., Hughes, M., Rowsell, R., Cockerell, R., Pipingas, A., Crewther, S., & Crewther, D. (2014). Omega-3 supplementation improves cognition and modifies brain activation in young adults. *Human Psychopharmacology, 29*(2), 133–144. https://doi.org/10.1002/hup.2379

Bearse, J. L., McMinn, M. R., Seegobin, W., & Free, K. (2013). Barriers to psychologists seeking mental health care. *Professional Psychology: Research and Practice, 44*(3), 150–157. https://doi.org/10.1037/a0031182

Beck, A. T. (1976). *Cognitive therapy and the emotional disorders*. International Universities Press.

Beckman, H., Regier, N., & Young, J. (2007). Effect of workplace laughter groups on personal efficacy beliefs. *The Journal of Primary Prevention, 28*(2), 167–182. https://doi.org/10.1007/s10935-007-0082-z

Behnke, S. (2009). Ethics from a developmental perspective. *Monitor on Psychology, 40*(1), 68. https://www.apa.org/monitor/2009/01/ethics

Ben-Zur, H., & Michael, K. (2007). Burnout, social support, and coping at work among social workers, psychologists, and nurses: The role of challenge/control appraisals. *Social Work in Health Care, 45*(4), 63–82. https://doi.org/10.1300/J010v45n04_04

Bercelli, D. (2005). *Trauma-releasing exercises (TRE): A revolutionary new method for stress/trauma recovery*. Booksurge Publishing.

Bergan, A., & McConatha, J. T. (2001). Religiosity and life satisfaction. *Activities, Adaptation and Aging, 24*(3), 23–34. https://doi.org/10.1300/J016v24n03_02

Berk, L., Tan, S. A., & Berk, D. (2008). Cortisol and catecholamine stress hormone decrease is associated with the behavior of perceptual anticipation of mirthful laughter. *The FASEB Journal, 22*(S1), 946.11. https://doi.org/10.1096/fasebj.22.1_supplement.946.11

Bjelland, J. (2017). *Brain training for the highly sensitive person: Techniques to reduce anxiety and overwhelming emotions: An 8-week program*. CreateSpace Independent Publishing Platform.

Blustein, D. L. (n.d.). *The 21st century challenge balancing work, children, and aging parents*. American Psychological Association. https://www.apa.org/education-career/development/early/balance.pdf

Bodhi, B. (2005). *In the Buddha's words: An anthology of discourses from the Pali Canon*. Wisdom Publications.

Boero, M. E., Caviglia, M. L., Monteverdi, R., Braida, V., Fabello, M., & Zorzella, L. M. (2005). Spirituality of health workers: A descriptive study. *International Journal of Nursing Studies, 42*(8), 915–921. https://doi.org/10.1016/j.ijnurstu.2004.11.007

Bonanno, G. A. (2004). Loss, trauma, and human resilience: Have we underestimated the human capacity to thrive after extremely aversive events? *American Psychologist, 59*(1), 20–28. https://doi.org/10.1037/0003-066X.59.1.20

Bonnell, G. (2008). *EFT tapping procedure (The basic recipe)*. https://www.tapintoheaven.com.

Bonovitz, C. (2009). Looking back, looking forward: A reexamination of Benjamin Wolstein's interlock and the emergence of intersubjectivity. *The International Journal of Psycho-Analysis, 90*(3), 463–485. https://doi.org/10.1111/j.1745-8315.2008.00128.x

Bootzin, R. R., Epstein, D., & Wood, J. M. (1991). Case studies in insomnia. In P. J. Hauri (Ed.), *Stimulus control instructions* (pp. 19–28). Plenum.

Bowen, S., Chawla, N., & Marlatt, G. A. (2010). *Mindfulness-based relapse prevention for the treatment of substance use disorders: A clinician's guide*. Guilford Press.

Bowlby, J. (1982). *Attachment*. Basic Books.

Brach, T. (2004). *Radical acceptance: Embracing your life with the heart of a Buddha*. Random House.

Brach, T. (2020). *RAIN: A practice of radical compassion*. https://www.tarabrach.com/wp-content/uploads/pdf/TaraBrach_RAIN_A-Practice-of-Radical-Compassion.pdf

Breslin, S. (2020, March 26). *Telehealth best practices: Laws and ethical codes for therapists*. https://www.goodtherapy.org/for-professionals/software-technology/telehealth/article/telehealth-best-practices-laws-and-ethical-codes-for-therapists

Breus, M. (2016). *The power of when: Discover your chronotype—and the best time to eat lunch, ask for a raise, have sex, write a novel, take your meds, and more*. Little, Brown Spark.

Brickel, R. E. (2015, December 21). Using the power of clinical consultations for therapists. *Brickel & Associates, LLC*. https://brickelandassociates.com/using-the-power-of-clinical-consultations-for-therapists

Bride, B. E. (2007). Prevalence of secondary traumatic stress among social workers. *Social Work, 52*(1), 63–70. https://doi.org/10.1093/sw/52.1.63

Bronfenbrenner, U. (1977). Toward an experimental ecology of human development. *American Psychologist, 32*(7), 513–531. https://doi.org/10.1037/0003-066X.32.7.513

Bronfenbrenner, U., & Ceci, S. J. (1994). Nature–nurture reconceptualized in developmental perspective: A bioecological model. *Psychological Review, 101*(4), 568–586. https://doi.org/10.1037/0033-295X.101.4.568

Brown, B. (2010, June). *The power of vulnerability* [Video]. TED Conferences. https://www.ted.com/talks/brene_brown_the_power_of_vulnerability?language=en

Brown, B. (2018). *Dare to lead: Brave work. Tough conversations. Whole hearts*. Random House.

Brown, D. (2010, May 11). *Experts say posture matters: The good . . . and the bad*. Go Upstate. https://www.goupstate.com/article/NC/20100511/News/605153212/SJ

Bryant, L. (n.d.). *Turning toward ourselves and each other: The pivotal nature of clinician self-care* [Virtual webinar]. Trust PARMA. https://parma.trustinsurance.com/Workshops-Webinars/Virtual-Webinar-Series/clinician-self-care

Burchard, B. (2012). *The charge: Activating the 10 human drives that make you feel alive*. Free Press.

Bureau of Labor Statistics, U.S. Department of Labor. (2017, March 8). *Women's median earnings 82 percent of men's in 2016*. https://www.bls.gov/opub/ted/2017/womens-median-earnings-82-percent-of-mens-in-2016.htm

Burns, D. D. (1980). *Feeling good: The new mood therapy*. William Morrow & Co.

Bush, A. D. (2015). *Simple self-care for therapists: Restorative practices to weave through your workday*. W. W. Norton & Company.

Callaghan, P. (2004). Exercise: A neglected intervention in mental health care? *Journal of Psychiatric and Mental Health Nursing, 11*(4), 476–483. https://doi.org/10.1111/j.1365-2850.2004.00751.x

Callahan, R., & Callahan, J. (1996). *Thought field therapy (TFT) and trauma: Treatment and theory*. The Callahan Techniques.

Canadian Psychological Association. (2017). *Canadian code of ethics for psychologists* (4th ed.). https://cpa.ca/aboutcpa/committees/ethics/codeofethics/

Capital Group. (2018). *Confronting the money taboo.* https://www.capitalgroup.com/content/dam/cgc/shared-content/documents/reports/MFGEWP-062-1218O.pdf

Carmody, J., & Baer, R. A. (2008). Relationships between mindfulness practice and levels of mindfulness, medical and psychological symptoms and well-being in a mindfulness-based stress reduction program. *Journal of Behavioral Medicine, 31*(1), 23–33. https://doi.org/10.1007/s10865-007-9130-7

Caroll, M. (2006). *Awake at work*. Shambhala.

Carroll, L., Gilroy, P. J., & Murra, J. (1999). The moral imperative: Self-care for women psychotherapists. *Women & Therapy, 22*(2), 133–143. https://doi.org/10.1300/J015v22n02_10

Carter, L. A., & Barnett, J. E. (2014). *Self-care for clinicians in training: A guide to psychological wellness for graduate students in psychology*. Oxford University Press.

Carter, L. A., & Wise, E. H. (2021, March). *Therapist self-care in the pandemic and beyond*. http://www.societyforpsychotherapy.org/self-care-for-private-practitioners-in-2020-and-beyond

Case, P. W., & McMinn, M. R. (2001). Spiritual coping and well-functioning among psychologists. *Journal of Psychology and Theology, 29*(1), 29–40. https://doi.org/10.1177/009164710102900104

Centers for Disease Control and Prevention. (n.d.). *Sleep and sleep disorders*. https://www.cdc.gov/sleep/index.html

Centers for Disease Control and Prevention. (2016). *Sleep and sleep disorders: Tips for better sleep*. https://www.cdc.gov/sleep/about_sleep/sleep_hygiene.html

Centers for Disease Control and Prevention. (2020). *Prediabetes—Your chance to prevent Type 2 diabetes*. https://www.cdc.gov/diabetes/basics/prediabetes.html

Chamberlin, J. (2017). Secrets of a great group practice. *Monitor on Psychology, 48*(4), 54. https://www.apa.org/monitor/2017/04/group-practice

Chemtob, C., Hamada, R., Bauer, G., Kinney, B., & Torigoe, R. Y. (1988). Patients' suicides: Frequency and impact on psychiatrists. *American Journal of Psychiatry, 145*(2), 224–228. https://doi.org/10.1176/ajp.145.2.224

Chen, C. K. (2016). Defiance, denial, and defining limits: Helping family caregivers of individuals with dementia distinguish the tap-out from the cop-out. *Journal of Psychotherapy Integration, 26*(4), 353–365. https://doi.org/10.1037/int0000017

Chen, M. N., Chien, L. W., & Liu, C. F. (2013). Acupuncture or acupressure at the Sanyinjiao (SP6) acupoint for the treatment of primary dysmenorrhea: A meta-analysis. *Evidence-Based Complementary and Alternative Medicine, 2013*, Article 493038. https://doi.org/10.1155/2013/493038

Cheng, S. T., Tsui, P. K., & Lam, J. H. (2015). Improving mental health in health care practitioners: Randomized controlled trial of a gratitude intervention. *Journal of Consulting and Clinical Psychology, 83*(1), 177–186. https://doi.org/10.1037/a0037895

Chevalier, G., Sinatra, S. T., Oschman, J. L., Sokal, K., & Sokal, P. (2012). Earthing: Health implications of reconnecting the human body to the Earth's surface electrons. *Journal of Environmental and Public Health, 2012*, Article 291541. https://doi.org/10.1155/2012/291541

Chödrön, P. (2016). *When things fall apart: Heart advice for difficult times.* Shambhala.

Chödrön, P. (2018). *Comfortable with uncertainty: 108 teachings on cultivating fearlessness and compassion.* Shambhala Publications.

Christopher, J. C., & Maris, J. A. (2010). Integrating mindfulness as self-care into counselling and psychotherapy training. *Counselling & Psychotherapy Research, 10*(2), 114–125. https://doi.org/10.1080/14733141003750285

Church, D., & Brooks, A. J. (2010). The effect of a brief EFT (emotional freedom techniques) self-intervention on anxiety, depression, pain and cravings in healthcare workers. *Integrative Medicine, 9*, 40–44.

Church, D., Stapleton, P., & Sabot, D. (2020). App-based delivery of clinical emotional freedom techniques: Cross-sectional study of app user self-ratings. *Journal of Medical Internet Research, 8*(10), Article e18545. https://doi.org/10.2196/18545

Church, D., Yount, G., & Brooks, A. J. (2012). The effect of emotional freedom techniques on stress biochemistry: A randomized controlled trial. *The Journal of Nervous and Mental Disease, 200*(10), 891–896. https://doi.org/10.1097/NMD.0b013e31826b9fc1

Clarke, T. C., Barnes, P. M., Black, L. I., Stussman, B. J., & Nahin, R. L. (2018). Use of yoga, meditation, and chiropractors among U.S. adults aged 18 and over. *NCHS Data Brief,* (325), 1–8.

Clay, R. A. (2003). Researchers replace midlife myths with facts. *Monitor on Psychology, 34*(4), 36. https://www.apa.org/monitor/apr03/researchers

Clear, J. (2018). *Atomic habits: An easy & proven way to build good habits & break bad ones.* Avery.

Cloke, K. (2004). Journeys into the heart of conflict. *Pepperdine Dispute Resolution Law Journal, 4*(2), 219–249.

Cocchiara, R. A., Peruzzo, M., Mannocci, A., Ottolenghi, L., Villari, P., Polimeni, A., Guerra, F., & La Torre, G. (2019). The use of yoga to manage stress and burnout in healthcare workers: A systematic review. *Journal of Clinical Medicine, 8*(3), 284. https://doi.org/10.3390/jcm8030284

Collier, L. (2016, November). Growth after trauma. *Monitor on Psychology, 47*(10), 48. https://www.apa.org/monitor/2016/11/growth-trauma

Colodro, H., & Oliver, J. (2020). *A guide to self-care for practitioners in times of uncertainty.* New Harbinger Publications. https://d2tdui6flib2aa.cloudfront.

net/new-harbinger-wp/wp-content/uploads/2021/02/12000938/selfCare UncertainTimes_FINAL.pdf

Converse, A. K., Ahlers, E. O., Travers, B. G., & Davidson, R. J. (2014). Tai chi training reduces self-report of inattention in healthy young adults. *Frontiers in Human Neuroscience, 8,* Article 13. https://doi.org/10.3389/fnhum. 2014.00013

Cook-Cottone, C. P. (2006). The attuned representation model for the primary prevention of eating disorders: An overview for school psychologists. *Psychology in the Schools, 43*(2), 223–230. https://doi.org/10.1002/pits.20139

Cook-Cottone, C. P. (2015). *Mindfulness and yoga for self-regulation: A primer for mental health professionals.* Springer. https://doi.org/10.1891/9780826198631

Cook-Cottone, C. P., & Guyker, W. M. (2017). The development and validation of the Mindful Self-Care Scale (MSCS): An assessment of practices that support positive embodiment. *Mindfulness, 9*(1), 161–175. https://doi.org/10.1007/ s12671-017-0759-1

Cooper, N. A. (2009). *A closer look at distress, burnout, stressors, and coping in psychologists today.* Loyola University Maryland.

Coster, J. S., & Schwebel, M. (1997). Well-functioning in professional psychologists. *Professional Psychology: Research and Practice, 28*(1), 5–13. https:// doi.org/10.1037/0735-7028.28.1.5

Covey, S. (2020). *Seven habits of highly effective people* (30th anniversary ed.). Simon & Schuster.

Craig, G. (2008). *The EFT manual (Everyday EFT: Emotional freedom techniques).* Energy Psychology Press.

Csikszentmihályi, M. (2008). *Flow: The psychology of optimal experience.* Harper Perennial Modern Classics.

Cuddy, A. J. C., Schultz, S. J., & Fosse, N. E. (2018). P-curving a more comprehensive body of research on postural feedback reveals clear evidential value for power-posing effects: Reply to Simmons and Simonsohn (2017). *Psychological Science, 29*(4), 656–666. https://doi.org/10.1177/0956797617746749

Dahl, J. C., & Lundgren, T. L. (2006). Acceptance and commitment therapy (ACT) in the treatment of chronic pain. In R. A. Baer (Ed.), *Mindfulness-based treatment approaches: Clinician's guide to evidence based and applications* (pp. 285–306). Elsevier Academic Press. https://doi.org/10.1016/B978-012088519-0/50014-9

Daminger, A., Hayes, J., Barrows, A., & Wright, J. (2015). *Poverty interrupted: Applying behavioral science to the context of chronic scarcity.* http://www. ideas42.org/wp-content/uploads/2015/05/I42_PovertyWhitePaper_Digital_ FINAL-1.pdf

Daniller, A. (2021). *Majorities of Americans see at least some discrimination against Black, Hispanic and Asian people in the U.S.* Pew Research Center. https:// www.pewresearch.org/fact-tank/2021/03/18/majorities-of-americans-see-at-least-some-discrimination-against-black-hispanic-and-asian-people-in-the-u-s/

Dautovic, G. (2021). *American savings statistics: How much should you have in your savings account?* https://fortunly.com/statistics/american-savings-statistics/

Davidson, R. J., Kabat-Zinn, J., Schumacher, J., Rosenkranz, M., Muller, D., Santorelli, S. F., Urbanowski, F., Harrington, A., Bonus, K., & Sheridan, J. F. (2003). Alterations in brain and immune function produced by mindfulness meditation. *Psychosomatic Medicine, 65*(4), 564–570. https://doi.org/10.1097/01.PSY.0000077505.67574.E3

Davis, D. A., Mazmanian, P. E., Fordis, M., Van Harrison, R., Thorpe, K. E., & Perrier, L. (2006). Accuracy of physician self-assessment compared with observed measures of competence: A systematic review. *Journal of the American Medical Association, 296*(9), 1094–1102. https://doi.org/10.1001/jama.296.9.1094

Davis, D. E., Hook, J. N., Worthington, E. L., Jr., Van Tongeren, D. R., Gartner, A. L., Jennings, D. J., II, & Emmons, R. A. (2011). Relational humility: Conceptualizing and measuring humility as a personality judgment. *Journal of Personality Assessment, 93*(3), 225–234. https://doi.org/10.1080/00223891.2011.558871

Dawson, P., & Guare, R. (2016). *The smart but scattered guide to success: How to use your brain's executive skills to keep up, stay calm, and get organized at work and at home.* Guilford Press.

Dearing, R. L., Maddux, J. E., & Tangney, J. P. (2005). Predictors of psychological help seeking in clinical and counseling psychology graduate students. *Professional Psychology: Research and Practice, 36*(3), 323–329. https://doi.org/10.1037/0735-7028.36.3.323

Dekeyser, M., Raes, F., Leijssen, M., Leysen, S., & Dewulf, D. (2008). Mindfulness skills and interpersonal behaviour. *Personality and Individual Differences, 44*(5), 1235–1245. https://doi.org/10.1016/j.paid.2007.11.018

Delahanty, D. L., & Nugent, N. R. (2006). Predicting PTSD prospectively based on prior trauma history and immediate biological responses. *Annals of the New York Academy of Science, 1071*, 27–40. https://doi.org/10.1196/annals.1364.003

Deloitte. (2017). *2017 global mobile consumer survey: US edition.* https://www2.deloitte.com/content/dam/Deloitte/us/Documents/technology-media-telecommunications/us-tmt-2017-global-mobile-consumer-survey-executive-summary.pdf

Demerouti, E., Bakker, A. B., Nachreiner, F., & Schaufeli, W. B. (2001). The job demands–resources model of burnout. *Journal of Applied Psychology, 86*(3), 499–512. https://doi.org/10.1037/0021-9010.86.3.499

Desbordes, G., Gard, T., Hoge, E. A., Hölzel, B. K., Kerr, C., Lazar, S., Olendzki, A., & Vago, D. R. (2015). Moving beyond mindfulness: Defining equanimity as an outcome measure in meditation and contemplative research. *Mindfulness, 6*(2), 356–372. https://doi.org/10.1007/s12671-013-0269-8

Dettle, K. L. (2014). *Psychologist self-care, perceived stress, psychological distress, and coping self-efficacy across the career-span.* Seton Hall University Dissertations and Theses (ETDs). http://scholarship.shu.edu/dissertations/2000

Deutsch, C. J. (1984). Self-reported sources of stress among psychotherapists. *Professional Psychology: Research and Practice, 15*(6), 833–845. https://doi.org/10.1037/0735-7028.15.6.833

Deutsch, C. J. (1985). A survey of therapists' personal problems and treatment. *Professional Psychology: Research and Practice, 16*(2), 305–315. https://doi.org/10.1037/0735-7028.16.2.305

Didonna, F. (Ed.). (2009). *Clinical handbook of mindfulness.* Springer Science + Business Media. https://doi.org/10.1007/978-0-387-09593-6

Dientsmann, G. (2018). *Practical meditation.* DK.

Dishman, R. (2003). The impact of behavior on quality of life. *Quality of Life Research, 12,* 43–49. https://doi.org/10.1023/A:1023517303411

Dispenza, J. (2007). *Evolve your brain: The science of changing your mind.* HCI.

Dorff, T. A. (1997). *A needs assessment of the stressors and coping resources of graduate students in clinical psychology* [Unpublished doctoral dissertation]. Rutgers University.

Dorociak, K. E., Rupert, P. A., Bryant, F. B., & Zahniser, E. (2017). Development of a self-care assessment for psychologists. *Journal of Counseling Psychology, 64*(3), 325–334. https://doi.org/10.1037/cou0000206

Dorociak, K. E., Rupert, P. A., & Zahniser, E. (2017). Work life, well-being, and self-care across the professional lifespan of psychologist. *Professional Psychology: Research and Practice, 48*(6), 429–437. https://doi.org/10.1037/pro0000160

Duckworth, A. (2018). *Grit: The power of passion and perseverance.* Scribner.

Duhigg, C. (2014). *The power of habit: Why we do what we do in life and in business.* Random House Trade Paperbacks.

Dunning, D., Heath, C., & Suls, J. M. (2004). Flawed self-assessment: Implications for health, education, and the workplace. *Psychological Science in the Public Interest, 5*(3), 69–106. https://doi.org/10.1111/j.1529-1006.2004.00018.x

Dunning, D., Johnson, K., Ehrlinger, J., & Kruger, J. (2003). Why people fail to recognize their own incompetence. *Current Directions in Psychological Science, 12*(3), 83–87. https://doi.org/10.1111/1467-8721.01235

Durston, S. (2010). Imaging genetics in ADHD. *NeuroImage, 53*(3), 832–838. https://doi.org/10.1016/j.neuroimage.2010.02.071

Dweck, C. (2007). *Mindset: The new psychology of success.* Ballantine Books.

Earl E. Bakken Center for Spirituality and Healing, University of Minnesota. (n.d.). *What is spirituality?* https://www.takingcharge.csh.umn.edu/what-spirituality

Eden, D. (2008). *Energy medicine: Balancing your body's energies for optimal health, joy, and vitality.* Tarcher Perigee.

Eden, D. (2010). *The daily energy routine.* Innersource. http://www.innersource.net/em/images/stories/downloads/pdf_files/Five_Minute_Routine.pdf

Eden, D. (2021). *Donna's daily energy routine.* Innersource. https://edenenergy-medicine.com/donnas-daily-energy-routine/

Eden, D., & Feinstein, D. (2008). *Energy medicine for women: Aligning your body's energies to boost your health and vitality* (Rev. ed.). Tarcher Perigee.

Ekman, P. (1999). Basic emotions. In T. Dalgleish & M. J. Power (Eds.), *Handbook of cognition and emotion* (pp. 45–60). Wiley. https://www.paulekman.com/wp-content/uploads/2013/07/Basic-Emotions.pdf

Eldringhoff, S., & MacEwan, M. (2005). *The rapid relief energy sweep.*

El-Ghoroury, N. H., Galper, D. I., Sawaqdeh, A., & Bufka, L. F. (2012). Stress, coping, and barriers to wellness among psychology graduate students. *Training and Education in Professional Psychology, 6*(2), 122–134. https://doi.org/10.1037/a0028768

Elliott, D. M., & Guy, J. D. (1993). Mental health professionals versus non-mental-health professionals: Childhood trauma and adult functioning. *Professional Psychology: Research and Practice, 24*(1), 83–90. https://doi.org/10.1037/0735-7028.24.1.83

Ellis, A. (1984). The essence of RET. *Journal of Rational-Emotive Therapy, 2*(1), 19–25. https://doi.org/10.1007/BF02283005

Elman, N. S., & Forrest, L. (2007). From trainee impairment to professional competence problems: Seeking new terminology that facilitates effective action. *Professional Psychology: Research and Practice, 38*(5), 501–509. https://doi.org/10.1037/0735-7028.38.5.501

Emmons, R. (2008). *Thanks!: How practicing gratitude can make you happier.* Mariner Books.

Enright, R. D., & Fitzgibbons, R. P. (2014). *Forgiveness therapy: An empirical guide for resolving anger and restoring hope.* American Psychological Association.

Essex, M. J., Boyce, W. T., Hertzman, C., Lam, L. L., Armstrong, J. M., Neumann, S. M. A., & Kobor, M. S. (2013). Epigenetic vestiges of early developmental adversity: Childhood stress exposure and DNA methylation in adolescence. *Child Development, 84*(1), 58–75. https://doi.org/10.1111/j.1467-8624.2011.01641.x

Estrella, K. (2010). Class in context: A narrative inquiry into the impact of social class mobility and identity on class consciousness in the practice of psychotherapy. *Dissertation Abstracts International: B. The Sciences and Engineering, 70*(9-B), 5816.

Eva, K. W., Rosenfeld, J., Reiter, H. I., & Norman, G. R. (2004). An admissions OSCE: The multiple mini-interview. *Medical Education, 38*(3), 314–326. https://doi.org/10.1046/j.1365-2923.2004.01776.x

Fagan, T. J., Ax, R. K., Liss, M., Resnick, R. J., & Moody, S. (2007). Professional education and training: How satisfied are we? An exploratory study. *Training and Education in Professional Psychology, 1*(1), 13–25. https://doi.org/10.1037/1931-3918.1.1.13

Faller, G. (2021, September/October). Talking about the nightmare. *The Psychotherapy Networker,* 45–47.

Farb, N. A., Anderson, A. K., Mayberg, H., Bean, J., McKeon, D., & Segal, Z. V. (2010). "Minding one's emotions: Mindfulness training alters the neural expression of sadness": Correction to Farb et al. (2010). *Emotion, 10*(2), 215. https://doi.org/10.1037/a0019263

Farb, N. A., Segal, Z. V., Mayberg, H., Bean, J., McKeon, D., Fatima, Z., & Anderson, A. K. (2007). Attending to the present: Mindfulness meditation reveals distinct neural modes of self-reference. *Social Cognitive and Affective Neuroscience, 2*(4), 313–322. https://doi.org/10.1093/scan/nsm030

Farber, B. A. (1983). The effects of psychotherapeutic practice upon psychotherapists. *Psychotherapy: Theory, Research, & Practice, 20*(2), 174–182. https://doi.org/10.1037/h0088488

Farber, B. A. (1990). Burnout in psychotherapists: Incidence, types, and trends. *Psychotherapy in Private Practice, 8*(1), 35–44. https://doi.org/10.1300/J294v08n01_07

Farber, B. A., & Heifetz, L. J. (1981). The satisfactions and stresses of psychotherapeutic work: A factor analytic study. *Professional Psychology: Research and Practice, 12*(5), 621–630. https://doi.org/10.1037/0735-7028.12.5.621

Farber, B. A., Manevich, I., Metzger, J., & Saypol, E. (2005). Choosing psychotherapy as a career: Why did we cross that road? *Journal of Clinical Psychology, 61*(8), 1009–1031. https://doi.org/10.1002/jclp.20174

Faunce, P. (1990). Self-care and wellness of feminist therapists. In H. Lerman & N. Porter (Eds.), *Feminist ethics in psychotherapy* (pp. 123–130). Springer.

Feinstein, D. (2019). Energy psychology: Efficacy, speed, mechanisms. *EXPLORE, 15*(5), 340–351. https://doi.org/10.1016/j.explore.2018.11.003

Fidelity Investments. (2018). *Top findings from the 2018 Fidelity Investments Couples & Money Study.* https://www.fidelity.com/bin-public/060_www_fidelity_com/documents/pr/couples-fact-sheet.pdf

Fields, R. (2012). *A year of living mindfully: Quotes and weekly mindfulness practices.* FACES Conferences.

Figley, C. R. (Ed.). (2002). *Psychosocial stress series, no. 24. Treating compassion fatigue.* Brunner-Routledge.

Fischer, J., Kumar, S., & Hatcher, S. (2007). What makes psychiatry such a stressful profession? A qualitative study. *Australasian Psychiatry, 15*(5), 417–421. https://doi.org/10.1080/10398560701439699

Fisher, J. (2021, September/October). Learning the art of being. *The Psychotherapy Networker,* 44–45.

Fleming, N. D., & Mills, C. (1992). Not another inventory, rather a catalyst for reflection. *To Improve the Academy, 11*, 136–149. https://digitalcommons.unl.edu/podimproveacad/246

Floyd, M., Myszka, M. T., & Orr, P. (1998). Licensed psychologists' knowledge and utilization of a state association colleague assistance committee. *Professional Psychology: Research and Practice, 29*(6), 594–598. https://doi.org/10.1037/0735-7028.29.6.594

Flückiger, C., Del Re, A. C., Wampold, B. E., & Horvath, A. O. (2018). The alliance in adult psychotherapy: A meta-analytic synthesis. *Psychotherapy: Theory, Research, & Practice, 55*(4), 316–340. https://doi.org/10.1037/pst0000172

Fogg, B. J. (2021). *Tiny habits: The small changes that change everything.* Mariner Books.

Follette, V. M., Polusny, M. M., & Milbeck, K. (1994). Mental health and law enforcement professionals: Trauma history, psychological symptoms, and impact of providing services to child sexual abuse survivors. *Professional Psychology: Research and Practice, 25*(3), 275–282. https://doi.org/10.1037/0735-7028.25.3.275

Ford, M. T., Heinen, B. A., & Langkamer, K. L. (2007). Work and family satisfaction and conflict: A meta-analysis of cross-domain relations. *Journal of Applied Psychology, 92*(1), 57–80. https://doi.org/10.1037/0021-9010.92.1.57

Fossum, I. N., Nordnes, L. T., Storemark, S. S., Bjorvatn, B., & Pallesen, S. (2014). The association between use of electronic media in bed before going to sleep and insomnia symptoms, daytime sleepiness, morningness, and chronotype. *Behavioral Sleep Medicine, 12*(5), 343–357. https://doi.org/10.1080/15402002.2013.819468

1440 Multiversity. (2017, April 10). *Jeremy Hunter on mindfulness and leadership* [Video]. YouTube. https://www.youtube.com/watch?v=ku9bgcti5CQ

Fredrickson, B. L. (2001). The role of positive emotions in positive psychology. The broaden-and-build theory of positive emotions. *American Psychologist, 56*(3), 218–226. https://doi.org/10.1037/0003-066X.56.3.218

Freedenthal, S. (2021, September/October). When therapists struggle with suicidality: Releasing ourselves from stigma and shame. *Psychotherapy Networker.* https://www.psychotherapynetworker.org/magazine/article/2576/when-therapists-struggle-with-suicidality

The Free Dictionary. (n.d.). Privilege. In *The Free Dictionary.com.* https://www.thefreedictionary.com/privilege

Freudenberger, H. J. (1975). The staff burn-out syndrome in alternative institutions. *Psychotherapy: Theory, Research, & Practice, 12*(1), 73–82. https://doi.org/10.1037/h0086411

Fuchs, E., & Flügge, G. (2014). Adult neuroplasticity: More than 40 years of research. *Neural Plasticity, 2014*, Article 541870. https://doi.org/10.1155/2014/541870

Gach, M. R., & Henning, B. A. (2004). *Acupressure emotional healing.* Bantam.

Gallant, S. N. (2016). Mindfulness meditation practice and executive functioning: Breaking down the benefit. *Consciousness and Cognition, 40*, 116–130. https://doi.org/10.1016/j.concog.2016.01.005

Gallo, F. P. (1998). *Energy psychology: Explorations at the intersection of energy, cognition, behavior, and health.* CRC Press.

Garis, M. G. (2021, January 12). 20 joyful activities to make play a priority in your self-care routine. *Well+Good.* https://www.wellandgood.com/joyful-activities-play/

Gilbert, P. (Ed.). (2005). *Compassion: Conceptualisations, research and use in psychotherapy.* Routledge. https://doi.org/10.4324/9780203003459

Gilbert, P. (2013). *The compassionate mind: A new approach to life's challenges.* Constable.

Gillespie, P. G., & Walker, R. G. (2001). Molecular basis of mechanosensory transduction. *Nature, 413*(6852), 194–202. https://doi.org/10.1038/35093011

Gilroy, P. J., Carroll, L., & Murra, J. (2002). A preliminary survey of counseling psychologists' personal experiences with depression and treatment. *Professional Psychology: Research and Practice, 33*(4), 402–407.

Glock, C. Y., & Stark, R. (1965). *Religion and society in tension*. Rand McNally and Company.

Godin, S. (2014, August 3). Short term, long term. *Seth's Blog*. https://seths.blog/2014/08/short-term-long-term

Goel, N., Rao, H., Durmer, J. S., & Dinges, D. F. (2009). Neurocognitive consequences of sleep deprivation. *Seminars in Neurology, 29*(4), 320–339. https://doi.org/10.1055/s-0029-1237117

Goldman, D. (2007). Faking it. *Contemporary Psychoanalysis, 43*(1), 17–36. https://doi.org/10.1080/00107530.2007.10745894

Goldstein, A., & Hastings, O. P. (2019). Buying in: Positional competition, schools, income inequality, and housing consumption. *Sociological Science, 6*(16), 416–445. https://doi.org/10.15195/v6.a16

Golem, K. (2018, July 8). *How your smartphone might sabotage your relationship*. The Gottman Institute. https://www.gottman.com/blog/smartphone-might-sabotage-relationship/

Good, G. E., Thoreson, R. W., & Shaughnessy, P. (1995). Substance use, confrontation of impaired colleagues, and psychological functioning among counseling psychologists: A national survey. *The Counseling Psychologist, 23*(4), 703–721. https://doi.org/10.1177/0011000095234010

Gordon, A. (2013). 5 ways gratitude can backfire. *Berkeley Science Review*. https://greatergood.berkeley.edu/article/item/five_ways_giving_thanks_can_backfire

Gordon, R. (1991). Intersubjectivity and the efficacy of group psychotherapy. *Group Analysis, 24*(1), 41–51. https://doi.org/10.1177/0533316491241008

Greason, P. B., & Cashwell, C. S. (2009). Mindfulness and counseling self-efficacy: The mediating role of attention and empathy. *Counselor Education and Supervision, 49*(1), 2–19. https://doi.org/10.1002/j.1556-6978.2009.tb00083.x

Green, A. G., & Hawley, G. C. (2009). Early career psychologists: Understanding, engaging, and mentoring tomorrow's leaders. *Professional Psychology: Research and Practice, 40*(2), 206–212. https://doi.org/10.1037/a0012504

Greenberg, L. (2009). *Emotion-focused therapy*. American Psychological Association.

Grepmair, L., Mitterlehner, F., Loew, T., Bachler, E., Rother, W., & Nickel, M. (2007). Promoting mindfulness in psychotherapists in training influences the treatment results of their patients: A randomized, double-blind, controlled study. *Psychotherapy and Psychosomatics, 76*(6), 332–338. https://doi.org/10.1159/000107560

Grise-Owens, E., Miller, J. J., & Eaves, M. (Eds.). (2016). *The A to Z self-care handbook for social workers and other helping professionals*. The New Social Worker Press.

Grossman, P., Niemann, L., Schmidt, S., & Walach, H. (2004). Mindfulness-based stress reduction and health benefits. A meta-analysis. *Journal of Psychosomatic Research, 57*(1), 35–43. https://doi.org/10.1016/S0022-3999(03)00573-7

Guenther, J. (2021). *Eight reasons you should go to therapy that you haven't considered before*. Therapy Den. https://www.therapyden.com/blog/eight-reasons-you-should-go-to-therapy-that-you-havent-considered-before

Gunaratana, B. (2011). *Mindfulness in plain English.* Wisdom Publications.

Guttmann, A. C. (2021). *Self-care and restoration. How energy psychology practices can enhance your self-care routine.* https://acepblog.org/2021/09/22/%EF%BF%BCself-care-and-restoration-how-energy-psychology-practices-can-enhance-your-self-care-routine/

Guy, J., Poelstra, P., & Stark, M. (1989). Personal distress and therapeutic effectiveness: National survey of psychologists practicing psychotherapy. *Professional Psychology: Research and Practice, 20*(1), 48–50. https://doi.org/10.1037/0735-7028.20.1.48

Haden, J. (2018). *The motivation myth: How high achievers really set themselves up to win.* Portfolio Penguin.

Haidt, J. (2000). The positive emotion of elevation. *Prevention & Treatment, 3*(1), Article 3c. https://doi.org/10.1037/1522-3736.3.1.33c

Hakked, C. S., Balakrishnan, R., & Krishnamurthy, M. N. (2017). Yogic breathing practices improve lung functions of competitive young swimmers. *Journal of Ayurveda and Integrative Medicine, 8*(2), 99–104. https://doi.org/10.1016/j.jaim.2016.12.005

Hall, J. E., & Boucher, A. P. (2003). Professional mobility for psychologists: Multiple choices, multiple opportunities. *Professional Psychology: Research and Practice, 34*(5), 463–467. https://doi.org/10.1037/0735-7028.34.5.463

Halliwell, E. (2020). *Why mindfulness meditation begins with the breath.* Mindful. https://www.mindful.org/6-reasons-why-mindfulness-begins-with-the-breath/

Hallowell, E. (2019, March 7). *ADHD: 2 times . . . now and not now* [Video]. YouTube. https://www.youtube.com/watch?v=faMeR0aoWP8

Hallowell, E. M. (2007). *CrazyBusy: Overstretched, overbooked, and about to snap! Strategies for handling your face-paced life.* Ballantine Books.

Hallowell, E. M. (2018). *Because I come from a crazy family: The making of a psychiatrist.* Bloomsbury Publishing.

Hallowell, E. M., & Hallowell, S. G. (2010). *Married to distraction: Restoring intimacy and strengthening your marriage in an age of interruption.* Ballantine Books.

Hallowell, E. M., & Ratey, J. J. (2021). *ADHD 2.0: New science and essential strategies for thriving with distraction—from childhood through adulthood.* Ballantine Books.

Handelsman, M. M., Knapp, S., & Gottlieb, M. C. (2009). Positive ethics: Themes and variations. In C. R. Snyder & S. J. Lopez (Eds.), *Oxford handbook of positive psychology* (2nd ed., pp. 105–113). Oxford University Press.

Handwerker, W. P. (2002). The construct validity of cultures: Cultural diversity, culture theory, and a method for ethnography. *American Anthropologist, 104*(1), 106–122. https://doi.org/10.1525/aa.2002.104.1.106

Hanson, R. (2009a). *Buddha's brain: The practical neuroscience of happiness, love, and wisdom.* New Harbinger Publications.

Hanson, R. (2009b, November 1). Taking in the good. *Greater Good Magazine.* https://greatergood.berkeley.edu/article/item/taking_in_the_good

Hanson, R. (2018). *Resilient: How to grow an unshakable core of calm, strength, and happiness.* Harmony.

Harris, D. (2018). *Meditation for fidgety skeptics: A 10% happier how-to book.* Harmony.

Harris, D. (2019). *10% happier revised edition: How I tamed the voice in my head, reduced stress without losing my edge, and found self-help that actually works—A true story.* Dey Street Books.

Harris, R. (2008). *The happiness trap: How to stop struggling and start living: A guide to ACT.* Trumpeter.

Harvard Health Publishing. (2019, November 5). *The sweet danger of sugar.* http://health.harvard.edu/heart-health/the-sweet-danger-of-sugar

Harvard Health Publishing. (2020, July 7). *Blue light has a dark side.* https://www.health.harvard.edu/staying-healthy/blue-light-has-a-dark-side

Harvard Health Publishing. (2021, April 19). *The gut–brain connection.* https://www.health.harvard.edu/diseases-and-conditions/the-gut-brain-connection

Hawkey, E., & Nigg, J. T. (2014). Omega-3 fatty acid and ADHD: Blood level analysis and meta-analytic extension of supplementation trials. *Clinical Psychology Review, 34*(6), 496–505. https://doi.org/10.1016/j.cpr.2014.05.005

Hayes, S. (2005). *Get out of your mind and into your life.* New Harbinger.

Hayes, S. C., Strosahl, K. D., & Wilson, K. G. (2012). *Acceptance and commitment therapy: The process and practice of mindful change* (2nd ed.). Guilford Press.

Hays, P. A. (2008). *Addressing cultural complexities in practice: Assessment, diagnosis, and therapy* (2nd ed.). American Psychological Association. https://doi.org/10.1037/11650-000

Heart Math Institute. (2012, August 20). *Heart-focused breathing.* https://www.heartmath.org/articles-of-the-heart/the-math-of-heartmath/heart-focused-breathing/

Helmreich, R. J., Shiao, S. Y. P. K., & Dune, L. S. (2006). Meta-analysis of acu-stimulation effects on nausea and vomiting in pregnant women. *EXPLORE, 2*(5), 412–421. https://doi.org/10.1016/j.explore.2006.06.002

Henderson, K., & Ainsworth, B. (2001). Researching leisure and physical activity with women of color: Issues and emerging questions. *Leisure Sciences, 23*(1), 21–34. https://doi.org/10.1080/01490400150502225

Henry, W. E., Sims, J. H., & Spray, S. L. (1971). *The fifth profession: Becoming a psychotherapist.* Jossey-Bass.

Herron, J. (2019, July 17). How many Americans with $1 million feel wealthy? Fewer than you may think. *USA Today.* https://www.usatoday.com/story/money/2019/07/17/what-wealthy-its-not-necessarily-becoming-millionaire/1744408001/

Hersh, M. A. (2014, July 8). *Clarifying client values using the "true north" act-based exercise.* The Thriving Therapist. http://www.thethrivingtherapist.org/clarifying-client-values-true-north-act-exercise/

Hersh, M. A. (2017). *Your signature stress experience: Enhancing your mindful awareness of the sources, experiences, and impacts of stress.* The Thriving Therapist. https://s3.amazonaws.com/thrivingtherapistresources/Signature+Stress+Experience+Handout.pdf

Hersh, M. A., & Richardson, T. (2016). *Essential mind–body practices to ground and rebound: Practitioners' daily self-care guide.* The Thriving Therapist. https://www.thethrivingtherapist.org/essential-mind-body-practices/

Hershfield, J., & Nicely, S. (2017). *Everyday mindfulness for OCD: Tips, tricks, and skills for living joyfully.* New Harbinger Publications.

Hill, C. E., Lystrupa, A., Klinea, K., Gebrua, N. M., Birchlera, J., Palmera, G., Robinson, J., Uma, M., Griffina, S., Lipskya, E., Knox, S., & Pinto-Coelhoa, K. (2013). Aspiring to become a therapist: Personal strengths and challenges, influences, motivations, and expectations of future psychotherapists. *Counselling Psychology Quarterly, 26*(3–4), 267–293. https://doi.org/10.1080/09515070.2013.825763

His Holiness The Dalai Lama, & Cutler, H. (2020). *The art of happiness: A handbook for living.* Riverhead Books.

Holdcroft, B. (2006). What is religiosity? *Catholic Education: A Journal of Inquiry and Practice, 10*(1), 89–103. https://doi.org/10.15365/joce.1001082013.

Hölzel, B. K., Carmody, J., Vangel, M., Congleton, C., Yerramsetti, S. M., Gard, T., & Lazar, S. W. (2011). Mindfulness practice leads to increases in regional brain gray matter density. *Psychiatry Research: Neuroimaging, 191*(1), 36–43. https://doi.org/10.1016/j.pscychresns.2010.08.006

Honos-Webb, L. (2018). *Brain hacks: Life-changing strategies to improve executive functioning.* Althea Press.

Hotchkiss, J. T. (2018). Mindful self-care and secondary traumatic stress mediate a relationship between compassion satisfaction and burnout risk among hospice care professionals. *American Journal of Hospice & Palliative Medicine, 35*(8), 1099–1108. https://doi.org/10.1177/1049909118756657

Howell, A. (2019, January 13). *Why can't Yoga Journal get it right?* Bad Yogi. http://www.badyogi.com/blog/yoga-journal-dual-covers/

Howes, R. (2010, August 5). Therapist on vacation? *Psychology Today.* https://www.psychologytoday.com/us/blog/in-therapy/201008/therapist-vacation

Huddleston, C. (2019). *Survey: 69% of Americans have less than $1000 in savings.* https://www.yahoo.com/now/survey-69-americans-less-1-171927256.html

Hummel, C. E. (2013). *Tyranny of the urgent: Revised and expanded.* InterVarsity Press.

Hyman, M. (2018). *How to feed your gut.* https://drhyman.com/blog/2018/04/13/how-to-feed-your-gut/

Jablow, M. M. (2017, July 11). *Compassion fatigue: The toll of being a care provider.* Association of American Medical Colleges. https://www.aamc.org/news-insights/compassion-fatigue-toll-being-care-provider

Jackson, K. (2014). Social worker self-care—The overlooked core competency. *Social Work Today, 14*(3), 14.

Jackson, P. (2002). *The Lord of the Rings: The two towers* [Film]. New Line Home Entertainment.

Jaeger, B. (2005). *Making work work for the highly sensitive person.* McGraw Hill.

James, M. (2016). 8 beliefs that you should have about money. *Psychology Today.* https://www.psychologytoday.com/us/blog/focus-forgiveness/201604/8-beliefs-you-should-have-about-money

Janis, I. L., & Mann, L. (1977). *Decision making: A psychological analysis of conflict, choice, and commitment.* Free Press.

Jazaieri, H., Jinpa, G. T., McGonigal, K., Rosenberg, E. L., Finkelstein, J., Simon-Thomas, E., Cullen, M., Doty, J. R., Gross, J. J., & Goldin, P. R. (2013). Enhancing compassion: A randomized controlled trial of a compassion cultivation training program. *Journal of Happiness Studies, 14*(4), 1113–1126. https://doi.org/10.1007/s10902-012-9373-z

Jelleyman, C., Yates, T., O'Donovan, G., Gray, L. J., King, J. A., Khunti, K., & Davies, M. J. (2015). The effects of high-intensity interval training on glucose regulation and insulin resistance: A meta-analysis. *Obesity Reviews, 16*(11), 942–961. https://doi.org/10.1111/obr.12317

Jha, A. P., Stanley, E. A., Kiyonaga, A., Wong, L., & Gelfand, L. (2010). Examining the protective effects of mindfulness training on working memory capacity and affective experience. *Emotion, 10*(1), 54–64. https://doi.org/10.1037/a0018438

Jiménez-Maldonado, A., Rentería, I., García-Suárez, P. C., Moncada-Jiménez, J., & Freire-Royes, L. F. (2018). The impact of high-intensity interval training on brain derived neurotrophic factor in brain: A mini-review. *Frontiers in Neuroscience, 12*, Article 839. https://doi.org/10.3389/fnins.2018.00839

Johnson, W. B., & Barnett, J. E. (2011). Preventing problems of professional competence in the face of life-threatening illness. *Professional Psychology: Research and Practice, 42*(4), 285–293. https://doi.org/10.1037/a0024433

Johnson, W. B., Barnett, J. E., Elman, N. S., Forrest, L., & Kaslow, N. J. (2012). The competent community: Toward a vital reformulation of professional ethics. *American Psychologist, 67*(7), 557–569. https://doi.org/10.1037/a0027206

Johnson, W. B., Barnett, J. E., Elman, N. S., Forrest, L., & Kaslow, N. J. (2013). The competence constellation model: A communitarian approach to support professional competence. *Professional Psychology: Research and Practice, 44*(5), 343–354. https://doi.org/10.1037/a0033131

Johnson, W. B., & Ridley, C. R. (2008). *The elements of ethics for professionals.* St. Martin's Publishing Group.

Joinson, C. (1992). Coping with compassion fatigue. *Nursing, 22*(4), 116–121, 118–119, 120. https://doi.org/10.1097/00152193-199204000-00035

Judith, A. (2004). *Eastern body, Western mind: Psychology and the chakra system as a path to the self.* Celestial Arts.

Kabat-Zinn, J. (2005a). *Coming to our senses: Healing ourselves and the world through mindfulness.* Hachette Books.

Kabat-Zinn, J. (2005b). *Wherever you go, there you are: Mindfulness meditation in everyday life* (10th ed.). Hachette Books.

Kabat-Zinn, J. (2013). *Full catastrophe living: Using the wisdom of your body and mind to face stress, pain, and illness* (Rev. ed.). Bantam.

Karver, M. S., De Nadai, A. S., Monahan, M., & Shirk, S. R. (2018). Meta-analysis of the prospective relation between alliance and outcome in child and adolescent psychotherapy. *Psychotherapy, 55*(4), 341–355. https://doi.org/10.1037/pst0000176

Kaslow, N. J., Borden, K. A., Collins, F. L., Jr., Forrest, L., Illfelder-Kaye, J., Nelson, P. D., Rallo, J. S., Vasquez, M. J. T., & Willmuth, M. E. (2004). Competencies conference: Future directions in education and credentialing in professional psychology. *Journal of Clinical Psychology, 60*(7), 699–712. https://doi.org/10.1002/jclp.20016

Kaufman, S. B. (2019). The evolution and cultivation of compassion for the dark side: A Q&A with Paul Gilbert. *Scientific American.* https://blogs.scientificamerican.com/beautiful-minds/the-evolution-and-cultivation-of-compassion-for-the-dark-side-a-q-a-with-paul-gilbert/

Kelley, T. M. (2005). Natural resilience and innate mental health. *American Psychologist, 60*(3), 265. https://doi.org/10.1037/0003-066X.60.3.265a

Keltner, D., & Haidt, J. (2003). Approaching awe, a moral, spiritual, and aesthetic emotion. *Cognition and Emotion, 17*(2), 297–314. https://doi.org/10.1080/02699930302297

Keng, S. L., Smoski, M. J., & Robins, C. J. (2011). Effects of mindfulness on psychological health: A review of empirical studies. *Clinical Psychology Review, 31*(6), 1041–1056. https://doi.org/10.1016/j.cpr.2011.04.006

Khan, A. (2019, August 16). Getting killed by the police is a leading cause of death for young black men in America. *Los Angeles Times.* https://www.latimes.com/science/story/2019-08-15/police-shootings-are-a-leading-cause-of-death-for-black-men

Killingsworth, M. A., & Gilbert, D. T. (2010, November 12). A wandering mind is an unhappy mind. *Science, 330*(6006), 932. https://doi.org/10.1126/science.1192439

King James Bible. (1989). World Bible Publishers.

Kingsbury, E. (2009). The relationship between empathy and mindfulness: Understanding the role of self-compassion. *Dissertation Abstracts International: Section B. The Sciences and Engineering, 70*(5-B), 3175.

Klammer, S. (2020, March 2). *Emotional check-in exercise.* https://www.shelleyklammer.com/post/emotional-check-in-exercise

Klimecki, O. M., Leiberg, S., Lamm, C., & Singer, T. (2013). Functional neural plasticity and associated changes in positive affect after compassion training. *Cerebral Cortex, 23*(7), 1552–1561. https://doi.org/10.1093/cercor/bhs142

Klimecki, O., & Singer, T. (2012). Empathic distress fatigue rather than compassion fatigue? Integrating findings from empathy research in psychology and social neuroscience. In B. Oakley, A. Knafo, G. Madhavan, & D. S. Wilson (Eds.), *Pathological altruism* (pp. 368–383). Oxford University Press.

Knüppel, A., Shipley, M. J., Llewellyn, C. H., & Brunner, E. J. (2017). Sugar intake from sweet food and beverages, common mental disorder and depression: Prospective findings from the Whitehall II study. *Scientific Reports, 7*, Article 6287. https://doi.org/10.1038/s41598-017-05649-7

Kornfield, J. (1993). *A path with heart: A guide through the perils and promises of spiritual life*. Bantam.

Kornfield, J. (2009). *The wise heart: A guide to the universal teachings of Buddhist psychology*. Bantam.

Kramen-Kahn, B. (2002). Do you "walk your talk"? *The Maryland Psychologist, 44*(3), 12.

Kramen-Kahn, B., & Hansen, N. D. (1998). Rafting the rapids: Occupational hazards, rewards, and coping strategies of psychotherapists. *Professional Psychology: Research and Practice, 29*(2), 130–134. https://doi.org/10.1037/0735-7028.29.2.130

Kroese, F. M., De Ridder, D. T. D., Evers, C., & Adriaanse, M. A. (2014). Bedtime procrastination: Introducing a new area of procrastination. *Frontiers in Psychology, 5*, Article 611. https://doi.org/10.3389/fpsyg.2014.00611

Kruger, J., & Dunning, D. (1999). Unskilled and unaware of it: How difficulties in recognizing one's own incompetence lead to inflated self-assessments. *Journal of Personality and Social Psychology, 77*(6), 1121–1134. https://doi.org/10.1037/0022-3514.77.6.1121

Kushner, H. (1997). *How good do we have to be? A new understanding of guilt and forgiveness*. Back Bay Books.

Kvarfordt, C. L., Sheridan, M. J., & Taylor, O. (2017). Religion and spirituality in social work curriculum: A survey of Canadian educators. *British Journal of Social Work, 48*(5), 1469–1487. https://doi.org/10.1093/bjsw/bcx069

Laliotis, D. A., & Grayson, J. H. (1985). Psychologist heal thyself. What is available for the impaired psychologist? *American Psychologist, 40*(1), 84–96. https://doi.org/10.1037/0003-066X.40.1.84

Lamb, D. H., Presser, N. R., Pfost, K. S., Baum, M. C., Jackson, V. R., & Jarvis, P. A. (1987). Confronting professional impairment during the internship: Identification, due process, and remediation. *Professional Psychology: Research and Practice, 18*(6), 597–603. https://doi.org/10.1037/0735-7028.18.6.597

Lazar, S. W. (2005). Mindfulness research. *Mindfulness and Psychotherapy, 22*, 220–238.

Lazar, S. W. (2013). The neurobiology of mindfulness. In C. K. Germer, R. D. Siegel, & P. R. Fulton (Eds.), *Mindfulness and psychotherapy* (2nd ed., pp. 282–294). Guilford Press.

Lee, J., Lim, N., Yang, E., & Lee, S. M. (2011). Antecedents and consequences of three dimensions of burnout in psychotherapists: A meta-analysis. *Professional Psychology: Research and Practice, 42*(3), 252–258. https://doi.org/10.1037/a0023319

Lee, K. (2014). *RESET: Make the most of your stress: Your 24–7 plan for well-being*. iUniverse.

Lee, K. (2018). *Mentalligence: A new psychology of thinking—Learn what it takes to be more agile, mindful, and connected in today's world*. Health Communications.

Leiter, M. P., & Maslach, C. (1999). Six areas of worklife: A model of the organizational context of burnout. *Journal of Health and Human Services Administration, 21*(4), 472–489.

LeJeune, J., & Luoma, J. B. (2019). *Values in therapy: A clinician's guide to helping clients explore values, increase psychological flexibility, and live a more meaningful life.* Context Press.

LeJeune, J. T., & Luoma, J. B. (2015). The integrated scientist–practitioner: A new model for combining research and clinical practice in fee-for-service settings. *Professional Psychology: Research and Practice, 46*(6), 421–428. https://doi.org/10.1037/pro0000049

Levine, P. (2010). *In an unspoken voice: How the body releases trauma and restores goodness.* North Atlantic Books.

Lin, T. W., & Kuo, Y. M. (2013). Exercise benefits brain function: The monoamine connection. *Brain Sciences, 3*(1), 39–53. https://doi.org/10.3390/brainsci3010039

Lindstrom, C., Levi, J., Murphy, L. R., & Sauter, S. L. (Eds.). (2011). *Encyclopaedia of occupational health and safety.* International Labour Organization.

Linton, S. J. (2004). Does work stress predict insomnia? A prospective study. *British Journal of Health Psychology, 9*(2), 127–136. https://doi.org/10.1348/135910704773891005

Lombardo, E. (2014). *Better than perfect: 7 strategies to crush your inner critic and create a life you love.* Seal Press.

Lounsbury, J. W., Steel, R. P., Gibson, L. W., & Drost, A. W. (2008). Personality traits and career satisfaction of human resource professionals. *Human Resource Development International, 11*(4), 351–366. https://doi.org/10.1080/13678860802261215

Lounsbury, J. W., Sundstrom, E., Loveland, J. M., & Gibson, L. W. (2003). Intelligence, "Big Five" personality traits, and work drive as predictors of course grade. *Personality and Individual Differences, 35*(6), 1231–1239. https://doi.org/10.1016/S0191-8869(02)00330-6

Lowen, A. C., Mubareka, S., Steel, J., & Palese, P. (2007). Influenza virus transmission is dependent on relative humidity and temperature. *PLOS Pathogens, 3*(10), Article e151. https://doi.org/10.1371/journal.ppat.0030151

Luoma, J. B., & Villatte, J. L. (2012). Mindfulness in the treatment of suicidal individuals. *Cognitive and Behavioral Practice, 19*(2), 265–276. https://doi.org/10.1016/j.cbpra.2010.12.003

Lustyk, M. K., Widman, L., Paschane, A. A., & Olson, K. C. (2004). Physical activity and quality of life: Assessing the influence of activity frequency, intensity, volume, and motives. *Behavioral Medicine, 30*(3), 124–132. https://doi.org/10.3200/BMED.30.3.124-132

Lutz, A., Slagter, H. A., Rawlings, N. B., Francis, A. D., Greischar, L. L., & Davidson, R. J. (2009). Mental training enhances attentional stability: Neural and behavioral evidence. *The Journal of Neuroscience, 29*(42), 13418–13427. https://doi.org/10.1523/JNEUROSCI.1614-09.2009

MacIntosh, B. J., Crane, D. E., Sage, M. D., Rajab, A. S., Donahue, M. J., McIlroy, W. E., & Middleton, L. E. (2014). Impact of a single bout of aerobic exercise on regional brain perfusion and activation responses in healthy young adults. *PLOS ONE, 9*(1), Article e85163. https://doi.org/10.1371/journal.pone.0085163

MacIntyre, A. (1999). *Dependent rational animals: Why human beings need the virtues.* Chicago.

Mahoney, M. J. (1997). Psychotherapists' personal problems and self-care patterns. *Professional Psychology: Research and Practice, 28*(1), 14–16. https://doi.org/10.1037/0735-7028.28.1.14

Mahony, D. L., Burroughs, W. J., & Lippman, L. G. (2002). Perceived attributes of health-promoting laughter: A cross-generational comparison. *The Journal of Psychology, 136*(2), 171–181. https://doi.org/10.1080/00223980209604148

Margison, F. (1997). Stress and psychotherapy: An overview. In V. P. Varma (Ed.), *Stress in psychotherapists* (pp. 210–234). Routledge.

Marquez-Castillo, R. L. (2013). *Martial arts and ADHD: A meta-analysis.* ProQuest Dissertations Publishing.

Marsh, H. W., Nagengast, B., & Morin, A. J. S. (2013). Measurement invariance of big-five factors over the life-span: ESEM tests of gender, age, plasticity, maturity, and la dolce vita effects. *Developmental Psychology, 49*(6), 1194–1218. https://doi.org/10.1037/a0026913

Martinez, G. M., Daniels, K., & Febo-Vazquez, I. (2018). Fertility of men and women aged 15–44 in the United States: National Survey of Family Growth, 2011–2015. *National Health Statistics Reports, no. 113.* National Center for Health Statistics. https://www.cdc.gov/nchs/data/nhsr/nhsr113.pdf

Maslach, C., & Jackson, S. (1981). The measurement of experienced burnout. *Journal of Organizational Behavior, 2*(2), 99–113. https://doi.org/10.1002/job.4030020205

Maslach, C., & Leiter, M. P. (2005). Reversing burnout: How to rekindle your passion for your work. *Stanford Social Innovation Review, 3,* 42–49. http://graphics8.nytimes.com/packages/pdf/business/06.BURNOUT.FINAL.pdf

Maslach, C., & Leiter, M. P. (2016). Understanding the burnout experience: Recent research and its implications for psychiatry. *World Psychiatry, 15*(2), 103–111. https://doi.org/10.1002/wps.20311

Maslach, C., Schaufeli, W. B., & Leiter, M. P. (2001). Job burnout. *Annual Review of Psychology, 52*(1), 397–422. https://doi.org/10.1146/annurev.psych.52.1.397

Maté, G. (2021, September/October). The helper syndrome: When are we enough? https://www.psychotherapynetworker.org/magazine/article/2577/helper-syndrome

Mazereeuw, G., Lanctôt, K. L., Chau, S. A., Swardfager, W., & Herrmann, N. (2012). Effects of omega-3 fatty acids on cognitive performance: A meta-analysis. *Neurobiology of Aging, 33*(7), 1482.e17–1482.e29. https://doi.org/10.1016/j.neurobiolaging.2011.12.014

McCann, I. L., & Pearlman, L. A. (1990). Vicarious traumatization: A framework for understanding the psychological effects of working with victims. *Journal of Traumatic Stress, 3*(1), 131–149. https://doi.org/10.1002/jts. 2490030110

McCormack, B., Borg, M., Cardiff, S., Dewing, J., Jacobs, G., Janes, N., Bengt, K., McCance, T., Mekki, T., Porock, D., Lieshout, F., & Wilson, V. (2015). Person-centredness—The 'state' of the art. *International Practice Development Journal, 5*(Suppl. 1), 1–15. https://doi.org/10.19043/ipdj.5SP.003

McCormack, H. M., MacIntyre, T. E., O'Shea, D., Herring, M. P., & Campbell, M. J. (2018). The prevalence and cause(s) of burnout among applied psychologists: A systemic review. *Frontiers in Psychology, 9*, Article 1897. https://doi.org/10.3389/fpsyg.2018.01897

McCormick, R. M. (2003). *Joy: A dharma talk.* Lotus Sutra Commentaries. https://pounceatron.dreamhosters.com/nichirenscoffeehouse.net/Ryuei/Joy.html

McCoy, J. G., & Strecker, R. E. (2011). The cognitive cost of sleep lost. *Neurobiology of Learning and Memory, 96*(4), 564–582. https://doi.org/10.1016/j.nlm.2011.07.004

McCrae, R. R., & Costa, P. T., Jr. (1987). Validation of the five-factor model of personality across instruments and observers. *Journal of Personality and Social Psychology, 52*(1), 81–90. https://doi.org/10.1037/0022-3514.52.1.81

McEntee, D. J., & Halgin, R. P. (1996). Therapists' attitudes about addressing the role of exercise in psychotherapy. *Journal of Clinical Psychology, 52*(1), 48–60. https://doi.org/10.1002/(SICI)1097-4679(199601)52:1<48::AID-JCLP7>3.0.CO;2-S

McIntosh, P. (2003). White privilege: Unpacking the invisible knapsack. In S. Plous (Ed.), *Understanding prejudice and discrimination* (pp. 191–196). McGraw-Hill.

McIntosh, P. (2020). White privilege and male privilege: A personal account of coming to see correspondences through work in women's studies. In P. McIntosh (Ed.), *On privilege, fraudulence, and teaching as learning: Selected essays 1981–2019* (pp. 12–28). Routledge.

McKay, M., Forsyth, J. P., & Eifert, G. H. (2010). *Your life on purpose.* New Harbinger.

McNeill, D. P., Morrison, D. A., Nouwen, H. J. M., & Filártiga, J. (1982). *Compassion, a reflection on the Christian life.* Doubleday.

Meghani, D. (2019). Self-care together: Strategies that benefit early career psychology faculty and psychology doctoral trainees. *Psychotherapy Bulletin, 54*(2), 5–12. https://societyforpsychotherapy.org/self-care-together/

Merriam-Webster. (n.d.-a). Mental health day. In *Merriam-Webster.com dictionary.* https://www.merriam-webster.com/dictionary/mental%20health%20day

Merriam-Webster. (n.d.-b). Stewardship. In *Merriam-Webster.com dictionary.* https://www.merriam-webster.com/dictionary/stewardship

Mestayer, C. (2021, September/October). Surviving the post-partum storm. *Psychotherapy Networker,* 48–49.

Michalski, D., Kohout, J., Wicherski, M., & Hart, B. (2011). *2009 doctoral employ-ment survey*. American Psychological Association. https://www.apa.org/workforce/publications/09-doc-empl/report.pdf

Mischke-Reeds, M. (2018). *Somatic psychotherapy toolbox: 125 worksheets and exercises to treat trauma & stress*. PESI.

Miyake, A., Friedman, N. P., Emerson, M. J., Witzki, A. H., Howerter, A., & Wager, T. D. (2000). The unity and diversity of executive functions and their contri-butions to complex 'frontal lobe' tasks: A latent variable analysis. *Cognitive Psychology, 41*, 49–100. https://doi.org/10.1006/cogp.1999.0734

Moore, A., & Malinowski, P. (2009). Meditation, mindfulness and cognitive flex-ibility. *Consciousness and Cognition, 18*(1), 176–186. https://doi.org/10.1016/j.concog.2008.12.008

Morse, G., Salyers, M. P., Rollins, A. L., Monroe-DeVita, M., & Pfahler, C. (2012). Burnout in mental health services: A review of the problem and its remedi-ation. *Administration and Policy in Mental Health, 39*(5), 341–352. https://doi.org/10.1007/s10488-011-0352-1

Muraven, M., Collins, R. L., Morsheimer, E. T., Shiffman, S., & Paty, J. A. (2005). The morning after: Limit violations and the self-regulation of alcohol con-sumption. *Psychology of Addictive Behaviors, 19*(3), 253–262. https://doi.org/10.1037/0893-164X.19.3.253

Murray, M. W. (2009, July 14). *Laughter is the best medicine for your heart*. University of Maryland Medical Center.

N'Diaye, S. (2021, September/October). Learning into grief. *Psychotherapy Networker*, 47–48.

Neff, K. (2003). Self-compassion: An alternative conceptualization of a healthy attitude toward oneself. *Self and Identity, 2*(2), 85–101. https://doi.org/10.1080/15298860309032

Neff, K. (2015). *Self-compassion. The proven power of being kind to yourself*. William Morrow.

Neff, K., & Germer, C. (2018). *The mindful self-compassion workbook: A proven way to accept yourself, build inner strength, and thrive*. Guilford Press.

Neimeyer, G. J., Minniti, A., & Taylor, J. M. (2019). Critical conversations in continuing education: Contemporary memes, themes, and dreams. *Professional Psychology: Research and Practice, 50*(2), 63–69. https://doi.org/10.1037/pro0000237

Neimeyer, G. J., & Taylor, J. M. (2019). Advancing the assessment of professional learning, self-care, and competence. *Professional Psychology: Research and Practice, 50*(2), 95–105. https://doi.org/10.1037/pro0000225

Nelms, J. A., & Castel, L. (2016). A systematic review and meta-analysis of randomized and nonrandomized trials of clinical emotional freedom tech-niques (EFT) for the treatment of depression. *EXPLORE, 12*(6), 416–426. https://doi.org/10.1016/j.explore.2016.08.001

Nestor, J. (2020). *Breath: The new science of a lost art*. Riverhead Books.

Nhat Hanh, T. (1999). *The miracle of mindfulness*. Beacon Press.

Nhat Hanh, T. (2020). *How to connect*. Parallax Press.

Nigrinis, A., Hamp, A., Stamm, K., & Christidis, P. (2014). Does the gender pay gap in psychology differ by work setting? *Monitor on Psychology, 45*(11).

Norcross, J. C. (2000). Psychotherapist self-care: Practitioner-tested, research-informed strategies. *Professional Psychology: Research and Practice, 31*(6), 710–713. https://doi.org/10.1037/0735-7028.31.6.710

Norcross, J. C., & Farber, B. A. (2005). Choosing psychotherapy as a career: Beyond "I want to help people." *Journal of Clinical Psychology, 61*(8), 939–943. https://doi.org/10.1002/jclp.20175

Norcross, J. C., & Guy, J. (2007). *Leaving it at the office: A guide to psychotherapist self-care*. Guilford Press.

Norcross, J. C., & Lambert, M. (2011). Evidence-based therapy relationships. In J. C. Norcross (Ed.), *Psychotherapy relationships that work: Evidence-based responsiveness* (pp. 3–21). Oxford University Press. https://doi.org/10.1093/acprof:oso/9780199737208.003.0001

Norcross, J. C., & VandenBos, G. R. (2018). *Leaving it at the office: A guide to psychotherapist self-care* (2nd ed.). Guilford Press.

Northrup, C. (2019). *Why the psoas muscle is the most vital muscle in the body*. https://www.drnorthrup.com/psoas-muscle-vital-muscle-body/

Nutrition Coalition. (2018, June 20). New survey shows changes in American diet trends. https://www.nutritioncoalition.us/news/2018/6/20/new-survey-shows-changes-in-american-diet-trends

O'Connor, M. (2001). On the etiology and effective management of professional distress and impairment among psychologists. *Professional Psychology: Research and Practice, 32*(4), 345–350. https://doi.org/10.1037/0735-7028.32.4.345

Office for the Coordination of Humanitarian Affairs. (2020). *Self-care manual for front-line workers*. https://www.humanitarianresponse.info/en/operations/lebanon/document/lebanon-national-self-care-manual-enar

Ogden, P. (2015). *Sensorimotor psychotherapy: Interventions for trauma and attachment*. W. W. Norton & Company.

Omin, R. R. (2020). To reveal or not to reveal: When the therapist has a serious illness. *Psychotherapy Networker, 44*(1), 40–45.

Ong, J. C., Shapiro, S. L., & Manber, R. (2008). Combining mindfulness meditation with cognitive-behavior therapy for insomnia: A treatment-development study. *Behavior Therapy, 39*(2), 171–182. https://doi.org/10.1016/j.beth.2007.07.002

Orsillo, S. M., & Roemer, L. (2011). *The mindful way through anxiety: Break free from chronic worry and reclaim your life*. Guilford Press.

Ortner, A. (2020). *The tapping solution planner*. Hay House.

Ortner, C. N. M., Kilner, S. J., & Zelazo, P. D. (2007). Mindfulness meditation and reduced emotional interference on a cognitive task. *Motivation and Emotion, 31*(4), 271–283. https://doi.org/10.1007/s11031-007-9076-7

Ota, A., Masue, T., Yasuda, N., Tsutsumi, A., Mino, Y., Ohara, H., & Ono, Y. (2009). Psychosocial job characteristics and insomnia: A prospective cohort study using the Demand-Control-Support (DCS) and Effort–Reward Imbalance

(ERI) job stress models. *Sleep Medicine, 10*(10), 1112–1117. https://doi.org/ 10.1016/j.sleep.2009.03.005

Pacheco, D. (2020). *Light therapy for insomnia sufferers.* https://www.sleep foundation.org/light-therapy

Page, S. E. (2007). *The difference: How the power of diversity creates better groups, firms, schools, and societies.* Princeton University Press.

Painter, E., & Woodside, M. (2016). Vicarious trauma: Emotional disruption and approaches to coping. *Counseling and Wellness Journal, 5,* 1–12.

Pandit, G. (2020). *Buddha at work: Finding purpose, balance, and happiness at your workplace.* Bright Hart Books.

Pappas, S. (2020). How to encourage student self-care. *Monitor on Psychology, 51*(5), 64. https://www.apa.org/monitor/2020/07/student-self-care

Parker, E. K. (1983). *Infinite insights into Kenpo: Vol. 2. Physical analyzation I.* Kam IV.

Parloff, M. B., Waskow, I. E., & Wolfe, B. E. (1978). Research on therapist variables in relation to process and outcome. In S. Garfield & A. E. Bergin (Eds.), *Handbook of psychotherapy and behavior change* (2nd ed., pp. 233–282). Wiley.

Pearlin, L. I., Lieberman, M. A., Menaghan, E. G., & Mullan, J. T. (1981). The stress process. *Journal of Health and Social Behavior, 22*(4), 337–356. https:// doi.org/10.2307/2136676

Pearlman, L. A., & Saakvitne, K. W. (1995). Treating therapists with vicarious traumatization and secondary traumatic stress disorders. In C. R. Figley (Ed.), *Compassion fatigue: Coping with secondary traumatic stress disorder in those who treat the traumatized* (pp. 150–177). Brunner/Mazel.

Peelen, M. V., & Kastner, S. (2014). Attention in the real world: Toward understanding its neural basis. *Trends in Cognitive Sciences, 18*(5), 242–250. https:// doi.org/10.1016/j.tics.2014.02.004

Pew Research Center. (2014a). *Attendance at religious services.* https://www. pewforum.org/religious-landscape-study/attendance-at-religious-services/

Pew Research Center. (2014b). *Frequency of prayer.* https://www.pewforum.org/ religious-landscape-study/frequency-of-prayer/

Pew Research Center. (2021). *Mobile fact sheet.* https://www.pewresearch.org/ internet/fact-sheet/mobile/#who-owns-cellphones-and-smartphones

Pica, M. (1998). The ambiguous nature of clinical training and its impact on the development of student clinicians. *Psychotherapy: Theory, Research, & Practice, 35*(3), 361–365. https://doi.org/10.1037/h0087840

Pickering, G., Mazur, A., Trousselard, M., Bienkowski, P., Yaltsewa, N., Amessou, M., Noah, L., & Pouteau, E. (2020). Magnesium status and stress: The vicious circle concept revisited. *Nutrients, 12*(2), Article 3672.

Pink, D. (2011). *Drive: The surprising truth about what motivates us.* Riverhead Books.

Pinsker, J. (2020, March 2). Why so many Americans don't talk about money. *The Atlantic.* https://www.theatlantic.com/family/archive/2020/03/americans-dont-talk-about-money-taboo/607273/

Pipes, R. B., Holstein, J. E., & Aguirre, M. G. (2005). Examining the personal–professional distinction: Ethics codes and the difficulty of drawing a boundary. *American Psychologist, 60*(4), 325–334. https://doi.org/10.1037/0003-066X.60.4.325

Polk, K. L., Schoendorff, B., Webster, M., & Olaz, F. O. (2016). *The essential guide to the ACT matrix: A step-by-step approach to using the ACT matrix model in clinical practice.* Context Press.

Pollak, S. M. (2017, October). Equanimity: A practice for troubled times: The secret ingredient in mindfulness. *Psychology Today.* https://www.psychologytoday.com/us/blog/the-art-now/201710/equanimity-practice-troubled-times

Pollak, S. M. (2019a). *The clinical application of compassion* [Continuing education lecture]. NICABM.

Pollak, S. M. (2019b). *Self-compassion for parents: Nurture your child by caring for yourself.* Guilford Press.

Pope, K. S., & Feldman-Summers, S. (1992). National survey of psychologists' sexual and physical abuse history and their evaluation of training and competence in these areas. *Professional Psychology: Research and Practice, 23*(5), 353–361. https://doi.org/10.1037/0735-7028.23.5.353

Pope, K. S., Keith-Spiegel, P., & Tabachnick, B. G. (2006). Sexual attraction to clients: The human therapist and the (sometimes) inhuman training system. *Training and Education in Professional Psychology, S*(2), 96–111. https://doi.org/10.1037/1931-3918.S.2.96

Pope, K. S., Sonne, J. L., & Greene, B. (2006). *What therapists don't talk about and why: Understanding taboos that hurt us and our clients.* American Psychological Association. https://doi.org/10.1037/11413-000

Pope, K. S., & Tabachnick, B. G. (1994). Therapists as patients: A national survey of psychologists' experiences, problems, and beliefs. *Professional Psychology: Research and Practice, 25*(3), 247–258. https://doi.org/10.1037/0735-7028.25.3.247

Pope, K. S., Tabachnick, B. G., & Keith-Spiegel, P. (1987). Ethics of practice. The beliefs and behaviors of psychologists as therapists. *American Psychologist, 42*(11), 993–1006. https://doi.org/10.1037/0003-066X.42.11.993

Porges, S. W. (2018). Polyvagal theory: A primer. In S. W. Porges & D. Dana (Eds.), *Clinical applications of the polyvagal theory: The emergence of polyvagal-informed therapies* (pp. 50–69). W. W. Norton.

Posluns, K., & Gall, T. L. (2020). Dear mental health practitioners, take care of yourselves: A literature review on self-care. *International Journal for the Advancement of Counseling, 42*(1), 1–20. https://doi.org/10.1007/s10447-019-09382-w

Price, M. (2001). *Secondary traumatization: Vulnerability factors for mental health professionals* [Unpublished doctoral dissertation]. University of Texas.

Prochaska, J. O., & DiClemente, C. C. (1983). Stages and processes of self-change of smoking: Toward an integrative model of change. *Journal of Consulting and Clinical Psychology, 51*(3), 390–395. https://doi.org/10.1037/0022-006X.51.3.390

Procyk, A. (2018). *Nutritional treatments to improve mental health disorders: Non-pharmaceutical interventions for depression, anxiety, bipolar & ADHD.* PESI.

Puder-York, M. (2005). *The office survival guide.* McGraw-Hill Education.

Race, K. (2016). *Mindful parenting: Simple and powerful solutions for raising creative, engaged, and happy kids in today's hectic world.* Griffin.

Racusin, G. R., Abramowitz, S. I., & Winter, W. D. (1981). Becoming a therapist: Family dynamics and career choice. *Professional Psychology, 12*(2), 271–279. https://doi.org/10.1037/0735-7028.12.2.271

Radeke, J. T., & Mahoney, M. J. (2000). Comparing the personal lives of psychotherapists and research psychologists. *Professional Psychology: Research and Practice, 31*(1), 82–84. https://doi.org/10.1037/0735-7028.31.1.82

Raghuraj, P., & Telles, S. (2008). Immediate effect of specific nostril manipulating yoga breathing practices on autonomic and respiratory variables. *Applied Psychophysiology and Biofeedback, 33*(2), 65–75. https://doi.org/10.1007/s10484-008-9055-0

Ram, S., Seirawan, H., Kumar, S. K. S., & Clark, G. T. (2010). Prevalence and impact of sleep disorders and sleep habits in the United States. *Sleep and Breathing, 14*(1), 63–70. https://doi.org/10.1007/s11325-009-0281-3

Ramirez, J. M., Doi, A., Garcia, A. J., III, Elsen, F. P., Koch, H., & Wei, A. D. (2012). The cellular building blocks of breathing. *Comprehensive Physiology, 2*(4), 2683–2731. https://doi.org/10.1002/cphy.c110033

Rantanen, J., Metsäpelto, R.-L., Feldt, T., Pulkkinen, L., & Kokko, K. (2007). Long-term stability in the Big Five personality traits in adulthood. *Scandinavian Journal of Psychology, 48*(6), 511–518. https://doi.org/10.1111/j.1467-9450.2007.00609.x

Ratey, J. J., with Hagerman, E. (Collaborator). (2008). *Spark: The revolutionary new science of exercise and the brain.* Little, Brown and Co.

Roberts, G. L. (2021, February 18). *Work–life blend: The new work–life balance.* LinkedIn. https://www.linkedin.com/pulse/work-life-blend-new-balance-gemma-leigh-roberts-1e

Roberts, J. A., & David, M. E. (2016). My life has become a major distraction from my cell phone: Partner phubbing and relationship satisfaction among romantic partners. *Computers in Human Behavior, 54,* 134–141. https://doi.org/10.1016/j.chb.2015.07.058

Robinson, P. A. (Director). (1989). *Field of dreams.* [Film]. Gordon Company.

Robison, J. (2005). Health at every size: Toward a new paradigm of weight and health. *Medscape General Medicine, 7*(3), 13.

Rogers, C. R. (1995). *On becoming a person: A therapist's view of psychotherapy.* Houghton Mifflin.

Rolfsen, G. D. (2016, May 2). *How to start changing an unhealthy work environment* [Video]. YouTube. https://www.youtube.com/watch?v=eYLb7WUtYt8

Rome, D. (2014). *Your body knows the answer: Using your felt sense to solve problems, effect change, and liberate creativity.* Shambhala.

Rosenzweig, S., Reibel, D. K., Greeson, J. M., Brainard, G. C., & Hojat, M. (2003). Mindfulness-based stress reduction lowers psychological distress in medical students. *Teaching and Learning in Medicine, 15*(2), 88–92. https://doi.org/10.1207/S15328015TLM1502_03

Rubin, D. I. (2007). Epidemiology and risk factors for spine pain. *Neurologic Clinics, 25*(2), 353–371. https://doi.org/10.1016/j.ncl.2007.01.004

Rupert, P. A., Hartman, E. R. T., & Miller, A. S. O. (2013). Work demands and resources, work–family conflict, and family functioning among practicing psychologists. *Professional Psychology: Research and Practice, 44*(5), 283–289. https://doi.org/10.1037/a0034494

Rupert, P. A., & Kent, J. S. (2007). Gender and work setting differences in career-sustaining behaviors and burnout among professional psychologists. *Professional Psychology: Research and Practice, 38*(1), 88–96. https://doi.org/10.1037/0735-7028.38.1.88

Rupert, P. A., Miller, A. O., & Dorociak, K. E. (2015). Preventing burnout: What does the research tell us? *Professional Psychology: Research and Practice, 46*(3), 168–174. https://doi.org/10.1037/a0039297

Rupert, P. A., Miller, A. O., Tuminello Hartman, E. R., & Bryant, F. B. (2012). Predictors of career satisfaction among practicing psychologists. *Professional Psychology: Research and Practice, 43*(5), 495–502. https://doi.org/10.1037/a0029420

Rupert, P. A., & Morgan, D. (2005). Work setting and burnout among professional psychologists. *Professional Psychology: Research and Practice, 36*(5), 544–550. https://doi.org/10.1037/0735-7028.36.5.544

Rupert, P. A., Stevanovic, P., Hartman, E., Bryant, F., & Miller, A. (2012). Predicting work–family conflict and life satisfaction among professional psychologists. *Professional Psychology: Research and Practice, 43*(4), 341–348. https://doi.org/10.1037/a0026675

Rupert, P. A., Stevanovic, P., & Hunley, H. (2009). Work–family conflict and burnout among practicing psychologists. *Professional Psychology: Research and Practice, 40*(1), 54–61. https://doi.org/10.1037/a0012538

Saakvitne, K. W., Gamble, S., Pearlman, L. A., & Tabor Lev, B. (2001). *Relational teaching experiential learning: The teaching manual for the Risking Connection curriculum.* Sidran Press.

Salzberg, S. (2002). *Lovingkindness: The revolutionary art of happiness.* Shambhala.

Salzberg, S. (2013). *Real happiness at work: Meditations for accomplishment, achievement, and peace.* Workman Publishing Group.

Sandercock, G. R., Bromley, P. D., & Brodie, D. A. (2005). Effects of exercise on heart rate variability: inferences from meta-analysis. *Medicine and Science in Sports and Exercise, 37*(3), 433–439. https://doi.org/10.1249/01.mss.0000155388.39002.9d

Sapienza, B. G., & Bugental, J. F. T. (2000). Keeping our instruments finely tuned: An existential-humanistic perspective. *Professional Psychology: Research and Practice, 31*(4), 458–460. https://doi.org/10.1037/0735-7028.31.4.458

Sarkis, S. M. (2018). *Executive function difficulties in adults: 100 ways to help your clients live productive and happy lives*. PESI.

Scaletta, S. (2021, May 3). *Helping the helpers: Mindful self-care, compassion fatigue, burnout, and compassion satisfaction among Utah mental health professionals* [Poster presentation]. American Psychological Association Annual Convention [Virtual].

Schauben, L. J., & Frazier, P. A. (1995). Vicarious trauma: The effects on female counselors of working with sexual violence survivors. *Psychology of Women Quarterly, 19*(1), 49–64. https://doi.org/10.1111/j.1471-6402.1995.tb00278.x

Schiraldi, G. R. (2017). *The resilience workbook*. New Harbinger.

Schlarb, A. A., Reis, D., & Schröder, A. (2012). Sleep characteristics, sleep problems, and associations to quality of life among psychotherapists. *Sleep Disorders, 2012*, Article 806913. https://doi.org/10.1155/2012/806913

Schoener, G. R. (1999). Practicing what we preach. *The Counseling Psychologist, 27*(5), 693–701. https://doi.org/10.1177/0011000099275003

Schoener, G. R. (2007). Do as I say, not as I do. *Professional Psychology: Research and Practice, 38*(6), 610–612.

Schulz, R., Hebert, R. S., Dew, M. A., Brown, S. L., Scheier, M. F., Beach, S. R., Czaja, S. J., Martire, L. M., Coon, D., Langa, K. M., Gitlin, L. N., Stevens, A. B., & Nichols, L. (2007). Patient suffering and caregiver compassion: New opportunities for research, practice, and policy. *The Gerontologist, 47*(1), 4–13. https://doi.org/10.1093/geront/47.1.4

Schutte-Rodin, S., Broch, L., Buysse, D., Dorsey, C., & Sateia, M. (2008). Clinical guideline for the evaluation and management of chronic insomnia in adults. *Journal of Clinical Sleep Medicine, 4*(5), 487–504. https://doi.org/10.5664/jcsm.27286

Schwartz-Mette, R. A., & Shen-Miller, D. S. (2018). Ships in the rising sea? Changes over time in psychologists' ethical beliefs and behaviors. *Ethics & Behavior, 28*(3), 176–198. https://doi.org/10.1080/10508422.2017.1308253

Scott, B. A., & Judge, T. A. (2006). Insomnia, emotions, and job satisfaction: A multilevel study. *Journal of Management, 32*(5), 622–645. https://doi.org/10.1177/0149206306289762

Sebastian, B., & Nelms, J. (2017). The effectiveness of Emotional Freedom Techniques in the treatment of posttraumatic stress disorder: A meta-analysis. *EXPLORE, 13*(1), 16–25. https://doi.org/10.1016/j.explore.2016.10.001

Segal, Z. V., Williams, M., & Teasdale, J. (2018). *Mindfulness-based cognitive therapy for depression* (2nd ed.). The Guilford Press.

Seligman, M. (2006). *Learned optimism: How to change your mind and your life*. Vintage.

Seneca the Younger. (1917). *The epistles of Seneca*. Loeb Classical Library. https://doi.org/10.4159/DLCL.seneca_younger-epistles.1917

Sentell, T., Pingitore, D., Scheffler, R., Schwalm, D., & Haley, M. (2001). Gender differences in practice patterns and income among psychologists in professional practice. *Professional Psychology: Research and Practice, 32*, 607–617. https://doi.org/10.1037/0735-7028.32.6.607

Sentell, T., Pingitore, D., Schwalm, D., & Haley, M. (2001). Gender differences in practice patterns and income among psychologists in professional practice. *Professional Psychology: Research and Practice, 32*(6), 607–617. https://doi.org/10.1037/0735-7028.32.6.607

Shannahoff-Khalsa, D. (1991). Lateralized rhythms of the central and autonomic nervous systems. *International Journal of Psychophysiology, 11*(3), 225–251. https://doi.org/10.1016/0167-8760(91)90017-R

Shapiro, S. L., Astin, J. A., Bishop, S. R., & Cordova, M. (2005). Mindfulness-based stress reduction for health care professionals: Results from a randomized trial. *International Journal of Stress Management, 12*(2), 164–176. https://doi.org/10.1037/1072-5245.12.2.164

Shapiro, S. L., Brown, K. W., & Biegel, G. M. (2007). Teaching self-care to caregivers: Effects of mindfulness-based stress reduction on the mental health of therapists in training. *Training and Education in Professional Psychology, 1*(2), 105–115. https://doi.org/10.1037/1931-3918.1.2.105

Shapiro, S. L., Schwartz, G. E., & Bonner, G. (1998). Effects of mindfulness-based stress reduction on medical and premedical students. *Journal of Behavioral Medicine, 21*(6), 581–599. https://doi.org/10.1023/A:1018700829825

Sharma, A., Madaan, V., & Petty, F. D. (2006). Exercise for mental health. *Primary Care Companion to the Journal of Clinical Psychiatry, 8*(2), 106. https://doi.org/10.4088/PCC.v08n0208a

Sharma, V. K., Trakroo, M., Subramaniam, V., Rajajeyakumar, M., Bhavanani, A. B., & Sahai, A. (2013). Effect of fast and slow pranayama on perceived stress and cardiovascular parameters in young health-care students. *International Journal of Yoga, 6*(2), 104–110. https://doi.org/10.4103/0973-6131.113400

Shaw, Z. (2020, September 10). Therapists share their top tips for self-care. *Psychology Today.* https://www.psychologytoday.com/us/blog/the-color-wellness/202009/therapists-share-their-top-tips-self-care

Sherman, M. (1996). Distress and professional impairment due to mental health problems among psychotherapists. *Clinical Psychology Review, 16*(4), 299–315. https://doi.org/10.1016/0272-7358(96)00016-5

Sherman, M. D., & Thelen, M. H. (1998). Distress and professional impairment among psychologists in clinical practice. *Professional Psychology: Research and Practice, 29*(1), 79–85. https://doi.org/10.1037/0735-7028.29.1.79

Siegel, D. (2007). Mindfulness training and neural integration: Differentiation of distinct streams of awareness and the cultivation of well-being. *Social Cognitive and Affective Neuroscience, 2*(4), 259–263. https://doi.org/10.1093/scan/nsm034

Siegel, D. J. (2016). *Mind: A journey to the heart of being human.* W. W. Norton & Company.

Siegel, D. J. (2018). *Aware: The science and practice of presence—The groundbreaking meditation practice.* TarcherPerigee.

Siegel, J. (2019, October 23). *The 3 most important questions you need to ask before starting a mindfulness practice.* Jeff Siegel Wellness. https://jeffsiegelwellness.

com/the-3-most-important-questions-you-need-to-ask-before-starting-a-mindfulness-practice/

Sim, W., Zanardelli, G., Loughran, M. J., Mannarino, M. B., & Hill, C. E. (2016). Thriving, burnout, and coping strategies of early and later career counseling center psychologists in the United States. *Counselling Psychology Quarterly, 29*(4), 382–404. https://doi.org/10.1080/09515070.2015.1121135

Simionato, G. K., & Simpson, S. (2018). Personal risk factors associated with burnout among psychotherapists: A systematic review of the literature. *Journal of Clinical Psychology, 74*(9), 1431–1456. https://doi.org/10.1002/jclp.22615

Skovholt, T. M. (2001). *The resilient practitioner: Burnout prevention and self-care strategies for counselors, therapists, teachers, and health professionals.* Allyn & Bacon.

Sliwinski, M. J., Smyth, J. M., Hofer, S. M., & Stawski, R. S. (2006). Intra-individual coupling of daily stress and cognition. *Psychology and Aging, 21*(3), 545–557. https://doi.org/10.1037/0882-7974.21.3.545

Smith, L. (2016). *The art of compassionate self-care.* Connectfulness. https://connectfulness.com/blog/the-art-of-compassionate-self-care/

Sodeke-Gregson, E. A., Holttum, S., & Billings, J. (2013). Compassion satisfaction, burnout, and secondary traumatic stress in UK therapists who work with adult trauma clients. *European Journal of Psychotraumatology, 4*(1), Article 21869. https://doi.org/10.3402/ejpt.v4i0.21869

Soots, L. (n.d.). *Flourishing.* The Positive Psychology People. http://www.thepositivepsychologypeople.com/flourishing

Spielman, A. J., Saskin, P., & Thorpy, M. J. (1987). Treatment of chronic insomnia by restriction of time in bed. *Sleep, 10*(1), 45–56.

Sprang, G., Clark, J. J., & Whitt-Woosley, A. (2007). Compassion fatigue, compassion satisfaction, and burnout: Factors impacting a professional's quality of life. *Journal of Loss and Trauma, 12*(3), 259–280. https://doi.org/10.1080/15325020701238093

Stapleton, P. (2019). *The science behind tapping: A proven stress management technique for the mind and body.* Hay House.

Stapleton, P., Buchan, C., Mitchell, I., McGrath, Y., Gorton, P., & Carter, B. (2019). An initial investigation of neural changes in overweight adults with food cravings after emotional freedom techniques. *OBM Integrative and Complementary Medicine, 4*(1), 14. https://doi.org/10.21926/obm.icm.1901010

Starling, L. (2019). *Be still: Spiritual self-care for mental health professionals.* Grace Psychological Health Services.

Statista Research Department. (2021). *Number of social network users worldwide from 2017–2025.* https://www.statista.com/statistics/278414/number-of-worldwide-social-network-users/

Stefanov, M., Potroz, M., Kim, J., Lim, J., Cha, R., & Nam, M. H. (2013). The primo vascular system as a new anatomical system. *Journal of Acupuncture and Meridian Studies, 6*(6), 331–338. https://doi.org/10.1016/j.jams.2013.10.001

Stessman, E. (2021, February 23). *5 Black wellness experts share how they practice self-care*. Today. https://www.today.com/shop/self-care-black-women-t209593

Stevanovic, P., & Rupert, P. A. (2004). Career-sustaining behaviors, satisfactions, and stresses of professional psychologists. *Psychotherapy: Theory, Research, & Practice, 41*(3), 301–309. https://doi.org/10.1037/0033-3204.41.3.301

Stone, D. M., Holland, K. M., Bartholow, B. N., Crosby, A. E., Davis, S. P., & Wilkins, N. (2017). *Preventing suicide: A technical package of policies, programs, and practice*. Division of Violence Prevention, U.S. National Center for Injury Prevention and Control. https://www.cdc.gov/violenceprevention/pdf/suicideTechnicalPackage.pdf

Stone, R. (2020, September 10). Therapists share their top tips for self-care. *Psychology Today*. https://www.psychologytoday.com/us/blog/the-color-wellness/202009/therapists-share-their-top-tips-self-care

Strosahl, K., Robinson, P., & Gustavsson, T. (2012). *Brief interventions for radical change: Principles and practice of focused acceptance and commitment therapy*. New Harbinger Publications.

Sünbül, Z. A., Malkoç, A., Gördesli, M. A., Arslan, R., & Çekici, F. (2018). Mindful self-care dimensions as agents of well-being for students in mental health fields. *European Journal of Education Studies, 5*(5), 33–41. https://doi.org/10.5281/zenodo.1469657

Suni, E. (2020, July 30). *Healthy sleep tips*. Sleep Foundation. https://www.sleepfoundation.org/sleep-hygiene/healthy-sleep-tips

SVYASA. (2006). *Scientific research on laughter yoga: Effects of laughter yoga on stress in the workplace? Bangalore Study 2006* [PowerPoint presentation]. Laughter Yoga University. https://laughteryoga.org/bangalore-study/

Tart, C. T. (Ed.). (1992). *Transpersonal psychologies*. Harper Collins.

Tartakovsky, M. (2012, December 13). *What it means to have a healthy relationship with money*. PsychCentral. https://psychcentral.com/blog/what-it-means-to-have-a-healthy-relationship-with-money/

Tartakovsky, M. (2016, June 23). *Self-care: Living life according to your values*. Dr. Erin Olivio. http://www.erinolivo.com/in-the-news/self-care-living-life-according-to-your-values/

Team Tony. (n.d.-a). *Discover the 6 human needs*. https://www.tonyrobbins.com/mind-meaning/do-you-need-to-feel-significant/

Team Tony. (n.d.-b). *5 money tips from Marie Forleo*. https://www.tonyrobbins.com/wealth-lifestyle/5-money-tips-from-marie-forleo/

Telles, S., Nagarathna, R., & Nagendra, H. R. (1994). Breathing through a particular nostril can alter metabolism and autonomic activities. *Indian Journal of Physiology and Pharmacology, 38*(2), 133–137.

Thich Nhat Hanh Quote Collective. (2018). *Sometimes your joy is the source of your smile* . . . https://thichnhathanhquotecollective.com/2018/07/22/sometimes-your-joy-is-the-source-of-your-smile/

Thoreau, H. D. (1971). *Walden* (J. Lyndon Shanley, Ed.). Princeton University Press.

Thoreson, R. W., Miller, M., & Krauskopf, C. J. (1989). The distressed psychologist: Prevalence and treatment considerations. *Professional Psychology: Research and Practice, 20*(3), 153–158. https://doi.org/10.1037/0735-7028.20.3.153

Tolle, E. (2004). *The power of now: A guide to spiritual enlightenment.* New World Library.

Toussaint, L., Shields, G. S., Dorn, G., & Slavich, G. M. (2016). Effects of lifetime stress exposure on mental and physical health in young adulthood: How stress degrades and forgiveness protects health. *Journal of Health Psychology, 21*(6), 1004–1014. https://doi.org/10.1177/1359105314544132

Toussaint, L. L., Shields, G. S., & Slavich, G. M. (2016). Forgiveness, stress, and health: A 5-week dynamic parallel process study. *Annals of Behavioral Medicine, 50*(5), 727–735. https://doi.org/10.1007/s12160-016-9796-6

Toussaint, L. L., Worthington, E. L., Jr., & Williams, D. R. (Eds.). (2015). *Forgiveness and health: Scientific evidence and theories relating forgiveness to better health.* Springer Science + Business Media. https://doi.org/10.1007/978-94-017-9993-5

Trauer, J. M., Qian, M. Y., Doyle, J. S., Rajaratnam, S. M., & Cunnington, D. (2015). Cognitive behavioral therapy for chronic insomnia: A systematic review and meta-analysis. *Annals of Internal Medicine, 163*(3), 191–204. https://doi.org/10.7326/M14-2841

Tseng, J., & Poppenk, J. (2020). Brain meta-state transitions demarcate thoughts across task contexts exposing the mental noise of trait neuroticism. *Nature Communications, 11*(1), 3480. https://doi.org/10.1038/s41467-020-17255-9

Tuckman, A. (2009). *More attention, less deficit: Success strategies for adults with ADHD.* Specialty Press.

Tuckman, A. (2012). *Understand your brain, get more done: The ADHD executive functions workbook.* Specialty Press.

Turner, E. (2021, September/October). Confessions of a racing mind: My silent battle with OCD. *The Psychotherapy Networker, 50–51,* 60.

Uddin, L. Q., Kelly, A. M., Biswal, B. B., Castellanos, F. X., & Milham, M. P. (2009). Functional connectivity of default mode network components: Correlation, anticorrelation, and causality. *Human Brain Mapping, 30*(2), 625–637. https://doi.org/10.1002/hbm.20531

University of Maryland Medical Center. (2005, March 19). University of Maryland School of Medicine study shows laughter helps blood vessels function better. *ScienceDaily.* https://www.sciencedaily.com/releases/2005/03/050309111444.htm

U.S. Department of Health and Human Services. (2018). *Physical activity guidelines for Americans, 2nd edition.* https://health.gov/sites/default/files/2019-09/Physical_Activity_Guidelines_2nd_edition.pdf

Van Der Kolk, B. (2015). *The body keeps the score: Brain, mind, and body in the healing of trauma*. Penguin Publishing Group.

Varghese, M. (Host). (2015–present). *Selling the couch* [Audio podcast]. https://selling-the-couch.captivate.fm/

Vazire, S., & Carlson, E. N. (2011). Others sometimes know us better than we know ourselves. *Current Directions in Psychological Science, 20*(2), 104–108. https://doi.org/10.1177/0963721411402478

Velicer, W. F., Fava, J. L., Prochaska, J. O., Abrams, D. B., Emmons, K. M., & Pierce, J. P. (1995). Distribution of smokers by stage in three representative samples. *Prevention Medicine, 24*(4), 401–411. https://doi.org/10.1006/pmed.1995.1065

Wachs, K., & Cordova, J. V. (2007). Mindful relating: Exploring mindfulness and emotion repertoires in intimate relationships. *Journal of Marital and Family Therapy, 33*(4), 464–481. https://doi.org/10.1111/j.1752-0606.2007.00032.x

Walker, L. J. (2003). Morality, religion, spirituality—The value of saintliness. *Journal of Moral Education, 32*(4), 373–384. https://doi.org/10.1080/0305724032000161277

Walsh, R. (2011). Lifestyle and mental health. *American Psychologist, 66*(7), 579–592. https://doi.org/10.1037/a0021769

Walsh, R., & Shapiro, S. L. (2006). The meeting of meditative disciplines and Western psychology: A mutually enriching dialogue. *American Psychologist, 61*(3), 227–239. https://doi.org/10.1037/0003-066X.61.3.227

Walsh, S., Nichols, K., & Cormack, M. (1991). Self-care and clinical psychologists: A threatening obligation? *Clinical Psychology Forum, 37*, 5–7.

Wang, S. J. (2007). Mindfulness meditation: Its personal and professional impact on psychotherapists. *Dissertation Abstracts International: B. The Sciences and Engineering, 67*(7-B), 4122.

Warren, L., Abblett, M., & Willard, C. (2018). *Anti-burnout card deck: 54 mindfulness and compassion practices to refresh your clinical work*. PESI Publishing & Media.

Webb, J. (2012). *Running on empty: Overcome your childhood emotional neglect*. Morgan James Publishing.

Weber, M. (2017). *The Protestant work ethic and the spirit of capitalism*. Vigeo Press.

Wegner, D. M. (1994). Ironic processes of mental control. *Psychological Review, 101*(1), 34–52. https://doi.org/10.1037/0033-295X.101.1.34

Wehrenberg, M. (2018). *The 10 best-ever anxiety management techniques: Understanding how your brain makes you anxious and what you can do to change it* (2nd ed.). W. W. Norton & Company.

Weiner-Davis, M. (2021, September/October). First, make the bed: A gentle path through depression. *Psychotherapy Networker*, 52–53.

Weir, K. (2017, January). Forgiveness can improve mental and physical health. *Monitor on Psychology, 48*(1), 30. https://www.apa.org/monitor/2017/01/ce-corner

Wicks, R. (2008). *The resilient clinician*. Oxford University Press.

Wigal, S. B., Emmerson, N., Gehricke, J. G., & Galassetti, P. (2013). Exercise: Applications to childhood ADHD. *Journal of Attention Disorders, 17*(4), 279–290. https://doi.org/10.1177/1087054712454192

Willams, M., Teasdale, J., Segal, Z. V., & Kabat-Zinn, J. (2007). *The mindful way through depression: Freeing yourself from chronic unhappiness*. Guilford Press.

Willard, C. (2016, March 22). Before you scroll, try this mindful social media practice. *Greater Good Magazine*. https://greatergood.berkeley.edu/article/item/before_you_scroll_try_this_mindful_social_media_practice

Willard, C., & Weisser, O. (2020). *The breathing book*. Sounds True.

Williams, J. M. (2010). Mindfulness and psychological process. *Emotion, 10*(1), 1–7. https://doi.org/10.1037/a0018360

Williams-Nickelson, C. (2001). Mentoring and leadership: lessons learned for women balancing professional and personal roles. *APAGS Newsletter, 13*(1).

Williams-Nickelson, C. (2006). Balanced living through self-care. In J. Worell & C. D. Goodheart (Eds.), *Handbook of girls' and women's psychological health: Gender and well-being across the lifespan* (pp. 183–191). Oxford University Press.

Wilmer, H. H., Sherman, L. E., & Chein, J. M. (2017). Smartphones and cognition: A review of research exploring the links between mobile technology habits and cognitive functioning. *Frontiers in Psychology, 8*, Article 605. https://doi.org/10.3389/fpsyg.2017.00605

Winerman, L. (2016). The debt trap. *Monitor on Psychology, 47*(4), 44.

Wise, E. H., & Barnett, J. E. (2016). Self-care for psychologists. In J. C. Norcross, G. R. VandenBos, D. K. Freedheim, & L. F. Campbell (Eds.), *APA handbook of clinical psychology: Education and profession* (pp. 209–222). American Psychological Association. https://doi.org/10.1037/14774-014

Wise, E. H., Hersh, M. A., & Gibson, C. M. (2011). Ethics and self-care: A developmental lifespan perspective. *Register Report, 37*, 20–29.

Wise, E. H., Hersh, M. A., & Gibson, C. M. (2012). Ethics, self-care and well-being for psychologists: Reenvisioning the stress–distress continuum. *Professional Psychology: Research and Practice, 43*(5), 487–494. https://doi.org/10.1037/a0029446

Wise, E. H., & Reuman, L. (2019). Promoting competent and flourishing lifelong practice for psychologists: A communitarian perspective. *Professional Psychology: Research and Practice, 50*(2), 129–135. https://doi.org/10.1037/pro0000226

Wittbrodt, M. T., & Millard-Stafford, M. (2018). Dehydration impairs cognitive performance: A meta-analysis. *Medicine and Science in Sports and Exercise, 50*(11), 2360–2368. https://doi.org/10.1249/MSS.0000000000001682

Wonders, L. (2020, December 5). *51 simple self-care practices*. https://wonderscounseling.com/51-simple-self-care-practices/

Wong, R. A. (2015, September 22). *Therapist's guide to clinical consultation in private practice*. PsychCentral. https://pro.psychcentral.com/kickstart/2015/09/clinical-consultation-private-practice/

Wong, Y. J., Owen, J., Gabana, N. T., Brown, J. W., McInnis, S., Toth, P., & Gilman, L. (2018). Does gratitude writing improve the mental health of psychotherapy clients? Evidence from a randomized controlled trial. *Psychotherapy Research, 28*(2), 192–202. https://doi.org/10.1080/10503307.2016.1169332

Wood, B. J., Klein, S., Cross, H. J., Lammers, C. J., & Elliott, J. K. (1985). Impaired practitioners. *Professional Psychology: Research and Practice, 16*(6), 843–850. https://doi.org/10.1037/0735-7028.16.6.843

Worthington, E. (2008). *Steps to REACH Forgiveness and to Reconcile.* Pearson Learning Solutions.

Wurst, F. M., Mueller, S., Petitjean, S., Euler, S., Thon, N., Wiesbeck, G., & Wolfersdorf, M. (2010). Patient suicide: A survey of therapists' reactions. *Suicide & Life-Threatening Behavior, 40*(4), 328–336. https://doi.org/10.1521/suli.2010.40.4.328

Xie, L., Kang, H., Xu, Q., Chen, M. J., Liao, Y., Thiyagarajan, M., O'Donnell, J., Christensen, D. J., Nicholson, C., Iliff, J. J., Takano, T., Deane, R., & Nedergaard, M. (2013, October 18). Sleep drives metabolite clearance from the adult brain. *Science, 342*(6156), 373–377. https://doi.org/10.1126/science.1241224

Yazdani, M., Esmaeilzadeh, M., Pahlavanzadeh, S., & Khaledi, F. (2014). The effect of laughter Yoga on general health among nursing students. *Iranian Journal of Nursing and Midwifery Research, 19*(1), 36–40.

Young, C. M. (1999). *Vicarious trauma in psychotherapists who work with physically or sexually abused children* [Unpublished doctoral dissertation]. The California School of Professional Psychology, Alameda.

Young, S. (2016, December). *A pain-processing algorithm.* https://www.shinzen.org/wp-content/uploads/2016/12/art_painprocessingalg.pdf

Youngstedt, S. D., & Kripke, D. F. (2004). Long sleep and mortality. Rationale for sleep restriction. *Sleep Medicine Review, 8*(3), 159–174. https://doi.org/10.1016/j.smrv.2003.10.002

Zahniser, E., Rupert, P. A., & Dorociak, K. E. (2017). Self-care in clinical psychology graduate training. *Training and Education in Professional Psychology, 11*(4), 283–289. https://doi.org/10.1037/tep0000172

Zeff, T. (2004). *The highly sensitive person's survival guide: Essential skills for living well in an overstimulating world.* New Harbinger Publications.

Zeidner, M., Hadar, D., Matthews, G., & Roberts, R. D. (2013). Personal factors related to compassion fatigue in health professionals. *Anxiety, Stress, and Coping, 26*(6), 595–609. https://doi.org/10.1080/10615806.2013.777045

Zelazo, P. D., Blair, C. B., & Willoughby, M. T. (2016). *Executive function: Implications for education.* National Center for Education Research. https://files.eric.ed.gov/fulltext/ED570880.pdf

Ziede, J. S., & Norcross, J. C. (2020). Personal therapy and self-care in the making of psychologists. *The Journal of Psychology, 154*(8), 585–618. https://doi.org/10.1080/00223980.2020.1757596

Zur Institute. (n.d.). *Humor in therapy: Using it effectively and responsibly*. https://www.zurinstitute.com/clinical-updates/humor-in-therapy/

Zur, O. (2007). *Boundaries in psychotherapy: Ethical and clinical considerations*. American Psychological Association. https://doi.org/10.1037/11563-000

Zylowska, L. (2012). *The mindfulness prescription for adult ADHD: An 8-step program for strengthening attention, managing emotions, and achieving your goals*. Trumpeter.

Index

About the Author

Matthew A. Hersh, PhD, is a licensed clinical psychologist who incorporates mindfulness, self-compassion, and energy psychology into his private practice with teens and adults. He is a certified Koru mindfulness teacher and a Diplomate of comprehensive energy psychology. Dedicated to sustainable self-care for therapists, Matt founded *The Thriving Therapist,* an online resource for mental health practitioners' self-care cultivation and burnout prevention. Matt is a longtime mindfulness meditation practitioner who also incorporates an array of subtle energy practices into his daily life. In his spare pockets of time, he loves taking endless landscape and sunset photos, playing and writing music, and dethatching his lawn. Matt recently stumbled upon the realization that therapist self-care is slightly easier in theory as he blends energy toward work, personal care, family life, and a very fluffy but energetic dog. Visit his website (https://www.TheThrivingTherapist.org) for additional resources for psychotherapist self-care.